W9-CAE-323

A FIELD GUIDE TO

REPTILES & AMPHIBIANS

EASTERN AND CENTRAL NORTH AMERICA

❧

ROGER CONANT

and

JOSEPH T. COLLINS

Illustrated by
ISABELLE HUNT CONANT
and TOM R. JOHNSON

THIRD EDITION, *Expanded*

SPONSORED BY THE NATIONAL AUDUBON SOCIETY,
THE NATIONAL WILDLIFE FEDERATION, AND
THE ROGER TORY PETERSON INSTITUTE

HOUGHTON MIFFLIN COMPANY
BOSTON   NEW YORK

LIBRARY OF CONGRESS CATALOGING-IN-PUBLICATION DATA

Conant, Roger, 1909–
A field guide to reptiles & amphibians : eastern and central North America /
Roger Conant and Joseph T. Collins ; illustrated by
Isabelle Hunt Conant and Tom R. Johnson. —3rd ed., expanded.
p. cm. — (The Peterson field guide series ; 12)
"Sponsored by the National Audubon Society, the National Wildlife
Federation, and the Roger Tory Peterson Institute."
Includes bibliographical references (p.   ) and index.
ISBN 0-395-90452-8
1. Reptiles—United States—Identification.   2. Amphibians—United States
—Identification.   3. Reptiles—Canada—Identification.   4. Amphibians—
Canada—Identification. I. Collins, Joseph T.   II. Title.   III. Series.
QL651 .C65 1998
597.9'097 — dc21   98-13622

Book design by Anne Chalmers
Typeface: Linotype-Hell Fairfield; Futura Condensed (Adobe)

PRINTED IN THE UNITED STATES OF AMERICA
RMT 10 9 8 7 6 5 4 3

This book is dedicated to

ISABELLE

without whose talents as photographer and artist

it never would have been attempted

and to

SUZANNE

without whose support and patience

this edition never would have

been completed.

❦

EDITOR'S NOTE

Amateur naturalists who are interested in herpetology, the science of reptiles and amphibians, have a distinct advantage over their fellows. Unlike most bird watchers, they can catch and handle these animals, and unlike botanists and entomologists, who must dry and mount their specimens in order to preserve them, herpetologists can keep their captives alive, often for long periods of time. They can study them and enjoy them as pets. The keeping of live reptiles and amphibians has become an important adjunct of the biology classroom and of the summer camp.

Roger Conant and Joseph T. Collins, keenly aware of this because of the thousands of questions they have received, have included a section in this book on how to house and feed reptiles and amphibians, and sprinkled through their text are numerous other hints. Hence this Field Guide serves a double purpose — it enables the reader to identify a specimen and then tells him or her how to care for it.

This book is far from being strictly technical. It contains information that the professional herpetologist needs to identify species and subspecies, but its language will be clear to everyone.

Roger Conant, Director and Curator of Reptiles Emeritus of the Philadelphia Zoological Garden, is now an adjunct professor in the Department of Biology at the University of New Mexico. He has written 10 books and more than 200 technical and semipopular papers, chiefly on reptiles and amphibians. Recently he completed, with the late Howard K. Gloyd, a lengthy book on the venomous snakes of the genus *Agkistrodon* on a worldwide basis. He also wrote the *Reptile Study* merit badge pamphlet for the Boy Scouts of America.

Joseph T. Collins is currently herpetologist emeritus at the Natural History Museum of the University of Kansas, Lawrence. He has written or co-edited 20 books and another 200 technical and semipopular papers on reptiles and amphibians. He recently co-edited a book entitled *Snakes: Ecology and Evolutionary Biology.*

The late Isabelle Hunt Conant, illustrator of the first and second editions of this Field Guide, and who was Mrs. Roger Conant, was the official photographer at the Philadelphia Zoo for 10 years. Scores of popular and technical publications reproduced her pictures. A very large number of her illustrations are included here.

Tom R. Johnson is the new illustrator for this edition. He is the herpetologist for the Missouri Department of Conservation and is an accomplished photographer as well as an artist. He recently authored *The Amphibians and Reptiles of Missouri*, a splendid book richly illustrated with his drawings and color photographs. He had the lengthy and arduous task of transforming the black-and-white plates of the previous editions of this Field Guide into color. To Johnson also fell the charge of keeping specimen animals alive and healthy, sometimes for extended periods, while the photographic illustrations were being prepared.

Standardization of vernacular names of North American birds was begun in 1886 and is now reaching stabilization. Joseph T. Collins recently authored the third edition of *Standard Common and Current Scientific Names for North American Amphibians and Reptiles*, published by the Society for the Study of Amphibians and Reptiles. These names are now reaching stability across the continent and are used throughout this book.

Many colleges and universities selected the first and second editions of this Field Guide as a text for their courses in herpetology. It has also served as a stimulus to amateur herpetological societies, members of which have provided the authors with much new information on range extensions, maximum sizes, etc.

The addition of many West Indian lizards that are now established in Florida and the discovery of many new species increase the number of full species covered in this third edition to 379. The distribution maps have all been updated and redrawn.

Roger Conant and Joseph T. Collins have produced a Field Guide that we are very proud to have in the series. Don't leave it on the library shelf. Put it in the glove compartment of your car, in your knapsack, or in your pocket when you travel about the countryside.

ROGER TORY PETERSON

ACKNOWLEDGMENTS

Since the publication of the second edition of this Field Guide in 1975, many letters have been sent to us, a great number from strangers, offering information on range extensions, new maximum lengths, suggestions for adjustments and improvements of the text, figures, and color plates, and a wealth of other data. All of this has been very helpful, and a large portion of the refinements and improvements in this third edition are the result of the interest and thoughtfulness of colleagues, their students, and a host of herpetologists and naturalists who have made contributions to the cause. We apologize for insisting that many of them send us firm evidence about specimens in order to substantiate their claims of range extensions. For the most part, we required voucher specimens (or photographs) to be deposited in institutional collections before we would accept such records. For this third edition we did not demand to see animals alleged to break size or weight records, but generally did require that they also be deposited in an institutional collection, where they would be more available for others to examine.

Many more non-native species, particularly West Indian and Central American lizards, are now firmly established in southern Florida. Additionally, some European forms now have breeding colonies in more temperate areas of the eastern and central United States. Users of this book may encounter them, so these have been added in text, map, and, sometimes, picture.

To all those persons who have helped we are deeply grateful, but we also are embarrassed. Space limitations preclude the listing of all their names. Their contributions, however, are carefully recorded in our workbooks, our files, and on our base maps, and their findings, properly accredited, are available on request.

To our new Field Guide artist, Tom R. Johnson, goes our special thanks. The new color plates in this edition are eloquent testimony to his professional skill, without which the value of this book would be greatly diminished. James A. Cooper provided him with invaluable technical assistance in the production of black-and-white prints, and Freida E. Fisher, Missouri Department of Conservation, gave him the secretarial support so necessary in an endeavor of this magnitude.

Our new graphics artist, Laura Poracsky, labored long on the 333 range maps. Her crisp and exact work demonstrates her professional ability, for which we are most grateful. Larry Rosche worked many long hours transferring the maps to electronic format and changing the ranges from textures to colors for this new design. Ann M. Musser skillfully drew the Mimic Glass Lizard in Figure 53. Keith Coldsnow (Keith Coldsnow Ltd., Kansas City, Missouri) was especially helpful in supplying us with graphics material for production of the maps, and to him we are much indebted.

Some persons have contributed considerable effort in responding to our requests for information, reading portions of the text, checking preliminary maps submitted for their critical review, or rendering other favors. In particular, we thank Darrel R. Frost, Richard Highton, John B. Iverson, and Paul E. Moler. Without their professional help and patient counsel, our task of producing this edition would have been much more difficult.

A number of herpetologists generously sent us copies of their unpublished manuscripts so we could preview them and, in some cases, incorporate taxonomic changes they were proposing. Others checked selected sections of the text or provided detailed information that was helpful in revising accounts of various genera and species. For their contributions in this manner, we are grateful to Ralph W. Axtell, James P. Bogart, David C. Cannatella, Charles J. Cole, Thomas R. Jones, Alvan A. Karlin, James C. List, Leslie A. Lowcock, John D. Lynch, D. Bruce Means, Michael A. Morris, William M. Palmer, George R. Pisani, Dwight R. Platt, Douglas A. Rossman, Eric M. Rundquist, David M. Sever, Samuel S. Sweet, Stephen G. Tilley, Stanley E. Trauth, Joseph P. Ward, and John W. Wright.

In the preparation of the distribution maps for this edition, we have had help from innumerable people, especially from those who were compiling unpublished records for specific states, provinces, or other areas. Among this group special credit must be given to: Earl L. Hanebrink, Flavius Killebrew, Michael V. Plummer, Henry W. Robison, David A. Saugey, Stanley E. Trauth, and Glyn Turnipseed (Arkansas), Ernest A. Liner (Coahuila, Nuevo León, and Tamaulipas), Paul E. Moler, Ray E. Ashton, Jr., David L. Auth, and John B. Iverson (Florida), Charles W. Seyle, Jr.

(Georgia), Michael A. Morris (Illinois), James L. Christiansen (Iowa), John MacGregor and Robert E. Todd, Jr. (Kentucky), Harold A. Dundee, Ernest A. Liner, and Douglas A. Rossman (Louisiana), Carroll B. Knox (Maine), William B. Preston (Manitoba), Herbert S. Harris, Jr. and Robert W. Miller (Maryland), James H. Harding and Arnold G. Kluge (Michigan), Jeffrey W. Lang and John J. Moriarty (Minnesota), Ronald Altig, J. William Cliburn, Edmund D. Keiser, Jr., Terry L. Vandeventer, and Robert A. Young (Mississippi), Tom R. Johnson (Missouri), Jeffrey Black (Montana), John D. Lynch (Nebraska), Terry E. Graham and James D. Lazell, Jr. (New England), William G. Degenhardt, Randy D. Jennings, and Charles W. Painter (New Mexico), Alvin R. Breisch (New York), Alvin L. Braswell and William M. Palmer (North Carolina), Paul M. Daniel, David M. Dennis, Floyd L. Downs, and Eric Juterbock (Ohio salamanders), Jeffrey Black, Charles C. Carpenter, George R. Cline, William Fesperman, Richard L. Lardie, Patrick S. Mulvaney, Stephen M. Secor, and Gregory and Lynnette Sievert (Oklahoma), Michael J. Oldham and Frederick W. Schueler (Ontario), Clarence J. McCoy (Pennsylvania), J. Whitfield Gibbons (South Carolina), William Redmond (Tennessee amphibians), Ralph W. Axtell, Jonathan A. Campbell, James R. Dixon, Jerry D. Johnson, William W. Lamar, and Thomas Vermersch (Texas), Joseph C. Mitchell and Christopher A. Pague (Virginia), Robert W. Henderson, Albert Schwartz, and Richard Thomas (West Indies), N. Bayard Green and Thomas K. Pauley (West Virginia), and Gary S. Casper (Wisconsin). A select group of herpetologists critiqued the distribution maps for a number of species having a pan-continental distribution. They are Edmund D. Brodie, Jr., R. Bruce Bury, Stephen Corn, Harry W. Greene, Randy D. Jennings, Ronald A. Nussbaum, and Andrew H. Price.

The gift or loan of live specimens was crucial to the preparation of this edition, because we needed living examples of the many alien species that had been introduced and are now established in the area covered by this Field Guide. Further, conversion of the black-and-white plates in the 1975 edition to the color versions in this edition required more live amphibians and reptiles. One of us (JTC) was accompanied by Kelly J. Irwin and Larry Miller on a three-week expedition during 1985 throughout the southeastern United States to obtain many of the needed animals. To these two field companions we give our sincere thanks. We are most grateful also for the efforts of Joseph Slowinski and Louis W. Porras, who, sometimes on very short notice, diligently supplied us with many lizards from the introduced populations in southern Florida. A host of other experienced field naturalists responded to our requests for living animals or assisted in acquiring the desired specimens. They include John S. Applegarth, David L. Auth, Alvin L. Braswell, Clinton Collins, Jerry D. Collins, Brian I. Crother, Tom Dillenbeck, Michael Dixon, James D. Florian, Daniel H. Gist, Richard Highton, Scott Hillard, Errol Hooper, Jr., Malcolm Hunter, Kris M. Irwin, Gwen Keller, W. Kenneth King, James L. Knight, Julian C. Lee, William B. Loftus, Jonathan B. Losos, Paul E. Moler, Lewis D. Ober, Stephen M. Reilly, David A. Saugey, Richard A. Seigel, Jay Smith, Katherine Trefethen, Robert Wilkinson, and Larry Zuckerman.

Conversion of the black-and-white plates from the 1975 edition to the color versions in this edition also created a need for color slides, and many colleagues responded to our requests for slides of the rarer species or subspecies. These are George M. Ferguson, Carrol L. Henderson, William W. Lamar, John Mac-Gregory, Larry Miller, Paul E. Moler, Louis W. Porras, Steven B. Reichling, and Raymond D. Semlitsch. The illustrations of tadpoles were expertly drawn by Tom R. Johnson. Eight of them are from his book, *The Amphibians and Reptiles of Missouri* (copyright 1987), and are reprinted with permission of the Conservation Commission of the State of Missouri.

For a wide variety of favors, including the loan of museum specimens, supplying miscellaneous information or locality records, checking selected maps, or helping in other ways, we are indebted to the following: Steven D. Aird, Mary L. Anderson, Bob Bader, Richard J. Baldaug, John Behler, Dale Belcher, Ellin Beltz, Charles R. Belm, Charles M. Bogert, Ronald A. Brandon, Kurt A. Buhlmann, Carleton Burke, Ray D. Burkett, Stephen D. Busack, Ellen J. Censky, Steven P. Christman, Charles J. Cole, Francis R. Cook, William Cooper, Ronald I. Crombie, Marc R. Des Meules, John E. DiOrio, C. Kenneth Dodd, Jr., Neil H. Douglas, William E. Duellman, David A. Easterla, David L. Edwards, Arthur C. Echternacht, John H. Epler, Carl H. Ernst, Michael A. Ewert, Henry S. Fitch, Neil B. Ford, Darrel R. Frost, John Frost, Frederick R. Gehlbach, John Gilhen, Daniel H. Gist, Ronald R. Goellner, David A. Good, David M. Green, Harry W. Greene, Arnold B. Grobman, Geoffrey A. Hammerson, Michael W. Hammock, James H. Harding, David L. Hardy, Julian R. Harrison III, John L. Hawken, S. Blair Hedges, Max Hensly, Dennis W. Herman, W. Ronald Heyer, David M. Hillis, Wayne Hoffman, Errol Hooper, Jr., Kelly J. Irwin, Jeffrey J. Jackson, James S. Jacob, Robert G. Jaeger, Robert Johnson, Robert L. Jones, Thomas R. Jones, Daryl Karns, David A. Kizirian, Michael W. Klemens, James J. Krupa, Mathias Lang, Karl W. Larsen, Michael Laturno, Robin Lawson, Carl S. Lieb, Allan D. Linder, James C. List, Jeff Lovich, Leslie A.

Lowcock, W. H. Martin, Edward J. Maruska, Hymen Marx, Chris T. McAllister, Nancy Glover McCartney, Michael J. McCoid, James R. McCranie, Hugh K. McCrystal, Roy W. McDiarmid, Joel McKinney, D. Bruce Means, Philip A. Medica, Peter Meylan, Kenneth Mierzwa, Larry Miller, Sherman A. Minton, Richard R. Montanucci, Scott M. Moody, Kevin Moore, Michael Morrison, Randall Morrison, Robert H. Mount, James B. Murphy, Henry R. Mushinsky, Charles W. Myers, Max A. Nickerson, Lewis D. Ober, Robert Owen, Lawrence M. Page, Ray Pawley, Jerry A. Payne, James W. Petranka, Jeff Pfeiffer, George R. Pisani, Frank Pitelka, Dwight R. Platt, Louis W. Porras, Robert Powell, Gregory K. Pregill, Andrew H. Price, Peter C. H. Pritchard, Al Redmond, Norman Reichenback, Howard K. Reinert, Robert P. Reynolds, Steven M. Roble, Eric M. Rundquist, William Sanderson, Cecil R. Schwalbe, Floyd Scott, Norman J. Scott, Jr., Michael E. Seidel, Richard A. Seigel, David Seigler, Kyle Selcer, Mark A. Sellers, David M. Sever, Jr., Bradley H. Shaffer, Kate Shaw, Mark Simmonds, John E. Simmons, Hobart M. Smith, Emmett Snellings, Jr., David H. Snyder, Dan W. Speake, David L. Stephan, J. D. Stewart, Margaret M. Stewart, Peter Strimple, Charles D. Sullivan, Samuel S. Sweet, Wilmer W. Tanner, Robert A. Thomas, Thomas A. Titus, Bern W. Tryon, R. Wayne Van Devender, Laurie J. Vitt, Allan W. Volkmann, David B. Wake, Joseph P. Ward, Robert G. Webb, Jeffrey Whipple, John Wiens, E. O. Wiley, Kenneth L. Williams, Michael A. Williamson, Larry David Wilson, Al Winstel, Addison Wynn, Doug Wynn, Robert T. Zappalorti, George R. Zug, and Richard G. Zweifel.

Kathryn Johns Gloyd devoted hundreds of hours to assisting with proofreading and typing chores during the preparation and editing of the manuscript for this book.

One of us (JTC) owes a debt of thanks to Philip S. Humphrey, Frank B. Cross, and E. O. Wiley, of the Museum of Natural History at the University of Kansas. Their patience during the writing of this book has been great, and they have been most supportive. Rebecca L. Alden and Tamara Wallace, students at the University of Kansas, cheerfully handled endless paperwork and other tasks associated with producing this book, and to them we give our thanks.

We extend our deep appreciation to the editorial staff of Houghton Mifflin Company. Harry L. Foster, Field Guide Editor, has given us repeated help and encouragement. Barbara Stratton aided us during early stages of work on this book, and she provided type for the relabeling of plates, maps, and text drawings. Anne P. Chalmers designed the book and assisted in perfecting the maps and art work. Susan W. Kunhardt, our copy editor, reviewed the manuscript with great thoroughness, made many excellent suggestions for improvement, and skillfully supervised the innumerable details that were inherent to seeing this Field Guide through the press.

Credit must also be given to the hundreds of herpetologists whose published works have been consulted, often repeatedly, and whose names would appear frequently if this were a documented, scientific publication. We are deeply grateful to them, but there is room to list only relatively few of their works on the pages devoted to references.

ROGER CONANT
JOSEPH T. COLLINS

CONTENTS

ILLUSTRATIONS

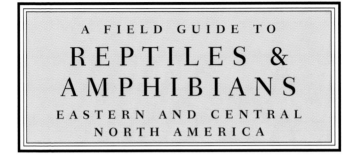

A FIELD GUIDE TO

REPTILES &
AMPHIBIANS

EASTERN AND CENTRAL
NORTH AMERICA

INTRODUCTION

Interest in herpetology continues to proliferate on two broad fronts—among scientists who are using reptiles and amphibians ever more frequently for studies on many subjects, including life history, behavior, demography, and life functions of the animals themselves, and among individuals who derive pleasure and knowledge from observing these animals in the field or keeping them in home terrariums. For both groups accurate identification of species is essential, and it is largely for them and the field naturalist in general that this book has been written.

This third edition of the *Field Guide to Reptiles and Amphibians* covers the same territory as its predecessors (see map on page ii). Many more alien lizards are now established in Florida, and new species and subspecies have been described or discovered, partly through the use of sophisticated laboratory techniques, since the second edition was published in 1975. We are now concerned with 379 species distributed as follows: Three crocodilians, 47 turtles, 74 lizards, one amphisbaenian, 91 snakes, 99 salamanders, and 64 toads and frogs. When all species and subspecies are counted, 595 different kinds of reptiles and amphibians are included, and the vast majority of these are illustrated. There are 656 reproductions of photographs in full color on 48 plates grouped together in the book. In addition, to show features that are useful in the identification of various species and subspecies, there are 384 line drawings, which are scattered through the text and legend pages in Figures 2 through 124. There are also 333 distribution maps accompanying the species accounts. Counting all these, the frontispiece map, the 101 color photographs, and the nine black-and-white photographs in Figure 1, the illustrations in this Field Guide total 1484.

Time was when the only good snake was a dead one, but that unfortunate attitude is now almost a thing of the past except among ignorant or intolerant people, and the pitiful, sadistic vandals who kill anything that moves. Most young persons, as a result of exposure to reptiles at summer camps or in science classrooms, have discovered that a snake is a useful creature and, in most varieties, quite harmless. Further, a 1988 survey revealed that less than half of the adults responding were afraid of snakes, probably a much lower percentage than even a few decades ago. This new attitude has also helped to reduce the antipathy toward lizards and frogs and other animals whose skins are moist or covered with scales. There is now conclusive proof that fear of these animals has to be learned by children, usually from parents or other persons, some of whom may be prejudiced or simply ignorant.

USING THIS BOOK: Anyone familiar with Roger Tory Peterson's Field Guides to birds will have no trouble consulting this book, for the general approach is the same. Most often, however, the reader will have a specimen at hand before attempting identification. The Boy Scout with his lizard, the biology student with her frog or salamander, or the angler or hunter with a freshly killed snake will bring book and animal together for comparison, or will refer to this Field Guide immediately after returning to their bases. Except for the basking turtle and an occasional other specimen, the techniques employed in bird watching will have little application. The vast majority of reptiles and amphibians are hiders, not likely to be seen at all by day unless one goes hunting for them. Even those that prowl are apt to be mere streaks in the grass. Accurate identification, for the most part, depends on a careful, close-range check.

Naturally, you will turn to the pictures first, and many times your specimen will closely match one of them. If it doesn't, then select the illustration it most nearly resembles and consult the text for that species—page references appear directly opposite each plate. Read about the key characters, the points of difference that are diagnostic for each separate kind, and also check the subentry **SIMILAR SPECIES** to eliminate others that may resemble the one in hand. Details of anatomy and pattern are shown in the line drawings to which there are references in the text. Time spent studying the illustrations on pages 138–141 of this book will be well invested, for it will help you to understand the things for which to look.

In trying to make identifications, remember that animals are not cut out by die-stamping machines or patterned by a trip through a printing press. Variation is a normal part of nature, and some species may show bewildering modifications of coloration and pattern. Occasional specimens may lack one or more of the pigment components of the skin and may be reddish, yellowish, bluish, or even albinistic (white or whitish) instead of exhibiting their normal colorations. Melanistic (all black) specimens are also occasionally found. Bear in mind, also, that frogs and lizards may change colors; a brown one, for example, may turn to green a short time later. We have tried to include the major variations by mentioning them in the text, and a few are shown on the color plates. Aberrant specimens or hybrids between species are found occasionally, and they may even confound experts. If you have real trouble in trying to make sure what you have caught, take it to the nearest natural history museum, zoo, or university support-ing a zoology or biology department and ask for help.

Only a few snakes are dangerous, and all venomous species known from within our area are illustrated on Pls. 30, 34, 35, and 36. Learn to recognize them on sight and let them strictly alone unless you have been given professional training on how to han-dle them. Also be cautious about picking up most turtles and large harmless snakes; they can and will bite in self-defense. Examples of how to handle big turtles are shown in Figure 1.

AREA: Since reptiles and amphibians lack the mobility of birds and rarely leave their normal habitats, geography is of major impor-tance in making accurate identifications. All reptiles and amphib-ians known to occur in the area covered by this book are includ-ed. The area covered includes all of the United States and Canada from the Eastern Seaboard to the western limits of Texas, Oklahoma, Kansas, Nebraska, the two Dakotas, Manitoba, and the District of Keewatin (see map, p. ii). This is an artificial boundary, but it was designed to meet the eastern edge of the ter-ritory embraced by Robert C. Stebbins's *Field Guide to Western Reptiles and Amphibians.* Our area thus includes a large part of the Great Plains as well as a portion of the Chihuahuan Desert in Trans-Pecos Texas, in which there is a strong representation of Mexican species.

By way of explanation for those not familiar with Canadian geography, Keewatin is actually the District of Keewatin, a part of the Northwest Territories, and is not politically equivalent to a province such as Manitoba. Further, Labrador is not politically equivalent to a province. It is actually a part of the Province of Newfoundland. The Province of Newfoundland consists of both the Island of Newfoundland and Labrador on the mainland.

RANGE: Knowing where a specimen was collected can be of great impor-tance in making identifications. Reptiles and amphibians lack the mobility of birds and seldom wander far from their natural habi-tats. Some of them, like salamanders, would die from desiccation if they left their caves or mountain streams. So note the origin of your specimen. If you take it to a herpetologist and ask for help, the first question probably will be, "Where did it come from?"

The ranges are stated in brief at the end of each species or subspecies discussion, but they are shown in detail on the maps.

MAPS: The general range of each species and subspecies is shown by a color on the maps, but don't expect to find any reptile or amphibian evenly distributed throughout the areas indicated. A water snake, for example, seldom wanders far from stream or pond or brook, and, toward the west, where rivers are far apart, many miles may separate localities in which to look for specimens. Obviously, on maps small enough to fit into a Field Guide it would be impossible to show all details. The range maps in this guide reflect, wherever possible, the known historical range based on voucher specimens (those preserved in a museum or university).

You may chance upon a specimen outside the known range of its species. There are several reasons why this may happen. For example:

1. People have a well-meaning but misguided (and often cruel) habit of turning loose any pets that become a burden. Turtles and horned lizards often fall into this category, and so do an astounding number of other amphibians and reptiles. Most die quickly in their new and alien environments, but sometimes the waifs establish themselves in their new locations, at least for a time. The Red-eared Slider has done so in a number of states, and the Texas Horned Lizard in Florida and elsewhere. A particularly acute problem involves frogs and toads, which are introduced as tadpoles, often in parks and wildlife refuges, during fish-stocking efforts by governmental agencies or private fish-farming operations. These tadpoles normally metamorphose and survive a single warm season, and then die with the onset of winter, but some may become at least temporarily established. Finally, a large number of tropical species have been introduced, most of them accidentally, into Florida or other southern states, and some kinds have developed temporary colonies only to die out after periods of heavy frost or other adverse conditions. The exotic species that seem now to be well established are included in this book.

2. You may discover a *bona fide* range extension. Many amphibians and reptiles are so secretive they are readily overlooked, and, although herpetology has acquired a legion of new adherents in recent years, there are still many areas that have been surveyed sketchily or not at all. If your outlander seems to be in a proper habitat and especially if it occurs in colonies, you may have something worth reporting.

3. On rare occasions you may find a specimen that tends to look like a distant subspecies instead of matching the race you

would expect in your immediate vicinity. This phenomenon is an expression of relationship. Related subspecies have had common ancestors, and it is not surprising to find the inherited characteristics of one race appearing occasionally in populations of another. This type of phenomenon may be commonplace within areas of intergradation—where two subspecies of the same species share a common boundary. There may be a nearly perfect blending of the two races with some individual specimens showing one or more characteristics of *both* subspecies. Care must be taken in trying to identify such specimens, and it is perfectly correct to refer to them as intergrades or intermediates. The areas of intergradation vary greatly in size; they are usually narrow in regions of sharp physiographic changes, such as along an escarpment or where grasslands give way to forests. But they may be very wide where changes in the environment are less pronounced. Only a few of the broader areas of intergradation are shown on the distribution maps, and these are indicated by the overlapping of patterns (spotting, hatching, etc.). Bear in mind that intergradation may take place for varying distances on both sides of any common boundary between subspecies. In some cases subspecies that once were probably connected through intergrades now occupy completely separate ranges; some retain enough similarity to be considered as races, but they could just as logically be considered distinct species.

Crosses between species, or hybrids, occur in nature, but such mismatings are almost always between animals of closely related species, and they may take place at various localities within their common ranges. Hybrids are frequently infertile, like a mule, the cross between a horse and an ass. Intergrades, on the other hand, are members of freely interbreeding populations and are restricted to geographical regions where the ranges of two or more subspecies come together.

Much time and effort were expended toward making the maps of this edition as complete and accurate as possible. The maps occupied our attention constantly as work progressed and, during the combined effort on all three editions, the maps were assembled, corrected, and updated over a period of two decades. They were submitted to many specialists for checking and criticism, and scores of herpetologists reviewed them. We make no claim to perfection, however, for it would take several lifetimes to run down every possible locality reference and to check the vast numbers of specimens preserved in museums. Some states have been much more thoroughly explored herpetologically than others, or the data about their reptiles and amphibians are much better organized or more readily accessible. As predicted in the first edition of this Field Guide in 1958, the appearance of the distribution maps resulted in literally hundreds of range extensions being reported in the scientific literature or in correspondence. Such a smoking-out process is a healthy sign of interest and is the usual by-product whenever a large collection of range maps appears in print. We expect this process to continue with the appearance of the maps in this edition.

The maps may be used to prepare a personal check list. Just tabulate or check off the species occurring in your own state or region. They also may be used for a life list by placing a check mark after the name of each species or subspecies you encounter.

ILLUSTRATIONS: We have illustrated this book the difficult way. Instead of making paintings, we have depended on photography combined with color illustration, an art in which the late Isabelle Hunt Conant was remarkably skilled and which has been admirably mastered by Tom R. Johnson, our new Field Guide artist. The process involved taking black-and-white photographs of each reptile or amphibian to be illustrated in color. Then a toned black-and-white print was prepared of each and was colored by hand, using the living animal as a model. This was a time-consuming task, but it enabled the artists to record both the colors and precise dimensions of each form with great accuracy. Also, by enlarging the original black-and-white prints to the proper dimensions before coloring them, it was relatively simple to group all the animals on any one plate (or portion of a plate) to the proper scale so that comparison between large and small animals was facilitated.

This book was the first of the Peterson Field Guides concerned with zoology to be illustrated directly from life. There is only one dead animal portrayed in the entire lot of photographs—a Leatherback turtle, a marine species that few herpetologists have ever seen alive. For the photograph of it we are indebted to The American Museum of Natural History. We have borrowed one other photograph, that of the Tennessee Cave Salamander, from Edward McCrady. Some of the rattlesnake pictures were made through the close cooperation of the late Carl F. Kauffeld.

Obtaining the animals alive has given us the extraordinary opportunity of getting acquainted with them firsthand, and we have not had to depend nearly so much on faded, stained, or distorted preserved specimens for data as would otherwise have been the case.

The color plates are supplemented by more than 100 sets of line drawings showing, for the most part, key characters that are useful in distinguishing among genera or between species or subspecies. These were executed by Isabelle Hunt Conant, with a few additions or alterations for this third edition by Ann Musser.

Many of these drawings are original, but others have been adapted from figures appearing in numerous scientific publications. The excellent drawings of frog and toad tadpoles by Tom R. Johnson (Figures 110–124) are a new feature for this edition, and are included in response to a growing interest in this phase of the lives of amphibians.

SCIENTIFIC NAMES: It will be quickly apparent to longtime users of this book that there have been many changes in scientific names since publication of the second edition in 1975. Herpetological nomenclature is still a long way from achieving stability. Some of the groups of reptiles and amphibians have not yet been subjected to intensive investigation, and there is considerable disagreement on how some of them should be classified.

Changes come about in a variety of ways. Careful study may reveal that what once appeared to be a single species may actually be two, as in the case of the Gray Treefrog. Conversely, two or more apparently different species or subspecies are now one. Hurter's and the Eastern Spadefoot, which were previously thought to be distinct, are now thought to be subspecies of a single species, although there is controversy regarding this arrangement. Another example concerns the various color and pattern variations of Jordan's Salamander (*Plethodon jordani*). They have been shown to intergrade in so many different ways and in so many different localities that they must be defined as one extremely variable species rather than as a collection of numerous subspecies. Alterations in nomenclature resulting from such studies usually receive wide acceptance among herpetologists.

In other cases, as soon as changes are proposed (published) by one or more herpetologists, they are vigorously opposed by others. This is particularly true at the generic level (the first unit of any scientific name and the one that is always capitalized). Should the Texas Earless Lizard be split off from *Holbrookia* and placed in another genus (*Cophosaurus*) by itself? One of the problems is that there is no general agreement on the definition of a genus, and the net result is often a switching back and forth of names that may cause endless confusion. The situation is acute in the enormous snake family, the Colubridae, and particularly in the subdivision of it that includes the water snakes and their allies. This group still defies classification even though many competent taxonomists have worked on it on a worldwide basis for decades.

Some generic name changes are not in dispute. For example, the Eastern Newts are now *Notophthalmus* instead of *Diemictylus* as a result of a decision by The International Commission on Zoological Nomenclature, a sort of Supreme Court to which problems concerning taxonomy may be referred for action. There are additional changes that are not in controversy and which the majority of herpetologists have accepted.

Other changes are still being debated. Future study and appeals to the International Commission may result in settling some of them, but others are likely to be argued pro and con for years. Rather than trying to anticipate the outcome, and in order to preserve some semblance of stability, we have often taken the conservative view in this book and have retained the same generic names that appeared in the second edition in those cases where there is controversy and confusion.

Generic names in this third edition that differ from those used in the second edition are as follows: *Chrysemys* has been divided into *Chrysemys*, *Pseudemys*, and *Trachemys*; *Trionyx* has been changed to *Apalone*; *Crotaphytus* has been split into *Crotaphytus* and *Gambelia*; *Holbrookia* has been split into *Holbrookia* and *Cophosaurus*; *Natrix* has been changed to *Nerodia* and divided into *Nerodia*, *Regina*, and *Clonophis*; *Liodytes* has been combined with *Regina*; *Elaphe* has been divided into *Elaphe* and *Bogertophis*; *Hylactophryne* has been combined with *Eleutherodactylus*; *Limnaoedus* has been combined with *Pseudacris*; and *Hyla* has been divided into *Hyla* and *Osteopilus*.

A number of other generic changes have been proposed in print, but are still controversial. Thus we have not adopted dividing *Gopherus* into *Gopherus* and *Xerobates*, *Anolis* into *Anolis*, *Ctenonotus*, and *Norops*, and *Scaphiopus* into *Scaphiopus* and *Spea*. Further, we reject combining *Sternotherus* into *Kinosternon*, and *Thamnophis* into *Nerodia* (or vice versa).

COMMON NAMES: The common names, but not all the scientific names, used in this book follow Collins (1990, third edition), published by the Society for the Study of Amphibians and Reptiles. This list is now widely accepted as the standard for common names for the United States and Canada.

In many instances the common names of the animals honor a herpetologist or general naturalist who is now deceased; for example, Jordan's Salamander and Blanding's Turtle. In these cases there is a brief identifying statement about the person in question.

SUBSPECIES: For those readers of the Field Guide who are being exposed to subspecies for the first time, the following should be borne in mind: the scientific name is the clue. If there are three parts to the name (a trinomial), then there are one or more additional related subspecies, each of which bears the same first two names. For example, *Lampropeltis getula nigra* (Black Kingsnake), and *Lampropeltis getula holbrooki* (Speckled Kingsnake), and *Lampropeltis getula getula* (Eastern Kingsnake) are all subspecies of the same species. The repetition of *getula* in the name for the Eastern Kingsnake shows that it was the first member of the group to receive scientific description. In this book the words "subspecies" and "race" are considered to be synonyms and are used interchangeably. If there are only two parts to a scientific name (a binomial), then no subspecies are known or recognized. The term "form" is used to designate any population of reptiles or amphibians that bears a scientific name and regardless of whether a species or subspecies is involved.

The problem of what to do about subspecies had to be resolved early in the planning stages of the first edition of this book.

In the case of birds only a relatively few subspecies can be identified with accuracy through binoculars. The detection of minor details is difficult, especially since many avian subspecies are based on differences that require examination in the laboratory rather than in the field. The situation with reptiles and amphibians is quite another matter, for, with the specimen at hand, accurate identification to subspecies is often quite possible.

A uniformly black snake, a yellow one with dark stripes, and others with bold spotted patterns look quite different, but all the serpents on Pl. 28 from the Black Rat Snake to the Gray Rat Snake (excluding the Baird's Rat Snake) are members of the same species. To illustrate just one and bury the others in the text would be unfair—both to the amateur naturalist and to these distinctively marked animals.

There are many other examples. Some of the subspecies (races) of the harmless Milk Snake strongly resemble the Coral Snake, and one is almost a perfect visual mimic of that dangerous species (Pl. 30). Some of the races of the Fence Lizard are striped longitudinally; others have wavy dark crossbands and no well-defined stripes.

So subspecies are included in this Field Guide, along with the problems that go with them. Some subspecies are separated from their closest relatives by minutiae that will bore the field person, but the data are briefly summarized for those who wish to know. We have tried to include, on the plates or among the line drawings, illustrations of the species *and subspecies* that are visually different and can be told apart without recourse to the microscope, complicated scale counts, checks on internal anatomy, or sophisticated laboratory techniques.

If a subspecies is visually distinct enough to warrant inclusion on the color plates, it also normally rates a separate main entry in the text. Less easily defined subspecies (and a few rare ones) are included under those they most closely resemble. Our methods of presenting or listing subspecies are variable and unorthodox, but the various races are included. It should be borne strongly in mind that most persons will refer to the illustrations first and the text afterward. Hence, the text has been made to fit the pictures and *not* vice versa.

Zoological taxonomists (persons who classify animals) are far from agreement as to what constitutes a subspecies. It is the general practice to recognize those races that have been defined as such by the author of a review or monograph of a genus or species. In less well-studied groups, opinions tend to differ. It is well known that most animal populations are subject to clinal variations. A cline is a geographical trend in which a certain structural, color, or pattern characteristic shows a gradual change from one part of the range to another. For example, Wood Frogs have long hind legs in the northeastern states, but very short ones in northern Canada and Alaska. The populations at opposite ends of the range are so different that they easily could be classified as different subspecies or even distinct species—if it were not for the gradually changing populations in between them. Often two or more clines are involved, and these may manifest themselves in different directions, one cline progressing from south to north, while another *in the same species* progresses from east to west. Many of the disputes concerning subspecies result from differences of opinion in the interpretation of clines. One taxonomist might consider all Wood Frogs as belonging to a single full species devoid of subspecies; a less conservative one might divide them into two or three or even more subspecies. Another problem is the use of ventral and subcaudal scale counts as the sole characteristics to define subspecies in snakes. Because the subspecies that have been described for the two kinds of Green Snakes (*Opheodrys*) and the Lined Snake (*Tropidoclonion*) have neither coloration nor pattern differences correlated with variations in scutellation, we have not included them. Trying to make subcaudal and ventral counts on live snakes, especially small ones, is difficult and can even be fatal to them if too much pressure is applied in an effort to render them immobile for counting. It is best not to try making such counts on small snakes unless it is absolutely necessary to clinch identifications.

Suffice it to say, without becoming deeply involved in this controversial subject, that no two books or lists that include subspecies are likely to be quite in agreement. More stability will undoubtedly be achieved as study material accumulates from critical localities and becomes available to the research worker. In preparing this Field Guide we have endeavored to bear the layman's problems in mind and have stressed the subspecies that *look* different. This means that from the taxonomic point of view we have been quite conservative in many instances but distinctly radical in others.

The subspecies, carefully defined and backed by detailed study, is a useful taxon (a classification unit). It provides a name for distinctive populations and helps point out evolutionary trends and the responses of species to habitats that may differ distinctively in concordance with the various physiographic regions inhabited by the species as a whole. The subspecies has been abused in the past, with a tendency for some taxonomists to assign names to fragmentary or splinter populations. Such extremism has now largely disappeared. On the other hand, we disagree with herpetologists who would ignore subspecies entirely and who refer to annectent populations as that portion of the species which is black in coloration, or the one that has a distinctive spotted pattern. How much simpler it is to refer to each fraction of the full species by a subspecific and standard common name that is applicable to the animals in question.

SIZE: Reptiles and amphibians may continue to grow as long as they live, rapidly at first but more slowly after maturity. Hence, giant specimens may be encountered on very rare occasions. The greatest length that we believe to be authentic is given for each animal included in this book. Longer measurements will be called to our attention, no doubt, and some of these may be accurate. Evaluating claims is not easy, for some snake hunters are as notorious as certain anglers. Serpents, like fishes, shrink remarkably in size when stretched along a rule or measuring tape. Hearsay "evidence" about big snakes is not difficult to find. The longest serpent native to the United States is the Eastern Indigo Snake, with a maximum known length of 103½ inches, or a little less than 9 feet (2.629 meters).

Because reptiles and amphibians do not attain standard lengths and then stop growing, their sizes, in most instances, are expressed in this book by three measurements. For the Ringed Salamander, to use an example, the following figures (omitting metric measurements for the moment) appear directly after **IDENTIFICATION:** 5¼–7; record 9⅜, and they indicate that average adults vary from 5¼ to 7 inches in length, whereas the largest specimen on record had a total length of 9⅜ inches. In the case of lizards, which so frequently lose their tails and then grow new but shorter ones, the maximum head–body lengths are also included. Among certain species, notably some of the turtles, females not only grow bigger than males but they also look different, so for them there are separate measurements for the two sexes. Approximate sizes of young reptiles at the time of hatching or birth are also given in most instances. Sizes at transformation of amphibians from the larval to adult form are not included for two reasons: there is a dearth of such information for many species, and variations in size are considerable and subject to environmental conditions. If a pond dries up, for example, tadpoles may transform into toadlets or froglets at a much smaller size than if the pond remained filled with water.

The proper methods of taking measurements of animals in each major group are illustrated on page 141.

Acceptance and use of the metric system in the United States has been sporadic. Nonetheless, both the U.S. measurements and their approximate metric equivalents are given for each of the many reptiles and amphibians included in this book. (Canada is on the metric system.)

VOICE: Toads and frogs are quite vociferous, at least in season, but only a few other amphibians and reptiles of our area produce sounds. The crocodilians grunt, roar, and bellow, and some of the geckos make mouselike squeaks. Kissing, squeaking, popping, and yelping noises have been reported occasionally in salamanders, but the sounds in this last group are usually produced when air is suddenly exhaled through the lips.

Each kind of toad or frog has its own distinctive call, and many can be readily identified by ear after a little practice. The calls normally are associated with the breeding season when males of most species assemble in or near shallow water and start singing lustily for their mates. Some choruses are enormous and may be composed of several species all singing at the same time. Local weather conditions are of paramount importance in stimulating frogs into calling and breeding, and even human activities may start them off, such as when areas are flooded during irrigation and temporary ponds or puddles are formed. Choruses, usually weak, without the enthusiasm of mating time, and composed largely or wholly of young frogs, may sometimes be heard out of season. A few southern species may be vocal at almost any time of year, and treefrogs call intermittently throughout the summer months. The onset and duration of the breeding season varies greatly, depending on locality, latitude, and weather conditions. The times mentioned in the text are only approximations. Certain migratory birds arrive at any given locality on almost the same day every year, but toads and frogs, which are cold-blooded animals and at the mercy of the weather, are highly irregular.

CONSERVATION: As is the case with so many kinds of animals, reptiles and amphibians are under great pressure, and they are rapidly disappearing from many areas where formerly they were abundant. The senseless slaughter that still continues, the massive destruction of habitats resulting from the activities of humankind, and the exploitation of these animals for the pet trade all take a heavy toll.

Despite educational efforts in their behalf and the realization by great numbers of people that they are useful creatures, amphibians and reptiles are still destroyed because of human ignorance or vandalism. Snakes are bombarded by rocks, clubbed to death, or run over, sometimes deliberately, by truck and automobile drivers. Basking turtles, frogs, and lizards are used for target practice by children with slingshots and their adult counterparts with guns. The plight of the alligator, which was relentlessly poached so that thoughtless, wealthy persons could have fancy wallets, handbags, and shoes, made national headlines. Because of public outcry, the alligator received protection and has made a comeback throughout most of its range.

Ruination of habitats and pollution are probably the worst enemies of reptiles and amphibians. Every new housing, factory, or shopping center development in rural areas decimates the local wildlife populations. The dumping of solid wastes in swamps or marshes also destroys habitats. So does the pollution of streams with industrial and organic sewage. For years we sprayed the countryside with deadly DDT and other long-lasting chlorinated hydrocarbons.

An aroused public, now keenly aware of the ecological-environmental crises that plague so many parts of the world, is bringing pressure to bear that may halt or at least decelerate many of these abuses, but the proliferation of the human population with its attendant demands for land may soon relegate many reptiles and amphibians to wildlife reservations and probably bring about the extinction of many species, or at least exterminate them in and near every megalopolis.

Another insidious threat is the pet trade. During one year in the late 1980s, more than a million reptiles and almost a third of a million amphibians were imported legally, a very large percentage of them for sale as pets. The pressure on our native species is even greater. Whatever their source, they are handled in such great numbers that individual care is impossible, and many vendors treat them as so much merchandise, like cans or boxes on a grocer's shelf. Many buyers acquire them as novelties or on sudden impulse, and the losses, in general, are appalling. There is no harm in keeping amphibians and reptiles as pets, at least those that are not rare or endangered in nature, but lay pet owners are usually totally unprepared to cope with the needs of a new purchase. To help you—and them—we have included a chapter on Care in Captivity.

In response to these various problems, many laws have been

passed protecting reptiles and amphibians. Mere possession of a protected species may earn you a heavy fine or a jail sentence. Don't collect any threatened or endangered species, and steadfastly refuse to buy specimens of such kinds from anyone. Check with your state wildlife department to learn which species are protected by law.

Concentrate on studying reptiles and amphibians in the field. You can make valuable contributions about behavior and population dynamics through a program of continuous observations of local populations. Also, if you employ techniques for harmlessly marking individual specimens for future positive identification, data on rates of growth, longevity, and movements from one habitat to another can be accumulated. (Similar work with birds, by placing numbered bands on their legs, has yielded an enormous amount of information on migration, duration of life, etc.) If you are seriously interested in undertaking such a project, any competent curator of reptiles in a zoo or museum, or a university professor who does research in herpetology, can give you references on how to mark reptiles and amphibians, and might even be willing to help you get started.

Another subject that has been neglected, except by a few specialists, is the photographing of reptiles and amphibians under field conditions. By comparison with the vast array of extraordinarily fine bird pictures that are now available, herpetology is far behind. If you have skill with a camera, here lies a big opportunity for you. Even an average photographer can soon accumulate a photo album collection of reptiles and amphibians, a collection that is permanent, needs no cleaning or feeding, and is not destructive to wild populations.

Don't maintain these animals as pets just for the novelty of having them. If you keep them in captivity, initiate a program of study or observation and make records of what you see.

Be kind to habitats. Some species, such as certain salamanders, occur only in restricted areas. By ripping up all the rocks and other shelters, you may do irreparable damage or even exterminate the colony. Replace rocks, logs, and boards after you overturn them. Mind your outdoor manners, and leave the countryside in the same or better condition than that in which you find it. If you discover a colony of any rare or unusual species, keep the information to yourself. Like telling a secret, the news may soon reach the ears of an unscrupulous person who, for private gain, may raid the colony for the pet market.

INTRODUCTIONS: Our herpetological fauna is changing. Besides the several destructive factors mentioned in the paragraphs above, there is the insidious problem of the introduction of exotic species or the transplantation of some of our native amphibians and reptiles into areas where they do not naturally occur. The Giant Toad and the Bullfrog are now well established in many localities where they don't belong, and their large size and voracious appetites have resulted in their decimating or even extirpating some of our native species. A great many amphibians and reptiles have been introduced into Florida, a number of which are reproducing and thriving. Others may become established, or colonies that apparently had vanished may be found to have survived. For example, the introduced Spinytail Iguana, *Ctenosaura pectinata,* still occurs at Brownsville, Texas, even though it apparently had disappeared from there some years ago. If you find an exotic that seems to be doing well, report it to the nearest zoo or museum, or to us at the Museum of Natural His-tory, Dyche Hall, University of Kansas, Lawrence, Kansas 66045.

FOR THE SERIOUS STUDENT: If you have a deep interest in herpetology you may wish to read further on the subject or even join one of the organizations devoted to the study of reptiles and amphibians. Reference books and papers are listed on pp. 585–594. If there is a report available on any or all of these animals for your own state or region, get a copy and keep it handy for ready reference. Reptile and amphibian organizations and societies have been established in many cities, and information about them can be obtained by inquiring at your local zoo or natural history museum. General information on herpetology for students and amateurs is available from the Secretary, Division of Reptiles and Amphibians, National Museum of Natural History, Washington, D.C. 20560.

There are three major American societies devoted to herpetology. These are: The Society for the Study of Amphibians and Reptiles, publishers of *Herpetological Review, Journal of Herpetol-ogy,* and *Catalogue of American Amphibians and Reptiles;* the Herpetologists' League, publishers of *Herpetologica* and *Herpetological Monographs;* and the American Society of Ichthyologists and Herpetologists, publishers of *Copeia.* For information about these write to the Natural History Museum, Dyche Hall, The University of Kansas, Lawrence, Kansas 66045.

Making and Transporting
the Catch

Before you make any attempt to collect reptiles and amphibians, or even to keep them in captivity, you should check with your state authorities — the Fish and Game, Nongame, or Wildlife Department in your state capital or regional office. They can give you a list of the species that are protected and tell you about any restrictions of which you should be aware. Also they can provide you with a list of endangered or threatened reptiles and amphibians that are protected by federal regulations.

Rules and restrictions vary from state to state. In some states you may need a permit to collect. The number and kinds of specimens you can take may be stipulated. There may be closed seasons of a month or more for certain species. Transporting reptiles and amphibians across state lines may be prohibited, and so also may be the buying or selling of them. You may even need a permit to keep your catch as pets in your home. Some states are far more liberal than others, but it is wise to find out all about the rules that apply to you so you will not get into trouble.

Once you have this basic information, the following suggestions will be helpful.

Your own two hands are the best tools for catching reptiles and amphibians. Most kinds can just be grabbed, but you had better be quick about it, for they are adept at slipping away. But *never try to catch a venomous snake unless you have received training on how to do it.* Learn to recognize the dangerous species instantly.

Large, harmless snakes can be caught without equipment after a little practice. One method is to immobilize the snake by stepping on it gently while you reach for the nearest stick with which to pin down its head. Or, if you are good at balancing yourself, you can use your other foot instead of a stick. Once the head is under control, you can pick up the serpent by grasping it firmly but gently behind the jaws. Use your thumb and middle finger to do the grasping, and place your index finger on top of the snake's head. Another method requires more skill and nerve. This consists of seizing the snake by tail or body and slinging it quickly, but gently, between your legs, meantime clamping your legs together to hold the reptile as in a vise. By pulling the snake slowly forward —tail first, of course—you will eventually come to the head and can grasp it in the approved fashion. Wear blue jeans or clothe yourself in some other tough fabric before you try this, however. Some nonvenomous snakes can bite hard, and you will be exposed to attack from the rear.

A slapping-down technique can be used for those lizards and frogs that freeze in place instead of dashing away. This consists of slapping your flattened hand over them and pinning them down while you grasp a leg (or legs) with your other hand. Don't slap too hard, or there will be casualties. You will have less difficulty in stalking your quarry if you *don't look directly at it.* Move in at an angle, watching it out of the corner of your eye.

Numerous other tricks are used to catch amphibians and reptiles by hand, and you may invent some of your own. Tools are essential for some purposes, though, particularly since considerable field work consists of overturning rocks and other objects beneath which reptiles and amphibians may have taken shelter. Each herpetologist has an opinion about what implements are best. Here are some of the important tools and their uses.

SNAKE STICK (OR SNAKE HOOK): This is an L-shaped instrument with the long arm serving as a handle; the short arm consists of a piece of metal flattened at the bottom and suitable for pinning a snake to the ground (Fig. 2). A golf putter that has been filed down makes a good snake stick. So also does a forged and tempered metal hook securely fastened to a wooden handle. A more simple and easily constructed type consists of an angle iron screwed to the end of a square stick, but it may break or bend if you use it for turning rocks. You will want to experiment, especially in deciding what handle length is best suited to your own stature and techniques. The traditional forked stick is of little value. If the fork is too large, small snakes will slip right through it; if too small, it may severely injure the neck of a large snake.

SNAKE TONGS: A mechanical device 3 or 4 feet (90 cm or 1.2 m) long that depends upon spring action. By pressing a hand grip, jaws can be made to grasp the body of a snake. Releasing the grip frees the snake. Such tongs are available commercially.

CAUTION: Don't attempt to catch or handle venomous snakes unless you have received professional training and are prepared to suffer the consequences of a snakebite accident. The photographs on the opposite page show safe ways to hold and transport amphibians and reptiles. Always use common sense when carrying these creatures — do not expose them to the hot sun or to cold temperatures.

1. **A BULLFROG,** like other amphibians, is slippery. Encircle its waist with your fingers so it won't kick itself free. Any large- or medium-sized frogs may be held in the same way, but small frogs are best grasped by the hind legs.

2. **A SNAPPING TURTLE'S TAIL** makes a good handle, but keep the head aimed away from your leg.

3. **LARGE SALAMANDERS** should be held firmly but gently with the entire hand. Let the head protrude. Small salamanders can be caged briefly within your clenched fist.

4. **LIZARDS** are best immobilized by holding their feet, but the body should also be gripped to prevent sudden lunges. Make it a practice *never* to grab or hold a lizard by the tail, for it may break right off in your hands.

5. **SOFTSHELLS** are difficult to hold. Pressing against the neck with your fingers will help keep the head from protruding far enough to turn around and bite at you. Also watch out for flailing legs with their sharp claws.

6. **CARRYING A SNAKE BAG.** With your hand held well above the knot and the bag held away from your leg, a venomous snake may be safely transported. In the case of harmless species, the knot and the empty part of the bag may be thrust upward under your belt, letting the snake dangle there until you return to your car or base. This leaves both hands free.

7. **GLASS JARS** are safest for transporting small, fragile specimens. They retain moisture and may save your catch from injury. More than one collector has sat or stepped on a collecting bag with fatal consequences to the specimens inside.

8. **A STEVEDORE'S HOOK** works well on logs, boards, and smaller rocks, but it requires stooping. An advantage is that it can be thrust under your belt when not in use. A small handpick is very good for most flat rocks, even large ones, but it must be carried.

9. **A POTATO RAKE** or similar tool is useful for overturning rocks. The long handle lets you stand erect and keeps you well away if by chance you should uncover a venomous snake.

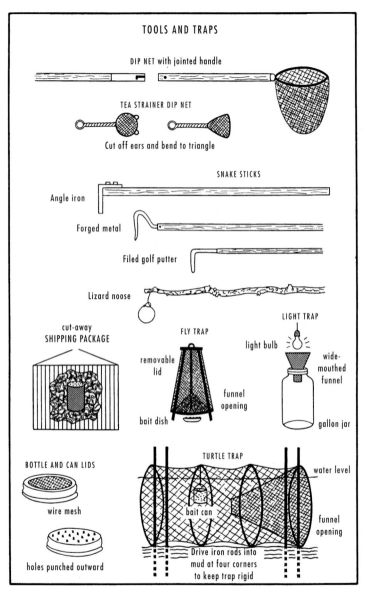

Fig. 2. *Tools used in catching and transporting reptiles and amphibians. Fly and light traps are useful for gathering live insects to feed captive lizards, toads, treefrogs, etc.*

POTATO RAKE AND STEVEDORE HOOK: See Fig. 1 for use of these tools.

COLLECTING BAGS: These are available commercially, or you, possibly with the help of some member of your family, can make your own. Unbleached muslin or any other sturdy kind of fabric will do. It is well to have two or three different sizes of bags: a large one measuring roughly 20 by 36 inches (50 by 90 cm), a medium one of perhaps 12 by 24 inches (30 by 60 cm), and a small one of about 8 by 16 inches (20 by 40 cm). Pillowcases are acceptable, but beware of castoffs that have worn thin and will rip the instant they touch a briar or any other snag in the field.

Loop one or two large bags through your belt to have them handy, and carry little ones in your pocket. Bagging small snakes is generally easy, but with large ones it is best to have your companion hold the bag while you drop in your catch. If the snake is venomous be sure to carry it in a bag in the manner shown in Fig. 1. Incidentally, it is prudent practice never to go snake hunting alone. Trying to bag a venomous snake all by yourself is not recommended. If you are bitten, you will need someone else to help get you to a doctor.

After a specimen has been caught and placed inside a cloth bag, the simplest way to confine it is to tie an overhand knot in the top (Fig. 1). Be careful not to tie the knot around the neck of a snake that may be crawling upward in its efforts to escape! The use of string for tying bags is not recommended—it is something extra to carry with you, it might work loose, and both large and small snakes, in struggling to get out, have been known to push string right off the neck of a bag.

If you catch amphibians, wet the bottoms of the bags and throw in a handful of moss, wet leaves, or other damp vegetation. Putting these animals in plain bags will dry them out, and they will die of desiccation. Even reptiles will survive better if their environment is slightly moist. Remove all livestock from bags as soon as possible; otherwise they may develop sore noses and feet from trying to escape. Wash bags thoroughly before using them again.

Plastic bags are also favored for field work—not the type you use in a refrigerator, but bags fashioned from heavy, sturdy plastic. These are translucent (even almost transparent) so you can see your catch, and lizards cannot climb upward as they frequently do in cloth bags. These bags are excellent for holding amphibians during the spring collecting season. Unacceptable bags are those made of canvas, which are too heavy and too closely woven for most purposes, and those made of burlap, which are useless for almost all amphibians and reptiles: the weave is so open and loose they can get through it with little effort.

GLASS JARS AND CANS: Punch holes in lids with points *aimed outward*. A tidier job can be done by soldering wire screening to the inner side of a screw-top lid, the kind that is open in the center and is little more than a rim. Both jars and cans have advantages and disadvantages. Glass jars can be broken, but you can see their contents. Cans will stand being dropped, but they will rust (unless they are made of aluminum), and you cannot tell in advance whether the animal is ready to leap out the moment you remove the lid. Jars made of opaque plastic are also dangerous for the same reason.

DIP NET: An ordinary crabbing net will do as a starter, but a deeper, finer-mesh bag will be necessary for holding baby turtles. The original handle will be too long to fit comfortably into the average automobile. Cut the handle in half and provide it with a ferrule and locking device for quick assembling or dismounting (Fig. 2).

TEA STRAINER DIP NET: An ordinary tea strainer, bent to triangular shape and with its ears lopped off or folded out of the way, makes a handy gadget for catching salamanders. These slippery and elusive amphibians, which normally hide or scurry away when rocks are overturned along tumbling brooks, can often be worked into a tea strainer dip net. When one gets in, clap your hand over the top and you've made your capture.

TURTLE TRAP: There are several different ways to trap turtles, but a simple, efficient device can be made from three sturdy wire hoops and a supply of stout corded fisherman's netting with a mesh of one inch (2.5 cm) or slightly smaller. Make the hoops 30 inches (75 cm) in diameter, give or take a little. (Measure the trunk of your car or your storage closet to see what size will fit conveniently.) Tie netting to the hoops to form a collapsible, barrel-shaped trap about 4 or 5 feet (1.2 or 1.5 m) long. At one end fashion a narrow, slitlike throat extending into the trap and through which a turtle can enter readily (Fig. 2). The other end of the barrel can be netted over solidly, or another throat can be installed. For the bait, select a can with a tight-fitting lid and about the same size as an ordinary drinking tumbler. Punch numerous holes through the can, through lid, sides, and bottom. Fill the can with freshly chopped raw fish or chicken entrails and hang it from the top of the trap so the bait is completely submerged. The trap can be kept rigidly in place by driving iron bars or rods (the rods used for reinforcing concrete are ideal) down through the ends of the trap and into the mud. Or, the trap can be made to float by attaching it to two logs or two pieces of timber, one along each side. When placing the trap, be sure its top extends above the surface of the water. Unless they can get air, turtles entering it may drown.

HEADLAMPS AND FLASHLIGHTS: Amphibians, especially frogs and toads in chorus, are easily found after dark with the aid of a flashlight. So are aquatic snakes, salamanders, and certain other amphibians and reptiles. For many purposes a headlamp, strapped around your forehead and powered by batteries fastened to your belt, is superior, particularly since it leaves both hands free for grabbing. Headlamps can be purchased from sporting goods stores or camp outfitters.

LIZARD CATCHERS: Using a noose is an excellent way to catch lizards without harming them. Attach a small noose of nylon fishing leader or fine thread to the end of a pole measuring a few feet in length. (If you use cotton or nylon thread, rub the noose frequently with paraffin to keep it stiff while you are in the field.) Walk up slowly and quietly and slip the noose over the lizard's head and let it come to rest around the neck. Jerk the pole quickly upward, and the lizard is yours! This method requires practice but is quite efficient when mastered.

Drift fences and pitfall traps are also useful in catching lizards, especially fast-running terrestrial ones. Drive stakes into the ground at intervals in a straight line, and attach small-mesh netting, wire, or hardware cloth, leaving no openings under it. The fence should be at least 18 inches (45 cm) high and as long as convenient. One of us (RC) used lengths in excess of 50 feet (15 m) collecting Whiptails in arid western Texas. At both ends of the fence bury a smooth-sided metal container, such as a large open-topped storage can, 18 inches or more deep, so that its rim is level with the surface of the ground. Several collectors working together a few yards or meters apart can walk slowly toward the fence, driving the lizards ahead of them. Once the reptiles reach the barrier they will turn and run along the fence and then fall into one of the cans. Pitfall traps, using even smaller cans or large, wide-mouthed glass jars, may be similarly buried and covered with a flat rock or board set a little above ground level so that small animals can run under it. In areas well populated by wildlife, such pitfall traps may yield an amazing variety of specimens, including not only lizards but also frogs, toads, and small snakes.

SHIPPING CONTAINERS: It occasionally may be necessary or desirable to send specimens to a friend or an institution such as a zoo or museum. Large snakes or turtles should be bagged and then placed inside a strong wooden box provided with numerous small holes to permit the flow of air to the inmates. In the case of venomous snakes, wrapping the entire container in stout wire hardware cloth provides a safeguard against escape if the box should be crushed or broken in transit.

Smaller amphibians and reptiles require special packing. Use a plastic storage container (of the type sold for use in refrigerator-freezers) with air holes in the lid, nearly fill it with slightly damp paper towels (moister for amphibians than for reptiles), and place the animals inside. The towels will not only prevent desiccation but will keep the travelers from getting shaken up too much. Nest the plastic storage container in the center of a cardboard box or Styrofoam cooler filled with excelsior (Fig. 2), shredded paper, or crumpled newspapers. Allow at least three inches of packing material on all sides of the plastic container. This material will help serve as insulation against heat or cold, and the space between its components becomes a reservoir of air during shipping. The package may be sealed on the outside if desired. Mark it "perishable" and use air or overnight express service if the recipient is some distance away. Snakes and turtles are barred from the U.S. mails. They and, in fact, all reptiles and amphibians are best sent by express or some other common carrier.

All of these instructions apply to shipment within the United States. Do *not* ship any live amphibians or reptiles to another country. A special federal permit, usually issued only to zoos and research institutions, is required.

As a good conservationist you will sort your catch in the field, select only the specimens you need for your studies, and liberate the others. Don't be a game hog!

Be sure to keep a record of the source of your material. If you should find something unusual or wish to tell a professional herpetologist about it, he or she will need certain basic information —the exact locality in which it was found, the date, collector's name and address, a description of the habitat, notes on the animal's behavior, and other pertinent data.

3

CARE IN CAPTIVITY

After you catch a snake or frog or turtle, what do you do with it? If you are the average outdoor enthusiast you will hold it briefly, check its identity, admire its coloration and pattern, perhaps photograph it, and then turn it loose. But you may wish to keep it for a time. Some reptiles and amphibians are relatively easy to maintain in captivity. They are fun to watch, and the surest way to learn something about them is to keep them close at hand, but, unless you plan special studies or observations, they should be liberated *where you found them* in not more than two or three weeks.

HOUSING THE CATCH: The most versatile of all cages is a home aquarium. Perhaps you have one left over from a former interest in mollies, guppies, or other tropical fishes. If not, aquariums are relatively inexpensive to buy. Get a roomy one—15 inches (38 cm) or more in length and at least 8 to 10 inches (20 to 25cm) in both width and height, and preferably with a custom-made, tight-fitting lid. If your purchase does not come with such a lid, then make a tight, heavy one of wire screening tacked onto a wooden frame. A secure lid is very important, for reptiles and amphibians can crawl, leap, or push their way out with startling agility. Even salamanders, because of the natural adhesion of their wet bodies against the glass, can readily walk up and out. If you are planning to keep lizards or treefrogs, build your own lid with two hinged doors so you can get your hand inside to service half their quarters at a time (Fig. 3). Don't try to catch these little animals and remove them every time their cage needs cleaning. And that brings up an important rule: Don't handle any specimen more than is necessary. Most of them will settle down and thrive best when they are undisturbed.

Once it is equipped with a lid, your aquarium is ready to serve as a terrarium, a cage, or as a true aquarium for aquatic species.

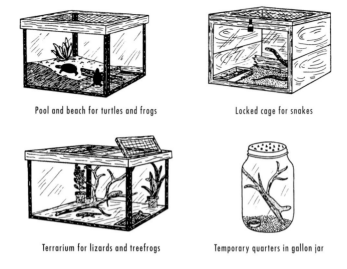

Pool and beach for turtles and frogs

Locked cage for snakes

Terrarium for lizards and treefrogs

Temporary quarters in gallon jar

Fig. 3. Living quarters for smaller reptiles and amphibians are easily made from old aquariums, wooden boxes, and glass one-gallon pickle, mustard, and mayonnaise jars.

PREPARING A TERRARIUM: Attractively planted terrariums make excellent homes for many kinds of amphibians, lizards, and small turtles. Fill the bottom of an aquarium with small, clean pebbles to a depth of an inch (2.5 cm) to provide drainage. Cover them with 2 to 3 inches of standard greenhouse potting soil to help keep the soil sweet. Then add about an inch of sandy soil. Small plants can be rooted in this, but it is easier and much more practical simply to put the plants in a flower pot, and place the pot (or pots) in the terrarium with its base resting on the soil or pebble layer. When you clean up, you lift out the pot instead of having to uproot the plants each time. Treefrogs and lizards of some kinds like to cling to the sides of a pot. Typical hothouse plants should be selected, ones that will stand watering two or three times a week. When they are sprinkled the lizards will lap up the drops. (Many lizards will *not* drink regularly from a water dish.) Other terrarium residents, such as frogs and toads, need a shallow water container made of glass, plastic, or nonrusting or noncorroding metal. Small branches may be placed in the cage for specimens that like to climb.

For lizards from arid habitats, the terrarium should be floored with pea-sized pebbles, and potted cactus plants may be used as an appropriate decoration. Such plants cannot stand a daily sprinkling, but water for the lizards can be provided by filling a shallow container to the brim and letting a little of the water spill over to provide a circle of damp pebbles around the dish.

Snakes normally do not make good terrarium animals, for they may burrow down out of sight and uproot plants, soil, and pebbles. Many toads and turtles may do likewise. Such specimens, if they are to be seen at all, are best kept on bare pebbles, but potted plants and shelters may be added.

Hiding places are a necessity, particularly for snakes and salamanders. A piece of bark with its concave side down makes a good shelter under which the residents may secrete themselves; natural cork bark, procurable from most first class florist shops, is ideal. Small, flat stones may be piled up to make a miniature cave, but they must be stacked carefully so they will not collapse on the animals. Small, flattish cardboard boxes, with their lids in place and with holes cut through their sides, may also be used, but in the damp environment of a terrarium they may disintegrate; they are better suited for dry cages. Plastic butter tubs, with an opening cut on the side at floor level, make good hiding places. They do not degrade and are easily cleaned.

THE SEMIAQUATIC TERRARIUM: Water-loving turtles, newts, and the more aquatic types of frogs often do best if they have a choice of wet and dry environments. This can be accomplished by inserting a partition across the center of the aquarium and piling pebbles on one side of it. The partition can be of stone or slate, or, if these are not at hand, a piece of wood may be used with its ends held firmly by small wooden wedges inserted between the wood and the glass. The pebbles provide a beach on which a potted plant and a shelter may be placed; the other half of the aquarium may be left in open water. Baby turtles may need a ramp, perhaps a small rough stone or piece of bark, on which to climb ashore.

THE TRUE AQUARIUM: Only a few kinds of reptiles and amphibians can live in water in straight-sided aquariums with no place to crawl out. These include mud, musk, and softshell turtles, rainbow, mud, and swamp snakes, aquatic newts, sirens, amphiumas, mudpuppies, waterdogs, and hellbenders. All of these should have a stone cave at the bottom of the aquarium to serve as a retreat. Aquatic vegetation may be used with most of them, and, in fact, some plant growth to furnish resting and hiding places is almost essential for the smaller kinds.

THE CAGE: The simplest type of cage is, once again, the home aquarium. For snakes and some kinds of terrestrial lizards, fold or cut sheets of newspaper (about four or five pages in thickness) to fit the bottom of the aquarium exactly. These will serve to absorb excess moisture, and when they become soiled they are easily discarded and replaced. More substantial cages are not difficult to construct. The one illustrated in Fig. 3 has wooden sides, back, and bottom, a glass front, and a screened top. The top is hinged at the back and is provided with hasp and staple for a lock. No air holes are necessary at the sides if the top is completely screened; in fact, snakes will rub their noses sore on any rough objects, such as wire tacked over air holes at cage-floor level.

Install a water dish large enough for the snake to submerge itself completely but heavy enough so it cannot be tipped over. Also provide a hiding place. Bark or stones will do, but here is where the cardboard box with a hole in its side serves to perfection. With the snake inside the box it is a simple matter to lift out the serpent and its house while the cage is cleaned. Most snakes, including water snakes, thrive best if their quarters are kept completely dry except for the contents of the water dish. When conditions are too damp snakes often develop skin blisters and infections.

TEMPORARY QUARTERS: A wide-mouthed one-gallon glass jar can serve as a temporary home for almost any small or medium-sized reptile or amphibian. This can be equipped with stones, sticks, etc., but plain crumpled paper towels are more practical. These can be dampened slightly (for lizards and snakes) or wet thoroughly (for amphibians and turtles). Not only do the towels supply moisture, but they also serve as hiding places. The jar should be cleaned at least every other day, and before replacing the towels a small amount of cool (not cold) water should be poured in to give the animals a chance to get a drink. In general, temporary quarters should not be used for much more than a week or so. Transfer their inmates to permanent cages or terrariums as quickly as possible.

TEMPERATURES: Reptiles and amphibians are cold-blooded animals whose temperatures, unless they are exposed to sunlight or heatlamps, closely approximate the temperatures of the room or cages in which you keep them. When they are cold, body functions slow down and appetites are poor or nonexistent. When they are too warm they suffer distress; too much heat will kill them. Temperatures of about 75° to 85° Fahrenheit (24°C to 30°C) are best for the majority of reptiles; most amphibians will thrive under somewhat cooler conditions, usually below 70°F (21°C).

In summer, specimens may be kept in any comparatively cool place, such as a well-ventilated camp building or in the basement of your home. Some sunshine is usually essential for lizards and turtles; snakes can get along with less of it if they eat well and are given good food. If you keep your reptiles indoors, provide them with an alternative to sunlight, such as a fluorescent Vita-Lite. If kept outside, provision must be made so that the animals can bask or retreat to the shade in accordance with their own desires. Hence, outdoor cages should be roomy and supplied with hiding places. Never set a cage wholly in the sunshine or in a spot where the sun may strike it later in the day and roast your captives.

In winter, normal room temperatures (without too much nightly chilling) are suitable for most amphibians. Reptiles, if they are to be active, need to be kept warmer. During the cooler months your herpetological collection should be installed in a warm part of the house, and the best location can be determined by running a few tests with a thermometer for a day or two. Check for the ideal temperatures mentioned above. Avoid too much drop at night. For example, don't place cages in a bedroom where the window normally would be opened at night.

Supplementary heat may be needed, especially for lizards, and this can be supplied by placing a sunlamp (not infrared) with a reflector atop the cage in such a way as to direct the heat downward. If the cage is large, the sunlamp should be mounted at an end or side so the reptiles may retreat to a cooler spot if they wish. If the cage is small, the sunlamp should be left on only for limited periods of time. Many lizards enjoy temperatures of 95°F (35°C) for a few hours daily, but such readings are too high for most other reptiles and amphibians. Test with a thermometer and adjust your heat source by moving it closer or farther away to produce the proper temperature. Basking places for most lizards, in the form of twigs or small branches, should be provided. Feed the lizards when they are well warmed up.

Don't expect your captives to eat with the same avidity in the winter as they do in warm weather, even when they are well supplied with heat. Some of them, turtles and crocodilians in particular, will go off feed for weeks or months at a time. When hunger strikes are prolonged, it is often best to transfer the fasters to cooler quarters with temperatures in the fifties (10° to 15°C) until spring, but they must be provided with water.

FOOD: The very large majority of reptiles and amphibians are carnivorous or insectivorous. A few eat vegetable matter.

Nearly all kinds of turtles (except the vegetarian Gopher and Texas Tortoises) may be fed canned dog food, but be sure to choose a brand that is nearly all meat. It is advisable to add vitamins and minerals even though the label on the can may indicate the contents have been fortified. The simplest method is to use a drop or two of a vitamin-mineral concentrate and a pinch of bone meal or dicalcium phosphate powder (for extra calcium) to the dog food or to lean ground meat, and then stir it in thoroughly. Mold the mixture into small rounded pellets and place them at the water's edge—not in it. The turtles will then take a piece at a time. (Of course, if they are in straight-sided aquariums, you will have to drop the food right in with them, but do it sparingly and with due regard for their appetites. There is no point in fouling the water unnecessarily.) Most turtles will also eat chopped fish (be sure to include entrails) and any natural food such as insects, worms, or freshly killed tadpoles. Do not feed them crayfish (crawdads)—these may transmit diseases to the turtles.

Turtles of almost all kinds will also eat some vegetable matter, with lettuce being the least nutritious. A piece of spinach, kale, beet tops, or other leafy vegetable should be given at least once each week. Lawn cuttings are savored by some. Tortoises and box turtles should have greens as well as a variety of soft fruits and berries. Even though they may show a preference for vegetable matter, box turtles should be given a chance to eat meat occasionally. However, the diet of Gopher and Texas Tortoises should be almost all vegetable matter.

A good labor-saving practice is to train your turtles to eat in a feeding bowl or pan supplied with shallow water. Place the turtles gently in it and then drop the food near their mouths. Once they get used to this procedure they will eat and strew their food around in an easily cleaned container rather than in their home aquarium. Rinse the turtles off with tepid water before putting them back.

Some kinds of reptiles and amphibians require live insects or other invertebrates. Toads and frogs and most lizards and salamanders are in this category, and the motion of their prey serves as a triggering mechanism that induces them to spring into action. Some of these animals will starve to death even if surrounded by platoons of dead insects. Drop in a live one and it will be seized at once.

Supplying live insects is not difficult during the warmer months. Examine window screens at night for beetles and moths attracted by the lights inside. The simplest method for collecting them consists of placing a jelly glass over the insect, and then sliding a card between the rim and the screen. The same apparatus can be used for imprisoning spiders you may find in basements, under eaves, or other lurking places. A light trap is an efficient way of obtaining nocturnal insects in quantity. Get a one-gallon glass jar and solder a wide-mouthed kitchen funnel to a large hole cut through its lid. Screw on the lid, place the jar on the ground outdoors at night, and set an electric light bulb an inch or two (2.5 to 5 cm) above the mouth of the funnel (Fig. 2). Insects will fly to the light and then tumble into the jar. A fly trap, for use in daytime, can be made on the same general pattern, but upside down and of wire (also see Fig. 2). This is set an inch (2.5 cm) or so above a dish of meat or fish. The flies are attracted to the bait, but in leaving it they fly upward. They strike the wire funnel, walk up it, pass through its neck, and then enter the wire cage above. Never use insects that have been exposed to fly sprays or chemicals. Your captives may be killed if they eat them.

Obtaining insects in winter is another matter, at least if you live in Canada or the northern states. Live crickets may be purchased from bait supply houses, as well as tropical-fish stores. If you intend keeping lizards and frogs in any quantity you will have to raise flies and meal worms or other insects, and you will have to start weeks or months ahead of time. Consult any experienced zoo reptile keeper or your government department of entomology for instructions.

Small salamanders and frogs will eat tiny crickets, which you can buy through tropical-fish dealers. Until fairly recently live brine shrimp and live tubifex worms were also widely available from the same source, but these are now freeze-dried or frozen for feeding aquarium fishes. Larger amphibians eat earthworms, which you can probably dig up for yourself except in the coldest weather. There are a few large biological supply houses, however, that still sell brine shrimp and tubifex worms alive or which also can supply white or red worms. If you need such small live foods in quantity, ask your local tropical-fish store to order them for you.

Snakes have specialized feeding habits, and their food is mentioned in the text for each group or species.

A SUGGESTION: Keeping reptile and amphibian pets is an interesting pastime, but it does take time and effort. In most instances you will find it practical to hold specimens for only a few days or weeks, studying them until you grow quite familiar with them and then liberating them where you caught them. Do not turn them loose in a strange environment. In any event do not keep them after it is obvious they are deteriorating for lack of food or for some other reason. If by any chance you should acquire an exotic reptile or amphibian from another state or even another country and no longer want it, give it to a zoo or museum. Don't be cruel by liberating it in a strange place where it almost certainly will die.

PET STORES: In general, we recommend that you do not buy reptiles or amphibians from pet stores but that you catch your own. After all, the capture is at least half the fun and excitement, and also teaches you about the behavior and habitats of these animals.

Further, the sale by pet stores of turtles with shells less than four inches in length is prohibited by federal regulation because of Salmonella, a bacterial infection that can cause serious illness. You should establish personal procedures to prevent or control Salmonella in your own collection. Keeping the water clean by frequent changes is helpful. Don't let children play with turtles, especially if they are still young enough to cram all sorts of objects into their mouths. Wash your hands thoroughly after handling turtles. If you follow these rules, there is little likelihood of having trouble.

LARVAL AMPHIBIANS: Tadpoles and salamander larvae are fairly easy to maintain in aquariums. Tadpoles are largely vegetarian during their early stages, and they should be supplied daily with freshly boiled lettuce and a pinch of commercial flaked fish food. Older tadpoles and salamander larvae are carnivorous and will usually thrive on canned dog food or ground beef that has been fortified with vitamins and minerals. As the time approaches for transformation to the adult stage, a floating object, such as natural cork bark, should be placed in the aquarium so the animals can crawl out when they so desire. Aquatic salamanders should be fed brine shrimp (available in frozen form) and insects.

WORDS OF CAUTION: Remember that many persons dislike reptiles, snakes especially. Your neighbors may resent your keeping such creatures unless you can assure them that your pets are under strict control at all times. Lock all snake cages to forestall escapes and to prevent the younger members of your family from getting into mischief. *Under no circumstances should venomous snakes be kept in a private home or apartment.*

AND A FINAL WORD: If you plan to keep harmless amphibians and reptiles as pets, consult your local zoo, regional or state herpetological society, nature center, wildlife rehabilitation center, or natural history museum for advice on how to maintain them. Be informed in advance, and the rewards of keeping amphibians and reptiles will be greatly enhanced for you.

IN CASE OF SNAKEBITE

In almost all parts of our area snakebite is a rarity, and in many states there have been no fatalities from that cause for decades. Bites still occur, however, and knowing what to do and what not to do should be part of the mental equipment of anyone who spends much time out-of-doors in places where venomous snakes are found. Here are a few brief suggestions.

1. Wear protective clothing. Rubber or knee-high leather boots are of some help. Use sturdy, high shoes for hiking or climbing on rocks, not sneakers or low shoes. Watch where you put your hands and feet when you are in rough country. Don't thrust hands under rock ledges, logs, or stumps that might harbor serpents. Stay on paths or trails, and watch where you walk. Obey the cardinal rule for hiking in wild or wilderness areas — never go off alone and always stay within call of your companions.

2. Be familiar with the venomous snakes of the area where you are. Study the illustrations on Pls. 30 and 34 to 36 and the text and maps associated with them. Learn to recognize the various kinds on sight. Also learn to recognize the "mimics," the nonvenomous snakes that resemble the dangerous ones. Milk or other snakes frequently are mistaken for copperheads and water snakes for cottonmouths; several harmless serpents resemble coral snakes. If you can be sure that a nonvenomous species did the biting, it will put your mind and those of your companions at ease. Large numbers of persons are bitten by harmless snakes each year.

3. If you are bitten by a venomous snake, get to the nearest hospital or medical facility as quickly as possible and, if you can, ask someone to telephone ahead that you are coming. This will give the attending physician time to prepare and to call the nearest poison information center for advice, if needed. A leading expert has stated that the most effective snakebite first aid kit consists of car keys and some coins with which to call a hospital.

4. If you are with someone who is bitten by a venomous snake, immobilize the limb and carry the person to your car, if you are able to do so. Urge him or her to keep calm and point out that, with proper care, the possibility of a fatality is virtually zero.

The old, oft-repeated "first-aid" instructions about making cuts through or near the site of the bite and then applying suction have been largely abandoned. Lacerations by untrained persons are apt to sever nerves or major blood vessels, thus leading to complications that may result in amputation of toes or fingers. Also, tourniquets are no longer recommended; those applied too tightly have been known to cause serious problems.

The universally accepted treatment for snakebite is the use of antivenom or snakebite serum. It should be administered only by a doctor. By law it can be dispensed only through prescription, and it may not always be available. A few hospitals and drug supply houses in some of the larger cities keep it in stock, particularly in the South where the most numerous and especially serious bites may occur. In these days of rapid transportation, however, it usually can be flown, under emergency conditions, to wherever needed.

Most cases of snakebite occur within an hour of medical help. You may have a summer home or cabin, however, from which travel may be much greater, and you may wish to prepare yourself for a possible emergency. Only two devices are recommended as this book goes to press. First is the Sawyer Extractor (Sawyer Products, Long Beach, California), a small, lightweight, durable kit that may help in extracting some of the snake's venom. Its use will also permit you to feel you are doing something to help. Second, an elastic bandage for use in the rare case of *coral snake bite only*. It can be applied to the bitten limb as you would wrap a sprained ankle, but don't wrap it too tightly. Do not use it for pit viper (copperhead, cottonmouth, or rattlesnake) bites.

The time-honored practice of killing the snake involved and taking it with you still has merit. Care must be exercised, however. Use a long stout stick, and handle the snake with extreme caution. Reflex action may last a long time and supposedly dead pit vipers have been known to bite. One of us (RC), who was the recognized "snake man" in a very large metropolitan area, received close to a hundred telephone calls over a period of some decades, from doctors in hospitals who wanted to be sure whether the snake was venomous or not before initiating treatment. When questioned about details of pattern and scutellation and the presence or absence of facial pits in the dead snake at hand, the result was that only a single venomous one, a copperhead, was involved. All others were harmless.

Snake venom is a liquid, usually yellowish in color, secreted by glands on the sides of the head and injected into a victim by grooved or hollow fangs. Venoms, which vary from species to species, are complex mixtures of chemicals capable of producing many destructive changes in body tissues and fluids. The effects vary, as well as the amount of venom injected. This is another reason why getting to a doctor is so important. He can follow clinical procedures that may be required, and he can determine whether a "dry" bite occurred, i.e., one in which no venom was actually injected.

The best advice is to avoid all venomous snakes. Just look at them in the field from a safe distance. Don't try to catch them unless you have had professional coaching on how to do it. A few kinds are now so rare that they are protected by law in some states.

Under no circumstances should you keep dangerous snakes as pets, especially in your home. Some people still take the extraordinary risk of keeping cobras, vipers, and other very dangerous snakes as pets. Let zoo and museum curators and research scientists maintain live captives of such snakes. They fully understand how to care for them properly and safely.

The Arizona Poison and Drug Information Center in Tucson, Arizona, serves as a national clearinghouse for data on snakebite. It also maintains an up-to-date list of which types of foreign antivenoms are available in different zoos across the country, and can advise a doctor which zoo to call in the event of a bite from an exotic venomous snake. The Center's telephone number is (520) 626-6016. Regional Poison Information Centers can also help.

Sherman A. Minton, M.D., and David L. Hardy, M.D., leading experts on snakebite treatment, contributed to and reviewed the information on this subject.

Symbols and Explanation of Scale

♂ means male and ♀ means female

These symbols, universally used in zoology and appearing frequently on the plates and legend pages that follow, are borrowed from astronomy. The ♂ represents the shield and spear of Mars and the ♀ the looking glass of Venus. Both symbols have long been used in referring to the planets bearing those two names.

Ssp. (for subspecies)

This designation signifies that the species (or subspecies) illustrated has one or more additional races that are not shown on the plates but that are discussed in the text. Some subspecies look so very much alike that recourse must be made to scale counts or other anatomical details to tell them apart. In such cases, only one subspecies is illustrated. Many of the reptiles and amphibians of the eastern and central United States and Canada have extralimital subspecies, the ranges of which are indicated in part on the maps as Western or Mexican subspecies.

Scale

All the animals depicted on any one plate are shown in scale with one another. But a black line across a plate denotes a change in scale, as in the case of the young crocodilians on Plate 1, which are shown proportionately larger than the adults.

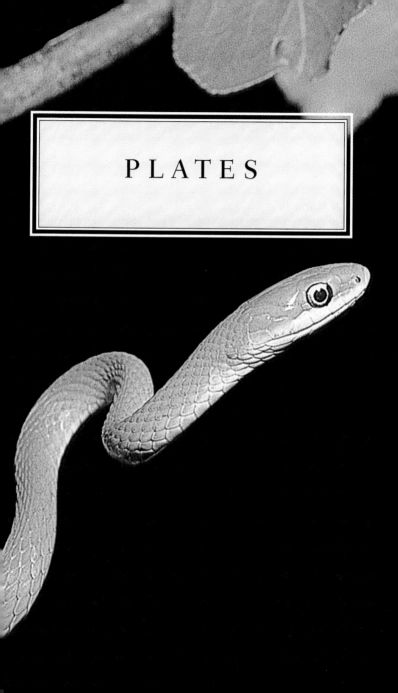

PLATES

PLATE 1

CROCODILIANS

YOUNG

AMERICAN ALLIGATOR, *Alligator mississippiensis*   **P. 143**
> Black with yellowish lines. Head smooth in front of eyes (as in adult Alligator shown on plate).

SPECTACLED CAIMAN, *Caiman crocodilus*   **P. 144**
> Gray with dark brown crossbands. A curved, bony, crosswise ridge in front of eyes (Fig. 4).

AMERICAN CROCODILE, *Crocodylus acutus*   **P. 142**
> Gray or greenish gray with black crossbands or rows of spots. Head tapering toward snout (as in adult Crocodile shown on plate).

ADULTS

AMERICAN CROCODILE   **P. 142**
> Tapering head; 4th tooth of lower jaw fitting into a groove in upper jaw and remaining visible when mouth is closed (Fig. 4). General coloration paler than that of Alligator.

AMERICAN ALLIGATOR   **P. 143**
> Broadly rounded snout; dark-colored, virtually black.

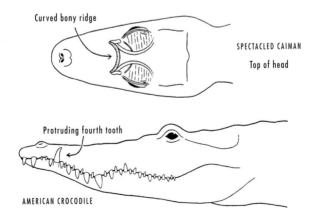

Curved bony ridge

SPECTACLED CAIMAN

Top of head

Protruding fourth tooth

AMERICAN CROCODILE

Fig. 4. *Head characteristics of Crocodilians.*

PLATE 1

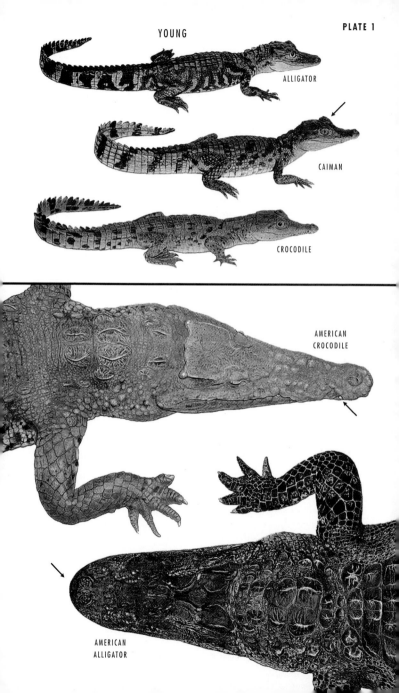

YOUNG

ALLIGATOR

CAIMAN

CROCODILE

AMERICAN
CROCODILE

AMERICAN
ALLIGATOR

PLATE 2

MUSK TURTLES (*Sternotherus*)

COMMON MUSK TURTLE, S. *odoratus*   P. 150
   Two light lines on head; plastron small. ♂: Large areas of skin between plastral scutes; large, stout tail. ♀: Plastral scutes close together.

STRIPENECK MUSK TURTLE, S. *minor peltifer*   P. 152
   Head and neck striped; a dorsal keel (Fig. 28).

RAZORBACK MUSK TURTLE, S. *carinatus*   P. 151
   Head spotted; strong dorsal keel (Fig. 28).

FLATTENED MUSK TURTLE, S. *depressus*   P. 153
   Netlike head pattern; shell flattened (Fig. 28).

LOGGERHEAD MUSK TURTLE, S. *minor minor*   P. 152
   ♂: Very large head. ♀: Head moderate; shell streaked, spotted, or blotched. *Young:* Shell streaked; three keels (Fig. 28).

MUD TURTLES (*Kinosternon*)

STRIPED MUD TURTLE, K. *baurii*   P. 155
   Shell and head usually striped—see text.

MISSISSIPPI MUD TURTLE, K. *subrubrum hippocrepis*   P. 155
   Two light lines on head; plastron large.

EASTERN MUD TURTLE, K. *subrubrum subrubrum*   P. 153
   Nondescript; rounded shell; plastron large.

YELLOW MUD TURTLE, K. *flavescens* (ssp.)   P. 156
   Throat plain yellow; 9th marginal higher than 8th; pectoral scutes narrowly in contact (Fig. 29).

BIG BEND MUD TURTLE, K. *hirtipes murrayi*   P. 157
   Head spotted; 10th marginal higher than 9th; pectoral scutes broadly in contact (Fig. 29).

GOPHER TORTOISES (*Gopherus*)

GOPHER TORTOISE, G. *polyphemus*   P. 188
   Foot elephant-like; shell relatively long.

TEXAS TORTOISE, G. *berlandieri*   P. 189
   Foot elephant-like; shell relatively short.

PLATE 2

COMMON MUSK

plastron ♀

plastron ♂

STRIPENECK MUSK

RAZORBACK MUSK

FLATTENED MUSK

young

♂

old ♀

LOGGERHEAD MUSK

STRIPED MUD

MISSISSIPPI MUD

EASTERN MUD

plastron

YELLOW MUD

BIG BEND MUD

GOPHER TORTOISE

TEXAS TORTOISE

PLATE 3

YOUNG TURTLES (1)

COMMON MUSK TURTLE, *Sternotherus odoratus*   P. 150
    Light head lines; edge of shell with light spots.

LOGGERHEAD MUSK TURTLE, *Sternotherus minor minor*   P. 152
Three keels along top of shell. *Plastron:* Pink.

EASTERN MUD TURTLE, *Kinosternon subrubrum subrubrum*   P. 153
    No lines on head. *Plastron:* Orange to pale yellow, dark at center.

COMMON MAP TURTLE, *Graptemys geographica*   P. 167
    Yellow spot behind eye; maplike lines on shell. *Plastron:* Dark
    lines along seams.

MISSISSIPPI MAP TURTLE, *Graptemys kohnii*   P. 170
    Yellowish crescent behind eye. *Plastron:* Broad dark markings
    with open centers.

BARBOUR'S MAP TURTLE, *Graptemys barbouri*   P. 168
    Saw-backed; broad light area behind eye and another across chin.

WOOD TURTLE, *Clemmys insculpta*   P. 159
    Shell rough; head dark, unmarked; long tail.

BLANDING'S TURTLE, *Emydoidea blandingii*   P. 188
    Light marks on head; chin yellow; long tail.

FLORIDA BOX TURTLE, *Terrapene carolina bauri*   P. 161
    Yellow middorsal stripe; mottled pattern.

EASTERN BOX TURTLE, *Terrapene carolina carolina*   P. 160
    Light spot in each large scute. *Plastron:* Dark pigment concen-
    trated toward center.

SPOTTED TURTLE, *Clemmys guttata*   P. 158
    Light spot in each large scute *and spots on head. Plastron:* Dark
    pigment toward center.

ALLIGATOR SNAPPING TURTLE, *Macroclemys temminckii*   P. 148
    Shell extremely rough; beak strongly hooked; long tail.

SNAPPING TURTLE, *Chelydra serpentina*   P. 146
    Shell rough, edged with light spots; long tail.

PLATE 3

COMMON MUSK

LOGGERHEAD MUSK

EASTERN MUD

COMMON MAP

MISSISSIPPI MAP

BARBOUR'S MAP

WOOD

BLANDING'S

FLORIDA BOX

EASTERN BOX

SPOTTED

ALLIGATOR SNAPPER

SNAPPER

PLATE 4

YOUNG TURTLES (2)

WESTERN PAINTED TURTLE, *Chrysemys picta bellii*   **P. 186**
Pale, wormlike markings. *Plastron:* Dark area large and with outward extensions.

MIDLAND PAINTED TURTLE, *Chrysemys picta marginata*   **P. 185**
No bold markings. *Plastron:* Dark central blotch.

SOUTHERN PAINTED TURTLE, *Chrysemys picta dorsalis*   **P. 186**
Broad red, orange, or yellow stripe.

EASTERN PAINTED TURTLE, *Chrysemys picta picta*   **P. 185**
The large scutes have light borders. *Plastron:* Usually unmarked.

NORTHERN DIAMONDBACK TERRAPIN, *Malaclemys terrapin terrapin*   **P. 165**
Dark lines parallel edges of scutes (both shells).

RED-EARED SLIDER, *Trachemys scripta elegans*   **P. 176**
Red patch or stripe behind eye. *Plastron:* Circular markings large and involving all parts of shell.

YELLOWBELLY SLIDER, *Trachemys scripta scripta*   **P. 176**
Large yellow patch behind eye. *Plastron:* Circular markings on forepart of shell.

PENINSULA COOTER, *Pseudemys floridana peninsularis*   **P. 182**
Curved lines on shell. *Plastron:* Unmarked. Dark spots on anterior marginals.

HIEROGLYPHIC RIVER COOTER, *Pseudemys concinna hieroglyphica*   **P. 180**
Markings circular, especially on marginals. *Plastron:* Markings chiefly along seams.

CHICKEN TURTLE, *Deirochelys reticularia*   **P. 187**
Network of light lines; has striped "pants" (Fig. 7, opp. Pl. 7).

FLORIDA SOFTSHELL, *Apalone ferox*   **P. 199**
Head striped; large round spots. *Plastron:* Dark.

EASTERN SPINY SOFTSHELL, *Apalone spinifera spinifera*   **P. 195**
Small circular spots. *Plastron:* Light and nearly matching underside of carapace.

SMOOTH SOFTSHELL, *Apalone mutica*   **P. 194**
Indistinct dots and dashes. *Plastron:* Light. (Underside of carapace brown.)

PLATE 4

WESTERN PAINTED

MIDLAND PAINTED

SOUTHERN PAINTED

EASTERN PAINTED

NORTHERN DIAMONDBACK

RED-EARED

YELLOWBELLY

PENINSULA COOTER

HIEROGLYPHIC
RIVER COOTER

CHICKEN

FLORIDA SOFTSHELL

EASTERN SPINY SOFTSHELL

SMOOTH
SOFTSHELL

PLATE 5

BOX, WOOD, AND SPOTTED TURTLES; DIAMONDBACK TERRAPINS

ORNATE BOX TURTLE, *Terrapene ornata ornata*   **P. 162**
   Carapace: Flattened or depressed on top; radiating light lines.
   Plastron: Transverse hinge; bold light lines.

EASTERN BOX TURTLE, *Terrapene carolina carolina* (ssp.)   **P. 160**
   Carapace: High, domelike; yellow, orange, or olive markings on
   dark brown or black. *Plastron:* Transverse hinge; pattern variable.

FLORIDA BOX TURTLE, *Terrapene carolina bauri*   **P. 161**
   Shell arched, highest toward rear, and with radiating light lines;
   two yellow stripes on head.

THREE-TOED BOX TURTLE, *Terrapene carolina triunguis*   **P. 162**
   Orange on head (and often on forelimbs); three toes on *hind* foot;
   shell pattern much reduced or absent.

BOG TURTLE, *Clemmys muhlenbergii*   **P. 159**
   Orange head patch; small size.

SPOTTED TURTLE, *Clemmys guttata*   **P. 158**
   Scattered yellow spots; orange or yellow spots on head.

BLANDING'S TURTLE, *Emydoidea blandingii*   **P. 188**
   Carapace: Profuse light spots. *Plastron:* Transverse hinge. *Bright
   yellow throat.*

WOOD TURTLE, *Clemmys insculpta*   **P. 159**
   Orange on neck and legs; shell rough, sculptured.

ORNATE DIAMONDBACK TERRAPIN,   **P. 165**
Malaclemys terrapin macrospilota (ssp.)
   Orange or yellow in center of each large scute. Salt and brackish
   water only.

NORTHERN DIAMONDBACK TERRAPIN,   **P. 165**
Malaclemys terrapin terrapin (ssp.)
   Concentric rings on each large scute. Salt and brackish water
   only.

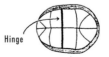

*Fig. 5. Blanding's and Box Turtles have a hinge across the plastron
(lower shell).*

PLATE 5

ORNATE BOX

plastron

EASTERN BOX

plastron

FLORIDA BOX

THREE-TOED BOX

BOG

BLANDING'S

SPOTTED

plastron

WOOD

NORTHERN DIAMONDBACK

ORNATE DIAMONDBACK

PLATE 6

MAP TURTLES (*Graptemys*)

Females of all species grow larger than males.

TEXAS MAP TURTLE, *G. versa*   **P. 172**
Horizontal or J-shaped line behind eye; anterior scutes of carapace distinctly convex (examine closely).

BLACK-KNOBBED MAP TURTLE, *G. nigrinoda*   **P. 173**
Rounded, black knobs; narrow light rings.

RINGED MAP TURTLE, *G. oculifera*   **P. 172**
Broad light rings.

ALABAMA MAP TURTLE, *G. pulchra*   **P. 169**
Broad, light bars on marginals; longitudinal light bar under chin (Fig. 32). ♀: Large and big-headed like Barbour's Map Turtle.

YELLOW-BLOTCHED MAP TURTLE, *G. flavimaculata*   **P. 173**
Solid orange or yellow spots.

BARBOUR'S MAP TURTLE, *G. barbouri*   **P. 168**
Narrow, light markings on marginals; a *curved* or transverse bar under chin (Fig. 32). *Mature* ♀: Very large; head enormous; pattern obscure.

MISSISSIPPI MAP TURTLE, *G. kohnii*   **P. 170**
Yellow crescent, cutting off neck stripes from eye.

FALSE MAP TURTLE, *G. pseudogeographica* (ssp.)   **P. 170**
Yellow spot behind eye; neck stripes reach eye; middorsal spines conspicuous.

COMMON MAP TURTLE, *G. geographica*   **P. 167**
Yellowish spot behind eye; maplike pattern, middorsal spines not prominent.

Fig. 6. A basking False Map Turtle.

PLATE 6

TEXAS

BLACK-KNOBBED

RINGED

ALABAMA

YELLOW-BLOTCHED

BARBOUR'S

MISSISSIPPI

FALSE

COMMON

PLATE 7

PAINTED AND CHICKEN TURTLES;
SLIDERS AND REDBELLY

See Pl. 4 for the young of many of these turtles.

MIDLAND PAINTED TURTLE, *Chrysemys picta marginata*   **P. 185**
    Large scutes arranged in alternating fashion.

EASTERN PAINTED TURTLE, *Chrysemys picta picta*   **P. 185**
    Large scutes with broad olive edges and arranged more or less in straight rows *across* back.

WESTERN PAINTED TURTLE, *Chrysemys picta bellii*   **P. 186**
    Light, wormlike or netlike lines on carapace; bars on marginals.

SOUTHERN PAINTED TURTLE, *Chrysemys picta dorsalis*   **P. 186**
    Broad red or orange stripe (sometimes yellowish).

YELLOWBELLY SLIDER, *Trachemys scripta scripta*   **P. 176**
    Yellow head blotch; vertical yellowish bars on shell; leg stripes *narrow*; has striped "pants" (Fig. 7).

CHICKEN TURTLE, *Deirochelys reticularia* (ssp.)   **P. 187**
    Long striped neck; light network on shell; leg stripe broad; has striped "pants" (Fig. 7).

RED-EARED SLIDER, *Trachemys scripta elegans* (ssp.)   **P. 176**
    ♀ *and young:* Reddish stripe behind eye. ♂: Reddish stripe reduced; completely obscured in old specimens (see text).

REDBELLY TURTLE, *Pseudemys rubriventris*   **P. 182**
    ♀: Vertical, reddish markings (persisting even in very dark specimens). ♂: Dark; markings irregular (see text).

YELLOWBELLY
Narrow leg stripes

BOTH
Striped "pants"

CHICKEN
Broad leg stripe

Fig. 7. Pattern characteristics of Yellowbelly Slider and Chicken Turtle.

PLATE 7

MIDLAND PAINTED

EASTERN PAINTED

WESTERN PAINTED

SOUTHERN PAINTED

YELLOWBELLY

CHICKEN

♂

♀

old ♂

RED-EARED

♀

♂

REDBELLY

PLATE 8

COOTERS, RIVER COOTERS, AND FLORIDA REDBELLY (*Pseudemys*)

PENINSULA COOTER, *P. floridana peninsularis* **P. 182**
 "Hairpins" on head; dark marginal smudges; plastron unmarked.

FLORIDA REDBELLY TURTLE, *P. nelsoni* **P. 183**
 Light vertical band; few stripes on head (Fig. 8).

EASTERN RIVER COOTER, *P. concinna concinna* **P. 178**
 A figure C; undersurfaces heavily marked.

FLORIDA COOTER, *P. floridana floridana* **P. 181**
 No "hairpins"; hollow circles on marginals; plastron as in Peninsula Cooter.

TEXAS RIVER COOTER, *P. texana* **P. 180**
 Broad head markings; undersurfaces basically like Eastern River Cooter's but reduced to narrow dark lines.

SUWANNEE RIVER COOTER, *P. concinna suwanniensis* **P. 179**
 A figure C; carapace dark; plastron like Eastern River Cooter's.

HIEROGLYPHIC RIVER COOTER, *P. concinna hieroglyphica* (ssp.) **P. 180**
 A figure C; shell pinched inward in front of hind legs; undersurfaces like Eastern River Cooter's.

FLORIDA
REDBELLY

Arrowhead at snout

Second scute
Broad line

Mouth. Cusps
flank notch

PENINSULA
COOTER

Light "hairpins"

Second scute
Narrow lines

Mouth. No notch,
no cusps

No arrow; no "hairpins"

SUWANNEE
RIVER COOTER

Second scute
Light figure "C"

Fig. 8. Head and scute patterns of three southeastern turtles.

Note: Patterns, often obscure in large specimens, are best seen if the turtle is submerged in water. The illustrations of the Eastern River Cooter and Texas River Cooter are of relatively young individuals, chosen to show the distinctive markings that fade or even disappear in old adults. These two turtles are reproduced at the scale of large adults. Note that their heads are disproportionately large.

PLATE 8

PENINSULA COOTER

plastron

FLORIDA REDBELLY

EASTERN RIVER COOTER

plastron

FLORIDA COOTER

SUWANNEE RIVER COOTER

TEXAS RIVER COOTER

HIEROGLYPHIC RIVER COOTER

PLATE 9

SNAPPING TURTLES

ALLIGATOR SNAPPING TURTLE, *Macroclemys temminckii* **P. 148**
Extra row of scutes at side of carapace; three prominent ridges along back; head very large, beaks strongly hooked.
SNAPPING TURTLE, *Chelydra serpentina* (ssp.) **P. 146**
Long, saw-toothed tail.

SEA TURTLES

LOGGERHEAD, *Caretta caretta* **P. 192**
Reddish brown; five (or more) costal plates, 1st touching the nuchal; 3 or 4 bridge scutes.
ATLANTIC RIDLEY, *Lepidochelys kempii* **P. 192**
Gray; five costal plates, 1st touching the nuchal; an interanal scute; usually four bridge scutes (Fig. 9).
GREEN TURTLE, *Chelonia mydas* **P. 191**
Four costal plates, 1st *not* touching the nuchal; one pair of plates between eyes (Fig. 37).
LEATHERBACK, *Dermochelys coriacea* **P. 193**
Prominent ridges along back; no scutes; smooth skin.
ATLANTIC HAWKSBILL, *Eretmochelys imbricata imbricata* **P. 191**
Tortoiseshell pattern; scutes overlap (varies—see text); two pairs of plates between eyes (Fig. 37).

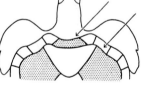

GREEN and HAWKSBILL
Nuchal separated from costal

LOGGERHEAD and RIDLEY
Nuchal touches first costal

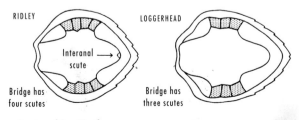

RIDLEY

Interanal → scute

Bridge has four scutes

LOGGERHEAD

Bridge has three scutes

Fig. 9. Scutes of Sea Turtles.

PLATE 9

ALLIGATOR SNAPPER

SNAPPER

LOGGERHEAD

GREEN

RIDLEY

HAWKSBILL

LEATHERBACK

PLATE 10

SOFTSHELLS *(Apalone)*

Consult text for descriptions of females not illustrated.

WESTERN SPINY SOFTSHELL, *A. spinifera hartwegi*   **P. 197**
    ♂: Shell with dark spots and small, eyelike marks; feet strongly streaked and spotted. Top of shell rough; feels like sandpaper, at least toward rear.

SMOOTH SOFTSHELL, *A. mutica* (ssp.)   **P. 194**
    Feet *not* strongly patterned. Shell smooth; no spines or bumps. No ridge in nostril (Fig. 10). ♂: Vague dots and dashes. ♀: An indefinite, mottled pattern.

EASTERN SPINY SOFTSHELL, *A. spinifera spinifera*   **P. 195**
    Feet strongly patterned. ♂: Large, eyelike spots; top of shell sand-papery. ♀: Pattern vague (see text); spines at front of shell.

GULF COAST SPINY SOFTSHELL, *A. spinifera aspera*   **P. 197**
    ♂: Two or more rows of curved black lines bordering rear edge of shell. Light lines on head usually meet (Fig. 38).

GUADALUPE SPINY SOFTSHELL,   **P. 198**
A. spinifera guadalupensis (ssp.)
    ♂: Numerous light dots.

FLORIDA SOFTSHELL, *A. ferox*   **P. 199**
    Shell proportionately longer than in other species. Anterior surface of shell with numerous small bumps in form of flattened hemispheres.

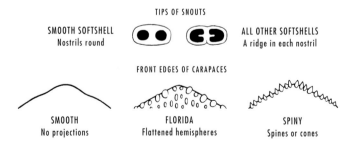

TIPS OF SNOUTS

SMOOTH SOFTSHELL
Nostrils round

ALL OTHER SOFTSHELLS
A ridge in each nostril

FRONT EDGES OF CARAPACES

SMOOTH
No projections

FLORIDA
Flattened hemispheres

SPINY
Spines or cones

Fig. 10. Nostrils and carapaces (upper shells) of Softshells.

PLATE 10

WESTERN SPINY ♂

SMOOTH ♂

♀

EASTERN SPINY ♀

♂

GULF COAST SPINY ♂

GUADALUPE SPINY ♂

FLORIDA ♂

♀

PLATE 11

GECKOS

ASHY GECKO, *Sphaerodactylus elegans elegans*   **P. 204**
    Adult: Tiny *light* spots on a dark ground color. *Young:* Dark crossbands; reddish tail.

FLORIDA REEF GECKO, *Sphaerodactylus notatus notatus*   **P. 204**
    Dark markings on a lighter ground color. ♂: Numerous small, dark spots. ♀: *Dark* head stripes; often two light spots on shoulder.

OCELLATED GECKO, *Sphaerodactylus argus argus*   **P. 205**
    Numerous white spots; tail light brown or reddish.

YELLOWHEAD GECKO, *Gonatodes albogularis fuscus*   **P. 206**
    Adult ♂: Yellowish head; body bluish (or black). ♀ *and young:* Light collar; body mottled.

TEXAS BANDED GECKO, *Coleonyx brevis*   **P. 206**
    Light crossbands (or mottlings) on a brown ground color; *movable eyelids.*

MEDITERRANEAN GECKO, *Hemidactylus turcicus turcicus*   **P. 203**
    Toe pads *broad* (Fig. 11); dorsum warty.

INDO-PACIFIC GECKO, *Hemidactylus garnotii*   **P. 204**
    Toe pads broad like those of Mediterranean Gecko (Fig. 11); dorsum smooth; belly lemon-yellow; pale red under tail.

ROUGHTAIL GECKO, *Cyrtopodion scabrum*   **P. 202**
    Rough, enlarged, keeled scales on tail; sand-colored with dark brown spots.

TOKAY GECKO, *Gekko gecko*   **P. 202**
    Pale bluish gray with numerous *brick red to orange* spots; prominent wartlike bumps cover head, body, legs, and tail; enlarged toe pads (see text).

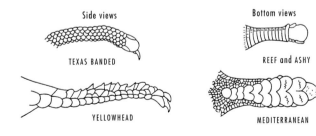

Fig. 11. *Toes of Geckos.*

PLATE 11

ASHY
adult
young

♂ FLORIDA REEF ♀

OCELLATED

YELLOWHEAD

♀ ♂

TEXAS BANDED

MEDITERRANEAN

INDO-PACIFIC

ROUGHTAIL

TOKAY

PLATE 12

WALL AND CURLYTAIL LIZARDS; BASILISK AND LARGE IGUANIDS

COMMON WALL LIZARD, *Podarcis muralis*　　　　　　　　**P. 246**
　Often with dark markings on the throat and *blue spots* on the shoulder; six rows of belly scales.

ITALIAN WALL LIZARD, *Podarcis sicula*　　　　　　　　**P. 247**
　Throat usually uniform white or gray; six rows of belly scales; often with *green* dorsum.

NORTHERN CURLYTAIL LIZARD, *Leiocephalus carinatus armouri*　　**P. 244**
　Low raised crest of scales down middle of back; dull gray or brown in color with dark bands on tail. Curls tail over back when prowling.

RED-SIDED CURLYTAIL LIZARD, *Leiocephalus schreibersii schreibersii* **P. 245**
　Low crest of scales down middle of back; tan to sandy in color with *light* spots on back; side with *reddish orange streaks*. Curls tail.

SPINYTAIL IGUANA, *Ctenosaura pectinata*　　　　　　　**P. 216**
　Lacks a single large smooth scale on throat below ear; a low *crest* of scales from head down middle of back to base of tail; tail strongly spined (see text).

BROWN BASILISK, *Basiliscus vittatus*　　　　　　　　**P. 215**
　♂: Large rounded or triangular crest on head; ♀: Small lobe at back of head.

GREEN IGUANA, *Iguana iguana*　　　　　　　　　　**P. 217**
　Large, round, smooth *scales on throat below ear opening*; row of spines down back onto tail, strongly developed in ♂, less so in ♀; large dewlap under chin, spiny along its anterior edge.

PLATE 12

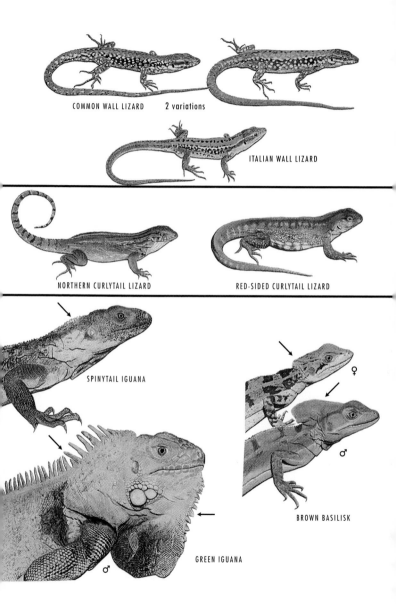

COMMON WALL LIZARD   2 variations

ITALIAN WALL LIZARD

NORTHERN CURLYTAIL LIZARD

RED-SIDED CURLYTAIL LIZARD

SPINYTAIL IGUANA

BROWN BASILISK

GREEN IGUANA

PLATE 13

ANOLES (*Anolis*)

BROWN ANOLE, *A. sagrei*　　　　　　　　　　　　　　　**P. 211**
　　Always brown. ♂: Vertical rows of yellowish spots. ♀: Light mid-
　　dorsal stripe with scalloped edges.

BARK ANOLE, *A. distichus*　　　　　　　　　　　　　　**P. 214**
　　Crossbanded tail and dark line between eyes (Fig. 41).

GREEN ANOLE, *A. carolinensis*　　　　　　　　　　　　**P. 209**
　　Green or brown or mottled with both.

PUERTO RICAN CRESTED ANOLE, *A. cristatellus cristatellus*　　**P. 213**
　　Light brown to greenish gray. ♂: Crest on body and tail; some-
　　times with dark body bands. ♀: Light middorsal stripe bordered by
　　thinner dark stripes.

LARGEHEAD ANOLE, *A. cybotes cybotes*　　　　　　　　**P. 214**
　　Some shade of brown; never wholly green. ♂: Often with green-
　　ish stripes on side. ♀: Usually plain orange-brown with middorsal
　　light stripe.

JAMAICAN GIANT ANOLE, *A. garmani*　　　　　　　　　**P. 212**
　　Leaf green to brown. ♂: Large; prominent crest on back of head
　　and neck; nine or more body bands (sometimes faint). ♀: Small;
　　row of dorsal spots.

KNIGHT ANOLE, *A. equestris equestris*　　　　　　　　　**P. 210**
　　Large size; yellowish lines on shoulder and from beneath eye to
　　ear opening.

THROAT FANS OF MALE ANOLES

BROWN ANOLE　　　　　　　　　　　　　　　　　　　**P. 211**
　　Orange-red with whitish border.

BARK ANOLE　　　　　　　　　　　　　　　　　　　　**P. 214**
　　Yellow with pale orange blush.

GREEN ANOLE　　　　　　　　　　　　　　　　　　　**P. 209**
　　Pink.

PUERTO RICAN CRESTED ANOLE　　　　　　　　　　　**P. 213**
　　Olive, yellow, or orange-yellow with orange border.

LARGEHEAD ANOLE　　　　　　　　　　　　　　　　　**P. 214**
　　Pale yellow or grayish yellow, sometimes with pale orange center.

JAMAICAN GIANT ANOLE　　　　　　　　　　　　　　　**P. 212**
　　Lemon yellow with orange center.

KNIGHT ANOLE　　　　　　　　　　　　　　　　　　　**P. 210**
　　Pink.

See also Fig. 40.

PLATE 13

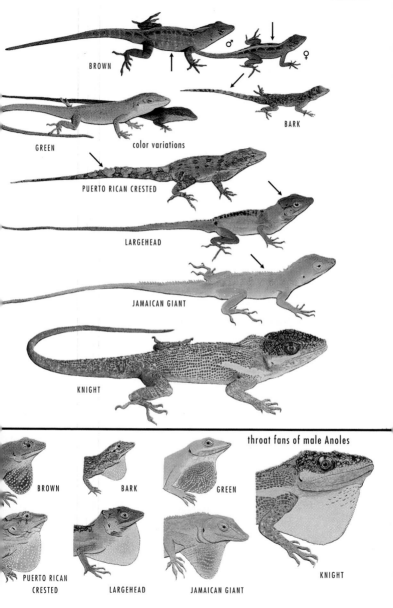

BROWN ♂ ♀

BARK

GREEN color variations

PUERTO RICAN CRESTED

LARGEHEAD

JAMAICAN GIANT

KNIGHT

throat fans of male Anoles

BROWN

BARK

GREEN

PUERTO RICAN CRESTED

LARGEHEAD

JAMAICAN GIANT

KNIGHT

PLATE 14

EARLESS, SIDE-BLOTCHED, AND HORNED LIZARDS

TEXAS EARLESS LIZARD, *Cophosaurus texanus texanus*   **P. 222**
Black crossbars under tail. ♂: Two black lines on lower side near groin and invading a blue field on belly.

SOUTHWESTERN EARLESS LIZARD, *Cophosaurus texanus scitulus*   **P. 223**
Black ventrolateral bars broad; body color different from that of hind legs and tail.

SPOT-TAILED EARLESS LIZARD, *Holbrookia lacerata* (ssp.)   **P. 225**
Dark dorsal blotches with light borders; dark streaks at edge of belly; dark spots under tail (Fig. 43).

KEELED EARLESS LIZARD, *Holbrookia propinqua propinqua*   **P. 226**
Tail long. ♂: Two short, black lines near armpit. ♀: Markings absent or indistinct; variable (see text).

NORTHERN EARLESS LIZARD, *Holbrookia maculata maculata*   **P. 223**
Tail short. ♂: Two short lines near armpit; faint longitudinal stripes; pale specklings faint and indistinct.

EASTERN EARLESS LIZARD, *Holbrookia maculata perspicua*   **P. 224**
♀: Distinct blotches or spots on back; suggestion of black lines near armpit; faint longitudinal stripes.

SPECKLED EARLESS LIZARD, *Holbrookia maculata approximans*   **P. 225**
Tail short. No light lines on body; dorsum with pale specklings, especially prominent in male.

DESERT SIDE-BLOTCHED LIZARD, *Uta stansburiana stejnegeri*   **P. 239**
Black spot posterior to armpit.

MOUNTAIN SHORT-HORNED LIZARD,   **P. 243**
Phrynosoma douglassii hernandesi
Horns little more than nubbins (Fig. 45); bright colors on head and body.

EASTERN SHORT-HORNED LIZARD, *Phrynosoma douglassii brevirostre*   **P. 242**
Horns little more than nubbins (Fig. 45); coloration dull.

TEXAS HORNED LIZARD, *Phrynosoma cornutum*   **P. 241**
Two central horns greatly elongated (Fig. 45).

ROUNDTAIL HORNED LIZARD, *Phrynosoma modestum*   **P. 243**
Tail crossbanded and round in cross section; large horns all about the same length (Fig. 45).

PLATE 14

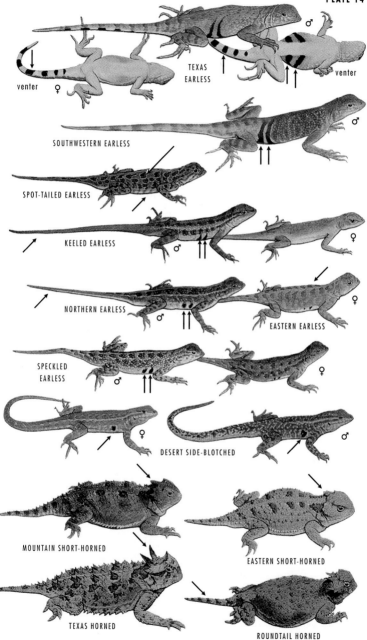

venter

TEXAS EARLESS

venter

♂

♀

SOUTHWESTERN EARLESS ♂

SPOT-TAILED EARLESS

KEELED EARLESS ♂ ♀

NORTHERN EARLESS ♂ EASTERN EARLESS ♀

SPECKLED EARLESS ♂ ♀

DESERT SIDE-BLOTCHED ♀ ♂

MOUNTAIN SHORT-HORNED

EASTERN SHORT-HORNED

TEXAS HORNED

ROUNDTAIL HORNED

PLATE 15

TREE AND SPINY LIZARDS (*Urosaurus* and *Sceloporus*)

(See also Pl. 16)

Males of most species have a blue patch at each side of belly.

TREE LIZARD, *U. ornatus* (ssp.)   **P. 238**
> Irregular dark spots; dorsal scales variable—some large, some tiny; a fold across throat (Fig. 12, below).

ROSEBELLY LIZARD, *S. variabilis marmoratus*   **P. 228**
> Row of dark spots bordered below by a light stripe; a pocket at rear of thigh (Fig. 44). ♂: Dark spot above armpit; large *pink* patch on each side of belly.

MESQUITE LIZARD, *S. grammicus microlepidotus*   **P. 228**
> Wavy, dark crosslines (in ♀); scales at sides of neck much smaller than scales on nape (Fig. 44).

FENCE LIZARD, *S. undulatus hyacinthinus* (ssp.)   **P. 232**
> ♀: Wavy, dark crosslines. ♂: Nearly unicolored above; dark blue throat patch surrounded by black.

PRAIRIE LIZARD, *S. undulatus garmani* (ssp.)   **P. 233**
> A row of small, dark spots bordered below by a *bold* light stripe; secondary light stripe along lower side of body.

CANYON LIZARD, *S. merriami* (ssp.)   **P. 237**
> A vertical black bar in front of foreleg; a partially developed throat fold (Fig. 42).

DUNES SAGEBRUSH LIZARD, *S. graciosus arenicolous*   **P. 236**
> Pale, nearly unicolored; small, granular scales on rear surface of thigh.

NORTHERN SAGEBRUSH LIZARD, *S. graciosus graciosus*   **P. 236**
> Four rows of dark longitudinal spots that may coalesce to form stripes; small, granular scales on rear of thigh.

FLORIDA SCRUB LIZARD, *S. woodi*   **P. 235**
> A prominent dark *brown* lateral stripe. ♀: Dark, wavy lines across back.

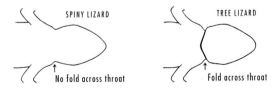

SPINY LIZARD — No fold across throat

TREE LIZARD — Fold across throat

Fig. 12. *Throat fold in two genera of lizards—present in Tree Lizard, absent in Spiny Lizards.*

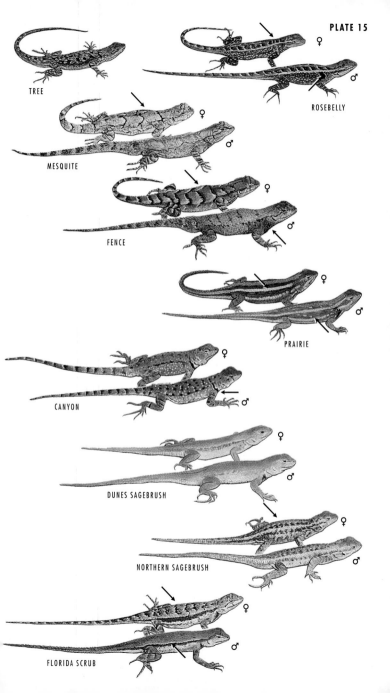

PLATE 15

TREE

ROSEBELLY ♀ ♂

MESQUITE ♀ ♂

FENCE ♀ ♂

PRAIRIE ♀ ♂

CANYON ♀ ♂

DUNES SAGEBRUSH ♀ ♂

NORTHERN SAGEBRUSH ♀ ♂

FLORIDA SCRUB ♀ ♂

PLATE 16

LARGE SPINY LIZARDS (*Sceloporus*)

(See also Pl. 15)
Males have a blue or blue-green patch at each side of belly.

TEXAS SPINY LIZARD, S. *olivaceus*   **P. 231**
 Pale, longitudinal, light stripe not sharply defined.

TWIN-SPOTTED SPINY LIZARD, S. *magister bimaculosus*   **P. 230**
 Black wedge or blotch on shoulder; twin spots on back not
 sharply defined.

CREVICE SPINY LIZARD, S. *poinsettii poinsettii*   **P. 229**
 Dark collar; tail strongly patterned near tip. ♀ *and young:* Dark
 bands across back.

BLUE SPINY LIZARD, S. *serrifer cyanogenys*   **P. 230**
 Dark collar; tail markings not clear-cut.

SOME FLORIDA INTRODUCTIONS

GIANT AMEIVA, *Ameiva ameiva*   **P. 260**
 Like an enormous Whiptail Lizard but with 12 rows of large rectangular plates on belly.

RAINBOW WHIPTAIL, *Cnemidophorus lemniscatus* complex **P. 259**
 Dark middorsal stripe; two narrow, indistinct, light dorsolateral
 stripes. Side of head and tail blue, the latter becoming greenish;
 flank golden yellow to yellowish brown with light spots.

PLATE 16

TEXAS SPINY

TWIN-SPOTTED SPINY ♀

♂

CREVICE SPINY ♀

♂

BLUE SPINY ♀

♂

GIANT AMEIVA

RAINBOW WHIPTAIL

PLATE 17

LEOPARD AND COLLARED LIZARDS
(*Gambelia* and *Crotaphytus*)

LONGNOSE LEOPARD LIZARD, *G. wislizenii wislizenii*   **P. 220**
    Profusion of brown spots; whitish crosslines often prominent on smaller specimens; head medium in size.

RETICULATE COLLARED LIZARD, *C. reticulatus*   **P. 219**
    Conspicuous black spots; head large.

EASTERN COLLARED LIZARD, *C. collaris collaris* (ssp.)   **P. 218**
    Two black collars across neck; head large.

WORM, GLASS, AND ALLIGATOR LIZARDS
(*Rhineura, Ophisaurus,* and *Gerrhonotus*)

FLORIDA WORM LIZARD, *R. floridana*   **P. 280**
    Like an earthworm; head scales distinctly evident when examined at close range.

SLENDER GLASS LIZARD, *O. attenuatus* (ssp.)*   **P. 276**
    No legs; dark middorsal stripe; dark stripes on lower sides.

EASTERN GLASS LIZARD, *O. ventralis**   **P. 275**
    No legs; no distinct dark middorsal stripe; greenish coloration. (Tip of tail regenerated.)

TEXAS ALLIGATOR LIZARD, *G. liocephalus infernalis*   **P. 279**
    Large scales; irregular light crosslines.

---

*There are four species of Glass Lizards, all confusingly alike. See text and Fig. 53.

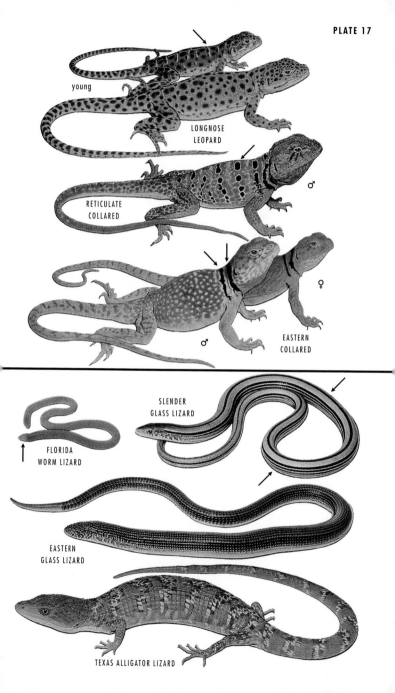

PLATE 17

young

LONGNOSE
LEOPARD

RETICULATE
COLLARED

♂

♂

♀

EASTERN
COLLARED

SLENDER
GLASS LIZARD

FLORIDA
WORM LIZARD

EASTERN
GLASS LIZARD

TEXAS ALLIGATOR LIZARD

PLATE 18

RACERUNNERS AND WHIPTAILS (*Cnemidophorus*)

SIX-LINED RACERUNNER, *C. sexlineatus sexlineatus*   P. 250
Six light stripes; dark stripes solid. (Only native member of genus occurring east of Mississippi R.)

PRAIRIE RACERUNNER, *C. sexlineatus viridis*   P. 250
Bright green coloration.

PLATEAU SPOTTED WHIPTAIL, *C. septemvittatus septemvittatus*   P. 257
Rump and base of tail rust-colored.

TEXAS SPOTTED WHIPTAIL, *C. gularis gularis*   P. 254
Prominent light spots in the dark lateral fields. Tail pink, pale orange-brown, or reddish.

DESERT GRASSLAND WHIPTAIL, *C. uniparens*   P. 253
Six light stripes; no light spots in dark fields.

NEW MEXICO WHIPTAIL, *C. neomexicanus*   P. 255
Seven light stripes, the center one *wavy*. Obscure light spots in dark fields.

TRANS-PECOS STRIPED WHIPTAIL, *C. inornatus heptagrammus*   P. 254
Blue tail. ♂: Blue on belly and side of head.

CHIHUAHUAN SPOTTED WHIPTAIL, *C. exsanguis*   P. 251
Six light stripes; pale spots on *both* the dark fields *and* light stripes. *Young:* Light stripes in strong contrast with dark fields.

MARBLED WHIPTAIL, *C. marmoratus marmoratus* (ssp.)   P. 258
A "gray" Whiptail. Highly variable; pattern may be striped, cross-banded, mottled, etc. (see text).

CHECKERED WHIPTAIL, *C. tesselatus* complex   P. 256
Black spots or squares on a tan or yellowish ground color.

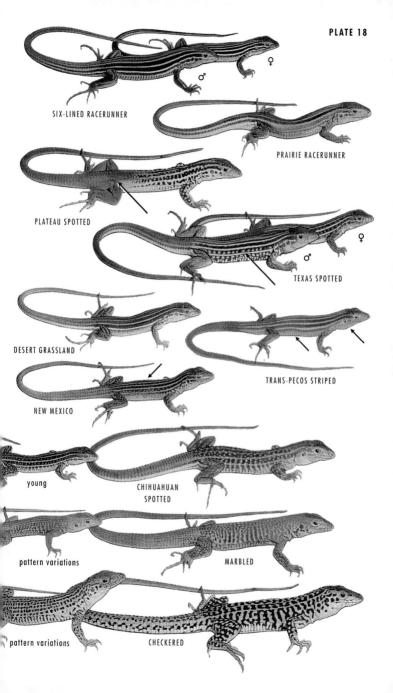

PLATE 18

SIX-LINED RACERUNNER

PRAIRIE RACERUNNER

PLATEAU SPOTTED

TEXAS SPOTTED

DESERT GRASSLAND

TRANS-PECOS STRIPED

NEW MEXICO

young

CHIHUAHUAN SPOTTED

pattern variations

MARBLED

pattern variations

CHECKERED

PLATE 19

SKINKS (*Eumeces, Neoseps,* and *Scincella*)

GREAT PLAINS SKINK, *E. obsoletus* **P. 266**
Dark-edged scales; suggestion of striping. *Young:* Black; bright head spots; blue tail.

SAND SKINK, *N. reynoldsi* **P. 274**
Tiny legs; only one or two toes.

GROUND SKINK, *S. lateralis* **P. 262**
Dark stripe; no light stripes.

MOLE SKINKS, *E. egregius* (ssp.) **P. 272–274**
Slender bodies; short legs. Variable (see text). Representatives of three subspecies illustrated; **PENINSULA,** *onocrepis;* **FLORIDA KEYS,** *egregius;* **BLUETAIL,** *lividus.*

SHORT-LINED SKINK, *E. tetragrammus brevilineatus* **P. 267**
Light stripes end at shoulder. *Young:* Blue tail.

FOUR-LINED SKINK, *E. tetragrammus tetragrammus* **P. 267**
Light stripes end near hind legs.

COAL SKINK, *E. anthracinus* (ssp.) **P. 268**
Light stripes extend onto tail; broad, dark stripe 2½ to 4 scales wide.

SOUTHERN PRAIRIE SKINK, *E. septentrionalis obtusirostris* **P. 270**
Middorsal area plain or only weakly patterned; broad, dark stripe not more than two scales wide.

NORTHERN PRAIRIE SKINK, *E. septentrionalis septentrionalis* **P. 269**
Stripes in middorsal area; broad, dark stripe not more than two scales wide.

NORTHERN MANY-LINED SKINK, *E. multivirgatus multivirgatus* **P. 271**
Light middorsal stripe flanked by bold, dark stripes; tail swollen at base.

VARIABLE SKINK, *E. multivirgatus epipleurotus* **P. 271**
Unicolored or striped. Variable (see text).

SOUTHEASTERN FIVE-LINED SKINK, *E. inexpectatus* **P. 264**
♀: Five light stripes, middle one narrow. ♂ *and young:* Similar to Five-lined Skink.

FIVE-LINED SKINK, *E. fasciatus* **P. 262**
♀: Five broad, light stripes. ♂: Traces of stripes; reddish on head. *Young:* Blue tail.

BROADHEAD SKINK, *E. laticeps* **P. 263**
♂: Body olive-brown; head reddish; grows very large. ♀ *and young:* Like Five-lined Skink.

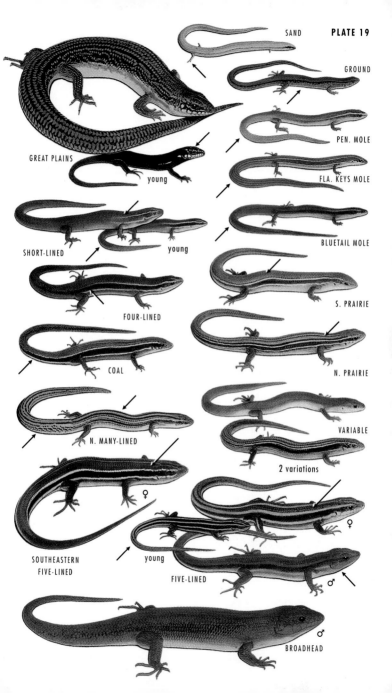

PLATE 19

SAND

GROUND

PEN. MOLE

FLA. KEYS MOLE

BLUETAIL MOLE

GREAT PLAINS

young

SHORT-LINED

young

FOUR-LINED

S. PRAIRIE

COAL

N. PRAIRIE

N. MANY-LINED

VARIABLE

2 variations

SOUTHEASTERN
FIVE-LINED

♀

♀

young

FIVE-LINED

♂

BROADHEAD

♂

PLATE 20

WATER SNAKES (NERODIA)

(See also Pl. 21)

Keeled scales and divided anal plates. The rectangles show belly colors and patterns.

BLOTCHED WATER SNAKE (young)   P. 292
  Dark spots on neck alternate with dorsal blotches.

NORTHERN WATER SNAKE (young)   P. 293
  Dark spots on neck join dorsal blotches to form crossbands.

MIDLAND WATER SNAKE, N. sipedon pleuralis   P. 295
  Dark markings narrower than lighter spaces between them, the latter usually more than 2½ scales wide. Belly: Double row of half-moons or crescents.

NORTHERN WATER SNAKE, N. sipedon sipedon (ssp.)   P. 293
  Dark markings wider than lighter spaces between them, the latter usually less than 2½ scales wide. Belly: Highly variable; half-moons paired, scattered, or virtually absent.

FLORIDA WATER SNAKE, N. fasciata pictiventris   P. 296
  Eye stripe (Fig. 55); black, brown, or red crossbands; often secondary dark spots on side. Belly: Wavy, wormlike crosslines.

BANDED WATER SNAKE, N. fasciata fasciata   P. 295
  Eye stripe (Fig. 55); black, brown, or red crossbands throughout length of body. Even in the darkest variations usually some red showing on sides. Belly: Largest markings squarish.

BROAD-BANDED WATER SNAKE, N. fasciata confluens   P. 297
  Eye stripe (Fig. 55); dark crossbands much wider than light interspaces. Belly: Large, squarish markings, red to black in coloration.

REDBELLY WATER SNAKE, N. erythrogaster erythrogaster (ssp.)   P. 291
  Plain brown above. Belly: Red or orange.

BLOTCHED WATER SNAKE, N. erythrogaster transversa   P. 292
  Dark lateral spots alternate with dorsal blotches throughout the length of body. Belly: Yellow with faint suggestions of spots.

YELLOWBELLY WATER SNAKE, N. erythrogaster flavigaster   P. 292
  Plain gray or greenish above. Belly: Yellow.

PLATE 20

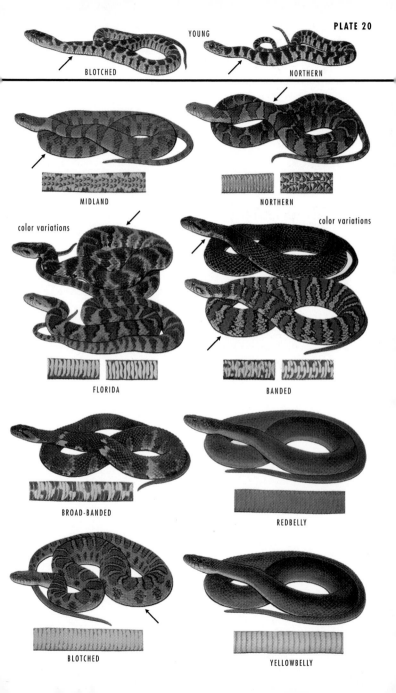

YOUNG

BLOTCHED

NORTHERN

MIDLAND

NORTHERN

color variations

FLORIDA

color variations

BANDED

BROAD-BANDED

REDBELLY

BLOTCHED

YELLOWBELLY

PLATE 21

WATER AND SALT MARSH SNAKES *(Nerodia)*

(See also Pl. 20)

Keeled scales and divided anal plates. The rectangles show belly colors and patterns.

GULF SALT MARSH SNAKE, *N. clarkii clarkii (ssp.)*   **P. 298**
Two *dark* stripes on each side of body. *Belly:* A row of light spots (sometimes *three* rows).

MANGROVE SALT MARSH SNAKE, *N. clarkii compressicauda*   **P. 299**
Irregular dark markings above and below; highly variable (see text). *Red variation:* Red or orange-red on both back and belly.

HARTER'S WATER SNAKE, *N. harteri* (ssp.)   **P. 299**
Two rows of spots on each side of body. *Belly:* Pink center; row of dark dots down each side, but inconspicuous or even absent in one subspecies (see text).

MISSISSIPPI GREEN WATER SNAKE, *N. cyclopion*   **P. 287**
No distinctive pattern; a row of scales between lip plates and eye (Fig. 55). *Belly:* Light half-moons on dark ground.

FLORIDA GREEN WATER SNAKE, *N. floridana*   **P. 288**
No distinctive pattern; a row of scales between lip plates and eye (Fig. 55). *Belly:* Light, virtually unicolored.

DIAMONDBACK WATER SNAKE, *N. rhombifer rhombifer*   **P. 290**
Dark chainlike pattern (Fig. 56). *Belly:* Yellow, largest dark spots concentrated chiefly at sides.

BROWN WATER SNAKE, *N. taxispilota*   **P. 289**
Dark middorsal blotches separate from lateral blotches (Fig. 56). *Belly:* Heavy, dark markings on yellow ground color.

PLATE 21

GULF SALT MARSH

2 variations

2 variations

HARTER'S

MANGROVE SALT MARSH

MISSISSIPPI GREEN

FLORIDA GREEN

DIAMONDBACK

BROWN

PLATE 22

CRAYFISH, EARTH, BROWN, AND SWAMP SNAKES

All have divided anal plates. The rectangles show belly colors and patterns.

GRAHAM'S CRAYFISH SNAKE, *Regina grahamii* **P. 301**
Broad, yellowish stripe. *Belly:* Plain or with a central row of dark spots; scales *keeled.*

QUEEN SNAKE, *Regina septemvittata* **P. 300**
Yellowish stripe. *Belly:* Four brown stripes; scales *keeled.*

GLOSSY CRAYFISH SNAKE, *Regina rigida* (ssp.) **P. 303**
Shiny, often with traces of stripes. *Belly:* Double row of large, black half-moons; scales *keeled.*

STRIPED CRAYFISH SNAKE, *Regina alleni* **P. 303**
A broad, yellowish stripe on lower side; a dark stripe down back and another on side of body; scales *smooth. Belly:* Plain yellow or orange or with a midventral row of dark spots (see text).

KIRTLAND'S SNAKE, *Clonophis kirtlandii* **P. 305**
Two rows of large, dark spots on each side of body; scales *keeled. Venter:* Brick red with flanking rows of black spots.

SMOOTH EARTH SNAKE, *Virginia valeriae* (ssp.) **P. 324**
Tiny, black dots on a plain gray or brown dorsum; loreal scale horizontal and touching eye (Fig. 13); scales *smooth* or *weakly keeled.*

ROUGH EARTH SNAKE, *Virginia striatula* **P. 325**
Head pointed; loreal scale horizontal and touching eye (Fig. 13); scales *keeled.*

NORTHERN BROWN SNAKE, *Storeria dekayi dekayi* (ssp.) **P. 306**
Dark downward streak on side of head; no loreal (Fig. 13); scales *keeled. Young:* Light band across neck.

FLORIDA BROWN SNAKE, *Storeria dekayi victa* **P. 308**
Light band across head; no loreal (Fig. 13); scales *keeled.*

REDBELLY SNAKE, *Storeria occipitomaculata* (ssp.) **P. 309**
Light spots on nape; coloration highly variable (see text); scales *keeled. Venter:* Normally bright red or orange-red, but sometimes jet black.

BLACK SWAMP SNAKE, *Seminatrix pygaea* (ssp.) **P. 305**
Shiny black; scales *smooth* but with pale streaks that *look* like keels. *Belly:* Red; black encroaching on ends of ventral scales.

EARTH SNAKE *(Virginia)*
Loreal scale horizontal
and touching eye

BROWN SNAKE *(Storeria)*
No loreal; postnasal scale
touches preocular

GROUND SNAKE *(Sonora)*
A loreal scale between
postnasal and preocular

Fig. 13. Loreal scales in three genera of small snakes—present or absent.

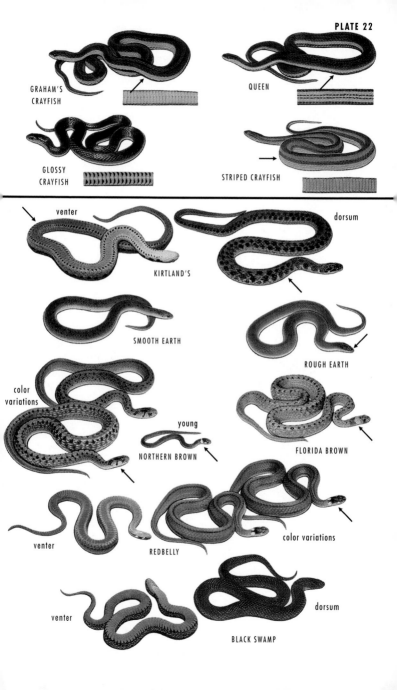

PLATE 22

GRAHAM'S
CRAYFISH

QUEEN

GLOSSY
CRAYFISH

STRIPED CRAYFISH

venter

dorsum

KIRTLAND'S

SMOOTH EARTH

ROUGH EARTH

color
variations

young
NORTHERN BROWN

FLORIDA BROWN

venter

REDBELLY

color variations

venter

BLACK SWAMP

dorsum

PLATE 23

GARTER AND RIBBON SNAKES (*Thamnophis*)

(*See also Pl. 24*)

Keeled scales and single anal plates. Ribbon Snakes are slender, and their lateral stripes are on scale rows 3 and 4.

EASTERN GARTER SNAKE, *T. sirtalis sirtalis* (ssp.) **P. 311**
   Stripe on rows 2 and 3; either stripes or spots may predominate. Some specimens are stripeless.

CHICAGO GARTER SNAKE, *T. sirtalis semifasciatus* **P. 313**
   Black bars cross lateral stripe in neck region.

BLUESTRIPE GARTER SNAKE, *T. sirtalis similis* **P. 314**
   Blue stripe on rows 2 and 3.

BUTLER'S GARTER SNAKE, *T. butleri* **P. 316**
   Small head; stripe on rows 2, 3, 4; scale rows 19.

SHORTHEAD GARTER SNAKE, *T. brachystoma* **P. 316**
   Very small head; scale rows 17.

EASTERN RIBBON SNAKE, *T. sauritus sauritus* (ssp.) **P. 319**
   Long, slender tail; stripe on rows 3 and 4; a brown ventrolateral stripe (see text).

WESTERN RIBBON SNAKE, *T. proximus proximus* (ssp.) **P. 321**
   Like Eastern Ribbon Snake; middorsal stripe often bright orange (see text).

REDSTRIPE RIBBON SNAKE, *T. proximus rubrilineatus* **P. 322**
   Red middorsal stripe.

BLUESTRIPE RIBBON SNAKE, *T. sauritus nitae* **P. 321**
   Blue stripe on rows 3 and 4; an obscure middorsal stripe sometimes present.

PENINSULA RIBBON SNAKE, *T. sauritus sackenii* **P. 320**
   Dorsal stripe fainter than lateral stripes, or even lacking.

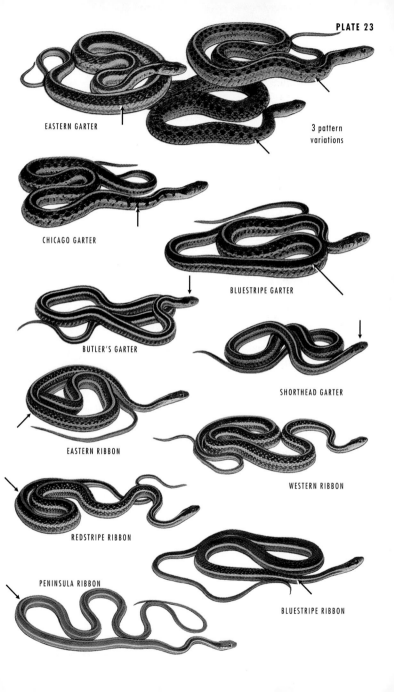

PLATE 23

EASTERN GARTER

3 pattern variations

CHICAGO GARTER

BLUESTRIPE GARTER

BUTLER'S GARTER

SHORTHEAD GARTER

EASTERN RIBBON

WESTERN RIBBON

REDSTRIPE RIBBON

PENINSULA RIBBON

BLUESTRIPE RIBBON

PLATE 24

WESTERN GARTER SNAKES (*Thamnophis*)

(*See also Pl. 23*)

Keeled scales and single anal plates.

RED-SIDED GARTER SNAKE, *T. sirtalis parietalis*　　　　**P. 313**
　　Red or orange bars; stripe on rows 2 and 3.

TEXAS GARTER SNAKE, *T. sirtalis annectens*　　　　**P. 314**
　　Broad, orange dorsal stripe; stripe on rows 2, 3, 4.

NEW MEXICO GARTER SNAKE, *T. sirtalis dorsalis*　　　　**P. 313**
　　Red subdued and largely confined to skin between scales.

PLAINS GARTER SNAKE, *T. radix* (ssp.)　　　　**P. 314**
　　Black bars on lips; stripe on rows 3 and 4.

CHECKERED GARTER SNAKE, *T. marcianus marcianus*　　　　**P. 317**
　　Checkerboard of black spots; light, curved band behind mouth
　　followed by broad black blotch.

WESTERN BLACKNECK GARTER SNAKE, *T. cyrtopsis cyrtopsis*　　　　**P. 318**
　　Black blotch at side of neck; lateral stripe on rows 2 and 3.

EASTERN BLACKNECK GARTER SNAKE, *T. cyrtopsis ocellatus*　　　　**P. 318**
　　Large black spots on neck; lateral stripe wavy.

WANDERING GARTER SNAKE, *T. elegans vagrans*　　　　**P. 319**
　　Eight upper labials and 21 scale rows at midbody. Variable; may
　　be striped or spotted (see text).

LINED SNAKE, *Tropidoclonion lineatum*　　　　**P. 323**
　　Double row of black half-moons on belly; small head; stripe on
　　rows 2 and 3.

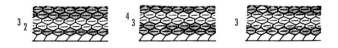

Fig. 14. *Positions of lateral stripes in Garter Snakes. Numbers refer to scale rows.*

PLATE 24

RED-SIDED GARTER

TEXAS GARTER

NEW MEXICO GARTER

PLAINS GARTER

CHECKERED GARTER

W. BLACKNECK GARTER

E. BLACKNECK GARTER

2 pattern variations

WANDERING GARTER

dorsum

LINED

venter

PLATE 25

RINGNECK, WORM, GREEN, PINE WOODS, HOGNOSE, MUD, AND RAINBOW SNAKES

SOUTHERN RINGNECK SNAKE, *Diadophis punctatus punctatus* (ssp.) **P. 331**
Prominent row of black spots; ring interrupted. (Hind part of snake turned upside down.)

NORTHERN RINGNECK SNAKE, *Diadophis punctatus edwardsii* **P. 330**
Belly plain yellow; ring complete. (Hind part of snake turned upside down.)

EASTERN WORM SNAKE, *Carphophis amoenus amoenus* (ssp.) **P. 333**
Brown back; light pink belly.

WESTERN WORM SNAKE, *Carphophis vermis* **P. 334**
Black back; bright pink belly.

SMOOTH GREEN SNAKE, *Opheodrys vernalis* **P. 347**
Plain green; *smooth* scales.

ROUGH GREEN SNAKE, *Opheodrys aestivus* **P. 346**
Plain green; *keeled* scales; body and tail very slender.

PINE WOODS SNAKE, *Rhadinaea flavilata* **P. 335**
Dark line through eye; *smooth* scales.

SOUTHERN HOGNOSE SNAKE, *Heterodon simus* **P. 328**
Snout sharply upturned; belly unpatterned or mottled with grayish brown (Fig. 59).

WESTERN HOGNOSE SNAKE, *Heterodon nasicus* (ssp.) **P. 328**
Snout sharply upturned; belly chiefly black (Fig. 59).

EASTERN HOGNOSE SNAKE, *Heterodon platirhinos* **P. 327**
Snout upturned; coloration highly variable; underside of tail lighter than belly (Fig. 59). *Dark variation:* Dark gray to black above; usually trace of broad, dark neck stripes.

MUD SNAKE, *Farancia abacura* (ssp.) **P. 335**
Dorsum: Shiny black or dark gray; red or pink of belly encroaches on sides. *Chin and neck* (at larger scale): Black spots continuous with black of dorsum.

RAINBOW SNAKE, *Farancia erytrogramma* (ssp.) **P. 336**
Dorsum: Red and black stripes. *Chin and neck* (at larger scale): Rounded black spots in double row.

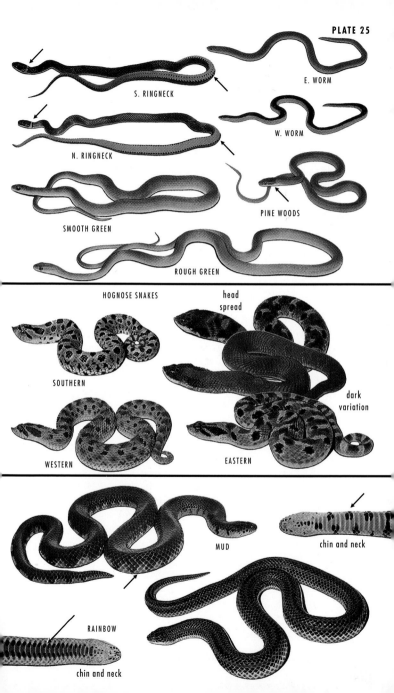

PLATE 25

E. WORM

S. RINGNECK

W. WORM

N. RINGNECK

PINE WOODS

SMOOTH GREEN

ROUGH GREEN

HOGNOSE SNAKES

head spread

SOUTHERN

dark variation

WESTERN

EASTERN

MUD

chin and neck

RAINBOW

chin and neck

PLATE 26

RACERS, COACHWHIPS, AND WHIPSNAKES
(*Coluber* and *Masticophis*)

All have smooth scales and divided anal plates.

NORTHERN BLACK RACER (young)   **P. 338**
  Dark middorsal blotches.

WESTERN COACHWHIP (young)   **P. 342**
  Dark crosslines.

NORTHERN BLACK RACER, *C. constrictor constrictor* (ssp.)   **P. 338**
  Plain black above and below; some white on chin.

BLUE RACER, *C. constrictor foxii* (ssp.)   **P. 339**
  Blue above, belly paler; dark area on side of head. (Everglades
  Racer may be very similar.)

EASTERN YELLOWBELLY RACER, *C. constrictor flaviventris* (ssp.)   **P. 340**
  Belly yellow; dorsal coloration variable (see text).

BUTTERMILK RACER, *C. constrictor anthicus* (ssp.)   **P. 341**
  Irregular white, buff, or blue spots.

WESTERN COACHWHIP, *M. flagellum testaceus*   **P. 342**
  Essentially plain brown above, but varying (see text); reddish in
  some parts of the range, as in Texas Big Bend region. Tail like a
  braided whip.

EASTERN COACHWHIP, *M. flagellum flagellum*   **P. 342**
  Head and body black or dark brown, changing to light brown posteriorly, but varying (see text). *Black variation:* Traces of light pattern; reddish on tail (see text).

CENTRAL TEXAS WHIPSNAKE, *M. taeniatus girardi* (ssp.)   **P. 343**
  Longitudinal white patches on sides.

SCHOTT'S WHIPSNAKE, *M. taeniatus schotti*   **P. 344**
  Striped on sides; reddish on neck; dorsal scales with light edges
  (Fig. 63).

RUTHVEN'S WHIPSNAKE, *M. taeniatus ruthveni*   **P. 345**
  Suggestion of stripes on sides; dorsal scales with light edges (Fig.
  63).

YOUNG

PLATE 26

N. BLACK RACER

W. COACHWHIP

BLUE RACER

N. BLACK RACER

E. YELLOWBELLY RACER

BUTTERMILK RACER

2 variations

W. COACHWHIP

2 variations

E. COACHWHIP

CENTRAL TEXAS WHIPSNAKE

SCHOTT'S WHIPSNAKE

RUTHVEN'S WHIPSNAKE

PLATE 27

PINE, BULL, GLOSSY, AND INDIGO SNAKES

All have single anal plates.

TEXAS GLOSSY SNAKE, *Arizona elegans arenicola* (ssp.)   **P. 362**
    Brown blotches on ground of cream or buff; superficially like
    Bullsnake; scales *smooth.*

NORTHERN PINE SNAKE, *Pituophis melanoleucus melanoleucus*   **P. 363**
    Dark blotches on white, yellowish, or pale gray; scales *keeled.*

BLACK PINE SNAKE, *Pituophis melanoleucus lodingi*   **P. 364**
    Nearly uniformly black or dark brown; scales *keeled.*

FLORIDA PINE SNAKE, *Pituophis melanoleucus mugitus*   **P. 364**
    Rusty brown or brownish gray; blotches obscure toward front of
    body; scales *keeled.*

LOUISIANA PINE SNAKE, *Pituophis melanoleucus ruthveni*   **P. 364**
    Forty or fewer dark body blotches, these obscure and dark toward
    front of body, but clear-cut on and near tail; no conspicuous head
    markings; scales *keeled.*

BULLSNAKE, *Pituophis melanoleucus sayi*   **P. 365**
    Dark line from eye to angle of jaw; 41 or more black or brown
    body blotches on a ground color of yellow; scales *keeled.*

TEXAS INDIGO SNAKE, *Drymarchon corais erebennus*   **P. 350**
    Black lines on upper lip; traces of pattern on forepart of body;
    scales *smooth.*

EASTERN INDIGO SNAKE, *Drymarchon corais couperi*   **P. 349**
    Plain shiny bluish black (chin and sides of head may be reddish-
    or orange-brown); scales *smooth.*

GLOSSY SNAKE
Two prefrontals

BULL and PINE SNAKES
Four prefrontals

*Fig. 15. Prefrontal scales in two genera of snakes (*Arizona *and*
Pituophis*).*

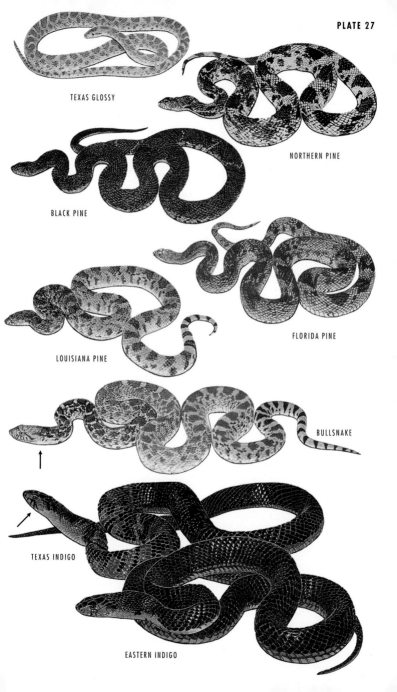

PLATE 27

TEXAS GLOSSY

NORTHERN PINE

BLACK PINE

LOUISIANA PINE

FLORIDA PINE

BULLSNAKE

TEXAS INDIGO

EASTERN INDIGO

PLATE 28

RAT SNAKES (*Elaphe*)

All have weakly keeled scales and divided anal plates.

CORN SNAKE, *E. guttata guttata*   **P. 354**
Reddish blotches with black borders of varying intensity on a ground of gray, tan, yellow, or orange. Highly variable.

GREAT PLAINS RAT SNAKE, *E. guttata emoryi*   **P. 355**
Brown blotches on a gray ground; neck lines unite to form a spearpoint on head (Fig. 67).

FOX SNAKE, *E. vulpina* (ssp.)   **P. 356**
Dark brown blotches on a yellowish ground; no spearpoint on head (Fig. 67).

BLACK RAT SNAKE, *E. obsoleta obsoleta*   **P. 357**
Uniform black or with faint traces of spotted pattern; throat light. *Young:* Patterned like Gray Rat Snake (below).

RAT SNAKE "INTERGRADE"   **P. 358**
(*E. obsoleta obsoleta* × *E. obsoleta quadrivittata*)
Four dark stripes on a ground of dark olive-gray.

YELLOW RAT SNAKE, *E. obsoleta quadrivittata*   **P. 358**
Four dark stripes on a ground of yellow to olive.

EVERGLADES RAT SNAKE, *E. obsoleta rossalleni*   **P. 358**
Four dark stripes on a ground of orange.

BAIRD'S RAT SNAKE, *E. bairdi*   **P. 360**
Four poorly defined dark stripes on a dark ground.

TEXAS RAT SNAKE, *E. obsoleta lindheimerii*   **P. 359**
Brownish- or bluish black blotches on a ground color of yellow or gray.

GRAY RAT SNAKE, *E. obsoleta spiloides*   **P. 359**
Grayish in general appearance, but coloration variable (see text).

Fig. 16. *Diagrammatic cross sections of snakes.*

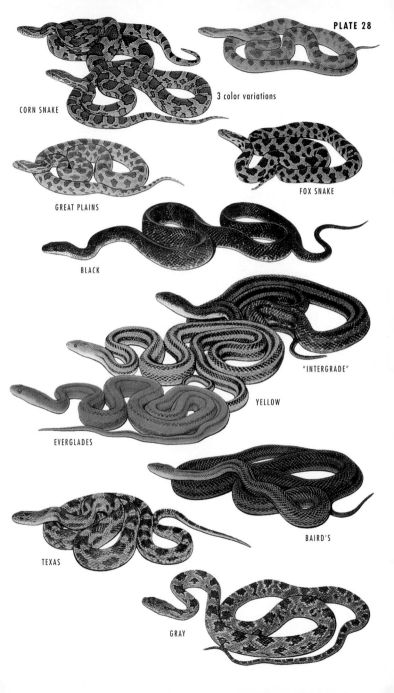

PLATE 28

CORN SNAKE

3 color variations

GREAT PLAINS

FOX SNAKE

BLACK

"INTERGRADE"

YELLOW

EVERGLADES

BAIRD'S

TEXAS

GRAY

PLATE 29

KINGSNAKES (*Lampropeltis*)

All have smooth scales and single anal plates.

PRAIRIE KINGSNAKE, *L. calligaster calligaster*　　　　　　**P. 376**
　　Spotted variation: Brown or reddish brown blotches arranged in middorsal and flanking rows. *Dark variation:* Pattern similar but obscure; a slight suggestion of dark longitudinal stripes.

MOLE KINGSNAKE, *L. calligaster rhombomaculata*　　　　　**P. 376**
　　Uniformly brown or with well-separated, dark, often reddish spots; variable (see text).

EASTERN KINGSNAKE, *L. getula getula* (ssp.)　　　　　　**P. 367**
　　Shiny black or dark brown with a bold, light, chainlike pattern.

BLOTCHED "INTERGRADE" (*L. getula getula* × *L. getula floridana*)　**P. 368**
　　Light bands very wide; dark blotches broad and few in number. (Northern Fla. and extr. s. Ga.)

PENINSULA "INTERGRADE" (*L. getula getula* × *L. getula floridana*)　**P. 368**
　　Dark blotches small and numerous; highly variable (see text). (Fla. peninsula)

FLORIDA KINGSNAKE, *L. getula floridana*　　　　　　　**P. 368**
　　Pale coloration; crosslined pattern only faintly indicated.

SPECKLED KINGSNAKE, *L. getula holbrooki*　　　　　　**P. 369**
　　Salt-and-pepper effect.

BLACK KINGSNAKE, *L. getula nigra*　　　　　　　　　**P. 368**
　　Shiny black with a pattern faintly or incompletely indicated by white or yellow dots.

DESERT KINGSNAKE, *L. getula splendida*　　　　　　　**P. 370**
　　Black or dark brown dorsal blotches; sides of body speckled.

PLATE 29

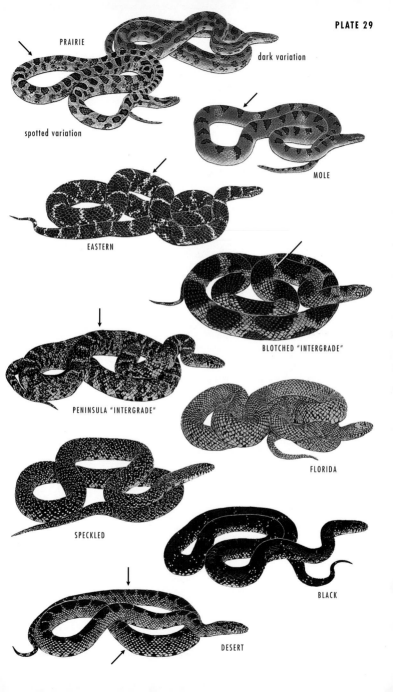

PRAIRIE

dark variation

spotted variation

MOLE

EASTERN

BLOTCHED "INTERGRADE"

PENINSULA "INTERGRADE"

FLORIDA

SPECKLED

BLACK

DESERT

PLATE 30

MILK SNAKES (*Lampropeltis triangulum*)

All have smooth scales and single anal plates.

EASTERN MILK SNAKE, *L. triangulum triangulum*   **P. 370**
   A light Y or V at back of head; large dorsal blotches alternating
   with smaller lateral ones. *Young:* Blotches red.

MILK SNAKE "INTERGRADE"   **P. 371**
(*L. triangulum triangulum* × *L. triangulum elapsoides*)
   A light collar; dorsal blotches reach belly scales on forepart of
   body; highly variable. (Mid-Atlantic region)

RED MILK SNAKE, *L. triangulum syspila*   **P. 371**
   A light collar; lateral blotches greatly reduced or absent. (Midwest)

LOUISIANA MILK SNAKE, *L. triangulum amaura*   **P. 374**
   Red rings broad (13–25 in number); head black, snout normally
   light.

MEXICAN MILK SNAKE, *L. triangulum annulata*   **P. 373**
   Red rings broad (14–26 in number); snout black; belly chiefly
   black.

CENTRAL PLAINS MILK SNAKE, *L. triangulum gentilis* (ssp.)   **P. 371**
   Reddish rings narrow (20–39 in number); head black, snout light.

CORAL SNAKE AND "MIMICS"

EASTERN CORAL SNAKE, *Micrurus fulvius fulvius*   **P. 395**
   VENOMOUS. Red and yellow rings touch; snout black.

SCARLET SNAKE, *Cemophora coccinea* (ssp.)   **P. 379**
   Red and yellow separated by black; belly whitish, unpatterned;
   snout red. (See also Pl. 31.)

SCARLET KINGSNAKE, *Lampropeltis triangulum elapsoides*   **P. 374**
   Red and yellow rings separated by black; rings enter upon or cross
   belly; snout red.

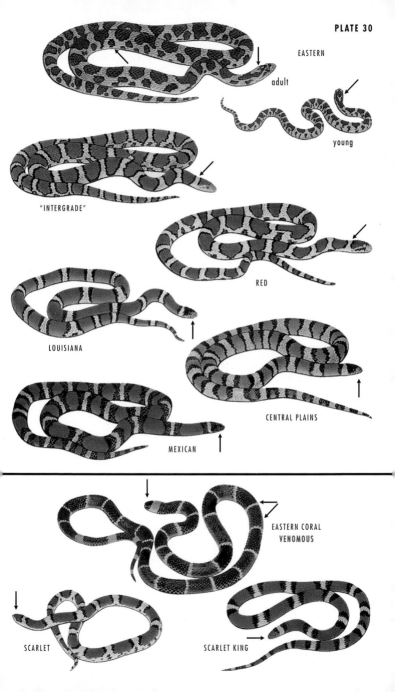

PLATE 30

EASTERN
adult

young

"INTERGRADE"

RED

LOUISIANA

CENTRAL PLAINS

MEXICAN

EASTERN CORAL
VENOMOUS

SCARLET

SCARLET KING

PLATE 31

GROUND, SHORT-TAILED, SCARLET, AND LONGNOSE SNAKES

GROUND SNAKE, *Sonora semiannulata* **P. 382**
Small, shiny, and with extremely variable pattern; sometimes almost uniform in color, sometimes with numerous crossbands (see text).

MOLE KINGSNAKE, **P. 376**
Lampropeltis calligaster rhombomaculata (young)
Dark markings small, well separated, often red.

SHORT-TAILED SNAKE, *Stilosoma extenuatum* **P. 381**
Dorsal blotches separated by areas of orange, red, or yellow; body very slender. (Fla. only)

SCARLET SNAKE, *Cemophora coccinea* (ssp.) **P. 379**
Red saddles bordered by black; head largely reddish; belly whitish, unpatterned. (See also Pl. 30.)

TEXAS LONGNOSE SNAKE, *Rhinocheilus lecontei tessellatus* **P. 380**
Crossbanded; red areas speckled with black; black areas speckled with yellow; head largely black; *subcaudals in single row.*

PATCHNOSE SNAKES (*Salvadora*)

All have a slightly projecting flap at each side of rostral.

BIG BEND PATCHNOSE SNAKE, *S. deserticola* **P. 352**
Narrow dark line on 4th scale row on forepart of body; two or three scales between posterior chin shields (Fig. 65).

MOUNTAIN PATCHNOSE SNAKE, *S. grahamiae grahamiae* **P. 351**
No narrow, dark lateral line; posterior chin shields touch or have only one scale between them (Fig. 65).

TEXAS PATCHNOSE SNAKE, *S. grahamiae lineata* **P. 351**
Both a broad and narrow dark lateral line, the latter on 3rd scale row on forepart of body; posterior chin shields touch or have only one scale between them (Fig. 65).

PLATE 31

GROUND

5 variations

MOLE KING
young

SCARLET

SHORT-TAILED

TEXAS LONGNOSE

PATCHNOSE SNAKES

BIG BEND

TEXAS

MOUNTAIN

PLATE 32

SOME SOUTH TEXAS SNAKES

TRANS-PECOS RAT SNAKE, *Bogertophis subocularis*   **P. 360**
    Head unicolored; black stripes on neck; dark blotches posteriorly.
    (Most of w. Texas) *Blond variation:* Uniformly light-colored with
    dark pattern reduced or absent. (Lower Pecos R. Valley of sw.
    Texas)

GRAY-BANDED KINGSNAKE, *Lampropeltis alterna*   **P. 377**
    Gray crossbands; varying amounts of red or orange (these colors
    sometimes absent). (W. Texas) *Dark variation:* Gray crossbands
    very dark.

TEXAS LYRE SNAKE, *Trimorphodon biscutatus vilkinsonii*   **P. 386**
    Dark brown saddles on a light brown (or gray) ground color. Pupil
    elliptical in daylight. (Chihuahuan Desert)

NORTHERN CAT-EYED SNAKE,   **P. 386**
Leptodeira septentrionalis septentrionalis
    Body crossed by bold, black (or dark brown) saddles; ground color
    often yellow, but variable from cream to reddish tan. Pupil ellipti-
    cal in daylight. (Extr. s. Texas)

SPECKLED RACER, *Drymobius margaritiferus margaritiferus*   **P. 348**
    Scales with light centers; dark stripe behind eye; a few middorsal
    rows of scales with faint keels. (Extr. s. Texas)

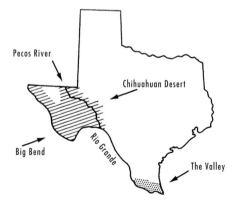

*Fig. 17. Several Mexican snakes enter Texas in the Chihuahuan Desert
of the Pecos R. and Big Bend regions, and in The Valley of the Rio
Grande in the extreme south.*

PLATE 32

TRANS-PECOS
RAT SNAKE

2 variations

GRAY-BANDED
KINGSNAKE

3 pattern variations

TEXAS LYRE SNAKE

NORTHERN
CAT-EYED SNAKE

SPECKLED RACER

PLATE 33

BLIND AND REAR-FANGED SNAKES

All have smooth scales.

TEXAS BLIND SNAKE, *Leptotyphlops dulcis* (ssp.)   **P. 284**
    Wormlike; tail blunt; belly scales same size as those on dorsum.

WESTERN HOOKNOSE SNAKE, *Gyalopion canum*   **P. 385**
    Snout upturned; head strongly crossbanded.

MEXICAN HOOKNOSE SNAKE, *Ficimia streckeri*   **P. 384**
    Snout upturned; head virtually unpatterned.

FLATHEAD SNAKE, *Tantilla gracilis*   **P. 390**
    Head nearly same color as body or only slightly darker; upper labials usually six.

SOUTHEASTERN CROWNED SNAKE, *Tantilla coronata*   **P. 387**
    Light band across rear of head.

CENTRAL FLORIDA CROWNED SNAKE, *Tantilla relicta neilli*   **P. 389**
    No light band; black cap extends far back of head scales.

PLAINS BLACKHEAD SNAKE, *Tantilla nigriceps*   **P. 391**
    Black pigmentation rounded or pointed on nape and normally without dark downward extensions; upper labials usually seven.

BLACKHOOD SNAKE, *Tantilla rubra cucullata*   **P. 394**
    Black hood covers both dorsal and ventral surfaces of head. Also has a variation with a light neck ring interrupted middorsally (see text). (Trans-Pecos Texas)

DEVIL'S RIVER BLACKHEAD SNAKE, *Tantilla rubra diabola*   **P. 394**
    Light band across rear of head. (W. Texas)

MEXICAN BLACKHEAD SNAKE, *Tantilla atriceps*   **P. 393**
    Rear of short black cap runs straight across. The Southwestern Blackhead Snake (*Tantilla hobartsmithi*) is almost identical in appearance, but it differs internally (see text).

TEXAS NIGHT SNAKE, *Hypsiglena torquata jani*   **P. 385**
    Dark neck spot; many dark spots; pupil elliptical in daylight.

BLACK-STRIPED SNAKE, *Coniophanes imperialis imperialis*   **P. 383**
    Three black (or dark brown) stripes on a ground color of light brown; belly bright red or orange.

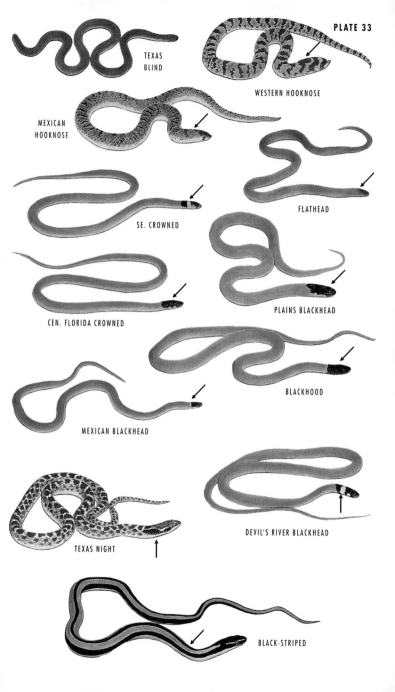

PLATE 33

TEXAS BLIND

WESTERN HOOKNOSE

MEXICAN HOOKNOSE

FLATHEAD

SE. CROWNED

CEN. FLORIDA CROWNED

PLAINS BLACKHEAD

BLACKHOOD

MEXICAN BLACKHEAD

TEXAS NIGHT

DEVIL'S RIVER BLACKHEAD

BLACK-STRIPED

PLATE 34

COPPERHEADS AND COTTONMOUTHS (*Agkistrodon*)

SOUTHERN COPPERHEAD, *A. contortrix contortrix*   P. 399
Bands narrow along midline of back, often failing to meet; ground color pale.

OSAGE COPPERHEAD, *A. contortrix phaeogaster*   P. 398
Bands similar to Northern Copperhead, but often edged with white.

NORTHERN COPPERHEAD, *A. contortrix mokasen*   P. 397
Coppery red head; bands wide at sides of body, narrow across back.

BROAD-BANDED COPPERHEAD, *A. contortrix laticinctus*   P. 400
Bands broad, nearly as wide across back as on sides.

TRANS-PECOS COPPERHEAD, *A. contortrix pictigaster*   P. 400
Pale area at base of each broad band; belly strongly patterned.

FLORIDA COTTONMOUTH (young)*   P. 402
Yellow tail tip; *broad* dark band through eye.

NORTHERN COPPERHEAD (young)   P. 397
Yellow tail tip; *narrow* dark line through eye.

FLORIDA COTTONMOUTH, *A. piscivorus conanti**   P. 402
Head markings well defined.

WESTERN COTTONMOUTH, *A. piscivorus leucostoma**   P. 403
Head markings obscure or absent; general coloration usually dark and body pattern indistinct.

EASTERN COTTONMOUTH, *A. piscivorus piscivorus**   P. 401
Head markings obscure; coloration variable—may be brown, black, or olive.

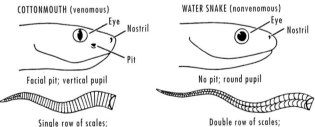

Fig. 18. *Heads and undersides of tails of a Cottonmouth and a typical Water Snake* (Nerodia).

*Cottonmouths resemble many of the Water Snakes. On dead or captive specimens check heads and undersurfaces of tails (Fig. 18).

PLATE 34

COPPERHEADS   ALL VENOMOUS

SOUTHERN

OSAGE

BROAD-BANDED

NORTHERN

TRANS-PECOS

YOUNG

FLORIDA COTTONMOUTH   NORTHERN COPPERHEAD

FLORIDA

WESTERN

EASTERN

COTTONMOUTHS
ALL VENOMOUS

PLATE 35

RATTLESNAKES (*Sistrurus* and *Crotalus*)

(See also Pl. 36)

WESTERN PIGMY RATTLESNAKE, S. *miliarius streckeri*　　**P. 407**
　　Tiny rattle; slender tail; dark bars.

DUSKY PIGMY RATTLESNAKE, S. *miliarius barbouri*　　**P. 407**
　　Tiny rattle; slender tail; rounded spots; dusty appearance.

CAROLINA PIGMY RATTLESNAKE, S. *miliarius miliarius*　　**P. 406**
　　Tiny rattle; slender tail; markings clear-cut; gray or reddish (see text).

WESTERN MASSASAUGA, S. *catenatus tergeminus* (ssp.)　　**P. 405**
　　Large rounded spots on a *pale* ground color; belly light (Fig. 75).

EASTERN MASSASAUGA, S. *catenatus catenatus*　　**P. 404**
　　Large rounded spots on a *medium to dark gray* ground color; belly mostly black (Fig. 75).

EASTERN DIAMONDBACK RATTLESNAKE, C. *adamanteus*　　**P. 410**
　　Large, clear-cut, strongly outlined diamonds.

TIMBER RATTLESNAKE, C. *horridus*　　**P. 408**
　　Highly variable, but always with dark crossbands (except in all-black individuals). *Western variation:* Generally gray; orange-red middorsal stripe; dark markings often edged with white; reddish-brown postocular line. *Southern variation:* Generally gray to pinkish; reddish-brown middorsal stripe; dark postocular line (Fig. 76). *Yellow variation:* No head markings (ne. part of range; Fig. 76). *Black variation:* Black predominates (often all black; ne. part of range).

Button

Young rattle, tapering in size, button still retained

Old rattle, terminal joints broken off

Cross section showing interlinking arrangement

Fig. 19. The rattle—hallmark of the group.

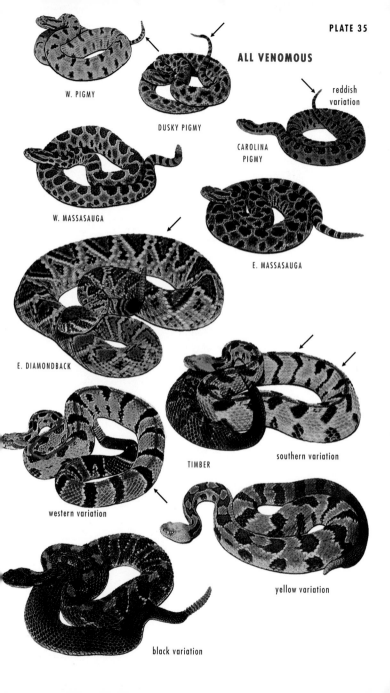

PLATE 35

ALL VENOMOUS

W. PIGMY

DUSKY PIGMY

reddish
variation

CAROLINA
PIGMY

W. MASSASAUGA

E. MASSASAUGA

E. DIAMONDBACK

TIMBER

southern variation

western variation

yellow variation

black variation

PLATE 36

WESTERN RATTLESNAKES *(Crotalus)* AND CORAL SNAKE

(See also Pl. 35)

BANDED ROCK RATTLESNAKE, *C. lepidus klauberi*　　　　**P. 415**
Conspicuous dark crossbars throughout length of body; no dark stripe from eye to angle of mouth.

MOTTLED ROCK RATTLESNAKE, *C. lepidus lepidus*　　　　**P. 414**
Dark crossbars conspicuous only on rear of body; dark stripe from eye to angle of mouth; coloration variable (see text).

BLACKTAIL RATTLESNAKE, *C. molossus molossus*　　　　**P. 413**
Black tail in strong contrast with body coloration.

PRAIRIE RATTLESNAKE, *C. viridis viridis*　　　　**P. 413**
Dark crossbars on rear of body; light postocular line passes *above* corner of mouth (Fig. 76).

MOJAVE RATTLESNAKE, *C. scutulatus scutulatus*　　　　**P. 412**
Black rings on tail much narrower than white rings; postocular light line passes *above* corner of mouth (Fig. 76).

WESTERN DIAMONDBACK RATTLESNAKE, *C. atrox*　　　　**P. 411**
Black tail rings relatively broad; diamonds not clear-cut; postocular light line ends on upper lip *in front of angle of mouth* (Fig. 76).

TEXAS CORAL SNAKE, *Micrurus fulvius tener*　　　　**P. 396**
Red and yellow rings touch; snout black. (See also Pl. 30.)

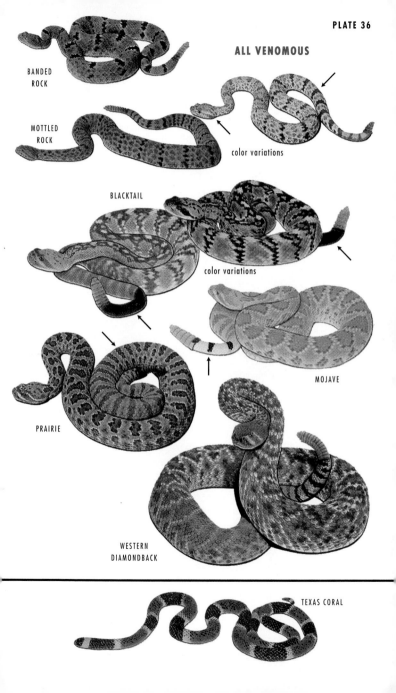

PLATE 36

ALL VENOMOUS

BANDED ROCK

MOTTLED ROCK

color variations

BLACKTAIL

color variations

MOJAVE

PRAIRIE

WESTERN DIAMONDBACK

TEXAS CORAL

PLATE 37

GIANT SALAMANDERS

WATERDOGS AND MUDPUPPY (*Necturus*)

All have external gills and four well-developed legs, each with four toes.

GULF COAST WATERDOG, N. *beyeri*   P. 423
     Dark spots numerous and close together.

DWARF WATERDOG, N. *punctatus*   P. 424
     Almost uniformly dark above; paler below.

MUDPUPPY, N. *maculosus* (ssp.)   P. 419
     Dark spots few and well separated.

SIRENS AND AMPHIUMAS

Eel-like salamanders with two or four legs.

LESSER SIREN, *Siren intermedia* (ssp.)   P. 428
     Tiny front legs; external gills; small size (see text).

GREATER SIREN, *Siren lacertina*   P. 426
     Small front legs; external gills; large size.

AMPHIUMA, *Amphiuma*   P. 425, 426
     Tiny front *and* hind legs; no external gills. (Three species, all virtually identical in gross appearance—count number of toes on any one foot—see text.)

HELLBENDERS (*Cryptobranchus*)

Broad, flat heads; folds of skin along sides.

EASTERN HELLBENDER, C. *alleganiensis alleganiensis*   P. 418
     Dark markings few and small.

OZARK HELLBENDER, C. *alleganiensis bishopi*   P. 419
     Dark markings large and blotchlike.

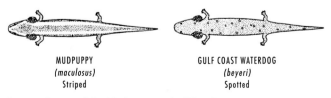

MUDPUPPY
(*maculosus*)
Striped

GULF COAST WATERDOG
(*beyeri*)
Spotted

Fig. 20. Larvae of the Mudpuppy and a Waterdog.

GULF COAST WATERDOG

DWARF WATERDOG

MUDPUPPY

PLATE 37

LESSER SIREN

GREATER SIREN

AMPHIUMA

EASTERN HELLBENDER

OZARK HELLBENDER

PLATE 38

MOLE SALAMANDERS (*Ambystoma*)

FLATWOODS SALAMANDER, *A. cingulatum*   P. 435
   Variable: (a) irregularly "frosted," (b) narrow light rings, or (c) tendency to form a netlike pattern.

MOLE SALAMANDER, *A. talpoideum*   P. 432
   Short, chunky body; large head.

MABEE'S SALAMANDER, *A. mabeei*   P. 436
   Profuse light speckling on side; small head.

MARBLED SALAMANDER, *A. opacum*   P. 433
   White or silvery crossbars; black on lower sides and belly.

SMALLMOUTH SALAMANDER, *A. texanum*   P. 436
   Very short snout; pattern variable. *Dark variation:* Markings indistinct. *Speckled variation:* Profuse lichenlike markings. (See also text for Streamside Salamander.)

BLUE-SPOTTED SALAMANDER, *A. laterale*   P. 438
   Long toes; numerous blue or bluish-white spots and flecks.

JEFFERSON SALAMANDER, *A. jeffersonianum*   P. 437
   Long toes; long snout; a few bluish flecks on side.

RINGED SALAMANDER, *A. annulatum*   P. 434
   Bold yellow crossbands; light ventrolateral stripe; small head.

SPOTTED SALAMANDER, *A. maculatum*   P. 439
   Round yellow to orange spots in irregular dorsolateral row.

BARRED TIGER SALAMANDER, *A. tigrinum mavortium* (ssp.)   P. 440
   Large light bars or blotches.

EASTERN TIGER SALAMANDER, *A. tigrinum tigrinum*   P. 440
   Light markings small, not forming definite pattern.

Fig. 21. Neotenic form ("axolotl") of the Barred Tiger Salamander.

PLATE 38

FLATWOODS   pattern variations

MOLE

MABEE'S

MARBLED

SMALLMOUTH

speckled variation

dark variation

BLUE-SPOTTED

JEFFERSON

RINGED

SPOTTED

BARRED TIGER

EASTERN TIGER

PLATE 39

NEWTS (*Notophthalmus*)

RED-SPOTTED NEWT, *N. viridescens viridescens*   **P. 442**
Red spots in all phases. *Red Eft* (land form): Red or orange, transforming to dark olive (or other colors—see text). *Aquatic ♀:* Olive, belly yellow, spotted with black. Aquatic ♂: (in breeding condition): High tail fin; black horny growths on hind legs and toes.

BLACK-SPOTTED NEWT, *N. meridionalis meridionalis*   **P. 445**
Large, scattered black spots; irregular yellowish stripes; orange belly.

STRIPED NEWT, *N. perstriatus*   **P. 444**
Red stripe.

BROKEN-STRIPED NEWT, *N. viridescens dorsalis*   **P. 444**
Red stripe broken into dots and dashes.

CENTRAL NEWT, *N. viridescens louisianensis*   **P. 443**
Dorsal and ventral coloration in sharp contrast; normally no red markings.

PENINSULA NEWT, *N. viridescens piaropicola*   **P. 444**
Dorsum very dark; belly peppered with black.

NEOTENIC SALAMANDERS

TEXAS BLIND SALAMANDER, *Typhlomolge rathbuni*   **P. 497**
Toothpick legs; pale coloration; gills evident.

GROTTO SALAMANDER, *Typhlotriton spelaeus*   **P. 498**
Pale coloration; no gills. *Larva:* High tail fin; longitudinal streaks on side; gills evident.

SAN MARCOS SALAMANDER, *Eurycea nana*   **P. 495**
Brown; a row of small, light spots; gills evident.

TEXAS SALAMANDER, *Eurycea neotenes*   **P. 495**
Yellowish; rows of light spots; gills evident.

OKLAHOMA SALAMANDER, *Eurycea tynerensis*   **P. 495**
Gray above, lighter below; gills evident.

SLENDER DWARF SIREN, *Pseudobranchus striatus spheniscus* (ssp.)   **P. 430**
Tiny forelimbs; no hind limbs; gills evident; yellowish side stripes; darker stripes above.

NARROW-STRIPED DWARF SIREN, *Pseudobranchus striatus axanthus*   **P. 430**
Similar to Slender Dwarf Siren, but general coloration grayish with faint stripes.

TENNESSEE CAVE SALAMANDER, *Gyrinophilus palleucus* (ssp.)   **P. 483**
Flesh-colored; gills evident; large tail fin.

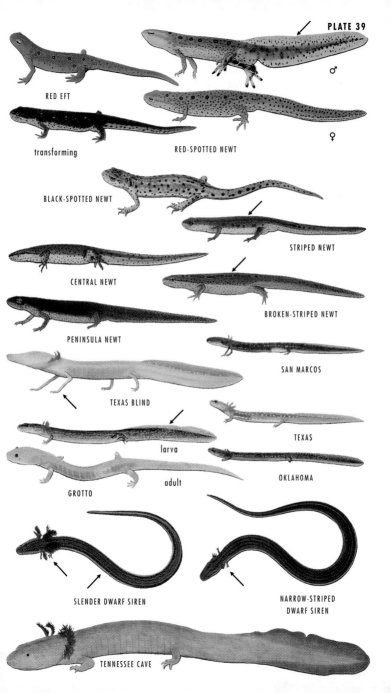

PLATE 39

RED EFT

transforming

RED-SPOTTED NEWT

♂

♀

BLACK-SPOTTED NEWT

STRIPED NEWT

CENTRAL NEWT

BROKEN-STRIPED NEWT

PENINSULA NEWT

SAN MARCOS

TEXAS BLIND

TEXAS

larva

OKLAHOMA

GROTTO

adult

SLENDER DWARF SIREN

NARROW-STRIPED
DWARF SIREN

TENNESSEE CAVE

PLATE 40

WOODLAND SALAMANDERS (Chiefly *Plethodon*)

JORDAN'S SALAMANDER, *P. jordani*　　　　　　　　　**P. 477**
　　Extremely variable. Includes Clemson, Metcalf's, Redleg, Red-cheek, and other less distinct pattern and color variations.

IMITATOR SALAMANDER, *Desmognathus imitator*　　　　**P. 456**
　　Light cheek patch; suggestion of line from eye to angle of jaw.

WELLER'S SALAMANDER, *P. welleri*　　　　　　　　　**P. 467**
　　Gold or silver blotches.

CHEAT MOUNTAIN SALAMANDER, *P. nettingi*　　　　　**P. 467**
　　Numerous small, gold flecks; belly *black*.

REDBACK SALAMANDER, *P. cinereus*　　　　　　　　　**P. 462**
　　Salt-and-pepper effect on belly (Fig. 90). *Redback variation:* Straight-edged middorsal stripe. *Leadback variation:* Dorsum nearly plain dark.

SOUTHERN REDBACK SALAMANDER, *P. serratus*　　　　**P. 464**
　　Narrow, straight-edged or serrated middorsal stripe extends well onto tail.

EASTERN ZIGZAG SALAMANDER, *P. dorsalis dorsalis* (ssp.)　**P. 468**
　　Zigzag or irregular middorsal stripe.

CADDO MOUNTAIN SALAMANDER, *P. caddoensis*　　　　**P. 476**
　　Salt-and-pepper effect. Identify by range.

FOURCHE MOUNTAIN SALAMANDER, *P. fourchensis*　　**P. 476**
　　Two irregular dorsal rows of large white spots.

RICH MOUNTAIN SALAMANDER, *P. ouachitae*　　　　　**P. 475**
　　Chestnut with white specks; variable (see text).

YONAHLOSSEE SALAMANDER, *P. yonahlossee*　　　　　**P. 474**
　　Dorsum red or chestnut; light lateral stripe. *Bat Cave Variation:* Red or chestnut color reduced; light ventrolateral stripe bordered above chiefly by dark pigment.

PLATE 40

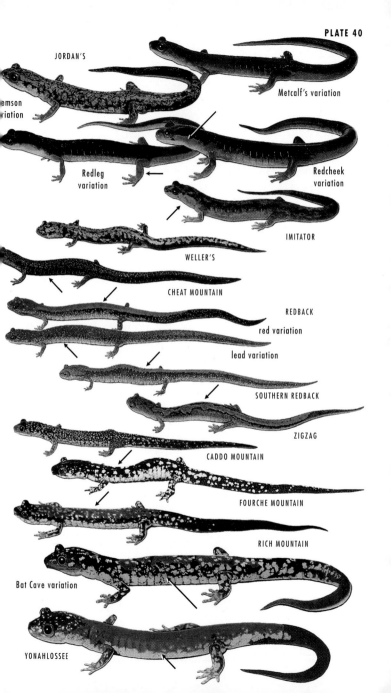

JORDAN'S

Metcalf's variation

emson
riation

Redleg
variation

Redcheek
variation

IMITATOR

WELLER'S

CHEAT MOUNTAIN

REDBACK

red variation

lead variation

SOUTHERN REDBACK

ZIGZAG

CADDO MOUNTAIN

FOURCHE MOUNTAIN

RICH MOUNTAIN

Bat Cave variation

YONAHLOSSEE

PLATE 41

WOODLAND AND DUSKY SALAMANDERS

WOODLAND SPECIES (*Plethodon*)

Most of these are blackish with light markings.

WEHRLE'S SALAMANDER, *P. wehrlei* **P. 469**
  White, bluish-white, or yellow spots along side. *Dixie Caverns variation:* Small white flecks and bronzy mottling on purplish-brown background.

RAVINE SALAMANDER, *P. richmondi* **P. 465**
  Long, slender body; no conspicuous markings; belly dark (Fig. 90).

PIGEON MOUNTAIN SALAMANDER, *P. petraeus* **P. 474**
  Dorsum reddish brown or brown; sides with white or yellowish spots; belly black.

NORTHERN SLIMY SALAMANDER, *P. glutinosus* **P. 471**
  Numerous white spots or brassy flecks or both; throat dark.

DUSKY (*Desmognathus*) AND ALLIED SPECIES

Usually a light diagonal line behind eye in most species.

SEAL SALAMANDER, *D. monticola* **P. 453**
  Heavy, dark markings on dorsum; venter pale.

NORTHERN DUSKY SALAMANDER, *D. fuscus fuscus* **P. 447**
  Markings extremely variable (see text); venter lightly pigmented.

BLACKBELLY SALAMANDER, *D. quadramaculatus* **P. 454**
  Two rows of light dots on side; venter black.

SHOVELNOSE SALAMANDER, *Leurognathus marmoratus* **P. 460**
  Spotted or blotched, but markings extremely variable (see text). Check internal openings of nostrils if in doubt (Fig. 88).

RED HILLS SALAMANDER, *Phaeognathus hubrichti* **P. 461**
  Very long body; small legs; uniformly very dark brown with no markings of any kind.

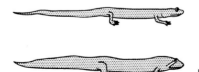

WOODLAND
Legs approximately same size

DUSKY
Hind legs larger than forelegs;
light line from eye to angle of jaw

Fig. 22. *Basic differences between Woodland* (Plethodon) *and Dusky* (Desmognathus) *Salamanders.*

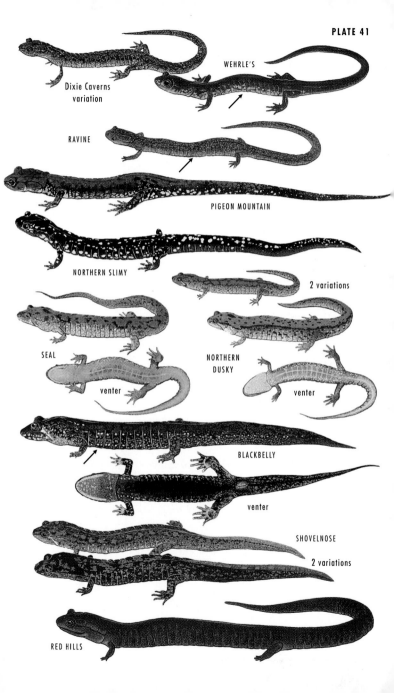

PLATE 41

Dixie Caverns variation

WEHRLE'S

RAVINE

PIGEON MOUNTAIN

NORTHERN SLIMY

2 variations

SEAL

NORTHERN DUSKY

venter

venter

BLACKBELLY

venter

SHOVELNOSE

2 variations

RED HILLS

PLATE 42

DUSKY SALAMANDERS *(Desmognathus)*

MOUNTAIN DUSKY SALAMANDER, *D. ochrophaeus*   **P. 454**
Coloration and pattern highly variable; young brightly colored, old adults dark with faint markings. *Northern variation:* Middorsal light stripe with nearly straight edges. *Southern variation:* Borders of middorsal stripe wavy, irregular, or interrupted. (See also Imitator Salamander on Pl. 40.)

PIGMY SALAMANDER, *D. wrighti*   **P. 458**
Tiny adult size; herringbone pattern; terrestrial.

SPOTTED DUSKY SALAMANDER, *D. fuscus conanti*   **P. 448**
Six to eight pairs of golden spots.

OUACHITA DUSKY SALAMANDER, *D. brimleyorum*   **P. 451**
Nondescript; confined to Ouachita Mountains of Arkansas and Oklahoma.

RED AND MUD SALAMANDERS *(Pseudotriton)*

NORTHERN RED SALAMANDER, *P. ruber ruber* (ssp.)   **P. 485**
Black spots numerous, irregular, and often running together; *eye yellow. Old adult:* Spots large but indistinct; ground color dark.

BLACKCHIN RED SALAMANDER, *P. ruber schencki*   **P. 486**
Heavy black pigment on chin.

SOUTHERN RED SALAMANDER, *P. ruber vioscai*   **P. 486**
Small white flecks, especially on head.

EASTERN MUD SALAMANDER, *P. montanus montanus* (ssp.)   **P. 484**
Black spots round, few in number, and remaining separate; *eye brown.*

RUSTY MUD SALAMANDER, *P. montanus floridanus*   **P. 485**
Markings obscure; dark streaks on side.

SPRING SALAMANDERS *(Gyrinophilus porphyriticus)*

NORTHERN SPRING SALAMANDER,   **P. 481**
G. porphyriticus porphyriticus (ssp.)
Eye lines and pattern not clear-cut.

BLUE RIDGE SPRING SALAMANDER, *G. porphyriticus danielsi* (ssp.)   **P. 482**
Light *and* dark line, eye to nostril; black spots.

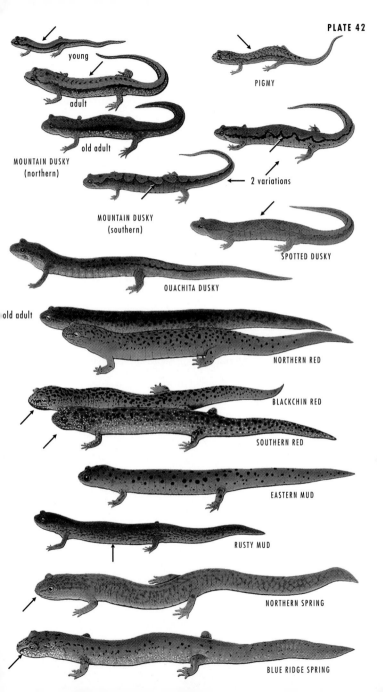

PLATE 42

young

adult

old adult

MOUNTAIN DUSKY
(northern)

PIGMY

2 variations

SPOTTED DUSKY

MOUNTAIN DUSKY
(southern)

OUACHITA DUSKY

old adult

NORTHERN RED

BLACKCHIN RED

SOUTHERN RED

EASTERN MUD

RUSTY MUD

NORTHERN SPRING

BLUE RIDGE SPRING

PLATE 43

BROOK AND FOUR-TOED SALAMANDERS
(*Eurycea* and *Hemidactylium*)

BLUE RIDGE TWO-LINED SALAMANDER, *E. wilderae* **P. 489**
Bright coloration; dark lines clear-cut. ♂: Conspicuous downward projection from nostril.

NORTHERN TWO-LINED SALAMANDER, *E. bislineata* **P. 488**
Dark line from eye to tail; belly yellow.

BROWNBACK SALAMANDER, *E. aquatica* **P. 490**
Brown back; dusky-black sides; relatively short tail.

MANY-RIBBED SALAMANDER, *E. multiplicata multiplicata* **P. 491**
Light spots in dark lateral stripe (see text).

GRAYBELLY SALAMANDER, *E. multiplicata griseogaster* **P. 491**
Dark belly; trace of tan on dorsum (see text).

DWARF SALAMANDER, *E. quadridigitata* **P. 494**
Four toes on each *hind* foot; dark dorsolateral stripe.

FOUR-TOED SALAMANDER, *Hemidactylium scutatum* **P. 479**
Four toes on each hind foot; constriction at base of tail; belly white with black spots (Fig. 90).

CAVE SALAMANDER, *E. lucifuga* **P. 493**
Tail long; black spots on orange or reddish ground color.

LONGTAIL SALAMANDER, *E. longicauda longicauda* **P. 491**
Tail long, with "dumbbells" or herringbone pattern.

DARK-SIDED SALAMANDER, *E. longicauda melanopleura* **P. 493**
Tail long; sides marked with gray and yellow.

THREE-LINED SALAMANDER, *E. longicauda guttolineata* **P. 492**
Tail long; a middorsal dark stripe.

GREEN AND MANY-LINED SALAMANDERS

GREEN SALAMANDER, *Aneides aeneus* **P. 479**
Green, lichenlike markings.

MANY-LINED SALAMANDER, *Stereochilus marginatus* **P. 479**
Light and dark streaks on lower sides; small head; short tail.

PLATE 43

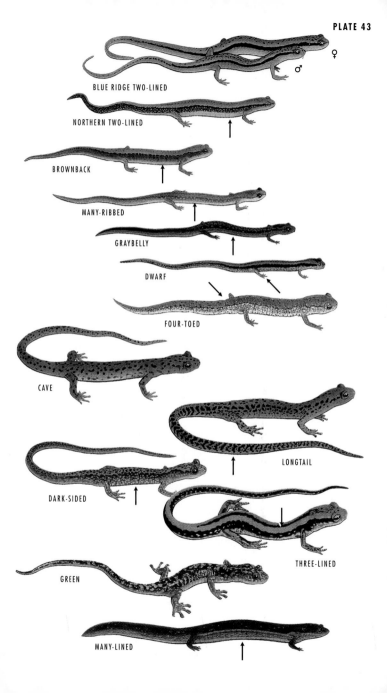

BLUE RIDGE TWO-LINED

♀

♂

NORTHERN TWO-LINED

BROWNBACK

MANY-RIBBED

GRAYBELLY

DWARF

FOUR-TOED

CAVE

LONGTAIL

DARK-SIDED

THREE-LINED

GREEN

MANY-LINED

PLATE 44

SPADEFOOTS (*Scaphiopus*)

A single sharp-edged spade under each hind foot.

COUCH'S SPADEFOOT, *S. couchii*   **P. 505**
  Dark, irregular pattern on yellowish or greenish ground color; variable (see text).

HURTER'S SPADEFOOT, *S. holbrookii hurterii*   **P. 504**
  Light dorsal lines; boss between eyes (Fig. 96).

EASTERN SPADEFOOT, *S. holbrookii holbrookii*   **P. 503**
  Light lines in the form of a lyre.

PLAINS SPADEFOOT, *S. bombifrons*   **P. 505**
  Faint, light, longitudinal stripes; boss between eyes (Fig. 96).

NEW MEXICO SPADEFOOT, *S. multiplicatus*   **P. 506**
  Gray, green, or brown with small, dark markings.

TRUE TOADS (*Bufo*)

(See also Pl. 46)
Two tubercles under hind foot — spadelike in some species.

SOUTHERN TOAD, *B. terrestris*   **P. 515**
  Prominent cranial knobs (Fig. 99)

AMERICAN TOAD, *B. americanus* (ssp.)   **P. 513**
  One or two large warts in each dark spot.

CANADIAN TOAD, *B. hemiophrys hemiophrys*   **P. 517**
  Boss between eyes (Fig. 96).

GULF COAST TOAD, *B. valliceps*   **P. 521**
  Broad, dark lateral stripe bordered above by light stripe.

FOWLER'S TOAD, *B. woodhousii fowleri*   **P. 520**
  Three or more warts in each dark spot.

WOODHOUSE'S TOAD, *B. woodhousii woodhousii* (ssp.)   **P. 518**
  Warts in dark spots variable in number (see text).

RED-SPOTTED TOAD, *B. punctatus*   **P. 524**
  Parotoid gland rounded; no light middorsal stripe.

TEXAS TOAD, *B. speciosus*   **P. 523**
  Parotoid gland oval; no light middorsal stripe.

GREAT PLAINS TOAD, *B. cognatus*   **P. 523**
  Large, dark blotches with light borders.

GIANT TOAD, *B. marinus*   **P. 526**
  Parotoid gland enormously enlarged.

SPADEFOOTS

PLATE 44

COUCH'S

HURTER'S

EASTERN

PLAINS

NEW MEXICO

SOUTHERN

AMERICAN

CANADIAN

GULF COAST

FOWLER'S

WOODHOUSE'S

RED-SPOTTED

TEXAS

GREAT PLAINS

GIANT

PLATE 45

NARROWMOUTH TOADS AND TROPICAL FROGS

GREAT PLAINS NARROWMOUTH TOAD, *Gastrophryne olivacea*　　**P. 553**
　　Plain gray, tan, or greenish and with or without small black spots.

EASTERN NARROWMOUTH TOAD, *Gastrophryne carolinensis*　　**P. 551**
　　Broad, light dorsolateral stripe; center of back dark. *Key West variations:* Dorsolateral stripe reddish; dorsum brown or tan.

SHEEP FROG, *Hypopachus variolosus*　　**P. 554**
　　Yellow streak down back.

MEXICAN BURROWING TOAD, *Rhinophrynus dorsalis*　　**P. 501**
　　Rotund body; orange middorsal stripe (buff in young).

SPOTTED CHIRPING FROG, *Syrrhophus guttilatus*　　**P. 511**
　　Dark bar between eyes; dark, wormlike pattern. (Big Bend of Texas)

CLIFF CHIRPING FROG, *Syrrhophus marnockii*　　**P. 510**
　　Pale greenish; numerous dark markings but no definite pattern; skin smooth.

RIO GRANDE CHIRPING FROG, *Syrrhophus cystignathoides campi*　　**P. 511**
　　Usually grayish brown or grayish olive; dark shadow from eye to nostril; legs crossbarred.

GREENHOUSE FROG, *Eleutherodactylus planirostris planirostris*　　**P. 509**
　　Reddish; pattern striped or spotted.

EASTERN BARKING FROG, *Eleutherodactylus augusti latrans*　　**P. 508**
　　Toadlike but no warts; very large forearm; a lateral fold.

PUERTO RICAN COQUI, *Eleutherodactylus coqui*　　**P. 509**
　　Uniform brown or grayish brown with highly variable pattern of light stripes or bands (see text).

WHITE-LIPPED FROG, *Leptodactylus labialis*　　**P. 508**
　　Light line on lip; a ventral disc (Fig. 97).

PLATE 45

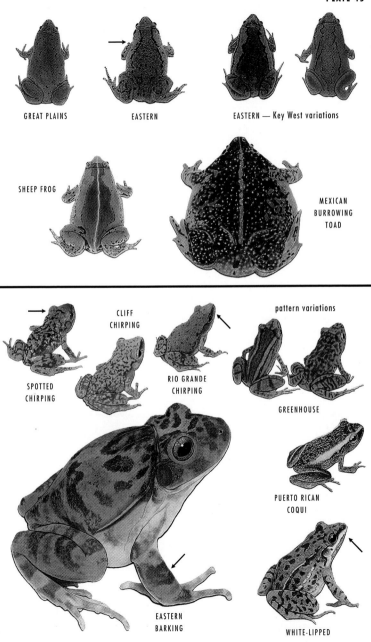

GREAT PLAINS

EASTERN

EASTERN — Key West variations

SHEEP FROG

MEXICAN BURROWING TOAD

SPOTTED CHIRPING

CLIFF CHIRPING

RIO GRANDE CHIRPING

pattern variations

GREENHOUSE

EASTERN BARKING

PUERTO RICAN COQUI

WHITE-LIPPED

PLATE 46

CHORUS FROGS (*Pseudacris*)

BOREAL CHORUS FROG, *P. triseriata maculata*   **P. 544**
 Pattern striped; leg short.

WESTERN CHORUS FROG, *P. triseriata triseriata* (ssp.)   **P. 542**
 Pattern striped (Fig. 102); leg long.

BRIMLEY'S CHORUS FROG, *P. brimleyi*   **P. 546**
 Side stripe black; dorsal stripes brown or gray; dark spots on chest.

SPRING PEEPER, *P. crucifer* (ssp.)   **P. 540**
 Dark X-shaped mark on back.

UPLAND CHORUS FROG, *P. triseriata feriarum*   **P. 544**
 Pattern spotted or weakly striped (Fig. 102).

SOUTHERN CHORUS FROG, *P. nigrita nigrita*   **P. 545**
 White line on lip; dorsal stripes broad but broken.

FLORIDA CHORUS FROG, *P. nigrita verrucosa*   **P. 545**
 Three rows of black spots; lip spotted black and white.

LITTLE GRASS FROG, *P. ocularis*   **P. 550**
 Tiny size; dark line through eye; pattern and coloration variable (see text).

MOUNTAIN CHORUS FROG, *P. brachyphona*   **P. 547**
 Dorsal stripes curved and bending toward center (Fig. 102); triangle between eyes.

ORNATE CHORUS FROG, *P. ornata*   **P. 548**
 Bold black spots on side and near groin.

SPOTTED CHORUS FROG, *P. clarkii*   **P. 546**
 Markings green; triangle between eyes; pattern usually spotted, rarely striped.

STRECKER'S CHORUS FROG, *P. streckeri* (ssp.)   **P. 549**
 Dark spot below eye; foreleg very stout.

CRICKET FROGS (*Acris*)

NORTHERN CRICKET FROG, *A. crepitans crepitans* (ssp.)   **P. 528**
 Short leg; dark triangle between eyes.

SOUTHERN CRICKET FROG, *A. gryllus gryllus*   **P. 528**
 Long leg; dark triangle between eyes.

BLANCHARD'S CRICKET FROG, *A. crepitans blanchardi*   **P. 530**
 Plump, stocky body; dark triangle between eyes.

TRUE TOADS (BUFO)

WESTERN GREEN TOAD, *B. debilis insidior*   **P. 525**
 Green or yellowish green; a black, netlike pattern on at least part of body; skin warty.

EASTERN GREEN TOAD, *B. debilis debilis*   **P. 525**
 Green, spotted with black and yellow; skin warty.

OAK TOAD, *B. quercicus*   **P. 522**
 Paired black spots; light middorsal stripe.

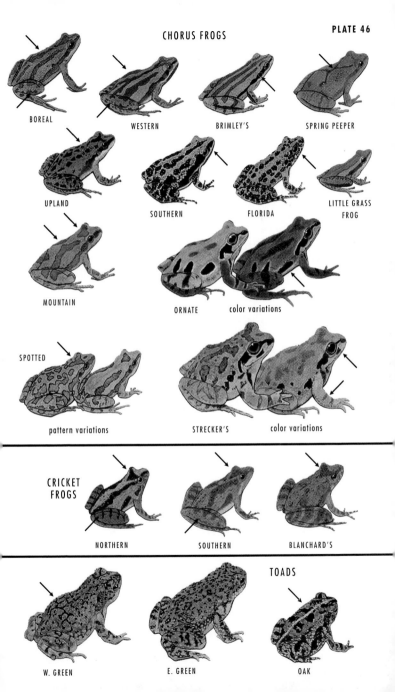

PLATE 46

CHORUS FROGS

BOREAL

WESTERN

BRIMLEY'S

SPRING PEEPER

UPLAND

SOUTHERN

FLORIDA

LITTLE GRASS FROG

MOUNTAIN

ORNATE

color variations

SPOTTED

pattern variations

STRECKER'S

color variations

CRICKET FROGS

NORTHERN

SOUTHERN

BLANCHARD'S

TOADS

W. GREEN

E. GREEN

OAK

PLATE 47

TREEFROGS (Chiefly *Hyla*)

PINE WOODS TREEFROG, *H. femoralis*   **P. 534**
Dark dorsal blotches; light spots on concealed surface of thigh (Fig. 100).

SQUIRREL TREEFROG, *H. squirella*   **P. 535**
Green or brown or combinations of both; highly variable (see text).

PINE BARRENS TREEFROG, *H. andersonii*   **P. 531**
Whitish (or yellowish) and purplish stripes.

GREEN TREEFROG, *H. cinerea*   **P. 532**
Light stripe on body highly variable in length; completely absent in some individuals.

GRAY TREEFROG, *H. versicolor* and *H. chrysoscelis*   **P. 536**
Light spot below eye; concealed surfaces of hind legs washed with orange. See text for comments on these two sibling species.

BIRD-VOICED TREEFROG, *H. avivoca*   **P. 537**
Light spot below eye; concealed surfaces of hind legs washed with green or yellowish white.

CANYON TREEFROG, *H. arenicolor*   **P. 538**
Dark bar below eye. (Trans-Pecos Texas)

BARKING TREEFROG, *H. gratiosa*   **P. 533**
Profusion of dark, rounded spots.

CUBAN TREEFROG, *Osteopilus septentrionalis*   **P. 538**
Large toe discs; warty skin.

MEXICAN TREEFROG, *Smilisca baudinii*   **P. 539**
Light spot below eye; black patch on shoulder behind eardrum.

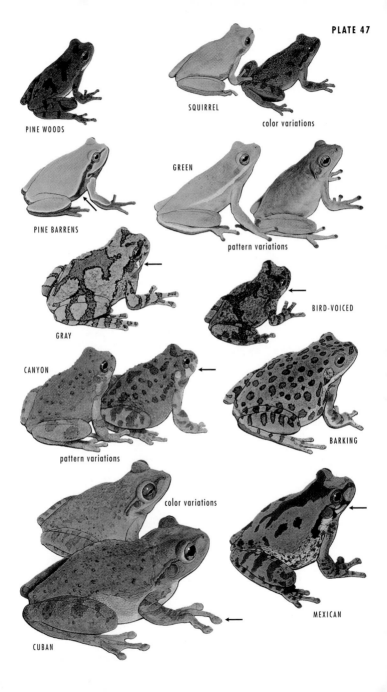

PLATE 47

PINE WOODS

SQUIRREL

color variations

PINE BARRENS

GREEN

pattern variations

GRAY

BIRD-VOICED

CANYON

pattern variations

BARKING

color variations

CUBAN

MEXICAN

PLATE 48

TRUE FROGS (*Rana*)

Most of these have dorsolateral ridges—see page 140.

FLORIDA BOG FROG, *R. okaloosae* **P. 559**
  Small size; dorsum unspotted; prominent ridges; 4th toe extends well beyond webbing on hind foot.

MINK FROG, *R. septentrionalis** **P. 562**
  Mottled or spotted pattern (Fig. 107); often no ridges; musky odor.

CARPENTER FROG, *R. virgatipes** **P. 558**
  Two golden-brown lateral stripes.

WOOD FROG, *R. sylvatica* **P. 563**
  Dark mask through eye.

NORTHERN LEOPARD FROG, *R. pipiens* **P. 566**
  Rounded dark spots; unbroken ridges (Fig. 108).

SOUTHERN LEOPARD FROG, *R. utricularia* **P. 567**
  Often a light spot on eardrum; pointed snout; unbroken ridges (Fig. 108).

RIO GRANDE LEOPARD FROG, *R. berlandieri* **P. 569**
  Pallid coloration; ridges inset medially just before groin (Fig. 108).

PLAINS LEOPARD FROG, *R. blairi* **P. 568**
  Brown; rarely with green color dorsally; ridges broken and inset medially just before groin (Fig. 108).

PICKEREL FROG, *R. palustris* **P. 569**
  Squarish dark spots; bright yellow or orange on concealed surfaces of hind legs.

FLORIDA GOPHER FROG, *R. capito aesopus* **P. 572**
  Stubby; irregular markings on light ground.

DUSKY GOPHER FROG, *R. capito sevosa* (ssp.) **P. 572**
  Stubby, dark; belly spotted (Fig. 109).

CRAWFISH FROG, *R. areolata* (ssp.) **P. 571**
  Stubby; dark spots rounded and with light borders; belly mostly without markings (Fig. 109).

BRONZE FROG, *R. clamitans clamitans** **P. 560**
  General bronzy coloration.

GREEN FROG, *R. clamitans melanota** **P. 561**
  Bright green and brown; highly variable (see text).

RIVER FROG, *R. heckscheri** **P. 556**
  Dark appearance; white spots on lip; no ridges; river-swamp habitat. (See also Fig. 106.)

PIG FROG, *R. grylio** **P. 557**
  Pointed snout; 4th toe extends only slightly beyond webbing (Fig. 105); no ridges.

BULLFROG, *R. catesbeiana** **P. 555**
  Blunt snout; 4th toe extends well beyond webbing (Fig. 105); no ridges; pattern variable (see text).

* The tympanum (eardrum) is larger than the eye in males, and only the size of the eye or smaller in females.

PLATE 48

FLORIDA BOG

MINK

CARPENTER

WOOD

N. LEOPARD

S. LEOPARD

RIO GRANDE LEOPARD

PLAINS LEOPARD

PICKEREL

FLORIDA

GOPHER

DUSKY

CRAWFISH

BRONZE

GREEN

RIVER

PIG

BULLFROG

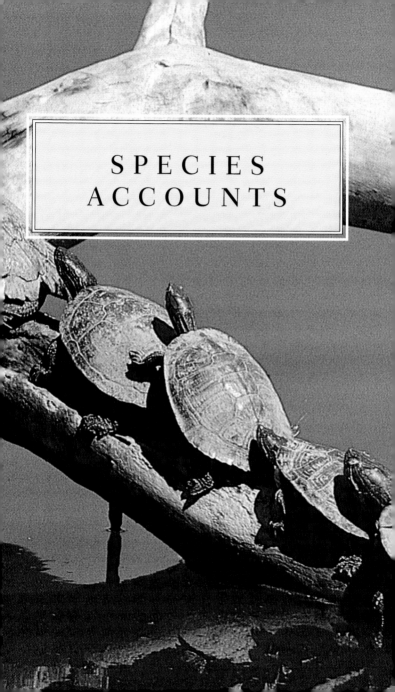

SPECIES
ACCOUNTS

What Is a Reptile?
And What Is an Amphibian?

Until about a century ago it was customary to classify all the animals listed in this book simply as "reptiles," and a few people still think of them in that way. Actually they form two natural groups, the Classes Reptilia and Amphibia among the vertebrates (back-boned animals), and they are placed below the birds and mammals and above the fishes. They are cold-blooded, deriving heat from outside sources and controlling their body temperatures by moving to cooler or warmer environments as necessary.

The following definitions will apply to all the species found in our area:

REPTILES are clad in scales, shields, or plates, and their toes bear claws. (The clawless Leatherback sea turtle is an exception. Soft-shell turtles have only a few scales on their limbs.) Young reptiles are miniature replicas of their parents, in general appearance if not always in coloration and pattern. To the Class Reptilia belong the crocodilians, turtles, lizards, amphisbaenians, and snakes—as well as the only surviving member of another group, the tuatara, which is now confined to tiny islets off the coast of New Zealand.

AMPHIBIANS have moist, glandular skins, and their toes are devoid of claws. Their young pass through a larval, usually aquatic stage (for instance, the tadpole stage of the frog) before they metamorphose into the adult form. The word *amphibious* is based upon Greek words and means "living a double life." Belonging to the Class Amphibia are the salamanders (including newts) and the toads and frogs. A third group occurs in the tropics, consisting of about 170 species of the burrowing, or aquatic, snake-shaped caecilians.

TURTLES

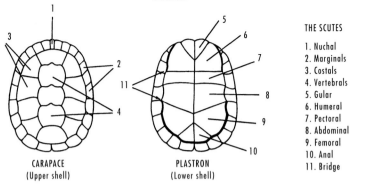

CARAPACE
(Upper shell)

PLASTRON
(Lower shell)

THE SCUTES

1. Nuchal
2. Marginals
3. Costals
4. Vertebrals
5. Gular
6. Humeral
7. Pectoral
8. Abdominal
9. Femoral
10. Anal
11. Bridge

LIZARDS

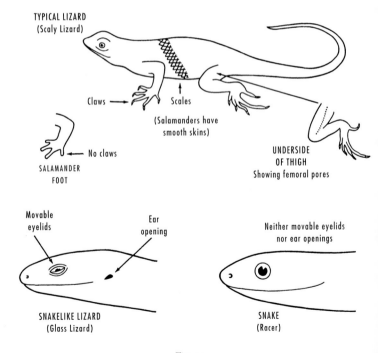

TYPICAL LIZARD
(Scaly Lizard)

Claws

Scales

(Salamanders have smooth skins)

No claws

SALAMANDER
FOOT

UNDERSIDE
OF THIGH
Showing femoral pores

Movable
eyelids

Ear
opening

SNAKELIKE LIZARD
(Glass Lizard)

Neither movable eyelids
nor ear openings

SNAKE
(Racer)

Fig. 23

SNAKES

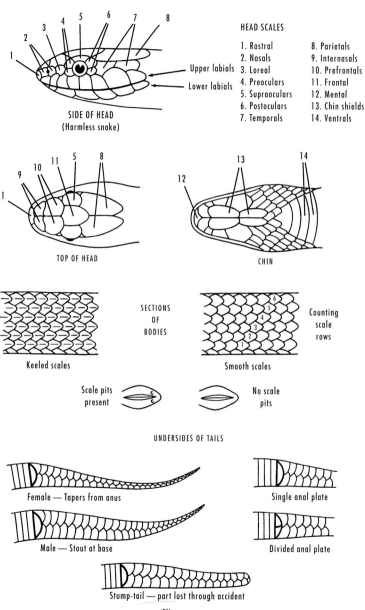

HEAD SCALES

1. Rostral	8. Parietals
2. Nasals	9. Internasals
3. Loreal	10. Prefrontals
4. Preoculars	11. Frontal
5. Supraoculars	12. Mental
6. Postoculars	13. Chin shields
7. Temporals	14. Ventrals

Upper labials
Lower labials

SIDE OF HEAD
(Harmless snake)

TOP OF HEAD

CHIN

SECTIONS
OF
BODIES

Counting
scale
rows

Keeled scales

Smooth scales

Scale pits
present

No scale
pits

UNDERSIDES OF TAILS

Female — Tapers from anus

Single anal plate

Male — Stout at base

Divided anal plate

Stump-tail — part lost through accident

Fig. 24

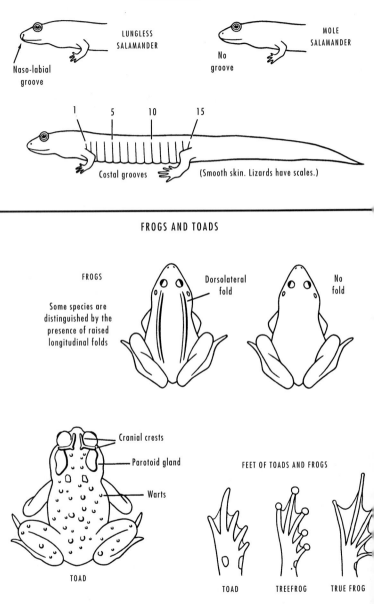

SALAMANDERS

LUNGLESS SALAMANDER

Naso-labial groove

MOLE SALAMANDER

No groove

1 5 10 15

Costal grooves   (Smooth skin. Lizards have scales.)

FROGS AND TOADS

FROGS

Some species are distinguished by the presence of raised longitudinal folds

Dorsolateral fold

No fold

Cranial crests

Parotoid gland

Warts

TOAD

FEET OF TOADS AND FROGS

TOAD   TREEFROG   TRUE FROG

Fig. 25

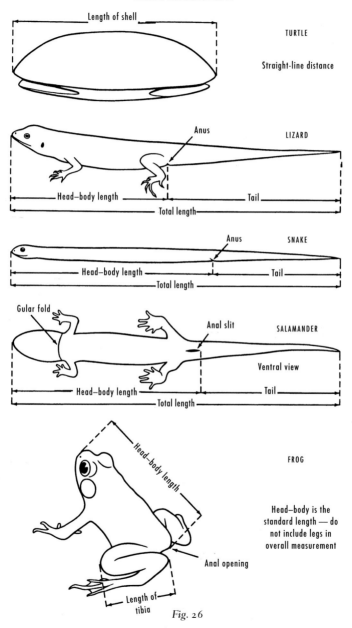

TAKING MEASUREMENTS

Length of shell

TURTLE

Straight-line distance

Anus

LIZARD

Head—body length

Tail

Total length

Anus

SNAKE

Head—body length

Tail

Total length

Gular fold

Anal slit

SALAMANDER

Ventral view

Head—body length

Tail

Total length

Head—body length

FROG

Head—body is the standard length — do not include legs in overall measurement

Anal opening

Length of tibia

Fig. 26

CROCODILIANS

ORDER CROCODYLIA

Huge, lizardlike reptiles that occur in many of the warmer parts of the world. Twenty-one species are known to science; of these, only two, the American Alligator and the American Crocodile, are native to the United States. A third species, the Spectacled Caiman, has been introduced in extreme southern Florida, where it is locally common.

CROCODILE: FAMILY CROCODYLIDAE

AMERICAN CROCODILE *Crocodylus acutus*   PL. 1

IDENTIFICATION: 7½–12 ft. (2.3–3.7 m); record 15 ft. (4.6 m) in U.S. to 23 ft. (7 m) in South America. The *long, tapering snout* is the hallmark of the American Crocodile. General overall coloration gray to tannish gray or dark greenish gray with dusky markings. A large tooth (4th) in lower jaw shows prominently when mouth is closed (Fig. 4, opp. Pl. 1). This is visible only at close range and is not well developed in young individuals. *Young:* Gray or greenish gray with narrow black crossbands or rows of spots; about 8½–10 in. (21.5–25.4 cm) when hatched.

The Crocodile, now rare in the United States, is confined chiefly to Florida Bay in the Everglades National Park, Biscayne Bay, and the Florida Keys. Any crocodilian seen in salt or brackish water from Miami southward and along the Keys will *probably* be this species. The Alligator rarely leaves fresh water, but is known to occur on Big Pine and other Keys. Although neither of these big reptiles normally attacks human beings, large adults should not be approached. Wounded ones are very dangerous, especially the Crocodile, which is a savage fighter when aroused or captured. Eggs are buried in sand or marl, which may be scooped into low mounds; nests normally are left unguarded, although the females may return to them more or less regularly at night. **SIMILAR SPECIES:** (1) Alligator has broadly rounded snout and no boldly conspicuous tooth in lower jaw. (2) Spectacled Caiman has curved bony ridge in front of eyes (Fig. 4, opp. Pl.1). **VOICE:** *Male:* A low rumble or growl, less intense than and without the penetrating power

of the Alligator's roar. *Young:* A high-pitched grunt. **RANGE:** Extr. s. Fla. and the Keys, occasionally wandering north at least to Sarasota and Palm Beach counties on Florida's west and east coasts, respectively. Greater Antilles; s. Mexico to Colombia and Ecuador.

ALLIGATOR AND CAIMAN: FAMILY ALLIGATORIDAE

AMERICAN ALLIGATOR *Alligator mississippiensis* PL. 1

IDENTIFICATION: 6–16½ ft. (1.8–5 m); record 19 ft. 2 in. (5.84 m). The *broadly rounded snout* will distinguish this big reptile from the American Crocodile of s. Fla., the only species with which a large adult Alligator could possibly be confused. General coloration black, but light markings of young may persist (not too conspicuously) into adulthood. *Young:* Bold yellowish crossbands on black ground color; about 8¼–9 in. (21.5–23 cm) at hatching.

The Alligator is a characteristic resident of the great river swamps, lakes, bayous, marshes, and other bodies of water of Fla. and the Gulf and Lower Atlantic Coastal Plains. All sizes bask. Watch for eyes, heads, or snouts protruding from water surface of 'gator holes along wilder waterways of the South. Nests, mounds of vegetable debris 4–7 ft. (1–2 m) in diameter, 18–36 in. (45–90 cm) high, and in which the eggs are buried, should be approached with caution from spring to early autumn, when there may be a guarding female in attendance nearby. **SIMILAR SPECIES:** (1)

An American Alligator moving at night through a longleaf pine forest. The demand for articles made from their hides caused overhunting of these huge reptiles, but with protection they have made a good comeback.

American Crocodile has tapering snout and, except in small individuals, the 4th lower jaw tooth protrudes conspicuously upward near snout (Fig. 4, opp. Pl. 1). (2) Spectacled Caiman has curved, bony, crosswise ridge in front of eyes (Fig. 4, opp. Pl. 1). **VOICE:** *Adult male:* A throaty, bellowing roar with great carrying power. *Adult female:* Bellows like the male but less loudly; grunts like a pig when calling to her young, which she actively protects from predators. The female uncovers hatchlings in the nest and gently carries them in her mouth to the safety of water. Under some circumstances the young may remain with her until the spring after they hatch. *Young:* A moaning grunt, like saying *umph-umph-umph* with mouth closed and in a fairly high key. Alligators of all sizes hiss. **RANGE:** Coastal N.C. to extr. s. Fla. and sporadic on the Keys; west to cen. Texas; probably introduced in the lower Rio Grande Valley. Extermination over large areas, because of poaching and the drastic alteration of habitats by human activities, makes preparation of an accurate range map very difficult. We have shown what we believe is the historical natural range.

Under protection, the Alligator has prospered and reoccupied wild areas where it had long been absent. Unfortunately, it has unwisely been released outside its known native range by government agencies.

SPECTACLED CAIMAN *Caiman crocodilus*   **PL. 1**
   IDENTIFICATION: 3½–6 ft. (1.1–1.8 m); record 8 ft. 8 in. (2.64 m). Ground color greenish-, yellowish-, or brownish gray with dark brown crossbands. *Bony ridge in front of eyes* (Fig. 4, opp. Pl. 1) may be broken or irregular, but it is by far the best means of identification. *Young:* About 8 in. (20.3 cm) at hatching. **SIMILAR SPECIES:**

(1) Adult Alligators are black, and their young have *yellow* crossbands on a black ground color. (2) American Crocodiles have a narrower snout, and in adults the 4th lower tooth protrudes conspicuously upward near the snout. **RANGE:** *Not native.* This reptile has escaped or has been deliberately released in Dade Co., Fla., where it is locally thriving; a nonbreeding, isolated population in Palm Beach Co.; introduced in e. P.R., and on the Isla de la Juventud (Isle of Pines) of Cuba. Natural range is from s. Mexico to n. Argentina.

SPECTACLED CAIMAN
Caiman crocodilus

6

TURTLES

ORDER TESTUDINES

Turtles occur in all the continents except Antarctica. They rove the open seas, survive in arid deserts, and are particularly abundant in eastern North America. Worldwide there are more than 240 species.

Some have good field marks that are visible through binoculars, but a great many kinds must be caught for positive identification. Check the number and arrangement of the scutes on the plastron (lower shell) and whether or not it is hinged. The markings of the soft parts may also require examination. To get a bashful turtle to stick out its neck and legs, put it temporarily in an aquarium or large glass jar full of water and wait quietly; usually the head and neck will soon be extended.

Bear in mind that turtles often turn up in strange places, sometimes far outside their natural ranges. Pets escape, and turtles may be caught, transported, and subsequently liberated unwisely by well-meaning persons.

SNAPPING TURTLES: FAMILY CHELYDRIDAE

Large freshwater turtles with short tempers and long tails; of economic value and ranging collectively from Canada to South America.

SNAPPING TURTLE *Chelydra serpentina*   PLS. 3, 9
IDENTIFICATION: 8–14 in. (20.3–36 cm); record 19⅜ in. (49.4 cm). Weight of average adults 10–35 lbs. (4.5–16 kg), but up to 75 lbs. (34 kg) for one wild-caught individual, and 86 lbs. (39 kg) for fattened captive ones. Ugly both in appearance and disposition, this

freshwater "loggerhead" is easily recognized by its large head, small plastron, and long tail, which is *saw-toothed* along the upper side. Carapace in adults varies from almost black to light horn-brown. *Young* (Pl. 3): Blackish or dark brown, a light spot at edge of each marginal scute. Carapace very rough and with three fairly well defined longitudinal keels. (The rugose condition becomes less prominent as turtle grows older; adults tend to become smooth, but usually retain traces of the keels.) Tail as long as carapace or longer. Carapace about ¾–1¼ in. (1.9–3.2 cm) at hatching.

SNAPPING TURTLES
Chelydra serpentina

■ COMMON
▨ FLORIDA

Any permanent body of fresh water, large or small, is a potential home for a snapper; it even enters brackish water. Snappers *rarely bask* as most other turtles do. Under water they are usually inoffensive, pulling in their heads when stepped on. They often bury themselves in mud in shallow water with only eyes showing. On land they may strike repeatedly; a favorite maneuver is to stand with hindquarters elevated and jaws agape and then lunge forward. Small and medium-sized specimens may be carried by their tails (Fig. 1). Keep plastron side toward your leg. Omnivorous—food includes various small aquatic invertebrates, fish, reptiles, birds, mammals, carrion, and a surprisingly large amount of vegetation. Economically important; large numbers are caught for making soups and stews. **SIMILAR SPECIES:** (1) Alligator Snapper has an extra row of scutes between marginals and costals. (2) Mud and Musk Turtles have short tails and (adults) smooth shells. **RANGE:** S. Canada to Gulf of Mexico; Atlantic Ocean to Rocky Mts., and introduced farther west; isolated records in n. Me. and s. Canada. **SUBSPECIES:** COMMON SNAPPING TURTLE, *Chelydra s. serpentina* (Pls. 3 and 9). As described above and with range as stated. FLORIDA SNAPPING TURTLE, *Chelydra s. osceola*. Similar, but with the knobs on the keels more toward the centers of the large scutes; upper surface of neck with long pointed tubercles (rounded, wartlike tubercles on neck of Common Snapper); averages smaller, the record size is 17¼ in. (43.8 cm); record weight 47½ lbs. (21.6 kg). *Young:* Chestnut brown; keels and ridges very prominent. Carapace about 1–1¼ in. (2.5–3 cm) at hatching. Peninsular Fla. and extr. s. Ga. Additional subspecies occur from s. Mexico to Ecuador.

An adult female Alligator Snapping Turtle from Montgomery County, Kansas. This is the largest freshwater turtle in North America.

ALLIGATOR SNAPPING TURTLE

Macroclemys temminckii

IDENTIFICATION: 15–26 in. (38–66 cm); record 31½ in. (80 cm). Weight 35–150 lbs. (16–68 kg); record 251 lbs. (113.9 kg) for a specimen maintained in captivity for nearly 50 years; 316 lbs. (143.3 kg) for a wild-caught example. Look for the *huge head* with its strongly *hooked beaks*, the prominent dorsal keels, and the *extra row of scutes* on each side of the carapace. Likely to be confused only with Snapping Turtles. *Young* (Pl. 3): Brown, shell exceedingly rough; tail very long. About 1¼–1¾ in. (3–4.4 cm) at hatching.

This gigantic freshwater turtle, our largest and one of the largest in the world, often lies at bottom of lake or river with mouth held open. A curious pink process on floor of mouth resembles a worm, wriggles like one, and serves as a lure for fish.

ALLIGATOR SNAPPING TURTLE
Macroclemys temminckii

SIMILAR SPECIES: Snapping Turtle has a saw-toothed tail and a smaller head, and also lacks the extra row of scutes between costals and marginals. **RANGE:** Sw. Ga. and n. Fla. to e. Texas; north in Mississippi Valley to Kans., Iowa, and sw. Ky.; an isolated record in cen. Tenn.

These are the "stinkpots," the "skillpots," and the "stinking-jims" that often take a fisherman's hook. Such inelegant names derive from a musky secretion exuded at the time of capture from two glandular openings on each side of the body. These are situated where the skin meets the bridge between the plastron and the carapace.

"Bottom crawlers" would be a good way to describe these reptiles. They are strongly aquatic, the musk turtles especially, and rarely leave the water except during rains or in the nesting season. They bask in the open occasionally, but are more likely to take the sun in shallow water with only part of the shell exposed above the surface. Catch them if you can, for identification is difficult without flipping them over for a look at the plastron. Use a net or hold the shell far back—their jaws are strong, necks are long, and many are very short-tempered.

The musk turtles (*Sternotherus*) have relatively small plastrons that offer little protection for the legs. The anterior lobe is movable on a transverse hinge situated between the 2nd and 3rd *pairs* of plastral scutes (Fig. 27), but the hinge usually is not apparent to the eye. It may be demonstrated, however, by moving the front tip of the plastron gently up and down. The pectoral scutes are squarish. This genus ranges from southern Ontario south to and through the Gulf States.

The mud turtles (*Kinosternon*) have much larger plastrons equipped with two readily discernible transverse hinges (Fig. 27). The pectoral scutes are usually triangular in shape in most of our species. *Kinosternon* ranges from Long Island to northern Argentina.

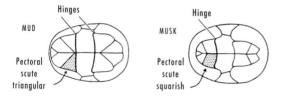

Fig. 27. Plastrons (lower shells) of Mud (Kinosternon) *and Musk* (Sternotherus) *Turtles.*

The two genera share the following characteristics: (a) there are barbels (downward fleshy projections) on the chin and smaller ones on the neck; and (b) the marginal scutes, including the nuchal, are almost always 23 in number (most other turtles have 25). At hatching, the young of most species vary from about ⁹⁄₁₆–1⅛ in. (1.4–2.8 cm) in carapace length.

These turtles are often mistaken for young snappers, but the Snapping Turtles have long tails with saw-toothed projections on top. Musk and Mud Turtles have short tails that are useful in distinguishing sexes. Males have longer, stouter tails, usually with a clawlike tip; in females the tails may be little more than nubbins. Males of most species also have two rough patches of skin on each hind leg; the patches touch each other when the knee is flexed.

COMMON MUSK TURTLE   *Sternotherus odoratus*   PLS. 2, 3

IDENTIFICATION: 2–4¼ in. (5.1–11.5 cm); record 5⅜ in. (13.7 cm). The only musk turtle occurring north of "Dixie." Two characteristics distinguish it from all other musk turtles: (a) two light stripes on head; and (b) barbels on chin *and* throat. Dark pigment may at least partly obscure the head stripes, and in extreme cases the head may be uniformly black. The smooth carapace varies from light olive brown to almost black and may be irregularly streaked or spotted with dark pigment. Plastron *small* and with *single* hinge. *Male:* Broad areas of soft skin showing between scutes of plastron; tail thick and terminating in a blunt, horny nail. *Female:* Only small areas of skin showing between plastral scutes; tail very small and with or without a sharp, horny nail. *Young:* Carapace length ⅞–1 in. (2.2–2.5 cm), dark gray to black, rough in texture, and with a prominent middorsal keel; a smaller keel on each side varying in size from a mere trace to as prominent as in Loggerhead Musk Turtle (Fig. 28); keels gradually disappear with age; head stripes prominent; light spot on each marginal (Pl. 3).

Extraordinarily abundant in many bodies of water, but not often observed except in shallow, clear-water lakes, ponds, and rivers. In these it may be seen leisurely patrolling the bottom in search of food, its shell looking like a rounded stone. This illusion is heightened by the green algae that grow on many specimens. Still waters are preferred.

If a turtle ever falls on your head or drops into your canoe, it probably will be this or one of the other musk turtles. Slanting boles of relatively slender trees are occasionally ascended by several species of turtles in wooded swamps, along watercourses, or at edges of marshes, where horizontal basking places are at a premium. Because of small size of plastron and consequent greater mobility of legs, members of the genus *Sternotherus* can most easily negotiate such difficult ascents, and among them the Common Musk Turtle has been recorded as climbing the highest, sometimes 6 or more feet (2 m) above the surface of the water. Sleepy ones may not drop off until your boat passes below them. **SIMILAR SPECIES:**(1) All other Musk Turtles share the following: (a)

COMMON MUSK TURTLE
Sternotherus odoratus

heads with *dark* spots, stripes, or streaks on a light ground color; and (b) barbels on *chin only*. (2) Mud Turtles have large *plastrons with two hinges*. (3) Snapping Turtles have long, stout tails. **RANGE:** New England and s. Ont. to s. Fla.; west to Wisc. and Texas. The Common Musk Turtle occurs in many of the larger, more sluggish streams that penetrate the eastern mountains but is lacking at the higher elevations.

RAZORBACK MUSK TURTLE

PL. 2; FIGS. 28, 30

Sternotherus carinatus

IDENTIFICATION: 4–5 in. (10–12.5 cm); record 6¹⁵⁄₁₆ in. (17.6 cm). The upper shell reminds one of the legendary razorback hog. A keel is present in *all* turtles of this species, from newest hatchling to oldest adult, and sides of carapace slope down like a tent (Fig. 28). Head with dark spots, streaks, or blotches; old adults may lose their patterns and become almost plain horn-colored; scutes slightly overlapping. Plastron *small*; a *single* hinge; usually *no* gular scute. Barbels on *chin only*. *Young:* A sharp middorsal keel; shell toothed along each side (Fig. 30).

A turtle of the streams and great river swamps of the mid-South. Basks much more frequently than other musk turtles. Margins of carapace are often irregular where bone and overlying tissue have crumbled away. Erosion also occurs in Loggerhead Musk Turtle. In both species it may result from combat between male turtles or from the invasion of damaged tissue by algae or fungi.

MUSK TURTLES

RAZORBACK
Sternotherus carinatus

FLATTENED
Sternotherus depressus

SIMILAR SPECIES: (1) Common Musk Turtle normally has two light lines on head; also has barbels on *throat* as well as chin. (2) Mud Turtles have *large* plastrons with *two* hinges. **RANGE:** Se. Miss. to e.-cen. Texas; north to cen. Ark. and se. Okla.

LOGGERHEAD MUSK TURTLE
Sternotherus minor minor   **PLS. 2, 3; FIG. 28**

IDENTIFICATION: 3–4¼ in. (7.5–11.5 cm); record 5⅝ in. (14.5 cm). This musk turtle has *three distinct keels* (Fig. 28), and distinguishing it would be easy if one could stop right there. But, alas, the keels vanish in old adults, and young Common Musk Turtles sometimes have three well-developed keels. Check the following things first and then allow for sex and age: (a) plastron *small* with *one* hinge and one gular scute; (b) barbels on *chin only*; (c) head normally marked with dark spots on a light ground color. *Old male:* Head enormously enlarged. *Female:* Carapace streaked, spotted, or *blotched*. *Young:* Three keels that normally persist into adulthood; carapace length ⅞–1⅛ in. (2.2–2.8 cm), and strongly streaked with dark rays; hatchling with *pink* plastron (Pl. 3).

A common turtle of large, clear Florida springs. Like the Common Musk Turtle, it may climb up snags or cypress knees a considerable distance above the water. **SIMILAR SPECIES:** (1) Common Musk Turtle has barbels on chin *and neck,* and normally has two light lines on each side of head. (2) Stripeneck Musk Turtle has only one keel. (3) Mud Turtles have *large* plastrons with *two* hinges. **RANGE:** N.-cen. Ga. to extr. se. Ala. and n.-cen. Fla.

STRIPENECK MUSK TURTLE
Sternotherus minor peltifer   **PL. 2; FIG. 28**

IDENTIFICATION: 3–4 in. (7.5–10 cm); record 4⅝ in. (11.7 cm). Dark stripes on sides of head and neck. A single middorsal keel, promi-

RAZORBACK	STRIPENECK	LOGGERHEAD	FLATTENED
(carinatus)	*(peltifer)*	*(minor)*	*(depressus)*
One keel,	One keel,	Three keels	Blunt keel,
sharp slope	gentle slope		low shell

Fig. 28. Transverse cross sections of young Musk Turtles (Sternotherus).

nent in young (Fig. 28), but
disappearing in older specimens. Carapace gray or brown
with dark streaks or spots.
Plastron *small*, with *one* hinge;
a single gular scute. Barbels on
chin only. Young: Traces of an
additional keel may be evident
on each side of carapace.

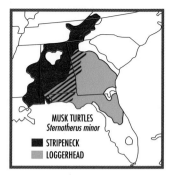

MUSK TURTLES
Sternotherus minor

■ STRIPENECK
▨ LOGGERHEAD

At home in many streams
and rivers of the mid-South.
Ascends clear, shallow creeks
to elevations of approximately
1,000 ft. (300 m) at the edges of mountains. Feeds chiefly on
small snails and insects. **SIMILAR SPECIES:** (See Fig. 28 for shapes of
shells.) (1) Sides of head in both Razorback and Loggerhead
Musk Turtles are marked with dark spots on a light ground color;
also, Razorback has *no* gular scute. (2) Common Musk Turtle has
two light lines on each side of head and barbels on chin *and*
throat. (3) Mud Turtles have *large* plastrons with *two* hinges.
RANGE: Extr. sw. Va. and e. Tenn. to the Gulf and the Pearl R., Miss.

FLATTENED MUSK TURTLE *Sternotherus depressus*   PL. 2

IDENTIFICATION: 3–4 in. (7.5–10 cm); record 4⅝ in. (11.7 cm). An
extraordinary little turtle that looks almost as though a person
with a heavy foot had trod upon it. In comparison with other
Musk Turtles the carapace is quite flattened, even in old adults.
In the young there is a blunted dorsal keel and the carapace flares
out at sides (Fig. 28); older specimens have flat shells rounded at
edges. Head and neck with network of dark lines on light ground
color. Scutes of carapace slightly overlapping. Plastron *small*, a
gular scute present. Barbels on *chin only. Young:* Carapace length
about 1 in. (2.5 cm). **RANGE:** Black Warrior R. system of n. Ala.

EASTERN MUD TURTLE   PLS. 2, 3; FIG. 29
Kinosternon subrubrum subrubrum

IDENTIFICATION: 2¾–4 in. (7–10 cm); record 4⅞ in. (12.4 cm). Adults
have no distinctive field marks, but throughout most of its range
this is the only mud turtle. Carapace smooth and some shade of
brown, varying from olive horn color to almost black. The large
double-hinged plastron may be plain yellowish brown or slightly
to heavily marked with black or dark brown. A broad bridge
between the upper and lower shells. Head spotted, mottled, or
irregularly streaked with yellow. *Young* (Pl. 3): Carapace length
¹¹⁄₁₆–1¹⁄₁₆ in. (1.7–2.6 cm), rough, black, or very dark brown, and

with a middorsal keel; an imperfect additional keel on each side. Plastron usually black in center and along the sutures (sometimes virtually solid black); lighter parts yellow, orange, or reddish; a bright spot on each marginal.

A semiaquatic reptile that wanders away from water much more often than the Common Musk Turtle. Shallow water preferred—ditches, wet meadows, small ponds, marshes, etc. This Mud Turtle has a strong tolerance for brackish water, and is often abundant at inner edges of tidal marshes and on many offshore islands. **SIMILAR SPECIES:** (1) Striped Mud Turtle has striped head and carapace. (2) Yellow Mud Turtle has 9th marginal scute much higher than 8th. (3) Musk Turtles have *small* plastrons with only a *single* hinge. **RANGE:** Long Island and extr. ne. N.J., and sw. Ind. to Gulf Coast; isolated colony in nw. Ind.

FLORIDA MUD TURTLE   FIG. 29
Kinosternon subrubrum steindachneri

IDENTIFICATION: 3–4 in. (7.5–10 cm); record 4¾ in. (12.1 cm). Like the Eastern Mud Turtle but with two main differences: (a) movable hind lobe of plastron is short, often shorter than front lobe;

EASTERN
(subrubrum)
Rear lobe large, bridge
broad at abdominal scute

FLORIDA
(steindachneri)
Rear lobe short, bridge
narrow at abdominal scute

YELLOW
(flavescens)
Pectorals pointed,
narrowly in contact

BIG BEND
(murrayi)
Pectorals blunt,
broadly in contact

Fig. 29. *Plastrons (lower shells) of Mud Turtles (Kinosternon).*

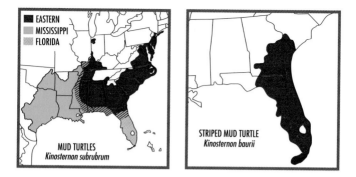

EASTERN
MISSISSIPPI
FLORIDA

MUD TURTLES
Kinosternon subrubrum

STRIPED MUD TURTLE
Kinosternon baurii

and (b) bridge connecting plastron to carapace is quite narrow (Fig. 29). Hence, plastron is proportionately smaller than in any other Mud Turtle and almost as small as the plastron of a Musk Turtle. Another point of similarity: many adult males have greatly enlarged heads, rivaling those of big male Loggerhead Musk Turtles.

Drainage ditches, marshes, sloughs, ponds, and other small bodies of water. More aquatic than Eastern Mud Turtle, with which it intergrades in northern Florida. **SIMILAR SPECIES:** (1) Striped Mud Turtle has light stripes on head and carapace. (2) Musk Turtles have only *one* plastral hinge. **RANGE:** Peninsular Fla. and Key Largo.

MISSISSIPPI MUD TURTLE   PL. 2
Kinosternon subrubrum hippocrepis

IDENTIFICATION: 3–4¾ in. (7.5–12.1 cm). The distinctive characters of two very different turtles are combined in this Mud Turtle. It has the *double-hinged plastron* of its genus but also sports *two light head stripes* on each side, like the Common Musk Turtle. Otherwise, similar to Eastern Mud Turtle, with which it intergrades chiefly east of the Mississippi R. *Young:* Carapace length ¹⁵⁄₁₆–1 in. (2.3–2.5 cm) at hatching.

A common turtle of bayous, lagoons, and great swamps of the lower Mississippi Valley. **SIMILAR SPECIES:** In Yellow Mud Turtle the 9th marginal scute is much higher than the 8th. **RANGE:** Se. Mo. to e.-cen. Okla. and south to the Gulf; Miss. to cen. Texas.

STRIPED MUD TURTLE *Kinosternon baurii*   PL. 2
IDENTIFICATION: 3–4 in. (7.5–10 cm); record 5 in. (12.7 cm). The *three light stripes on the shell* (one down center and another at each side) may be obscure, particularly in older turtles. If in

doubt, also check the *head* for *two light stripes* on each side. In some specimens scutes of carapace are so nearly transparent that vague outlines of underlying bony structure may be seen through them. *Young:* A narrow middorsal keel; carapace length ⁹⁄₁₆–1 in. (1.4–2.5 cm); carapace rough; a light spot on each marginal.

Habitats vary from deep drainage canals, sloughs, ponds, and "lettuce" lakes in cypress swamps to wet meadows, ditches, and other small, shallow bodies of water. Often prowls on land, even during the daytime. One of these turtles was reported to have lived nearly 50 years in captivity. **SIMILAR SPECIES:** Musk Turtles have small plastrons with only one hinge. **RANGE:** S.C. to the Lower Fla. Keys.

YELLOW MUD TURTLE *Kinosternon flavescens*   PL. 2; FIG. 30

IDENTIFICATION: 4–5 in. (10–12.5 cm); record 6⅜ in. (16.2 cm). The *yellowish chin and throat,* which sometimes may be seen from a distance when the turtle is prowling in shallow water or basking at the surface, is a good field character (at least for the wide-ranging western subspecies). But the 9th marginal scute makes identification positive. This scale is distinctly higher than the 8th marginal (10th marginal is also high). Carapace, usually flat or even depressed on top, is olive-brown to olive-green. Pectoral scutes of plastron pointed and only narrowly in contact (Fig. 29). Head and neck olive above. *Young:* 9th and 10th marginals as low as 8th (or even lower), except that 9th is always distinctly *peaked* dorsally, with the peak rising above the upper edge of both the 8th and 10th. The 9th and 10th marginals begin to enlarge when shell reaches a length of about 2¼ in. (6.4 cm). Small specimens have *bold black dots* at posterior borders of scutes of carapace

YELLOW MUD
(K. flavescens)
Dark spot on each
large scute; shell
smooth and rounded

RAZORBACK MUSK
(S. carinatus)
A middorsal keel;
shell toothed
along each side

Fig. 30. Carapaces (upper shells) of baby Mud (Kinosternon) *and Musk* (Sternotherus) *Turtles.*

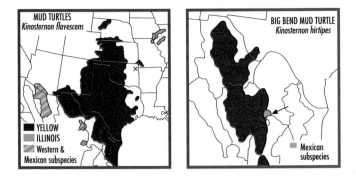

MUD TURTLES
Kinosternon flavescens

YELLOW
ILLINOIS
Western & Mexican subspecies

BIG BEND MUD TURTLE
Kinosternon hirtipes

Mexican subspecies

(Fig. 30); hatchlings have a bold yellow and black plastron; carapace length ¹³⁄₁₆–1³⁄₁₆ in. (2.1–3 cm) at hatching.

A common turtle throughout much of its range, occurring in a wide variety of bodies of water including temporary pools, but usually those with muddy bottoms. Toward the west it also utilizes such artificial habitats as cattle tanks, irrigation ditches, cisterns, and sewer drains. May appear on land during rains, while migrating when pools are drying up, or when merely foraging. During periods of drought, it can burrow into mud, there to await more favorable weather. **SIMILAR SPECIES:** (1) In all our other Mud Turtles, 9th marginal scute is same height or only slightly higher than 8th. (2) Musk Turtles have *small* plastrons with only *one* hinge. (3) In western Texas also see Big Bend Mud Turtle. **RANGE:** Ill. and Neb. to n. Mexico. **SUBSPECIES:** YELLOW MUD TURTLE *Kinosternon f. flavescens* (Pl. 2). As described above. S. Neb. to n. Mexico and west to extr. se. Ariz.; isolated colonies in sw. Mo. and adj. Kans., nw. Nebr., and e. Texas; an isolated record in ne. Okla. Mexican subspecies. ILLINOIS MUD TURTLE *Kinosternon f. spooneri.* Similar but with soft parts black or dark gray, carapace dark brown, and yellow pigment restricted to barbels and front half of lower jaw. Sand prairies of cen. and nw. Ill.; adj. Iowa and Mo.

BIG BEND MUD TURTLE *Kinosternon hirtipes murrayi*   **PL. 2**
IDENTIFICATION: 3¾–6¹¹⁄₁₆ in. (9.5–17 cm); record 7¼ in. (18.2 cm). Superficially similar to the Eastern Mud Turtle, but larger and more elongated. *Tenth marginal scute distinctly higher than all other marginals.* A faint middorsal keel at all ages. Carapace olive-brown to almost black, each scute narrowly bordered by black. Plastron yellowish; seams bordered by black or dark brown; pectoral scutes broadly in contact (Fig. 29). Head brown or olive, profusely marked with small dark spots and streaks.

This Mexican turtle barely enters western Texas, where it has been found in spring-fed cattle tanks. It probably also occurs in the Rio Grande. Unlike the Yellow Mud Turtle, this species requires permanent water. **SIMILAR SPECIES:** Yellow Mud Turtle has a yellow throat, a flattened carapace, the *9th marginal distinctly higher than the 8th*, and the pectoral scutes meeting at a point or only narrowly in contact (Fig. 29). **RANGE:** Alamito Creek drainage in Presidio Co., Texas; the Río Conchos and desert basin drainages of n. Chihuahua south to Morelos. Mexican subspecies.

BOX AND WATER TURTLES: FAMILY EMYDIDAE

The largest of all turtle families, with representatives in every habitable continent except Australia, and with many kinds in the eastern and central United States and Canada (genera *Clemmys,* this page, to *Emydoidea,* p. 188, inclusive).

SPOTTED, BOG, AND WOOD TURTLES: GENUS *Clemmys*

These are residents chiefly of the Northeast; related members of the family occur in Europe, Asia, and North Africa, and one other member of the genus lives in our Pacific states.

SPOTTED TURTLE *Clemmys guttata*   PLS. 3, 5

IDENTIFICATION: 3½–4½ in. (9–11.5 cm); record 5 in. (12.7 cm). The "polka-dot turtle." The *yellow spots* are extremely variable in number. Hatchlings usually have one spot on each large scute, but older turtles may be well sprinkled, their dots totaling 100 or more. Conversely, spots on carapace may be few or (rarely) lacking entirely. In such cases, examine head and neck for several yellow or orange spots. *Male:* Horny portion of both jaws almost completely covered with dark pigment. *Female:* Horny portion of both jaws yellowish and virtually unmarked. *Young* (Pl. 3): About 1⅛ in. (2.8 cm) at hatching.

SPOTTED TURTLE
Clemmys guttata

At home in marshy meadows, bogs, swamps, small ponds, ditches, or other shallow bodies of water. Seldom in a hurry. Basking specimens usually enter the water rather leisurely when disturbed, hiding themselves nearby in mud or debris at bottom. *Much more frequently seen in spring than at other seasons.* **SIMILAR SPECIES:** (1) Bog Turtle has a large orange head patch. (2) Blanding's Turtle has great numbers of yellow spots and a *hinged plastron*. **RANGE:** S. Me. to extr. ne. Ill.; south in the East to cen. Fla.; isolated colonies in s. Que., s. Ont., cen. Ill., and sw. N.C. and adj. S.C.; an isolated record in nw. Vt.

BOG TURTLE
Clemmys muhlenbergii

BOG TURTLE
Clemmys muhlenbergii   **PL. 5**

IDENTIFICATION: 3–3½ in. (7.5–9 cm); record 4½ in. (11.4 cm). Formerly called "Muhlenberg's turtle." The *head patch*, normally orange, sometimes is yellow or split in two parts. Large scutes of carapace may have yellowish or reddish centers. *Young:* Carapace length 1–1¼ in. (2.5–3.2 cm) at hatching.

Although the Bog Turtle still occurs in certain areas, it is rare or completely absent in many regions where it once was fairly abundant. Sphagnum bogs, swamps, and clear, slow-moving meadow streams with muddy bottoms are preferred. The human propensity for draining and reclaiming such habitats has contributed to its disappearance. **SIMILAR SPECIES:** Spotted Turtles, a rare few of which completely lack yellow dots on their shells, have many separate yellow or orange spots on their heads and necks. **RANGE:** N.Y. to w. N.C. and extr. ne. Ga. in disjunct colonies; from near sea level in the North to 4,000 ft. (1200 m) in the southern mountains.

WOOD TURTLE
Clemmys insculpta   **PLS. 3, 5**

IDENTIFICATION: 5½–8 in. (14–20 cm); record 9³⁄₁₆ in. (23.4 cm). The "sculptured turtle." *Shell very rough*; each large scute in the form of an irregular pyramid rising upward in series of concentric grooves and ridges. *Orange on neck and limbs* led to vernacular name of "redleg" when this turtle was sold for human food during the early years of the 20th century. *Young* (Pl. 3): Shell broad and low, brown or grayish brown; no orange on neck or legs; tail

WOOD TURTLE
Clemmys insculpta

almost as long as carapace; 1 ⅛–1 ⅝ in. (2.8–4.1 cm) at hatching.

Next to gopher tortoises and box turtles, this is our most terrestrial turtle. Although quite at home in water and hibernating there, it frequently wanders far afield, through woods and meadows, across farmlands, and—often with fatal results—on roads and highways. **SIMILAR SPECIES:** (1) Both other "land turtles" occurring within the range of Wood Turtle (Blanding's and Eastern Box) have strongly *hinged* plastrons. (2) Adult Diamondback Terrapins are also sculptured, but are restricted to maritime marshes and their environs along the coast; baby Diamondbacks are strongly patterned (Pl. 4). **RANGE:** Nova Scotia to e. Minn.; south in the East to the Virginias; an isolated colony in ne. Iowa; isolated records in s. Que. and n. N.Y.

Box Turtles: Genus *Terrapene*

These are the "dry-land turtles" that close their shells tightly when danger threatens. Their hallmark is a broad hinge across the plastron, providing movable lobes both fore and aft (Fig. 5, opp. Pl. 5); these fit so neatly against the upper shell that in many individuals not even a knife blade could be inserted between them. With such close-fitting armor, box turtles are well adapted for a terrestrial life, even though they are much more closely related to some of the water turtles than to the gopher tortoises they superficially resemble. The upper jaw ends in a down-turned beak. In hatchlings—average 1 ⅛–1 ⅜ in. (2.8–3.5 cm)—the hinge is not functional. The young have a median dorsal ridge, evidences of which may persist in adults. Box turtles, which are strictly North American, range widely over the eastern and central United States and into the Southwest, and they also occur in many parts of Mexico. They are often captured and kept as temporary pets, only to be released well outside their native range. We have not attempted to map such records.

As adults, box turtles are kept more frequently as pets than any other turtles. Most adapt themselves readily to captivity, requiring only a backyard or a box of dirt for digging and a shallow pan of water for an occasional soaking. They are omnivorous, and are fond of fruits, berries, and raw hamburger. Canned dog food is a good staple diet. Ages of 30 and 40 years are common, and a few have been reported to reach the century mark.

EASTERN BOX TURTLE *Terrapene carolina carolina*   **PLS. 3, 5**

IDENTIFICATION: 4½–6 in. (11.5–15.2 cm); record 7 13/16 in. (19.8 cm). A "land turtle" with a high, domelike shell and an extremely variable coloration and pattern. Both upper and lower shells may be yellow, orange, or olive on black or brown; either dark or light colors may predominate. Four toes on each hind foot. *Male:* Rear lobe of plastron with central concave area; eyes sometimes red. *Female:* Plastron flat or slightly convex; eyes normally brown. *Young* (Pl. 3): Shell much flatter; mostly plain grayish brown, but with spot of yellow on each large scute.

BOX TURTLES
Terrapene carolina
■ THREE-TOED ■ EASTERN
■ GULF COAST ■ FLORIDA

Although essentially terrestrial, these turtles sometimes soak themselves by the hour (or day) in mud or water. During hot, dry weather they burrow beneath logs or rotting vegetation, but sharp summer showers usually bring them out of hiding, often in numbers. **SIMILAR SPECIES:** (1) Top of carapace is flattened in Ornate Box Turtle. (2) Gopher Tortoises have no plastral hinges. (3) Blanding's Turtle has flatter shell, profusion of light dots, and plastral lobes that don't shut tight. Obese Box Turtles also cannot close tight (thus leaving themselves vulnerable to enemies); but, by pushing down one lobe at a time with the fingers, you can check on whether the closure in the turtle's younger and slimmer days would have been complete. **RANGE:** Ne. Mass. to Ga., west to Mich., Ill., and Tenn. Within the U.S. this and all other races of *Terrapene carolina* intergrade with one another in most areas where their ranges come in contact; two other races occur in Mexico. **SUBSPECIES:** GULF COAST BOX TURTLE *Terrapene c. major.* Largest of living Box Turtles—record 8½ in. (21.6 cm). Rear margin of carapace flaring outward and sometimes turning upward to form a gutter instead of extending almost straight downward as in Eastern Box Turtle. Has four toes on each hind foot, but no distinctive pattern of its own; some individuals resemble Florida or Three-toed Box Turtles; some adults have white or white-blotched heads. Deep concavity in plastron of males. Young: Carapace length 1¼–1⅜ in. (3.1–3.5 cm); carapace uniform dark brown or black with yellow spot on each costal; pronounced middorsal keel with yellow stripe. Occurs in coastal marshes and palmetto-pine forests. Lower Apalachicola region of Fla. panhandle. The influence of *major* is evident along a large part of the Gulf Coast where it intergrades with other races.

FLORIDA BOX TURTLE *Terrapene carolina bauri*   **PLS. 3, 5**
IDENTIFICATION: 5–6½ in. (12.5–16.5 cm); record 7⁷⁄₁₆ in. (18.7 cm). The *light, radiating lines* may be broken or irregular, at least on some scutes. Also the *two head lines* may be interrupted or incom-

plete. Usually three toes on each hind foot. Deep concavity in plastron of males. *Young:* Yellowish middorsal stripe, involving keel; pattern mottled, yellowish or greenish on dark brown (see Pl. 3). **RANGE:** Fla. peninsula and some of the Keys.

THREE-TOED BOX TURTLE   **PL. 5**
Terrapene carolina triunguis

IDENTIFICATION: 4½–5 in. (11.5–12.5 cm); record 7 in. (17.9 cm). Don't depend entirely on the toes—it sometimes has four! The Florida Box Turtle also usually has only three toes on each hind foot, and so do occasional specimens of all other subspecies. Concavity in plastron of males very shallow or absent. A marked tendency for pattern to be replaced (sometimes completely) by plain olive- or horn-colored areas; plastron often plain yellow or horn-colored. Orange or yellow spots usually conspicuous on both head and forelimbs. **SIMILAR SPECIES:** In Ornate Box Turtle carapace is flattened on top and the pattern of radiating yellow lines is quite constant. Habitat will often separate the two: Ornate most often occurs in open, treeless areas; Three-toed, like its related subspecies, in woodlands, thickets, etc., particularly in the heat of summer. **RANGE:** Mo. to Texas and s.-cen. Ala.

ORNATE BOX TURTLE *Terrapene ornata ornata*   **PL. 5; FIG. 31**
IDENTIFICATION: 4–5 in. (10–12.5 cm); record 6⅛ in. (15.4 cm). *Well ornamented above and below* and showing far less variation in pattern and coloration than other Box Turtles. Light lines radiate downward from three centers on each side of carapace; 5 to 9 light stripes on 2nd costal scute (Fig. 31), but these are sometimes broken into rows of light spots. The strong plastral pattern

An adult Three-toed Box Turtle. Note the three toes on the hind foot.

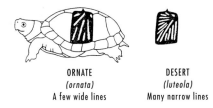

ORNATE
(ornata)
A few wide lines

DESERT
(luteola)
Many narrow lines

*Fig. 31. Radiating lines on second costal scute in subspecies of the
Ornate Box Turtle* (Terrapene ornata).

is characteristic. Other features distinguishing the Ornate from
the *carolina* Box Turtles are: (a) carapace flat on top, sometimes
dished-in, and seldom with any traces of a keel; and (b) plastron
large, usually as long as, or longer than, carapace. *Male:* Inner
hind toe capable of turning inward at a sharp angle and used in
clasping shell of female during mating. Males of *carolina* Box Turtles
lack this feature.

A turtle of the plains and prairies, often found in sandy areas
and able to tolerate more arid conditions than its eastern relatives.
Burrows to escape heat; rain storms sometimes result in the
sudden appearance of large numbers. Feeds largely on insects,
including those found in cattle dung. Reaches a natural longevity
of at least 30 years. SIMILAR SPECIES: (1) Three-toed and (2) Eastern
Box Turtles, aside from their different patterns, also have high,
arched shells and usually retain evidences of a dorsal keel. RANGE:
Ind. to se. Wyo., south through Texas and into the coastal prairies
of La.; range discontinuous toward northeast.

*An adult female
Ornate Box Turtle.
This creature was formally
designated the
official state reptile of
Kansas by the state
legislature in 1986.
These turtles are estimated
to reach an age
of 30 years.*

ORNATE ■
DESERT ■

BOX TURTLES
Terrapene ornata

DESERT BOX TURTLE

Terrapene ornata luteola **FIG. 31**

IDENTIFICATION: 4–5 in. (10–12.5 cm); record 5⅞ in. (14.9 cm). Also called "yellow box turtle," a name derived from the tendency for specimens to lose their patterns and to become uniformly yellowish, straw-, or horn-colored with age. Younger specimens (and some adults) have an abundance of radiating lines that number 11 to 14 on the 2nd costal scute (Fig. 31). In other respects this race resembles Ornate Box Turtle.

A resident of arid grasslands, oak-savannah habitats, and (occasionally) the edges of forests with open herbaceous vegetation. **RANGE:** Northern portions of the Chihuahuan and Sonoran deserts; intergrades with the Ornate Box Turtle in e.-cen. N.M. and through the Big Bend region of Texas.

DIAMONDBACK TERRAPINS: Genus *Malaclemys*

Most celebrated of American turtles. Its succulent flesh, when properly (and laboriously) prepared, rates high on the gourmet's list. During the heyday of the terrapin fad, market hunting seriously reduced it in numbers, but its popularity has waned and it has made a strong comeback in many areas. The Diamondback Terrapin is a reptile of the coastal marshes, rarely straying from salt or brackish water. Its food includes fish, crustaceans, mollusks, and insects. Seven races are recognized, all of a single species, and ranging, collectively, from Massachusetts at least to southern Texas.

Concentric grooves and ridges or concentric dark and light markings on each of the large scutes of the carapace are characteristic. So are the flecked or spotted heads and legs. The carapace has a central keel, low and inconspicuous in the Atlantic Coast races, but prominent and often knobbed in the subspecies along the Gulf of Mexico. Individual variation is great, and some forms are confusingly alike; therefore it is well to lean heavily on geography (the place where the turtle is found) in making identifications.

Females grow considerably larger than males. The sizes given in the text are the standard full lengths of the carapace (see drawing p. 141). Terrapin marketers used a different system—the length of the *plastron* from its front end to the bottom of the notch at the rear.

NORTHERN DIAMONDBACK TERRAPIN PLS. 4, 5
Malaclemys terrapin terrapin

IDENTIFICATION: Adult females 6–9 in. (15.2–22.9 cm); males 4–5½ in. (10–14 cm). The salt-marsh or brackish-water habitat is a good field character. *Concentric rings or ridges* and *spotted head and limbs* clinch identification when turtle is at hand. Coloration extremely variable: some specimens have carapace boldly patterned with dark rings on a ground of light gray or light brown, others have shell uniform black or dark brown; plastron orange or yellowish- to greenish gray, and with or without bold dark markings. In this race the carapace is wedge-shaped when viewed from above, with widest part in rear half; plastron has nearly parallel sides. *Young* (Pl. 4): More brightly patterned than most adults; about 1–1¼ in. (2.5–3.2 cm) at hatching.

Coastal marshes, tidal flats, coves, estuaries, inner edges of barrier beaches—in general, any sheltered and unpolluted body of salt or brackish water. **SIMILAR SPECIES:** (1) The rough-shelled Wood Turtle has orange on neck and limbs, and it avoids salt water. (2) Snappers and Mud Turtles frequently enter brackish water; Snappers have a long, saw-toothed tail, Mud Turtles have hinged plastrons. **RANGE:** Coastal strip, Cape Cod to Cape Hatteras. **SUBSPECIES:** CAROLINA DIAMONDBACK TERRAPIN, *Malaclemys t. centrata.* Very similar, but with sides of carapace more nearly parallel, and sides of plastron tending to curve inward toward rear. Coastal strip, Cape Hatteras to n. Fla. FLORIDA EAST COAST TERRAPIN, *Malaclemys t. tequesta.* Carapace dark or horn-colored and without a pattern of concentric circles; centers of large scutes only a little lighter than areas surrounding them. East coast of Fla. MANGROVE DIAMONDBACK TERRAPIN. *Malaclemys t. rhizophorarum.* Dark spots on neck fused together, producing boldly streaked appearance; bulbous bumps on dorsal keel; some specimens have striped "pants." The Fla. Keys, chiefly among mangroves.

ORNATE DIAMONDBACK TERRAPIN PL. 5
Malaclemys terrapin macrospilota

IDENTIFICATION: Adult females 6–8 in. (15.2–20.3 cm); males 4–5½ in. (10–14 cm). The *orange or yellow centers of the large scutes* distinguish this diamondback from all other races. Bulbous bumps or tubercles on middorsal keel are evident in many specimens, juveniles and males especially. *Young:* Entire shell light horn color, except that dorsal scutes are narrowly bordered with

DIAMONDBACK TERRAPINS
Malaclemys terrapin

A. NORTHERN
B. CAROLINA
C. FLORIDA EAST COAST
D. MANGROVE
E. ORNATE
F. MISSISSIPPI
G. TEXAS

black; tubercles also black.

At home in salt or brackish coastal streams and passes, especially those bordered by mangroves. Also may wander offshore or take refuge in the tall stiff grasses that characterize many Gulf beaches. **RANGE:** Fla. west coast, Flor-ida Bay to the panhandle. **SUBSPECIES:** MISSISSIPPI DIAMONDBACK TERRAPIN, *Malaclemys t. pileata.* A dark turtle; carapace usually uniform black or brown; skin very dark; plastron yellow, often clouded with a dusky shade; a strongly tuberculate central keel; edges of shell orange or yellow and turned upward; most males and some females with a black "mustache" on upper jaw. Averages larger, the record size (an enormous female) 9⅜ in. (23.8 cm). Marshes and estuaries of Gulf Coast from Fla. panhandle to w. La. TEXAS DIAMONDBACK TERRAPIN, *Malaclemys t. littoralis.* Similar to Mississippi Diamondback, but with a deeper shell that has its highest point toward rear of carapace; skin greenish gray, heavily marked with black spots; plastron nearly white; "mustache" usually missing. Coast of Texas.

MAP TURTLES: GENUS *Graptemys*

These are lake and river turtles. They are shy, quick to plunge from their basking places, and usually difficult to capture. Among them are some of our most beautifully marked and grotesquely adorned turtles. There are ten species, all found in the eastern United States, but several are confined to single river systems emptying into the Gulf of Mexico. All have dorsal keels; in some there are projections upward from the keel, and these are known locally in several parts of their ranges as "sawbacks." Hatchling size varies from 1–1½ in. (2.5–3.8 cm). In the young, the patterns are brightest and the spines best developed; males tend to retain most of the juvenile characteristics; females lose many of them and are often smudged with dark pigment. The heads of adults are quite broad in four species (Common Map, Mississippi, Alabama, and Barbour's); adult females of the last two have enormously enlarged heads that are efficient machines for crushing the shells of snails and freshwater clams.

The limbs and heads of these turtles are patterned with what may seem at first glance to be a veritable maze of light and dark stripes, whorls, and curlicues. The light head markings, which often take the form of spots or crescents, are useful in making identifications, and so also, in some species, are the light markings on the chins. Although they are subject to considerable individual variation, the chin markings diagrammed on Fig. 32 are usually evident. Note that in several of them the characteristic light figures are bordered by *double* dark lines.

The populations of several species of *Graptemys* have been severely decimated by the pollution or channelization (or both) of many southern rivers, and young turtles (in the past) suffered commercial exploitation for the pet trade.

COMMON MAP TURTLE *Graptemys geographica*   PLS. 3, 6

IDENTIFICATION: Adult females 7–10¾ in. (18–27.3 cm); males 3½–6¼ in. (9–15.9 cm). A young or well-marked specimen carries a map on its back; the light markings resemble an intricate system of canals or waterways laid out on a chart. Shell moderately low; keel may have mere suggestions of knobs on it. A more or less longitudinal *yellow spot behind eye*, variable in size and shape but usually largest in specimens from southern part of range. *Female:* Head considerably enlarged; pattern obscure. *Young:* Dorsal keel pronounced; plastral pattern consisting of dark lines bordering seams between the scutes (see Pl. 3). Adults have virtually plain plastrons.

The Common Map Turtle prefers large bodies of water — rivers rather than creeks and lakes rather than ponds. A confirmed but wary basker; slow to retreat into hibernation. In northern lakes it may sometimes be seen walking about in slow motion under ice

An adult male Common Map Turtle from Missouri, displaying the distinctive yellow spot on the head behind the eye.

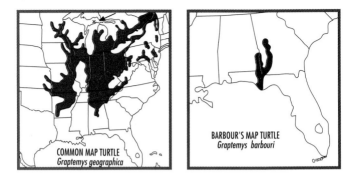

COMMON MAP TURTLE
Graptemys geographica

BARBOUR'S MAP TURTLE
Graptemys barbouri

after early cold snaps. Snails and crayfish are the chief foods. **SIMILAR SPECIES:** (1) In False Map Turtle traces of upward projections are usually evident along keel, and head is relatively small. (2) Mississippi Map Turtle has yellow crescent behind eye. (3) Painted Turtles have *un*keeled shells. (4) In Cooters and Sliders, the crushing surface in roof of mouth is ridged (smooth in Common Map Turtle). Tap turtle gently on snout to make it open mouth. Use a stick, *not* your fingers! **RANGE:** Extr. s. Que. to cen. Ala., west to cen. Minn., e. Kans., and much of Ark.; apparently absent in the Mississippi R. Valley from cen. Ill. southward; distribution in the Northeast consists of scattered colonies, including one in the Delaware R.

BARBOUR'S MAP TURTLE *Graptemys barbouri*   PLS. 3, 6

IDENTIFICATION: Adult females 7–12⅞ in. (18–32.7 cm); males 3½–5 in. (9–12.7 cm). The male is a dwarf compared with his mate. Females attain really imposing dimensions, and their heads are enormously enlarged. Adult males retain most markings of young, but big females become smudged and blotched with dark pigment that effectively hides their patterns. *Young:* Strong sawteeth on back; small longitudinal keel on each costal plate; *broad olive area between and behind eyes. Light markings on marginals,* if present, are *narrow;* all the light curved markings on carapace of juvenile illustrated on Pl. 3 are reduced or completely absent in many specimens. Light bar *across* or paralleling curve of chin (Fig. 32). Half-grown individuals have *deep* plastrons (viewed in profile). Plastral spines present. Carapace length 1¼–1½ in. (3.2–3.8 cm) at hatching.

Named for Thomas Barbour, herpetologist and long director of Harvard's Museum of Comparative Zoology. **SIMILAR SPECIES:** (1) Alabama Map Turtle has *longitudinal* light bar running back from point of chin (Fig. 32), *broad* light markings on marginals, and no plastral spines. (2) Mississippi Map Turtle has narrow light crescent behind eye. **RANGE:** Apalachicola R. system (Fla. Panhandle and adj. Ga. and extr. se. Ala.).

ALABAMA MAP TURTLE *Graptemys pulchra*   **PL. 6; FIG. 32**

IDENTIFICATION: Adult females 7–11¼ in. (18–29.2 cm); males 3½–5 in. (9–12.7 cm). Big females have grotesquely enlarged heads and strongly resemble females of Barbour's Map Turtle, even to being smudged and blotched with dark pigment. Adult males retain most markings of juveniles. *Young:* A middorsal black line involving the spines; a *broad* olive area between and behind eyes. Light markings on marginals *wide and prominent*. A *longitudinal* light bar running back from point of chin (Fig. 32). Half-grown specimens have *shallow* plastrons (viewed in profile).

This and other map turtles feed to a large extent on snails and other mollusks, the shells of which are crushed by the broad surfaces of the jaws. Aquatic insects also figure largely in the diet, especially of males, which do not have such powerful shell crackers as females. **SIMILAR SPECIES:** (1) Barbour's Map Turtle has a light bar across or following the curve of chin (Fig. 32), and the light markings on marginals are narrow or obscure. (2) Mississippi Map Turtle has narrow light crescent behind eye. **RANGE:** Streams flowing into Gulf of Mexico — from the Escambia and Alabama R. systems to the Pearl R. system (extr. w. Fla. to extr. e. La.) and well northward into Miss., Ala., and nw. Ga.

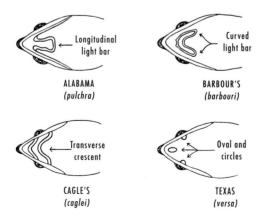

ALABAMA
(pulchra)
Longitudinal light bar

BARBOUR'S
(barbouri)
Curved light bar

CAGLE'S
(caglei)
Transverse crescent

TEXAS
(versa)
Oval and circles

Fig. 32. Chins of Map Turtles (Graptemys).

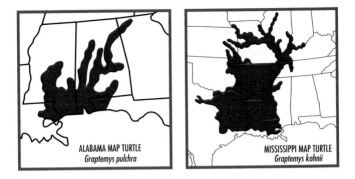

ALABAMA MAP TURTLE
Graptemys pulchra

MISSISSIPPI MAP TURTLE
Graptemys kohnii

MISSISSIPPI MAP TURTLE *Graptemys kohnii*   PLS. 3, 6

IDENTIFICATION: Adult females 6–10 in. (15.2–25.4 cm); males 3½–5 in. (9–12.7 cm). The *crescent behind the eye* is the best feature. This sometimes is broken into 2 or 3 parts, but fragmented or whole it cuts off the narrow yellow head stripes from the eye. The eye, on gross inspection, is a wide white ring with black center. *Head large*, especially in females. Toenails on forefeet of large males are elongated. *Young:* These and young of the False Map Turtle, although they have brownish carapaces, long had the name of "graybacks" in the pet trade. (It is now illegal to sell all live baby turtles because of possible disease transmission to children.) Babies are saw-backed, the rear margin of the carapace is toothed, and there is an intricate design of double dark lines on the plastron (Pl. 3). **SIMILAR SPECIES:** (1) In races of the False Map Turtle one or more light neck stripes reach eye. (2) In Texas Map Turtle the enlarged light postocular stripe extends *backward*. **RANGE:** N. cen. Ill. to La., west to cen. Texas and e. Kans. **NOTE:** The relationships of the turtles of the *Graptemys kohnii-G.pseudogeographica* complex are confusing and controversial. The two species live together and maintain their identities in many areas, notably in Kans., Mo., Tenn., Texas, and parts of La., but elsewhere they may hybridize, showing a combination of characters of both species in local populations. A thorough study of the status of this complex is badly needed.

FALSE MAP TURTLE *Graptemys pseudogeographica*   PL. 6

IDENTIFICATION: Adult females 5–10¾ in. (12.5–27.3 cm); males 3½–5¾ in. (9–14.6 cm). Variable, but usually with this combination of characters: (a) carapace brown; (b) middorsal keel with suggestions of knobs; and (c) light spot or line behind eye. Some of the light neck stripes *reach eye*. Head relatively small.

Male: Greatly elongated toenails on forefeet. *Young*: Carapace 1–1⅜ in. (2.5–3.5 cm) at hatching, saw-backed, spines black; rear of carapace toothed; a well-developed plastral pattern. Adults retain indications of the spines, but the teeth of the shell and the plastral pattern become much reduced as turtles grow older.

MAP TURTLES
Graptemys pseudogeographica

■ OUACHITA
▨ FALSE
▨ SABINE

These reptiles and their close relatives often choose basking spots shunned by other turtles, attempting seemingly impossible climbs up slippery snags that rise at steep angles from the surface of the water. **SIMILAR SPECIES:** (1) In Mississippi Map Turtle a light crescent prevents neck stripes from reaching the eye. (2) In Common Map Turtle the keel is lower, and knobs are weak or lacking; head broader and plastral pattern much reduced or absent. **RANGE:** Mississippi drainage from Ohio, Wisc., Minn., and s. N.D. to La.; Sabine R. drainage, Texas and La. Distribution disjunct toward the Northeast; isolated records in n. Ind. **SUBSPECIES:** OUACHITA MAP TURTLE, *Graptemys p. ouachitensis* (Pl. 6). A prominent squarish or rectangular light spot behind eye; 1 to 3 light neck lines reach the eye; a pair of light spots on jaws, one under the eye and another similar one on chin (Fig. 33). Occupies most of the range of the species. SABINE MAP TURTLE, *Graptemys p. sabinensis*. Similar, but with postocular light spot oval or elongate; 5 to 9 light neck stripes reach eye; transverse bands under chin; plastron (in juveniles) with more and finer lines. Sabine R. and adj. drainages in w. La. and e. Texas. FALSE MAP TURTLE, *Graptemys p. pseudogeographica*. Yellow postocular line narrow; no enlarged spots on mandibles; fewer lines on legs. Attains maximum size of the species; the other races average con-

OUACHITA MAP
TURTLE
Light spot behind the
eye and two below it

(*Graptemys p. ouachitensis*)

BIG BEND SLIDER
A large light spot on
side of head, small
one back of eye

(*Trachemys gaigeae*)

Fig. 33. *Heads of two aquatic turtles.*

TEXAS MAP TURTLE
Graptemys versa

CAGLE'S MAP TURTLE
Graptemys caglei

siderably smaller. Missouri R. system from nw. Mo., to N.D., Minn., and Wisc. in the Mississippi R. drainage; w. Ind.; intergrades with the Ouachita Map Turtle throughout a large area. **NOTE:** The subspecies of this turtle are poorly defined, partly because of individual variation and partly because of hybridization with *Graptemys kohnii*. (See **NOTE** under that species.)

TEXAS MAP TURTLE *Graptemys versa*   PL. 6; FIG. 32

IDENTIFICATION: Adult females 4–8⅜ in. (10–21.4 cm); males 2¾–4½ in. (7–11.5 cm). A light yellow or orange line (often J-shaped) extending *backward* from eye. Chin marked with a light oval near its point and a small, light, round spot farther back on each side (Fig. 32). The more anterior plates of carapace have a quilted effect; they are high and rounded at their centers, the sutures forming rather deep grooves between them. **SIMILAR SPECIES:** Texas Slider has broad light stripes, spots, or vertical bars on its head. **RANGE:** Colorado R. system, Texas.

CAGLE'S MAP TURTLE *Graptemys caglei*   FIG. 32

IDENTIFICATION: Adult females to 7¹⁵⁄₁₆ in. (20.2 cm); males 2¾–5 in. (7–12.6 cm). Similar in general appearance to Texas Map Turtle, but with a dark-edged, cream-colored crescent or band across chin (Fig. 32). A bold light V-shaped marking on top of head, each arm of which often forms a crescent behind eye (as in Mississippi Map Turtle). Carapace predominantly green (olive in Texas Map Turtle). *Male:* Usually with black flecking on light parts of plastron.

Named for Fred R. Cagle, an authority on turtles and a former administrator of Tulane University. **RANGE:** San Antonio-Guadalupe R. system of s.-cen. Texas.

RINGED MAP TURTLE *Graptemys oculifera*   PL. 6

IDENTIFICATION: Adult females 5–8½ in. (12.5–21.6 cm); males 3–4 in. (7.5–10.2 cm). *Broad* light rings on costal plates of carapace. Head has a clownish appearance, as though smeared with greasepaint—light mandibles, large postocular yellow spot, and two broad light neck stripes entering eye. This and the next two species are the spiniest of our turtles. Dorsal spines very conspicuous in the young and adult males, somewhat less so in large females. Also in big females, the light rings may be partially obscured by dark pigment. In juveniles the rear corners of the marginals project outward to give shell a saw-toothed appearance.

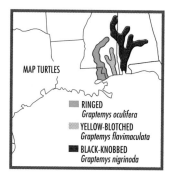

The jaws, scissorlike in action, are useful in dismembering insects, which, with mollusks, constitute the principal food of this and the next two species. **SIMILAR SPECIES:** The head markings are similar in (1) Black-knobbed and (2) Yellow-blotched Map Turtles, but their names describe those two. In Black-knobbed, spines are widened and flattened, and the rings on carapace are narrow. In Yellow-blotched, light shell markings are of solid colors or are invaded by ground color of shell; they do not form a series of broad, symmetrical rings. **RANGE:** Pearl R. system, s. Miss. and adj. La.

YELLOW-BLOTCHED MAP TURTLE PL. 6
Graptemys flavimaculata
IDENTIFICATION: Adult females 4–6⅞ in. (10–17.5 cm); males 3–4 in. (7.5–10.2 cm). *Solid* areas of yellow or orange in each of the large scutes of the carapace. These may be invaded by or surround areas of the dark ground color, but they do not form a series of symmetrical rings. Head markings and gross anatomy are similar to those of Ringed Map Turtle. **RANGE:** Pascagoula R. system, Miss.

BLACK-KNOBBED MAP TURTLE *Graptemys nigrinoda* PL. 6
IDENTIFICATION: Adult females 4–7½ in. (10–19.1 cm); males 3–4½ in. (7.5–11.5 cm). The spines are *broadly knobbed* at their tips, like metal spikes struck by a heavy hammer. Light rings on carapace are *narrow*.

This turtle, and the Ringed and Yellow-blotched, are most common in streams with moderate current, a bottom of sand or clay, and an abundance of brush, logs, and flood-stranded debris. **RANGE:** Alabama-Tombigbee-Black Warrior R. systems, Ala. and ne. Miss. **SUBSPECIES:** BLACK-KNOBBED MAP TURTLE, *Graptemys n. nigrinoda* (Pl. 6). Head, legs, and overall appearance of skin mostly light-colored; dark plastral figure covers 30% or less of lower shell; crescent-shaped, strongly *recurved* postorbital mark; female carapace to 6⅟₁₆ in. (15.5 cm). Restricted in Ala. to the Coosa, Tallapoosa, Cahaba, and Alabama rivers from the Fall Line southward to the Wilcox-Monroe county line. DELTA MAP

TURTLE, *Graptemys n. delticola*. Head, legs, and overall appearance of skin mostly black; dark plastral figure covers 60% or more of lower shell; *linear or angular* postorbital mark; female carapace to 7⅝ in. (19.5 cm). Restricted in Ala. to the delta of the Mobile and Tensaw R. systems north of Mobile Bay in Baldwin and Mobile counties. **NOTE:** Because the two races intergrade throughout most of the range of the species, no effort was made to show subspecific distributions on the map.

SLIDERS, COOTERS,* REDBELLIES, AND PAINTED TURTLES: GENERA *Trachemys, Pseudemys,* AND *Chrysemys*

Except for the Map Turtles, many of which are equally addicted to taking the sun, members of these genera are usually the most conspicuous and abundant of all our basking turtles. In spring or autumn, or at any time when the weather is not too hot or too cold, they may rest by the hour on logs, stumps, snags, or rocks. If such "hauling out" places are at a premium, they may stack themselves two and three deep as the late comers climb atop their fellows. A few kinds can be identified through binoculars, especially if their heads are outstretched, but details of carapacial patterns become inconspicuous as their shells dry out in the sun. Check them from a distance or from your car. If you step out the door or approach too closely on foot, the entire assemblage will plunge into the water and out of sight.

The genus *Chrysemys* consists of the Painted Turtles (see pp. 184–186), whereas the genera *Trachemys* and *Pseudemys* are composed of big basking turtles, an abundant group in the ponds and streams of the Southeast and the Mississippi Valley. These large turtles are brown or olive in general appearance with streaks, whorls, or circles of brown or black on a lighter ground color. The carapaces of adults are usually wrinkled with numerous, chiefly longitudinal furrows, and their rear margins are sawtoothed. The head stripes are usually yellowish. Only a few have good field marks. Even in hand they are sometimes difficult to identify, particularly since hybridization between species occasionally occurs. There are four groups of big basking turtles, as follows:

1. Sliders (*Trachemys*). Usually a prominent patch (or patches) of red or yellow on side of head. Lower jaw rounded (flat in all other groups—see Fig. 34). Includes Yellowbelly, Red-eared, Cumberland, and Big Bend Sliders.

2. River Cooters (*Pseudemys concinna* and *P. texana*). A light C-

---

* Derived from *kuta,* a word for turtle in several African dialects and brought to America during early slave days.

shaped figure on the second costal scute (Fig. 35). Undersurfaces with numerous dark markings on plastron, bridge, and marginals. Includes Eastern, Missouri, Rio Grande, Suwannee, and Texas River Cooters, although the Texas species does not have a light C-shaped figure on the carapace.

3. Cooters (*Pseudemys floridana*). Light vertical line (or lines) on 2nd costal scute (Fig. 8, opp. Pl. 8). Plastron unmarked or only lightly patterned; dark markings on bridge and marginals fewer and less conspicuous than in the river species. Includes Florida and Peninsula Cooters.

4. Redbelly Turtles (*Pseudemys rubriventris* group). Plastron usually red, orange, or coral, at least around the edges. Light arrow (Fig. 8, opp. Pl. 8) at front of head (also shared by the Sliders). Sharp notch at tip of upper jaw bordered on each side by a pronounced cusp (Fig. 8, opp. Pl. 8). Cutting edges of jaws sawtoothed. Includes Redbelly, Florida Redbelly, and Alabama Redbelly Turtles.

Adult males have greatly elongated nails on their forelimbs (except in Big Bend Slider—p. 178), and their shells are rather

SLIDERS
(*Trachemys*)
Rounded lower jaw

COOTERS AND RED-
BELLIES
(*Pseudemys*)
Flattened lower jaw

Fig. 34. *Jaws of Sliders and Cooters.*

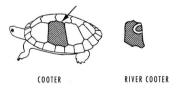

COOTER   RIVER COOTER

Fig. 35. *Second costal scute (arrow). River Cooter* (Pseudemys concinna *ssp.*) *has a light "C" on this scute; Cooter* (P. floridana *ssp.*) *lacks it.*

flat compared with the well-arched shells of females. Males, especially of Sliders and Redbelly Turtles, also tend to become dark and to lose their patterns at a smaller size than their mates. Females grow the larger. Hatchlings have a carapace length ranging from about ⅞–1½ in. (2.2–3.8 cm); the babies are strongly and colorfully marked and were once popular in the pet trade, but are no longer sold because of the chance of bacterial contamination when children handle them.

All cooters and sliders are largely vegetarian. Captives will eat natural aquatic plants or, in their absence, lettuce, carrot tops, or other greens. Most of them will also eat raw meat, fishes, shellfish, worms, and insects.

The genera *Trachemys, Pseudemys,* and *Chrysemys* range from southern Canada to Argentina and Uruguay. Because so many of them are similar in appearance, it is advisable to rely heavily on geography when trying to identify them (see Maps on pp. 177, 179, 181, 183, and 185).

YELLOWBELLY SLIDER *Trachemys scripta scripta*   PLS. 4, 7
IDENTIFICATION: 5–8 in. (12.5–20.3 cm); record 11⅜ in. (28.9 cm). The *yellow blotch behind the eye* is the most conspicuous field mark, but this is strongly evident only in the young and in many females. Vertical yellow bands on carapace show best when shell is wet. Yellow underside of both shells marked with round dusky smudges, one toward rear of each marginal and others on forward part of plastron. These markings may be reduced or obscure in older individuals, especially in adult males, which may lose their original patterns, becoming dark and mottled like old male Red-eared Sliders. Vertical stripes on "seat of the pants," and *narrow* yellow stripes along front surface of forelegs (Fig. 7, opp. Pl. 7). *Young* (Pl. 4): Smudges or eyelike spots on marginals, bridge, and forepart of plastron. Such markings may appear all over the plastron, but in that case the anterior ones are darker and better formed. Carapace length 1⅛–1⁵⁄₁₆ in. (2.8–3.3 cm).

A common turtle of the Southeast. Utilizes a wide variety of habitats, including rivers, ditches, sloughs, lakes, and ponds. **SIMILAR SPECIES:** (1) Chicken Turtle also has striped "pants," but yellow stripe on each foreleg is *broad,* and carapace is long and narrow. (2) See also introductory section on Cooters and Sliders above. **RANGE:** Se. Va. to n. Fla. Intergrades with Red-eared Slider through most of Ala. and parts of adj. states.

RED-EARED SLIDER *Trachemys scripta elegans*   PLS. 4, 7
IDENTIFICATION: 5–8 in. (12.5–20.3 cm); record 11⅜ in. (28.9 cm). The broad *reddish stripe* behind the eye is unique among North American turtles, but not all Red-ears have it. Rarely, the red is

replaced by yellow. Most trouble will result in trying to identify adult specimens in which development of dark pigment (melanism) is advanced. This is a phenomenon in which black appears on both shells in the form of bars, spots, or blotches. These spread and run together, obliterating details of original pattern, and in extreme cases producing a nearly uniformly black or very

dark turtle. Even limbs, head, and tail become dark. Change may start at any age from young adulthood onward, but males are more susceptible to melanism than females. *Young:* Carapace green and with a low keel; plastron profusely marked with dark, eyelike spots (see Pl. 4); carapace length 1⅛–1¼ in. (2.8–3.3 cm).

The Red-eared Slider prefers quiet water with a muddy bottom and a profusion of vegetation. Basks on logs or other projections above water or in masses of floating plants; occasionally hauls out on banks, particularly in the western part of its range. **SIMILAR SPECIES:** See introductory section on Cooters and Sliders (pp. 174–176). **RANGE:** W. Va. to N.M. and south to the Gulf and extr. ne. Mexico; relict colony in Ohio; introduced and established over a large area in n. Md. Through the escape or liberation of captives, it has been found in many localities outside its native range, but most of these are not established colonies and are not mapped. **SUBSPECIES:** CUMBERLAND SLIDER, *Trachemys s. troosti.* Similar but with a narrower yellow stripe behind eye, and fewer

A young adult male Red-eared Slider showing its namesake head stripe.

and much wider stripes on legs, neck, and head; dark spots under marginals smaller in diameter than light spaces between them. Extr. sw. Va. and ne. Tenn.

BIG BEND SLIDER *Trachemys gaigeae* FIG. 33

IDENTIFICATION: 5–8 in. (12.5–20.3 cm); record 8¾ in. (22.2 cm). A large *black-bordered orange spot* on the side of the head is a good field character. A second much smaller spot directly behind eye (Fig. 33). Carapace pale olive-brown with numerous pale orange curved lines, including one on each marginal. Plastron pale orange and olive with a median series of elongated, concentric dark lines; eyelike spots on underside of marginals. Melanism develops rapidly with age, and large adults, males especially, may have the pattern largely or completely obliterated. The pale head spot may remain in evidence, however. Nails on the forelimbs of males are not enlarged.

The common slider of the upper Rio Grande and some of its tributaries, occurring in the streams themselves, where there is permanent water; also in nearby ponds, tanks, sloughs, and canals. **SIMILAR SPECIES:** In Western Painted Turtle there is no large head spot, and plastron is marked with a large dark figure. **RANGE:** Rio Grande in Big Bend region of Texas and Río Conchos system in Chihuahua; Rio Grande Valley in s.-cen. N.M.

EASTERN RIVER COOTER PL. 8
Pseudemys concinna concinna

IDENTIFICATION: 9–12 in. (23–30.6 cm); record 12¾ in. (32.4 cm). The *light C on the 2nd costal scute* (Fig. 35) rarely can be picked out through binoculars, especially if the turtle has basked long enough for its shell to dry. It must be at hand for accurate check-

An adult female Eastern River Cooter in Meriwether County, Georgia.

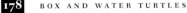

ing. Concentric circles are usually well developed in conjunction with the C as well as on the other scutes. Five light stripes between the eyes. The dark plastral pattern tends to follow the seams between the plastral scutes. All (or almost all) marginals have dark spots under them, usually doughnut-shaped, and some may touch the dark markings on the bridge between the shells.

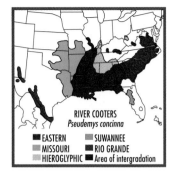

RIVER COOTERS
Pseudemys concinna

■ EASTERN ■ SUWANNEE
■ MISSOURI ■ RIO GRANDE
■ HIEROGLYPHIC ■ Area of intergradation

Young: Carapace 1⅜–1⅝ in. (3.5–4.1 cm) at hatching.

Indigenous to streams of the Piedmont and following such streams to the Atlantic Coast. Intergradation among three of the four easternmost races of river cooters takes place over a large area, from cen. Ga. and the Fla. panhandle almost to e. Texas, and north in the Mississippi Valley to s. Ill. Turtles of this species found in this area may exhibit a bewildering array of characteristics from any or all three subspecies, and should simply be called River Cooters. **SIMILAR SPECIES:** See Florida Cooter. **RANGE:** E. Va. to e. Ga.; isolated colonies in W. Va., Ky., and Tenn.

SUWANNEE RIVER COOTER   PL. 8
Pseudemys concinna suwanniensis

IDENTIFICATION: 9–13 in. (23–33 cm); record 17¼ in. (43.7 cm). Darkest and largest of the cooters. Out of water, upper shell may look virtually plain black. Ground color of legs and head also very dark, but head stripes are whitish- to greenish yellow and number five between the eyes. Characteristic ventral markings of the river cooters are strongly evident, with marginal dark spots in contact with dark markings on bridge. Ground color of plastron usually yellow, but brightly tinged with orange in some parts of range. *Young:* Hatchling has dark gray blotches on a pale gray ground, but blotches change within a few days to brownish green separated by a network of yellowish green. *Pale C clearly defined.* Plastron citron-colored with pattern of grayish brown along seams.

A turtle of the clear spring runs of Florida's upper west coast, and sometimes wandering into the big springs themselves. Also occurs in Gulf of Mexico in the turtle-grass flats off mouths of streams, and occasionally appears far out in the Gulf, its shell encrusted with barnacles. **SIMILAR SPECIES:** (1) Peninsula Cooter has light "hairpins" on head (Fig. 8, opp. Pl. 8) and *lacks a C;* also, its ventral markings are greatly reduced. (2) Florida Redbelly Turtle also *lacks a C;* there is an arrow on its head, and the upper jaws

have a notch and cusps (Fig. 8, opp. Pl. 8). (3) See also Sliders.
RANGE: Suwannee R. region of the upper Fla. Gulf Coast south to
vicinity of Tampa Bay.

HIEROGLYPHIC RIVER COOTER PLS. 4, 8
Pseudemys concinna hieroglyphica

IDENTIFICATION: 9–13 in. (23–33 cm); record 14¾ in. (37.5 cm). The
Tennessee R. representative of the River Cooter. A *light C* (Fig.
35) and a strong plastral pattern are in evidence. Many individuals have shell "pinched in" anterior to hind legs. Five light stripes
between eyes.

Like other basking turtles, this one slips into the water at the
least sign of danger. **SIMILAR SPECIES:** (1) Red-eared Sliders have an
oval reddish patch on side of head; old darkened Red-ears may be
distinguished by rounded shape of lower jaw (flat in River Cooters
—see Fig. 34). (2) Map Turtles have strong keels or projections
down their backs. (3) In Painted Turtles, rear margin of carapace
is smooth (not notched or saw-toothed). **RANGE:** S. Ill. to ne. Miss.,
east to se. Tenn. and nw. Ga.; isolated colony in W. Va. **SUBSPECIES:**
MISSOURI RIVER COOTER, *Pseudemys c. metteri.* The northwestern representative of the River Cooters. Somewhat smaller,
females up to 13⅜ in. (34 cm). Distinguished by its lack of a postorbital spot and lack of concentric whorls in the 2nd costal scute,
which may or may not contain a light C (Fig. 35). Pattern of dark
lines along the seams of the plastron. From s.-cen. Mo. and adj.
se. Kans., south through e. Okla., w. Ark., extr. nw. La., and e.
Texas to the Gulf of Mexico. RIO GRANDE RIVER COOTER,
Pseudemys c. gorzugi. An isolated race of River Cooter with 4 or 5
distinct concentric whorls in the 2nd costal scute. Centers of
whorls light yellow. Pattern on plastron of narrow dark lines along
the anterior edge of the seams and the midline. Restricted to the
Rio Grande Valley from the Gulf to Del Rio, and a short distance
n. in the Pecos and Devil's rivers, Texas; isolated populations in s.
N.M. and adj. Texas in the Pecos R. system.

TEXAS RIVER COOTER *Pseudemys texana* PL. 8

IDENTIFICATION: 7–10 in. (18–25.5 cm); record 12½ in. (31.9 cm).
Variable yellow head markings with many lateral stripes, a vertical
bar on each side of the head near the angle of the jaws, and a
small, round postorbital spot. Lateral head stripes curve above
the bar near the angle of the jaws. *Second costal scute contains 5
or 6 concentric whorls with dark centers.* Plastron with dark lines
along both sides of the seams. Upper jaw has a notch flanked by a
cusp at each side, as in Florida Redbelly Turtle (Fig. 8, opp. Pl.
8). *Old Male:* Shell, head, and limbs rather uniformly mottled,

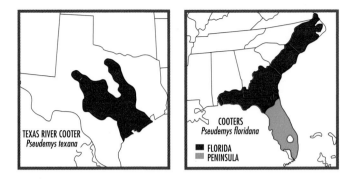

TEXAS RIVER COOTER
Pseudemys texana

COOTERS
Pseudemys floridana
■ FLORIDA
■ PENINSULA

completely obscuring original pattern. (Some females approach this mottled condition.) A pair of swollen ridges extends downward from nostrils and terminates in the cusps.

Rivers constitute the chief habitat, but this turtle is also found in ditches and cattle tanks. **SIMILAR SPECIES:** (1) Red-eared and Big Bend Sliders have rounded lower jaws (flat in River Cooters — see Fig. 34). (2) Texas Map Turtle has keel down back and carapace has a quilted effect. (3) See also Cagle's Map Turtle. **RANGE:** Most of cen. Texas, from San Antonio Bay and Galveston on the Gulf, west in the Colorado, Brazos, Guadalupe, and San Antonio river drainages.

FLORIDA COOTER *Pseudemys floridana floridana* PL. 8

IDENTIFICATION: 9–13 in. (23–33 cm); record 15⅝ in. (39.7 cm). The unmarked plastron and the dark "doughnuts" or thick, hollow ovals on underside of the marginals are characteristic. Numerous stripes on head, but they normally do not join to form "hairpins" except in regions where intergradation takes place with Peninsula Cooter. One or more vertical light stripes on 2nd costal scute, as in *peninsularis* (Fig. 8, opp. Pl. 8). *Young:* Carapace 1¼–1⅜ in. (3.2–3.5 cm).

A turtle of the Coastal Plain, residing in permanent bodies of water — ponds, lakes, big swamps or marshes, *and* rivers. (Except in times of flood, Coastal Plain streams are quiet and sluggish, and similar to lakes in many respects.) This turtle will frequently be seen basking, but it is extremely wary and is seldom caught. **SIMILAR SPECIES:** (1) Eastern and Suwannee River Cooters have heavy ventral markings (Pl. 8), five light stripes between the eyes, and a C on the 2nd costal scute (Fig. 35). (2) Yellowbelly Slider has striped "pants" (Fig. 7, opp. Pl. 7), and there may be a large yellow patch on side of head. (3) Chicken Turtle also has striped "pants," and its carapace is marked with a network of light lines. (4) Red-eared Slider has a reddish oval on each side of head. (5) In Painted Turtles the rear margin of carapace is smooth (not notched or saw-toothed). **RANGE:** Coastal Plain from extr. se. Va. to s. Ala., but excluding peninsular Fla.

PENINSULA COOTER PLS. 4, 8
Pseudemys floridana peninsularis

IDENTIFICATION: 9–13 in. (23–33 cm); record 15⅞ in. (40.3 cm). The only cooter with a pair of *light "hairpins"* atop the head (Fig. 8, opp. Pl. 8). One or both of these may be broken or incomplete. (Submerge turtle in water to make its head come out.) Plastron usually completely unmarked, but marginal spots may be stronger and more numerous than shown on Pl. 8. *Young* (Pl. 4): Plastron yellow or with slight tinge of orange; never strongly orange or reddish.

A turtle of lakes, sloughs, wet prairies, canals, and Florida's great springs and spring runs; also lives in the Everglades north of and along the Tamiami Trail. Although extremely wary at or above water's surface, it can be closely approached when submerged. Divers equipped with face masks usually find this and other turtles easy to observe in clear streams and springs. **SIMILAR SPECIES:** (1) Suwannee River Cooter has all the characteristics of River Cooters and Sliders—a light C on 2nd costal (Fig. 35) and heavy dark ventral markings. (2) Florida Cooter has dark "doughnuts" on the marginals. (3) Plastron of Florida Redbelly Turtle is reddish, orange, or coral and almost always marked with at least some dark pigment. Peninsula Cooter occasionally hybridizes with both Suwannee River Cooter and Florida Redbelly, and it intergrades with Florida Cooter where their respective ranges meet. **RANGE:** Fla. peninsula, excluding extr. sw. tip.

REDBELLY TURTLE *Pseudemys rubriventris* PL. 7; FIG. 36

IDENTIFICATION: 10–12½ in. (25.4–32 cm); record 15¾ in. (40 cm). The only big *basking turtle* throughout most of its range. Much larger than Painted Turtles, with which it often suns on logs and snags. A notch in upper jaw is flanked by a cusp at each side as in Florida Redbelly (Fig. 8, opp. Pl. 8). Adult females with vertical reddish line on each of first three costal scutes. Old males mottled with reddish brown. Coloration and pattern highly variable, and melanism is almost universal among large adults in some areas, notably in southern New Jersey. Even among the virtually black specimens, the reddish markings usually persist, although they may be quite vague. (You may have to wet the shell to see them.) Ground color of plastron yellow, marked with large gray smudges and bordered by a wash of pink or orange-red. Plastrons of old males often mottled with pink and light charcoal-gray. *Young:* Carapace length 1–1¼ in. (2.5–3.2 cm), with slight keel and patterned (with yellow or olive on green) in same basic design as in adult female illustrated. Plastron with large dark pattern on coral-red ground color (Fig. 36), and often strongly resembling that of Western Painted Turtle (see Pl. 4).

■ REDBELLY TURTLE
Pseudemys rubriventris
■ ALABAMA REDBELLY TURTLE
Pseudemys alabamensis
■ FLORIDA REDBELLY TURTLE
Pseudemys nelsoni

A turtle of ponds, rivers, and, in general, relatively large bodies of fresh water. **SIMILAR SPECIES:** (1) In both Eastern River Cooter and Florida Cooter, upper jaw is rounded and lacks both notch and cusps. (2) In Painted Turtles there are two bright yellow spots on each side of head. **RANGE:** S. N.J. and extr. e. W.Va. to ne. N.C.; Plymouth Co., Mass.

FLORIDA REDBELLY TURTLE *Pseudemys nelsoni*   PL. 8

IDENTIFICATION: 8–12 in. (20.3–30.6 cm); record 14¾ in. (37.5 cm). Many of these turtles have a distinctly reddish appearance (quite noticeable when submerged in clear water) that contrasts with the darker Peninsula Cooter and Suwannee River Cooter. Other specimens may be darker and more somber, but plastron is almost always strongly tinted with orange, red, or coral, at least around margins. Light vertical band on the 2nd costal is variable in width from quite wide (Fig. 8, opp. Pl. 8) to relatively narrow. The light head stripes are few in number, but they include a *slender arrow*

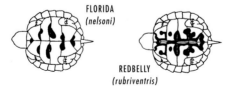

FLORIDA
(*nelsoni*)

REDBELLY
(*rubriventris*)

Fig. 36. *Plastral (lower shell) patterns of baby Redbelly Turtles (Pseudemys).*

with its shaft between the eyes and its point at the turtle's snout; also the notch in upper jaw is flanked by a strong cusp on each side (Fig. 8, opp. Pl. 8). *Young:* Plastron orange to scarlet-orange (rarely yellow); dark plastral markings tend to be in form of solid semicircles with flat sides along seams between scutes (Fig. 36).

A turtle of streams, ponds, lakes, ditches, sloughs, marshes, and mangrove-bordered creeks. **SIMILAR SPECIES:** (1) Peninsula Cooter and (2) Suwannee River Cooter *lack:* (a) notch and cusps; and (b) arrow on head. **RANGE:** Fla. Peninsula north to extr. se. Ga.; isolated colony in Apalachicola region of Fla. panhandle.

ALABAMA REDBELLY TURTLE   NOT ILLUS.
Pseudemys alabamensis

IDENTIFICATION: 8–12 in. (20.3–30.6 cm); record 13¼ in. (33.5 cm). A big, robust turtle with a yellow or red bar on the 2nd costal scute. *Plastron reddish,* usually with a pattern of dark bars and light-centered dark figures. Head olive to black with few yellow stripes, but look for the *slender arrow* with its shaft between the eyes and its point at the turtle's snout. Upper jaw with notch flanked by cusps (Fig. 8, opp. Pl. 8). Carapace brown to olive (adults) or greenish (young).

A turtle fond of basking on logs over fresh to moderately brackish water. Prefers an abundance of submerged aquatic vegetation, its principal food. **SIMILAR SPECIES:** (1) In the Eastern River Cooter, the upper jaw lacks both notch and cusps. (2) Florida Cooter has plain plastron, with hollow circles on the marginals. (3) Map Turtles have strong keels or projections down their backs. **RANGE:** Restricted to Mobile Bay drainage in Baldwin, Mobile, and Monroe cos., Ala.

PAINTED TURTLES: THE RACES OF *Chrysemys picta*

These are readily identified by their *smooth, unkeeled shells* and attractive patterns of *red, yellow,* and *black* (or olive). They live chiefly where the water is shallow, the aquatic vegetation profuse, and the bottom soft and muddy—in ponds, marshes, ditches, edges of lakes, backwaters of streams, and (westward) in prairie sloughs, cattle tanks, and river pools. Their food in nature consists largely of aquatic vegetation, insects, crayfish, and small mollusks.

The shells often become encrusted with a red or brownish deposit (easily scraped away by thumbnail or knife) that may hide the true coloration. Females average larger than their mates. Fully adult males have very long nails on their forefeet. Hatchlings are usually ⅞–1⅛ in. (2.2–2.8 cm) in upper shell length; their carapaces *are keeled.*

There is only one species, but four distinct subspecies. Where the ranges of these approach one another there are broad areas of overlap in which individual turtles may combine the characteristics of different subspecies.

Painted Turtles range from coast to coast (although not continuously) through the northern states and southern Canada, but they also occur southward virtually (in fresh water) to the Gulf of Mexico from Louisiana to extreme southwestern Alabama. In many northern localities they are the only conspicuous basking turtles.

EASTERN PAINTED TURTLE *Chrysemys picta picta* PLS. 4, 7

IDENTIFICATION: 4½–6 in. (11.5–15.2 cm); record 7⅛ in. (18.1 cm). A unique turtle, only one in which the large scutes of the carapace are in more or less *straight rows* across the back. In other turtles the scutes are arranged in alternating fashion across the back. The olive front edges of the large scutes collectively form light bands across the carapace—a good field mark easily seen through binoculars when the turtle floats at the surface in clear water. Look also for bright yellow spots on head (two on each side). For basking specimens, red and black margins of shell are also good checks. Plastron is plain yellow or with a small dark spot or two. (See Pl. 4 for young.) **RANGE:** Nova Scotia to Ga., but intergrading with the Midland Painted Turtle throughout a large area in the Northeast.

MIDLAND PAINTED TURTLE PLS. 4, 7
Chrysemys picta marginata

IDENTIFICATION: 4½–5½ in. (11.5–14 cm); record 7⅝ in. (19.5 cm). Very similar to Eastern Painted Turtle but with large scutes of back alternating instead of running straight across. There is also a dark plastral blotch that is variable in size, shape, and intensity from one turtle to the next. Typically it is oval, involves all, or nearly all, of the scutes, is half or less than width of plastron, and does not normally send out extensions along the seams. (See Pl. 4 for young.) **RANGE:** S. Que. and s. Ont. to Tenn., extr. nw. Ga., and extr. ne. Ala.

A young adult male Western Painted Turtle from Lyon County, Kansas; this is the most attractive of the races of this species.

SOUTHERN PAINTED TURTLE PLS. 4, 7
Chrysemys picta dorsalis

IDENTIFICATION: 4–5 in. (10–12.5 cm); record 6⅛ in. (15.6 cm). A *broad* red or orange stripe down the back and normally a plain yellow plastron. Stripe is sometimes yellow; plastron may show one or two small black spots. (See Pl. 4 for young.) **RANGE:** Extr. s. Ill. to the Gulf; sw. Ala. to extr. se. Okla.; absent from n.-cen. Ala. and s. Miss. and adj. La.; isolated colony in cen. Texas.

WESTERN PAINTED TURTLE *Chrysemys picta bellii* PLS. 4, 7

IDENTIFICATION: 3½–7 in. (9–18 cm); record 9⅞ in. (25.1 cm). Largest of the Painted Turtles and the one with the most intricate pattern. Not much red on marginals; light, irregular lines appear on carapace, these sometimes so extensive as to form a netlike pattern. Males from North Dakota sometimes have a fine black reticulation superimposed over the normal pattern. Most of plastron occupied by a large, dark figure that sends branches out along seams of scutes. (See Pl. 4 for young.) **RANGE:** Sw. Ont. and s. Mo. to the Pacific Northwest; absent from much of Mont.; disjunct colonies in the Southwest; isolated record in n. Chihuahua.

CHICKEN AND BLANDING'S TURTLES:
GENERA *Deirochelys* AND *Emydoidea*

Despite the marked differences in their patterns, coloration, and plastrons, these two genera may be closely related. Their members have the longest necks of any of our turtles except the Softshells, and the first vertebral scute is in contact with four marginals and the nuchal. In all other members of the Family

Emydidae within our area only two marginals and the nuchal normally are in broad contact with the first vertebral. The Chicken Turtle is southern in distribution, and it has a rigid plastron. Blanding's Turtle is northern, and its plastron is hinged, an adaptation that has developed in turtles of many genera in many parts of the world.

CHICKEN TURTLES
Deirochelys reticularia
■ EASTERN
■ WESTERN
■ FLORIDA

CHICKEN TURTLE *Deirochelys reticularia* PLS. 4, 7

IDENTIFICATION: 4–6 in. (10–15.2 cm); record 10 in. (25.4 cm). The *light, netlike pattern* on the carapace and the *extra-long, strongly striped neck* are good characters, but they may be invisible if the shell is coated with mud or algae or if the turtle refuses to stick out its neck. In the case of timid specimens, look at the "seat of the pants." The hind legs are *vertically striped* (Fig. 7, opp. Pl. 7). Also look at the forelegs; each one has a *broad* yellow stripe along its front surface. Many specimens have a longitudinal dark bar, spot, or spots on bridge. Carapace is sculptured with small, line-like ridges, is much longer than wide, and is widest over the hind legs. *Young* (Pl. 4): Carapace with a slight keel; 1⅛–1¼ in. (2.8–3.2 cm) at hatching.

An inhabitant of still water—ponds, marshes, sloughs, and ditches. Frequently walks about on land. **SIMILAR SPECIES:** Yellowbelly Turtle also has striped "pants," but yellow lines on forelegs are *narrow* and carapace is much rounder. **RANGE:** Chiefly the Coastal Plain from se. N.C. to e. Texas; an isolated colony in extr. se. Va. **SUBSPECIES:** FLORIDA CHICKEN TURTLE, *Deirochelys r. chrysea* (Pl. 7). Netlike pattern orange or yellow, bold and broad in younger specimens but less conspicuous in old ones; rim of carapace boldly edged with orange; plastron orange or bright yellow, unpatterned. Fla. peninsula. EASTERN CHICKEN TURTLE, *Deirochelys r. reticularia* (young illustrated on Pl. 4). Similar but with the netlike lines greenish or brownish and much narrower; entire turtle less brightly colored. N.C. to Mississippi R.; well established, isolated colony (introduced?) in Virginia Beach region of se. Va.; isolated record in N.C. WESTERN CHICKEN TURTLE, *Deirochelys r. miaria*. This race has a rather flat appearance; netlike lines broad but only a little lighter than the ground color between them; plastron with dark markings along seams; underside of neck unpatterned in adults. Extr. se. Mo. and se. Okla. south to La. and e. Texas.

BLANDING'S TURTLE
Emydoidea blandingii

BLANDING'S TURTLE

Emydoidea blandingii **PLS. 3, 5**
IDENTIFICATION: 5–7 in. (12.5–18 cm); record 10¾ in. (27.4 cm). The "semi-box turtle." Hinge across plastron permits the movable lobes to be pulled well upward toward carapace, but closure is far less complete than in Box Turtles. The profuse light spots often tend to run together, forming bars or streaks. *Bright yellow* on chin and throat is a good field character that is easily seen through binoculars when turtle basks or floats at water's surface. *Young* (Pl. 3): Carapace virtually plain gray or grayish brown; plastron blackish with an edging of yellow; tail much longer proportionately than in adults; 1–1¼ in. (2.5–3.8 cm) at hatching.

Essentially aquatic, but often wanders about on land, although seldom far from marshes, bogs, lakes, or small streams. Usually hisses sharply when picked up in the field. Named for William Blanding, an early Philadelphia naturalist. **SIMILAR SPECIES:** (1) Spotted Turtle has fewer and well-separated spots and no plastral hinge. (2) Box Turtles can close up tightly, and they have hooklike beaks. **RANGE:** Nova Scotia to Neb.; range discontinuous and spotty east of Ohio and Ont.; extirpated in Pa.; isolated records in se. S.D. and nw. Mo.

GOPHER TORTOISES: FAMILY TESTUDINIDAE

The only tortoises native to the United States. The feet are stumpy, the hind ones elephantlike. The heavily scaled forelimbs, when folded, close the opening of the shell and provide good protection for the head and neck. Carapace high and rounded, each scute with or without a light center. Captives eat grass, lettuce, and a variety of other vegetables and fruit; some show interest in meat. May reach ages in excess of 50 years. Of the four known species, one is confined to the Southeast, two are shared by the United States and Mexico, and one occurs only in arid north central Mexico. The family is represented on all the continents except Australia, and it includes the giant Galápagos and Aldabra tortoises.

GOPHER TORTOISE *Gopherus polyphemus*   **PL. 2**

IDENTIFICATION: 6–9½ in. (15.2–24 cm); record 15 in. (38.1 cm). This is the "gopher" of the Deep South. The *stumpy feet,* completely without webs, and the rigid, unhinged plastron make identification easy. Carapace brown or tan; plastron dull yellowish, soft parts grayish brown. Old adults are virtually smooth, but younger ones have conspicuous growth rings. Compared with the Texas Tortoise, the Gopher Tortoise's carapace is longer and lower in proportion to its width, its hind feet are smaller, and the front

GOPHER TORTOISE
Gopherus polyphemus

of its head, when viewed from above, is rounded (wedge-shaped in Texas Tortoise). *Young:* Considerable orange or yellow on soft parts, plastron, and marginals; each large carapace scute yellowish but bordered by brown; 1–2 in. (2.5–5.1 cm) at hatching.

An accomplished burrower. Its tunnels slope downward from the surface and then usually level off underground. An excavation may be as long as 35 ft. (about 10 m), and wide enough so the turtle can turn around at any point along its length. Many other animals seek shelter or live permanently in "gopher" burrows, these running the gamut from insects to burrowing owls, raccoons, and opossums. Gopher Frogs, Indigo Snakes, and Diamondback Rattlers are frequent guests — a good point to remember before you start probing into a tunnel.

Tortoises emerge daily in warm weather, usually in the morning before the heat is too great, to forage on grass, leaves, and such wild fruits or berries as they can find. **SIMILAR SPECIES:** Box Turtles have a hinge across plastron. **RANGE:** Sandy regions of Coastal Plain from extr. s. S.C. to extr. e. La. and most of Fla.; introduced on Cumberland I., Ga.

TEXAS TORTOISE *Gopherus berlandieri*   PL. 2

IDENTIFICATION: 5½–8 in. (14–20.3 cm); record 8¾ in. (22.2 cm). The rounded carapace may be nearly as broad as it is long, and its coloration varies from tan to dark brown. Specimens showing growth rings have a finely sculptured appearance. *Feet stumpy;* plastron rigid. Gular scutes of plastron may be *greatly elongated,* forked, and curved upward, especially in adult males, which are thus equipped with a weapon useful in overturning masculine opponents during breeding activities. *Young:* Each large scute of carapace with a yellow center, and each marginal edged with same color; about 1½–2 in. (3.8–5.1 cm) at hatching (both lengthwise and crosswise).

An arid-land counterpart of the Gopher Tortoise that prowls

TEXAS TORTOISE
Gopherus berlandieri

actively in hot weather, usually in early morning or late afternoon. Burrows sometimes are constructed in sandy soil, but Texas Tortoises normally spend their resting time in shallow forms or pallets made by scraping away the ground litter and soil at the base of a bush or clump of grass or cactus. Such simple shelters may conceal them only partially, but they often enter mammal burrows. Food consists mainly of grass and the pads, flowers, and fruits *(tunas)* of the prickly pear, but other vegetation also is eaten. **SIMILAR SPECIES:** Box Turtles have a hinge across plastron. **RANGE:** S. Texas and ne. Mexico.

SEA TURTLES:
FAMILIES CHELONIIDAE AND DERMOCHELYIDAE

Large turtles of tropical seas whose limbs are modified into flippers. They may turn up on beaches, in bays, or at sea, and some kinds nest along the Gulf and Atlantic shores of our southern states. Some are swept northward through the warm waters of the Gulf Stream to North Carolina and then continue up the coast to appear during the summer months offshore and in estuaries as far north as New England, Nova Scotia, and Newfoundland. Some apparently ride or accompany the Stream to northern Europe. All five kinds occur in or have relatives in the Pacific Ocean.

Measurements and weights for larger specimens are often unreliable because of the difficulty of lifting and maneuvering such huge animals, varying techniques of measuring, and estimates which, although sheer guesswork when made, get mellowed by time and repetition and are finally accepted as truth. Adult sea turtles often are battered or encrusted with barnacles, making identification more difficult. If in doubt, be sure to check the scute and headplate diagrams (Fig. 37 and Fig. 9, opp. Pl. 9). Be careful in handling or approaching large specimens. They bite, and their flippers can deliver punishing blows.

All the sea turtles are in trouble because of overhunting, the frequency with which they are caught and drowned in nets used in commercial fishing and by shrimp trawlers, and the destruction of enormous numbers of their eggs for human food and for use as an imagined aphrodisiac. As a result, all are protected by

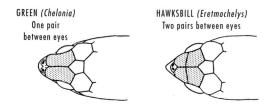

GREEN *(Chelonia)*
One pair
between eyes

HAWKSBILL *(Eretmochelys)*
Two pairs between eyes

Fig. 37. *Head plates of Sea Turtles.*

U.S. law and in many other countries, but poaching and drownings continue. A number of turtle nesting beaches, both in this country and in the tropics, are guarded and patrolled during the nesting season.

GREEN TURTLE *Chelonia mydas*   **PL. 9**

IDENTIFICATION: 36–48 in. (90–122 cm); record 60⅜ in. (153 cm). Weight 250–450 lbs. (113–204 kg); record 650+ lbs. (295+ kg). General coloration brown. (This turtle's name derives from the greenish fat of the body.) Carapace light or dark brown, sometimes shaded with olive; often with radiating mottled or wavy dark markings or large dark brown blotches. Only four costal plates on each side of carapace, the 1st not touching the nuchal. *One* pair of prefrontal plates between eyes (Fig. 37). Large scutes of carapace do not overlap. *Young:* Dorsum dark brown; venter white except for ends of flippers, which are black but edged with white; a keel down center of back and a pair of keels down plastron; 1⅝–2⅜ in. (4.1–6 cm) at hatching. Hatchlings are black above, but they become much paler by the age of 6 months.

A turtle greatly reduced in numbers because of its succulent flesh and its possession of "calipee" and "calipash." These two ingredients, esteemed for producing a gelatinous consistency in green-turtle soup, are derived from cartilaginous portions of the shell. **SIMILAR SPECIES:** (1) Hawksbill has *two pairs* of prefrontals and large scutes on carapace may overlap. (2) In both Loggerhead and Ridley the 1st costal touches the nuchal. **RANGE:** In the Western Atlantic, from Mass. to n. Argentina.

ATLANTIC HAWKSBILL   **PL. 9**
Eretmochelys imbricata imbricata

IDENTIFICATION: 30–35 in. (76–89 cm); record 36+ in. (90+ cm). Weight 95–165 lbs. (43–75 kg); record 280 lbs. (127 kg). The large scutes of the carapace overlap, except in very old individuals in which they lie side by side as in most other turtles. A keel down center of carapace. General coloration brown. Some specimens, smaller ones especially, show a tortoiseshell pattern. Four costal plates on each side of carapace, the 1st not touching the nuchal; two *pairs* of prefrontals between eyes (Fig. 37). *Young:* Black or very dark brown above and below except for raised ridges, edges of shell, and areas on neck and flippers—all of which are light brown; one middorsal and two plastral keels; about 1½–1⅞ in. (3.8–4.8 cm) at hatching.

Source of the tortoiseshell of commerce, still in demand as a luxury item even though plastics have replaced many of its former uses. **SIMILAR SPECIES:** (1) Green Turtle has only *one pair* of prefrontals between eyes, and scutes do not overlap (except in very young). (2) In Loggerhead and Ridley there are 5 or more costals on each side of carapace, the 1st touching the nuchal. **RANGE:** In the Western Atlantic, from s. New England to s. Brazil.

LOGGERHEAD *Caretta caretta* PL. 9

IDENTIFICATION: 31–45 in. (79–114 cm); record 48+ in. (122+ cm). Weight 170–350 lbs. (77–159 kg); record 500+ lbs. (227+ kg). Reddish brown coloration offers quickest clue, but also check arrangement of the scutes. Number of costals on each side of carapace is five or more, and the 1st one always *touches* the nuchal. There are three (usually) or four large scutes on bridge between shells (see Fig. 9, opp. Pl. 9), but these are poreless. There is also a middorsal keel, but this becomes low and inconspicuous in large specimens. *Young:* Brown above and whitish, yellowish, or tan beneath; three dorsal keels and two plastral keels; 1⅝–1⅞ in. (4.1–4.8 cm) at hatching. **SIMILAR SPECIES:** (1) The Ridley is smaller, has an almost circular olive-green carapace (gray in young specimens), usually has an interanal scute, and almost always has four large, pored scutes on bridge. (2) In both Hawksbill and Green Turtles the 1st costal does *not* touch the nuchal. **RANGE:** In the Western Atlantic, from the Canadian Maritime Provinces to Argentina. Nests regularly north to the beaches of the Carolinas and (rarely) to Md. and N.J.

ATLANTIC RIDLEY *Lepidochelys kempii* PL. 9

IDENTIFICATION: 23–27½ in. (58–70 cm); record 29½ in. (74.9 cm). Weight 80–100 lbs. (36–45 kg); record 110 lbs. (49.9 kg). Our only sea turtle with an almost circular carapace; olive green above and yellow below (gray above in smaller specimens). Five costals on each side of carapace, the 1st one *touching* the nuchal. Almost invariably *four* (rarely five) enlarged scutes on bridge, *each* *pierced by a pore near the posterior edge;* usually an interanal scute (Fig. 9, opp. Pl. 9) at posterior tip of plastron. *Young:* Almost completely dark gray; a short streak of light gray along rear edge of front flipper; three tuberculate dorsal ridges and four plastral ones; about 1½–1¾ in. (3.8–4.4 cm) at hatching.

Smallest of the Atlantic sea turtles and widely known as the "bastard turtle" because of the erroneous belief it is a hybrid between the Loggerhead and Green Turtle. **SIMILAR SPECIES:** (1) The much larger Loggerhead is reddish brown, lacks an interanal scute, and the three or four large scutes on bridge are poreless. (2) In both the Hawksbill and Green Turtles the 1st costal does *not* touch the nuchal. **RANGE:** Chiefly Gulf of Mexico, but immatures often appear in summer and fall along the Atlantic Coast as far north as New England and Nova Scotia. **NOTE:** The Pacific Ridley, *Lepidochelys olivacea*, may eventually appear in Florida waters. Nesting colonies, apparently derived from migrants across the Atlantic Ocean from West Africa, occur along several beaches of the Guianas and Trinidad, and stray specimens are known from Puerto Rico and the northern coast of Cuba. In *olivacea* there are usually six or seven costals (sometimes as many as nine) on each side of the carapace, instead of the usual five as in *kempii;* the middle marginals are mostly wider than long in *kempii* (longer than wide in *olivacea*).

LEATHERBACK *Dermochelys coriacea* PL. 9

IDENTIFICATION: 53–70 in. (135–178 cm); record 74¼ in. (189 cm). Weight 650–1,200 lbs. (295–544 kg); record 2,016 lbs. (916 kg). Largest of all living turtles. *Seven prominent longitudinal ridges on carapace.* Five similar ridges on plastron. Carapace and plastron have no scutes but are covered instead by a smooth, slate-black, dark bluish, or dark bluish black skin. Irregular patches of white or pink may appear almost anywhere; white predominates on the plastron. *Young:* Black and white and much more conspicuously marked than adults; covered with great numbers of small, beady scales, which later are shed; tail keeled above; about 2⅜–3 in. (6–7.5 cm) at hatching.

This strong and powerful swimmer, the only member of the Family Dermochelyidae, uses its jaws and flippers with telling effect if attacked or restrained. When hurt it emits cries that have been likened to groans, roars, and bellows. Despite its great size the Leatherback feeds chiefly on jellyfish. Long, backward-projecting spines that line both the mouth and esophagus help in swallowing such soft and slimy food. This turtle has the extraordinary ability to maintain its deep body temperature at a considerably higher level than that of the cold water in which it is sometimes found along our northern coasts during summer. **RANGE:** In the Western Atlantic, from Newf. to Argentina, frequently appearing in New England waters during the summer months. Nests along the Atlantic Coast as far north as N.C. and on several beaches around the Gulf of Mexico.

SOFTSHELL TURTLES: FAMILY TRIONYCHIDAE

These animated pancakes belie the traditional slowness of the turtle. They are powerful swimmers, and they can run on land with startling speed and agility. The shell is soft and leathery, bends freely at the sides and rear, and is completely devoid of scales or scutes. Vague outlines of the underlying bony structure often show through the skin of the plastron.

All species are aquatic. They may bask ashore, but only where they can slide or dash into the water in literally a split second. A frequent habit is to lie buried in mud or sand in shallow water with only the eyes and snout exposed and where, when the long neck is extended, the nostrils can reach the surface for a breath of air. The Florida Softshell lives chiefly in lakes; all the others are river turtles to a large degree.

Identification is hampered by changes associated with age and sex. Young softshells are about as well patterned as they will ever be. Males tend to retain the juvenile pattern and coloration, but the females, which grow very large in comparison with their mates, undergo marked changes, the original pattern being replaced and eventually obliterated completely by mottlings and blotches. (An exception to the general rule is the Florida Softshell, in which both sexes become drab and retain only traces of pattern.) Males have much longer and stouter tails than females. The young in all our species average about 1¼–2 in. (3.2–5.1 cm) at hatching time.

Handle softshells with caution. Their sharp claws and mandibles deserve respect.

The Family Trionychidae occurs in Africa, Asia, and the East Indies as well as in North America.

SMOOTH SOFTSHELL *Apalone mutica*   **PLS. 4, 10**

IDENTIFICATION: Adult females 6½–14 in. (16.5–35.6 cm); males 4½–7 in. (11.5–17.8 cm). Sometimes called the "spineless softshell," which is not very complimentary to a turtle that can bite and scratch with vigor, but this is a good way to remember an important fact. Our only softshell *without* spines, bumps, or sandpapery projections on carapace. Shell is quite smooth. Also, only softshell *without* ridges in nostrils (see Fig. 10, opp. Pl. 10). To complete the roster of negative characters, the feet are not strongly streaked or spotted. *Male and young:* Carapace olive-gray or brown, marked with dots and dashes only a little darker than ground color. *Adult female:* Mottled with various shades of gray, brown, or olive. *Young:* Plastron paler than underside of carapace (see Pl. 4).

SMOOTH SOFTSHELLS
Apalone mutica
■ MIDLAND
▨ GULF COAST

Essentially a river turtle, an inhabitant of streams ranging in size from creeks to the mighty Mississippi. Occurs in lakes less frequently than Spiny Softshells, and often is missing where they are abundant, and vice versa. **SIMILAR SPECIES:** (1) Florida Softshell has a bumpy carapace, and (2) all races of the Spiny Softshell have shells that are either sandpapery or with spines on front edge of carapace, or both. (3) All softshells except Smooth have a ridge in each nostril. **RANGE:** Cen. U.S.; Ohio, Mississippi, and Missouri rivers and their tributaries; streams draining to the Gulf of Mexico, from extr. w. Fla. to e. Texas. **SUBSPECIES:** MIDLAND SMOOTH SOFTSHELL, *Apalone m. mutica* (Pls. 4 and 10). Ill-defined pale stripes usually evident on snout in front of eyes; pale postocular stripes with narrow, dark borders; otherwise as described above. W. Pa. to extr. n. Ala., w. Miss., and much of La.; west to Texas, and north to Minn. and N.D. Isolated in Canadian R. of ne. N.M. Apparently absent from a large area in s. Mo., se. Kans., and ne. Okla.; extirpated from Pa. GULF COAST SMOOTH SOFTSHELL, *Apalone m. calvata.* Carapace of young has large, circular, dusky spots that disappear in adult females but persist at least indistinctly in adult males. No stripes on dorsal surface of snout; pale postocular stripe with thick black borders. Smaller; females up to 11¼ in. (28.7 cm). Streams of Miss. and Ala. draining to the Gulf of Mexico, from the Escambia R. of extr. w. Fla. west to the Pearl R. and the Florida Parishes of La.

EASTERN SPINY SOFTSHELL
PLS. 4, 10

Apalone spinifera spinifera

IDENTIFICATION: Adult females 7–17 in. (18–43.2 cm); males 5–9¼ in. (12.5–23.5 cm). Check three items: (a) *feet strongly streaked and spotted*; (b) a *ridge* in each nostril (Fig. 10, opp. Pl. 10); and (c) look or feel for *projections* on upper surface of carapace as described for the two sexes. *Male:* Dark eyelike spots (ocelli) on

SPINY SOFTSHELLS
Apalone spinifera

■ PALLID ▨ WESTERN ■ EASTERN
■ GUADALUPE ▨ TEXAS ▨ GULF COAST

carapace, especially toward center. These are quite variable in size—on same turtle and from one specimen to the next. Ground color olive-gray to yellowish brown. Tiny projections on entire surface of carapace in adult males make shell feel like sandpaper; anterior edge of shell has small, spinelike projections. *Female:* The circular markings, characteristic of juveniles, begin to break up as female approaches maturity; they are replaced by blotches of brown or olive-brown of varying sizes that produce a camouflage effect. Surface of carapace smooth, but spines or enlarged tubercles are present on and near forward edge of carapace (Fig. 10, opp. Pl. 10), and raised protuberances may appear on other parts of shell. *Young* (Pl. 4): Small, dark spots or circular markings on a pale yellowish brown ground color.

Essentially a river turtle but also occurring in lakes and other quiet bodies of water where sand and mud bars are available. Sometimes floats at surface, where shape identifies it as a softshell. Over a large part of the range this is the only member of the group, but in areas where Smooth Softshells also occur it is usually necessary to capture specimens to be sure of identification. **SIMILAR SPECIES:** See Smooth Softshell. **RANGE:** W. N.Y. to Wisc. and south to the Tennessee R.; intergrading with other races in the lower Mississippi Valley virtually to the Gulf. A disjunct area in Lake Champlain and lower part of Ottawa R., Canada; an isolated record from e.-cen. N.Y., and introduced and well established in Maurice R. system of s. N.J.

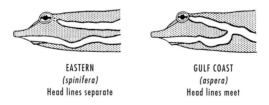

EASTERN
(spinifera)
Head lines separate

GULF COAST
(aspera)
Head lines meet

Fig. 38. *Head patterns of two subspecies of the Spiny Softshell* (Apalone spinifera).

Western Spiny Softshell. In this widespread subspecies the dark spots and ocelli on the carapace are greatly reduced in size and sometimes are almost completely absent in large adults, especially females such as this.

WESTERN SPINY SOFTSHELL   PL. 10
Apalone spinifera hartwegi

IDENTIFICATION: Adult females 7–18 in. (18–45.7 cm); males 5–7¼ in. (12.5–18.4 cm); record 20½ in. (52.3 cm). A western subspecies characterized by the smallness of the dark markings on the carapace; these are only slightly enlarged toward the center of shell. In other characteristics like Eastern Spiny Softshell.

In western parts of range, where arid or semiarid conditions prevail, rivers offer the only suitable natural habitats for softshells. Farther east a variety of bodies of water are utilized. **SIMILAR SPECIES:** See Smooth Softshell. **RANGE:** Minn. to Ark. and west to se. Wyo., e. Colo., and ne. N.M.; an isolated record in e. Wyo., and a large disjunct area in Missouri R. drainage in Mont. This race intergrades with Eastern Spiny Softshell through a broad area paralleling the Mississippi R.

GULF COAST SPINY SOFTSHELL   PL. 10
Apalone spinifera aspera

IDENTIFICATION: Adult females 7–17⅞ in. (18–45.4 cm); males 5–8 in. (12.5–20.3 cm). The southern representative of the Spiny Softshells. Two items of pattern set this race apart from other subspecies: (a) *two or more dark lines* (or broken lines) parallel the rear margin of shell—in all other races there is only a single dark line; (b) the two light lines on head, one extending backward from eye and the other from the jaw, usually unite on side of head (Fig. 38)—in Eastern Spiny Softshell the light lines normally fail to join. All these markings are best seen in juvenile and male specimens; they are obscure or even lacking in old females. In many of the latter, spines on forward part of shell are developed to a remarkable degree.

A resident of southern rivers and ponds or oxbows associated with rivers. **SIMILAR SPECIES:** (1) Florida Softshell has: (a) bumps on carapace in form of flattened hemispheres; (b) general coloration dark in both sexes; and (c) a carapace that, proportionately, is considerably longer than wide; young Florida Softshell is patterned with large, dark spots separated by a network of light areas (Pl. 4). (2) See Smooth Softshell. **RANGE:** S.-cen. N.C. to n. Fla.; west to Miss. and e. La. Four races of the species (Eastern, Western, Pallid, and Gulf Coast) come together in the great plexus of rivers and bayous of the lower Mississippi Valley in Ark., La., and Miss., and all contribute their characters to a general Spiny Softshell melting pot. Specimens from those areas should be considered as intergrades.

GUADALUPE SPINY SOFTSHELL PL. 10
Apalone spinifera guadalupensis

IDENTIFICATION: Adult females 7–16⅝ in. (18–42.2 cm); males 5–8½ in. (12.5–21.6 cm). Small, white spots are present on almost all parts of the carapace, and each spot is often tightly surrounded by a narrow black ring. This is a member of a complex of three subspecies of the Spiny Softshell that are characterized by small white spots on the brown or olive carapace. (See Subspecies below for ways to distinguish the other two races.) Among all three the spots are usually conspicuous in the young and in many adult males; females, which become mottled like females of our other softshells, usually lack them. Males may be quite sandpapery, but females usually do not have the spines so well developed as in other races of the Spiny Softshell.

One might think, from their western distribution, that these turtles are adept at threading their way through arid country by following the streams. That is probably true in some cases, but geological evidence indicates that a large part of the range formerly was much more moist than at present. The turtles have survived only in the more permanent streams and by estivating in mud during periods of drought. **SIMILAR SPECIES:** See Smooth Softshell. **RANGE:** S.-cen. Texas; drainage systems of the Guadalupe-San Antonio and Nueces rivers; intergrades with the Pallid Spiny Softshell in the Colorado R. system. **SUBSPECIES:** PALLID SPINY SOFTSHELL, *Apalone s. pallida*. White spots more or less confined to posterior half of carapace and not ringed with black. Largest of the races, with females up to 21¼ in. (54 cm). W. La., s. Okla., and most of n. and e. Texas. TEXAS SPINY SOFTSHELL, *Apalone s. emoryi*. White spots confined to rear third of carapace; pale rim of carapace conspicuously widened along rear edge, 4 or 5 times wider than pale rim of lateral edges. Rio

Grande and Pecos R. drainages and south to the Río Purificación, Tamaulipas; also the Gila-Colorado R. system (into which it may have been introduced through human agency) from sw. N.M. and extr. sw. Utah to the delta at the head of the Gulf of California; isolated colony in e.-cen. Ariz.

FLORIDA SOFTSHELL
Apalone ferox

FLORIDA SOFTSHELL
Apalone ferox   **PLS. 4, 10**

IDENTIFICATION: Adult females 11–24¾ in. (28–62.8 cm); males 6–12¾ in. (15.2–32.4 cm). Heaviest and bulkiest of North American softshells, but the species with the smallest range. General appearance is dark brown or dark brownish gray, nearly uniform in coloration or with vague suggestions of large dark spots. There are numerous small bumps on the carapace (Fig. 10, opp. Pl. 10), usually occupying a crescentic area involving the front of the shell and back along its sides as far as the forelegs. The bumps are flattened hemispheres—not spines or conical projections. A ridge in each nostril (Fig. 10, opp. Pl. 10), just as there is in the various subspecies of the Spiny Softshell. *Young:* Carapace with large dark round spots separated by network of light areas; bright lines and spots on an otherwise dark head (see Pl. 4).

The lake dweller among the softshells—at home in lakes, ponds, big springs, canals, and roadside ditches, and occasionally in quiet portions of rivers. Largely because of the nature of its habitat, this softshell is the most conspicuous member of the genus, at least when submerged. Often seen moving about in clear water. **SIMILAR SPECIES:** Gulf Coast Spiny Softshell has spines or cone-shaped projections on carapace, and in large individuals these may be strongly present; males and young are easily identified by yellowish brown carapace and dark lines or broken lines paralleling rear margin of shell. **RANGE:** All of Fla. mainland, plus a colony (introduced?) on Big Pine Key; s. S.C. to Mobile Bay, Ala.

LIZARDS

ORDER SQUAMATA*
SUBORDER LACERTILIA

Lizards are abundant in the tropics and many temperate regions, and collectively they range from above the Arctic Circle (in the Old World) to the southern tips of Africa, Australia, and South America. They have also reached many islands—even remote ones—to which they were transported on floating vegetation or inadvertently in the cargoes or personal belongings of humankind. Vertically, they occur from sea level to in excess of 16,000 feet (4900 m) in both the Andes and Himalayan Mountains. There are over 3700 species, but only two are venomous—the Beaded Lizard, which is confined to Mexico, and the Gila Monster of Mexico and our own Southwest. The latter ranges eastward only to extreme southwestern New Mexico. There are no poisonous lizards in the area covered by this Field Guide.

Many kinds of lizards must be caught for accurate identification, a real challenge in the cases of the more alert, active, and elusive varieties. Nooses, traps, or other devices are often indispensable. Be careful when seizing any lizard to avoid grasping the tail, which, in a great many of our species, may break off at the slightest pinch. The tails, unless they are severed close to the body, soon regenerate, but the new ones are never so long nor so perfectly formed as the originals. Tails are so frequently incomplete that professional herpetologists, when assembling data for their studies, usually measure the *snout-vent length*, the distance

---

* The Order Squamata includes the vast majority of all living reptiles. Subdivisions (Suborders) are Lacertilia (lizards), Amphisbaenia (amphisbaenians), and Serpentes (snakes).

from the tip of the snout to the anus. The total length (tip of snout to end of the tail) is better for visualizing the *real* size of a lizard, and is of more interest to readers of this Field Guide. Both measurements are included in the text accounts that follow.

Superficially, salamanders look like lizards, but salamanders completely lack scales, and there are no claws on their toes.

GECKOS:
FAMILIES GEKKONIDAE AND EUBLEPHARIDAE

A large and diverse group of lizards, widespread through the tropics and subtropics of both New and Old Worlds. Geckos are notorious for their ability to establish themselves around buildings and old docks in tropical seaports, and seven of the ten species in our area are immigrants that arrived fortuitously, presumably in cargoes of fruit, produce, lumber, etc., in Key West, Florida, and other localities in our southern states.

Eight of our ten species have immovable eyelids, and their eyes, like those of snakes, are open all the time. Some kinds are diurnal or crepuscular. Others prowl at night, and in these, the pupil of the eye, which is a mere vertical slit in bright light, expands widely in the dark. Gecko food includes insects, spiders, and other arthropods.

Many kinds of geckos are as good as flies at walking up and down smooth walls and even across ceilings. This they can do by virtue of their expanded toes, which are covered by brushlike pads or lamellae that bear myriads of tiny bristles or setae. Each bristle (and there may be a million of them in at least one Old World species) ends in as many as 100 to 1000 suction cups so extremely small they are clearly visible only under a scanning electron microscope. No wonder some geckos are marvelous acrobats, with so many "plumber's helpers" to assist them! On rough surfaces, the claws are also useful in climbing.

Geckos as a whole are noted for their vocalizations, and the group derives both its common and scientific names from an oriental species whose cry sounds like *geck'-o*. Coloration may vary considerably in the same individual specimen, at least in some species, in response to such factors as temperature, humidity, amount of light, and degree of activity. The tails of most geckos are *very* easily detached.

Representatives of two families are found in our area: (1) the House Geckos (*Gekko, Cyrtopodion, Gonatodes, Hemidactylus,* and *Sphaerodactylus* of the Family Gekkonidae); and (2) Banded Geckos (*Coleonyx* of the Family Eublepharidae). Banded Geckos have movable eyelids; the others do not.

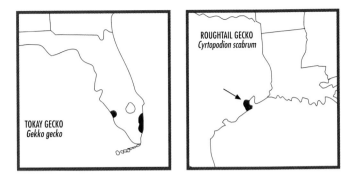

TOKAY GECKO *Gekko gecko*   PL. 11

IDENTIFICATION: 8–14 in. (20.3–36 cm); head-body max. 7 in. (18 cm). Largest of the geckos in our area. Pale bluish gray ground color with numerous white and brick-red to orange spots across the dorsum. Prominent tubercles (wartlike bumps) on head, body, legs, and tail; enlarged toe pads with up to 20 cross ridges underneath. Strong jaws on a broad massive head. *Young:* about 3 9/16–3 15/16 in. (9.1–9.9 cm) at hatching; tail with alternating bands of dark blue and white, the dark bands broader than the white ones.

Often released in homes within its native tropical range to control cockroaches and other insects; these colorful, aggressive geckos also eat other lizards. **VOICE:** Nocturnal and quite vocal. The call often begins with a preliminary cackle followed by *to-kay* or *tuk-koo* repeated about a half dozen times, but dropping off in loudness at the end. **SIMILAR SPECIES:** (1) Larger than other Floridian geckos, and the only one with brick-red spots on the dorsum. (2) All Floridian lizards other than geckos have movable eyelids. **RANGE:** Established in s. Fla., in the Miami area along the Atlantic Coast in Dade and Broward cos., and in Lee Co. along the Gulf coast. Occurs naturally in se. Asia and the Malay Archipelago.

ROUGHTAIL GECKO *Cyrtopodion scabrum*   PL. 11

IDENTIFICATION: 3–4⅜ in. (7.5–11.7 cm); head-body max. 2 in. (5.1 cm). A medium-sized gecko, sand-colored above with dark brown spots arranged in a fairly regular pattern down the back; belly white; toes with "adhesive" lamellae. Tail with dark brown crossbands or spots, and covered with prominent *enlarged, keeled scales. Young:* About 1⅝–2⅜ in. (4.1–6 cm) at hatching.

Like other House Geckos, this lizard is nocturnal and lives in and on buildings, where it feeds largely on insects. **SIMILAR SPECIES:** (1) Mediterranean Gecko has a paler pattern and lacks rough, keeled scales on the tail. (2) Except for the Mediterranean Gecko, all other lizards along the Texas Gulf Coast have movable eyelids. **RANGE:** Established along the commercial shipping docks of Galveston, Texas. Occurs naturally from Egypt southward to Sudan and east to nw. India.

MEDITERRANEAN GECKO
Hemidactylus turcicus turcicus

IDENTIFICATION: 4–5 in. (10–12.7 cm); head-body max. 2⅜ in. (6 cm). A pale, ghostly lizard with very large eyes, and *broad toe pads* extending nearly full length of toes (Fig. 11, opp. Pl. 11). Prominent tubercles (wartlike bumps) on head, body, legs, and tail. Both light and dark spots on a pale ground. Dark spots may be brown or gray; pale areas variable from bright pinkish ivory to very pale or whitish. *Young:* Head-body length ¾–1¼ in. (2–3cm).

Almost completely nocturnal. On warm evenings, look for it on buildings, window screens, or near lights where insects congregate. It makes itself quite at home around human habitations. **VOICE:** A faint, mouselike squeak repeated at more or less regular intervals. Dominant males may emit a series of clicking noises in rapid succession. **RANGE:** Established at many localities in the se. and s. cen. states and ne. Mexico, and now known throughout much of s. Texas; also introduced into s. Ariz., s. Calif., Cuba, P.R., Panama, and other parts of Mexico. An Old World gecko that ranges from w. India and Somali, chiefly in coastal areas and around both sides of the Mediterranean Basin, to Spain, Morocco, and the Canary Is. The speed with which this gecko has expanded its range in the southern U.S. in recent years may be attributed to both the lizards and their communal egg clutches being transported, chiefly inadvertently, by humankind.

MEDITERRANEAN GECKO
Hemidactylus turcicus

INDO-PACIFIC GECKO
Hemidactylus garnotii

INDO-PACIFIC GECKO *Hemidactylus garnotii*

IDENTIFICATION: 4–5¼ in. (10–13.3 cm); head-body max. 2½ in. (6.4 cm). A brownish gray lizard with small, ovoid dorsal scales and large toe pads (as in the Mediterranean Gecko, Fig. 11, opp. Pl. 11), but *no large tubercles*. Dorsum almost uniformly colored or marbled with darker brown; small, whitish dorsal spots that vary in size and shape. *Belly lemon yellow;* underside of tail pale red. *Young:* About 1⅝–2⅛ in. (4.1–5.4 cm) at hatching.

Like many of the whiptail lizards, this gecko is unisexual. Males are unknown, and reproduction is by parthenogenesis (development of an unfertilized egg). **SIMILAR SPECIES:** Mediterranean Gecko is pinkish or whitish and has conspicuous tubercles on the dorsal surfaces. **VOICE:** Emits an attack squeak during combats with others of its kind. **RANGE:** Established in Fla. from Seminole Co. on the Atlantic Coast south to Miami and Key Largo, and north on the Gulf Coast to Charlotte Co.; native to se. Asia, the East Indies, and many islands of the South Seas; also established in Hawaii.

ASHY GECKO *Sphaerodactylus elegans elegans*

PL. 11; FIG. 11

IDENTIFICATION: 2¾–2⅞ in. (7–7.3 cm); head-body max. 1⁷⁄₁₆ in. (3.7 cm). A wraith of a lizard that appears on building walls, window screens, or near lights on warm evenings in search of insects attracted by the illumination. Check dorsal pattern. Upper surfaces with a profusion of tiny white or yellow spots on a darker ground color that varies from reddish brown to pale grayish brown. The spots often tend to run together and form light lines on head. Snout pointed and slightly flattened. Dorsal scales *small and granular.* Small round pad at tip of each toe (Fig. 11, opp. Pl. 11). *Young:* The dark crossbands and reddish tail disappear with age.

Chiefly crepuscular, but active at night near houses and street lights; hides in crevices or under debris or vegetation during daylight hours. Often found in or on walls of cisterns and outhouses. **SIMILAR SPECIES:** (1) Florida Reef and (2) Ocellated Geckos are brown with *dark* markings, and their dorsal scales are strongly *keeled.* Ocellated Gecko also has light stripes on head and white spots on nape. **RANGE:** Introduced on Key West from where it has spread to other Lower Florida Keys; native to Cuba and adj. islands.

FLORIDA REEF GECKO *Sphaerodactylus notatus notatus* PL. 11

IDENTIFICATION: 2–2¼ in. (5.1–5.7 cm); head-body max. 1³⁄₁₆ in. (3 cm). A tiny, chubby, brown lizard with a pointed, slightly flattened snout. Dorsal scales *strongly keeled,* 41 to 48 around midbody.

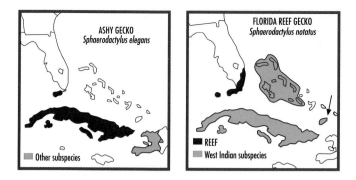

Small round pad at tip of each toe (Fig. 11, opp. Pl. 11). *Male:* Entire dorsal surface with small dark spots. Old males may be uniformly brown. *Female:* Three broad, dark, light-centered, longitudinal stripes on head. A pair of light spots on the shoulder may or may not be present. *Young:* Like adult female (not strongly crossbanded as in Ashy Gecko).

The Florida Reef Gecko quickly scurries for the next nearest cover when its shelter (a board, stone, trash, or other debris) is lifted. Chiefly crepuscular. Occurs in pinelands, hammocks, vacant lots, and around buildings. **SIMILAR SPECIES:** (1) Ashy Gecko has *light* spots on dark ground color and small *granular* dorsal scales. (2) Ocellated Gecko has many *pale* spots on nape and *light lines on head.* **RANGE:** Native. The Dry Tortugas, the Florida Keys, and extr. se. mainland Fla.; other races in Cuba, the Bahamas, and on Little Swan I. in western part of Caribbean Sea.

OCELLATED GECKO *Sphaerodactylus argus argus* **PL. 11**

IDENTIFICATION: 1⅞–2⅜ in. (4.8–6 cm); head-body max. 1⁵⁄₁₆ in. (3.3 cm). The tiny, white eyelike spots (ocelli) on the nape are far fewer than the hundred eyes of the Argus of mythology, but they give this lizard its scientific name and furnish a quick clue to identification. The ocelli may continue onto the back and some may fuse with one another longitudinally or with the *light lines on the head.* Some specimens are virtually patternless. Dorsal coloration brown to olive-brown, tail brown or reddish. Dorsal scales *keeled,* 57–73 around midbody. Small round pad at tip of each toe (as in Florida Reef and Ashy Geckos, Fig. 11, opp. Pl. 11). *Young:* Like adults but tending to have a more lineate body pattern; about 1¹⁄₁₆ in. (2.6 cm) at hatching. **SIMILAR SPECIES:** (1) Florida Reef Gecko has only two light spots on nape or none at all, head stripes (if present) are dark, and dorsal scales around midbody are 48 or

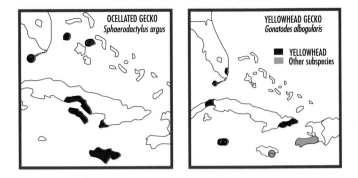

fewer. (2) Ashy Gecko has granular dorsal scales. **RANGE:** Introduced on Key West, Fla., the Biminis and Nassau in the Bahamas, the Yucatán Peninsula of Mexico, and mainland Panama; native to Jamaica, the south coast of Cuba and adj. offshore islets, and the Corn Is. (Nicaragua). Another subspecies occurs on the Isla de San Andrés in the sw. Caribbean Sea.

YELLOWHEAD GECKO *Gonatodes albogularis fuscus*   PL. 11

IDENTIFICATION: 2½–3½ in. (6.4–8.9 cm); head-body max. 1⁹⁄₁₆ in. (4 cm). *Adult males:* Head yellow; body, legs, and tail uniformly dark, almost black in sunlight, but bluish (as illustrated) at night or in heavy shade. *Female and young:* Mottled with brown, gray, and yellow; a *narrow light collar* usually present on *one or both sides of neck.* In this species there are no expanded pads on toes (Fig. 11, opp. Pl. 11), and pupils of eyes are round. Tip of tail, unless regenerated, is whitish.

Largely diurnal, in contrast with our other geckos. Occurs in and about abandoned buildings and docks and among debris on vacant land. A favorite habit is to cling upside down beneath a log, board, or other shelter. **RANGE:** Introduced on Key West and in Coconut Grove, Miami, Fla.; Cuba (possibly introduced), Grand Cayman I., Central America, and Colombia. Subspecies in s. Mexico, the West Indies, and n. South America.

TEXAS BANDED GECKO *Coleonyx brevis*   PL. 11; FIG. 39

IDENTIFICATION: 4–4⅞ in. (10–12.4 cm); head-body max. 2⁵⁄₁₆ in. (5.9 cm). A gecko with *functional eyelids.* No toe pads (Fig. 11, opp. Pl. 11). Scales tiny. A considerable *change in pattern* is associated with age. Juveniles are strongly marked by broad chocolate crossbands that alternate with narrower bands of cream or yellow. But as they grow older, dark pigment appears in the light bands and,

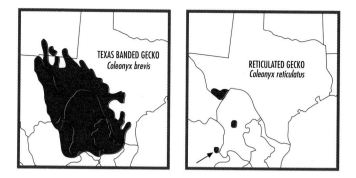

conversely, light areas develop in the chocolate bands. This produces a mottled effect that increases with age. In many adults the original pattern can be made out only with difficulty. *Young:* See above; about 1¾ in. (4.4 cm) at hatching.

Texas Banded Geckos are terrestrial, climbing but little in comparison with their more acrobatic cousins in the Family Gekkonidae. They prefer rocky areas, such as canyons, where they can take shelter during daylight hours beneath stones or in crevices. One of the thrills of nighttime driving in Banded Gecko country is to see these pale, delicate lizards standing out conspicuously against the blacktop paving as they cross the highway during their nocturnal prowlings. **SIMILAR SPECIES:** See Reticulated Gecko. **VOICE:** A faint squeak, often heard when a specimen is first picked up or when it is actively moving about in a terrarium. **RANGE:** S. N.M. to se. Texas and south to Nuevo León and ne. Durango.

ETICULATED GECKO *Coleonyx reticulatus* FIG. 39

IDENTIFICATION: 5½–6¾ in. (14–17.2 cm); head-body max. 3⁹⁄₁₆ in. (9 cm). Superficially like the Texas Banded Gecko, but differing as follows: (a) enlarged tubercles scattered among the tiny scales of the back (Fig. 39); (b) dorsum marked with brown spots or streaks on a light brown ground color and often arranged to suggest a light reticulated (netlike) pattern; (c) attains a much larger size. The *eyelids are functional. Young:* Total length at hatching about 3⅛ in. (8 cm); body and tail with distinct chocolate brown bands on a pinkish ground. Nocturnal and secretive. Apparently prefers cliff crevices, a habitat where its prehensile tail is used to good advantage. **VOICE:** Specimens may squeak when captured. **RANGE:** Brewster and Presidio cos. in the Big Bend of Texas; isolated records in Mexico.

RETICULATED
(reticulatus)
Enlarged tubercles

TEXAS BANDED
(brevis)
All scales small

Fig. 39. *Scales of the back in Geckos* (Coleonyx).

IGUANIAN LIZARDS

Herpetologists have long suspected that the former large Family Iguanidae, which contained about 550 species, was a composite of several groups. It was subdivided in 1989 into eight separate families, four of which are native to our area; members of two other families have been introduced into Florida. The iguanines as a whole include all the lizards from *Anolis* to *Leiocephalus*. The six families are: (1) the Anoles and their relatives (Family Polychridae), ranging from southern North America to southern South America, (2) the Iguanas, Spinytail Iguanas, and Chuckwallas (Family Iguanidae) which occur from the southwestern United States to south-central South America, on the Galápagos Islands, and on the Indo-Pacific islands of the Tonga and Fiji groups, (3) the Casquehead Lizards (Family Corytophanidae), native from southern Mexico to northwestern South America, (4) the Collared and Leopard Lizards (Family Crotaphytidae) of central and southwestern North America, (5) the Spiny, Sand, Tree, and Horned Lizards (Family Phrynosomatidae) of temperate and tropical North America, and (6) the Neotropical Ground Lizards (Family Tropiduridae), native to temperate and tropical South America and many of the islands of the West Indies.

ANOLES: FAMILY POLYCHRIDAE

The Anoles, with more than 250 species, constitute the largest genus of lizards in the world. They are especially abundant in the tropics, and extend southward to Bolivia and Paraguay. Only one species, the Green Anole, is native to the continental United States; six West Indian species are now well established in Florida. All seven belong to the genus *Anolis*.

A striking feature is the throat fan (Pl. 13). A flap of skin, attached to the throat and extending onto the chest in some species, is swung forward and downward by a flexible rod of cartilage attached near the middle of the throat. As the fan flares out, the scales become widely separated and a bright color (often red, orange, or yellow) flashes into view. Males have large throat fans; in females they are small or rudimentary. The fan is displayed, often to the accompaniment of push-ups and head-bobbing, during courtship and in defense of territory.

The ability to change color is well developed. The changes are the result of the movement of pigment granules within the cells of the skin and in response to such stimuli as temperature, humidity, emotion, and activity. Our single native (and six introduced) species, taken collectively, are capable of exhibiting browns, grays, and greens. The measurements that appear in the text immediately following Identification are for males; females are smaller.

Anoles have pads on their toes that aid in climbing, but they are less adept at negotiating smooth vertical surfaces than some of the geckos. All our Anoles are arboreal, but they also forage on the ground. Their food consists largely of insects and spiders.

GREEN ANOLE *Anolis carolinensis* PL. 13; FIG. 40
IDENTIFICATION: 5–8 in. (12.5–20.3 cm); head-body max. 2¹⁵⁄₁₆ in. (7.5 cm). The misnamed "chameleon" often sold in pet stores. The plain *green hue* and *pink throat fan* (Pl. 13; Fig. 40), combined with overall small size, distinguish it from all our other lizards. Coloration varies: individuals are green at one time, mottled green and brown at another, and all brown at still another. There may be indications of pattern in the form of dark streaks or spots.

A Green Anole eating a caterpillar. This small lizard, which is widely distributed through the southeastern United States, feeds principally on insects, spiders, and other arthropods that can be gulped down whole.

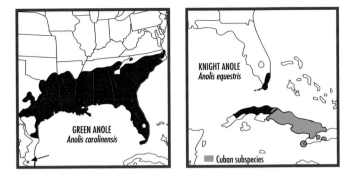

GREEN ANOLE
Anolis carolinensis

KNIGHT ANOLE
Anolis equestris

Cuban subspecies

Color-changing abilities are poor compared with true chameleons of the Old World. *Young:* About 2⅟₁₆–2⅝ in. (5.2–6.7 cm) at hatching.

An abundant lizard in the South; often seen on fences, around old buildings, on shrubs and vines, or (less often) on ground. Green Anoles climb high into trees, out of which they may tumble —especially when chasing one another—without harmful effects. Easily caught at night when, asleep on leaf or vine, the lizard stands out vividly in the beam of a flashlight. **RANGE:** N.C. to Key West, Fla.; west to se. Okla. and cen. Texas, and established in lower Rio Grande Valley; an isolated record in Tamaulipas. **NOTE:** Males from southern Florida are variable. They may be longitudinally streaked with slate gray on the nape and anterior part of the trunk. Throat fans vary from virtually white through pinks and magentas to blues and purples. Whether these anomalies represent variation within the species or whether a sibling complex of two or more species is involved is unknown at this time.

KNIGHT ANOLE *Anolis equestris equestris* PL. 13

IDENTIFICATION: 13–19⅜ in. (33–49.2 cm); head-body max. 7 in. (18 cm). This colorful and impressive lizard is one of the giant Cuban Anoles, the largest members of the genus. *Sheer size,* the enormous *pink throat fan* of the male, and the arboreal habits are sufficient to distinguish this lizard from others within its limited Floridian range. The presence of two white or yellowish longitudinal lines, one on the shoulder and the other extending from below the eye to the ear opening, are also helpful field marks. General coloration bright or apple-green, but sometimes changing to dull grayish brown. Yellow areas may appear and disappear, especially across the tail. Small crest on nape can be raised at will.

At home in shade trees along the streets of some areas of Miami;

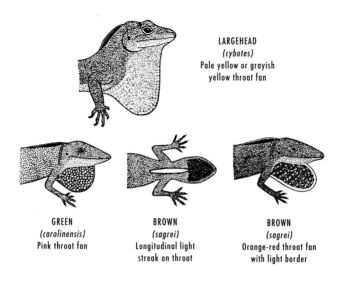

LARGEHEAD
(cybotes)
Pale yellow or grayish
yellow throat fan

GREEN
(carolinensis)
Pink throat fan

BROWN
(sagrei)
Longitudinal light
streak on throat

BROWN
(sagrei)
Orange-red throat fan
with light border

Fig. 40. Heads of Anoles (Anolis).

erroneously called "iguanas" by local residents. **RANGE:** Introduced into metropolitan Miami, Fla.; native to Habana Province and vicinity in Cuba; related subspecies in other parts of Cuba.

BROWN ANOLE *Anolis sagrei*   **PL. 13; FIG. 40**

IDENTIFICATION: 5–8⅜ in. (12.5–21.3 cm); head-body max. 2½ in. (6.4 cm). *Male:* A *brown or gray* lizard with a *white streak* down center of throat, although not always so prominent as in Fig. 40. The streak is the underside of the throat fan, which, when extended, may range in color from mustard yellow to chocolate to brilliant orange-red with a whitish border sometimes flecked with dark brown. Both throat fan and white streak are good field marks easily seen through binoculars. General coloration and pattern vari-

BROWN ANOLE
Anolis sagrei

■ West Indian
subspecies

The Brown Anole, an abundant species on many islands of the West Indies, was introduced long ago into southern states, especially Florida, where it is now well established. It is more terrestrial than the Green Anole.

able; same individual may change from pale gray to very dark brown. Small yellow spots, arranged in six or more vertical rows, are visible in some specimens. Some males may have a pronounced crest along top of tail. *Female: Narrow, yellowish stripe down center of back, flanked on each side by a row of dark brown half-circles.*

"Ground anoles" would be a good name for these lizards. They climb but are far less arboreal than the other Anoles in Florida. When cornered, they make short, erratic hops in their efforts to escape. **SIMILAR SPECIES:** (1) Green Anoles turn bright green, whereas Brown Anoles are always some shade of brown or gray. (2) Bark Anole is geckolike and has crossbands on tail. (3) See also Largehead Anole. **RANGE:** Introduced and established in most of peninsular Fla. and at isolated localities in se. Texas; also in coastal localities from s. Mexico to Honduras; Cuba, Jamaica, and the Bahamas. **NOTE:** Although two subspecies, *Anolis s. sagrei* and *Anolis s. ordinatus,* were originally introduced into southern Fla., they no longer can be distinguished. Further, the characteristics of the introduced Fla. populations now are such that they apparently differ from either of the two original colonizing races. Thus, the Fla. form is given no subspecific designation and is mapped as distinct from the Cuban and Bahaman races, pending further study.

JAMAICAN GIANT ANOLE *Anolis garmani*   PL. 13
IDENTIFICATION: 5⅞–10⅝ in. (15–27 cm); head-body max. 5¼ in. (13.3 cm). A large, muscular anole with slender limbs and considerable differences between sexes. *Male:* Leaf green to brown, sometimes with nine or more straw-colored bands; *prominent*

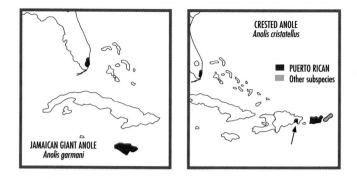

Map labels: JAMAICAN GIANT ANOLE *Anolis garmani*

CRESTED ANOLE *Anolis cristatellus*

■ PUERTO RICAN
▨ Other subspecies

crest on body and neck; head enlarged; throat fan lemon with orange center. *Female:* Similar ground color, but with a row of dorsal spots instead of bands; smaller, head-body length up to 3¾ in. (9.5 cm); throat fan small and dusky-colored.

Arboreal, rarely descending to the ground except to hide among rocks. Feeds on insects and some plant matter. **SIMILAR SPECIES:** (1) Largehead Anole is brown (never wholly green), sometimes with longitudinal stripes; (2) Knight Anole has a pink throat fan; (3) Other Floridian anoles lack the enlarged head in males. **RANGE:** Introduced and established in Miami, Fla.; native to Jamaica.

UERTO RICAN CRESTED ANOLE PL. 13
nolis cristatellus cristatellus

IDENTIFICATION: 4–7 in. (10–18 cm); head-body max. 3 in. (7.5 cm). *Male:* Light brown to greenish gray, sometimes with darker bands on body and tail; *crest on body and tail;* much larger than female; throat fan variable, from plain olive, yellow, or orange-yellow to olive green or mustard with an orange border. *Female:* Ground color similar but with a light middorsal stripe bordered by thinner, dark stripes (smaller males may also have this pattern); head-body length to 2¼ in. (5.7 cm).

Arboreal, preferring perch sites such as walls and fence posts in open areas, from where it forages for insects, spiders, and small fruits. **SIMILAR SPECIES:** (1) Knight Anole and Jamaican Giant Anole are much larger; (2) Green Anole is normally plain green or brown with pink throat fan; (3) The remaining three species of Floridian anoles have throat fans with different combinations of colors and patterns (see Pl. 13). **RANGE:** Introduced and established in Miami, Fla., and se. coast of the Dominican Republic; native to P.R. and the Virgin Is.; subspecies on the islands of the e. Puerto Rican Bank.

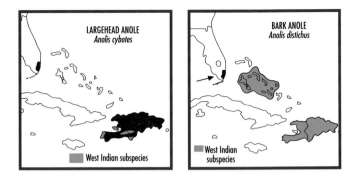

LARGEHEAD ANOLE *Anolis cybotes cybotes* **PL. 13; FIG. 40**
IDENTIFICATION: 7–8 in. (18–20.3 cm); head-body max. 2¹⁵⁄₁₆ in. (7.4 cm). Females considerably smaller than males. A large-headed, stockily built anole. General coloration brown (never wholly green), but varying through several shades of brown to tan. *Male:* Changeable—often with a pair of greenish longitudinal stripes on each side of body and dark brown crossbands on body, legs, and at least base of tail. An *erectile dorsal and nuchal crest,* the nuchal one especially prominent. Throat fan pale yellow or grayish yellow, sometimes with a central area of pale orange. *Female:* Nearly plain orange-brown except for a light middorsal stripe that may be smooth-sided or with scalloped or notched edges posteriorly; a pair of small yellowish spots on back and shoulder; head not enlarged. **SIMILAR SPECIES:** (1) Brown Anole (male) has white streak on throat (absent in *cybotes*). (2) Bark Anole has a small head and paired rows of snout scales. **RANGE:** Established in Dade Co., Fla.; Hispaniola and some of its satellite islands. Additional subspecies on Hispaniola.

BARK ANOLE *Anolis distichus* **PL. 13; FIG. 41**
IDENTIFICATION: 3½–5 in. (9–12.7 cm); head-body max. 2¼ in. (5.7 cm). Resembles a piece of lichen-covered bark that scurries away when approached. Coloration and pattern changeable, but always some shade of gray, brown, or green. When at rest or asleep, this lizard may appear putty-colored or almost white; at other times it varies from pale gray to green to mahogany brown to almost black. A *dark line* across and between eyes and a *crossbanded tail* (most pronounced near tip) are almost always present. A frequently occurring pattern consists of two small, eyelike spots at back of head and four vague chevrons pointing rearward on dor-

Fig. 41. *Dorsal view of the Bark Anole* (Anolis distichus). *Faint chevronlike pattern.*

sum (Fig. 41). Throat fan yellow, sometimes with an extensive pale orange blush.

This highly arboreal lizard is geckolike in its actions. Once aroused, it can be extremely elusive and difficult to catch. **RANGE:** Miami, Fla. area; related subspecies in Hispaniola and the Bahamas.

CASQUEHEAD LIZARDS: FAMILY CORYTOPHANIDAE

This lizard family, consisting of nine species in three genera, is not native to the area covered by our Field Guide, but a single species of the genus *Basiliscus* is now established in southern Florida. The Florida colony is probably from animals imported for the commercial animal trade. Whether it resulted from escapees or deliberate releases may never be known, but because of its spectacular appearance, the Brown Basilisk is now a noteworthy part of our lizard fauna.

BROWN BASILISK *Basiliscus vittatus* PL. 12

IDENTIFICATION: 11–27 in. (28–68.8 cm); head-body max. 6⅞ in. (17.5 cm). A slender lizard with long legs, a long tail, and an overall ground color of brown to olive-brown, sometimes with a body pattern of 6 or 7 dark brown or black crossbands or blotches. Smaller individuals have two light-colored stripes dorsolaterally from the head onto each side of the body, the upper one more distinct on the head and sometimes reaching the groin; older adults are more uniformly colored. Scales keeled on the light-colored cream to gray belly; chin and lips of upper jaws lighter than top of head. Tail a lighter brown with dark bands. *Male:* Larger than female, with a *triangular-shaped crest* on the head and a low mid-

BROWN BASILISK
Basiliscus vittatus

dorsal body crest. *Female:* Lacks pronounced crest on head and body but has a *hood-like lobe* on the neck.

A lizard of open areas near water, where it hunts for insects and small vertebrates. Young have fringes on the toes of their hind feet, which spread out when wet and allow them to run across the water's surface, using the long tail as a counterbalance; adults have more difficulty in doing so. Because of this habit, members of the genus are sometimes called "Jesus Christ Lizards" in their Latin American homeland because they "walk on water." **RANGE:** Introduced in extr. se. Fla. from Davie, Broward Co., to Miami, where it lives along sparsely vegetated canals. Occurs naturally from Jalisco and Tamaulipas, Mexico, south on both coasts through Central America to Colombia.

IGUANAS AND SPINYTAIL IGUANAS: FAMILY IGUANIDAE

This family of large, omnivorous lizards, composed of 25 species in eight genera, is not native to the area covered by this Field Guide, but two species, one from each of two genera (*Ctenosaura* and *Iguana*), are now established in southern Florida, and one of these is also established in extreme southern Texas. Both are probably from animals imported for the commercial animal trade. Because of their large size, both are now conspicuous, although localized, members of our lizard fauna. Both are native to the New World tropics.

SPINYTAIL IGUANA *Ctenosaura pectinata* PL. 12

IDENTIFICATION: 12–48 in. (30.6–122 cm); head-body max. 13⅞ in. (34.8 cm). A large, robust lizard with a *raised crest* of scales down the back to the base of the tail. Small, smooth scales on body contrasting with large, rough, keeled spines ringing the tail. Adults are gray, brown, or yellowish brown with ill-defined, broad, darker crossbands on the body. Upper part of head and neck usually brown, legs uniformly darker, and belly yellowish olive. Tail with wide bands of yellow and brown. *Young:* Bright green with brown and gold markings.

A lizard that prefers open sandy or rocky areas with holes and

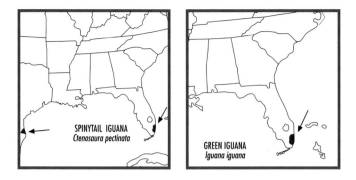

SPINYTAIL IGUANA
Ctenosaura pectinata

GREEN IGUANA
Iguana iguana

crevices in which to hide. Wood, rock, and trash piles, rock walls, tree hollows, and abandoned dwellings are favored haunts. Feeds mostly on leaves and fruits but will also eat small animals. Its powerful claws can inflict nasty scratches. **RANGE:** Introduced in extr. s. Texas at and near Brownsville, Cameron Co., and along Biscayne Bay in Miami, Fla. Native of w. Mexico, from Sinaloa southward to the Isthmus of Tehuantepec; found also on the Tres Marías Is. off the coast of Nayarit.

GREEN IGUANA *Iguana iguana* PL. 12

IDENTIFICATION: 30–79 in. (76–201 cm); head-body max. 21 ⅝ in. (55 cm). An introduced species, and the largest lizard now known to occur within the borders of the U.S. *An enlarged, round, smooth, dark-edged scale* on each side of throat below ear opening. Highly variable in color and pattern. Adults tend to darken and become more uniform with age, but younger ones may have a ground color of green, brown, tan, or gray with darker bands across the shoulder and around the tail; a row of fleshy, gray spines down the back and onto the tail. *Male:* A massive head and jaws, and well-developed spines. *Female:* Usually with a dull green ground color. *Young:* Bright emerald green; head-body 2½–3⅜ in. (6.4–8.6 cm) at hatching.

At home in tall trees with dense canopies near water, where it can bask in the sun, but it adapts well to more open areas. It is an excellent swimmer and will dive beneath the surface to escape enemies. Eats leaves, flowers, and fruits, but also consumes insects, small vertebrates, and carrion. Caution is advised in handling adults, which will bite, scratch, and lash with their muscular tails. **RANGE:** Introduced and breeding in se. Fla. in Miami and on Virginia Key and Key Biscayne. Ranges naturally from n. Mexico south (excluding much of the Yucatán Peninsula) through

Central America into South America as far south as the Tropic of Capricorn in Paraguay and se. Brazil; also found on numerous islands off the Pacific, Gulf, and Atlantic coasts; introduced on ne. coast of P.R.

COLLARED AND LEOPARD LIZARDS: FAMILY CROTAPHYTIDAE

Despite the marked differences in head shapes—narrow in the Leopard Lizards *(Gambelia)* and almost grotesquely enlarged in the Collared Lizards *(Crotaphytus)*—the members of these two genera are closely related. All are alert, elusive, and pugnacious. The two genera, consisting of seven species, range as a whole from eastern Missouri to the Pacific States and well south into western Mexico, including virtually all of Baja California and several islands off its coast, both in the Gulf of California and the Pacific Ocean. Only three species are found in our area.

EASTERN COLLARED LIZARD PL. 17
Crotaphytus collaris collaris

IDENTIFICATION: 8–14 in. (20.3–35.6 cm); head-body max. 4½ in. (11.5 cm). The "mountain boomer," a gangling, big-headed, long-tailed lizard that runs on its hind legs like a miniature dinosaur. The *two black collar markings* (often broken at nape) are constant, but coloration and pattern are variable. Body scales very small; 10 or fewer upper labials. *Male:* General coloration yellowish, greenish, brownish, or bluish; throat yellow or orange-yellow; dorsal pattern consisting of a profusion of light spots and (at least in younger specimens) a series of dark crossbands. Very old specimens may lose all their markings except for the black collars and light spots. *Female:* Similar but less brilliantly colored; in gravid specimens red spots or bars appear on sides of body, and similar spots may appear on sides of neck. *Young:* Broad, dark crossbands consisting of rows of dark spots alternating with yellowish crossbands (at hatching; later, young of both sexes may develop red bars on body like gravid females; the red is lost when a head-body length of about 3 in. (7.5 cm) is attained. Total length about 3–3¼ in. (7.5–9 cm) at hatching.

This reptile has no voice. The name "mountain boomer" is an unfortunate misnomer, and may have originated from someone's having seen an Eastern Collared Lizard on top of a rock while some other animal, possibly a Barking Frog, called from beneath the same rock. A resident of hilly, rocky, often arid or semiarid regions. Seldom found on the plains, except on rocky hills or in gullies traversing them. Limestone ledges or rock piles, both offering an abundance of hiding places, are favorite habitats. Col-

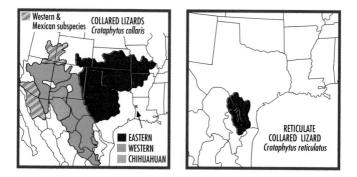

Western & Mexican subspecies

COLLARED LIZARDS
Crotaphytus collaris

■ EASTERN
■ WESTERN
▨ CHIHUAHUAN

**RETICULATE
COLLARED LIZARD**
Crotaphytus reticulatus

lared Lizards are wary and quick to take cover. When surprised in the open, however, they run first on all fours, not assuming the upright, bipedal type of locomotion until they have attained considerable speed. They are pugnacious, nip hard when caught, and when on the defense hold their mouths open in readiness to bite, exposing the black throat lining to view. Insects of many kinds are eaten; so also are small lizards, including Horned Lizards. Don't house Collared Lizards with other reptiles smaller than themselves. **SIMILAR SPECIES:** Both (1) Blue and (2) Crevice Spiny Lizards have only *one* black band (collar) across the neck, and their dorsal scales are very large and spiny. **RANGE:** E. and s.-cen. Mo. through cen. Texas; north into e. N.M. and se. Colo. **SUBSPECIES:** WESTERN COLLARED LIZARD, *Crotaphytus c. baileyi*. Resembles Eastern Collared Lizard but lacks yellow or orange-yellow on the throat; 11 or more upper labials. Adults, especially males, greenish or bluish above; head yellow or whitish. Throats of males west of the Continental Divide often bluish. From n. Ariz. and N.M., south through parts of ne. Sonora, s. Chihuahua, and w. Texas to n. San Luis Potosí. Western and northern subspecies. CHIHUAHUAN COLLARED LIZARD, *Crotaphytus c. fuscus*. Lacks the greens and yellows of the eastern and western races. A cream ground color above and below, with a dull brown and black pattern on neck; head light to cream-colored with no yellow. Restricted to sw. N.M., extr. w. Texas, and n.-cen. Chihuahua

RETICULATE COLLARED LIZARD   PL. 17
Crotaphytus reticulatus
IDENTIFICATION: 8–16¾ in. (20.3–42.5 cm); head-body max. 5⅜ in. (13.7 cm). Reticulate means netlike, and the light markings on the dorsum of this large lizard form an open, though often broken, network. This, in conjunction with a series of large black

spots across the back, makes identification easy, although the *net-like pattern* temporarily disappears in specimens chilled by cold weather. *Male:* A bright golden yellow suffusion on chest during breeding season. *Female:* No vertical black bars on neck; during breeding season vertical, brick-red bars may appear between lateral rows of black spots, and throat may have a pinkish suffusion. *Young:* Hatchlings are light gray, marked with 4 to 6 yellow or yellow-orange crossbands interspersed with transverse rows of black spots. About 3½–4 in. (9–10 cm) at hatching.

An alert, active lizard most often seen sunning atop rocks or found hiding beneath rocks or debris or in packrat nests. A resident of thornbrush deserts. Habits similar to those of Eastern Collared Lizard. **RANGE:** Rio Grande Valley in s. Texas and adj. Mexico.

LONGNOSE LEOPARD LIZARD PL. 17
Gambelia wislizenii wislizenii

IDENTIFICATION: 8½–15⅛ in. (21.5–38.4 cm); head-body max. 5¼ in. (13.2 cm). Unlike its mammalian namesake, this "leopard" can change its spots—or at least their coloration. Spots vary from black through several shades of brown, all in the same lizard, depending on such factors as temperature and activity. Ground color gray or brown, darkest when lizard is cool. In darker phases, narrow, whitish lines extend upward on each side of body, from neck to base of tail, usually meeting their partners to form crosslines; they are especially prominent in juveniles. Throat streaked with gray. *Female:* Flanks and underside of tail have salmon-red spots and streaks for a short period before laying eggs in spring or summer. *Young:* Spots often reddish. A curved yellow line above each eye, in combination with pale spots on lips, creates the illusion the lizard is wearing spectacles. About 4–5⅛ in. (10–13 cm) at hatching.

LONGNOSE LEOPARD LIZARD
Gambelia wislizenii

Western & Mexican subspecies

A large, speedy resident of arid or semiarid flats where vegetation occurs in clumps with ample running space between them. Almost always found on loose, sandy or gravelly soil, and frequently close to a burrow. Characteristically flattens it-self after running, and the spotted pattern usually blends so well with the ground that the lizard is difficult to see. Feeds on a large variety of insects and spiders; also eats lizards smaller than itself. Bites hard. **SIMILAR SPECIES:** Large size and strongly spotted or cross-banded pattern distinguish this species from all other lizards within our area. (1) Eastern Collared Lizard has two black collars and a much wider head. (2) Most other spotted lizards have spots in rows, not scattered. **RANGE:** Extr. w. Texas, west to e. Calif., north to Nev. and n. Utah, and south into nw. Sonora and n. Chihuahua; large disjunct populations in w. Texas, Coahuila, and Durango. Western and Mexican subspecies.

EARLESS, SPINY, TREE, SIDE-BLOTCHED, AND HORNED LIZARDS: FAMILY PHRYNOSOMATIDAE

Within our area, lizards in this family consist of three main groups: (1) the Earless Lizards (*Cophosaurus* and *Holbrookia*), (2) the Spiny, Tree, and Side-blotched Lizards (*Sceloporus, Urosaurus,* and *Uta),* and (3) the Horned Lizards (*Phrynosoma*). Display patterns, consisting of head-bobbing, nodding, and push-ups and which serve to declare territory, establish sex, aid in species discrimination, or enable a male to challenge another male, are characteristic and well-developed in many members of this family, which contains 10 genera with over 100 species.

EARLESS LIZARDS: GENERA *Cophosaurus* AND *Holbrookia*

These lizards have no visible ear openings. There are two folds across the throat, one strongly indicated, the other weak, irregular, or both (Fig. 42). Several of the species are adapted for life in regions of dry sandy or loamy soil. Their long legs and toes are useful for running on the surface, and their heads are shaped for quick burrowing in sand. They dive in head first and quickly bury themselves with a shimmying motion. The Texas and Southwest-

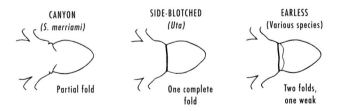

Fig. 42. Throat folds of several kinds of lizards.

ern Earless Lizards prefer rocky areas. Sexual dimorphism is pronounced, and males of most species are marked with a pair of bold black bars on their sides. Such bars are usually less distinct in adult females or may be lacking entirely. Females heavy with eggs may bear a bright overwash, often strong, of orange, reddish orange, pink, or yellow. Food includes insects and spiders. Members of the two genera occur well southward into Mexico.

Throughout the area covered by this Field Guide, the two most wide-ranging species (including their several subspecies, many of which are described below) are known as the Greater Earless Lizard (*Cophosaurus texanus*) and the Lesser Earless Lizard (*Holbrookia maculata*), respectively.

TEXAS EARLESS LIZARD *Cophosaurus texanus texanus* PL. 14

IDENTIFICATION: Males 3¼–7⅛ in. (8.3–18.1 cm); head-body max. 3¼ in. (8.3 cm). Females 2¾–5⅝ in. (7–14.3 cm); head-body max. 2¾ in. (7 cm). The *black bars under the tail* (Fig. 43) offer a conspicuous field mark, for this lizard often holds its tail curled over the back, especially when perched on top of a boulder. The bars are flashed when running, the tail is curled and waved from side to side as the lizard slows to a halt, or immediately after it stops. (Caution: Black bars are lacking under regenerated portions of tails.) Intensity of dark dorsal markings varies in same individual and from one lizard or one geographical locality to the next. Also, there is a tendency for the general coloration to resemble that of the habitat: those living in regions of gray soil are often grayish, those living on reddish soil are often reddish, etc. *Male:* The two bold, black, crescent-shaped lines near the groin (shared by the Southwestern Earless Lizard) are much longer than in other species of earless lizards. The blue field surrounding them on the belly is usually prominent. *Female:* No black lines or blue field. *Young:* About 2 in. (5.1 cm) at hatching.

Rocky streambeds, sandstone or limestone outcrops, and open

GREATER EARLESS LIZARDS
Cophosaurus texanus

TEXAS
SOUTHWESTERN
Mexican subspecies

rocky or gravelly areas in general are typical habitats of this race of the Greater Earless Lizard. Each lizard tends to remain in its own home range and may dash from one boulder to another and then back again when pursued. The protective coloration of the dorsum is spectacularly evident when one of these lizards runs just a short distance, settles down on a pale-colored rock or sand, and virtually disappears. **SIMILAR SPECIES:** Spot-tailed Earless Lizard has rounded dark spots under tail instead of crossbars (Fig. 43). **RANGE:** N.-cen. Texas south to ne. Mexico.

SOUTHWESTERN EARLESS LIZARD PL. 14
Cophosaurus texanus scitulus
IDENTIFICATION: Males 3½–7¼ in. (9–18.4 cm); head-body max. 3¼ in. (8.3 cm). Females 2⅜–5⁵⁄₁₆ in. (6.7–13.5 cm); head-body max. 2½ in. (6.4 cm). Similar to the Texas Earless Lizard, but males much more colorful, and so brilliant during the breeding season that ranchers of the Big Bend region call them "the lizard with the pink shirt and green pants." *Black bars under tail* (Fig. 43). A light-bordered *dark stripe on rear of thigh,* often clearly visible when lizard is approached from rear; conspicuous in females and young but much less so in large males. (This characteristic also shared by Texas Earless Lizard.) *Male:* Two prominent black ventro-lateral crescents bordered by blue or green on belly and by yellowish on flanks. Normal coloration gray with orange markings on forward part of body; hindquarters, legs, and tail green or yellowish. *Female:* Brown to gray, but with a rosy tint along the flanks when heavy with eggs; ventro-lateral crescents faint or absent.

A common and fast-running lizard of rocky desert flats and the vicinity of rocky cliffs and stream beds. **RANGE:** The Big Bend and adj. w. Texas to s.-cen. N.M. and se. Ariz.; south to ne. Zacatecas, adj. San Luis Potosí, and extr. w. Nuevo León; isolated records in w. Ariz. Mexican subspecies.

NORTHERN EARLESS LIZARD PL. 14
Holbrookia maculata maculata
IDENTIFICATION: 4–5 in. (10–12.7 cm); head-body max. 2⁷⁄₁₆ in. (6.2 cm). *Pale longitudinal stripes,* one extending from eye to base of tail and another faint one from armpit to groin. A single obscure middorsal stripe. *No black spots under tail. Male:* A pair of black bars behind armpit, often touched or surrounded by a small area

GREATER	SPOT-TAILED	KEELED and LESSER
(*C. texana*)	(*H. lacerata*)	(*H. propinqua* and *H. maculata*)
Black crossbars	Dark spots	No markings

Fig. 43. *Undersurfaces of tails of Earless Lizards* (Cophosaurus *and* Holbrookia).

An adult Northern Earless Lizard from Sumner County, Kansas. This lizard loves open areas with sand and loose soil, into which it burrows quite rapidly.

of blue; dorsal pattern blotched but not clear-cut; dorsum usually sprinkled with small white specks. *Female:* Slightly smaller in size and with lateral black bars much reduced and without blue borders; dorsal spots well defined but *not* surrounded by light pigment. Body strongly tinted with orange or orange-red when heavy with eggs, the color brightest on the two lateral stripes. *Young:* Like female in pattern and coloration; about 1½ in. (3.8 cm) at hatching.

This race of the Lesser Earless Lizard is a resident of sandy prairies, either open or with scant vegetational cover. Specific habitats include sandy grasslands, dry sandbars in streambeds, and fields under cultivation. These lizards are diurnal and during the heat of the day keep to shade afforded by bushes and other plants or take refuge in mammal or other burrows. **SIMILAR SPECIES:** (1) Texas and Spot-tailed Earless Lizards have black bars or spots under tail (Fig. 43). (2) Desert Side-blotched Lizard (*Uta*) has ear openings and only *one black spot* near armpit. (3) See also Keeled Earless Lizard. **RANGE:** S. S.D. to e.-cen. N.M. and through the Texas panhandle.

EASTERN EARLESS LIZARD   PL. 14
Holbrookia maculata perspicua

IDENTIFICATION: 4–5 in. (10–12.7 cm); head-body max. 2⅜ in. (6.1 cm). Similar to Northern Earless Lizard, but males lack white speckling. In many specimens of both sexes there is a strong tendency for the dark dorsal blotches to fuse together so there is only a *single* row of *broad* blotches down each side of body.

Occurs chiefly in tallgrass or modified tallgrass prairie with sandy or loamy soils. **RANGE:** Se. Kans. to cen. Texas.

SPECKLED EARLESS LIZARD PL. 14

Holbrookia maculata approximans

LESSER EARLESS LIZARDS
Holbrookia maculata

■ SPECKLED
▨ EASTERN
▨ NORTHERN
▨ Mexican subspecies

IDENTIFICATION: 4⅛–5⅛ in. (10.5–13 cm); head-body max. 2¾ in. (7 cm). *Dorsum strongly speckled,* especially in males. No longitudinal light stripes except on neck. Otherwise similar to Northern Earless Lizard. *No black spots under tail.*

A western race of the Lesser Earless Lizard that occurs chiefly in desert grasslands and outwash slopes of intermontane basins. **SIMILAR SPECIES:** Desert Side-blotched Lizard (*Uta*) has ear openings and *only one black spot near armpit.* **RANGE:** Trans-Pecos Texas, N.M. and Ariz. south to Jalisco and Guanajuato; an isolated record in n. Ariz. Western and Mexican subspecies, including a nearly uniformly white or ash-gray race confined to the White Sands region of N.M.

SPOT-TAILED EARLESS LIZARD *Holbrookia lacerata* PL. 14

IDENTIFICATION: 4½–6 in. (11.5–15.2 cm); head-body max. 2¹³⁄₁₆ in. (7.1 cm). Most conspicuously spotted of all earless lizards. Three separate sets of markings can be checked: (a) dark dorsal spots *surrounded* by light pigment; (b) about seven rounded dark spots under tail (Fig. 43); and (c) dusky to black oval streaks at edge of abdomen (these variable in number—from four to only one, or even absent). Sexes patterned alike. *Young:* Marked like adults; about 1¼ in. (3.8 cm) at hatching.

A species of arid, dark-soil flats, mesquite-prickly pear associations, and uplands of Edwards Plateau in cen. Texas. **SIMILAR SPECIES:** (1) Texas Earless Lizard has black *bars* extending completely across underside of tail. (2) In female Lesser Earless Lizards (races of *Holbrookia maculata*) the light pigment does *not* surround the dorsal spots and there are *no* dark spots under tail. **RANGE:** Cen. and s. Texas and adj. Mexico. **SUBSPECIES:** SOUTHERN EARLESS LIZARD, *Holbrookia l. subcaudalis* (Pl. 14). Two distinct rows of dark blotches down each side of back; femoral pores average 16 under each hind leg. S. Texas and adj. Mexico, but not in lower Rio Grande Valley. PLATEAU EARLESS LIZARD, *Holbrookia l. lacerata.* Dark blotches usually fused together in pairs, producing the effect of a single row on each side of back; femoral pores average 13. Northwestward from the Edwards Plateau region of cen. Texas.

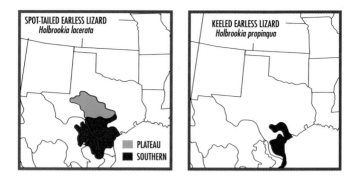

KEELED EARLESS LIZARD

PL. 14; FIG. 43

Holbrookia propinqua propinqua

IDENTIFICATION: 4½–5⁹⁄₁₆ in. (11.5–14.1 cm); head-body max. 2⅜ in. (6 cm). This is a *long-tailed* earless lizard. The full original tail is noticeably longer than the head-body length in males and as long or longer in females. Dorsal scales distinctly keeled but so small that a lens is necessary to see them. No dark spots under tail (Fig. 43). *Male:* Two black lines on side of body (behind armpit) *not* surrounded by blue; dorsal pattern variable and not clear cut— usually a combination of dark blotches and dark longitudinal stripes covered by many small light dots. *Female:* Specimens from near the coast lack any prominent markings, but inland females are darker and with blotches. *Young:* Well-defined pattern of paired blotches; about 1½ in. (3.8 cm) long at hatching.

A lizard indigenous to loose, wind-blown sands and dunes and barrier beach islands of s. Texas and the Mexican coast. **SIMILAR SPECIES:** Tail in Lesser Earless Lizards (races of *Holbrookia maculata*) is shorter—about as long as head and body combined or a little shorter. (*Caution:* Be sure the tail has not been regenerated. Comparisons must be made upon basis of full original tail and not on invariably shorter, newly grown replacement.) Lesser Earless males usually have a small patch of blue touching or surrounding the black bars near the armpit. Some Lesser Earless Lizards have keeled scales. The two species (*propinqua* and *maculata*) are most easily separated on basis of range. If in doubt, also check the femoral pores (10 to 21, average 14 or 15, under each hind leg in Keeled Earless Lizard; 5 to 15, average 11 or 12, in Lesser Earless Lizard). **RANGE:** S. Texas and south along the Gulf Coast of Mexico. Mexican subspecies.

A large and distinctive genus of lizards with *keeled* and pointed dorsal scales. Some species are so rough they seem almost like pine cones with legs and tails. Several were formerly called "swifts."

In gross appearance they resemble the Tree and Side-blotched Lizards (*Urosaurus* and *Uta*), but in those two genera there is a fold of skin across the throat (Fig. 42 and Fig. 12, opp. Pl. 15).

Most Spiny Lizards within our area are arboreal, at least to some extent. Rock outcrops or boulders and large rotting stumps or logs are also favorite habitats. They are best stalked by two persons working toward them from opposite directions, for they are adept at keeping a tree trunk or rock between themselves and a single observer.

These lizards are chiefly insectivorous, but they also eat spiders and other arthropods and even smaller lizards, baby mice, etc. Some kinds reproduce by laying eggs; others bear living young.

Sexual differences are usually well marked. Males of most species have a prominent blue patch at each side of the belly, and in many there is also some blue on the throat. Under certain conditions, such as during cool weather or before skin shedding, the blue may turn black. Females lack the blue areas or have them only slightly developed. Middorsal dark markings, which are often faint or reduced in size (or both) in males, are normally rather prominent in females.

Counting dorsal scales may be necessary in some cases to distinguish between members of this genus. Counts are stated in the text as the number of scales from "back of head to base of tail." Count in as direct a line as possible down middle of back, starting

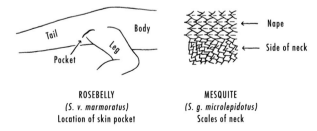

ROSEBELLY
(S. v. marmoratus)
Location of skin pocket

MESQUITE
(S. g. microlepidotus)
Scales of neck

Fig. 44. *Characteristics of two kinds of Spiny Lizards* (Sceloporus).

immediately behind the large head scales and terminating at a point opposite rear margin of thighs. Hold thighs at right angles to lizard's trunk to be sure of correct stopping point. (This is the most practical method. Counting to a point directly above the anal opening, the real base of the tail, is difficult because it is not visible from above and, in turning the specimen back and forth, one can easily lose one's place.)

The genus ranges from the Pacific Northwest and extreme southern New York to Panama.

ROSEBELLY LIZARD *Sceloporus variabilis marmoratus* PL. 15

IDENTIFICATION: 3¾–5½ in. (9.5–14 cm); head-body max. 2¼ in. (5.7 cm). Unique in two ways. Our only spiny lizard with: (a) pink belly patches and (b) a skin pocket behind the thigh (Fig. 44). Neither one is a good field mark; the reptile usually must be caught to see them. The *light dorsolateral stripe* and row of brown spots down each side of back are best points to check. General coloration buffy- to olive-brown. *Male:* Large area of pink at each side of belly bordered fore and aft and toward center of belly by dark blue; the dark color extends upward onto sides of body to form a *prominent dark spot in armpit* and another much smaller one in groin. *Young:* About 2 in. (5.1 cm) at birth.

An essentially terrestrial lizard of arid southern Texas. Often seen on fence posts and in clumps of cactus; occasionally on rocks or in mesquite or other scrubby trees. **SIMILAR SPECIES:** (1) Prairie and Fence Lizards lack skin pocket behind thigh, and color on belly, when present, is blue and not pink. (2) Mesquite Lizard lacks light dorsolateral line, and scales on side of neck are abruptly smaller than those on nape (Fig. 44). (3) Texas Spiny Lizard grows very large and has only 33 or fewer dorsal scales counted from back of head to base of tail (58 or more in Rose-belly Lizard). (4) Tree Lizard (*Urosaurus*) has fold of skin across throat (Fig. 12, opp. Pl. 15).
RANGE: S. Texas and ne. Mexico. Mexican and Cen. American subspecies.

MESQUITE LIZARD PL. 15; FIG. 44
Sceloporus grammicus microlepidotus

IDENTIFICATION: 4–6⅞ in. (10–17.5 cm); head-body max. 2⅞ in. (7.3 cm). An arboreal and remarkably camouflaged spiny lizard, best identified (at a distance) by habitat and habits. When caught, check on scalation. Only spiny lizard in southern Texas with scales on sides of neck abruptly *much* smaller than those on nape (Fig. 44). General coloration gray or olive-gray. *Male:* Dorsum sometimes with a metallic greenish luster; markings obscure; a

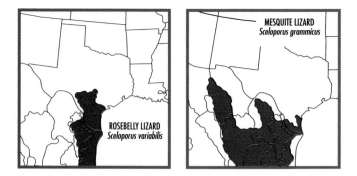

dark vertical line in front of arm; sides of belly pale blue, the blue bordered by black (toward center of belly); throat mottled with black except the center, which may be flesh color or pale blue. *Female:* four or five dark, wavy lines across back; foreleg distinctly barred. *Young:* About 1⅝–1¹⁵⁄₁₆ in. (4.1–4.9 cm) at birth.

Most quiet and unobtrusive of the spiny lizards. Protective coloration and the habit of dodging to the opposite side of tree limb or bole are so well developed that few people ever see this reptile. Usually retreats to uppermost branches while observer is still far away. Found chiefly in mesquite but also on other small, scrubby trees. **SIMILAR SPECIES:** (1) Rosebelly Lizard and Southern Prairie Lizards have a light dorsolateral stripe; both also are largely terrestrial. (2) Texas Spiny Lizard grows big and has large dorsal scales, numbering 33 or fewer from back of head to base of tail; dorsal scales are 50 or more in Mesquite Lizard. (3) Tree Lizard (*Urosaurus*) has fold of skin across throat (Fig. 12, opp. Pl. 15). **RANGE:** Extr. s. Texas and n. Mexico. Mexican subspecies.

CREVICE SPINY LIZARD *Sceloporus poinsettii poinsettii* **PL. 16**
IDENTIFICATION: 5–11½ in. (12.5–29.2 cm); head-body max. 5⅛ in. (13 cm). The *dark band across the neck* is an excellent field mark. Tail strongly barred, especially *near tip*. Young, at birth, boldly crossbanded with black from head to tip of tail. Females tend to retain these markings, but in adult males they may virtually disappear, except across neck and on tail. General dorsal coloration gray or greenish gray to orange or reddish. *Male:* Throat bright blue; sides of belly bright blue, the blue bordered on its inner side by a broad black band. *Young:* Sometimes a narrow, dark stripe connecting crossbands down center of back; 2¼–3 in. (6.4–7.5 cm) at birth.

Boulders and rocky outcrops are favorite habitats, and on these

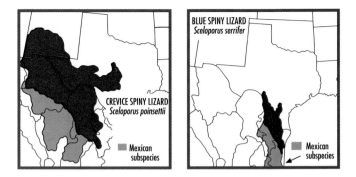

the lizards may stand out conspicuously—at binocular range. Difficult to approach and capture in such places, quickly darting to opposite side or into crevices. Prying them from hiding places unharmed is difficult; the slightest touch makes them wedge themselves even tighter. **SIMILAR SPECIES:** (1) In Blue Spiny Lizard the tail markings are *not* conspicuous toward tip; light spots are present on nape and back. (2) In Collared Lizards, there are *two* black lines on neck, and scales are very small and smooth. **RANGE:** Edwards Plateau of cen. Texas to sw. N.M.; south into Chihuahua and to s. Coahuila and w. Nuevo León. Mexican subspecies.

BLUE SPINY LIZARD *Sceloporus serrifer cyanogenys*   PL. 16
IDENTIFICATION: 5–14¼ in. (12.5–36.2 cm); head-body max. 5¹³⁄₁₆ in. (14.8 cm). Largest and bluest of the spiny lizards. The *dark band across neck,* bordered by white and in combination with light spots on nape and back, is a good field mark. Tail markings not conspicuous at tip. *Male:* A brilliant metallic greenish blue over a ground color of brown; upper sides of legs bronzy; entire throat bright blue; a large light blue patch at each side of belly bordered by a black band on inner side. *Female* (and young male): Gray or brown. *Young:* 2½–2¾ in. (6.4–7 cm) at birth.

    Habitats include boulders, rocky or earthen cliffs, stone bridges, and abandoned houses. **SIMILAR SPECIES:** (1) In Crevice Spiny Lizard the black bands are conspicuous near *tip* of tail. (2) Collared Lizards have *two* black lines across neck, and scales are smooth and very small. **RANGE:** S. Texas and ne. Mexico.

TWIN-SPOTTED SPINY LIZARD   PL. 16
Sceloporus magister bimaculosus
    IDENTIFICATION: 7½–13 in. (19–33 cm); head-body max. 5½ in. (14 cm). A relatively pale, stocky lizard with large, pointed scales, a

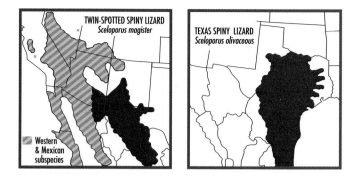

narrow dark line running back from lower corner of eye, and a *black wedge (or blotch) on each side of neck.* Twin spots on back not sharply defined. General coloration pale gray or brown to straw color; some scales on sides may be yellow. Legs finely striped longitudinally with pale and dark gray. *Male:* Groin black; blue-green throat patch; two elongated blue-green belly patches edged with black and often joined together. Mature males may have a wash of pale blue about five scales wide on forepart of back. *Female:* All blue pigment absent or only slightly indicated. *Young:* Markings much more prominent; black wedge bordered by yellow; four rows of black spots, a twin row on back and an extra row on each side of body. About 2⅞–3⅜ in. (7.3–8.6 cm) at hatching.

A wary but not especially speedy lizard of arid and semiarid country below 4000 ft. (1200 m) elevation. Seldom found far from dense thickets, rock piles, old buildings, burrows, or other refuges to which it darts when approached. Adults are chiefly terrestrial; young more arboreal. Large ones bite hard and, when held, may move their heads from side to side, forcing the sharp scales against one's fingers. **SIMILAR SPECIES:** Crevice Spiny Lizards have conspicuously crossbanded tails. **RANGE:** Trans-Pecos Texas; w.-cen. N.M. and se. Ariz. to w. Coahuila. Western and Mexican subspecies.

TEXAS SPINY LIZARD *Sceloporus olivaceus*   **PL. 16**

IDENTIFICATION: 7½–11 in. (19–27.9 cm); head-body max. 4¾ in. (12.1 cm). The "rusty lizard." Conspicuous field marks are lacking, but this is our only very large, very spiny, tree-inhabiting lizard. A rather vague light dorsolateral stripe (stronger in males) and wavy, dark lines across the back (more conspicuous in females). General dorsal coloration gray- to rusty-brown. The very large dorsal scales, counted from back of head to base of tail, are 33 or fewer (average 30). *Male:* Narrow light blue area at each side of belly and *without* a black border. *Young:* 2½–2⅝ in. (6.4–6.7 cm) at hatching.

Usually seen in trees—mesquite, live oak, cottonwood, cedar, etc. They are inconspicuous against the bark and are usually discovered when they move or by the noise they make in climbing. Although essentially arboreal, Texas Spiny Lizards also may be seen on fences, old bridges, abandoned houses, in patches of prickly pear, or in other places that offer shelter in the form of cracks or cavities. SIMILAR SPECIES: Fence Lizard usually has a fairly complete black line running along rear surface of thigh. In Northern Fence and Prairie Lizards the dorsal scales are small; from back of head to base of tail they number 35 or more. RANGE: N. Texas to ne. Mexico.

FENCE LIZARD *Sceloporus undulatus* (eastern subspecies) PL. 15
IDENTIFICATION: 4–7¼ in. (10–18.4 cm); head-body max. 3⅜ in. (8.6 cm). A small gray or brown spiny lizard with strong arboreal tendencies. Females chiefly gray and most conspicuously patterned on top; males usually brown and most heavily marked on bottom. Both sexes have a more or less complete dark line running along the rear surface of thigh. *Male:* Sides of belly hyacinth- to greenish blue, the bright color bordered by black toward center of belly; a broad bluish area at base of throat, the blue surrounded by black and often split in two parts; dorsal crosslines indistinct or absent. *Female:* A series of dark, wavy (undulating) lines across back; yellow, orange, or reddish at base of tail; belly whitish with scattered black flecks; small amounts of pale blue at sides of belly and throat. *Young:* Patterned like female but darker and duller; averaging 1⅝–2¼ in. (4.1–5.7 cm) at hatching.

Often seen on rail fences or on rotting logs or stumps. The only spiny lizard occurring throughout most of its range. (No other members of the genus are found north of Florida or east of Texas.) When surprised on the ground, Fence Lizards usually dash for a nearby tree, climb upward for a short distance, and then remain motionless on the opposite side of the trunk. If approached, they dodge to the opposite side again, but higher up. The performance may be repeated several times, and the lizard soon ascends out of reach. Often called "pine lizard" because of its frequent occurrence in open pine woods. SIMILAR SPECIES (AND SUBSPECIES): (1) Florida Scrub Lizard has a distinct *dark brown* lateral stripe. (2) Prairie Lizards have light longitudinal stripes, and are largely terrestrial in habits. (3) Texas Spiny Lizard grows much bigger, has very large dorsal scales, and lacks a dark line on rear of thigh. RANGE: S. N.J. to cen. Fla.; west to e. Kans. and e. Texas; iso-

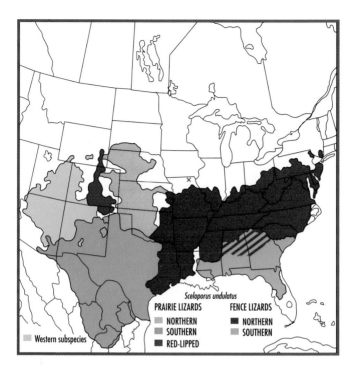

Sceloporus undulatus

PRAIRIE LIZARDS
- NORTHERN
- SOUTHERN
- RED-LIPPED

FENCE LIZARDS
- NORTHERN
- SOUTHERN

Western subspecies

lated colonies in se. N.Y. and ne. Pa.; isolated record in ne. Mo. **SUBSPECIES:** NORTHERN FENCE LIZARD, *Sceloporus u. hyacinthinus* (Pl. 15). As described above. All of general range except the deep Southeast. SOUTHERN FENCE LIZARD, *Sceloporus u. undulatus.* Similar, but averaging slightly larger and with black markings more intense. Undersurfaces of males may be almost entirely black, except for patches of blue. In females the ventral black flecks are more numerous than in the northern race, and some of them may form a broken black line down center of belly. Dorsal scales larger, usually 37 or fewer from back of head to base of tail. In Northern Fence Lizard they are usually 38 or more. S. S.C. to cen. Fla. and west to e. La.

PRAIRIE LIZARD
Sceloporus undulatus (western subspecies)
> **IDENTIFICATION:** 3½–7 in. (9–18 cm); head-body max. 3 in. (7.5 cm). The *light longitudinal stripes,* bold and usually clear-cut, are excellent field marks. (The lower stripe on each side may be less

An adult Northern Prairie Lizard. These lizards are very fast and are fond of hiding in thick brush and bushes.

conspicuous than in the specimens illustrated.) Dark dorsal markings, so prominent in other subspecies, are reduced to spots bordering the light dorsolateral stripe. Ground color light brown to reddish brown; a light brown stripe down center of back. *Male:* Two long, narrow, light blue patches, one at each side of belly, bordered medially with black and well separated from each other. Throat markings absent or consisting of two small, widely separated blue patches. *Female:* Uniform white below and without the black flecks of the Fence Lizards. *Young:* About 1 ¾–2 in. (4.4–5.1 cm) at hatching.

Essentially terrestrial, but occupying a wide variety of habitats —stabilized (nonblowing) sand dunes and other sandy areas, open prairies (but with weeds, brush, or mammal burrows for cover), brushy flatlands, etc. Often found under shocks of wheat. Forages widely for food but scurries to cover when approached. Northern sandhill-dwelling specimens are awkward at climbing, but southern prairie dwellers commonly ascend into yuccas and other low plants. **SIMILAR SPECIES (AND SUBSPECIES):** (1) In Fence Lizard, a light dorsolateral stripe is sometimes evident, but it is not well defined and is crossed by the dark markings of the back. Male Fence Lizards are conspicuously marked with black on throat and belly. (2) Texas Spiny Lizard grows much bigger, and its very large dorsal scales number only 33 or fewer counted from back of head to base of tail (35 or more in Prairie Lizards). (3) Racerunners, most Whiptail Lizards, and many of the Skinks have prominent light stripes, but none has large keeled scales. **RANGE:** S. S.D. to n. Mexico; west through N.M. to se. Ariz. **SUBSPECIES:** NORTHERN PRAIRIE LIZARD, *Sceloporus u. garmani* (Pl. 15). As described above but smaller. Gular patches absent or faint, not black-bordered. S. S.D. to cen. Okla. and ne. corner of Texas panhandle; isolated populations in extr. e. N.M. SOUTHERN PRAIRIE LIZARD, *Sceloporus u. consobrinus*. Similar but with the light stripes less prominent. Males have two large gular patches, blue and black-bordered, that often fuse together across throat; females usually have a small amount of blue on throat. Averages larger than the northern subspecies and attains a total length of about 7 in. (18 cm) and a head-body maximum of 3 in. (7.5 cm). A lizard of the plains and mountains (although it avoids the highest elevations). Especially common in rocky terrain that furnishes abundant hiding and basking places. Sw. Okla. to extr. se. Ariz. and well south into Mexico. Western subspecies, including a pale gray to almost white, virtually patternless race that is confined to the White Sands region of N.M.

RED-LIPPED PRAIRIE LIZARD   NOT ILLUS.
Sceloporus undulatus erythrocheilus

IDENTIFICATION: 4–7¼ in. (10–19.1 cm); head-body max. 3 in. (7.6 cm). A spiny lizard characterized by the orange or red coloration of the chin and lips anterior to the blue throat patches. The colors are more intense in males than females and may be bright rusty red during the breeding season. *Male:* Blue patches on throat meet at midline.

A rock face lizard, often found on cliffs, lava flows, gully banks, etc., where cover in the form of vegetation or cracks and fissures is available. **RANGE:** Barely enters our area in extr. w. Okla. Se. Wyo. south through e.-cen. Colo. to ne. N.M.

FLORIDA SCRUB LIZARD *Sceloporus woodi*   PL. 15

IDENTIFICATION: 3¹³⁄₁₆–5¹¹⁄₁₆ in. (9.7–14.4 cm); head-body max. 2⁹⁄₁₆ in. (6.5 cm). A spiny lizard with a *dark brown* lateral stripe. General coloration brown or gray-brown above, whitish below. *Male:* Mid-dorsal area has few, if any, markings. A long blue patch on each side of belly, bordered by black on inner side; a pair of blue spots at base of throat; rest of throat black except for median white stripe. *Female:* Seven to ten dark brown wavy lines across back; rarely, these may be fused or otherwise altered to form dark longitudinal lines. Dark spots often present on chest and undersurface of head; some blue on throat and sides of belly (not bordered by black). *Young:* Similar to female but paler and with the markings darkening with age; about 1¾ in. (4.4 cm) at hatching.

A lizard characteristic of sand-pine scrub but sometimes found in adjacent beach dune scrub, longleaf pine-turkey oak woodlands, or citrus groves where areas of open, sandy ground exist. More terrestrial than the Fence Lizard in foraging and escape

FLORIDA SCRUB LIZARD
Sceloporus woodi

behavior but commonly seen on lower tree trunks. **SIMILAR SPECIES:** In Southern Fence Lizard the undersurfaces are marked with considerable black pigment, and there may be a *black* lateral stripe, but it is not so clear-cut as the *brown* stripe in the Florida Scrub Lizard. Dorsal scales (counted from back of head to base of tail) in Florida Scrub Lizard average more than 40; in Southern Fence Lizard average is 34. **RANGE:** Restricted to four disjunct areas in cen. and s. Fla.

NORTHERN SAGEBRUSH LIZARD   PL. 15
Sceloporus graciosus graciosus

IDENTIFICATION: 4½–5⅞ in. (11.5–14.9 cm); head-body max. 2¾ in. (7 cm). A pale brown spiny lizard with four longitudinal rows of darker brown spots that may run together to suggest dark longitudinal stripes. Usually two pale dorsolateral stripes, one extending backward from each eye and terminating on the tail. Often an irregular black spot on shoulder. *Small granular scales on rear surface of thigh.* *Male:* A large elongated blue patch at each side of belly; no blue throat patches, although throat may be mottled with blue. *Young:* About 2¼ in. (6.4 cm) at hatching.

Often found in sagebrush but also occurs on rocks, in open forested areas, or in canyon bottoms. Essentially terrestrial, seldom climbs, and usually remains close to shelter. **SIMILAR SPECIES:** (1) Other Spiny Lizards have *large, keeled scales on rear of thigh.* (2) In Prairie Lizards (as among other members of the *S. undulatus* complex) there is a narrow, dark line between eyes. **RANGE:** Known in our area only from w. Neb. and w. N.D.; Mont. to nw. N.M. and west to the Pacific Coast. Western and Mexican subspecies.

DUNES SAGEBRUSH LIZARD   PL. 15
Sceloporus graciosus arenicolous

IDENTIFICATION: 4½–6 in. (11.5–15.2 cm); head-body max. 2¾ in. (7 cm). A relatively faint *grayish brown stripe,* extending from upper edge of ear opening to the tail, is the most conspicuous pattern feature of this very pale lizard. Dorsum light yellowish brown or light golden brown; venter white, cream-colored, or yellowish. *Small, granular scales on rear surface of thigh* instead of keeled

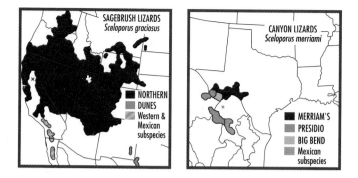

scales. *Male:* A large, elongated, bright blue patch at each side of belly, bordered midventrally by a band of deeper blue or black. No blue on throat in either sex. *Young:* About 1¾ in. (4.4 cm) at hatching.

A ghostly streak dashing across the sand dunes that usually comes to rest hidden or nearly hidden beneath patches of dwarf shin oak, sand sagebrush, prairie yuccas, or other plants. Most specimens match the sand so closely that they virtually disappear when they stop running. If closely pursued, they often hide in leaf litter or burrow in the sand beneath sheltering vegetation. **SIMILAR SPECIES:** (1) Other Spiny Lizards have large scales on rear surface of thigh. (2) The Side-blotched Lizard has a dark spot posterior to the arm. **RANGE:** Active sand dune areas from Andrews to Crane cos., Texas, and the Mescalero Sands of se. N.M.

CANYON LIZARD *Sceloporus merriami*　　　**PL. 15; FIG. 42**

IDENTIFICATION: 4½–6¼ in. (11.5–15.9 cm); head-body max. 2⁷⁄₁₆ in. (6.2 cm). A rock-dwelling spiny lizard that usually matches the general coloration of the cliffs and boulders on which it is found (gray, tan, reddish brown, etc.). Four rows of dark spots on back that are most conspicuous in the two westernmost subspecies. A *vertical black bar* on shoulder directly in front of foreleg, but this may be obscured by a fold of skin if the lizard turns its head toward you. *Scales at sides of body tiny* (granular); dorsal scales, although keeled, are small. Scales on sides of neck abruptly smaller than those on nape, comparable with change in Mesquite Lizard (Fig. 44). A partially developed throat fold (Fig. 42). *Male:* Belly with two large blue patches that are broadly margined midventrally and posteriorly with black; there may be a white midventral stripe, or the black markings may merge together from the two sides. Blue and black lines on throat. Crosslines may be present under tail. A small but rather conspicuous dewlap. *Female:* Ventral markings much less extensive than those in male; dewlap proportionately smaller. *Young:* About 2 in. (5.1 cm) at hatching.

Boulders, rocky outcrops, and the rocky walls of canyons are the favorite habitats of this small lizard. It is not very wary, and, if frightened, may reappear soon after taking refuge in a crack or crevice. **SIMILAR SPECIES:** (1) Other Spiny Lizards within range have large, keeled scales on sides of body. (2) Tree and Side-blotched Lizards have a fold of skin completely across throat. (3) Whiptail Lizards have tiny dorsal scales and broad rectangular belly plates. **RANGE:** W. Texas from Edwards to Presidio cos.; s.-cen. Coahuila, e. Chihuahua, and extr. n. Durango. **SUBSPECIES:** BIG BEND CANYON LIZARD, *Sceloporus m. annulatus* (Pl. 15). Dark dorsal spots well defined; usually 52 or fewer dorsal scales from back of head to base of tail. Ventral markings bold and extensive in males. Higher elevations of Big Bend region of w. Texas. MERRIAM'S CANYON LIZARD, *Sceloporus m. merriami.* A pale, ashen race with dorsal spots faint or absent; usually 58 or more dorsal scales; a narrow, white midventral stripe in males; dark ventral markings reduced. Named for C. Hart Merriam, originator and chief of the Bureau of Biological Survey, a forerunner of the U.S. Fish and Wildlife Service. W. Texas from Edwards and Crockett cos. to e.-cen. Presidio Co. and adj. Mexico. PRESIDIO CANYON LIZARD, *Sceloporus m. longipunctatus.* Dorsal spots comma-shaped, with tails of commas pointing outward; ventral markings paler and less extensive than in subspecies *annulatus*. S. Presidio Co., Texas and adj. ne. Chihuahua; also disjunct in extr. se. Chihuahua, w. Coahuila, and n. Durango; isolated record in w.-cen. Coahuila.

TREE AND SIDE-BLOTCHED LIZARDS:
GENERA *Urosaurus* AND *Uta*

Members of these two genera bear varying degrees of resemblance to the Spiny Lizards (*Sceloporus*) but may be recognized by the presence of a skin fold across their throats and by the absence of large, strongly keeled scales over most of their bodies. Both range widely through the southwestern U.S. and into Mexico, the Tree Lizards (*Urosaurus*) southward to Chiapas, and the Side-blotched Lizards (*Uta*) into the northern Mexican states.

TREE LIZARD *Urosaurus ornatus*   PL. 15
IDENTIFICATION: 4–5⅜ in. (10–13.7 cm); head-body max. 2 in. (5.1 cm). A small, gray or grayish brown lizard with arboreal tendencies. Back has irregular dark spots or crossbands, some narrowly

edged with blue. Check for three things: (a) a fold of skin running across the throat (Fig. 12, opp. Pl. 15); (b) dorsal scales variable in size—some large, some tiny; and (c) two long folds of skin on each side of body. The folds give the Tree Lizard a somewhat wrinkled appearance, as though the skin were a little too large for it. Throat yellow or pale orange in adults. *Male:* Three blue

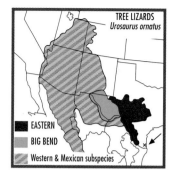

TREE LIZARDS
Urosaurus ornatus

■ EASTERN
■ BIG BEND
▨ Western & Mexican subspecies

patches—one centered under throat and another at each side of belly. *Young:* About 1¼–1¾ in. (3.2–4.4 cm) at hatching.

Almost always seen in trees or on rocks or stone or cinder-block walls and usually resting in a *vertical* position—"heads up" with tail dangling or the reverse with head pointing down. Trips to the ground, either to forage or to move from one tree or rock to another, are usually brief. A difficult reptile to observe or catch by hand. When motionless, camouflage is nearly perfect, but the lizard often may reveal itself by indulging in bobbing movements. When pursued, it is adept at dodging, keeping on opposite side of tree trunk or rock and climbing quickly out of reach. **SIMILAR SPECIES:** Various members of the Spiny Lizard genus (*Sceloporus*), although similar to Tree Lizard in gross appearance, have following distinctive features: (a) *no* fold completely across throat; and (b) dorsal scales all approximately *same size*. **RANGE:** Cen. Texas and Rio Grande Valley; west to se. Calif. and north to Utah and extr. sw. Wyo.; south in w. Mexico to s. Sinaloa. **SUBSPECIES:** EASTERN TREE LIZARD, *Urosaurus o. ornatus* (Pl. 15). Enlarged scales of the inner series on each side of dorsum about twice as large as those of outer series. Cen. Texas and Rio Grande Valley; an isolated record in extr. s. Texas. BIG BEND TREE LIZARD, *Urosaurus o. schmidti.* Inner series of enlarged dorsal scales *not* twice as large as outer ones. Usually seen on rocks and boulders and often associated with the Canyon Lizard in desert habitats, but utilizes trees in the mountains. Trans-Pecos Texas and adj. Mexico and N.M. Western and Mexican subspecies.

DESERT SIDE-BLOTCHED LIZARD PL. 14
Uta stansburiana stejnegeri

IDENTIFICATION: 4–5⅜ in. (10–13.7 cm); head-body max. 2⅛ in. (5.4 cm). Our only lizard with a blue-spangled back (chiefly in males) and a *single black spot posterior to the armpit.* Except in the very

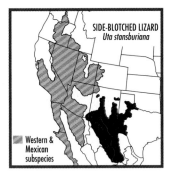

SIDE-BLOTCHED LIZARD
Uta stansburiana

Western & Mexican subspecies

young the spot may be readily seen with binoculars, at least at close range. General coloration brown, striped and spotted, or with a profusion of blue flecks on the back and yellow to pale orange-brown spots on the sides. With the lizard at hand check for two things: (a) a single fold of skin across the throat (Fig. 42); (b) middorsal scales keeled and larger than the small, smooth scales on the sides of the body (use a lens). *Female:* A pale, dark-bordered stripe from eye to base of tail and another stripe or series of pale spots from upper lip to groin. *Adult male:* Pale stripes greatly reduced or absent; throat and lower sides of body washed with pale blue or pale bluish gray. *Young:* About 2⁵⁄₁₆ in. (5.9 cm) at hatching.

An abundant lizard in many areas; often found in sandy regions and on desert flats and foothills. Chiefly terrestrial, but also climbs on rocks or boulders. Less speedy than many other lizards, and seldom wanders far from such shelters as crevices, mammal burrows, or clumps of vegetation. **SIMILAR SPECIES:** (1) Earless Lizards (*Holbrookia* and *Cophosaurus*) may show *two* dark spots behind the foreleg when viewed from the side, and they have *two folds* of skin under the throat (Fig. 42). (2) Spiny Lizards (*Sceloporus*) lack complete throat folds. **RANGE:** Trans-Pecos Texas, parts of the Texas panhandle, and extr. sw. Okla.; N.M. and extr. se. Ariz. to w. Coahuila and n. Durango; isolated colonies in nw. and ne. N.M. Western and Mexican subspecies.

HORNED LIZARDS: GENUS *Phrynosoma*

The misnamed "horned toads," the majority of them adorned like cactus plants, are the most bizarre of all our lizards. The arrangement of the spines, especially on the head, and the fringe scales at the sides of the abdomen offer the best clues to identification.

Horned Lizards are diurnal. They eat spiders, sowbugs, and insects—ants especially. Maintaining them in captivity requires special techniques. If you find a Horned Lizard, we recommend that you look at it carefully, perhaps photograph it, and then liberate it where you found it. These lizards are protected by law in many states.

An extraordinary habit is the occasional squirting of blood from the forward corners of the eyes for a distance of several feet. This is associated with increased blood pressure in the head, and the squirting occurs when a lizard is handled while blood pressure in the head is high. Some species lay eggs; others give birth to living young. Despite their spiny garb, horned lizards are eaten by certain birds, such as hawks and roadrunners, by such reptiles

TEXAS HORNED LIZARD
Phrynosoma cornutum

as whipsnakes and collared lizards, and by mammals, such as coyotes. The genus ranges from southern Canada to Guatemala and is particularly well represented in the Southwest and in Mexico.

TEXAS HORNED LIZARD *Phrynosoma cornutum* PL. 14

IDENTIFICATION: 2½–4 in. (6.4–10 cm); record 7⅛ in. (18.1 cm); head-body max. 5⅛ in. (13 cm). This lizard is the species most frequently carried home, often illegally, by tourists or visitors to the Southwest. The two central head spines are *much longer* than any of the others (Fig. 45). *Two rows* of fringe scales at each side of abdomen. The general coloration is usually some shade of brown —yellowish, reddish, grayish, or tan—but may sometimes be gray. Dark dorsal spots usually conspicuous and with light posterior borders. *Young:* About 1⅛–1¼ in. (2.8–3.2 cm) at hatching.

A lizard typically of flat, open terrain with sparse plant cover; often found in areas of sandy, rocky, or loamy soil. Occurs from

An adult Texas Horned Lizard. Note the prominent spines on the head, a formidable array that probably discourages some predators.

sea level to at least 6000 ft. (1800 m). Specimens are usually in evidence only on very warm days. They run surprisingly fast and seek refuge in mammal burrows, rock piles or ledges, or clumps of vegetation. **SIMILAR SPECIES:** (1) In Roundtail Horned Lizard: (a) the tail is slender and rounded but broadens abruptly near base; (b) all the longer horns are about equal in length; and (c) there are *no* fringe scales at edge of abdomen. (2) In Short-horned Lizards the horns are greatly reduced in size (Fig. 45), and there is *one row* of fringe scales. **RANGE:** Kans. and nw. La. to se. Ariz. and n. Mexico; introduced colonies and isolated records (not mapped) exist from ne. Kans., s. La., Ala., s. Ga., coastal S.C., and Fla.; apparently has disappeared from much of its former range in Texas.

EASTERN SHORT-HORNED LIZARD   PL. 14

Phrynosoma douglassii brevirostre

IDENTIFICATION: 2½–3¾ in. (6.4–9.5 cm); record 4½ in. (11.4 cm); head-body max. 3 in. (7.5 cm). Short, stubby horns (Fig. 45) and only a *single row* of fringe scales along each side of abdomen. Ground color brown or gray. *Young:* About 1¼ in. (3.2 cm) at birth.

Indigenous to semiarid, shortgrass portions of the northern Great Plains; usually found in rather rough terrain. **SIMILAR SPECIES:** See Texas Horned Lizard. **RANGE:** Western parts of the Dakotas and Neb.; Mont. and adj. Canada south to e. Colo. and ne. Utah. Western subspecies.

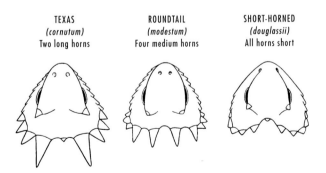

TEXAS
(cornutum)
Two long horns

ROUNDTAIL
(modestum)
Four medium horns

SHORT-HORNED
(douglassii)
All horns short

Fig. 45. Heads of Horned Lizards (Phrynosoma).

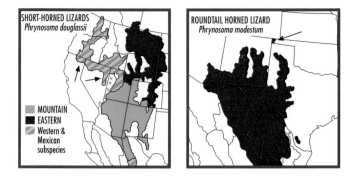

MOUNTAIN SHORT-HORNED LIZARD PL. 14; FIG. 45
Phrynosoma douglassii hernandesi

IDENTIFICATION: 3¾–5 in. (9.5–12.5 cm); record 6⅚ in. (15.9 cm); head-body max. 4⅜ in. (11.2 cm). Like the Eastern Short-horned Lizard but larger, and adults usually more colorful, often with much orange or reddish brown pigment on both dorsum and belly. Short horns and *one row of fringe scales. Young:* About 1½ in. (3.8 cm) at birth.

An upland race, found within our area only in or near forested portions of the Guadalupe and Davis mts., but it may occur in other forested mountains of w. Texas. **SIMILAR SPECIES:** See Texas Horned Lizard. **RANGE:** W. Texas and much of N.M.; Colo. and Utah south to ne. Sonora and nw. Chihuahua. Mexican subspecies.

ROUNDTAIL HORNED LIZARD PL. 14; FIG. 45
Phrynosoma modestum

IDENTIFICATION: 3–4⅛ in. (7.5–10.5 cm); head-body max. 2¹³⁄₁₆ in. (7.1 cm). Three distinct items to check: (a) tail round and slender but broadened abruptly near base; (b) four horns at back of head, all about equal in length (Fig. 45); and (c) *no* row of fringe scales along sides of abdomen. Coloration variable: general tone may be yellowish gray or ash-white or any of several shades of light brown, but adults usually closely match the dominant soil color of the immediate habitat; young and half-grown individuals are less likely to match. The ability to change color is marked, and the intensity of the dark blotches may vary from black to pale hues only a little darker than the ground color. *Young:* About 1¼–1½ in. (3.2–3.8 cm) at hatching.

This lizard is so well camouflaged that it can easily be overlooked. Normally it remains motionless when approached, with its body flattened so closely to the ground that it casts almost no shadow—a trait common to all our horned lizards. It may be almost stepped on before it moves. After a short dash, it stops abruptly, virtually vanishing against the background. Habitats include desert flats and washes, and arid and semiarid plains with shrubby vegetation. **SIMILAR SPECIES:** See Texas Horned Lizard. **RANGE:** W.-cen. Texas and much of N.M. to se. Ariz. and cen. Mexico; isolated colonies in extr. w. Okla., s. Texas, and an isolated record in w. Tamaulipas, not shown on map.

NEOTROPICAL GROUND LIZARDS: FAMILY TROPIDURIDAE

This family of lizards contains about 180 species in 14 genera. They are native to South America and many of the islands of the West Indies, and are similar in appearance and ecology to the North American Spiny Lizards (*Sceloporus*). One Antillean genus (*Leiocephalus*) has been introduced in southern Florida.

CURLYTAIL LIZARDS: GENUS *Leiocephalus*

Members of this genus, which consists of more than 20 species, superficially resemble Spiny Lizards but lack femoral pores on the underside of the thigh, a characteristic of all *Sceloporus*. The genus inhabits the West Indies, but two species have been introduced or escaped into southern Florida and have become established.

NORTHERN CURLYTAIL LIZARD   PL. 12
Leiocephalus carinatus armouri

IDENTIFICATION: 7–10½ in. (18–26 cm); head-body max. 4⅛ in. (10.5 cm). Resembles a large, robust spiny lizard. Ground color gray to dark brown, sometimes with small dark spots on back and lighter ones on the sides. Large, keeled, pointed scales on back form a *low raised crest* that extends onto the banded, slightly compressed tail. During the breeding season, males often curl the tail upward above the back like a scorpion in a display meant to attract females and discourage other males.

On their native West Indian islands, these lizards occupy a wide variety of habitats, from rocky coasts and beaches to scrub and pine woods. They even invade towns and villages. On islands where English is spoken they are called "lion lizards." In southern Fla., they are equally at home on the ground or in trees. Insects are the principal food. **SIMILAR SPECIES:** Male Red-sided Curlytail Lizards are much paler in ground color but are brightly colored laterally with light blue and reddish orange; females may have a

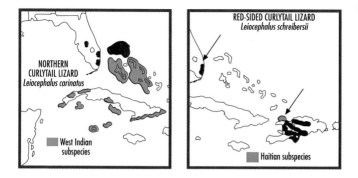

gray or black spot in each armpit. **RANGE:** Introduced in southern Fla. Known to occur in Dade Co. on Key Biscayne and Virginia Key, and at the Port of Miami; also reported from Boynton Beach, and Palm Beach I. and adj. mainland in Palm Beach Co.; found recently in Highlands Co. Native to Grand Bahama I., the Abacos, and associated keys of the Little Bahama Bank, Bahama Is. Numerous Cuban and Bahaman subspecies; other races on the Cayman and Swan Is. of the Caribbean Sea.

RED-SIDED CURLYTAIL LIZARD

Leiocephalus schreibersii schreibersii

IDENTIFICATION: 7–10½ in. (18–26 cm); head-body max. 4¼ in. (10.7 cm). This robust, active lizard has a pale tan to sandy ground color, with a low crest of raised scales down the back that become more pronounced as the crest extends onto the compressed tail; distinct folds of skin, composed of much smaller scales, on each side of body between fore and hind limbs; venter grayish or pale blue. *Males:* Dorsum sprinkled liberally with buffy, yellow, or golden dots, washed laterally on the body and tail with light blue; five *reddish orange streaks* along the side and belly; head and lips in front of eyes may be reddish orange; throat grayish to purplish with scattered pale blue to green scales; underside of tail bright orange, intermixed with pale blue or brick-red scales. *Females:* Smaller and duller, with a series of about eight dorsal grayish transverse bars, and often with a gray to black spot in each armpit; throat streaked or clouded with dark gray; head-body max. 3 in. (7.5 cm). Like male Northern Curlytail Lizards, males often curl their tails upward during the breeding season.

Within its native range, a lizard of hot, arid areas, where it often shuns shade and forages on rocky or sandy soils for insects. Found in towns and villages, where it seeks shelter in rock piles and abandoned walls and even beneath concrete slabs. **SIMILAR**

SPECIES: See Northern Curlytail Lizard. **RANGE:** Introduced and established in southern Fla., in Dade and Broward cos., from pet trade escapees originally captured on the north coast of Haiti. Native to Haiti, the Dominican Republic, and a few nearby islands; a subspecies on the I. de la Tortue.

WALL LIZARDS: FAMILY LACERTIDAE

A large family of lizards, comprising about 180 species, that occurs throughout much of Europe, Africa, and Asia. These are small, alert, active, diurnal lizards, usually with a head-body maximum of 3¼ in. (8 cm) or less, although a few kinds reach larger sizes. They are relatively slender, with long tails and well-developed legs, and dart about with quick jerking movements, similar to those of our native Racerunners and Whiptails *(Cnemidophorus)*. All but one species of this family reproduce by laying eggs. Although these lizards are not native to the New World, two species of one genus *(Podarcis)* have been introduced in at least four localities in the United States, and are still apparently established and breeding at three of them. Another member of this family, the Green Lacerta *(Lacerta viridis)* was once established in urban Topeka, Kans., but has not been found there for over a decade, and is not included in this Field Guide.

COMMON WALL LIZARD   *Podarcis muralis*   **PL. 12**
IDENTIFICATION: 5½–8⅛ in. (14–20.5 cm); head-body max. 3 in. (7.5 cm). A small, slender lizard, highly variable in coloration and pattern. Dorsum of body usually covered with fine, granular scales which are uniformly brown to gray (occasionally tinged with green). Usually a row of dark middorsal spots, which sometimes form a stripe; some individuals have a reticulate pattern with dark markings on the sides, with many scattered white spots that may be blue in the shoulder region. Tail brown, gray, or rusty red, and sometimes patterned with light and dark bars on sides. Belly with 6 rows of large, smooth, rectangular scales colored uniformly white to reddish, pink, or orange; dark markings may or may not be present on throat.

A lizard of rubble and ruins that apparently prefers an urban setting where it can run and hide among the crevices of crumbling rock walls and piles of debris. Feeds on insects. **RANGE:** Introduced and well-established along the terraced, rubble-strewn hillsides of the Ohio R. in metropolitan Cincinnati, Ohio, and on the Cincinnati Zoo grounds; an isolated record from Van Wert Co. in nw. Ohio. Native range is mainland Europe from central Spain to southern Belgium and the Netherlands, and east into northwestern Asia Minor.

ITALIAN WALL LIZARD

Podarcis sicula **PL. 12**

COMMON WALL LIZARD
Podarcis muralis

ITALIAN WALL LIZARD
Podarcis sicula

IDENTIFICATION: 5½–9½ in. (14–24 cm); head-body max. 3⅝ in. (9.1 cm). Like all members of the genus, highly variable in coloration and pattern. The head, neck, and upper body are most often green with a brown middorsal stripe or row of spots; some individuals may have an irregular reticulate pattern of dark markings on a ground color of light green, yellow, olive, or light brown. Blue spot or spots sometimes present on shoulder. Tail generally brown or gray, sometimes with light and dark markings on sides. Belly and throat uniform white or gray, normally without dark spots or pattern. Scales on upper body fine and granular, in contrast to the 6 rows of large, smooth, rectangular scales on the belly.

Inhabits urban areas, where it scurries from one pile of debris to the next, feeding on insects. Prefers nearby vegetation but can adapt to nearly any area with rock rubble, wood, or lumber piles, and may even retreat from danger beneath abandoned car bodies and ground-level air-conditioning units. **RANGE:** Introduced and currently established in and around West Hempstead on Long Island, N.Y., and in urban southwestern Topeka, Kans. Also known previously from Philadelphia but has not been seen there for decades. The natural range of this lizard is Italy and Mediterranean islands, with colonies in Spain and Turkey.

WHIPTAILS: FAMILY TEIIDAE

A large family, confined to the New World and especially abundant and diverse in South America. One genus (*Cnemidophorus*), containing about 55 species and occurring throughout much of North and South America, is native to the United States. Ten species are native to our area; all are diurnal and can be recognized as Whiptails by their long tails and active, nervous prowling. There are thousands of tiny scales (granules) on their backs and eight rows of large, rectangular scales on their bellies (Fig. 46). The tail is rough to the touch.

Distinguishing among the many species is very difficult, partly because some look confusingly alike and partly because their patterns change with age and growth. Positive identification often is impossible unless the specimen is in hand, and then the following must be checked: (a) How many light longitudinal stripes are

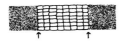
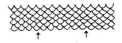

WHIPTAILS and RACERUNNERS
Rows of enlarged scales on belly

SKINKS
All scales approximately same size

Fig. 46. Back and belly scales of Whiptails and Racerunners (Cnemidophorus), and Skinks (Eumeces).

there? (b) Are there pale spots in the dark fields between the light stripes? (c) Do the small scales around the inner edge of the supraorbital scales (the supraorbital semicircles) penetrate far forward or do they stop before they reach the frontal plate (Fig. 47)? (d) Are the scales directly anterior to the gular fold abruptly enlarged? (e) Is there a patch of enlarged scales on the rear of the forearm (Fig. 48)? (f) How many granules are there across the back at midbody? (Use a strong lens or dissecting microscope, and count the granules all the way around the body in as straight a line as possible. Do *not* include the large belly scales.)

Five of the 10 kinds of native Whiptails found in the area covered by this Field Guide are unisexual; apparently the introduced

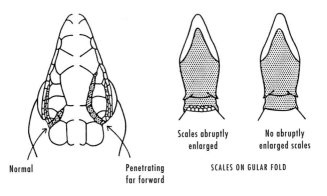

Normal | Penetrating far forward

Scales abruptly enlarged | No abruptly enlarged scales

SCALES ON GULAR FOLD

SUPRAORBITAL SEMICIRCLES

Fig. 47. Head characteristics of Whiptail Lizards (Cnemidophorus).

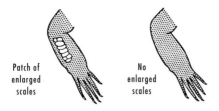

Patch of
enlarged
scales

No
enlarged
scales

Fig. 48. Rear of forearm in Whiptail Lizards (Cnemidophorus).

population of Rainbow Whiptails (*Cnemidophorus lemniscatus* complex) is bisexual. Unisexuals reproduce through parthenogenesis (development of an unfertilized egg). Males are completely unknown in some of these species; they have been reported in others, but there is some evidence to indicate that such males may be hybrids between the unisexual form and a bisexual species inhabiting the same area. Food consists chiefly of insects but also includes spiders, scorpions, and other small arthropods. Often these are dug from the ground, suggesting that the sense of smell or hearing may be useful in locating prey.

Although Whiptails can easily be observed through binoculars and often approach to within a few feet of a person, they are extremely difficult to catch by hand. Several collectors working together can drive them into a drift fence equipped with a trap; pitfall traps set beneath boards or flat stones may also be successful. Despite their narrow heads, they can be noosed if, as soon as they are snared, they are swung continuously until one's free hand can grab them.

In addition to the 10 native species, two other representatives of the Family Teiidae have been introduced and are now established in southern Fla. Because they were imported for the pet trade and subsequently were released, Rainbow Whiptails (*Cnemidophorus lemniscatus* complex), normally residents of lowland Central America and much of tropical South America, are now established in the Miami area. The Giant Ameiva (*Ameiva ameiva*) has been introduced also in at least a half dozen localities in Miami, Dade Co. Members of this genus are especially numerous in the West Indies, but they also range, collectively, from cen. Tamaulipas and Nayarit southward along both coasts of Mexico through Central and South America to Paraguay and se. Brazil.

RACERUNNERS
Cnemidophorus sexlineatus
■ SIX-LINED ■ PRAIRIE

SIX-LINED RACERUNNER   PL. 18

Cnemidophorus sexlineatus sexlineatus

IDENTIFICATION: 6–9½ in. (15.2–24.1 cm); head-body max. 3 in. (7.5 cm). The only member of the genus native to most of the U.S. east of the Mississippi R. *Six light stripes;* no spots in dark fields. Stripes yellow, white, pale gray, or pale blue. Dark fields some shade of brown, greenish brown, or sometimes almost black. A short, dark stripe on side of tail, extending backward from leg and bordered above by a light stripe. Scales anterior to gular fold conspicuously enlarged (Fig. 47); scales on rear of forearm only slightly enlarged or not at all (Fig. 48). Supraorbital semicircles normal (Fig. 47); 89–110 granules around midbody. Bisexual. *Male:* Stripes well defined; belly washed with blue. *Young:* Light blue tail; stripes yellow and sharply in contrast with dark fields; head-body length about 1⅛–1¼ in. (2.8–3.2 cm) at hatching.

An active lizard, conspicuous because of its boldness. Open, well-drained areas are preferred—those covered with sand or loose soil; fields, open woods, thicket margins, rocky outcrops, river floodplains, etc. Racerunners are well named, usually winning the race with the would-be collector. Called "field-streaks" in some parts of range and "sandlappers" in others. When pursued, they take refuge in vegetation, under boards or stones, or in burrows that are sometimes of their own making. **SIMILAR SPECIES:** Skinks are shiny, and their ventral scales are like their dorsal scales in size and shape. **RANGE:** Md. to Fla. Keys and west to Mo. and e. Texas; intergrades with Prairie Racerunner west of Mississippi R. from St. Louis to the Gulf Coast of w. La. and e. Texas.

PRAIRIE RACERUNNER   PL. 18

Cnemidophorus sexlineatus viridis

IDENTIFICATION: 6–10½ in. (15.2–26.7 cm); head-body max. 3⅜ in. (8.6 cm) in some females. Similar to the Six-lined Racerunner in lacking spots, but there are *seven light stripes* and the coloration is *bright green anteriorly.* Scutellation also similar, but dorsal granules are fewer (62–91 around midbody). Bisexual. *Male:* Belly pale blue. *Young:* Head-body length about 1³⁄₁₆–1¼ in. (3–3.2 cm) at hatching.

Occupies a variety of habitats—banks and floodplains of

An adult male Prairie Racerunner during the breeding season, showing the distinctive green color on the anterior of the body.

rivers, open grasslands with scattered bushes, and the vicinity of rock outcrops; occurs in both lowland and hilly terrain. **SIMILAR SPECIES:** Other Whiptails within its range have pale spots in the dark fields. (1) Texas Spotted Whiptail (*gularis*) lacks the short, dark stripe on side of tail, extending backward from hind leg and bordered above by a light stripe (a characteristic shared by both subspecies of Racerunners). (2) In Checkered Whiptail (*tesselatus* complex) the supraorbital semicircles extend far forward. (3) Trans-Pecos Striped Whiptail (*inornatus*) has a blue tail and a bluish suffusion over head and sides of body. **RANGE:** S. S.D. and se. Wyo. south to s. Texas; northeast through Mo. to extr. nw. Ind., and north in the Mississippi R. Valley into extr. se. Minn.

CHIHUAHUAN SPOTTED WHIPTAIL PL. 18
Cnemidophorus exsanguis

IDENTIFICATION: 9½–12⅜ in. (24–31.4 cm); head-body max. 3⅞ in. (9.8 cm). A distinctly brown or reddish brown Whiptail with *six light stripes*. Pale yellowish or whitish spots in the dark fields *and on the light stripes*. Dark fields brown or reddish brown; stripes pale brown or gray-brown, most conspicuous and often yellowish on sides of body. Tail dark, usually brown but often with a greenish tinge. Venter whitish or faintly bluish, unmarked. Enlarged scales along anterior edge of gular fold (Fig. 47) and on rear of forearm (Fig. 48). Supraorbital semicircles normal (Fig. 47); 62–86 granules around midbody. Unisexual. *Young:* Stripes yellow or whitish, clean-cut and sharply in contrast with the dark brown or blackish fields; paravertebral stripes wavy. *Pale reddish spots present in hatchlings.* A light middorsal stripe may be present on the nape; this disappears or is only vaguely indicated in adults.

CHIHUAHUAN SPOTTED WHIPTAIL
Cnemidophorus exsanguis

Tail blue or greenish. Head-body length about 1 ⁵⁄₁₆– 1 ⁹⁄₁₆ in. (3.3–4 cm) at hatching.

Habitats vary from desert grasslands to forested mountains. This whiptail is usually found in the open, but always near cover—on rocky hillsides, in canyon bottoms or dry washes, and, like other unisexual whiptails, most often in disturbed areas such as along draws or arroyos where flooding occurs periodically. **SIMILAR SPECIES:** (1) Texas Spotted Whiptail (*gularis*) is easily confused with Chihuahuan Spotted Whiptail in Trans-Pecos Texas. Upper side of tail is dark in Chihuahuan, but *pink* in Texas Spotted. Also, Texas Spotted Whiptail has pale spots largely confined to the lateral dark fields; spots occur in all dark fields in the Chihuahuan. Texas Spotted also has 7 or 8 light stripes, in contrast with 6 in the Chihuahuan Whiptail. Males of Texas Spotted have pink on chin and often black on chest. (2) In New Mexico Whiptail (*neomexicanus*) the light stripes are sharply in contrast with the dark fields at all ages, the middorsal light stripe is distinctly wavy, the pale spots in the dark fields are obscure, and the supraorbital semicircles penetrate far forward. **RANGE:** Trans-Pecos Texas to n.-cen. N.M. and west to se. Ariz.; through Chihuahua to extr. ne. Sonora.

LAREDO STRIPED WHIPTAIL · · · · · · · · · · NOT ILLUS.
Cnemidophorus laredoensis complex

IDENTIFICATION: 7⅜–11⅜ in. (18.7–28.9 cm); head-body max. 3½ in. (9 cm). A distinctly striped member of the genus with a dark green to greenish brown ground color and seven cream or whitish stripes on the body; vertebral stripe very narrow; small pale or indistinct spots are sometimes present on the posterior half to one third of the body. Upper surface of hind limbs with reticulate pattern of cream-colored, irregular lines. Venter white. Tail greenish brown above with dorsolateral stripes extending outward from the body for one-third the length; below light tan. Supraorbital semicircles normal (Fig. 47); 84–98 granules around midbody. Slightly enlarged scales on rear of forearm (Fig. 48). Unisexual. *Young:* Distinctly striped with spots confined to dark fields.

A lizard that inhabits semiarid regions near stream beds and hills with little vegetation, where it hunts for insects. **SIMILAR SPECIES:** (1) Trans-Pecos Striped Whiptail (*inornatus*) has a dis-

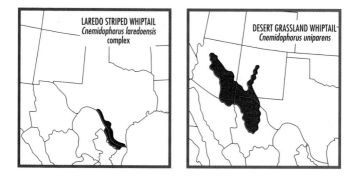

LAREDO STRIPED WHIPTAIL
Cnemidophorus laredoensis
complex

DESERT GRASSLAND WHIPTAIL
Cnemidophorus uniparens

tinctly blue tail, especially on its underside. (2) Texas Spotted Whiptail (*gularis*) has broad vertebral stripe. (3) Plateau Spotted Whiptail (*septemvittatus*) has distinct rusty red to orange rump, dorsal stripes terminating toward rear of body, and females with orange throat. (4) Prairie Racerunner (*viridis*) lacks spots on the dark fields, is bright green anteriorly, has fewer granules around midbody (62–91), and males have pale blue venter. **RANGE:** Lower Rio Grande Valley of Texas and adj. Mexico, from extr. se. Val Verde Co., to within a few miles of the Gulf Coast. **NOTE:** This is a complex of lizards composed of at least two unisexual forms, one of which, the Laredo Striped Whiptail (*Cnemidophorus laredoensis*), has been named. Because the other form has not yet received a scientific designation and the distributions and natural histories are still unknown, both forms are included here under a single name.

DESERT GRASSLAND WHIPTAIL   PL. 18
Cnemidophorus uniparens

IDENTIFICATION: 6½–9⅜ in. (16.5–23.8 cm); head-body max. 2¹⁵⁄₁₆ in. (7.4 cm). A small, six-striped whiptail with *no pale spots in the dark fields.* Usually a suggestion of a seventh (middorsal) light stripe, at least on the neck. Dark fields reddish brown to black. Stripes yellowish; whitish on sides of body. *Tail bluish green or olive-green.* Venter whitish and virtually unmarked; adults often with a bluish wash on chin and sides of neck. Enlarged scales along anterior edge of gular fold (Fig. 47) and on rear of forearm (Fig. 48). Supraorbital semicircles normal (Fig. 47); 59–78 granules around midbody. Unisexual. *Young:* Head-body length about 1⅜6–1⅝6 in. (3.3–4 cm) at hatching.

A whiptail of desert and mesquite grassland, but also ascending river valleys into lower mountainous areas. **SIMILAR SPECIES:** (1)

Trans-Pecos Striped Whiptail (*inornatus*) has a distinctly *blue tail*, especially on its underside. (2) In New Mexico Whiptail (*neomexicanus*), middorsal stripe is wavy, there are pale spots in the dark fields, and supraorbital semicircles extend far forward. **RANGE:** Vicinity of El Paso, Texas, and north in Rio Grande Valley to cen. N.M.; n. Chihuahua and ne. Sonora to cen. Ariz.

TEXAS SPOTTED WHIPTAIL PL. 18
Cnemidophorus gularis gularis

IDENTIFICATION: 6½–11 in. (16.5–27.9 cm); head-body max. 3½ in. (9 cm). A liberally spotted whiptail with 7–8 stripes. The vertebral (middorsal) stripe is very broad and often splits apart (to give a count of eight). Stripes normally whitish or yellowish, but often greenish anteriorly and brownish posteriorly. Pale spots prominent in *lateral* dark fields but faint or absent in paravertebral dark fields; spots white or pale yellow, changing to brownish toward rear of body. Tail pink, pale orange-brown, or reddish. Enlarged scales along anterior edge of gular fold (Fig. 47) and on rear of forearm (Fig. 48). Supraorbital semicircles normal (Fig. 47); 76–93 granules around midbody. Bisexual. *Male:* Chin pink, red, or orange; chest and belly blue, frequently also with a large, black patch. *Female:* Venter unmarked, whitish or cream throughout life. *Young:* Striped, but spotting faint or absent and confined to lateral dark fields when present; tail pink or reddish; rump reddish. Head-body length about 1⅜ in. (3.5 cm) at hatching.

A lizard of prairie grasslands, river floodplains and washes, grassland reverting to brush, and rocky hillsides. More deliberate in its movements than Prairie Racerunner and generally less wary. **SIMILAR SPECIES:** (1) Prairie Racerunner (*viridis*) is bright green anteriorly, lacks spots in dark fields, and has a short dark stripe extending backward from hind leg. (2) Chihuahuan Spotted Whiptail (*exsanguis*) has *six* light lines and an unmarked venter at all ages, and pale spots in paravertebral as well as lateral dark fields. Also check number of granules between paravertebral light stripes—10 to 21 in Texas Spotted Whiptail, 3 to 7 in Chihuahuan Spotted Whiptail. (3) In Plateau Spotted Whiptail (*septemvittatus*), dorsal stripes and dark fields both terminate on body. **RANGE:** S. Okla., Texas panhandle, and se. N.M. to n. Veracruz. Mexican subspecies.

TRANS-PECOS STRIPED WHIPTAIL PL. 18
Cnemidophorus inornatus heptagrammus

IDENTIFICATION: 6¼–9⅜ in. (16.5–23.8 cm); head-body max. 2¹³⁄₁₆ in. (7.1 cm). The "blue-tailed whiptail." *Tail bright blue to purplish blue* at all ages. The juvenile pattern of seven light stripes separa-

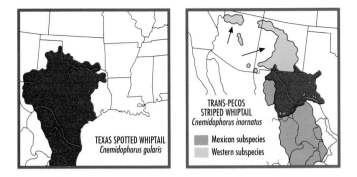

TEXAS SPOTTED WHIPTAIL
Cnemidophorus gularis

TRANS-PECOS
STRIPED WHIPTAIL
Cnemidophorus inornatus

- Mexican subspecies
- Western subspecies

ted by dark, *unspotted fields* is retained throughout life. Stripes yellow in young, whitish or cream in adults. Fields black in young, becoming grayish or brownish with age. Scales anterior to gular fold slightly enlarged (Fig. 47); approximately two rows of scales on posterior surface of forearm slightly enlarged (Fig. 48). Supraorbital semicircles normal (Fig. 47); 55–71 granules around midbody. Bisexual. *Male: Venter and sides of head bright blue* (bluish to bluish white in females). *Young:* Less blue below than in adults; head-body length about 1⅛ in. (2.8 cm) at hatching.

Primarily a lizard of the foothills in western Texas, most often found on rocky, grassy slopes and deteriorated grassland or where a rocky knoll pushes upward above flat mesa tops. Sometimes seen on alluvial flats or on sandy-silty soil. **SIMILAR SPECIES:** (1) Desert Grassland (*uniparens*) and New Mexico (*neomexicanus*) Whiptails have greenish tails. (2) Texas Spotted Whiptail (*gularis*) has pink tail. (3) New Mexico and Chihuahuan Spotted (*exsanguis*) Whiptails have pale spots in their dark fields. **RANGE:** Trans-Pecos Texas and adjacent portions of N.M., e. Chihuahua, and extr. n. Coahuila. Western and Mexican subspecies.

NEW MEXICO WHIPTAIL
PL. 18

Cnemidophorus neomexicanus

IDENTIFICATION: 8–11⅞ in. (20.3–30.2 cm); head-body max. 3⅜ in. (8.6 cm). A pattern of seven pale yellow stripes, all equally distinct but with the *middorsal stripe wavy.* Fields brown to black and obscurely spotted throughout life. Tail *greenish gray to bluish green.* Venter white to pale blue, unmarked. Usually no abruptly enlarged scales anterior to gular fold (Fig. 47) or on posterior surface of forearm (Fig. 48). *Supraorbital semicircles penetrating far forward* (Fig. 47); 71–85 granules around midbody. Unisexual.

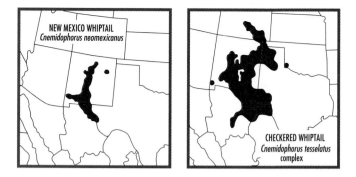

New Mexico Whiptail *Cnemidophorus neomexicanus* / Checkered Whiptail *Cnemidophorus tesselatus* complex

Young: Strongly striped, yellow on black, and with spots in the dark fields. Tail bright blue in hatchlings. Head-body length about 1⅜–1⅝ in. (3.5–4.1 cm) at hatching.

A lizard of disturbed areas; for example, where periodic flooding at the confluence of arroyos with the Rio Grande provides a perpetually disturbed, sandy habitat. Also occurs around the perimeter of playas, in open sandy places, such as washes and draws, and in terrain altered by human activities. **SIMILAR SPECIES:** (1) In Desert Grassland Whiptail *(uniparens)* light middorsal stripe is straight-edged and supraorbital semicircles are normal. (2) See also Chihuahuan Spotted Whiptail *(exsanguis)*, in which the spots are more numerous and the stripes less well defined. The New Mexico Whiptail occasionally hybridizes with other kinds, especially the Trans-Pecos Striped Whiptail *(inornatus)*. **RANGE:** Chiefly the Rio Grande Valley from Presidio Co., Texas, to north of Santa Fe, N.M.; isolated introduction in ne. N.M.

CHECKERED WHIPTAIL   PL. 18
Cnemidophorus tesselatus complex

IDENTIFICATION: 11–15½ in. (28–39.4 cm); head-body max. 4³⁄₁₆ in. (10.6 cm). Largest of our Whiptails. A variable complex—many individuals and some entire populations bear checkered patterns, others have rows of black spots, and some display an orange-brown rump. Ground color yellowish to cream. Tail brown to yellow. Venter plain whitish or with some black spots; chin usually unmarked. *Scales anterior to gular fold abruptly enlarged* (Fig. 47). No distinctly enlarged scales on rear of forearm (Fig. 48). *Supraorbital semicircles extending far forward* (Fig. 47) in most Texas specimens; 81–112 granules around midbody. Unisexual. *Young:* Number of light stripes highly variable, from as few as 6 up to 14 in different populations; small pale spots in dark fields.

Light midddorsal stripes (if present) often represented by a series of pale dots or dashes that may produce a wavy appearance. As the lizard grows, the light stripes become less conspicuous and may disappear altogether on sides of body, largely because they are invaded by black checks or spots. Head-body length about 1½–1¾ in. (3.8–4.4 cm) at hatching.

A lizard of many habitats — plains, canyons, foothill uplands, and river floodplains (as along the Rio Grande) — but almost always associated in one way or another with rocks. More than any other kind of Whiptail, this species occurs in isolated local populations or small groups of individuals. **SIMILAR SPECIES:** (1) In Marbled Whiptail (*marmoratus*), scales anterior to the gular fold are only slightly enlarged, underside of the tail is dark, and, in adults, there are black spots on the peach-colored chin, throat, and chest. (2) In Chihuahuan Spotted Whiptail (*exsanguis*), the supraorbital semicircles are normal and there is a patch of enlarged scales on the rear of the forearm. **RANGE:** Trans-Pecos Texas and Río Conchos drainage in Chihuahua north to se. Colo., and Okla. and Texas panhandles; isolated colonies in extr. sw. Okla. and sw. N.M. **NOTE:** The Checkered Whiptail is treated in this Field Guide as a species complex, composed of a number of unisexual entities, each independently derived from hybridization between the same "parental" species, and none of whose relationships, distributions, and natural histories are clearly known. One of these, the GRAY CHECKERED WHIPTAIL (*Cnemidophorus dixoni*), has a range restricted to sw. Presidio Co., Texas, with an isolated colony in extr. sw. N.M. Pending further resolution of the larger problem of relationships of these lizards, the Gray Checkered Whiptail is retained in this complex.

PLATEAU SPOTTED WHIPTAIL PL. 18
Cnemidophorus septemvittatus septemvittatus

IDENTIFICATION: 8–12½ in. (20.3–31.8 cm); head-body max. 4⅛ in. (10.5 cm). A brownish green lizard with two main pattern characteristics: (a) dorsal stripes terminating toward rear of body; and (b) *rump and base of tail rusty red or orange.* Hind legs may also be rust-colored. Vertebral stripe narrow. The young are patterned with 6 or 7 light stripes; adults retain this basic pattern, but the dark fields become spotted as the lizard grows. Tail brown or gray. Venter white or pale blue; a few black spots on chin and chest in some specimens. Enlarged scales along anterior edge of gular fold (Fig. 47) and on rear of forearm (Fig. 48). Supraorbital semicircles normal (Fig. 47); 77–98 granules around midbody. Bisexual. *Females:* Orange throat. *Young:* Light stripes inclined to be wavy, with the middorsal one intermittent; fields very dark with pale

PLATEAU SPOTTED WHIPTAIL
Cnemidophorus septemvittatus

Mexican subspecies

spots chiefly in lowermost dark field; tail blue or greenish. Head-body length about 1½ in. (3.8 cm) at hatching.

When prowling, this lizard moves slowly and deliberately in comparison with some of the other Whiptails. It often roots in ground litter, overturning sticks and stones with its snout. A resident of mountains and desert foothills, of lava flows and canyons; most frequently found in rocky situations with sparse vegetation. **SIMILAR SPECIES:** (1) The rusty rump distinguishes this species from all our other Whiptails. (2) In the Short-lined Skink, the light stripes terminate on the shoulder, and the belly scales are approximately same size as dorsal ones (Fig. 46). **RANGE:** Big Bend region of Texas; adj. Chihuahua and much of Coahuila. Mexican subspecies.

MARBLED WHIPTAIL *Cnemidophorus marmoratus*   PL. 18

IDENTIFICATION: 8–12 in. (20.3–30.5 cm); head-body max. 4⅛ in. (10.5 cm). Pattern extremely variable. Ground color brownish, sometimes with 4 to 8 yellowish white stripes (often obscured because they are broken and reticulated) on the top and sides of the body; laterally, light transverse bars invade dark fields and may be broken into spots. Some individuals virtually uniform. Venter chiefly white or pale yellow with black flecks anteriorly and laterally covering less than one half of the chest surface; washed with peach on throat and, in larger individuals, also on chest and sides of abdomen; chin and throat with round or irregularly shaped black flecks or spots (in adults). Scales anterior to gular fold slightly enlarged (Fig. 47), but separated from the fold by one or more rows of granules; no enlarged scales on rear of forearm (Fig. 48). *Supraorbital semicircles penetrating well forward* (Fig. 47), reaching or almost reaching frontal plate; 74–114 granules around midbody. Bisexual. *Young:* Numerous small, pale, often elongated spots arranged in longitudinal rows on a ground color of dark brown to black. Head-body length about 1⅜–1¾ in. (3.5–4.4 cm) at hatching.

At home on desert flats or sandy areas, where this lizard prowls incessantly beneath clumps of thorny vegetation in search of insects. When disturbed it darts into the open and races to another clump of vegetation, looking like a dark streak as it goes. If pursued, it flees in similar fashion from clump to clump, but eventually returns to a favorite spot where it may disappear down a

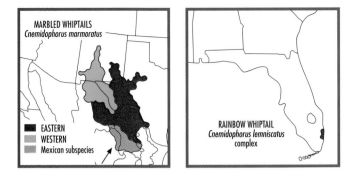

MARBLED WHIPTAILS
Cnemidophorus marmoratus

- **EASTERN**
- **WESTERN**
- Mexican subspecies

RAINBOW WHIPTAIL
Cnemidophorus lemniscatus
complex

burrow. One of the few lizards apt to be encountered at (shade) temperatures of 100° F (38° C) or more. **SIMILAR SPECIES:** Boldly marked individuals may be confused with Checkered Whiptails (*tesselatus* complex), but in the latter the scales anterior to the gular fold are abruptly enlarged, the chin is never peach-colored, and there are rarely any black spots on the chin. Other Whiptails retain at least two distinct pairs of longitudinal light stripes throughout life. **RANGE:** Chiefly the Chihuahuan Desert of w. Texas and adjacent parts of N.M., Chihuahua, and Coahuila. **SUBSPECIES:** WESTERN MARBLED WHIPTAIL, *Cnemidophorus m. marmoratus* (Pl. 18). Pattern on upper body of adults more reticulate than striped. Rio Grande drainage of w. N.M., and w. Texas including Presidio, Culberson, and El Paso cos., and adj. n. Chihuahua. EASTERN MARBLED WHIPTAIL, *Cnemidophorus m. reticuloriens* (Pl. 18). Pattern on upper body of adults more striped than reticulate. A patternless variation with a uniformly brownish gray dorsum and plain white venter is known from the Texas counties of Brewster, Crane, Presidio, Terrell, and Val Verde. Pecos R. drainage of se. N.M. and adj. Texas northeast to Fisher Co. and southeast to Webb Co., and parts of Chihuahua, Coahuila, and Nuevo León. Mexican subspecies.

RAINBOW WHIPTAIL

PL. 16

Cnemidophorus lemniscatus complex

IDENTIFICATION: 6½–13 in. (16.5–33 cm); head-body max. 4⅛ in. (10.5 cm). Introduced. A brightly and variably colored tropical member of the genus with a broad brown dorsal stripe bordered dorsolaterally by distinct dark stripes; flanks with light stripes or spots. Scales anterior to the gular fold enlarged and supraorbital semicircles normal (Fig. 47); 103–128 granules around midbody. Bisexual. *Male:* A broad, brown middorsal area bordered on each side of body by two stripes, the inner one narrow, light (often yellow), and fading out posteriorly, the outer one wider, green in coloration, and continuing onto tail; *flanks yellowish brown with light spots*. Tail and undersides of limbs blue, the hind limbs brownish above with light spots; *side of head blue*; chin, throat, and chest blue, but belly light gray. *Female:* Usually with numerous light dorsal stripes; *flanks with light stripes; side of head orangish*; chin, throat, lower surface of forelimbs, and anterior part of belly white; posterior part of belly, lower surface of hind limbs, and tail greenish yellow. Dorsum of hind limbs dark with light spots.

An active, sun-loving, ground-dwelling lizard that retreats to burrows when threatened. **SIMILAR SPECIES:** The Six-lined Racerunner has no spots on flanks, six light stripes on the dorsum, and a low number of granules around midbody (89–110). **RANGE:** Introduced and established near Hialeah and in Miami, Fla.; natural range from Guatemala south to Colombia, Venezuela, the Guianas, and n. Brazil; also known from a number of Caribbean islands. Subspecies. **NOTE:** Another member of the genus treated in this Field Guide as a complex. The Rainbow Whiptail may consist of at least four distinct forms, some bisexual, some unisexual, and some of which are still unnamed. Further, it is unknown whether the population introduced in the Miami area also includes unisexuals. It is best to treat this lizard simply as a complex until its variation and natural history are better understood.

GIANT AMEIVA *Ameiva ameiva* PL. 16

IDENTIFICATION: 15–25 in. (38–63.5 cm); head-body max. 8¼ in. (21 cm). A giant relative of the Whiptail Lizards, but with 10 or 12 rows of large rectangular plates on the belly instead of eight. A generally dark lizard, sometimes predominantly green but more often bluish; several vertical rows of yellowish, circular spots on sides of body and bluish spots on the two or three outermost rows

GIANT AMEIVA
Ameiva ameiva

of belly plates and anterior surface of hind leg. A brown or yellowish middorsal stripe may be present on posterior two-thirds of body.

An alert, elusive lizard. The introduced and scattered Florida populations are apparently composed of at least two races, *Ameiva a. ameiva* and *Ameiva a. petersi*. Evidently the two subspecies have not made contact with each other in Florida and do not intergrade there. RANGE: Introduced and established at various localities in Miami, Fla.; the species as a whole inhabits grasslands, savannahs, and other open areas in Panama and tropical South America, and it also occurs on Trinidad, Tobago, the I. de Margarita, and the I. de Providencia, the latter off the coast of Nicaragua.

SKINKS: FAMILY SCINCIDAE

Smooth, shiny, alert, and active lizards that are difficult to catch —and to hold. Yet in most instances they *must* be caught and examined carefully for accurate identification. Watch the tails; they break off *very* easily. The average Skink will try to bite, and large ones can pinch painfully hard.

In making identifications be sure to check *all* characters. Many Skinks change markedly in coloration and pattern as they grow older (as in the Five-lined species). Others (notably among the Mole Skinks) show a bewildering degree of individual variation. The positions of the longitudinal stripes are important. Count downward from the midline of the back. Thus, *stripe on 3rd row,* for example, indicates that stripes occupy the 3rd row of scales on each side of the midline. Rule out Whiptail Lizards by checking back and belly scales (Fig. 46).

Most Skinks are terrestrial, foraging actively by day but taking shelter (at night, in bad weather, or from high temperatures) under stones or in debris, decaying logs, abandoned packrat nests, etc. The Broadhead Skink and some others are often arboreal. Habitats usually include some evidence of moisture, such as in the form of nearby springs or swamps or underground humid retreats. Insects and other arthropods are the chief food, but large Skinks can also manage such sizable prey as baby mice or birds in the nest, or the eggs of such species as sparrows. Captives often do well on a diet of live insects and spiders and will sometimes take bits of meat dipped in raw, beaten egg. (Add vitamins and minerals!)

All but two of our Skinks belong to the big genus *Eumeces;* the exceptions are the Ground Skink (*Scincella*) and the curious Sand Skink (*Neoseps*). In some of the species of *Eumeces,* tones of red or orange appear on the heads (of males only) as a sex recognition characteristic during the breeding season; in others the bright colors are retained throughout the year. Females normally guard their eggs during the incubation period.

The family is very large and occurs in all the habitable continents, but the great majority of species are confined to the Eastern Hemisphere.

GROUND SKINK *Scincella lateralis*   **PL. 19**
    IDENTIFICATION: 3–5¾ in. (7.5–14.6 cm); head-body max. 2¼ in. (5.7 cm). The "brown-backed skink." A small, smooth, golden brown to blackish brown lizard with a *dark* dorsolateral stripe. Shade of brown varies from one locality to another—from reddish or chocolate to light golden brown. In darkest specimens, the dark stripe almost blends with ground color. Belly white or yellowish. A "window" in lower eyelid in form of a transparent disc through which lizard may see when eye is closed. *Young:* About 1¾ in. (4.4 cm) at hatching.

    An elfin reptile of the woodland floor, quietly but nervously searching for insects among leaves, decaying wood, and detritus, and taking refuge, when approached, beneath the nearest shelter. When running, it makes lateral, snakelike movements. Does not hesitate to enter shallow water to escape. Seldom climbs. Likely to appear almost anywhere in the Deep South, even in towns and gardens. **SIMILAR SPECIES:** (1) Two-lined Salamanders are similar in coloration and patterns, but they lack claws and scales. (2) Other small brown lizards either have rough scales, indications of *light* stripes, or both. **RANGE:** S. N.J. to Fla. Keys; west to e. Kans. and w.-cen. Texas; isolated records in cen. Ill., ne. Mo., and Coahuila.

FIVE-LINED SKINK *Eumeces fasciatus*   **PL. 19; FIGS. 49, 50**
    IDENTIFICATION: 5–8½ in. (12.5–21.5 cm); head-body max. 3⅜ in. (8.6 cm). Highly variable, depending on age and sex. Hatchlings have five white or yellowish stripes on a black ground color, and their tails are bright blue. As they grow older and larger, the pattern becomes less conspicuous—the stripes darken and the ground color lightens; the tail turns gray. Females almost always retain some indications of striped pattern, the broad dark band extending backward from eye and along the side of body remaining most prominent. Adult males usually show traces of stripes, but they tend to become nearly uniform brown or olive in coloration; orange-red appears on jaws during spring breeding season. *Young:* See above; about 2–2½ in. (5.1–6.4 cm) at hatching.

    Two other species, Broadhead and Southeastern Five-lined Skinks, are similarly patterned, undergo comparable changes, and have ranges broadly overlapping that of the Five-lined Skink. Therefore it is essential to check scale characters to be sure of identification. Eliminate Southeastern Five-lined Skink (*inexpectatus*) by looking under base of tail; all its scales are about same size (middle row enlarged in the other two species—see Fig. 49). This species (*fasciatus*) has: (a) 26–30 longitudinal rows of scales around center of body; (b) usually four labials anterior to the subocular; and (c) two enlarged postlabial scales (Fig. 50).

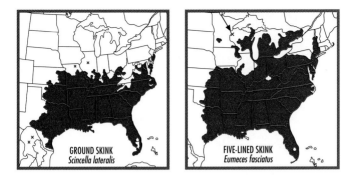

GROUND SKINK
Scincella lateralis

FIVE-LINED SKINK
Eumeces fasciatus

Cutover woodlots with many rotting stumps and logs, abandoned board or sawdust piles, rock piles, and decaying debris in or near woods are good places to look for these lizards. Habitat is usually damp. Over the greater part of its range, the Five-lined Skink is essentially terrestrial, but it occasionally ascends trees, especially dead and decaying snags where insects are abundant. In Texas, it is distinctly arboreal. **SIMILAR SPECIES:** (1) Broadhead Skink usually has: (a) 30–32 rows of scales at midbody; (b) five labials anterior to the subocular; and (c) no enlarged postlabials (Fig. 50). (2) See also Southeastern Five-lined Skink. **RANGE:** New England to n. Fla.; west to Wisc. and eastern parts of Kans., Okla., and Texas; isolated colonies in ne. Iowa and adj. parts of Wisc. and Minn., and sw. Minn.; an isolated record for nw. Wisc.

BROADHEAD SKINK *Eumeces laticeps*   **PL. 19; FIGS. 49, 50**

IDENTIFICATION: 6½–12¾ in. (16.5–32.4 cm); head-body max. 5⅝ in. (14.3 cm). The "red-headed scorpion" is our second largest Skink; only the Great Plains Skink attains a greater length and bulk. Big, olive-brown males, with their widely swollen jowls and orange-red heads, are impressive reptiles, although the orange-red head color fades by early summer. Pattern and color variations parallel those of the Five-lined Skink (*fasciatus*). Broadhead Skink has: (a) scale rows at midbody usually 30 or 32; (b) usually five (sometimes four on one side only) labials anterior to the subocular; and (c) no enlarged postlabials (Fig. 50). Middle row of scales under tail wider than others (Fig. 49). *Young:* Black with five yellow stripes and bright blue tail; in eastern part of range young may show *seven light stripes*; about 2¼–3⅜ in. (5.7–8.6 cm) at hatching.

Habitats vary from swamp forests to empty urban lots strewn with debris. This is essentially a woodland species, however, and the most arboreal of our Skinks. The lizards make use of hollow

An adult female Broadhead Skink from Cherokee County, Kansas, on the nest with her clutch of eggs.

trees and tree holes, and sometimes may be seen on rail fences or high among bare branches of dead or decaying trees. **SIMILAR SPECIES:** (1) Southeastern Five-lined Skink *(inexpectatus)* has the scales under tail all about same size. (2) Five-lined Skink *(fasciatus)* has: (a) scale rows at midbody 26–30; (b) usually four labials anterior to the subocular; and (c) two enlarged postlabials (Fig. 50). **RANGE:** Se. Pa. to cen. Fla.; west to e. Kans. and e.-cen. Texas.

SOUTHEASTERN FIVE-LINED SKINK   PL. 19; FIG. 49
Eumeces inexpectatus

IDENTIFICATION: 5½–8½ in. (14–21.6 cm); head-body max. 3½ in. (8.9 cm). The only one of the three Five-lined Skinks in which the rows of scales under the tail are all about the same size (Fig. 49). (Check only on an original part of tail—not a regenerated portion.) Pattern and coloration run same course of changes as in Five-lined Skink *(fasciatus)*. Light stripes, especially middorsal one, tend to be quite narrow. Dorsolateral stripe is on the 5th (or 4th and 5th) row of scales, counting from midline of back. Dark areas between light stripes are black in young, but become brown

SOUTHEASTERN
FIVE-LINED
(inexpectatus)
All scales about same size

FIVE-LINED and
BROADHEAD
(fasciatus and laticeps)
Middle row enlarged

Fig. 49. Undersurfaces of tails of Skinks (Eumeces).

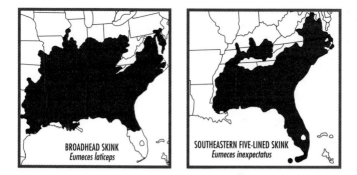

BROADHEAD SKINK
Eumeces laticeps

SOUTHEASTERN FIVE-LINED SKINK
Eumeces inexpectatus

in older specimens. *Young:* Five very narrow yellow or orange stripes that become brighter (often reddish orange) on head; often an additional faint light stripe at each side of belly; tail blue or purple. The juvenile coloration very frequently persists into adulthood, the orange head stripes remaining prominent and, in conjunction with the darker stripes, giving head an overall orange-brown appearance; purplish hues may be seen on tails of even rather large specimens. About 2½ in. (6.4 cm) at hatching.

Found in a great variety of habitats but able to tolerate drier conditions than the two other five-striped species. Thrives on many small seashore islands in the Southeast that have no fresh water and little vegetation. Climbs well but is also quite at home on the ground. **SIMILAR SPECIES:** In (1) Five-lined Skink *(fasciatus)* and (2) Broadhead Skink *(laticeps),* middle row of scales under tail is distinctly wider than other rows (Fig. 49). Also, the dorso-lateral light stripe is on the 3rd and 4th (or 4th only) rows of scales in both of those species. **RANGE:** S. Md., Va., and Ky. to the Fla. Keys and the Dry Tortugas; west to e. La.

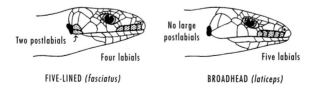

Two postlabials

Four labials

FIVE-LINED *(fasciatus)*

No large postlabials

Five labials

BROADHEAD *(laticeps)*

Fig. 50. Heads of Skinks (Eumeces).

An adult Great Plains Skink. This is the largest skink found in the area covered by this field guide.

GREAT PLAINS SKINK *Eumeces obsoletus* PL. 19; FIG. 51

IDENTIFICATION: 6½–13¾ in. (16.5–34.9 cm); head-body max. 5⅝ in. (14.3 cm). Largest of all Skinks occurring within our area, and unique in having scales on sides of body arranged *obliquely* instead of in horizontal rows (Fig. 51). The ground color varies from light tan to light gray, and basically each scale is edged with black or dark brown. Distribution of edging varies so that some specimens have strong indications of longitudinal stripes. Two postmental scales (Fig. 52). *Young:* Jet-black; tail blue; white and orange spots on head; about 2½ in. (6.4 cm) at hatching.

Chiefly a grassland species in the Great Plains, where it prefers fine-grained soil suitable for burrowing and with sunken rocks for shelter. In the arid Southwest and northern Mexico it occurs along watercourses and in other areas where there is permanent or semipermanent moisture. Secretive; seldom seen except when rock slabs or other places of concealment are overturned. Can inflict a painful bite. **SIMILAR SPECIES:** Young Southern Coal Skinks also may be virtually plain black; their snouts and lips may be reddish, but they lack bold white and orange head spots. Check chin

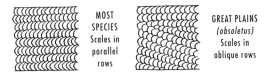

MOST SPECIES Scales in parallel rows   GREAT PLAINS (*obsoletus*) Scales in oblique rows

Fig. 51. Scales on sides of bodies of Skinks (Eumeces).

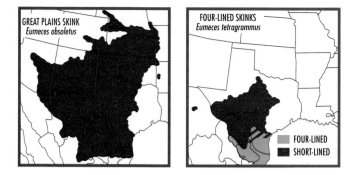

—Coal Skinks have only one postmental scale (Fig. 52). **RANGE:** S. Neb. and extr. w. Mo. southward, and including much of Texas; west to cen. Ariz.; southward to Chihuahua, Durango, and ne. Mexico; an isolated colony in Ark.

FOUR-LINED SKINK

Eumeces tetragrammus tetragrammus

IDENTIFICATION: 5–7⅞ in. (12.5–20 cm); head-body max. 3 in. (7.5 cm). Four light stripes that terminate in the region of the *groin*. A broad, black stripe between them on each side of body; dorsal coloration dark gray or gray-brown. In old individuals, pattern is less distinct, with dorsum changing to light brown and the black lateral stripe to brown. *Young:* Black with orange head and neck lines and tail bright blue (the adult pattern and coloration are gradually assumed); 1½ in. (3.8 cm) or more at hatching.

At home in the lower Rio Grande Valley, in brush- or grasslands, and in the gallery forest along the river. Hides under all sorts of debris. Sometimes found by peeling away the dried frond husks at the bases of palm trees. **SIMILAR SPECIES AND SUBSPECIES:** (1) In Southern Prairie Skink, light stripes extend onto tail, and the light lateral stripe passes *above* the ear opening onto the head (it crosses the ear opening in both races of *tetragrammus*). (2) In Short-lined Skink, light stripes terminate in *shoulder* region. **RANGE:** S. Texas to n. Veracruz and Querétaro; west to Coahuila. Intergrades with the Short-lined Skink in s. Texas.

SHORT-LINED SKINK

Eumeces tetragrammus brevilineatus

IDENTIFICATION: 5–7 in. (12.5–17.8 cm); head-body max. 2⅝ in. (6.7 cm). The light stripes terminate in the region of the *shoulder*. Dorsal coloration varies from brown or gray to olive- or grayish

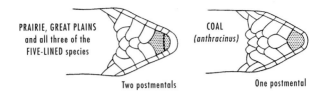

PRAIRIE, GREAT PLAINS
and all three of the
FIVE-LINED species

Two postmentals

COAL
(anthracinus)

One postmental

Fig. 52. Scales on chins of Skinks (Eumeces).

green. *Male:* Wash of orange at sides of throat. *Young:* Dark band extending backward from eye; tail bright blue; about 2 in. (5.1 cm) at hatching.

A resident of rough, hilly country (as on the Edwards Plateau), in brush- or grasslands with sandy soil, and riparian woodlands (as in the gallery forest of the Nueces R.). Elevations range from the Texas lowlands to 7500 ft. (2300 m) in the Chisos Mts. of the Big Bend region. Hides in, and forages near, brush and trash piles, clumps of cactus, or abandoned packrat nests. **SIMILAR SPECIES:** See Four-lined Skink. **RANGE:** Cen. and sw. Texas south through n. Coahuila and n. Nuevo León; an isolated colony in the Sierra del Nido, Chihuahua.

COAL SKINK *Eumeces anthracinus* PL. 19; FIG. 52

IDENTIFICATION: 5–7 in. (12.5–17.8 cm); head-body max. 2¾ in. (7 cm). A four-lined Skink but with the light stripes extending *onto tail.* Broad dark lateral stripe 2¼ to 4 scales wide. *No light lines on top of head.* Light dorsolateral stripe is on the edges of the 3rd and 4th scale rows, counting from midline of back. *One postmental scale* (Fig. 52). *Male:* Sides of head reddish during spring breeding season, at least in some parts of range. *Young:* Plain black in one subspecies; patterned like adults in the other; about 1⅞–2 in. (4.8–5.1 cm) at hatching.

The more humid portions of wooded hillsides are favorite habitats; also vicinity of springs and rocky bluffs overlooking creek valleys. When pursued, these lizards (as well as Skinks of some other species) do not hesitate to take refuge in shallow water, going to the bottom and hiding under stones or debris. **SIMILAR SPECIES:** (1) In the two Prairie Skinks the dark lateral stripe is not more than two scales wide, and the light dorsolateral stripe is on the 4th (or 4th and 5th) row of scales. (2) In Short-lined and

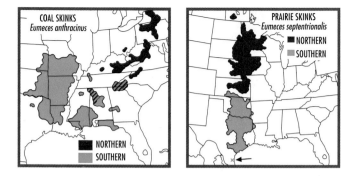

Four-lined Skinks light stripes do not extend onto tail. (3) In juveniles and young adults of the three species of Five-lined Skinks (*fasciatus, inexpectatus,* and *laticeps*) there are two light lines on head; in old adults of these, in which the stripes may have faded, check for presence of two *postmental scales* (Fig. 52). (4) The black young of the Great Plains Skink have bold white and orange spots on their heads; they also have two postmental scales (Fig. 52). **RANGE:** Discontinuous—see subspecies below. **SUBSPECIES:** SOUTHERN COAL SKINK, *Eumeces a. pluvialis* (Pl. 19). Posterior supralabials with light centers and dark edges, producing a spotted appearance. Rows of scales around middle of body 26 or more. Young are black and unpatterned but often with faint suggestions of light stripes or whitish labial spots or both; snout and lips may be reddish; tail blue. E. Kans. and Mo. to e. Texas and nw. La., but absent from the Mississippi Alluvial Plain; isolated colonies in Ga., the Fla. panhandle, cen. Ala., n.-cen. Miss., sw. Ky. and adj. Tenn., and a large disjunct area in se. La., s. Miss., and sw. Ala.; intergrades with Northern Coal Skink in scattered areas of the Southeast. NORTHERN COAL SKINK, *Eumeces a. anthracinus.* A continuous light stripe through posterior supralabials. Rows of scales around midbody usually 25 or fewer. Young with blue tail, but otherwise patterned like adults. Range disjunct from N.Y. to N.C. and Ky.; isolated colonies in Ohio and w.-cen. Ky.

NORTHERN PRAIRIE SKINK

PL. 19

Eumeces septentrionalis septentrionalis

IDENTIFICATION: 5¼–8¾ in. (13.3–22.4 cm); head-body max. 3½ in. (9 cm). A many-striped Skink but with the *light* dorsolateral stripe strongly bordered *both above and below* by dark stripes and extending onto the tail. This light stripe is on the 4th (or 4th and

An adult male Northern Prairie Skink during the breeding season, showing the reddish orange color on the lips and chin.

5th) row of scales, counting from midline of back. A pair of relatively faint dark lines down center of back, or a pale middorsal stripe, or both. Broadest dark stripe not more than *two scales wide*. Dorsal ground color olive to olive-brown. Two postmental scales (Fig. 52). *Male:* Deep reddish orange on sides of head during breeding season. *Young:* Tail bright blue; about 2 in. (5.1 cm) at hatching.

Seldom seen in the open but uses shallow burrows and excavations, often of its own making. Often occurs along stream banks in areas of soft sands or soils, frequently in gravelly glacial deposits or their sandy outwashes (in northern localities). Sometimes found in rock or sawdust piles or by overturning objects left undisturbed long enough to be well settled into surface of sod or soil. **SIMILAR SPECIES:** (1) In Many-lined Skink, the light dorsolateral stripe is confined to 3rd row of scales. (2) Coal Skink has: (a) broad dark lateral stripe, 2½ to 4 scales wide; (b) light dorsolateral stripe on edges of 3rd and 4th scale rows; and (c) a single postmental scale (Fig. 52). **RANGE:** Minn. and w. Wisc. to Kans.; an isolated area in s. Manitoba.

SOUTHERN PRAIRIE SKINK   PL. 19
Eumeces septentrionalis obtusirostris

IDENTIFICATION: 5–7 in. (12.5–17.8 cm); head-body max. 2¹⁵⁄₁₆ in. (7.5 cm). Similar to the Northern Prairie Skink but with the middorsal markings greatly reduced or absent. In extreme cases the dark line above the light dorsolateral stripe may even be missing. Occasionally the light stripe along lower sides also is lacking. Light dorsolateral line is on the 4th (or 4th and 5th) row of scales, counting from middorsal line. The broad dark lateral stripe is not more than *two scales wide*. Two postmental scales (Fig. 52).

Often seen foraging along dry stream beds or washes near bases of clumps of prickly pear or other vegetation into which it retreats at first sign of danger. **SIMILAR SPECIES:** (1) Coal Skink has: (a) the light dorsolateral stripe on edges of the 3rd and 4th scale rows; (b) only one postmental scale; and (c) the broad, dark lateral stripe is 2½ to 4 *scales wide.* (2) In Short-lined and Four-lined Skinks, light lines do not extend onto tail. **RANGE:** S.-cen. Kans. to e.-cen. Texas; an isolated record in extr. s. Texas.

MANY-LINED SKINKS
Eumeces multivirgatus

■ NORTHERN
■ VARIABLE

NORTHERN MANY-LINED SKINK   PL. 19
Eumeces multivirgatus multivirgatus

IDENTIFICATION: 5–7⅝ in. (12.5–19.4 cm); head-body max. 2⅞ in. (7.3 cm). Numerous light and dark stripes, some strong and well defined, others weak and appearing merely as rows of dark dots. This lizard and the southern race (*epipleurotus*) are the only Skinks of our area with a *prominent light stripe restricted to 3rd row of scales,* counting from midline of back. A well-defined *light* middorsal stripe flanked by *dark* stripes. Tail swollen at base. Stripeless or virtually stripeless individuals occur as rare variants. *Young:* Darker than adults; only the prominent lines present, and these rather dim; the fainter secondary stripes develop later; tail brilliant blue; about 2½ in. (6.4 cm) at hatching.

A lizard of the open plains and sand hills, often occurring in vacant lots and under debris in towns and settlements. Sometimes also found beneath cow chips, where it has taken shelter or is in search of insects. **SIMILAR SPECIES:** In Northern Prairie Skink, light dorsolateral stripe is on the 4th (or 4th and 5th) row of scales. **RANGE:** Sw. S.D. to e.-cen. Colo.

VARIABLE SKINK *Eumeces multivirgatus epipleurotus*   PL. 19
IDENTIFICATION: 5–7⅝ in. (12.5–19.4 cm); head-body max. 2⅞ in. (7.3 cm). A Skink with a highly variable pattern; both plain-colored and striped variants occur, and the striped ones change with age. Juveniles of the latter are dark, but they bear a well-defined light middorsal stripe and a vivid dorsolateral stripe on the 3rd row of scales, counting from midline of back. As the lizards grow, the ground color becomes paler, the middorsal stripe disappears, and the dark dorsal stripes are reduced to narrow zigzag lines, or they vanish altogether. Meanwhile, the broad, dark lateral stripe

Removing the cover of her hiding place revealed a mother Variable Skink and one of her newly hatched young. Females of many kinds of skinks use well-secreted nests and then remain with their eggs until they hatch.

is invaded by the pale ground color and is replaced by two or three dark lines. Tail may be swollen at base in large adults. *Young:* Tail bright blue; 2–2½ in. (5.1–6.4 cm) at hatching.

Habitats are as variable as the color pattern. They range from high mountains and plateaus, where the striped phase is common, to relatively low creosote-bush deserts, where the plain-colored variant is more abundant and blends better with the rocks and soils of the open, arid landscape. **RANGE:** Extr. s. Colo., se. Utah, and much of Ariz. to w. Texas; intergrades with Northern Many-lined Skink in se. Colo. and possibly also in w. Texas, although its taxonomic status in the latter area is not clear; isolated records in sw. Texas.

FLORIDA KEYS MOLE SKINK   PL. 19
Eumeces egregius egregius

IDENTIFICATION: 3½–6 in. (9–15.2 cm); head-body max. 2¼ in. (5.7 cm). A combination of red or brownish red tail plus light stripes that neither widen nor diverge to other scale rows. The lateral stripes usually continue to the groin, but the dorsolateral stripes may terminate much farther forward. Ground color varies from gray-brown to dark chocolate brown. Reddish color of tail *persists throughout life;* it does not fade as does the blue in other species of Skinks. Scales around middle of body usually 22 or more. *Male:* With a reddish or orange suffusion that extends onto the venter during the mating season.

Highly secretive; often found in piles of stones or debris. Also in driftwood and tidal wrack along shores of the islands. Mole Skinks in general feed largely on roaches and crickets, but other kinds of insects and spiders are also eaten. Small crustaceans constitute a large part of the diet of some of the insular populations. **RANGE:** Fla. Keys and the Dry Tortugas. **SUBSPECIES:** NORTHERN MOLE SKINK, *Eumeces e. similis.* Similar but with only six upper labials (most frequently seven in the other races). Scales around middle of body usually 21 or fewer. Tail red, orange, or reddish brown. Length of stripes highly variable. Habitat similar to that of Peninsula Mole Skink, except that dry, rocky areas are also utilized. N. Fla. and roughly the southern half of Ga. and adj. portions of Ala. CEDAR KEY MOLE SKINK, *Eumeces e. insularis.* Slightly larger in size — to 6⅜ in. (16.2 cm); head-body to 2–2½ in. (5.1–6.4 cm). Light dorsolateral stripes inconspicuous; 21 or fewer scale rows around middle of body. Hatchlings almost uniform black in coloration. Cedar and Seahorse Keys, Levy Co., Fla.

MOLE SKINKS
Eumeces egregius
■ PENINSULA
■ NORTHERN
■ CEDAR KEY
■ BLUETAIL
■ FLORIDA KEYS

PENINSULA MOLE SKINK *Eumeces egregius onocrepis* PL. 19
IDENTIFICATION: 3¼–6³⁄₁₆ in. (9–15.7 cm); head-body max. 2⁵⁄₁₆ in. (5.9 cm). A variable race in which the tail may be red, orange, yellow, pinkish, brown, or lavender. Light dorsolateral stripes widen posteriorly or diverge to a different scale row, or both. *Young* (of Mole Skinks in general): 1⅞–2⅜ in. (4.8–6 cm) at hatching.

The Mole Skinks are so slender and their legs are so short that they seem almost snakelike in appearance and actions. They are found chiefly in areas of sandy, well-drained soil that support sandhill scrub or dry hammock vegetation. They burrow in loose, dry sand and frequently "bask" just beneath the surface in mounds pushed up by pocket gophers. **RANGE:** Much of the Fla. peninsula.

BLUETAIL MOLE SKINK *Eumeces egregius lividus* PL. 19
IDENTIFICATION: 3¼–6¼ in. (9–16.5 cm); head-body max. 2⁷⁄₁₆ in. (6.2 cm). Distinguished from all other Mole Skinks by the bright blue tail of the young, a coloration that persists in some adults. Tail light blue to salmon in older specimens. Light dorsolateral stripes widen posteriorly or diverge to involve another scale row, or both; invariably seven upper labials on each side of head.

A sand burrower like the other members of its species. Discovery of this blue-tailed race suggested the advisability of using the more appropriate name of Mole Skinks for the group instead of "red-tailed skinks," by which they were previously known. **RANGE:**

SAND SKINK
Neoseps reynoldsi

Essentially confined to the Lake Wales Ridge of Polk and Highlands cos., Fla.

SAND SKINK   **PL. 19**
Neoseps reynoldsi
IDENTIFICATION: 4–5⅛ in. (10–13 cm); head-body max. 2⁹⁄₁₆ in. (6.5 cm). The legs are greatly reduced in size. Each foreleg fits into a groove on lower side of body; it bears only a *single toe* and is so tiny as to be easily overlooked. Hind legs are a little larger, and each has two digits. Other characteristics include a wedge-shaped snout, lower jaw partially countersunk into upper one, a flat or slightly concave belly that meets sides of body at an angle, a tiny eye with built-in "window" in lower lid, and no external ear opening. Coloration varies from dirty white to deep tan. *Young:* About 2⁵⁄₁₆ in. (5.9 cm) at hatching.

An adept burrower that "swims" through dry sand. The limbs, of little help underground, are in the evolutionary process of being lost. Food consists mainly of termites and beetle larvae, most of which are caught and eaten while burrowing. Largely restricted to areas of rosemary scrub, where moist sand underlies the dry surface sand at a depth of one to a few inches (2.5 cm or more). The Sand Skink may play 'possum when first caught, holding itself rigidly immobile, but it will flop over on its belly if placed upside down on a hard surface. **RANGE:** Apparently confined to a narrow corridor of the Fla. peninsula from Marion Co. to Highlands Co.

GLASS LIZARDS AND ALLIGATOR LIZARD: FAMILY ANGUIDAE

Members of this small but wide-ranging family have their scales reinforced with bony plates called osteoderms, a characteristic shared by the Skinks. Compensation for the resultant stiffening of the body is provided, among the Glass Lizards and our single form of Alligator Lizard, by the presence of a deep, flexible groove that runs along each side of the body. The groove is lined with granular scales, and it permits expansion when the body is distended with food or (in females) with eggs.

The legless Glass Lizards are easily mistaken for snakes. But, *unlike* snakes, they have *movable eyelids* and *external ear openings* (see page 138). To the touch they feel stiff, almost brittle, and they lack the suppleness of the serpent. Their tails are very long (up to 2.75 times the head-body length) and are so fragile in the wide-ranging species that full-tailed specimens are not common. The regenerated tip, sharply pointed and of a different color from the remaining part of the original tail, earns them the name of "horn snakes" among country folk. Some people even think such a tip is a stinger. If hit with a flat object, the tail may break in two or more pieces. This is the origin of the "joint snake" legend in which the animal, after fragmentation, is supposed to grow back together again — an obvious impossibility. (See Fracture planes in Glossary.)

Glass Lizards are good burrowers, and at least two of the kinds may spend much of their time below ground. Their food includes insects, spiders, snails, birds' eggs, and small snakes and lizards. Captives will usually accept a mixture of chopped raw meat and egg (add vitamins and minerals!). They should have gravel or soil in which to hide and should not be caged with other reptiles much smaller than themselves. The young average about 6–8 inches (15.2–20.3 cm) at hatching (smaller in *compressus*). Females normally guard their eggs during incubation.

We have four species of Glass Lizards. Other members of the genus occur in Mexico, Africa, Europe, and Asia.

In contrast with the members of the genus *Ophisaurus*, the Alligator Lizards, of which there are several genera ranging, collectively, from British Columbia to Panama, have four well-developed legs. The lateral groove is strongly evident in some of them but only weakly in others. North of Mexico they are confined to the West and only one, the Texas Alligator Lizard, occurs in our area.

The family as a whole ranges from extreme southwestern Canada to northern Argentina, and it is also represented in the West Indies and the Old World.

EASTERN GLASS LIZARD *Ophisaurus ventralis* **PL. 17; FIG. 53**

IDENTIFICATION: 18–42⅜ in. (45.7–108.3 cm); head-body max. 12 in. (30.6 cm). *No* dark lengthwise stripes below the lateral groove or under the tail; *no* distinct dark middorsal stripe (Fig. 53). White marks on neck, essentially vertical, are highly irregular in shape. White markings on *posterior corners of scales*. In older specimens there are numerous longitudinal dark lines or dashes on uppersides of body, and sometimes similar parallel lines occupy the entire middorsal area. An old adult (as shown on Pl. 17) may be greenish above and yellow below. *Only* Glass Lizard that may look green. Scales along lateral groove number 98 or more. *Young:*

Khaki-colored and normally with a broad, dark longitudinal stripe on each side of back.

Characteristically an inhabitant of wet meadows and grasslands and pine flatwoods; also occurs in tropical, hardwood hammocks in southern Florida. **SIMILAR SPECIES:** (1) Slender Glass Lizards may have a middorsal dark stripe or series of dashes, and at least traces of dark stripes below lateral groove. (2) Mimic Glass Lizard has a weak middorsal dark stripe and several lateral stripes above the groove. (3) See also Island Glass Lizard. **RANGE:** Extr. se. Va. to s. Fla., and west to e. La.

SLENDER GLASS LIZARD *Ophisaurus attenuatus* PL. 17

IDENTIFICATION: 22–42 in. (56–106.7 cm); head-body max. 11⅜ in. (28.9 cm). Narrow, dark longitudinal stripes *below* the lateral groove and under the tail (Fig. 53); these are black in the young, but paler and less prominent (sometimes considerably less) in adults. A dark middorsal stripe or series of dashes in young and medium-sized specimens. Old adults may be brown with irregular light (but dark-bordered) crossbands on the back and tail. White marks on scales occupy *middle* of scales. In some parts of range, females are strongly patterned, but males become flecked with whitish when nearing adult size. These markings become more prominent with age, and old males may have a salt-and-pepper appearance. Scales along lateral groove number 98 or more.

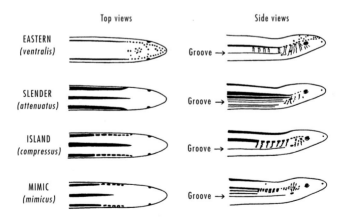

Fig. 53. Heads of Glass Lizards (Ophisaurus).

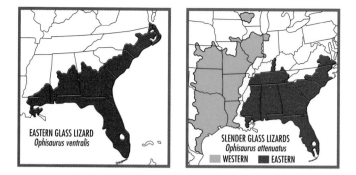

EASTERN GLASS LIZARD
Ophisaurus ventralis

SLENDER GLASS LIZARDS
Ophisaurus attenuatus
□ WESTERN ■ EASTERN

Found chiefly in dry grasslands or dry, open woods. Seldom burrows, except for hibernation. Very active when restrained, vigorously trying to escape and sometimes whipping back and forth somewhat as Racers and Whipsnakes do. Fully capable of snapping off the tail, even if held carefully by the body and when the tail is not touching anything. Glass Lizards of the other species are much less energetic in their efforts to escape. **SIMILAR SPECIES:** Both (1) Eastern and (2) Island Glass Lizards lack dark stripes below lateral groove and under tail. (3) Mimic Glass Lizard generally lacks dark stripes below lateral groove; if present, they are faint and indistinct. **RANGE:** Se. Va. to s. Fla.; west to cen. Texas and north in Mississippi Valley to se. Neb. and nw. Ind.; disjunct area in sw. Wisc. **SUBSPECIES:** WESTERN SLENDER GLASS LIZARD, *Ophisaurus a. attenuatus* (Pl. 17). Tail (when unregenerated) less than 2.4 times head-body length. Chiefly west of Mississippi R.,

An adult Slender Glass Lizard from Marshall County, Mississippi. Often mistaken for a snake, this legless lizard has ear openings and movable eyelids, characters that serpents lack.

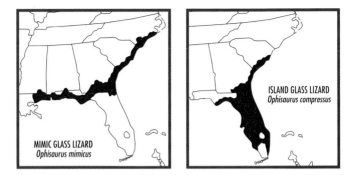

ISLAND GLASS LIZARD
Ophisaurus compressus

MIMIC GLASS LIZARD
Ophisaurus mimicus

but crossing into Ill. and adjacent states in the North. EASTERN SLENDER GLASS LIZARD, *Ophisaurus a. longicaudus*. Tail longer (when unregenerated), 2.4 or more times head-body length. Attains a greater length than western subspecies—to 46½ in. (118.1 cm); head-body max. 14¼ in. (35.9 cm). Se. Va. to s. Fla. and west to the Mississippi R.; a northward extension in Ky.

MIMIC GLASS LIZARD *Ophisaurus mimicus* FIG. 53

IDENTIFICATION: 15–25¾ in. (38–65.7 cm); head-body max. 7³⁄₁₆ in. (18.3 cm). The smallest of our Glass Lizards, similar in coloration and pattern to the Island and Slender Glass Lizards. Dark brown or black middorsal stripe present, weak anteriorly but more distinct posteriorly and onto the tail; *three or four dark stripes or rows of spots above the lateral groove separated by pale stripes*. Scales along lateral groove number 97 or fewer. One or two upper labials extend upward to the eye or are sometimes separated from it by very small scales. Fracture planes are present in the caudal vertebrae.

A resident of pine flatwoods and open woodlands, diurnal in habit and difficult to find. This species was long overlooked and was only recently described. **SIMILAR SPECIES:** (1) Eastern Glass Lizard lacks dark middorsal stripe. (2) Slender Glass Lizard has distinct stripes below the lateral groove and 98 or more scales along lateral groove. (3) Island Glass Lizard lacks fracture planes in the caudal vertebrae and has only *one lateral stripe,* which is above the groove. **RANGE:** In a narrow band from coastal N.C. to Ga., west across the Fla. panhandle to s. Miss.

ISLAND GLASS LIZARD *Ophisaurus compressus* FIG. 53

IDENTIFICATION: 15–24 in. (38–61 cm); head-body max. 7⅝ in. (19.5 cm). The *single* dark, solid stripe on each side of the body is situated on scale rows 3 and 4 above the lateral groove. A dark middorsal stripe present, but this is sometimes represented merely by a series of dark dashes (Fig. 53). *No dark stripes below the groove.* Undersurfaces pinkish buff or yellowish and unmarked. Numerous more or less vertical light bars on neck, more numerous and usually more conspicuous than those of Eastern Glass Lizard.

TEXAS ALLIGATOR LIZARD
Gerrhonotus liocephalus
▓ Mexican subspecies

In older specimens the top and sides of neck are mottled with bronze. Scales along lateral groove number 97 or fewer. One or two upper labials extend upward to the eye. Fracture planes are lacking in the caudal vertebrae, and the tail is not brittle. **SIMILAR SPECIES:** (1) Slender Glass Lizard has dark stripes below lateral groove. (2) Both Eastern and Slender Glass Lizards have 98 or more scales along lateral groove. (3) Mimic Glass Lizard has several lateral stripes above groove and has fracture planes in the caudal vertebrae. **RANGE:** Coastal areas and offshore islands of S.C., Ga., and Fla.; scrub pine regions and adj. flatwoods of peninsular Fla.

TEXAS ALLIGATOR LIZARD PL. 17
Gerrhonotus liocephalus infernalis

IDENTIFICATION: 10–16 in. (25.4–41 cm); record 20 in. (50.8 cm); head-body max. 8 in. (20.3 cm). Scales large and platelike (suggesting the alligator). Coloration variable from yellowish- to reddish brown. Broken, irregular, light lines cross back and tail. Check for flexible groove that runs along the side from neck to hind leg. Our only lizard with *both a lateral groove and legs.* (The alligator lizard illustrated on Pl. 17 has puffed itself up with air—a common reptilian habit—so the groove is stretched out nearly flat.) *Young:* Much more vividly marked than adults; ground color dark brown to black and crossed by narrow whitish crossbands; head tan; about 3½–4 in. (9–10 cm) at hatching.

Essentially terrestrial and usually slow and deliberate, in contrast with the quick, darting movements of most lizards. Tail is somewhat prehensile. Food includes insects, spiders, newborn mice, and small snakes and lizards. Never cage alligator lizards with smaller reptiles. Large specimens can bite painfully hard. **RANGE:** Edwards Plateau and Big Bend regions of Texas to San Luis Potosí; an isolated record in w. Tamaulipas.

8

Amphisbaenians

ORDER SQUAMATA
SUBORDER AMPHISBAENIA

Snakelike reptiles with rings of scales encircling body and tail. There are no external ear openings, and only a few members of the Suborder have visible limbs. Represented in Africa and adjacent parts of Europe and Asia, South America to Mexico, the West Indies, and Florida. There are about 150 species, but only one occurs in our area.

WORM LIZARD: FAMILY AMPHISBAENIDAE

FLORIDA WORM LIZARD *Rhineura floridana*   **PL. 17**
IDENTIFICATION: 7–11 in. (18–28 cm); record 16 in. (40.6 cm). Extraordinarily *similar to the common earthworm,* both in coloration and gross appearance. Body looks segmented, like the earthworm's, but this reptile has scales and a well-defined, lizardlike head, even though both ends of the animal look superficially alike. Lower jaw countersunk into upper, facilitating burrowing. There are no limbs, no ear openings, and most specimens lack external eyes (internally there are remnants of eyes). Upper surface of the very short tail is flattened and covered with numerous small bumps (tubercles), forming an effective stopper for the tunnels this reptile makes as it burrows through sand or soil. *Young:* About 4 in. (10 cm) at hatching.

Worm lizards remain underground virtually all their lives but are sometimes plowed or dug up or may be forced to the surface by heavy rains. Dry, sandy habitats are preferred. Earthworms, spiders, and termites are the principal foods.

Despite its common name, this reptile is an amphisbaenian and not a lizard. **RANGE:** Cen. and n. parts of Fla. peninsula.

FLORIDA WORM LIZARD
Rhineura floridana

Florida Worm Lizard. This reptile is neither a lizard nor a worm. It is our only member of the suborder Amphisbaenia, a group with representatives in many parts of the world. Note its similarity to an earthworm.

SNAKES

ORDER SQUAMATA
SUBORDER SERPENTES

Snakes, of which there are over 2300 species, are almost as widespread as lizards. They range northward above the Arctic Circle in Scandinavia and to the 60th parallel in North America. Southward they extend through Australia and into Tasmania, to the Cape Region of Africa, and very nearly to the tip of South America. They are absent, however, from many islands where lizards occur, including Ireland, New Zealand, and numerous South Sea archipelagos. Vertically, they range from sea level to 16,000 feet (4900 m) in the Himalayan Mountains of Asia.

Venomous snakes are widespread through the larger land masses and on many islands. No poisonous kinds occur on Madagascar, however, or on any of the West Indian islands except St. Lucia and Martinique. In Australia, venomous snakes predominate.

Many snakes are easily recognized by their patterns, behavior, or other characteristics, but a great number of kinds must be caught for close examination. Checking for the presence or absence of certain scales is sometimes necessary, and ventrals or subcaudals (or, occasionally, both) must be counted for positive identification. Be extremely careful in approaching poisonous snakes. Make no attempt to catch them unless you have had thorough training on how to do it. Learn to recognize venomous snakes on sight (study Pls. 30, 34, 35, and 36). If you are bitten, go immediately to the nearest physician or medical facility for treatment.

BLIND SNAKES:
FAMILIES TYPHLOPIDAE AND LEPTOTYPHLOPIDAE

Two large families of small, burrowing, wormlike snakes containing an estimated 250 species in four genera worldwide. The families are indistinguishable on the basis of external characters. The two genera of Blind Snakes (one from each family) known to occur in the United States possess vestigial eyes, extremely short tails, and are unique among snakes in our area in having *belly scales the same size as the dorsal scales.*

Which end is the head in these snakes? The blunt, rounded tail strongly resembles the head, but the latter may be recognized by two black dots that show where the eyes are buried beneath translucent scales. Despite its blunt appearance, the tail ends in a tiny spine. Food consists of termites and the larvae and pupae of ants.

The Family Leptotyphlopidae, represented in our area by the genus *Leptotyphlops*, ranges from the south-central United States to Argentina and also occurs in the West Indies, Africa, and southwestern Asia. The Family Typhlopidae, although not native to the United States, is represented by *Ramphotyphlops braminus,* a unisexual species that has been introduced in extreme southern Florida. Worldwide, this family is known from the New World tropics, the Mediterranean region, Madagascar, southern Asia, Australia, and Africa, as well as the West Indies, Hawaii, the Philippines, and many other South Pacific Is.

BRAHMINY BLIND SNAKE   NOT ILLUS.
Ramphotyphlops braminus

IDENTIFICATION: 4⅜–6½ in. (11.2–16.5 cm); record 6⅞ in. (17.3 cm). The smallest snake found in the area covered by this Field Guide. A very slender, wormlike serpent (a dark version of the genus *Leptotyphlops;* see Pl. 33) with a dark gray, dark brown, or black dorsum, and a lighter belly; snout, lower lips, chin, throat, tip of tail, and anal area may be white to buffy yellow. No constriction at neck. Ventral scales the same size as the dorsal scales. Vestigial eyes beneath translucent scales. Before shedding, the outer layer of skin loosens and turns light blue. Unisexual, as are several of the Whiptail Lizards. *Young:* Identical to adults; about 2¼ in. (6.4 cm) at hatching.

A burrower in loose, moist soil; without such habitat it will dry out and die. Lays from 2 to 8 eggs in moist earth. This tiny snake eats large quantities of termites, as well as other soft-bodied insects and their larvae. It is sometimes concealed in the roots of potted plants, and thus transported into areas where it is not

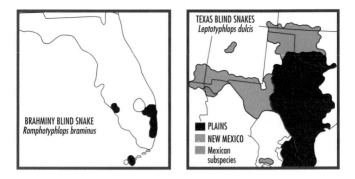

BRAHMINY BLIND SNAKE
Ramphotyphlops braminus

TEXAS BLIND SNAKES
Leptotyphlops dulcis

■ PLAINS
■ NEW MEXICO
▨ Mexican subspecies

native. **RANGE:** Introduced in southern Fla. at a number of localities in the area from Lake Okeechobee east to the Atlantic Coast and south to Miami and Homestead; also found on Big Pine Key and at Ft. Myers on the Gulf Coast. Its natural range may have been Asian, but through introductions it has spread rapidly to other tropical and subtropical parts of the world, including Mexico and Hawaii.

TEXAS BLIND SNAKE *Leptotyphlops dulcis*   **PL. 33**
IDENTIFICATION: 5–8 in. (12.5–20.3 cm); record 10¾ in. (27.3 cm). A wormlike snake, slender as a knitting needle, with no constriction at the neck, *no enlarged ventral scales,* and *three* small scales between the oculars (Fig. 54). Coloration pale shiny brown or reddish brown above, and whitish or pinkish below; no markings. May appear silvery after being caught (see below). *Young:* Smallest known specimen 2⁹⁄₁₆ in. (6.5 cm) in total length.

A largely subterranean resident of the plains and semiarid regions. Occurs on stony hillsides, prairies, and in sandy or rocky deserts, but almost always in areas where some moisture is available. Frequently found beneath stones and small boulders after rains. Most likely to prowl abroad in early evening. When first caught or when attacked by ants, these snakes tilt the individual scales, imparting a silvery appearance to their skins. Individuals protect themselves by writhing while they coat their bodies with feces and a clear, viscous liquid discharged from the anus. The coating serves to repel insects and permits the snake to enter columns of ants (and presumably their nests) in its search for food. **RANGE:** S.-cen. Kans. to ne. Mexico and west to se. Ariz. **SIMILAR SPECIES:** Trans-Pecos Blind Snake has only one scale between the oculars (Fig. 54). **SUBSPECIES:** PLAINS BLIND SNAKE, *Leptotyphlops d. dulcis* (Pl. 33). *A single* supralabial scale between the

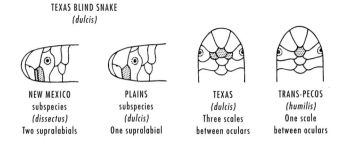

TEXAS BLIND SNAKE
(dulcis)

NEW MEXICO	PLAINS	TEXAS	TRANS-PECOS
subspecies *(dissectus)*	subspecies *(dulcis)*	*(dulcis)*	*(humilis)*
Two supralabials	One supralabial	Three scales between oculars	One scale between oculars

Fig. 54. Heads of Blind Snakes (Leptotyphlops).

enlarged ocular scale (the one containing the eye) and the lower nasal scale (the one containing the nostril) — see Fig. 54. S. Okla. to ne. Mexico. NEW MEXICO BLIND SNAKE, *Leptotyphlops d. dissectus.* *Two* supralabial scales between ocular and lower nasal scale (Fig. 54). Disjunct population in s.-cen. Kans., extr. se. Colo., cen. Okla., and n. Texas; another from w. Texas to se. Ariz. and ne. Sonora; isolated colonies in nw. N.M. and s. Coahuila. Mexican subspecies.

TRANS-PECOS BLIND SNAKE   FIG. 54
Leptotyphlops humilis segregus

IDENTIFICATION: 7–10 in. (18–25.4 cm); record 13⅛ in. (33.3 cm). Similar to our other Blind Snakes, but with only a *single* scale on top of the head between the ocular scales (Fig. 54). *Belly scales same size as dorsals.* Coloration brown or pale dull purplish above; venter paler but usually pink or purplish. *Young:* About 3½ in. (8.9 cm) at hatching.

A burrower that, like all our Blind Snakes, has the lower jaw countersunk into the upper one for easy progress through loose soil or sand. A resident of sandy and stony deserts, grassland-desert transition areas, and foothill canyons. By day it is most often found under rocks near streams, springs, or other areas where moisture is present. During warm weather

TRANS-PECOS BLIND SNAKE
Leptotyphlops humilis
Mexican subspecies

it often prowls in the open at night. SIMILAR SPECIES: In both races of Texas Blind Snake there are *three* scales on top of head between ocular scales (Fig. 54). RANGE: Sw. Texas, the Big Bend region, and w. Coahuila to se. Ariz.; an isolated record in cen. Coahuila.

COLUBRIDS: FAMILY COLUBRIDAE

To this enormous family belong approximately 75% of all the genera and 78% of the species of snakes of the entire world. Its members predominate on all the continents save Australia, where relatives of the cobras and coral snakes (Family Elapidae) are most numerous. An even greater preponderance is evident in our area, where the colubrids constitute about 85% of the genera and 84% of the species. All the snakes from *Nerodia* to *Tantilla,* inclusive, are currently placed in the Family Colubridae. They vary in form and size from the stout-bodied Hognose Snakes to the slender Short-tailed and Rough Green Snakes, and from the 7-foot-plus (2 m or more) Rat, Bull, and Indigo Snakes to the tiny Ground and Earth Snakes.

Most of our colubrids have solid teeth, but some species are equipped with grooved fangs in the rear portions of the upper jaws.

WATER SNAKES AND SALT MARSH SNAKES: GENUS *Nerodia*

Relatively large, thick-bodied, harmless, semiaquatic snakes often seen basking on logs, branches, or brush, from which they drop or glide into the water at the slightest alarm. They are adept at swimming and diving, and obtain most of their food, including frogs, salamanders, fish, and crayfish, in or near the water. Canned sardines or chopped raw fish (be sure to include the entrails) are readily accepted by captives of many species.

Water and Salt Marsh Snakes have been more maligned than any other non-poisonous serpents, partly because they strike and bite hard when cornered (even a rat would do as much), and partly because biased or uninformed persons resent their predation on fishes. They actually improve fishing by culling out sick and less vigorous fish and helping to thin out overpopulated lakes and ponds in which the fish otherwise would remain stunted in size.

Most persons confuse the large, stouter kinds of Water and Salt Marsh Snakes with the venomous Cottonmouth, and with good reason. They look much alike, and even the distinctive patterns may be obscured if the snake has been crawling in mud or is soon to shed its skin. Live Cottonmouths move more slowly, beating a more dignified retreat; cornered ones hold their mouths open wide in readiness to bite. Dead Cottonmouths can be checked for two things: (a) a single row of scales under the tail (double in Water and Salt Marsh Snakes); and (b) a deep pit between eye and nostril (absent in all harmless snakes—see Fig. 18, opp. Pl. 34). Be cautious about trying to catch any aquatic serpent within the range of the Cottonmouth (see map, p. 403).

Many Water and Salt Marsh Snakes flatten their bodies when alarmed. When first seized, they discharge copious quantities of foul-smelling musk from glands at the base of the tail. Females grow larger than males; many that are heavy with young are noticeably distended in girth. Dead or captive Water or Salt Marsh Snakes are often most quickly identified by flipping them over and examining their colorful and usually distinctive belly patterns.

The genus *Nerodia* contains nine species, three of which (the Northern Water Snake, *Nerodia sipedon*, Southern Water Snake, *Nerodia fasciata*, and Plainbelly Water Snake, *Nerodia erythrogaster*, have distributions greater than any of the others (see maps, pp. 294, 297, and 293). The genus is restricted to the eastern and central United States and Mexico; one of the species also occurs along the northern coast of Cuba.

MISSISSIPPI GREEN WATER SNAKE PL. 21; FIG. 55
Nerodia cyclopion

IDENTIFICATION: 30–45 in. (76–114 cm); record 50 in. (127 cm). Although they lack distinctive field marks, the two Green Water Snakes are unique among *Nerodia* in having a row of scales between the eye and lip scales (upper labials)—see Fig. 55. This makes identification positive and final, but it means having the

A Mississippi Green Water Snake eating a fish. In keeping with their semiaquatic habitats, water snakes of all kinds feed principally on animals that live in or near streams, marshes, lakes, and ponds.

snake in hand for close-up examination. General dorsal coloration may be greenish or brownish but usually with at least some faint suggestion of a dark pattern on a lighter ground. Belly marked with *light* spots or half-moons on a ground color of gray or brown. Scales *keeled;* anal *divided.* *Young:* About 9–11 in. (23–28 cm) at birth.

A species of quiet waters— edges of lakes and ponds, swamps, rice fields, or marshes, of bayous and other waterways. Occasionally found in brackish water. **SIMILAR SPECIES:** (1) Virtually all other large Water Snakes usually have strong indications of pattern—stripes, spots, or blotches— but these may not show well in a basking serpent unless it is wet. (2) Cottonmouth usually moves sluggishly, not dropping or diving into water as fast as Water Snakes. **RANGE:** Mississippi Valley from extr. s. Ill. to the Gulf; extr. sw. Ala. and adj. Fla. to se. Texas.

FLORIDA GREEN WATER SNAKE　　　　　PL. 21; FIG. 55
Nerodia floridana

IDENTIFICATION: 30–55 in. (76–140 cm); record 74 in. (188 cm). A large greenish or brownish serpent (sometimes reddish in southern Florida) without any distinctive markings. Belly plain whitish or cream-colored, except near anus and under tail, where it is patterned like the Mississippi Green Water Snake. A row of scales between eye and upper lip plates (Fig. 55). Scales *keeled;* anal

GREEN
(cyclopion and *floridana)*
Scales between eye and lip plates

BANDED, BROAD-BANDED, and **FLORIDA**
(fasciata subspecies)
Dark stripe from eye to angle of jaw

Fig. 55. *Heads of Water Snakes* (Nerodia).

divided. Young: Ground color brownish- or greenish olive with about 50 black or dark brown bars on each side of body and similar but less conspicuous markings on back; belly yellow, but with black markings near and under tail; 8¾–10 in. (22.4–25.4 cm) at birth.

Habitats include the Everglades and the Okefenokee region, as well as other swamps, marshes, and quiet bodies of water. Sometimes found in brackish water. **SIMILAR SPECIES:** (1) Most other Water Snakes have distinctive patterns, either on their backs or bellies or both. (2) Cottonmouth retreats slowly, and often holds mouth open in readiness to bite when closely approached. **RANGE:** Disjunct; a smaller northern population in s. S.C. and adj. extr. e. Ga.; a larger southern population in Fla. and adj. s. Ga.; absent along the Atlantic Coast from the Ga.-S.C. border to extr. ne. Fla.

BROWN WATER SNAKE *Nerodia taxispilota*   **PL. 21; FIG. 56**
IDENTIFICATION: 30–60 in. (76–152 cm); record 69½ in. (176.6 cm). Often called the "water-pilot," and one of the easiest of all water snakes to mistake for the venomous Cottonmouth. The pattern consists of a series of large, squarish, *dark brown blotches* down middle of back and a similar but alternating row on each side (Fig. 56). Many specimens are exceptionally dark, being deep chocolate brown in gross appearance and with blotches only a little darker than ground color. Belly yellow to brown and boldly marked with spots and half-moons of dark brown or black. The head in this species is distinctly wider than the neck, producing a heart-shaped or diamond-headed appearance (viewed from above) that is mistakenly alleged to occur only in venomous snakes. Scales *keeled;* anal *divided. Young:* 7½–14 in. (19–36 cm) at birth.

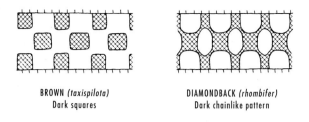

BROWN *(taxispilota)*
Dark squares

DIAMONDBACK *(rhombifer)*
Dark chainlike pattern

Fig. 56. Diagrammatic dorsal patterns of Water Snakes (Nerodia).

A species chiefly of clear, quiet waters. Largely diurnal and a characteristic resident of the great swamps and rivers of the South. An accomplished swimmer and climber, ascending trees to heights of 20 ft. (6 m) or more. Although they flee from people with alacrity, Brown Water Snakes are spirited fighters when seized or cornered. **SIMILAR SPECIES:** (1) Cottonmouth is either virtually plain dark brown or marked with broad crossbands on a lighter (often greenish or olive) ground color; often holds mouth open in readiness to bite when approached. (2) Mississippi and Florida Green Water Snakes have a row of scales between eye and upper labials (Fig. 55). (3) Southern Water Snakes *(fasciata)* often have red in their patterns, and usually show a dark stripe from eye to angle of jaw (Fig. 55). **RANGE:** Se. Va. to sw. Ala. and south to tip of Fla.; chiefly in Coastal Plain, but ascending streams into the Piedmont.

DIAMONDBACK WATER SNAKE   PL. 21; FIGS. 56, 57
Nerodia rhombifer rhombifer
IDENTIFICATION: 30–48 in. (76–122 cm); record 63 in. (160 cm). The light areas on the back may be vaguely diamond-shaped, but the pattern is best described as consisting of *dark brown chainlike markings* on a ground color of lighter brown or dirty yellow (Fig. 56). Belly yellow, marked with black or dark brown spots or half-moons. *Adult male:* Unique among serpents of our area in having numerous raised protuberances (papillae) under chin (Fig. 57). Scales *keeled;* anal *divided. Young:* Strongly patterned, belly often brightly tinged with orange; 8¼–13⅛ in. (21–33.2 cm) at birth.

Throughout most of its range this is a ubiquitous serpent, appearing in many types of aquatic habitats from big lakes and rivers to ditches and cattle tanks. Toward the west, it follows rivers far into otherwise arid terrain. During warm weather it becomes strongly nocturnal. **SIMILAR SPECIES:** Cottonmouth tends to move slowly and often holds mouth open when approached; adult Western Cottonmouths usually are plain black or dark brown, but younger ones are marked with wide dark crossbands on a lighter ground color. **RANGE:** Mississippi Valley from sw. Ind. and extr. se. Iowa to sw. Kans. and south to the Gulf and ne.

DIAMONDBACK WATER SNAKE
Nerodia rhombifer
■ Mexican subspecies

Mexico; absent from much of the Interior Highlands region in Mo. and Ark. Mexican subspecies.

REDBELLY WATER SNAKE

PL. 20

Nerodia erythrogaster erythrogaster

IDENTIFICATION: 30–48 in. (76–122 cm); record 62 in. (157.5 cm). *Belly plain red* or orange-red. Dorsum normally plain brown (pale reddish brown to rich chocolate brown), but often somewhat grayish or greenish on lower sides of body. Scales *keeled*; anal normally *divided* (single in about 10 percent of the specimens of all subspecies of *Nerodia erythrogaster*). *Young:* Boldly patterned, ground color usually pinkish as in young of Blotched Water Snake (top left figure, Pl. 20); lateral blotches *alternate* with larger middorsal ones all the way *forward to head* (or nearly so). Juvenile pattern disappears with age, but traces of it often persist well into young adulthood. About 8–12 in. (20.3–30.6 cm) at birth.

At home in the great river swamps and numerous other aquatic habitats of the Southeast. This serpent often wanders well away from water in hot, humid weather, a habit shared by the several subspecies of this snake. **SIMILAR SPECIES:** (1) Occasional Water Snakes of other species may be uniformly brown above, but they normally have strongly patterned bellies. (2) Certain small serpents, such as the Redbelly Snake and Black Swamp Snake, may have plain dark dorsal surfaces and crimson venters, but, when fully adult, they are of a size comparable with the well-patterned young of the Redbelly Water Snake. (3) Kirtland's Snake has a row of black spots down each side of the belly. **RANGE:** Se. Va. to n. Fla. and se. Ala.; also a population in s. Del. and adj. Md. **SUBSPECIES:** COPPERBELLY WATER SNAKE, *Nerodia e. neglecta*. Similar but darker above (sometimes black); belly often heavily invaded by dorsal ground color; young with the dorsal spots often irregular and running together. Prefers swampy woodlands or river bottoms. W. Ky. and adj. se. Ill. and sw. Ind.; disjunct populations, some now extirpated, in s. Mich., nw. Ohio, and ne. Ind.; isolated colonies in w.-cen. Ohio, s. Ind., n.-cen. Ky., and nw. Tenn.

YELLOWBELLY WATER SNAKE PL. 20
Nerodia erythrogaster flavigaster

IDENTIFICATION: 30–48 in. (76–122 cm); record 59 in. (149.9 cm). A "redbelly" without the red—essentially like the Redbelly Water Snake except in coloration. Dorsum gray or greenish gray, usually plain but sometimes with traces of pattern persisting as light (but dark-bordered) transverse bars across center of back as in the Blotched Water Snake (Fig. 57). Belly plain yellow, often washed with orange; occasionally with dark pigment on bases or ends of ventral scutes. Scales *keeled;* anal usually *divided. Young:* Strongly patterned like young of Blotched Water Snake (Pl. 20); about 9–12 in. (23–30.6 cm) at birth.

A snake of the wetlands of the lower Mississippi Valley and adjacent areas. Usually found in or near the larger, more permanent, bodies of water—in river bottoms, swamps, marshes, and edges of ponds and lakes. **SIMILAR SPECIES:** Adult Water Snakes of other species are sometimes plain dark above, but their bellies are usually boldly marked. **RANGE:** N.-cen. Ga. and w. Ill. to e. Texas and the Gulf; isolated colonies in se. Iowa, nw. Ill., and s.-cen. Mo.

BLOTCHED WATER SNAKE PL. 20; FIG. 57
Nerodia erythrogaster transversa

IDENTIFICATION: 30–48 in. (76–122 cm); record 58 in. (147.3 cm). A race of the "redbelly" in which the blotched pattern of the young persists into adulthood or even throughout life. An extremely vari-

BLOTCHED
(transversa)
Traces of dark-bordered but light
crossbars in middorsal area

DIAMONDBACK
(rhombifer)
Projecting papillae
on chin of male

Fig. 57. Characteristics of Water Snakes (Nerodia).

able snake; general coloration may be almost any shade of gray or brown but with markings darker than background. Occasionally the blotched pattern may virtually disappear, but traces of it remain in the form of short, light, but dark-bordered bars across center of back (Fig. 57). Belly virtually plain yellow, often with an orange tinge; bases of belly scales may be dark, or the dark

coloration of the dorsum may encroach onto edges of the scutes. Underside of tail unpatterned and usually *orange* or *reddish.* Scales *keeled;* anal usually *divided. Young:* Strongly blotched, lateral dark blotches (or spots) alternating with large middorsal blotches all the way forward to the head (or nearly so); 7½–12⅞ in. (19–32.7 cm) at birth.

Likely to be found wherever permanent or semipermanent water occurs—in ditches, cattle tanks, and along streams. Follows rivers, in western part of its range, into what is otherwise decidedly arid country. **SIMILAR SPECIES:** (1) In Northern Water Snake, the lateral blotches unite with the middorsal ones to form dark crossbands on neck and forepart of body; belly is usually strongly patterned with half-moons or other dark markings, and underside of tail is patterned. (2) In Broad-banded Water Snake, dorsal markings are quite large, the venter is boldly patterned, and the head bears a dark stripe from eye to angle of jaw (Fig. 55). **RANGE:** W. Mo. and Kans. to ne. Mexico. Intergrades with Yellowbelly Water Snake over a wide area where their ranges meet, especially in se. Texas and even into extr. sw. La. Mexican subspecies.

NORTHERN WATER SNAKE *Nerodia sipedon sipedon*   **PL. 20**
  IDENTIFICATION: 24–42 in. (61–106.7 cm); record 55⅛ in. (140.5 cm). The only large water snake in most of the northern states, a fortunate thing for northerners, because this reptile exhibits a bewildering array of variations. Farther south, where its range overlaps some of the other species of Water Snakes, one must check the chief diagnostic characters, which are: (a) dark *dorsal* markings on body from neck to anus usually are bands anteriorly, becoming alternating dorsal and lateral blotches posteriorly (rarely completely crossbanded), but total *dorsal* markings (bands plus blotches) on body, from neck to above the anus, usually 30 or more and separated by one scale row or less; (b) light spaces

NORTHERN WATER SNAKES
Nerodia sipedon

CAROLINA NORTHERN
LAKE ERIE MIDLAND

between lateral dark markings usually less than 2½ scale rows wide; (c) reddish- or brownish-centered half-moon and other distinct markings on belly extend past the 50th ventral scute (compare with Carolina Water Snake below); (d) dark pattern on posterior of belly continuous to tip of underside of tail; (e) first 3 to 15 tail markings (counting from the anal plate back) usually composed of alternating dorsal blotches and lateral bars. Ground color varies from pale gray to dark brown, markings from bright reddish brown to black. Adults tend to darken so that the pattern becomes obscure; it may disappear altogether, resulting in a plain black or dark brown serpent. (Putting snake in water will often reveal pattern details in what seems like a virtually unicolored specimen.) Half-moons on belly may be arranged in a regular pattern, scattered at random, represented merely by dusky areas, or be entirely absent. Some specimens have their bellies almost uniformly stippled with gray except for a yellow, orange, or pinkish midventral stripe. Scales *keeled*; anal *divided*. *Young:* Strongly patterned, black on a ground of pale gray or light brown; 7½–10¾ in. (19–27.3 cm) at birth.

A resident of virtually every swamp, marsh, or bog, of every stream, pond, or lake border within its range. Quiet waters are preferred, but swift-flowing streams and the environs of waterfalls also have their quotas of these water snakes—unless they have been exterminated by people or pollution! SIMILAR SPECIES: (1) Banded Water Snake has crossbands throughout length of body, a dark stripe from eye to corner of mouth (Fig. 55), and squarish spots on belly. (2) Copperbelly Water Snake has bright red or orange belly marked only with black or dark brown and usually just at edges of ventral scales, but the dark pigment may often heavily invade belly. (3) Blotched Water Snake has virtually plain yellowish belly, and underside of tail is unpatterned and usually orange or reddish. RANGE: Me. and s. Que. to extr. ne. N.C., including the n. Outer Banks; also the uplands of w. N.C. and adj. portions of Tenn. and Va.; west to e. Colo.; disjunct colonies in n. Colo. and e. Me. Intergrades with the Midland Water Snake over a broad area from se. Okla. to coastal N.C. SUBSPECIES: LAKE ERIE WATER SNAKE, *Nerodia s. insularum.* A pale race in which the pattern is much reduced or completely lacking. General coloration gray (often greenish or brownish); belly white or yellowish and sometimes with a pink or orange tinge down center. Pattern elements, when present, are like those of Northern Water Snake. Islands of Put-in-Bay Archipelago, Lake Erie. CAROLINA WATER SNAKE, *Nerodia s. williamengelsi*. A very dark race; many specimens are almost plain black above. Half-moons on belly solid black except anterior to 50th ventral scale, where some may have brown or reddish centers. Light spaces between dark lateral markings usually 1½ scales or less in width at midbody; on neck, 1½ scales wide. A snake adapted to seaside and estuarine conditions that avoids drinking salt water. S. Outer Banks of e. N.C. and mainland shores of Pamlico and Core sounds.

MIDLAND WATER SNAKE *Nerodia sipedon pleuralis* PL. 20

IDENTIFICATION: 22–40 in. (56–102 cm); record 59 in. (150 cm). Patterned basically like the Northern Water Snake—dark crossbands on the neck and alternating blotches further back. But the dark *dorsal* markings (bands and blotches) on the body, from the neck to above the anus, usually number 30 or less and are separated by more than one scale row, the light spaces between the dark lateral markings are usually more than 2½ scale rows wide, and the tail markings usually consist of complete rings. Occasionally, crossbands continue throughout length of body. General coloration may be brown or gray instead of red, and blotches may even be black. The belly markings tend strongly to be in pairs and do not so often break up and disappear as they do in Northern Water Snake. Scales *keeled*; anal *divided*. *Young:* 7½–12 in. (19–30.6 cm) at birth.

Throughout the bulk of its range, this snake utilizes a wide variety of habitats—streams, ponds, swales, marshes, etc. Toward the south, however, it follows river valleys, in some cases all the way to the Gulf Coast. **SIMILAR SPECIES:** In the Banded Water Snake, crossbands are present throughout the length of body, belly markings tend to be squarish and most prominent at sides, and there is a dark stripe from eye to angle of jaw (Fig. 55). **RANGE:** Midland America, from Ind. to ne. Ark. and the Gulf, and (southeast of the mountains) to the Carolinas.

BANDED WATER SNAKE *Nerodia fasciata fasciata* PL. 20

IDENTIFICATION: 24–42 in. (61–106.7 cm); record 60 in. (152.4 cm). Distinguished by three characteristics: (a) *dark crossbands* (often black-bordered); (b) squarish spots at sides of belly; and (c) dark stripe from eye to angle of jaw (Fig. 55). There is great variation in coloration; crossbands may be red, brown, or black and ground color gray, tan, yellow, or even reddish. Most specimens darken with age, and black pigment tends to obscure the markings, resulting, in extreme cases, in a virtually all-black snake. Even in one of these, however, patches of red or of other light colors usually appear on lower sides of body. Scales *keeled*; anal *divided*. *Young*: Crossbands very dark, usually black, and in strong contrast with pale ground color; 7½–9½ in. (19–24 cm) at birth.

Occupies virtually all types of freshwater habitats, including streams, ponds, lakes, and marshes. **SIMILAR SPECIES:** (1) Northern and Midland Water Snakes normally have dark crossbands only on *forepart* of body; their belly markings include dark or reddish half-moons. (2) See also Cottonmouth (Pl. 34 and Fig. 18). **RANGE:** Coastal Plain, N.C. to s. Ala. Hybridizes with the Northern and Midland Water Snakes in a few localities along the Fall Line in Ga. and the Carolinas and with the Carolina Water Snake in the Sounds region of e. N.C. Intergrades with Broad-banded Water Snake in sw. Ala. and adj. Miss.

FLORIDA WATER SNAKE *Nerodia fasciata pictiventris* **PL. 20**
IDENTIFICATION: 24–42 in. (61–106.7 cm); record 62½ in. (158.8 cm). The Florida member of the "banded" water snake group. As in the others, there are dark crossbands and a dark stripe from eye to angle of jaw (Fig. 55). But it differs in often having *secondary dark spots* on sides of body (between the prominent crossbands) and possessing *wormlike* red or black markings across belly. Coloration and pattern highly variable—black, brown, or reddish markings on a ground color of gray, tan, or reddish. In the redder specimens, black pigment is reduced or even lacking; in darker ones, black obscures the other colors, and virtually plain black specimens are not rare. Scales *keeled*; anal *divided*. *Young*: Red or black crossbands that are in bold contrast with a light ground color; 7½–10½ in. (19–26.6 cm) at birth.

An adult Florida Water Snake from Highlands County, Florida, in an aggressive stance. Members of the water snake genus Nerodia *bite readily, but none are venomous.*

A snake chiefly of shallow-water habitats, of Florida's swamps, marshes, flatwoods ponds, cypress bays, borders of lakes and ponds, rivers, and fresh water in general. **SIMILAR SPECIES:** (1) Florida Green Water Snake has a row of scales between eye and lip plates (Fig. 55). (2) See also Florida Cottonmouth. **RANGE:** Extr. se. Ga. to southern tip of Fla.; introduced in Cameron Co. in extr. s. Texas.

SOUTHERN WATER SNAKES
Nerodia fasciata
■ BROAD-BANDED
■ BANDED ▨ FLORIDA

BROAD-BANDED WATER SNAKE
Nerodia fasciata confluens

PL. 20

IDENTIFICATION: 22–36 in. (56–90 cm); record 45 in. (114.3 cm). None of our other water snakes has such *broad* dark crossbands or so few. They number only 11 to 17 on the body; every other North American *Nerodia* has at least 19 and normally many more than that. The dark crossbands are separated by areas of yellow, irregular in shape and arrangement, and they frequently run together; in coloration they vary from black through brown to rich red-brown (or combinations of these). In some parts of its range, either the yellow or red may be exceptionally prominent, as is reflected in such colorful local names as "yellow moccasin" and "pink flamingo snake." In the lower Mississippi Valley, dark hues predominate, and even the large, squarish belly markings are usu-

The Broad-banded Water Snake is well named. Usually it is easy to identify except in the extreme south where it occasionally hybridizes with the Gulf Salt Marsh Snake to form combinations of stripes and blotches.

ally black or very dark brown. A *dark stripe from eye to angle of mouth* (Fig. 55). Scales *keeled;* anal *divided. Young:* More brightly patterned; 7–9½ in. (18–24 cm) at birth.

A snake of the great watery wilderness of the Mississippi R. delta region, and of marshes, swamps, and shallow bodies of water in general throughout its range. Occurs to very edge of salt or brackish water along Gulf Coast. **SIMILAR SPECIES:** Cottonmouth has broad head and is a stouter, heavier snake with a single row of scales under tail. **RANGE:** Central lowlands from extr. s. Ill. to cen. Texas and Gulf Coast.

GULF SALT MARSH SNAKE *Nerodia clarkii clarkii* PL. 21
IDENTIFICATION: 15–30 in. (38–76 cm); record 36 in. (91.4 cm). The only *striped* water snake normally occurring in a salt- or brackish-water habitat. There are *two* dark brown stripes and *two* tan or yellowish ones on *each* side of body. The very distinctive belly pattern consists of a central row of large white or yellow spots on a ground color of brown or reddish brown; in some specimens there is an extra, smaller row of light spots on each side, making three rows in all. Dorsal scale rows 21 or 23. Scales *keeled;* anal *divided. Young:* 7¾–10½ in. (19.7–26.6 cm) at birth.

An abundant snake of Gulf coastal salt meadows, swamps, and marshes; only rarely enters freshwater habitats. **SIMILAR SPECIES:** (1) Queen Snake and Graham's Crayfish Snake do not have more than 19 dorsal scale rows. (2) Garter Snakes have *single* anal plates and only *one* light stripe on each side of body. **RANGE:** Gulf Coast from w.-cen. Fla. to s. Texas. Hybridizes with Banded and Broad-banded Water Snakes in areas where their freshwater habitats blend into brackish ones. **SUBSPECIES:** ATLANTIC SALT MARSH SNAKE, *Nerodia c. taeniata.* Dorsum striped anteriorly as in Gulf Salt Marsh Snake, but pattern on remainder of body consisting of dark blotches on a light ground color. A row of broad, light yellowish spots down center of belly. Smallest of the races; maximum length 23⅞ in. (60.9 cm). Restricted to Volusia County along the Atlantic Coast of n. Fla. **NOTE:** Water snakes from scattered localities in coastal regions may have aberrant patterns that combine the characteristics of two different species. Some, for example, may be partially blotched or spotted (as in the Banded Water Snakes) and partially striped (as in the Gulf Salt Marsh Snake), and the blotch-stripe combinations can occur at random on any part of the body. Such snakes are often members of hybrid swarms, which are the temporary byproducts of hurricanes that cause severe flooding inland. The consequent heavy runoff carries or rafts (on floating vegetation) freshwater species of *Nerodia* into salt- or brackish-water habitats where they hybridize with the Salt Marsh Snakes.

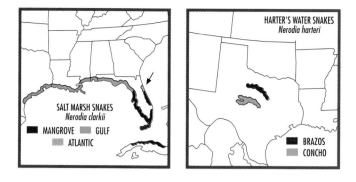

MANGROVE SALT MARSH SNAKE   PL. 21
Nerodia clarkii compressicauda

IDENTIFICATION: 15–30 in. (38–76 cm); record 36¾ in. (93.3 cm). A small snake of the mangrove swamps of Florida's lower coasts. Pattern and coloration extremely variable. Commonly there are *dark spots or crossbands* on a greenish ground color. Stripes may appear on the neck. Some specimens are almost plain black, others straw-colored, and one fairly common variant is virtually plain red or orange-red. Scales *keeled;* anal *divided. Young:* 7–9½ in. (18–24 cm) at birth.

Identification is often best accomplished on basis of habitat. Although it occasionally enters fresh water, as in some ponds on the Florida Keys, this is chiefly a serpent of salt and brackish water, an environment not often invaded by other water snakes native to southern Fla. **SIMILAR SPECIES:** Cottonmouth, which also sometimes occurs in brackish waters, is stout-bodied and has a broad head distinctly wider than neck; often opens mouth in readiness to bite when alarmed. **RANGE:** Both coasts of Fla., from Brevard Co. on the Atlantic to Citrus Co. on the Gulf, and on the Keys; north coast of Cuba. Intergrades with Gulf Salt Marsh Snake north of Tampa Bay, and sometimes hybridizes with Florida Water Snake where salt- and freshwater habitats meet.

HARTER'S WATER SNAKE   *Nerodia harteri*   PL. 21
IDENTIFICATION: 20–30 in. (51–76 cm); record 35½ in. (90.2 cm). Within its range this is the only water snake with *four rows of dark spots* on its back (two rows on each side) and a row of dark dots down each side of a pink or orange belly. (Kirtland's Snake, of the north-central region, is similarly patterned.) Dorsal spots brown on a brownish-gray or slightly greenish ground color. Usually two rows of small scales between the posterior chin shields. Scales

keeled; anal *divided. Young:* 6¾–1 o in. (1 7.2–2 5.4 cm) at birth.

A resident of isolated stream systems in central Texas, occurring in and near both still and fast-moving water. The young are often at shallow riffles where small fishes are easily caught. Named for Philip Harter, snake fancier and collector of Palo Pinto, Texas, who discovered the species. **RANGE:** Brazos and Concho R. systems in cen. Texas. **SUBSPECIES:** B R A Z O S   W A T E R   S N A K E , *Nerodia h. harteri* (Pl. 2 1). As described above. Brazos R. C O N - C H O   W A T E R   S N A K E , *Nerodia h. paucimaculata.* Similar but more reddish in coloration, the dorsal spots less prominent, and the dark dots on the belly inconspicuous or completely absent. A single row of scales between the posterior chin shields. Known only from the Concho-Colorado R. system in cen. Texas. Does not intergrade with the Brazos Water Snake.

CRAYFISH SNAKES: GENUS *Regina*

A group of slender, moderate- to small-sized, semiaquatic to aquatic snakes that live at the margins of streams, along sloughs, bayous, swamps, and bogs, and nearly any other habitat where they can find one of their favorite foods—crayfish (called crawdads in the South). These snakes are good swimmers, but, unlike their cousins the Water Snakes (*Nerodia*), they do not make good captives, often refusing to eat and frequently developing skin lesions when confined in enclosures that do not meet their precise requirements.

All four species of *Regina* have a more or less uniformly dark dorsum, relatively small head (when compared with the Water Snakes), and 1 9 dorsal scale rows, and all but one species has broad, light ventrolateral stripes. Like the Water Snakes, Crayfish Snakes will flatten their bodies when alarmed and, if seized, discharge a foul-smelling musk from glands at the base of the tail. They may bite when first caught, but, unlike the Water Snakes, cannot inflict a painful wound. Some are secretive and seldom seen.

This group of snakes is confined to the eastern U.S., from extreme southern Ontario to southern Fla., and west to the panhandle of Texas.

QUEEN SNAKE *Regina septemvittata* PL. 22

IDENTIFICATION: 1 5–2 4 in. (3 8–6 1 cm); record 3 6¼ in. (9 2.1 cm). A slender, brown aquatic snake with a *yellow stripe* along lower side of body (on 2 nd scale row and upper half of 1 st). Belly yellow but boldly marked with four brown stripes; the two outer stripes are the larger and are situated on the edges of the belly plates (plus lower half of 1st row of scales). Ventral stripes most prominent toward neck; farther back they tend to run together, especially in adults, and to be obscured by a darkening of the ground color. Three additional very narrow dark stripes run down the back but are difficult to see except in specimens that have recently shed their skins. Queen Snakes from the South tend to be nearly unicolored,

QUEEN SNAKE
Regina septemvittata

with indications of pattern remaining only in the neck region. Scales *keeled*; anal *divided*. *Young:* Belly stripes clearly defined, usually all the way to tail; about 6¹³⁄₁₆–10½ in. (17.3–26.6 cm) at birth.

The "willow snake" or "leather snake," as it sometimes is called, likes small stony creeks and rivers, especially those abounding in crayfish, but it is by no means confined to such habitats. Queen Snakes are not usually such conspicuous baskers as the water snakes, and they are more likely to be seen swimming or discovered beneath rocks or debris at the water's edge. They feed very largely on soft-shelled crayfish (ones that have just shed), and so are difficult to keep in captivity. SIMILAR SPECIES: (1) Garter Snakes have *single* anal plates and usually a *light middorsal stripe.* (2) Graham's Crayfish Snake has a broader yellow stripe (on scale rows 1, 2, and 3); its belly is either plain yellow or with a single dark area or row of spots down the center. (3) Glossy Crayfish Snake and Lined Snake each have a *double* row of black belly spots. (4) Gulf Salt Marsh Snake has brown or black belly with one or three rows of yellow spots down center. RANGE: S. Ont., sw. N.Y., and se. Pa. south to Gulf Coast at Fla.-Ala. border; west to se. Wisc. and e. Miss. A disjunct area in Ark. and sw. Mo., but it may be extinct in the latter state; an isolated colony in n. Mich.; an isolated record in extr. sw. Miss.

GRAHAM'S CRAYFISH SNAKE *Regina grahamii* **PL. 22**
IDENTIFICATION: 18–28 in. (45.7–71 cm); record 47 in. (119.4 cm). Look for two pattern characteristics: (a) *broad, yellow stripe* on scale rows 1, 2, and 3; and (b) narrow, black stripe where lowermost row of scales meets belly plates (stripe often zigzag or irregular). Sometimes a dark-bordered, pale stripe down center of back. Belly yellowish, either plain or marked with dark dots or a dull dark area down center. A dark color variant of this snake occurs in

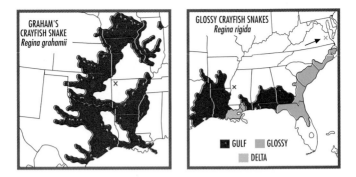

GRAHAM'S CRAYFISH SNAKE
Regina grahamii

GLOSSY CRAYFISH SNAKES
Regina rigida

■ GULF ■ GLOSSY
  DELTA

Iowa in which entire dorsal surface is brown and pattern details can be made out only with difficulty; belly is deep olive-buff, chin and throat yellow. Scales *keeled;* anal *divided. Young:* About 7½–10 in. (19–25.4 cm) at birth.

Found at margins of ponds and streams, along sloughs and bayous, and in swamps. Sometimes basks but is more apt to be found by overturning stones and debris at water's edge. May hide in holes in muddy stream banks or in crayfish chimneys. Food includes crayfish and other crustaceans, plus small amphibians and fish. Named for James Duncan Graham, a professional soldier and engineer, who was in the field with the U.S. and Mexican Boundary Survey in the early 1850s. **SIMILAR SPECIES:** (1) Queen Snake has four brown stripes down belly, and yellow side stripe is on scale rows 1 and 2. (2) Garter Snakes have *single* anal plates and usually a prominent light stripe down center of back. **RANGE:**

A subadult Graham's Crayfish Snake from Linn County, Kansas. This serpent feeds almost exclusively on crayfish.

Iowa and Ill. to La. and Texas; absent from much of the Interior Highlands region in Mo., Ark., and Okla.; an isolated colony in ne. Ill.; an isolated record in nw. Ark.

GLOSSY CRAYFISH SNAKE   *Regina rigida*   PL. 22

IDENTIFICATION: 14–24 in. (36–61 cm); record 31⅜ in. (79.7 cm). A *shiny* snake, more or less plain brown or olive-brown, but dark stripes may be faintly evident on back or (more strongly so) on lower sides of body. The two rows of black spots down the belly are bold and distinct even in large specimens, in which the center portion of belly may become clouded with dark pigment. Scales *keeled*; anal *divided*. *Young:* About 6½–9 in. (16.5–22.7 cm) at birth.

A secretive snake of the southern lowlands, rarely seen in the open except at night or after heavy rains. Decidedly aquatic, its habits resembling those of the Swamp Snakes. Food is predominantly crayfish, but some frogs, salamanders, and small fishes are also taken. **SIMILAR SPECIES:** (1) Garter Snakes, (2) Lined Snakes, (3) Striped Crayfish Snake, and (4) Salt Marsh Snakes have prominent *light* stripes. **RANGE:** Coastal Plain; N.C. to n.-cen. Fla. and west to e.-cen. Texas; isolated records in w.-cen. Miss. and e. Va. **SUBSPECIES:** GLOSSY CRAYFISH SNAKE, *Regina r. rigida* (Pl. 22). A pattern of narrow, dusky stripes following edges of scales on sides of throat; subcaudals usually 54 or fewer in females; 62 or fewer in males. Atlantic Coastal Plain from N.C. to n.-cen. Fla.; an isolated colony in e. Va. GULF CRAYFISH SNAKE, *Regina r. sinicola.* No pattern on sides of throat; subcaudals usually 55 or more in females; 63 or more in males. Two disjunct areas, one from Gulf Coastal Plain of sw. Ga. to se. Miss.; the other from most of La. west to e.-cen. Texas and se. Okla., and north to s. Ark.; isolated record in w.-cen. Miss. DELTA CRAYFISH SNAKE, *Regina r. deltae.* Only one preocular scale on at least one side of head (two on both sides in other races); number of subcaudals subtracted from number of ventrals usually 81 or more in females; 73 or more in males (fewer in other races). Se. La. and adj. Miss.

STRIPED CRAYFISH SNAKE   *Regina alleni*   PL. 22

IDENTIFICATION: 13–20 in. (33–51 cm); record 25¾ in. (65.4 cm). Shiniest of all the Crayfish Snakes. A brown, chiefly aquatic snake with a *broad, yellowish stripe* along the lower side of body. Three relatively inconspicuous dark stripes on back, one middorsal and the others lateral. Belly normally yellowish and virtually unmarked, but it may be orange or orange-brown instead, and the same color may also replace the yellow of the lateral stripe. Dark

STRIPED CRAYFISH SNAKE
Regina alleni

midventral markings, when present, may vary from a few scattered smudges to a long, well-defined row of spots. Head small in proportion to size of body; nasal scales on head arranged in unorthodox fashion; *only one internasal scute* and the two nasal scutes *meet each other* on the middorsal line of the snout. Scales *smooth* except in anal region and on top of tail, where they are keeled. Anal *divided. Young:* Like adults; 6¼–7 in. (15.9–18 cm) at birth.

At home in dense vegetation in shallow water. Sometimes found by hauling masses of water hyacinths ashore and then sorting through them. Habitats include sloughs and marshes, bayheads and sphagnum bogs. At twilight, especially on rainy or humid evenings, Striped Crayfish Snakes sometimes travel overland and may be seen on roads paralleling or traversing wet prairies or marshes. Food consists primarily of crayfish; the jaws are powerful enough to hold and engulf them even when hardshelled. **SIMILAR SPECIES:** (1) Garter and (2) Ribbon Snakes have *keeled* scales and *single* anal plates. **RANGE:** Extr. s. Ga. and peninsular Fla.

KIRTLAND'S AND SWAMP SNAKES: GENERA *Clonophis* AND *Seminatrix*

Two genera of small, secretive snakes, each with one species, both of which have red bellies. Kirtland's Snake, genus *Clonophis*, is a resident of meadows, seasonally marshy areas, and hillsides of the midwestern United States, and often is also found beneath debris in parks in urban areas. Once considered a relative of the Water Snakes, it is now placed in a genus of its own and is apparently more closely related to the Lined Snake and Brown Snakes. The Black Swamp Snake, genus *Seminatrix*, is a resident of coastal lowland swamps in the southeastern United States and is probably now more abundant than it was before the introduction of the water hyacinth from Venezuela in 1884. The enormous mats formed by these floating plants provide shelter among their roots and leaves for a veritable menagerie of small aquatic and semiaquatic animals, including several kinds of snakes, frogs, and salamanders.

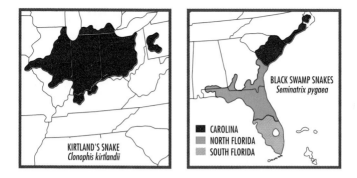

KIRTLAND'S SNAKE
Clonophis kirtlandii

BLACK SWAMP SNAKES
Seminatrix pygaea

- CAROLINA
- NORTH FLORIDA
- SOUTH FLORIDA

KIRTLAND'S SNAKE *Clonophis kirtlandii*   **PL. 22**

IDENTIFICATION: 14–18 in. (36–45.7 cm); record 24½ in. (62.2 cm). The reddish *belly with a prominent row of round, black spots* down each side is the best check. The four rows of dark spots on the back are not always conspicuous. They show best when the skin is stretched, when the body, for example, is distended by food or by pregnancy. In a relatively few specimens, the dark spots of the two central rows become small and indistinct, especially toward the rear of body, and the reddish-brown ground color may appear as a light middorsal stripe. Scales *keeled;* anal *divided. Young:* Dark and virtually unicolored above (unless skin is stretched); belly deep red; about 4½–6½ in. (11.5–16.5 cm) at birth.

Flattening of the body when alarmed, a trait shared by Water Snakes, Garter Snakes, Brown Snakes, and many other species found within the area encompassed by this Field Guide, is developed to a remarkable degree in this species. Some specimens can make themselves almost ribbonlike, and they may remain rigidly immobile until touched or otherwise disturbed. Often found in or near wet meadows and open swamp-forest habitats, but also on sparsely wooded slopes of hillsides and in adjacent meadows, particularly in parks in urban areas. Feeds on earthworms and slugs. Named for Jared P. Kirtland, early Ohio physician and naturalist. **SIMILAR SPECIES:** Northern Redbelly Snake lacks conspicuous black spots, either above or below. **RANGE:** Most of Ohio to ne. Mo.; s. Mich. to w.-cen. Ky.; large disjunct area in w. Pa.

BLACK SWAMP SNAKE *Seminatrix pygaea*   **PL. 22**

IDENTIFICATION: 10–15 in. (25.4–38 cm); record 18¼ in. (47 cm). A *shiny black* aquatic snake with a *red belly.* Scales *smooth,* but each scale of the 3 to 5 lowermost rows bears a light, longitudinal line that *looks* like a keel. Anal *divided. Young:* Like adults; 4¼–5¹⁵⁄₁₆ in. (10.7–15.1 cm).

Often common in areas where water hyacinths abound. Dragging hyacinths ashore is one way to search for them. They often hide under boards and debris at water's edge, and on rainy or dewy nights may wander overland. The environs of cypress ponds are a natural habitat, and probably were one of the most important before the pestiferous hyacinth was introduced. Food includes leeches, small fish, worms, tadpoles, Dwarf Sirens, and other small salamanders. **SIMILAR SPECIES:** Redbelly Snake has *keeled* scales. **RANGE:** Coastal N.C. to s. Fla. **SUBSPECIES:** NORTH FLORIDA SWAMP SNAKE, *Seminatrix p. pygaea* (Pl. 22). Belly plain red or with pair of black bars on base of each ventral scale; ventrals 118 to 124. N. Fla., extr. s. Ala., and s. Ga. SOUTH FLORIDA SWAMP SNAKE, *Seminatrix p. cyclas.* A short, triangular black mark at forward edge of each ventral scale; ventrals 117 or fewer. Southern half of Fla. peninsula. CAROLINA SWAMP SNAKE, *Seminatrix p. paludis.* A pair of black bars on each ventral scale; ventrals 127 or more. Chiefly the Coastal Plain of S.C. to extr. e. N.C.

BROWN SNAKES: GENUS *Storeria*

These are small, secretive snakes, usually brown but sometimes gray or reddish in dorsal coloration. Scales *keeled,* anal *divided,* and no loreal scale (Fig. 13, opp. Pl. 22). Several other small brown or gray snakes of other genera resemble them, so recourse to checking scale characteristics, especially whether a loreal is present or not, is often necessary.

Brown Snakes, like the Garter and Water Snakes to which they are related, may flatten their bodies when alarmed. They also use their anal scent glands when picked up, but the odor is not particularly offensive. Food includes slugs, earthworms, and soft-bodied insects. The genus ranges from Canada to Honduras.

NORTHERN BROWN SNAKE *Storeria dekayi dekayi*   PL. 22
IDENTIFICATION: 9–13 in. (23–33 cm); record 19⅜ in. (49.2 cm). Formerly called "DeKay's snake" after James Edward DeKay, an early naturalist of New York. This is the little brown snake with two parallel rows of blackish spots down the back. A few of the spots may be linked with their partners across the dorsum by narrow lines of dark pigment. General coloration varies from light yellowish brown or gray to dark brown or deep reddish brown. The middorsal area, for a width of about four scales, is almost always lighter in color than sides of body. The small, dark lateral spots

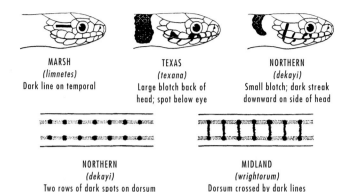

MARSH
(limnetes)
Dark line on temporal

TEXAS
(texana)
Large blotch back of
head; spot below eye

NORTHERN
(dekayi)
Small blotch; dark streak
downward on side of head

NORTHERN
(dekayi)
Two rows of dark spots on dorsum

MIDLAND
(wrightorum)
Dorsum crossed by dark lines

Fig. 58. *Head and dorsal patterns of subspecies of the Brown Snake* (Storeria dekayi).

may be inconspicuous unless skin is stretched. A *dark downward streak* on side of head (Fig. 58). Belly pale yellowish, brownish, or pinkish, unmarked except for one or more small black dots at side of each ventral scale. Scales *keeled* and in 17 rows; anal *divided*. *Young:* Conspicuous yellowish collar across neck; general coloration darker than in adults and with spotted pattern scarcely evident; 2¾–4⁷⁄₁₆ in. (7–11.3 cm) at birth.

Before the days of bad pollution and the massive use of pesticides, this reptile could almost have been called the "city snake" because of the frequency with which it turned up in parks, cemeteries, and beneath trash in empty lots, even in large urban centers. Although still a common snake in some areas, even in close proximity to people, it is so adept at hiding that few persons know it, and those who encounter it for the first time may mistake it for a baby Garter Snake. Habitats (away from cities) include environs of bogs, swamps, freshwater marshes, moist woods, hillsides, etc. **SIMILAR SPECIES:** (1) Earth Snakes (*Virginia*) have a long, horizontal loreal scale—see Fig. 13, opp. Pl. 22. (2) Ground Snake (*Sonora*) and Worm Snakes (*Carphophis*) have *smooth* scales. (3) Redbelly Snake has 15 scale rows and (normally) a red belly. (4) Garter Snakes have *single* anal plates and (usually) a light stripe on each side of body. (5) Ringneck Snake (easily confused with a young Brown Snake) has *smooth* scales. **RANGE:** S. Me. and s. Canada to N.C.; an isolated colony in sw. Va. Intergradation among the several races of this species occurs over such enormous areas that accurate delineation of the ranges is difficult. In some instances

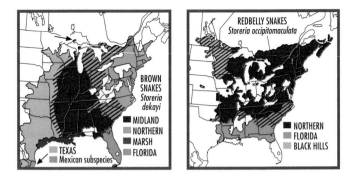

BROWN SNAKES
Storeria dekayi

- ■ MIDLAND
- ■ NORTHERN
- ■ MARSH
- ■ FLORIDA

TEXAS
Mexican subspecies

REDBELLY SNAKES
Storeria occipitomaculata

- ■ NORTHERN
- ■ FLORIDA
- ■ BLACK HILLS

it may be practical simply to designate specimens as Brown Snakes without attempting to assign them to subspecies. **SUB-SPECIES:** MIDLAND BROWN SNAKE, *Storeria d. wrightorum.* Record length 20¾ in. (52.7 cm). Very similar but with numerous dark crosslines (Fig. 58). E. Wisc. to the Carolinas and Gulf Coast; isolated colonies in the Upper Peninsula of Mich. TEXAS BROWN SNAKE, *Storeria d. texana.* Record length 18 in. (45.9 cm). Similar to the northern subspecies, with two rows of dark spots down back; no dark line on temporal scale, but a large dark spot under eye. Also, spot behind head is large and extends downward to belly scales (Fig. 58). W. Wisc. to Texas and ne. Mexico; isolated colony in w.-cen. Texas. MARSH BROWN SNAKE, *Storeria d. limnetes.* Record length 16⅕ in. (40.8 cm). A median dark line through the axis of temporal scale, and no dark markings on 6th and 7th upper or lower labials (Fig. 58). Restricted chiefly to the salt marshes from Mobile Bay, Ala. to Texas where it occurs on levees and in muskrat houses.

FLORIDA BROWN SNAKE *Storeria dekayi victa* **PL. 22**
IDENTIFICATION: 9–13 in. (23–33 cm); record 19 in. (48.3 cm). The broad, light band across the back of the head, heavy dark pigment on the lip scales below the eye, and a double row of small black spots at each side of the belly are all present in typical specimens, but this Brown Snake is subject to many variations. Some individuals closely resemble Midland Brown Snake in pattern and coloration, but others have the markings greatly reduced. *Most constant character* is number of dorsal scale rows — 15 as opposed to 17 in all other subspecies of *Storeria dekayi.* Florida Brown Snake also tends to be more slender than the others. Scales *keeled;* anal *divided. Young:* Similar to adults, but much darker; a prominent

light band across back of head; 3⁵⁄₁₆–4¼ in. (8.4–10.7 cm) at birth.

A resident of bogs and marshes, river-bottom swamps, and environs of ponds and sloughs, but also occurring in upland hammocks and the pineland-prairie region of s. Fla. Often hides among water hyacinths. Most likely to be seen abroad on warm, rainy, or humid nights on roads that traverse or parallel marshy bodies of water. **SIMILAR SPECIES:** (1) Pine Woods and Crowned Snakes have *smooth* scales. (2) Earth Snakes have a horizontal loreal scale (Fig. 13, opp. Pl. 22). (3) Florida Redbelly Snake (some of them do not have red bellies!) shows a light collar across neck (not back of head) and there is a light spot on the 5th upper lip (labial) scale. **RANGE:** Se. Ga. and peninsular Fla.; lower Keys.

REDBELLY SNAKE *Storeria occipitomaculata* **PL. 22**

IDENTIFICATION: 8–10 in. (20.3–25.4 cm); record 16 in. (40.6 cm). The two key characters—a plain *red belly* and *three pale-colored nape spots*—are usually present, but this small snake is subject to great variation. Dorsum normally plain brown except for indications of four narrow, dark stripes or a broad, fairly light middorsal stripe, or both. Many specimens are gray; a few are black, and in extreme cases the belly may be blue-black. The belly color, normally bright red, may vary through orange to pale yellow. The three light spots may fuse together (especially in the Florida subspecies) to form a light collar across neck. Two preoculars. Scales *keeled* and in 15 rows; anal *divided*. *Young:* Similar, but darker than adults; 2¾–4 in. (7–10 cm) at birth.

A secretive snake of spotty distribution, common in some localities but rare or lacking in others that seem to offer identical habitats. Particularly abundant in many mountainous or upland parts

An adult Redbelly Snake showing its namesake belly.

of the Northeast. Often found in or near open woods, but also occurring in or near sphagnum bogs from sea level to high in the mountains. **SIMILAR SPECIES:** (1) Kirtland's Snake has double row of black spots down belly. (2) Black Swamp Snake has *smooth* scales. **RANGE:** Nova Scotia to cen. Fla.; west to se. Sask., ne. N.D., e. S.D., and the eastern parts of Kans., Okla., and Texas; disjunct area in the Black Hills of S.D. and Wyo.; isolated colonies in s.-cen. Neb., ne. Mo., and nw. Ohio. Absent from large areas of the eastern U.S. **SUBSPECIES:** NORTHERN REDBELLY SNAKE, *Storeria o. occipitomaculata* (Pl. 22). The three light nape spots are usually well defined; moderate amount of black pigment on sides and back of head; a light mark on the 5th upper labial, which is *bordered below by black.* All of range except the Black Hills and the Southeast from n. Fla. to e. Texas; absent from much of w. Ohio, Ind., and Ill. FLORIDA REDBELLY SNAKE, *Storeria o. obscura.* Spots fused to form a light collar across neck; top and sides of head black; a light spot on 5th upper labial extending downward to edge of mouth. N. Fla. and s. Ga., west to e. Texas; absent from nw. Ala., cen. Miss., and ne. La. BLACK HILLS REDBELLY SNAKE, *Storeria o. pahasapae.* Light nape spots very small or lacking; no light spot on 5th upper labial. Wooded portions of the Black Hills in extr. w. S.D. and adj. Wyo.; intergrades extensively with Northern Redbelly Snake in Canada, ne. N.D., Minn., and nw. Iowa.

GARTER, RIBBON, AND LINED SNAKES: GENUS *Thamnophis* AND *Tropidoclonion*

Like the fancy garters that once were fashionable for supporting gentlemen's socks, most of these snakes are longitudinally striped. The positions of the light lateral stripes (one on each side of the body) and whether they are encroached upon by the dark pattern are useful in telling one species of Garter Snake from another. To locate the stripe accurately, count upward from the large belly scales (the ventrals). "Stripe on rows 3 and 4," for example, means that the light lateral stripe is on the 3rd and 4th rows of scales above the ventrals. (See Fig. 14, opp. Pl. 24.) Count ¼ of the way back on the body. Most garter snakes have two very small white or yellow spots on top of their heads.

When alarmed, many specimens flatten their bodies, making the pattern seem particularly vivid. When first captured, they discharge musk from glands at the base of the tail that has an unpleasant, sweetish odor. Many are docile, but others may strike and bite vigorously in self-defense.

Natural foods consist chiefly of frogs, toads, salamanders, fish, tadpoles, and earthworms, but other items, including leeches, small mammals, birds, and carrion, are eaten occasionally. Captives usually learn to accept chopped fresh fish. (Be sure to include the entrails.)

Garter and Ribbon Snakes are closely allied to the Water Snakes (*Nerodia*), but, unlike Water Snakes, they almost always have *single* anal plates. (See p. 139.) Members of the group are often found near water, especially in the arid or semiarid West, with the inevitable result of their being called "water snakes" by persons not acquainted with representatives of the genus *Nerodia*. In the more humid East, Garter (sometimes called "garden") Snakes may occur almost anywhere, from sea level to high in the mountains. The genus ranges from coast to coast across both southern Canada and the United States and southward to Costa Rica.

The diminutive Lined Snake, the only member of the genus *Tropidoclonion*, strongly resembles the Garter Snakes and shares most of their characteristics. It ranges widely across the plains and prairies of the central United States.

EASTERN GARTER SNAKE *Thamnophis sirtalis sirtalis* **PL. 23**
IDENTIFICATION: 18–26 in. (45.7–66 cm); record 48¾ in. (123.8 cm). The *only* Garter Snake throughout most of its range with lateral stripes *confined to rows 2 and 3*. Extremely variable in coloration and pattern; either stripes or spots may predominate. Normally three yellowish stripes, but they may be brownish, greenish, or bluish instead. Ground color black, dark brown, green, or olive. Usually a double row of alternating black spots between stripes, the spots sometimes very prominent and invading the stripes; occasional specimens are virtually stripeless. Belly greenish or yellowish, with two rows of indistinct black spots partially hidden under overlapping portions of ventrals. Some individuals, especially from western part of range, have red or orange on skin between dorsal scales. Jet-black (melanistic) specimens are found occasionally, especially near shores of Lake Erie. Scales *keeled*; anal *single*. *Young:* 5–9 in. (12.5–23 cm) at birth.

A well-known and common snake occupying a wide variety of habitats — meadows, marshes, woodlands, hillsides, along streams and drainage ditches, and sometimes even in city lots, parks, and cemeteries if pollution is not too severe. **SIMILAR SPECIES:** (1) All other Garter Snakes within the range have lateral stripes involving row 4, at least on neck —except Shorthead Garter Snake, which is distinguished by small head and low number (17) of scale rows (19 in Eastern Garter). (2) The Crayfish Snakes (*Regina*) and Gulf Salt Marsh Snake all have *divided* anal plates,

GARTER SNAKES
Thamnophis sirtalis

- ■ RED-SIDED
- EASTERN
- MARITIME
- TEXAS
- CHICAGO
- ■ BLUESTRIPE
- NEW MEXICO
- Western subspecies
- Mexican subspecies

and most of them have *strongly patterned* bellies. (3) Brown Snakes lack light *lateral* stripes and loreal scales (Fig. 13, opp. Pl. 22). **RANGE:** S. Canada north of the Great Lakes to Gulf of Mexico and west to Minn. and e. Texas. **SUBSPECIES:** MARITIME GARTER SNAKE, *Thamnophis s. pallidulus*. A resident of the extr. Northeast, this race reaches a maximum length of 36 in. (91.7 cm). Gray, tan, or yellow dorsal stripe often lacking or present only anteriorly and poorly developed; whitish, gray or tan lateral stripes more distinct but often merging into darker shade below with little contrast; dorsolateral ground color cinnamon brown, yellowish olive, or olive-gray with alternating rows of black or dark brown spots in a checkered pattern; belly whitish anteriorly, becoming dusky gray posteriorly. *Young:* 5⁵⁄₁₆–7½ in. (13.5–19 cm) at birth. S. Que., from the e. shore of James Bay east to the Gulf of St. Lawrence and Nova Scotia, and south in New England to extr. ne. Mass.

CHICAGO GARTER SNAKE
Thamnophis sirtalis semifasciatus

IDENTIFICATION: 18–26 in. (45.7–66 cm); record 35⅝ in. (90.5 cm). The lateral stripes on the forepart of the body are interrupted at regular intervals by *vertical black crossbars,* which are formed by the fusion of the black spots immediately above and below the light stripe. Also, in many specimens, one or more narrow, black lines may cross middorsal stripe in neck region. Otherwise similar to Eastern Garter Snake. **RANGE:** Ne. Ill. and small adj. portions of Ind. and Wisc.

RED-SIDED GARTER SNAKE
Thamnophis sirtalis parietalis

IDENTIFICATION: 16–26 in. (41–66 cm); record 48⅞ in. (124.1 cm). The *red or orange bars* vary in size and intensity, so some specimens are redder than others. In many, red is largely confined to skin between scales. General ground color olive, brown, or black, the dark pigment sometimes invading much of belly. Lateral stripes on rows 2 and 3; all three stripes may be yellow, orange-yellow, bluish, or greenish. Scales *keeled;* anal *single. Young:* 5⅚–8 in. (13.5–20.3 cm) at birth.

In the eastern part of the range, this snake is widespread and common in such habitats as prairie swales, along ditches paralleling railroads, the environs of ponds, etc. Farther west it may occur wherever water is found, and it follows watercourses, even intermittent ones, far into arid country. **SIMILAR SPECIES:** (1) All other Garter Snakes within the range of this one lack red bars. (2) Plains Garter Snake and Ribbon Snakes have the light lateral stripes on rows 3 and 4. **RANGE:** Extr. s. Dis. of Mack. of the N.W. Terr. and e.-cen. B.C. to Okla.; an isolated colony in sw. Sask. Western subspecies.

NEW MEXICO GARTER SNAKE
Thamnophis sirtalis dorsalis

IDENTIFICATION: 18–28 in. (45.7–71 cm); record 51⅛ in. (131.1 cm). Similar to the Red-sided Garter Snake but with the red more subdued and largely confined to the skin between the scales, which may be chiefly black in the middorsal region. In some specimens the red is reduced, the stripes are especially prominent, and the general appearance may be greenish. Lateral stripes on scale rows 2 and 3. Belly bluish or brownish, unmarked or with dark spots on edges. Scales *keeled;* anal *single. Young:* Similar but occasionally rusty orange in coloration; about 6–8 in. (15.2–20.3 cm) at birth.

Found in marshy swales and depressions and irrigation ditches, less often in running water. **RANGE:** Rio Grande Valley from extr. n.-

cen. N.M. south to vicinity of El Paso, Texas; disjunct population in ne. N.M. Mexican subspecies.

TEXAS GARTER SNAKE *Thamnophis sirtalis annectens* **PL. 24**
IDENTIFICATION: 18–25 in. (45.7–63.5 cm); record 42¾ in. (108.9 cm). The unusually *broad, orange middorsal stripe* is characteristic. On forward third of body the lateral stripes involve row 3, plus adjacent parts of rows 2 and 4. Scales *keeled*; anal *single*. *Young:* 6¹⁵⁄₁₆–8³⁄₁₆ in. (17.6–22.2 cm) at birth. **SIMILAR SPECIES AND SUBSPECIES:** In Red-sided Garter Snake, the lateral stripes do not include row 4. (2) Eastern Blackneck Garter Snake has *single* row of large black spots on each side of neck. (3) Western Ribbon Snake is more slender, and lateral stripes do not involve scale row 2. (4) Checkered Garter Snake has a light curved band behind mouth followed by a broad, dark blotch. **RANGE:** E.-cen. Texas; disjunct population in sw. Kans., adj. Okla., and Texas panhandle.

BLUESTRIPE GARTER SNAKE **PL. 23**
Thamnophis sirtalis similis
IDENTIFICATION: 20–26 in. (51–66 cm); record 39¼ in. (99.7 cm). An extraordinary "mimic" of the Bluestripe Ribbon Snake. They occur together, and positive identification often requires checking the position of the lateral stripe—on *rows 2 and 3* in the garter snake and 3 and 4 in the ribbon snake. Dorsum dark brown or *very* dark brown; middorsal stripe dull tan or yellowish; lateral stripes light blue or bluish white. Scales *keeled*; anal *single*. *Young:* 7¼–9⅛ in. (18.4–23.2 cm) at birth.

Occurs in marshes, pine flatwoods, etc. in the coastal lowlands of nw. peninsular Fla. Usually far less abundant than the Bluestripe Ribbon Snake. **RANGE:** W. Fla. from Wakulla Co. to the Withlacoochee R.

PLAINS GARTER SNAKE *Thamnophis radix* **PL. 24**
IDENTIFICATION: 15–28 in. (38–71 cm); record 43 in. (109.5 cm). This one may be troublesome. First check the stripe—it is on rows 3 and 4. Then look for black markings—*black bars on lips,* a double alternating row of black spots between stripes, a row of black spots *below* each lateral stripe, and a row of dark, often indefinite, spots down each side of belly. Dorsal ground color brown, greenish, or (rarely) reddish, but some specimens are so dark that part of the markings may be obscured. Dorsal stripe may be bright yellow or orange, lateral ones greenish or bluish. Scales *keeled* in a maximum of 21 rows; anal *single*. *Young:* 5¹⁵⁄₁₆–7½ in. (15.1–19 cm) at birth.

An abundant snake throughout much of its range, and especially common in river valleys and near prairie ponds and sloughs. Formerly common in open lots and parks in many large cities, but now greatly reduced in numbers in such habitats because of building activities and the widespread use of pesticides. **SIMILAR SPECIES:** (1) Lateral stripes involve row 2 and maximum number of scale rows is only 19 in most other Garter snakes (Eastern,

WESTERN
EASTERN

PLAINS GARTER SNAKES
Thamnophis radix

Red-sided, Butler's) occurring within the range of this one. (2) Checkered Garter Snake has a yellow curve or triangle behind mouth followed by a broad dark blotch. (3) Ribbon Snakes, with lateral stripes on rows 3 and 4, are slender and their tails are long —¼ or more of total length. (4) Wandering Garter Snake has lateral stripes on rows 2 and 3, and 21 rows of scales at midbody. **RANGE:** Nw. Ind. to Rocky Mts. and from s. Alberta to ne. N.M.; disjunct, relictual colonies in n.-cen. Ohio and on Mo.-Ill. border. **SUBSPECIES:** EASTERN PLAINS GARTER SNAKE, *Thamnophis r. radix* (Pl. 24). Ventral scales usually 154 or fewer; scale rows on neck usually 19. N.-cen. Ohio; nw. Ind. to Iowa and adj. states. WESTERN PLAINS GARTER SNAKE, *Thamnophis r. haydenii*. Similar but with black spots between stripes somewhat smaller. Ventral scales usually 155 or more; scale rows on neck usually 21. Minn., Iowa, and nw. Mo. to the Rockies; prairie parts of Canada to ne. N.M. and extr. n. Texas.

An adult Plains Garter Snake. Along the streams of the western areas covered by the field guide, this serpent replaces the more familiar water snakes of eastern North America.

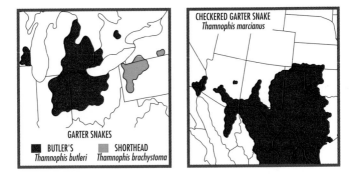

BUTLER'S GARTER SNAKE *Thamnophis butleri*   **PL. 23**

IDENTIFICATION: 15–20 in. (38–51 cm); record 27¼ in. (69.2 cm). A curious method of crawling when excited—as when trying to escape—is a good field character. The body wriggles vigorously from side to side, but the rather meager forward progress is out of all proportion to the amount of energy expended. *Head small;* lateral stripe (on neck) on row 3 and adjacent halves of rows 2 and 4. Lateral stripes may be orange. Dorsal ground color variable— olive-brown to black —and it may or may not show a double row of black spots between the stripes. Scales *keeled;* anal *single. Young:* 5–7 in. (12.5–18 cm) at birth.

Chiefly a snake of open, prairie-like areas. Common in some localities but rare or completely lacking over many parts of its range. Named for Amos Butler, early Indiana naturalist. **SIMILAR SPECIES:** (1) Eastern Garter Snake has lateral stripes on rows 2 and 3. (2) Plains Garter Snake has lateral stripes on rows 3 and 4, and there are usually prominent black spots both above *and* below the stripes. (3) See also Shorthead Garter Snake. **RANGE:** Ohio, extr. s. Ont., and e. Mich. to cen. Ind.; disjunct colonies in se. Wisc. and s. Ont.

SHORTHEAD GARTER SNAKE   **PL. 23**
Thamnophis brachystoma

IDENTIFICATION: 14–18 in. (36–45.7 cm); record 22 in. (55.9 cm). Smallest of the eastern Garter Snakes and the one with the most restricted range. *Head short* and no wider than neck. A tendency for each lateral stripe to be bordered by a narrow, dark line. Lateral stripe (on neck) on rows 2 and 3 but occasionally involving lower part of row 4. Dark spots between stripes, so common in many other kinds of garter snakes, are lacking or only faintly indicated. Scales *keeled;* anal *single. Young:* 4¹⁵⁄₁₆–6¼ in. (12.4–15.9 cm) at birth.

A snake of the Allegheny High Plateau. Low herbaceous cover, such as in meadows and old fields, is preferred. Food consists very largely of earthworms. **SIMILAR SPECIES:** Butler's Garter Snake has the lateral stripe on same scale rows, but head is somewhat larger and a trifle wider than neck; also, dark spots may appear between stripes. If any doubt remains, count dorsal scale rows; maximum number normally is 17 in Shorthead and 19 in both Butler's and Eastern Garter Snakes. The stripe in the latter does *not* involve row 4. **RANGE:** Sw. N.Y. and nw. Pa.; introduced and established at Pittsburgh, apparently also in Butler and Erie cos., Pa., and in s.-cen. N.Y.

CHECKERED GARTER SNAKE PL. 24
Thamnophis marcianus marcianus

IDENTIFICATION: 18–24 in. (45.7–61 cm); record 42½ in. (108 cm). The garter snake with the *checkerboard pattern.* Black, squarish spots often strongly invade the light stripes. On each side of head behind mouth there is a *yellowish curve or triangle,* followed by a large dark blotch. Lateral stripe on row 3 near head; on rows 2 and 3 farther back. Scales *keeled* in a maximum of 21 rows; anal *single. Young:* 6¼–9¼ in. (15.9–23.5 cm) at birth.

A snake of the southern plains and the Edwards Plateau; also widely distributed through the arid Southwest, where it seldom strays far from streambeds, springs, irrigation ditches, or other places where water may be present—at least beneath the surface. **SIMILAR SPECIES:** Plains Garter Snake may have a suggestion of a yellowish curve behind head, but lateral stripes involve row 4, and

An adult female Checkered Garter Snake from Comanche County, Kansas.

middorsal stripe is normally straight-edged (usually jagged-edged in Checkered Garter). **RANGE:** E.-cen. Texas to s. Kans. and west to s.-cen. Ariz.; south to nw. Zacatecas and extr. n. Veracruz; isolated colonies in e.-cen. Ariz., se. Calif., sw. Ariz. and adj. Mexico, and in the vicinity of Tehuantepec, Oaxaca. Mexican and Central American subspecies.

WESTERN BLACKNECK GARTER SNAKE   PL. 24
Thamnophis cyrtopsis cyrtopsis

IDENTIFICATION: 16–28 in. (41–71 cm); record 42³⁄₁₆ in. (107 cm). *A large black blotch at each side of neck,* usually separated from its partner by the middorsal stripe, which is orange anteriorly but fades to dull yellow posteriorly. Lateral stripes on scale rows 2 and 3; yellowish anteriorly, whitish or pale tan throughout most of length. Head gray (usually bluish gray), its color sharply set off from the black neck blotches. (Specimens from the Big Bend of Texas are chiefly black or very dark brown between the light stripes; large black spots appear when skin is stretched. Those from far western Texas are brown with smudgy black spots.) Belly unmarked, whitish or slightly brownish or greenish. Scales *keeled,* usually in 19 rows at midbody; anal *single. Young:* More brightly and contrastingly colored than adults; about 8 in. (20.3 cm) at birth.

Usually found near water, in permanent or intermittent streams, vicinity of springs, cattle tanks, etc., but often wandering into arid terrain during wet weather. Occurs from low desert flats to forested mountains. **SIMILAR SPECIES:** (1) Checkered Garter Snake usually has 21 rows of scales at midbody and lateral stripes involve *only scale row 3* near head. (2) New Mexico Garter Snake lacks prominent black blotches at sides of neck and has red on skin between scales. **RANGE:** Trans-Pecos Texas; se. Utah and s. Colo. south to Sonora, Zacatecas, and San Luis Potosí; isolated colonies in w. Ariz.; apparently absent from cen. Chihuahua. Mexican subspecies.

EASTERN BLACKNECK GARTER SNAKE   PL. 24
Thamnophis cyrtopsis ocellatus

IDENTIFICATION: 16–20 in. (41–51 cm); record 43 in. (109.2 cm). The *single row* of *large* dark spots on the neck sets this apart from our other garter snakes. The light lateral stripe on rows 2 and 3 is wavy from being partly invaded by the black spots both above and below it. Scales *keeled;* anal *single. Young:* 8–10½ in. (20.2–26.5 cm) at birth.

An inhabitant of rocky hillsides, limestone ledges, and cedar brakes. **RANGE:** Edwards Plateau of s.-cen. Texas west to the Big Bend.

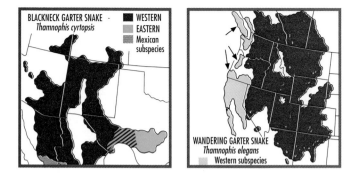

WANDERING GARTER SNAKE

PL. 24

Thamnophis elegans vagrans

IDENTIFICATION: 18–30 in. (45.7–76 cm); record 37 in. (94 cm). Despite the considerable variation in coloration and pattern, the light middorsal stripe is fairly well defined, the dark markings are rounded, and there are usually 8 upper labials and 21 rows of scales at midbody. General coloration brown, brownish green, greenish buff, or gray; belly often heavily marked with black posteriorly. Lateral light stripe on scale rows 2 and 3. Scales *keeled;* anal *single. Young:* about 7–8 in. (18–20.3 cm) at birth.

A wide-ranging western Garter Snake that barely enters our area. Normally found near water but also wanders well away from it. Food includes lizards, fish, frogs, tadpoles, salamanders, earthworms, slugs, and leeches. **SIMILAR SPECIES:** (1) Plains Garter Snake has lateral stripe on scale rows 3 and 4. (2) Skin between scales is red in Red-sided Garter Snake. (3) Checkered Garter Snake has lateral stripe confined to scale row 3 near head. **RANGE:** Black Hills of S.D.; extr. nw. Neb. and extr. nw. Okla.; west to B.C., Wash., Ore., Nev., and extr. e.-cen. Calif. Western and Mexican subspecies.

EASTERN RIBBON SNAKE

PL. 23

Thamnophis sauritus sauritus

IDENTIFICATION: 18–26 in. (45.7–66 cm); record 38 in. (96.5 cm). Ribbon Snakes are the slimmest, trimmest members of the genus. The three bright stripes are well set off against the dark slender body and tail; stripes normally yellow but middorsal one sometimes with an orange or greenish tinge. A double row of black spots may appear between the stripes when the skin is stretched. Lateral stripes on rows 3 and 4. A medium to light brown ventrolateral stripe, involving the two lowermost rows of scales and the outer edge of the belly. *Parietal spots on head, if present, are faint and do not touch each other,* a characteristic of this and all other races of the Eastern Ribbon Snake (*sauritus*). Lips unpatterned; normally 7 upper labials; belly plain yellowish or greenish. *Tail exceptionally long,* about ⅓ total length of snake. Scales *keeled;* anal *single. Young:* About 7¼–9 in. (18.4–23 cm) at birth.

This agile, nervous serpent is semiaquatic, seldom wandering far from streams, ponds, bogs, or swamps. Swims at surface instead of diving as water snakes do. Deep water normally is avoided, and fleeing Ribbon Snakes skirt the shore, threading their way through vegetation and getting lost from sight with amazing rapidity. Unlike other members of the genus, Ribbon Snakes usually will not eat earthworms but are fond of salamanders, frogs, and small fish. Captives remain nervous and may dart out of their cages the instant the lids are opened. **SIMILAR SPECIES:** Several other members of the genus have stripes that also involve row 4, but no other kinds are so thin and have such long tails. The tail in other species of *Thamnophis* and in the Crayfish Snakes (*Regina*) is generally less than ¼ of total length. **RANGE:** Southern half of New England to S.C.; southwest to extr. se. Ill., La., and the Fla. panhandle; isolated colonies in Ky.; absent from large areas in Pa., W. Va., Ohio, Ind., Ky., Tenn., Ala., Ga., N.C., and Va. **SUBSPECIES:** NORTHERN RIBBON SNAKE, *Thamnophis s. septentrionalis.* Similar but smaller and darker; dorsum velvety black or dark brown; yellow middorsal stripe often partly obscured by brown pigment; tail usually less than ⅓ the total length. Me. to Mich., south to Ind. and n. Ohio; isolated colonies in Nova Scotia and e. Wisc.

PENINSULA RIBBON SNAKE PL. 23
Thamnophis sauritus sackenii
IDENTIFICATION: 18–25 in. (45.7–63.5 cm); record 40 in. (101.6 cm). The "southern ribbon snake." On mainland Fla., a less-well-patterned counterpart of the other Ribbon Snakes. The general impression is of a tan or brown snake with a narrow light stripe on each side involving rows 3 and 4. Middorsal stripe less distinct than lateral ones and occasionally lacking altogether or represented only by a short line on neck. A broad, medium brown ventrolateral stripe; belly plain yellowish white. Upper labials 8. Tail very long. Scales *keeled;* anal *single.*

This abundant southern subspecies is semiaquatic and, like other ribbon snakes, often basks on vegetation overhanging water, dropping in at the slightest alarm. **SIMILAR SPECIES:** Queen, Glossy Crayfish, and Striped Crayfish Snakes have *divided* anals and series of dark markings on their bellies. **RANGE:** Extr. s. S.C., south

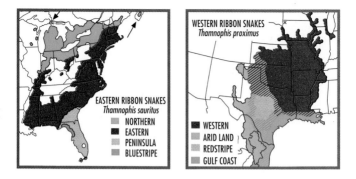

EASTERN RIBBON SNAKES
Thamnophis sauritus
- NORTHERN
- EASTERN
- PENINSULA
- BLUESTRIPE

WESTERN RIBBON SNAKES
Thamnophis proximus
- WESTERN
- ARID LAND
- REDSTRIPE
- GULF COAST

to southern tip of Fla. peninsula; the lower Keys (Big Pine and Cudjoe). **NOTE:** Snakes from the Lower Fla. Keys are exceptional in that they have a well-developed yellow or orange middorsal stripe bordered by two narrow black stripes and only 7 upper labials.

BLUESTRIPE RIBBON SNAKE   PL. 23
Thamnophis sauritus nitae

IDENTIFICATION: 18–25 in. (45.7–63.5 cm); record 29¾ in. (75.6 cm). Typically a velvety black snake with a *narrow, sky blue or bluish white stripe* on each side of body. Dorsum may be black or dark brown; lower sides (scale rows 1 and 2) often somewhat paler; an obscure middorsal stripe sometimes present; lateral stripe involving rows 3 and 4; upper labials 8; tail more than ⅓ of total length. Scales *keeled*; anal *single*. *Young:* About 7–9 in. (18–23 cm) at birth.

Found in and near marshes, pine flatwoods, and hammocks in the Gulf Coastal region of nw. peninsular Fla. **SIMILAR SPECIES:** See Bluestripe Garter Snake. **RANGE:** W. Fla. from e. Wakulla Co. to the Withlacoochee R.

WESTERN RIBBON SNAKE   PL. 23
Thamnophis proximus proximus

IDENTIFICATION: 20–30 in. (51–76 cm); record 37⅝ in. (95.6 cm). Very similar to the Eastern Ribbon Snake, but the *parietal spots on the head are large, brightly colored, and they touch each other.* Dorsum black; a narrow, orange vertebral stripe; lateral stripes light and on scale rows 3 and 4; ventrolateral stripes dark; belly unmarked. Upper labials usually 8. Tail long, but usually somewhat less than ⅓ total length. Scales *keeled*; anal *single*. *Young:* About 9–11 ¹³⁄₁₆ in. (23–29.8 cm) at birth.

An adult Western Ribbon Snake from Meade County, Kansas. This serpent spends much of its time around marshes and swamps, searching for small frogs, its favorite prey.

Semiaquatic and remaining close to streams and ditches, the edges of lakes and ponds, and other bodies of water. **SIMILAR SPECIES:** (1) Garter Snakes with a stripe on rows 3 and 4 have tails that are generally less than ¼ total length. (2) Glossy Crayfish Snake has a *divided* anal and bold black ventral markings. **RANGE:** Sw. Wisc. to cen. La., west to w. Kans., w. Okla., and ne. Texas; a disjunct colony in ne. Ill. and adj. se. Wisc. and nw. Ind.; isolated record in extr. nw. Iowa. **SUBSPECIES:** GULF COAST RIBBON SNAKE, *Thamnophis p. orarius.* Similar but with an olive-brown dorsum and a broad *gold* vertebral stripe. Gulf Coast, chiefly in the marshes from extr. sw. Miss. to s. Texas. ARID LAND RIBBON SNAKE, *Thamnophis p. diabolicus.* Record 48¼ in. (123.2 cm). Dorsum olive-gray to olive-brown; vertebral stripe *orange*; a narrow, brown ventrolateral stripe. Occurs in streams, cattle tanks, and other bodies of permanent or semipermanent water. Disjunct range, the main body from the Pecos River Valley of se. N.M. south to s. Nuevo León and extr. w. Tamaulipas, and a smaller area in ne. N.M. and adj. nw. Texas. Intergradation between two and even three subspecies is common over a wide area within the range of *Thamnophis proximus.*

REDSTRIPE RIBBON SNAKE   PL. 23
Thamnophis proximus rubrilineatus
IDENTIFICATION: 20–30 in. (51–76 cm); record 48 in. (121.9 cm). The *red vertebral stripe* may change to orange on the neck in some specimens or, rarely, may be orange throughout its length. Dorsal ground color olive-brown to olive-gray; a narrow, dark ventrolateral stripe sometimes present; lateral light stripe on rows 3 and 4. Scales *keeled*; anal *single*.

Confined chiefly to the vicinity of streams, springs, and cattle tanks, but occasionally wanders farther afield during rainy weather. **RANGE:** The Edwards Plateau of cen. Texas and intergrading with the adj. subspecies over a relatively broad area.

LINED SNAKE
Tropidoclonion lineatum

LINED SNAKE
Tropidoclonion lineatum **PL. 24**

IDENTIFICATION: 8¾–15 in. (22.4–38 cm); record 21½ in. (54.4 cm). It's "bottoms up" for checking this snake. The *double row of bold black half-moons* down the belly plus *single* anal plate should clinch identification. Middorsal stripe variable in coloration—whitish, yellow, orange, or light gray. Lateral stripe on rows 2 and 3. Scales *keeled*. *Young:* Averaging 3¾–4¾ in. (9.5–12.1 cm) at birth.

An abundant snake through much of its range, sometimes even appearing in city lots, parks, cemeteries, or abandoned trash dumps that have not been seriously affected by pollution or the use of pesticides. Also occurs on open prairies and in sparsely timbered areas. Usually found by overturning stones, boards, and debris, but it prowls at night or during the breeding season in spring. Earthworms are the favorite food. **SIMILAR SPECIES:** (1) Some of the Garter Snakes have dark spots on their bellies, but these are not so large, dark, or clearly defined as in the Lined Snake. (2) Glossy Crayfish Snake bears similar belly markings, but its dorsal

An adult Lined Snake. This reptile is a diminutive relative of the garter snakes, genus Thamnophis.

pattern, if any shows at all, consists of *dark* stripes, and its anal plate is *divided*. (3) Graham's Crayfish Snake also has *divided* anal. **RANGE:** Highly disjunct; Ill. to Colo. and N.M.; se. S.D. to s.-cen. Texas.

EARTH SNAKES: GENUS *Virginia*

These are small gray, brown, or reddish brown snakes virtually devoid of any distinctive markings. They must be caught and examined closely to verify identification. Any small nondescript serpent of an earthy color *may* belong to this genus. Earth Snakes are highly secretive and, in the North at least, seldom appear above ground except after cool, heavy rains, when they may be found, in addition to other places, hidden beneath stones that have been warmed by the sun. Food includes earthworms and soft-bodied insects and their larvae. The genus occurs only in the eastern United States, and a variety of names have been applied to its members—"ground snakes," "gray snakes," "little brown snakes," etc.

SMOOTH EARTH SNAKE *Virginia valeriae*   **PL. 22**

IDENTIFICATION: 7–10 in. (18–25.4 cm); record 15⅜ in. (39.3 cm). Any small gray or reddish brown snake virtually without markings may be this one (within its geographical range, of course). There may be an indication of a faint light stripe down the back, and many scales may have faint light lines on them that look like keels but aren't. Often a dark shadow from eye to nostril. Belly plain white or yellowish. Upper labials 6; a horizontal loreal scale (Fig. 13, opp. Pl. 22). Scales *smooth or weakly keeled* and in 15 or 17 rows (see subspecies below). Anal *divided. Young:* Without mark-

An adult Smooth Earth Snake from Shawnee County, Kansas. This is one of the most secretive serpents in North America.

ings; 3⅛–4½ in. (8–11.5 cm) at birth.

Although considered a rare reptile over much of its range, the Smooth Earth Snake is locally common and may be much more abundant than it seems. Adept at keeping out of sight. Habitats include abandoned fields and environs of trails and back roads, especially those in or near deciduous forests.

SMOOTH EARTH SNAKES
Virginia valeriae
■ EASTERN ■ WESTERN
▨ MOUNTAIN

SIMILAR SPECIES: (1) Brown Snakes have *strongly keeled* scales and no loreal (Fig. 13, opp. Pl. 22). (2) Rough Earth Snake has *strong keels* and only 5 upper labials. (3) Worm Snakes have *smooth* scales and a maximum of 13 scale rows. (4) Pine Woods Snake has a dark band running from snout through eye and to angle of jaw, and 7 upper labials. **RANGE:** N.J. to n. Fla.; west to Iowa, Kans., and Texas; disjunct colony in s. Fla., just nw. of Lake Okeechobee. **SUBSPECIES:** EASTERN EARTH SNAKE, *Virginia v. valeriae* (Pl. 22). Scale rows 15; scales mostly *smooth,* but faint keels are usually discernible on back near tail. Often there are tiny black spots on dorsum, more or less scattered or arranged in four rows. Coloration gray or light brownish gray. N.J. to n. Fla.; west to Ohio, extr. ne. Miss., and Ala.; an isolated colony in s. Fla. MOUNTAIN EARTH SNAKE, *Virginia v. pulchra*. Scales *weakly keeled,* in 15 rows anteriorly and 17 at midbody and posteriorly. Dorsum reddish brown to dark gray. Unglaciated mountains and high plateaus of w. Pa. and adj. Md. into ne. W. Va. WESTERN EARTH SNAKE, *Virginia v. elegans*. Scales *weakly keeled,* in 17 rows. Reddish- to grayish brown above; belly whitish, with a pale greenish yellow tint in adults. (Ground Snake, range of which overlaps range of Western Earth Snake, has *smooth* scales in 15 rows.) Cen. Ind. and s. Iowa to Miss. and e.-cen. Texas; apparently absent from much of the Mississippi R. floodplain.

ROUGH EARTH SNAKE *Virginia striatula*   PL. 22

IDENTIFICATION: 7–10 in. (18–25.4 cm); record 12¾ in. (32.4 cm). A cone-headed snake with a distinctly pointed snout. Plain light gray or brown to reddish brown in coloration. *Upper labials 5; a horizontal loreal scale* (Fig. 13, opp. Pl. 22); *internasals fused together into a single scale*. Scales *keeled;* anal normally *divided,* occasionally single. *Young:* Darker and grayer. The newborn young may have a pale gray to white band across the back of the head, which is lost as maturity is reached. They thus resemble

ROUGH EARTH SNAKE
Virginia striatula

young Brown or Ringneck Snakes both of which, however, have *two internasals* and 7 *or more upper labials*; 3⅛–4¾ in. (8–12.1 cm) at birth.

This small, secretive snake is locally common in the South. It feeds chiefly on earthworms. **SIMILAR SPECIES:** (1) Smooth Earth Snake has 6 upper labials and *smooth* or *weakly keeled* scales. (2) Brown Snakes have no loreal scale (Fig. 13, opp. Pl. 22). (3) Worm, Ringneck, and Pine Woods Snakes have *smooth* scales. **RANGE:** Va. to n. Fla.; west to w. Miss.; apparently absent from much of the Mississippi R. floodplain; west of the Mississippi R., from s. Mo. and La. west to se. Kans., Okla., and Texas.

HOGNOSE SNAKES: GENUS *Heterodon*

Serpents of extraordinary behavior. These are the "spreadheads" that flatten their heads and necks, hiss loudly, and inflate their bodies with air, producing a show of hostility that has earned them a bad reputation. If the intruder fails to retreat or prods the snake with a stick, it may soon roll on its back, open its mouth, give a few convulsive movements, and then lie still as though dead. Turn the snake right side up, and it promptly rolls over

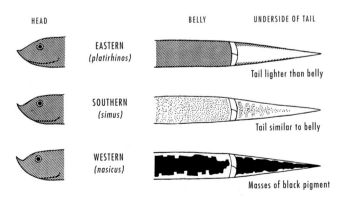

Fig. 59. *Head shapes and belly patterns of Hognose Snakes (Heterodon).*

again, giving the bluff away.

As a result of their behavior, these harmless snakes have earned such dangerous-sounding names as "hissing adder," "blow viper," "spreading adder," "hissing sand snake," and "puff adder."

The upturned snout (in combination with keeled scales) is also a good identification point. The tail is often held in a tight, flat coil. Toads are the principal food. The genus occurs only in North America.

EASTERN HOGNOSE SNAKE
Heterodon platirhinos

EASTERN HOGNOSE SNAKE *Heterodon platirhinos* PL. 25

IDENTIFICATION: 20–33 in. (51–84 cm); record 45½ in. (115.6 cm). The hissing, head- and neck-spreading, and playing 'possum are usually sufficient. Check for the *upturned snout*, which is keeled above. General coloration quite variable—yellow, brown, gray, olive, orange, or red may predominate. Normally a spotted snake, but jet black specimens or nearly plain gray ones are common in some areas. Belly mottled, gray or greenish (rarely black) on yellow, light gray, or pinkish. Underside of tail *lighter than belly*—easily checked when the snake is playing 'possum (see Fig. 59). Scales *keeled*; anal *divided*. *Young:* 5–10 in. (12.5–25.4 cm) at hatching.

Sandy areas are a favorite habitat. After a short period in captiv-

An adult Eastern Hognose Snake. Note the upturned snout, used for digging up toads, which are the favorite food of these reptiles.

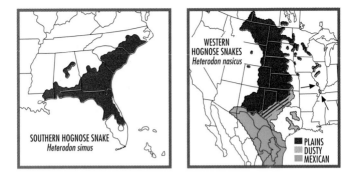

ity, most Hognose Snakes fail to "perform" any longer. Although toads are the mainstay, frogs also are eaten; a young snake may also eat crickets and other insects. **SIMILAR SPECIES:** (1) In Southern Hognose, underside of tail is *not* lighter than belly. (2) In all three races of the Western Hognose, the entire ventral surface is black with white or yellow patches (Fig. 59). **RANGE:** Extr. s. N.H. to s. Fla.; west to Minn., se. S.D., Kans., and Texas; an isolated colony in extr. nw. Pa.

SOUTHERN HOGNOSE SNAKE *Heterodon simus*   **PL. 25**

IDENTIFICATION: 14–20 in. (36–51 cm); record 24 in. (61 cm). Smallest of the hognose snakes. *Snout sharply upturned* (Fig. 59) and keeled above. Coloration fairly constant, not highly variable as in Eastern Hognose Snake. Underside of tail *not* conspicuously lighter than belly (Fig. 59). Scales *keeled;* anal *divided.*

Habitats include sandy woods, fields, and groves, dry river floodplains, and hardwood hammocks; occasionally plowed out of the ground. Upturned snout is used in burrowing and in digging for spadefoots and toads. **SIMILAR SPECIES:** In Eastern Hognose Snake, underside of tail is lighter than belly (Fig. 59). **RANGE:** Se. N.C. to s.-cen. Fla. and s. Miss.; disjunct colony in n. Ala.

WESTERN HOGNOSE SNAKE *Heterodon nasicus*   **PL. 25**

IDENTIFICATION: 15–25 in. (38–63.5 cm); record 39½ in. (100.6 cm). The sharply upturned snout, normally with a keel on top, marks this as a hognose snake, but the belly should be checked for positive species identification (Fig. 59). Large, jet black ventral areas, interspersed with white or yellow, are characteristic. Scales *keeled;* anal *divided. Young:* 5½–7¾ in. (14–19.7 cm) at hatching.

Partial to relatively dry prairie areas, especially sandy ones. The habit of head- and neck-spreading is not so well developed as in the Eastern Hognose Snake, but feigning of death and rolling

An adult Western Hognose Snake "playing dead," part of a defense behavior typical of all members of this genus.

over occurs almost as frequently. Some Western Hognose Snakes may crawl away without performing or may hide their heads beneath coils of their bodies. Called "prairie rooter" in some parts of range. Amphibians and lizards are the chief foods, but small mammals and ground-nesting birds are also eaten. **SIMILAR SPECIES:** (1) In Eastern Hognose, underside of tail is never black and is usually lighter than belly (Fig. 59). (2) The two kinds of Hooknose Snakes have smooth scales, and there is a depression instead of a raised keel behind the "hook." **RANGE:** Ill. to Alberta; south to se. Ariz. and cen. Mexico. Isolated, relict populations, indicative of a once much wider distribution, survive in suitable habitats both east and west of main part of range. **SUBSPECIES:** DUSTY HOGNOSE SNAKE, *Heterodon n. gloydi* (Pl. 25). Dark middorsal blotches, counted from head to a point directly above anus, are fewer than 32 in males; fewer than 37 in females. Extr. s. Kans. to s.-cen. Texas; isolated colonies in se. Mo., sw. Ill., and e. Texas. PLAINS HOGNOSE SNAKE, *Heterodon n. nasicus*. Similar but with markings darker and in sharper contrast with ground color. Dark body blotches more than 35 in males; more than 40 in females. Minn. to se. Alberta and south to N.M. and extr. w. Texas; isolated colonies in Manitoba, cen. Wyo., nw. Colo., ne. S.D., s. Minn., w. Iowa, and extr. nw. Mo. Intergrades between *nasicus* and *gloydi* occur from extr. se. N.M. to cen. Okla., and in isolated colonies in sand prairies of w. Ill. and adj. Iowa. MEXICAN HOGNOSE SNAKE, *Heterodon n. kennerlyi*. Like Dusty Hognose Snake in coloration and pattern, but distinguished by scalation. Two to six small scales in the group on top of head directly behind rostral plate. The Plains and Dusty subspecies have 9 or more such scales. (These are called azygous scales.) Extr. s. Texas to se. Ariz. and cen. Mexico.

Secretive snakes that are usually discovered by overturning boards, flat stones, or debris or by tearing apart decaying logs or stumps. The Ringneck Snake (*Diadophis*) has a yellow belly that, in many southern and western populations, turns to red under and near the tail. The presence or absence and arrangement of the black spots on the belly are useful in distinguishing among subspecies. Ringnecks are noted for the habit of twisting their tails into tight coils and elevating them to show the bright under-surfaces, thus earning the names of "corkscrew" and "thimble" snakes. Curiously, the display occurs only in populations with red tails—in Regal and Prairie Ringnecks, in Mississippi Ringnecks from extreme southern Mississippi, and Southern Ringnecks from the Florida Peninsula. Exceptions are where the two types of coloration occur together and where both red- and yellow-tailed snakes show this behavior. When a Ringneck is held, drops of saliva may appear at the corners of its mouth. The musk is pungent, clinging, and unpleasant.

Worm Snakes (*Carphophis*) and the Pine Woods Snake (*Rhadinaea*) are more plainly and less colorfully marked than the Ringneck Snake, and they neither twist their tails nor exhibit other spectacular behavior.

The range of the genus *Diadophis* extends from coast to coast except for large gaps in the arid West, where it is confined to uplands and the vicinity of streams; it also occurs far south into Mexico, where future studies will probably show it to be absent from most basin and lowland habitats. *Carphophis* occupies a large part of the eastern and central United States. Our lone representative of *Rhadinaea* is confined to the Southeast, but the genus as a whole, with over 40 species, ranges south through Mexico and the American tropics to Uruguay and northern Argentina.

NORTHERN RINGNECK SNAKE   PL. 25; FIGS. 60, 61
Diadophis punctatus edwardsii

IDENTIFICATION: 10–15 in. (25.4–38 cm); record 27¹¹⁄₁₆ in. (70.6 cm). A plain, dark, slender snake with a *golden collar* (Fig. 61). Dorsal coloration variable—bluish black, bluish gray, slate, or brownish. Belly uniform yellow (Fig. 60) or occasionally with a row or partial row of small black dots down center. Scales *smooth;* anal *divided. Young:* Darker than adults; 4–5½ in. (10–14 cm) at hatching.

A secretive woodland snake, usually most common in cutover

areas that include an abundance of hiding places in the form of stones, logs, bark slabs, or other rotting wood. Rocky, wooded hillsides are also favored. Many people believe Ringnecks are young Racers. Small salamanders are an important food, but earthworms and small snakes, lizards, and frogs also are eaten.

NORTHERN
PRAIRIE
REGAL
Mexican subspecies
SOUTHERN
MISSISSIPPI
KEY

RINGNECK SNAKES
Diadophis punctatus

SIMILAR SPECIES: Juvenile Brown Snakes have neck rings, but they also have *keeled* scales. (A lens may be needed to see them.) **RANGE:** Nova Scotia to ne. Minn.; south through uplands to n. Ga. and ne. Ala.; north in Mississippi Valley to Ill.; absent from large areas in Wisc., Ill., Ind., and Ohio; isolated records in Ind.

SOUTHERN RINGNECK SNAKE   PL. 25; FIGS. 60, 61
Diadophis punctatus punctatus

IDENTIFICATION: 10–14 in. (25.4–36 cm); record 18⅞ in. (48.2 cm). A ringneck with a spotted belly. The black spots are large, shaped like half-moons, and in a *central row* (Fig. 60). Neck ring normally interrupted by dark pigment (Fig. 61). Small black spots on chin and lower lips. Dorsal coloration light brown to nearly black; belly yellow, changing to red posteriorly and under tail in Fla. peninsula. Scales *smooth*; anal *divided*. Young: 3½–4¼ in. (9–10.7 cm) at hatching.

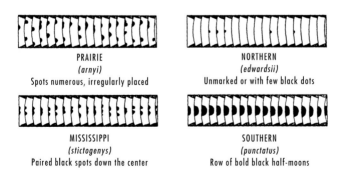

PRAIRIE
(*arnyi*)
Spots numerous, irregularly placed

NORTHERN
(*edwardsii*)
Unmarked or with few black dots

MISSISSIPPI
(*stictogenys*)
Paired black spots down the center

SOUTHERN
(*punctatus*)
Row of bold black half-moons

Fig. 60. Belly patterns of subspecies of the Ringneck Snake (Diadophis punctatus).

Although not aquatic, Ringnecks are most often found where there are evidences of moisture—near swamps, springs, on damp wooded hillsides, in flat, poorly-drained pine woods, etc.—but almost invariably under shelter. Prowling occurs chiefly at night. Specimens from peninsular Fla. twist tails, exposing their red undersurfaces. **RANGE:** S. N.J. to Upper Fla. Keys; west to the Appalachian Mts. in the South, and to sw. Ala. (The entire population in s. N.J. and the Delmarva Peninsula is intermediate between the northern and southern races.) **SUBSPECIES:** MISSISSIPPI RINGNECK SNAKE, *Diadophis p. stictogenys.* Neck ring narrow, often interrupted; belly spots irregular but usually grouped along midline in attached or separate pairs (Fig. 60). Extr. s. Ill. to the Gulf; w. Ala. to e. Texas. KEY RINGNECK SNAKE, *Diadophis p. acricus.* Virtually no neck ring; head pale grayish brown; chin and labials only faintly spotted; dorsum of body slate gray anteriorly but black posteriorly. Known only from Big Pine Key but may also occur on some of the other Lower Fla. Keys that support pine and scrub vegetation.

PRAIRIE RINGNECK SNAKE   FIG. 60
Diadophis punctatus arnyi

IDENTIFICATION: 10–14 in. (25.4–36 cm); record 16½ in. (41.9 cm). Dark head coloration extending around or across angle of jaw and slightly forward on lower jaw; neck ring sometimes interrupted; belly spots numerous and highly irregular (Fig. 60); scale rows usually 17 on forward part of body (normally 15 on the four eastern subspecies). Scales *smooth;* anal *divided. Young:* 4¹⁵⁄₁₆–5⅜ in. (12.5–13.5 cm) at hatching.

Rocky hillsides in open woods are a favorite habitat, but to the west they may be common under cover on treeless prairie uplands in spring. Like the Eastern and Southern Ringnecks, members of this race may occur in large colonies in some localities but may be

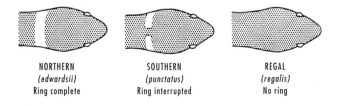

NORTHERN	SOUTHERN	REGAL
(edwardsii)	*(punctatus)*	*(regalis)*
Ring complete	Ring interrupted	No ring

Fig. 61. *Typical neck patterns in subspecies of the Ringneck Snake* (Diadophis punctatus).

rare or absent in others that seem to offer identical conditions for hiding and finding food. Twists tail, exposing red undersurface. Often feigns death, a behavior shared by the Regal Ringneck Snake. **RANGE:** Extr. sw. Wisc. and extr. se. S.D. to s.-cen. Texas and e. N.M.

REGAL RINGNECK SNAKE *Diadophis punctatus regalis* **FIG. 61**

IDENTIFICATION: 15–18 in. (38–45.7 cm); record 19¼ in. (48.9 cm); to 33⅝ in. (85.7 cm) west of our area. Neck ring usually absent but sometimes partially indicated or even complete (in Trans-Pecos Texas populations). Dorsum plain greenish, brownish, or pale slate gray; pale bluish gray in young. Yellow pigment on 1st scale row or 1st and 2nd rows. Belly yellow, irregularly spotted with black but turning to bright orange-red near and under tail. Scale rows usually 17 anteriorly and at midbody. (Strictly speaking, the entire Trans-Pecos population is intermediate between the subspecies *arnyi* and *regalis,* but closer to *regalis.)*

Less generally distributed than the eastern races. Partial to moist habitats—forested mountains, vicinity of watercourses, etc. Food consists chiefly of lizards, small snakes, and invertebrates. Twists tail into spiral when caught or pinned down, exposing the reddish coloration to view. **RANGE:** W.-cen. N.M. to w.-cen. Ariz. and south to Durango and San Luis Potosí; disjunct populations from Idaho to se. Calif. The large Regal Ringneck and smaller Prairie Ringneck apparently intergrade in w. and cen. Texas despite their disparity in size. The two occur together and maintain their identities in the Guadalupe Mts. of the Texas-N. M. border region. Western and Mexican subspecies.

EASTERN WORM SNAKE *Carphophis amoenus amoenus* **PL. 25**

IDENTIFICATION: 7½–11 in. (19–28 cm); record 13¼ in. (33.7 cm). A serpentine imitation of the common earthworm. Plain brown

EASTERN
(amoenus)
Prefrontals and
internasals
separate

MIDWEST
(helenae)
Each prefrontal
fused with the
corresponding
internasal

Fig. 62. Head scales of subspecies of the Worm Snake (Carphophis amoenus).

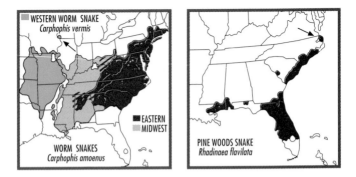

WESTERN WORM SNAKE
Carphophis vermis

EASTERN
MIDWEST

WORM SNAKES
Carphophis amoenus

PINE WOODS SNAKE
Rhadinaea flavilata

above; belly and adjacent 1 or 2 rows of dorsal scales pink. Head pointed. Two prefrontal and two internasal scales (Fig. 62). Scales *smooth and opalescent*; anal *divided. Young:* Darker than adults; 3¼–4 in. (8.3–10 cm) at hatching.

Almost never seen in the open. Usually discovered under stones or boards, in rotting logs, during digging operations, etc. Partial to moist earth, and disappears deep underground in dry weather. When held in the hand, worm snakes attempt to push their way between one's fingers with both the head and spinelike tail tip. Food includes earthworms and soft-bodied insects. **SIMILAR SPECIES:** Other small, brown snakes either have keeled scales or the belly color doesn't extend upward to involve a full row or more of dorsal scales. **RANGE:** S. New England to S.C., cen. Ga., and cen. Ala. **SUBSPECIES:** MIDWEST WORM SNAKE, *Carphophis a. helenae.* Very similar but with each prefrontal scale fused with corresponding internasal (Fig. 62). S. Ohio to s. Ill. and e. Ark.; south to the Gulf. Intergrades with subspecies *amoenus* in several broad areas where their ranges meet.

WESTERN WORM SNAKE *Carphophis vermis*   PL. 25; FIG. 62

IDENTIFICATION: 7½–11 in. (19–28 cm); record 15⅜ in. (39.1 cm). Plain purplish black above; pink of belly extends upward on the sides to the 3rd row of scales. Head pointed. Scales *smooth and opalescent*; anal *divided. Young:* About 4–4¾ in. (10–12.1 cm) at hatching.

Essentially a woodland snake that follows stream valleys westward through prairie areas. Secretive; usually found under moist logs, stones, etc. **RANGE:** Extr. s. Iowa, se. Neb., and w. Ill. to nw. La. and ne. Texas; isolated records in sw. Wisc. and se. Ark. Hybridizes with the Midwest Worm Snake *(helenae)* in a relictual, disjunct area in ne. La.

PINE WOODS SNAKE *Rhadinaea flavilata*

IDENTIFICATION: 10–13 in. (25–33 cm); record 15⅞ in. (40.3 cm). The "yellow-lipped snake." Dorsal coloration varying from rich golden brown to light reddish brown but becoming paler on the lower sides. Head darker. *Dark line through eye.* Often a suggestion of a narrow dark stripe down center of back and another on each side of body on scale rows 2 and 3 (3rd only toward tail). Belly plain white, pale yellow, or yellow-green. Lip (labial) scales virtually plain white or yellowish in most Florida specimens, but usually speckled with dark pigment in the western and especially the northern part of the range. Usually seven upper labials. Scales *smooth*; anal *divided. Young:* About 5¼–6¼ in. (14–16 cm) at hatching.

A snake of damp woodlands, chiefly pine flatwoods but also occasionally in hardwood hammocks and on coastal islands. Secretive; found under logs, boards, or leaves, in woodpiles or loose soil, but most frequently under bark and in the decaying interiors of pine logs and stumps. Food includes small frogs and lizards; captives also have eaten salamanders and small snakes. **RANGE:** Disjunct areas along a narrow coastal strip from N.C. to e. La., and most of Fla.

Mud and Rainbow Snakes: Genus *Farancia*

These large, smooth-scaled snakes are fully as aquatic as the keel-scaled Water Snakes *(Nerodia),* and they are best kept in aquariums. They are specialized for overpowering and eating slippery aquatic prey, eel-like salamanders and true eels in the cases of the Mud and Rainbow Snakes, respectively. The tongue is noticeably small for such large serpents, and, prior to shedding, the skin in both becomes a translucent blue that obscures the normal color pattern. Both are confined to the southeastern United States, where their ranges widely overlap each other.

MUD SNAKE *Farancia abacura*

IDENTIFICATION: 40–54 in. (102–137 cm); record 81½ in. (207 cm). A shiny, iridescent black and red (or pink) snake. Scales *smooth,* except in the supra-anal region, where they are keeled. Anal normally *divided,* occasionally single. *Young:* Tail tip sharp, in contrast with blunt tip of adult; 6¼–10⅝ in. (15.9–27 cm) at hatching.

A snake of southern swamps and lowlands. A burrower, but also thoroughly at home in water. Feeds chiefly on eel-like salamanders (Amphiumas). When Mud Snakes are first caught, the tail also may press against the collector's hands. This behavior earns

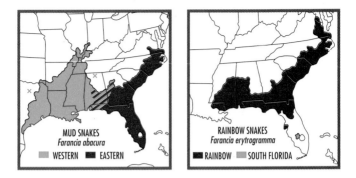

MUD SNAKES
Farancia abacura
■ WESTERN ■ EASTERN

RAINBOW SNAKES
Farancia erytrogramma
■ RAINBOW ■ SOUTH FLORIDA

it the names of "horn snake" and "stinging snake," and the habit of lying in a loose, horizontal coil associates this species with the fabled "hoop snake." Sirens, other amphibians, and fish also are eaten. **RANGE:** Southern lowlands (see subspecies below). **SUBSPECIES:** WESTERN MUD SNAKE, *Farancia a. reinwardtii* (Pl. 25). Belly color extends upward on lower sides to form 52 or fewer red bars with rounded tops. (Count on body only; omit tail.) Ala. to e. Texas and north in Mississippi Valley to s. Ill. and sw. Ind.; isolated records in n.-cen. Ala. and ne. Texas. EASTERN MUD SNAKE, *Farancia a. abacura.* Like the western subspecies but with red bars more numerous (53 or more), extending farther upward, and in the shape of triangles. In some, the young especially, the upward red extensions from the points of the triangles may cross back of neck. Se. Va. to s. Fla. and intergrading with the western subspecies in Ala. and adj. states.

RAINBOW SNAKE *Farancia erytrogramma* PL. 25

IDENTIFICATION: 27–48 in. (68.8–122 cm); record 66 in. (167.6 cm). An iridescent, glossy snake with *red and black stripes.* Often an extra row of small black spots between the two main rows on the belly. Scales *smooth,* but some specimens may have supra-anal keels. Anal normally *divided,* but sometimes single, especially in Virginia populations. *Young:* 7¾–11 in. (19.7–28 cm) at hatching.

This handsome snake is usually found in or near water; streams passing through cypress swamps are a favorite habitat. It swims well and is so adept at catching eels, its principal food, that many country people in the South call it the "eel moccasin." Young ones also eat small frogs, salamanders, and, especially, tadpoles. In the northern part of its range it burrows in sandy fields near water and is sometimes turned up by plowing. Specimens are usually inoffensive when handled, but when first caught the hind part of the body may thrash about, and the harmless tail may stab at the collector's hands. **RANGE:** S. Md. to s.-cen. Fla. and e. La. **SUBSPECIES:** R A I N B O W   S N A K E , *Farancia e. erytrogramma* (Pl. 25). As described above. All of range except for vicinity of Lake Okeechobee, Fla. S O U T H   F L O R I D A   R A I N B O W   S N A K E , *Farancia e. seminola.* Similar except that black pigment predominates on the venter and extends upward onto lower rows of dorsal scales. S.-cen. Fla.

R A C E R S   A N D   W H I P S N A K E S :
G E N E R A   *Coluber* A N D   *Masticophis*

These are slender, fast-moving snakes—often mere streaks in the grass as they dash away. Adults of most kinds are more or less uniformly colored or longitudinally striped. Young racers are blotched or spotted, juvenile coachwhips are crosslined, and baby whipsnakes, in general, resemble their parents. The scales are *smooth;* anal *divided.*

When alarmed or on the defensive, many of these snakes rapidly vibrate the tips of their tails, and, if they are in dry weeds or leaves, they produce a buzzing sound suggestive of a rattlesnake. When held by the neck with the body dangling, they characteristically lash vigorously back and forth in an effort to shake themselves free. All are diurnal; many are partially arboreal, ascending into shrubs, cactus, or low trees. Rodents, small birds, lizards, snakes, frogs, and insects are included on their menus. Food is not constricted. A loop of the body is thrown over the struggling victim, pressing it down. Eggs of whipsnakes, racers, and indigo

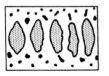

YOUNG RACERS
(C. constrictor)
of most subspecies.
Middorsal blotches

YOUNG MEXICAN RACER
(C. c. oaxaca)
Spots and crossbands

SCHOTT'S and RUTHVEN'S WHIPSNAKES
Scales of middorsal rows
with light edges

Fig. 63. Dorsal patterns of Racers (Coluber) and Whipsnakes (Masticophis). Each diagram shows a section of skin removed from the animal.

snakes are coated with small nodules resembling hard, dry grains of salt. Racers range from about 7½–14 in. (19–36 cm) at hatching; Coachwhips 11–16 in. (28–41 cm); and Whipsnakes 10–17 in. (25.4–43.2 cm).

These snakes are subject to considerable individual and local variation, especially in regions where two or more subspecies intergrade. Whipsnakes and Coachwhips (*Masticophis*) range from the United States to northern South America. Racers (*Coluber*) occur from southern Canada to Guatemala; there are related species in southern Europe, northern Africa, and parts of Asia.

NORTHERN BLACK RACER
Coluber constrictor constrictor

PL. 26

IDENTIFICATION: 36–60 in. (90–152 cm); record 73 in. (185.4 cm). A slender, satiny snake that is plain black *both* above and below. Usually some white on chin and throat. Iris of eye brown or dark amber. Scales *smooth*; anal *divided*. *Young:* Strongly patterned with a middorsal row of dark gray, brown, or reddish brown blotches on a ground color of gray or bluish gray; small dark spots on flanks and venter (Fig. 63); tail virtually unpatterned. As snake grows older, pattern becomes less distinct and uppersurface darkens; at length of 30 inches (76 cm) virtually all traces of pattern have usually disappeared.

An alert, active, locally abundant serpent that is quick to flee when approached but fights fiercely when cornered. Often retreats *upward* into bushes or low branches of trees when closely pursued. Normally makes a poor captive, seldom settling down and often falling victim to parasites and infections. **SIMILAR SPECIES:** (1) Black Rat Snake has *keels* on middorsal scales and is shaped like a loaf of bread in cross section (Fig. 16, opp. Pl. 28). (2) Black variant of Eastern Coachwhip may show slight indications of light pigment toward rear of dorsum, and sides of tail often are reddish; check number of scale rows just anterior to the tail—13 in Coachwhips, 15 in Racers. (3) Melanistic specimens of Eastern Garter Snake have *keeled* scales and *single* anal plates. (4) Young Rat Snakes have conspicuous dark blotches on tails. **RANGE:** S. Me. to ne. Ala. **SUBSPECIES:** SOUTHERN BLACK RACER, *Coluber c. priapus.* Very similar to Northern Black Racer but with internal anatomical differences. (Enlarged basal hemipenial spine three or more times length of its predecessor in same row. Spine is less than three times as long in Northern Black Racer.) Florida specimens usually have considerable white on chin and throat, and their irises may be bright red or orange. Young also similar to those of Northern Black Racer, but juveniles from Florida may have reddish dorsal blotches and their bellies may be reddish or

pinkish toward tail. Southeastern states and north and west in Mississippi Valley to s. Ind. and se. Okla.; Lower Fla. Keys. BROWNCHIN RACER, *Coluber c. helvigularis.* Uniform black above and below except for chin and lips, which are light tan or brown or mottled or suffused with those colors. Lower Chipola and Apalachicola R. valleys in Fla. panhandle and adj. Ga.

BLUE RACER *Coluber constrictor foxii*   PL. 26

IDENTIFICATION: 36–60 in. (90–152 cm); record 72 in. (182.9 cm). Plain blue above, the head darker and very often with an even darker area extending backward from the eye. Shade of blue varies; it may be greenish, grayish, or much darker than in the illustration. Chin and throat white, unspotted. Belly bluish, paler than back. Scales *smooth*; anal *divided. Young:* Similar to young of Northern Black Racer.

Prairies, open woodlands, environs of lakes and tamarack-sphagnum bogs, and more or less open habitats in general. **RANGE:**

Extr. s. Ont. and nw. Ohio to e. Iowa and se. Minn.; an isolated colony in Menominee Co., Mich. Intergrades through a broad area with Eastern Yellowbelly Racer. **SUBSPECIES:** EVERGLADES RACER, *Coluber c. paludicola*. A pale bluish-, greenish-, or brownish gray snake. Bluish ones look very much like Blue Racer of the north-central region, and they will check out to that subspecies when compared with Pl. 26. Belly whitish and usually with pale cloudy markings of whitish gray or powder blue. Iris of eye red or (rarely) yellow or reddish brown. *Young:* Similar to those of Black Racers but with a decidedly reddish cast; dorsal spots light chestnut, reddish, or pinkish; belly spots reddish or orange. The Everglades and the Miami rim rock of se. Fla. and the Upper Fla. Keys; also Cape Canaveral region of e. Fla.

EASTERN YELLOWBELLY RACER

PL. 26

Coluber constrictor flaviventris

IDENTIFICATION: 23–50 in. (58–127 cm); record 70 in. (177.8 cm). Averages considerably smaller than the Black or the Blue Racer. Highly variable in coloration. Dorsum plain brown, gray, olive, medium to pale dull green, or dull to dark blue. *Belly plain yellowish,* varying from pale cream in some parts of range to bright lemon-yellow in others. Scales *smooth;* anal *divided. Young:* Similar to young of Northern Black Racer.

At home in fields and grasslands, brushy areas, and open woods. More likely to forage actively through the day than most other snakes. Like other small animals of plains and prairies, it takes refuge in clumps of vegetation, glides into small mammal burrows, or hides in stone or rock piles. **SIMILAR SPECIES:** Could be mistaken for one of the Green Snakes: (1) Rough Green Snake

In the Eastern Yellowbelly Racer the dorsal coloration is highly variable. Some, like this one, may resemble the Blue Racer, but in others the upper surface may be plain brown, gray, olive, or medium to dull green.

has *keeled* scales. (2) Smooth Green Snake has a maximum of 15 rows of dorsal scales (17 in the Racer). Most confusion will occur with young. Scales must be checked; combination of *smooth* scales, *divided* anal, and maximum of 17 dorsal scale rows will distinguish juveniles from any of the several other spotted snakes occurring within its range. **RANGE:** Mont., w. N.D., east to Iowa and south to Texas and extr. sw. La.; isolated records in N.M. and Texas. **SUBSPECIES:** BLACKMASK RACER, *Coluber c. latrunculus.* Dorsum slate gray, belly grayish blue; a *black postocular stripe* like a mask. Bottomland hardwoods and cypress regions of se. La. north along the east side of the Mississippi R. to n. Miss.

MEXICAN RACER *Coluber constrictor oaxaca* FIG. 63

IDENTIFICATION: 20–40 in. (51–101.6 cm). The "dwarf" or "Rio Grande" subspecies. Middorsal area plain green or greenish gray, sides of body much lighter, and belly plain yellow to yellow-green. Upper labials usually 8 (normally 7 in Eastern Yellowbelly Racer). Scales *smooth;* anal *divided. Young:* Scattered small, dark spots on a greenish ground color, the spots joining together to form dark crossbands on neck and forward part of body (Fig. 63); body becoming uniform dark olive green toward tail.

Often arboreal, foraging in shrubs and bushes, where it may remain immobile when approached, and where its coloration makes detection difficult. **RANGE:** S. Texas and Tamaulipas to cen. Veracruz; isolated records in Nuevo León, Coahuila, Durango, Colima, Oaxaca, Chiapas, and Guatemala. Some isolated records from N.M. and Texas are intermediate between *oaxaca* and *flaviventris,* while others in both states are *flaviventris* only.

BUTTERMILK RACER *Coluber constrictor anthicus* PL. 26

IDENTIFICATION: 36–60 in. (90–152 cm); record 70 in. (177.8 cm). This Racer looks almost as though it had been spattered by a bleaching compound. Numerous scales are the "wrong" color — white, yellow, buff, or pale blue — and scattered about indiscriminately. No two specimens are marked alike; some are only slightly spotted, but others are heavily speckled. Ground color may be black, bluish, or olive. Scales *smooth;* anal *divided.*

Usually found in open areas, such as old fields, but also occurs at forest edges. **SIMILAR SPECIES:** (1) Speckled Kingsnake is shiny, has a *single* anal plate, and the specks are small (several would fit on one scale). (2) Speckled Racer has several rows of scales *weakly keeled.* **RANGE:** S. Ark., La., and e. Texas. **SUBSPECIES:** TAN RACER, *Coluber c. etheridgei.* Similar; the pale spots variable in number but with the dorsal ground color light tan. Longleaf pine flatwoods in extr. w.-cen. La. and adj. Texas.

Masticophis flagellum flagellum

IDENTIFICATION: 42–60 in. (106.7–152 cm); record 102± in. (259± cm). The marked change from black or dark brown "forward" to light brown "aft" is unique among our snakes, but the amount of dark pigment is variable. Some specimens have only their heads and necks dark, others may be half-and-half, and still others may show light pigment only on the tail and rear of body. Coloration of belly corresponds with that of back. Scalation of the long, slender tail suggests a braided whip. *Black variation:* In parts of nw. Ark. and adj. Okla., Kans., and Mo., Coachwhips may be virtually plain black all over, or with tail and rear of body distinctly reddish. Even in the blackest specimens, however, sides of tail are often reddish, and there may be traces of lighter pigment toward rear of dorsum, plus a considerable light area under tail. *Pale variation:* Coachwhips from several parts of s. Ga. and n. and w. Fla. have the dark pigment reduced to narrow, dark brown crossbands on a pale tan ground color. Minimum number of scale rows (just anterior to anus) is 13 (15 in Racers). Scales *smooth;* anal *divided.* *Young:* Similar to young of Western Coachwhip (see Pl. 26), but with dark crosslines closer together.

An active, fast-moving serpent that sometimes prowls with head raised well above ground. Normally escapes the would-be collector with a burst of speed, but fights savagely when cornered. Many habitats are utilized, ranging from dry, sandy flatwoods to swamps, creek valleys, and the rugged terrain of w. Ark. Coachwhips make nervous captives and are prone to strike repeatedly at persons passing their cages. In biting, they embed their teeth and then yank away, producing lacerations instead of puncture wounds. **RANGE:** N.C. to s. Fla. and west to Texas, Okla., and se. Kans.; apparently absent from a large portion of the lower Mississippi River Valley; an isolated colony in s.-cen. Ky.

WESTERN COACHWHIP *Masticophis flagellum testaceus* PL. 26

IDENTIFICATION: 42–60 in. (106.7–152 cm); record 80 in. (203.2 cm). A highly variable snake, light yellow-brown to dark brown in coloration and with head and neck same color as body and tail. Occurs in three distinct pattern variations: (a) unicolored, with virtually no markings; (b) narrow-banded, with narrow, dark crossbands like those seen in the young; and (c) broad-banded, marked with several broad crossbands, 10 to 15 scales wide, that are somewhat darker than and alternate with similar broad bands of the ground color. Among these the narrow-banded variant is the commonest and the broad-banded variant the least abundant. Some of the populations in Trans-Pecos Texas, east-central N.M., and southeastern Colo., include numerous reddish-colored individuals (see Pl. 26). Scales *smooth*; anal *divided*. *Young*: Dark crosslines one or two scales wide and separated from one another by about the width of three or more scales. Head often distinctly darker than body.

A snake of grasslands, mesquite savannahs, arid brushlands, and numerous other more or less open habitats. Called "prairie runner" in some

COACHWHIPS
Masticophis flagellum

WESTERN ■■ EASTERN
▨ Western & Mexican subspecies

parts of its range. **SIMILAR SPECIES:** (1) Racers have 15 dorsal scale rows immediately in front of anus; Coachwhips have 13. (2) Ruthven's Whipsnake has only 15 dorsal rows on forward part of body; Coachwhips have 17. **RANGE:** Sw. Neb., e. Colo., and w. Kans. to ne. Mexico. Western and Mexican subspecies. **NOTE:** Specimens from the vicinity of El Paso, Texas, may show some of the characteristics of the LINED COACHWHIP, *Masticophis f. lineatulus*, that occurs in adjacent Chihuahua. In these there may be a central longitudinal dark streak on each anterior dorsal scale, and the underside of the tail and posterior portion of the venter may be salmon pink.

CENTRAL TEXAS WHIPSNAKE   PL. 26
Masticophis taeniatus girardi

IDENTIFICATION: 42–60 in. (106.7–152 cm); record 72 in. (182.9 cm). The only "black snake" with longitudinal white patches on the sides. These are about equally spaced but are strongest on

A Western Coachwhip (red phase) with its head raised as it prowls in search of prey and to see potential enemies. An active, fast-moving snake that is difficult to follow when it scoots away through vegetation.

WHIPSNAKES
Masticophis taeniatus

■ DESERT STRIPED
CENTRAL TEXAS
SCHOTT'S
RUTHVEN'S
Mexican subspecies

neck and become gradually less prominent farther back. Effect is similar to that produced by an automobile tire that runs over a freshly painted white line on highway and then prints an ever weakening white spot with each turn of the wheel. In some parts of range, white markings may be strongly evident throughout length of body and may produce a crossbanded effect.

Large scales atop head usually outlined with light pigment. General dorsal coloration variable from black to reddish brown. Underside of tail bright coral pink. Scales *smooth*; anal *divided*. *Young:* No white patches, except for narrow, light crossband just behind head; longitudinal stripes present on lower sides, the most prominent being a light one on scale rows 3 and 4; usually a reddish overwash.

Also called "cedar racer" and "ornate whipsnake." An alert, fast-moving snake of brakes and valleys of Edwards Plateau and mountains and basins of Trans-Pecos Texas; occurs at least to 5800 ft. (1800 m). Retreats among rocks, thorny vegetation, or other shelter when approached. **RANGE:** Cen. and w. Texas; south on Mexican plateau to Guanajuato. Mexican subspecies. **SUBSPECIES:** DESERT STRIPED WHIPSNAKE, *Masticophis t. taeniatus.* Similar but with the white patches absent. Longitudinal white stripes strongly developed, two on each side of body, and the upper stripe actually a double one with the two halves separated by a black line that runs along center of 4th scale row. A western race that barely enters our area. Northern part of Trans-Pecos Texas; west and north to Calif. and Wash.

SCHOTT'S WHIPSNAKE *Masticophis taeniatus schotti* **PL. 26**
IDENTIFICATION: 40–56 in. (102–142 cm); record 66 in. (167.6 cm). The only *strongly striped* whipsnake in southern Texas. The two light longitudinal stripes on each side, one at edge of belly scales and the other on scale rows 3 and 4, are the most conspicuous features of the pattern. General coloration varies from bluish- to greenish gray. Sides of neck reddish orange. Belly whitish anteriorly, stippled with bluish gray farther back; underside of tail pink or salmon. The light anterior edgings of 7 or 8 middorsal rows of scales (Fig. 63) are best seen when scales are spread slightly apart (easily checked on living specimens). Scales *smooth*; anal *divided*. *Young:* Like adults but with reddish overwash.

The slender, colorful, big-eyed Schott's Whipsnake is as active and elusive as the coachwhips. It occurs in brush country—scattered creosote bush, mesquite, prickly pear, and desert grasses of extreme southern Texas.

An alert, elusive resident of the arid brush country of southern Texas. Named for Arthur Schott, who collected the type specimen while a member of the U.S. and Mexican Boundary Survey soon after the end of the Mexican War. **SIMILAR SPECIES:** (1) Texas Patchnose Snake has a light *middorsal* stripe flanked by dark stripes. (2) Ruthven's Whipsnake has only faint indications of light stripes. **RANGE:** Texas, south of San Antonio; west into adj. Mexico.

RUTHVEN'S WHIPSNAKE PL. 26; FIG. 63
Masticophis taeniatus ruthveni

IDENTIFICATION: 40–56 in. (102–142 cm); record 66⅛ in. (168 cm). Typical specimens show very little pattern except for traces of narrow, light stripes on neck or sides. Throat dotted with dark orange; belly bright yellow anteriorly, light bluish gray or olive at midbody, and pink posteriorly; underside of tail bright red. Light anterior edges on 7 or 8 of the middorsal rows of scales (Fig. 63). Scales *smooth*; anal *divided*. *Young:* Like adult but with neck stripes better indicated.

An agile serpent of arid brushlands. Named for Alexander Grant Ruthven, herpetologist and long-time president of the University of Michigan. **SIMILAR SPECIES:** (1) Mexican Racer has maximum of 17 scale rows; Whipsnakes have only 15. (2) Rough Green Snake has *keeled* scales. **RANGE:** Extr. s. Texas and ne. Mexico. Intergrades with Schott's Whipsnake in lower Rio Grande Valley. (Specimen illustrated on Pl. 26 is actually an intergrade and shows more indications of stripes than do typical individuals from Mexico.)

Two green snakes occur within our area, the terrestrial Smooth Green Snake and the more arboreal Rough Green Snake, which gets its name from its keeled scales. The bright green coloration changes quickly to blue after death, a good point to remember if you ever find a dull blue snake that has been run over on the road. The genus *Opheodrys* ranges from southern Canada to Florida and northeastern Mexico, and from the Maritime Provinces to the Rocky Mountains. It also occurs in Asia.

ROUGH GREEN SNAKE *Opheodrys aestivus*   PL. 25

IDENTIFICATION: 22–32 in. (56–81 cm); record 45⅝ in. (115.9 cm). The "vine snake." This dainty, slender serpent is plain light *green above* and plain white, yellow, or pale greenish below. Scales *keeled*; anal *divided*. *Young:* Grayish green; 6¾–8¹⁵⁄₁₆ in. (17.2–22.8 cm) at hatching.

An excellent climber that, when foraging amid vines or shrubs, blends with the background so well it is virtually invisible. At times it is almost semiaquatic, freely entering shallow bodies of water. A frequent habitat is in the dense growth of vegetation overhanging a stream or lake border. Crickets, grasshoppers, larvae of moths and butterflies, and spiders constitute the bulk of the food. **SIMILAR SPECIES:** (1) The very similar Smooth Green Snake has *smooth* scales; (2) So also does the greenish Mexican Racer. **RANGE:** S. N.J. to Fla. Keys; west to se. Kans. and Texas; south in Mexico to Tampico; isolated population in Coahuila; an isolated record in ne. Mo.

An adult Rough Green Snake blends with any verdant vegetation, making it difficult to observe.

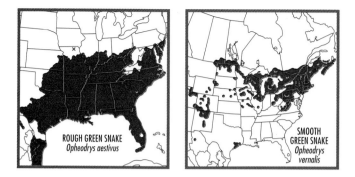

ROUGH GREEN SNAKE
Opheodrys aestivus

SMOOTH GREEN SNAKE
Opheodrys vernalis

SMOOTH GREEN SNAKE *Opheodrys vernalis*   **PL. 25**

IDENTIFICATION: 11⅞–20 in. (30.3–51 cm); record 26 in. (66 cm). The "green grass snake." A gentle little reptile that is plain bright *green above* and plain white or washed with pale yellow below. Scales *smooth;* anal *divided. Young:* Dark olive- or bluish gray; 3¹⁵⁄₁₆–6½ in. (8.4–16.5 cm) at hatching.

In eastern and far western parts of its range this is an upland snake, but it occupies the lowlands in the north-central portion of the country and in southeastern Texas. Largely terrestrial, showing little inclination to climb. Spiders and insects are eaten. **SIMILAR SPECIES:** (1) Rough Green Snake is more slender, grows to a much greater length, and has *keeled* scales; its range is more southern, only partially overlapping that of Smooth Green Snake.

An adult Smooth Green Snake from Beaver Island, Michigan. One of the few North American serpents with a boreal distribution.

(2) Greenish specimens of the Yellowbelly Racer are usually longer than the largest Smooth Green Snake by the time they become unicolored. If in doubt check the nostril. In Green Snakes (both species) the nostril is centered in a single scale; in Yellowbelly Racer it lies between two scales. **RANGE:** Apparently more or less continuous from the Maritime Provinces of Canada west to Minn. and se. Sask., and south to ne. Ill. and n. Va. Disjunct colonies are found in sw. Ohio, s. Ill., Iowa, n. Mo., the Dakotas, Neb., e. Wyo., ne. Utah, Colo., N.M., along the Gulf Coast of Texas, and in w. Chihuahua. Members of the disjunct population in the grasslands of se. Texas may be light brown with an olive wash instead of green. Occasional examples of an unusual tan variant of this snake have been found in Ill., Iowa, Mich., and Wisc.

SPECKLED RACER AND INDIGO SNAKES: GENERA *Drymobius* AND *Drymarchon*

Essentially these are tropical snakes. There are several species of *Drymobius,* and together, they range from extreme southern Texas to Peru and Venezuela. The genus *Drymarchon,* which includes the Indigo Snakes, has only a single species, but its many races extend, collectively, from the southeastern United States to Argentina. One subspecies *(melanurus)* attains a known length of 116⅛ in. (295 cm), the greatest measurement for any member of the Family Colubridae in the New World.

SPECKLED RACER   PL. 32
Drymobius margaritiferus margaritiferus

IDENTIFICATION: 30–40 in. (76–102 cm); record 50 in. (127 cm). A black stripe behind the eye, and a yellow spot near the center of each dorsal scale. Base of each scale *blue*. This, in combination with the *yellow spots,* produces the illusion of a greenish overwash along sides of body. Outer part of each scale black. Belly plain whitish or yellowish. Subcaudal scales black-edged posteriorly; ventrals may be similarly marked. Scales of several middorsal rows weakly *keeled*; outer rows smooth. Anal *divided. Young:* Similar but with colors less vivid; about 6–10⅛ in. (15.2–27.7 cm) at hatching.

A rarity north of the Rio Grande. May be found near water or in thickets of dense natural vegetation. Frogs are relished. **RANGE:** Low to moderate elevations from extr. s. Texas south along the Caribbean coast to n. S. America; an isolated record in Coahuila. Mexican and Cen. American subspecies.

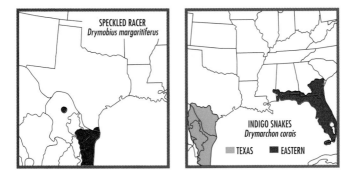

EASTERN INDIGO SNAKE *Drymarchon corais couperi* PL. 27

IDENTIFICATION: 60–84 in. (152–213 cm); record 103½ in. (262.9 cm). This large, handsome serpent is entirely *shiny bluish black*, belly included, except that chin and sides of head may be reddish- or orange-brown. Scales normally *smooth*, but some males, particularly larger individuals, have faintly keeled scales on as many as five middorsal rows, starting at about the second quarter of the body; anal *single*. Third from last upper labial wedge-shaped and cut off above by contact between adjacent labials (Fig. 64). *Young:* Like adults but often with much more reddish on head and forward part of belly; 17–24 in. (43.2–61 cm) at hatching.

When cornered, the Indigo Snake flattens its neck vertically (not horizontally as in the Hognose Snakes), hisses, and vibrates its tail, producing a rattling sound. When caught, it seldom attempts to bite. Captives are usually restless and keep on the move when handled. Food includes small mammals, birds, frogs, and snakes—even Cottonmouths and Rattlesnakes are eaten. Not a constrictor. A snake chiefly of large, unsettled areas.

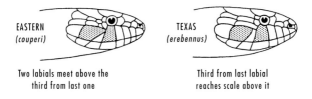

EASTERN
(couperi)

Two labials meet above the
third from last one

TEXAS
(erebennus)

Third from last labial
reaches scale above it

Fig. 64. *Heads of subspecies of the Indigo Snake* (Drymarchon corais).

Indigo Snakes of several races, including imported tropical ones, were long popular with snake charmers and carnival "pit" shows, in which they were exhibited as "blue bullsnakes" or "blue gophers." These names are still in use in some areas. **SIMILAR SPECIES:** All other plain black snakes within its range have *keeled* scales, a *divided* anal plate, or both. **RANGE:** Se. Ga., peninsular Fla. and lower Keys; west to se. Miss. Apparently released outside of its native range in extr. s. Miss. (Harrison and Marion cos.) by governmental agencies.

TEXAS INDIGO SNAKE *Drymarchon corais erebennus* PL. 27

IDENTIFICATION: 60–78 in. (152–198 cm); record 100¼ in. (254.6 cm). Like the Eastern Indigo Snake except for: (a) prominent *dark lines* downward from eye; (b) tendency for forepart of body to be brownish and with some indications of pattern; (c) 3rd from last upper labial reaching the scale above it (Fig. 64); and (d) almost always 14 rows of dorsal scales on hindmost part of body instead of 15 as in eastern race. Scales *smooth*; anal *single*. Hisses and vibrates tail. *Young:* About 18–26 in. (45.7–66 cm) at hatching. **RANGE:** Arid s. Texas to Veracruz and Hidalgo.

PATCHNOSE SNAKES: GENUS *Salvadora*

The curious snout, which may facilitate digging in loose sand, is characteristic of these diurnal snakes. The rostral is large, curved upward, and notched below, and has a free, slightly projecting flap at each side. The pale middorsal stripe, flanked by broad, dark stripes, will also distinguish the Patchnose Snakes from any other smooth-scaled species within our area. (Keels may appear, however, on a few scales above the anal region in adult males and large females). Some individuals strike repeatedly when first caught and may vibrate their tails. Food includes lizards and snakes (and their eggs) and small rodents. The young are pat-

BIG BEND
(*deserticola*)

Two or three scales between
posterior chin shields

MOUNTAIN
(*grahamiae*)
and TEXAS (*lineata*)

Posterior chin shields touching
or separated by only one scale

Fig. 65. *Chins of Patchnose Snakes* (Salvadora).

terned like the adults and are about 8¼ to 11 in. (21 to 28 cm) at hatching. Members of the genus occur from Texas to California and southward through Mexico to Chiapas.

PATCHNOSE SNAKES
Salvadora grahamiae

☐ TEXAS
☐ MOUNTAIN

MOUNTAIN PATCHNOSE SNAKE   PL. 31; FIG. 65
Salvadora grahamiae grahamiae

IDENTIFICATION: 22–30 in. (56–76 cm); record 37½ in. (95.3 cm). A pale gray or slightly olive or brownish snake with two fairly broad, dark olive-brown, often nearly black, dorsolateral stripes running the length of the body. Pale middorsal stripe matching or only a little brighter than coloration on sides of body. Some specimens have a *faint* narrow, dark line on the 3rd row of scales. Posterior chin shields touching each other or separated only by width of one scale (Fig. 65). Scales *smooth;* anal *divided.*

A snake of isolated mountain areas, foothills, and mesas. Usually occurs at higher elevations than the Big Bend Patchnose Snake. **SIMILAR SPECIES:** (1) Garter and Ribbon Snakes have *keeled* scales and single anals. (2) Big Bend Patchnose Snake has a dark stripe on *4th* row of scales and 2 or 3 small scales between posterior chin shields (Fig. 65). **RANGE:** Trans-Pecos region of Texas to n.-cen. N.M. and se. Ariz.; intergrades with Texas Patchnose Snake east of the Big Bend in Texas; disjunct colonies in Chihuahua and cen. Ariz.

TEXAS PATCHNOSE SNAKE   PL. 31; FIG. 65
Salvadora grahamiae lineata

IDENTIFICATION: 26–40 in. (66–102 cm); record 47 in. (119.4 cm). The middorsal stripe varies in coloration from one specimen to another through several tones of yellow or pale orange, and the broad, dark stripes that border it are brown to almost black. A narrow, sharply distinct, dark line on *3rd row of scales* (on 2nd row toward tail). Posterior chin shields touching each other or separated only by width of one scale (Fig. 65). Scales *smooth;* anal *divided.*

An essentially terrestrial snake that utilizes a variety of habitats, including prairies, rugged, rocky terrain of the Edwards Plateau in central Texas, arid brushlands farther south, and cultivated country of the lower Rio Grande Valley. **SIMILAR SPECIES:** Garter and Ribbon Snakes have *keeled* scales and *single* anals. **RANGE:** N.-cen.

BIG BEND PATCHNOSE SNAKE
Salvadora deserticola

Texas southward to Hidalgo; disjunct populations in Chihuahua, and along Chihuahua-Durango border.

BIG BEND PATCH-NOSE SNAKE

Salvadora deserticola   **PL. 31**
IDENTIFICATION: 24–32 in. (61–81 cm); record 40 in. (101.6 cm). Check for two things: (a) a narrow, dark line on the 4*th* row of scales (it may encroach on the 3rd anteriorly and shifts entirely to the 3rd near the tail); and (b) 2 or 3 small scales between the posterior chin shields (Fig. 65). Middorsal stripe varies from brownish orange in some specimens to tan in others; dark stripes black or dark brown. Lateral ground color pale gray but with orange-brown encroaching on anterior corner of each scale. Belly peach-colored. Scales *smooth;* anal *divided.*

At home on desert flats and washes but also ascending into the foothills and mesas surrounding the higher mountains. The habitats of this species and the Mountain Patchnose Snake overlap in some areas, and they occasionally are found together. **SIMILAR SPECIES:** (1) Garter and Ribbon Snakes have *keeled* scales and *single* anals. (2) In Mountain Patchnose Snake the narrow, dark line, if present, is on 3*rd* row of scales, and posterior chin shields are separated by width of only *one* scale (Fig. 65). **RANGE:** Big Bend region of Texas to se. Ariz.; south to s. Sinaloa; disjunct populations in s. Chihuahua.

RAT SNAKES: GENERA *Elaphe* AND *Bogertophis*

These large, handsome snakes are shaped, in cross section, like a loaf of bread, the flat belly meeting the sides of the body at an angle (Fig. 16, opp. Pl. 28). Adults have several of the middorsal rows of scales weakly *keeled* and the others smooth; keels are only slightly developed or lacking altogether in the young. The anal plate is *divided.*

Hatchling rat snakes are boldly patterned with dark spots or blotches; some kinds retain these markings throughout life, in others they vanish with age. Some develop four dark longitudinal stripes, and similar stripes may appear in individual specimens of kinds that normally are not striped at all. When cornered in the field, many of these snakes literally stand up and fight, with the

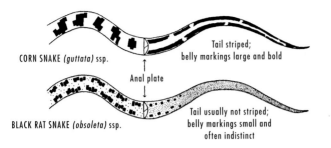

CORN SNAKE *(guttata)* ssp.

Anal plate

Tail striped;
belly markings large and bold

BLACK RAT SNAKE *(obsoleta)* ssp.

Tail usually not striped;
belly markings small and
often indistinct

Fig. 66. *Undersurfaces of young Rat Snakes* (Elaphe).

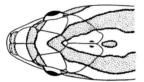

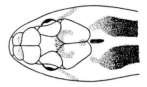

CORN SNAKE ssp. *(guttata)*
Dark neck lines unite to form a spearpoint between the eyes

FOX SNAKE ssp. *(vulpina)*
No spearpoint; head brown
or reddish

Fig. 67. *Heads of adult Rat Snakes* (Elaphe).

CORN SNAKE *(guttata)* ssp.
Postocular stripe has dark border,
extends onto neck

BLACK RAT SNAKE *(obsoleta)* ssp.
Postocular stripe entirely dark,
stops at mouth line

Fig. 68. *Heads of young Rat Snakes* (Elaphe).

fore portion of the body reared upward, the head drawn back in an S-curve, and the mouth held open in readiness to strike. Sometimes they hiss as they lunge forward. All the Rat Snakes vibrate their tails rapidly when alarmed. All are good climbers, the angles in their belly scales helping to grip irregularities on the boles of trees, faces of cliffs, etc. With proper care most of them thrive in captivity. They constrict mice, young rats, or small birds in their strong coils. Young Rat Snakes also eat lizards and frogs, treefrogs especially. Young of Fox and Corn Snakes vary from 7¹⁵⁄₁₆–15½ in. (20.2–39.4 cm) at hatching; Rat Snakes (*obsoleta*) and Baird's Rat Snake from about 10½–17 in. (26.6–43.2 cm).

The genus *Elaphe* ranges southward to Costa Rica and is also represented in the Old World. *Bogertophis* not only extends southward from Texas into adjacent Mexico, but it also has another species in Baja California and extr. s. California.

CORN SNAKE *Elaphe guttata guttata* PL. 28

IDENTIFICATION: 30–48 in. (76–122 cm); record 72 in. (182.9 cm). The "red rat snake." The belly is boldly checkered with black on whitish, and the underside of tail is usually striped (Fig. 66). A beautiful red or orange snake, but subject to considerable individual variation in color. Some specimens tend strongly to browns, especially those from upland habitats. Ground color variable from orange to gray. Dorsal spots and blotches boldly outlined with black. First blotch on neck divided into two branches that extend forward and meet in a *spearpoint* between eyes (Fig. 67). Dorsum occasionally with four dusky longitudinal stripes. Scales weakly *keeled*; anal *divided*. Corn Snakes from the Fla. Keys often exhibit reduced black pigment dorsally and a less intense checker-

A Corn Snake in a defensive posture. Body-bridging, raising part of the coils to present a larger target toward a potential enemy, is used by some snakes, especially rattlers when confronted by an aggressive kingsnake.

board pattern on the belly (Pl. 28). *Young:* Blotches dark, usually rich reddish brown; patches of orange between blotches along middorsal line. The stripe extending backward from the eye has dark borders and usually continues past mouth line and onto neck (Fig. 68).

The Corn Snake climbs well but is most likely to be found in terrestrial habitats — in pine barrens or wood lots, on rocky hillsides, etc. More common in many areas than it appears, spending much time underground, resting in or prowling through rodent burrows or other subterranean passageways. **SIMILAR SPECIES:** Milk Snake and Mole Kingsnake have *single* anal plates and *smooth* scales, and *lack* striping under tails. (2) In young Rat Snakes *(obsoleta)* and Baird's Rat Snake there is no dark spearpoint between the eyes, and the postocular dark stripe stops at the mouth line (Fig. 68). **RANGE:** Disjunct. A northern population in s. N.J., cen. parts of the Delmarva peninsula, and s. Md. and Va.; the bulk of the range from e. N.C. to s. Fla. and the Keys, and west to the Mississippi R. and s. La.; sizable disjunct colonies in Ky. and a smaller one in w. Md.; apparently absent from a large area in s. Va. and adj. n. N.C.; introduced on Grand Cayman I. south of Cuba.

GREAT PLAINS RAT SNAKE *Elaphe guttata emoryi*   PL. 28

IDENTIFICATION: 24–36 in. (61–91 cm); record 60¼ in. (153 cm). A western and rather drab subspecies of the Corn Snake, but similar in all essentials of pattern, including a *spearpoint* between the eyes (Fig. 67) and striping under tail (Fig. 66). In very old adults the head markings are usually faint. Four dusky longitudinal stripes may be present. Blotches dark gray, brown, or olive-brown on a ground color of light gray. (In northern part of range, blotches are much more numerous and so narrowed that they resemble transverse bands.) Scales weakly *keeled*; anal *divided*.

Secretive and essentially nocturnal during warm weather; hides beneath stones and in rock crevices, caves, etc., by day. More likely to be found in canyons or rocky draws or on hillsides than on open plains or prairies. Often occurs along watercourses or near springs in arid country. **SIMILAR SPECIES:** (1) Bullsnake has *strongly keeled* scales and a *single* anal plate. (2) Prairie Kingsnake and Glossy Snakes have *single* anals plus *smooth* scales. (3) Black, Texas, and Baird's Rat Snakes and Fox Snake (Fig. 67) all lack a spearpoint between eyes. **RANGE:** Sw. Ill. to se. Colo. and e. N.M. and south through Texas and n. Mexico to San Luis Potosí and n. Veracruz; a disjunct area in w. Colo. and adj. e. Utah, and an isolated record in extr. ne. Utah. Intergrades with the Corn Snake in extr. s. Ark., nw. La., and adj. e. Texas.

FOX SNAKE *Elaphe vulpina*   **PL. 28**

IDENTIFICATION: 36–54 in. (91–137 cm); record 70½ in. (179.1 cm). A boldly blotched snake of the north-central region. Ground color varies from yellowish to light brown, the dark spots and blotches from chocolate to black. The head, usually devoid of any really conspicuous markings (Fig. 67), varies from brown to distinctly reddish. Belly yellow, strongly checkered with black. Scales weakly *keeled;* anal *divided. Young:* Ground color paler than in adults; blotches rich brown and narrowly edged with black or dark brown; head markings bold, including a dark transverse line anterior to eyes and a dark line from eye to angle of jaw. Dark lines on head fade and become difficult to define as the snake approaches adulthood.

A serpent with many aliases—a "timber snake" in Ohio and parts of Michigan, a "pine snake" in Wisconsin and adjacent states, and a "spotted adder" to many who cannot think of a better name. The reddish head frequently causes it to be killed as a copperhead, and the black and yellowish coloration plus the habit of vibrating the tail cause it to be slain as a rattler. Actually harmless and normally quite inoffensive. Toward the west, it occurs in farmlands, prairies, stream valleys, woods, and dune country, but the eastern subspecies is essentially a resident of the extensive marshes bordering Lakes Erie and Huron and their immediate environs. **SIMILAR SPECIES:** (1) Corn Snake and Great Plains Rat Snake have a spearpoint atop head (Fig. 67). (2) Milk Snakes and Prairie Kingsnake have *smooth* scales and *single* anal plates. (3) Bullsnake, a great hisser, has pointed snout, *strongly keeled* scales, and a *single* anal. (4) Hognose Snakes have upturned snouts. (5) Juvenile Black Rat Snakes will be troublesome, for they are as strongly spotted as young Fox Snakes; only safe check is to count ventral scutes—221 or more in Black Rat Snake and 216 or fewer in Fox Snake. **RANGE:** S. Ont. to Neb.; upper peninsula of Mich. to cen. Ill. and n. Mo. **SUBSPECIES:** WESTERN FOX SNAKE, *Elaphe v. vulpina* (Pl. 28). Large dorsal blotches average 41 in number (counted on body only). Most of range outlined above. EASTERN FOX SNAKE, *Elaphe v. gloydi.* Dorsal blotches larger and fewer, averaging 34. Head very likely to be reddish. S. Ont., e. Mich., and n.-cen. Ohio.

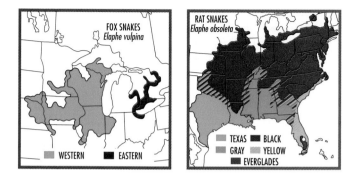

FOX SNAKES
Elaphe vulpina

WESTERN EASTERN

RAT SNAKES
Elaphe obsoleta

TEXAS BLACK
GRAY YELLOW
EVERGLADES

BLACK RAT SNAKE *Elaphe obsoleta obsoleta* PL. 28

IDENTIFICATION: 42–72 in. (106.7–183 cm); record 101 in. (256.5 cm). Typically a plain, shiny black snake, but sometimes showing traces of a spotted pattern when the skin is distended (as after a heavy meal) or in portions of the range near where intergradation takes place with related subspecies. Light areas, chiefly confined to *skin between scales*, may be white, yellow, orange, or red. Belly diffused or clouded with gray or brown on white or yellowish, but usually with some indications of checkerboarding, at least toward head. Chin and throat plain white or cream. Scales weakly *keeled*; anal *divided*. *Young:* Strongly patterned dorsally on *body and tail* with gray or brown blotches on a pale gray ground color and looking like the adult Gray Rat Snake illustrated on Pl. 28. Darkening occurs rapidly as the animal grows, and a specimen roughly 3 ft. (1 m) long may have only traces of pattern remaining. The dark stripe extending backward from eye normally terminates at mouth line (Fig. 68). Some young Black Rat Snakes may have indications of dark stripes beneath the tail, but these are usually not so prominent as those in the corn snake group (Fig. 66), and usually fade out rapidly as snake grows older and larger.

The so-called "pilot" or "mountain black snake." Occurs virtually at sea level and to considerable altitudes in parts of the Appalachian mountain chain. Habitats range from rocky, timbered hillsides to flat farmlands of the Coastal Plain. An excellent climber, sometimes establishing residence in cavities high up in hollow trees. **SIMILAR SPECIES:** (1) Black Racers and Coachwhips have *smooth* scales, and their bodies are round in cross section — not shaped like a loaf of bread (Fig. 16, opp. Pl. 28). Juvenile Racers have no pattern on tail, or only traces of one. (2) Water Snakes have *strongly keeled* scales, and many of them flatten their bodies when alarmed. (3) Fox Snakes have 216 or fewer ventrals (221 or more in Black Rat Snake). (4) Milk Snakes and Kingsnakes have *smooth* scales and *single* anal plates. (5) See also Hognose Snakes. Most confusion will occur in trying to identify young Black Rat Snakes. In young (and adults) of Corn Snake and Great Plains Rat Snake, there is a spearpoint on head (Fig. 67), and the postocular stripe continues onto neck (Fig. 68). **RANGE:** Sw. New England and s. Ont. to Ga. in the East; sw. Wisc. to Okla. and n. La. in the Midwest; a disjunct colony in e. Ont. and adj. N.Y.; an isolated record in the Okla. panhandle.

YELLOW RAT SNAKE *Elaphe obsoleta quadrivittata*   **PL. 28**
IDENTIFICATION: 42–72 in. (106.7–183 cm); record 87 in. (221 cm). The *four dark stripes* are always strongly defined, but the ground color is subject to considerable variation. The brightest, most golden-yellow specimens come from peninsular Fla.; from farther north they are darker, less brilliant yellow. (The Rat Snake "intergrade" on Pl. 28 is a greenish intergrade between the Black and Yellow Rat Snakes from along the extreme northern portion of latter's range.) *Tongue black.* Scales weakly *keeled*; anal *divided. Young:* Strongly blotched and similar in general appearance to an adult Gray Rat Snake (Pl. 28); stripes absent or only slightly indicated. Blotches fade, and the dark stripes develop as the young serpent grows.

A common and characteristic snake of the great river swamps of the South, foraging high into cypress and other trees. Also occurs in a wide variety of other habitats, including live-oak hammocks, cutover woods, fallow fields, and around barns and abandoned buildings. **NOTE:** Snakes of this race from the Florida Keys often exhibit both stripes and spots, with the stripes gray-brown to blackish and well defined; dorsal ground color tan, dull orange, or some shade of brown; dark dorsal spots, remnants of juvenile pattern, are usually distinctly evident; belly suffused with light gray, at least posteriorly. **SIMILAR SPECIES:** For ways of telling the blotched young from other blotched or spotted snakes see Black Rat Snake. **RANGE:** S. N.C. to s. Fla. and the Upper Keys.

EVERGLADES RAT SNAKE *Elaphe obsoleta rossalleni*   **PL. 28**
IDENTIFICATION: 48–78 in. (122–198 cm); record 87 in. (221 cm). "Orange rat snake" would be a good alternate name for this handsome serpent. The ground color, usually bright *orange,* may be orange-yellow or orange-brown instead. The grayish longitudinal stripes are not clear-cut and are often vague or almost lacking. Belly bright orange or orange-yellow. *Tongue red.* Scales weakly *keeled*; anal *divided. Young:* Ground color pinkish buff or pinkish

orange; blotches light grayish brown and not sharply in contrast with ground color.

A resident of the Kissimmee Prairie and the Everglades where it is found in the great waving seas of sawgrass, on open prairies within the 'Glades, in trees or shrubs, and along the waterways, taking readily to the water and swimming skillfully when alarmed. Often seen in the Australian pine *(Casuarina)* trees that have been planted along roads of the region. **RANGE:** S. Fla., chiefly in the Everglades.

GRAY RAT SNAKE *Elaphe obsoleta spiloides* PL. 28

IDENTIFICATION: 42–72 in. (106.7–183 cm); record 84¼ in. (214 cm). Called the "oak snake" in some parts of the South. This Rat Snake retains the strongly blotched juvenile pattern throughout life, but there is much variation in its intensity. The ground color may be dark or medium gray in some specimens but pale brown or gray, sometimes almost white, in others. Blotches may be either brown or gray and varying from pale to very dark, but always in contrast with the lighter ground color. Scales weakly *keeled*; anal *divided*.

Habits of this serpent are similar to those of the Black Rat Snake, which it replaces in the South. The two intergrade over a fairly broad zone where their ranges meet. Intergrades in some areas are often chocolate brown with the blotches not much darker than ground color; in other areas individuals may look like either the Black or Gray Rat Snake, but may be capable of producing young that, upon maturity, resemble the opposite type. **SIMILAR SPECIES:** See (1) Black Rat Snake and (2) general discussion of Rat Snakes. **RANGE:** Sw. Ga. to Miss. and north in Mississippi Valley to extr. s. Ill. and sw. Ind.

TEXAS RAT SNAKE *Elaphe obsoleta lindheimerii* PL. 28

IDENTIFICATION: 42–72 in. (106.7–183 cm); record 86 in. (218.4 cm). A blotched Rat Snake but often with less contrast between pattern and ground color than in Gray Rat Snake. Blotches usually brownish- or bluish-black; ground color gray or yellowish. Head often black. There may be red on the skin between scales, and this color often encroaches on edges of the scales themselves. This race is subject to considerable individual variation in both coloration and pattern. Scales weakly *keeled*; anal *divided. Young:* A pattern of bold dark blotches that are considerably larger than the spaces between them. Ground color gray — much darker than in the young of other races of *Elaphe obsoleta.*

A snake with a variety of habitats, ranging from bayou and swampy country of Louisiana and eastern Texas through woods and stream valleys to rocky canyons in western part of range. **SIMI-LAR SPECIES:** See (1) Black Rat Snake and (2) general section on Rat Snakes. **RANGE:** From the Pearl and Mississippi rivers west through La. to cen. and s. Texas.

BAIRD'S RAT SNAKE *Elaphe bairdi* PL. 28

IDENTIFICATION: 33–54 in. (84–137 cm); record 62 in. (157.5 cm). The *four longitudinal stripes*, all rather vague but with the two center ones darkest, are the most conspicuous markings in large adults. Traces of dorsal and lateral spots, remnants of the juvenile pattern, are often faintly discernible, but very large specimens may be patternless. The general dorsal coloration is grayish brown, but edges of the scales are yellow or orange-yellow on forepart of body and deeper orange toward rear, giving snake a rich overwash of bright coloration. Scales weakly *keeled*; anal *divided. Young:* 48 or more brown crossbands on back, and additional ones on tail; an alternating row of smaller dark spots along each side of body; a dark band across head anterior to eyes, and a dark postocular stripe that stops at mouth line.

A resident of rocky, wooded canyons and of forested uplands (as in Chisos Mountains of the Big Bend). Named for Spencer Fullerton Baird, zoologist and administrator of the Smithsonian Institution during the 19th century. **RANGE:** Cen. Texas to the Big Bend and adj. Coahuila; isolated colonies in cen. Coahuila, Nuevo León, and Tamaulipas.

TRANS-PECOS RAT SNAKE *Bogertophis subocularis* PL. 32

IDENTIFICATION: 36–54 in. (90–137 cm); record 66 in. (167.6 cm). A relatively slender, graceful Rat Snake that displays a variety of

The pattern of a typical Trans-Pecos Rat Snake consists of dark H-shaped markings, the long arms of which change to dark stripes on the neck. There are small scales between the large eye and the upper labial scales.

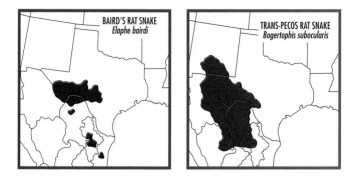

BAIRD'S RAT SNAKE
Elaphe bairdi

TRANS-PECOS RAT SNAKE
Bogertophis subocularis

patterns on a normally tan, yellow, or olive-yellow dorsum. Throughout much of its range, this snake possesses 21–28 large black or brown H-shaped dorsal body markings, the arms of the H's forming parts of two longitudinal stripes that, anteriorly, are bold and black and terminate on the neck. In the Lower Pecos R. drainage a form commonly referred to as the "blond" variant displays a lighter ground color and lacks much, if not all, of the dorsal pattern. In the Franklin Mountains near El Paso in extr. w. Texas these serpents may have a steel-gray ground color. No pattern of any kind on the olive or tan-colored head. Venter whitish, virtually unmarked except for indications of dusky stripes under tail. *A row of scales between eye and upper labials.* Scales *keeled;* anal *divided. Young:* Dorsal markings similar but paler; ground color yellow with a slightly grayish tinge; 11–14⅞ in. (28–37.8 cm) at hatching.

The Rat Snake of the Chihuahuan Desert. This large, slightly popeyed serpent is locally common in areas where it can hide by day in rock piles or mammal burrows. Like other residents of the desert, it prowls at night when the rodents that constitute the bulk of its food are abroad. It also feeds on bats and birds. Lizards are an important item in the diet of the young. **SIMILAR SPECIES:** Adults of Baird's Rat Snake have four rather vague dark stripes and no blotches; the young of that species are marked with rounded or rectangular (not H-shaped) blotches. **RANGE:** S. N.M. to Durango and Nuevo León.

GLOSSY SNAKES: GENUS *Arizona*

The genus *Arizona* includes only a single species, but there are many races, all of which are sometimes called "faded snakes"

Mexican subspecies · KANSAS
Western subspecies · TEXAS · PAINTED DESERT

GLOSSY SNAKES
Arizona elegans

because of their pale, washed-out appearance. The snakes of this group are related to the Bullsnake and Gopher Snakes, but they differ in being mainly nocturnal or crepuscular and in having smooth scales and only two prefrontals. (Some Mexican members of the genus *Pituophis* also have only two prefrontals.) The Glossy Snake ranges collectively from Nebraska, Kansas, Oklahoma, and southeastern Texas to California and south to San Luis Potosí, Aguascalientes, Sinaloa, and central Baja California.

TEXAS GLOSSY SNAKE *Arizona elegans arenicola*   PL. 27
IDENTIFICATION: 27–36 in. (68.8–90 cm); record 54⅝ in. (138.7 cm). A shiny, brownish "bullsnake." *Blotches brown* and dark-edged, usually 50 or fewer on body. *Ground color cream or buff*. In large adults the sides of the body may become so heavily suffused with brown or gray that the lateral spots are obscured, and the pale ground color may be restricted to small middorsal patches between the large blotches. Belly white or pale buff, *unmarked*. Pupil of eye slightly elliptical. Only two prefrontals (Fig. 15, opp. Pl. 27). Ventrals usually 212 or more in males and 221 or more in females. Scales *smooth*; anal *single*. *Young*: 9½–11 in. (24–28 cm) at hatching.

Chiefly nocturnal or crepuscular, but also may be abroad during morning hours. Vibrates tail when alarmed. Partial to sandy areas and adept at burrowing. Food includes small mammals and lizards. **SIMILAR SPECIES:** (1) Great Plains and Texas Rat Snakes have *keeled* scales and *divided* anals. (2) In Prairie Kingsnake, belly is normally marked with squarish blotches of brown on a yellowish ground color, but sometimes it is plain *except* that the lowermost lateral spots encroach on ends of ventrals. **RANGE:** S. Texas. **SUB-SPECIES:** KANSAS GLOSSY SNAKE, *Arizona e. elegans*. Similar but usually with more than 50 large body blotches; ventrals 211 or fewer in males and 220 or fewer in females; record size 55¾ in. (142 cm). Extr. sw. Neb. and cen. Kans. through w. Texas and southeast to Tamaulipas. PAINTED DESERT GLOSSY SNAKE, *Arizona e. philipi*. Maximum number of scale rows usually 27 (29 or more in eastern races); body blotches usually 62 or more. El Paso, Texas, region; Utah, N.M., Ariz., and extr. n. Chihuahua. Western and Mexican subspecies.

Large, powerful, constricting snakes that hiss loudly, vibrate their tails rapidly, and are apt to strike vigorously when first encountered. The head appears disproportionately small, especially among the Pine Snakes. In our species there are four prefrontal scales (Fig. 15, opp. Pl. 27) instead of two as in most other snakes of the Family Colubridae. The snout is somewhat pointed and the rostral plate extends upward between the internasals. Scales *keeled*; anal *single*.

Snakes of this group are good burrowers; they are chiefly diurnal except during hot weather and are useful in controlling rodents. Their food consists largely of small mammals, but they also eat birds and their eggs, and the smaller snakes prey on lizards. Some make good captives, but they tend to be nervous and wriggly when handled. The young vary from 12¼ to 21½ in. (32 to 54.9 cm) at hatching. Our single species (*melanoleucus*) occurs in a variety of subspecies ranging collectively from coast to coast; members are called Pine Snakes in the East, Bullsnakes from the plains and prairie states westward, and Gopher Snakes in the Pacific states. The genus *Pituophis* as a whole ranges from New Jersey, Wisconsin, Minnesota, and southwestern Canada to Guatemala and the southern tip of Baja California.

NORTHERN PINE SNAKE   PL. 27
Pituophis melanoleucus melanoleucus

IDENTIFICATION: 48–66 in. (122–168 cm); record 83 in. (210.8 cm). A large black and white snake with a *noisy hiss*. *Dark blotches* are black toward front of body, but they may be brown near and on tail. Ground color dull *white, yellowish, or light gray*. Scales *keeled*; anal *single*. *Young:* Pattern like that of adults, but with ground color paler and with a pink or orange tinge.

A snake of flat, sandy pine barrens, sandhills, and dry mountain ridges, most often in or near pine woods. Climbs occasionally but is much addicted to burrowing and is so secretive that its presence may be unsuspected even by persons who have lived in the same region with it for years. **SIMILAR SPECIES:** Gray Rat Snakes and juvenile Black Rat Snakes have divided anals and only two prefrontals (four in Pine and Bullsnakes—see Fig. 15, opp. Pl. 27). **RANGE:** Extr. s. N.C. west through S.C. to n. Ga., e. Tenn., and extr. se. Ky., and well south into Ala. Small disjunct colonies in s. N.J., w.-cen. Va. and adj. W. Va., cen. Ky., and sw. Tenn.; a larger one in w. Tenn., adj. sw. Ky. and n. Ala. Intergrades with Florida Pine Snake in S.C., Ga., and Ala.

FLORIDA PINE SNAKE *Pituophis melanoleucus mugitus* **PL. 27**
 IDENTIFICATION: 48–66 in. (122–168 cm); record 90 in. (228.6 cm).
A *tan or rusty-brown* snake with an indistinct pattern. Might be
likened to a Northern Pine Snake coated with a thin layer of dried
mud and through which dark markings are vaguely visible.
Amount of pattern quite variable, but the markings are never so
clean-cut and sharply defined as in the northern race. The dark
blotches are clearly distinct on only the hind part of the body and
on the tail. *Hisses loudly.* Scales *keeled*; anal *single. Young:*
Patterned much as in the Northern Pine Snake, but with the
blotches brown instead of black.

   Often found in dry, sandy areas, in stands of oak or pine, abandoned fields, etc. An accomplished burrower, adept at pursuing
pocket gophers, a favorite food. **SIMILAR SPECIES:** (1) Eastern Coachwhip has *smooth* scales and *divided* anal. (2) Rat Snakes have
divided anals and a few middorsal rows of scales *weakly* keeled.
RANGE: S. S.C. to Ga. and s. Fla.

BLACK PINE SNAKE *Pituophis melanoleucus lodingi*   **PL. 27**
 IDENTIFICATION: 48–64 in. (122–163 cm); record 76 in. (193 cm). A
melanistic Pine Snake. Plain (or nearly plain) *black or dark
brown,* both above and below. Faint indications of blotches may
be evident on or near tail, and a few irregular white spots may be
present on throat or belly. Snout and lips often dark russet-brown.
Hisses loudly. Scales *keeled*; anal *single. Young:* Dark anteriorly,
patterned posteriorly; venter tan to pink with some black
blotches. **SIMILAR SPECIES:** (1) Racers and Whipsnakes have *smooth*
scales and *divided* anals. (2) Eastern Indigo Snake has *smooth*
scales. **RANGE:** Chiefly in sandy areas of longleaf pine belt from sw.
Ala. to extr. e. La.

LOUISIANA PINE SNAKE   **PL. 27**
Pituophis melanoleucus ruthveni
 IDENTIFICATION: 48–56 in. (122–142 cm); record 70¼ in. (178.4 cm).
Markings conspicuously different at opposite ends of body: (a)
blotches *near head* dark brown, obscuring ground color and often
running together; and (b) blotches *near and on tail* brown or russet, clear-cut, and well separated. Total number of *body* blotches
(in middorsal row) 28 to 42. Ground color buff, changing to yellowish on and near tail. Head buff and profusely spotted or
splotched with dark brown. Belly boldly marked with black.
Hisses loudly. Scales *keeled*; anal *single.* **RANGE:** Chiefly sandy, longleaf pine woods of w.-cen. La. and e. Texas.

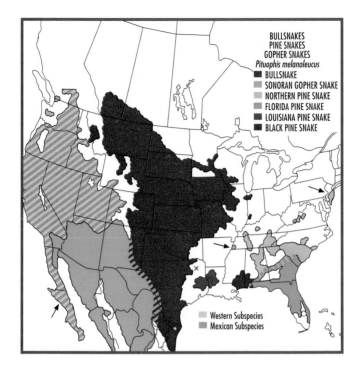

BULLSNAKES
PINE SNAKES
GOPHER SNAKES
Pituophis melanoleucus
■ BULLSNAKE
■ SONORAN GOPHER SNAKE
■ NORTHERN PINE SNAKE
■ FLORIDA PINE SNAKE
■ LOUISIANA PINE SNAKE
■ BLACK PINE SNAKE

Western Subspecies
Mexican Subspecies

BULLSNAKE *Pituophis melanoleucus sayi*   PL. 27

IDENTIFICATION: 37–72 in. (94.8–183 cm); record 100 in. (254 cm).
A large, yellowish snake marked with a series of black, brown, or
reddish brown dorsal blotches, which are darkest and in strongest
contrast with the ground color at *both* ends of the snake—near
the head and near and on the tail. Some specimens, especially
those from eastern part of range, have all the blotches dark; in
arid regions the general appearance is more pallid. *Body* blotches
(in middorsal row) usually 41 or more. Belly yellow with bold
black spots, especially toward sides. Usually a *dark band* extending from eye to angle of jaw, and with a parallel yellow band above
it. *Hisses loudly.* Scales *keeled*; anal *single.*

At home on plains and prairies; also occurring from sand
prairies in Illinois and Indiana southwestward to the desert and
semi-arid portions of southern and western Texas and adjacent
Mexico. Clumps of vegetation and mammal burrows are favorite
lurking places, both for the Bullsnake and its rodent food. Birds

An adult Bullsnake, one of the few kinds of North American serpents that can hiss loudly.

and their eggs are also eaten. **SIMILAR SPECIES:** Texas Rat Snake, Glossy Snake, and Prairie Kingsnake have only two prefrontals (four in the Bullsnake—see Fig. 15, opp. Pl. 27). **RANGE:** W. Ind. and Wisc. to s. Alberta, and south to Texas and ne. Mexico; an isolated record in ne. Texas.

SONORAN GOPHER SNAKE NOT ILLUS.
Pituophis melanoleucus affinis

IDENTIFICATION: 50–72 in. (127–183 cm); record 92 in. (233.7 cm). Similar to the Bullsnake but with the blotches all brown or reddish brown on the forepart of the body; the blotches are strikingly darker on and near the tail, where they may be almost black.

Some specimens are extraordinarily belligerent when first encountered. They raise and draw back their heads, inflate their throats, hiss and strike repeatedly, and glide toward a person, meanwhile beating a lively tattoo with their tails. Similar behavior occurs (rarely) in the Bullsnake. **RANGE:** W. Texas to se. Calif. and south to Zacatecas and s. Sinaloa. Western and Mexican subspecies.

KINGSNAKES AND MILK SNAKES: GENUS *Lampropeltis*

These are shiny snakes with *smooth* scales and *single* anal plates. All are powerful constrictors, and their killing and eating of other serpents, including venomous ones, is well known. They should not be kept with other reptiles smaller than themselves, even of their own species. In fact, they must be fed in separate cages or watched very closely. Otherwise two of them may start to eat at opposite ends of the same food animal and, when their heads meet, one snake will engulf the other! Besides snakes, they also eat lizards, rodents, small birds and their eggs, and turtle eggs.

Kingsnakes are essentially black (or dark brown) with white or yellowish spots on their scales, but the size and arrangement of the spots vary from one subspecies to the next. When first encountered they vibrate their tails rapidly and may hiss and strike but, once caught, the majority become calm almost immediately. Contrary to popular opinion, they do not prowl about looking for rattlers to fight. Any snake is simply a meal, but they apparently are immune to the venoms of our *native* poisonous snakes. Young Kingsnakes vary from about 9 to 12 in. (23 to 30.6 cm) at hatching.

Milk Snakes are basically tricolored, with red (or brown), black, and white (or yellow) in the form of transverse rings. In some kinds there are rows of blotches instead of rings, but in all cases the reddish parts of the pattern are surrounded by black. Milk Snakes also vibrate their tails and hiss and strike, but many remain belligerent in captivity; some have a habit, when handled, of biting without warning. The name of the group derives from the nonsensical old wives' tale that snakes milk cows. Milk Snakes feed largely on mice and are among our most beneficial serpents; small snakes and lizards also are eaten. Young Milk Snakes are about 5 to 11 in. (12.5 to 28 cm) at hatching.

The Prairie and Mole Kingsnakes are marked with brown or reddish brown blotches outlined with black on a ground color of light brown or tan. The Gray-banded Kingsnake has a gray ground color, black crossbands, and may or may not also have coral-colored markings.

The genus occurs from southeastern Canada and Montana to Ecuador, and so does the Milk Snake, *Lampropeltis triangulum*, which has one of the largest ranges of any species of snake in the world. It is also one of the most variable, with 25 races, including eight within our area and another 17 distributed, collectively, from Mexico to Ecuador.

ASTERN KINGSNAKE *Lampropeltis getula getula* PL. 29
IDENTIFICATION: 36–48 in. (90–122 cm); record 82 in. (208.3 cm). The "chain snake" —a shiny black serpent clad with large, bold *links* of white or cream. Specimens from southern part of range may be dark brown instead of black. Scales *smooth*; anal *single*. *Young:* Patterned like adults.

A handsome snake of the eastern seaboard's pine belt, but one that also crosses the Piedmont and even enters mountain valleys. Habitat is chiefly terrestrial, but it shows a distinct liking for streambanks and borders of swamps, possibly because Water Snakes and turtle eggs, two important foods, may be abundant there. Kingsnakes swim readily. They are often secretive, hiding under boards, logs, or debris; they bask in the open occasionally in spring or autumn, and may prowl by day, especially in early morning or at twilight, but are largely nocturnal in hot weather. Other vernacular names are "thunder snake" and "swamp wamper." **SIMILAR SPECIES:** (1) Northern Pine Snake has black or dark brown blotches on a *whitish* ground color and *strongly keeled* scales. (2) Young Black Rat Snakes and young Black Racers, which bear a superficial resemblance to young Kingsnakes, have *divided* anals. **RANGE:** S. N.J. to n. Fla.; west to the Appalachians and s. Ala. **SUBSPECIES:** OUTER BANKS KINGSNAKE, *Lampropeltis g. sticticeps.* Similar but usually brown instead of black; white speckles present in dark interspaces between chainlike markings; a robust, tapering head with the rostral exceptionally large (its dorsal length exceeds length of suture between internasal scales). Outer Banks of N.C. from Cape Hatteras to Cape Lookout.

FLORIDA KINGSNAKE *Lampropeltis getula floridana*   **PL. 29**
IDENTIFICATION: 36–48 in. (90–122 cm); record 69½ in. (176.3 cm). *Palest* of the large Kingsnakes. Each individual dorsal scale is yellowish or cream-colored at base and brown at apex. Indications of light crosslines are usually present, especially in neck region. Belly is cream to pale yellow with spots of tan or pinkish brown. Scales *smooth*; anal *single*. *Young:* A chainlike pattern similar to that of Eastern Kingsnake. Dorsal crossbands cream-colored, yellow, or reddish yellow on a ground color of brown; many scales in the dark dorsal areas have reddish brown centers; light areas on sides have bright red centers. **RANGE:** S. Fla. from vicinity of Tampa Bay to southern tip of peninsula; intergrades with the Eastern Kingsnake over much of Fla., including a large part of the peninsula and in disjunct areas in the panhandle and along the border with se. Ga. Two types of intergradation are illustrated on Pl. 29, one labeled the "peninsula intergrade" and the other, from the panhandle population, labeled the "blotched intergrade."

BLACK KINGSNAKE *Lampropeltis getula nigra*   **PL. 29**
IDENTIFICATION: 36–45 in. (90–114 cm); record 58 in. (147.3 cm). Similar to the Eastern Kingsnake, but with the chainlike pattern greatly reduced and indicated only by small white or yellowish spots. Some specimens are almost plain black; others, especially those from near the region of intergradation with the Speckled Kingsnake, may have numerous yellowish spots on sides of body.

KINGSNAKES
Lampropeltis getula

EASTERN
SPECKLED
DESERT
FLORIDA
BLACK
OUTER BANKS
Western &
Mexican subspecies

Scales *smooth*; anal *single. Young:* Chainlike pattern clearly distinct.

Habitats include dry, rocky hills, open woods, dry prairies, and stream valleys. **SIMILAR SPECIES:** Black Racers and Black Rat Snakes both have *divided* anal plates; Rat Snakes also have *keeled* scales. **RANGE:** S. Ohio and adj. W. Va. to se. Ill.; south to cen. Ala.

SPECKLED KINGSNAKE *Lampropeltis getula holbrooki* **PL. 29**
IDENTIFICATION: 36–48 in. (90–122 cm); record 72 in. (182.9 cm). The "salt-and-pepper snake" with a white or yellowish spot centered in each (or most) of the black or dark brown dorsal scales. The light spots often form narrow whitish rows across the back. Scales *smooth*; anal *single. Young:* Distinct light dorsal crossbands with little or no spotting between them; sides of body spotted.

This Kingsnake makes use of a greater variety of habitats than any of the related subspecies. It is at home in the great river swamps of the lower Mississippi Valley, in coastal marshes, in upland wooded areas like the Ozarks, and in stream valleys across the open plains and prairies. Shelters, such as logs, rocks, ledges, thick clumps of vegetation, etc., are utilized as hiding places. **SIMI-LAR SPECIES:** Buttermilk Racer has light spots that vary both in coloration and size, and its anal plate is *divided*. **RANGE:** S. Iowa south to the Gulf of Mexico; isolated record in nw. Kans.; intergrades with the Desert Kingsnake throughout a wide area from Neb. to Texas.

DESERT KINGSNAKE *Lampropeltis getula splendida*   PL. 29

IDENTIFICATION: 36–45 in. (90–114 cm); record 60 in. (152.4 cm). A profusion of white or yellowish dots on the sides, but with a mid-dorsal series of plain black or dark brown spots. Each such spot is separated from its neighbor by a row of light dots across the back. *Belly chiefly black*. Scales *smooth*; anal *single*. *Young:* Less dark pigment; middorsal dark spots boldly outlined with yellow; a row of dark spots on each side of body. The speckled flanks and overall dark appearance develop with age.

A Kingsnake of the arid Southwest which, in order to avoid high temperatures and desiccation, is largely nocturnal — like other serpents of the region. Often found near streams or irrigation ditches. **SIMILAR SPECIES:** Speckled Racer has *divided* anal plate and the middle rows of dorsal scales are *weakly* keeled. Also, Speckled Racer has conspicuously large eyes and a black stripe extending backward from eye. **RANGE:** Cen. Texas to extr. se. Ariz. and n.-cen. Mexico; isolated records in n. N.M. and s. Colo. Western and Mexican subspecies.

EASTERN MILK SNAKE   PL. 30; FIG. 69
Lampropeltis triangulum triangulum

IDENTIFICATION: 24–36 in. (61–90 cm); record 52 in. (132.1 cm). A rather slender, strongly blotched snake with a Y-shaped or V-shaped *light patch* on the nape. There are three (sometimes five) rows of brown or reddish brown, black-bordered blotches down the body, the middorsal ones quite large and alternating in position with the smaller lateral ones. Ground color gray to tan. Belly checkerboarded (often very irregularly) with black on white (Fig. 69). Not too much trust should be placed in the Y or V marking, because it is subject to variation; in extreme cases it may even be replaced by a light collar like those found in other races of Milk Snakes. Scales *smooth*; anal *single*. *Young:* Blotches bright red and forming basis for the name "red adder."

A frequent victim of the ridiculous belief that it milks cows. Also killed because of its superficial resemblance to the Copperhead — and the vernacular name "adder" doesn't help, either.

Sometimes called "house snake," but "barn snake" would be more descriptive, because it would reflect the frequency with which farm buildings are entered in search of rodents. Many habitats are utilized—fields, woodlands, rocky hillsides, river bottoms, etc., from virtually sea level to high up in mountains. Usually secretive and found hiding under logs, boards, stones, etc. **SIMILAR SPECIES:** (1) Copperhead has coppery, virtually unmarked head, single row of dorsal crossbands, and a belly that is *not* checkerboarded. (2) Water Snakes have *keeled* scales and *divided* anals. (3) Racers and Rat Snakes, the young of which are spotted, have *divided* anals. (4) Scarlet Snake has plain (unpatterned) belly. (5) Dark markings of Mole Kingsnake are well separated from one another (Pls. 29 and 31). **RANGE:** Me. to Minn.; south in uplands to n. Ala. Presumably intergrades with Scarlet Kingsnake from s. N.J. to ne. N.C.; specimens from that area exhibit a wide variety of patterns and various shades of reds and browns; one is illustrated on Pl. 30 as an intergrade.

RED MILK SNAKE *Lampropeltis triangulum syspila* PL. 30

IDENTIFICATION: 21–28 in. (53–71 cm); record 42 in. (106.7 cm). Also called "red snake" and "candy-cane snake." A reddish serpent with larger and fewer markings than Eastern Milk Snake. The middorsal blotches extend well down onto sides of body, and the lateral blotches are small or virtually absent, at least in the neck region. Whitish or yellowish collar usually conspicuous. Belly boldly checked with black on white. Scales *smooth;* anal *single.*

Habitats vary from woodlands and rocky hillsides to open farming country. **SIMILAR SPECIES:** (1) In Corn Snake and Great Plains Rat Snake there is a spearpoint between the eyes (Fig. 67), and underside of tail is striped (Fig. 66). (2) In Prairie Kingsnake, blotches are brown, and belly markings are brown or yellowish brown. (3) See also Similar species under Eastern Milk Snake (above). **RANGE:** Midland America from s. Ind. to nw. Miss. and west to a line extending from extr. se. S.D. to e. Okla.

CENTRAL PLAINS MILK SNAKE PL. 30; FIG. 69
Lampropeltis triangulum gentilis

IDENTIFICATION: 16–24 in. (41–61 cm); record 36 in. (91.4 cm). This "western Milk Snake" has a higher average number of red or orange rings (20–39) on the body than either the Louisiana Milk Snake or Mexican Milk Snake. The light rings vary from pale gray to yellow or greenish yellow, or are sometimes nearly white. The black pigment crosses the red rings on the belly (Fig. 69), and in some specimens it also cuts (sometimes completely) across the red rings middorsally, especially on posterior part of body. Head black; snout light. Scales *smooth,* in 21 or more rows at midbody; anal *single.*

Occupies a wide range of habitats—open prairies, wooded stream valleys, rocky canyons, mountain slopes, etc. **SIMILAR SPECIES:** (1) The two warning colors—red and yellow—touch in Coral Snakes. (2) Scarlet Snake has plain whitish belly. (3) Longnose Snake has broad black markings sprinkled with yellow spots, and its subcaudals are mostly in a single row (in two rows in Milk Snakes and most other snakes). (4) Ground Snake has 15 rows of scales at midbody. **RANGE:** Most of Kans., Okla., and extr. n.-cen. Texas to cen. Colo. **SUBSPECIES:** PALE MILK SNAKE, *Lampropeltis t. multistriata.* Similar but paler, the black areas reduced in size and the red replaced by orange (rings 22–38); snout orange, with scattered black flecks; midventral area immaculate white or whitish with only a few scattered black markings. An inhabitant of

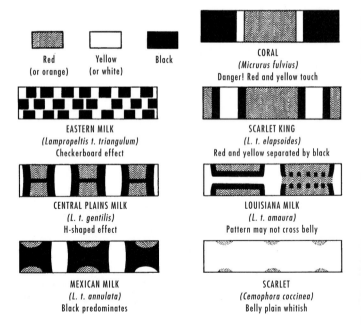

Red (or orange)	Yellow (or white)	Black

CORAL
(Micrurus fulvius)
Danger! Red and yellow touch

EASTERN MILK
(Lampropeltis t. triangulum)
Checkerboard effect

SCARLET KING
(L. t. elapsoides)
Red and yellow separated by black

CENTRAL PLAINS MILK
(L. t. gentilis)
H-shaped effect

LOUISIANA MILK
(L. t. amaura)
Pattern may not cross belly

MEXICAN MILK
(L. t. annulata)
Black predominates

SCARLET
(Cemophora coccinea)
Belly plain whitish

Fig. 69. Diagrammatic belly patterns of snakes boldly ringed or blotched with red, yellow, and black.

sand dunes, open prairies, and high plains. Most of Neb. to cen. Mont. NEW MEXICO MILK SNAKE, *Lampropeltis t. celaenops*. Black rings widen in middorsal area but normally do not cross venter; red rings 17 to 30; snout mottled with black and white. Occurs chiefly in wooded mountains, from shin oak associations to 7000 ft. (2100 m) in juniper-pinyon pine forests. Disjunct. One large area in the Big Bend Region of Texas north into cen. N.M., and a second in w. Texas and adj. e. and n. N.M. and adj. Colo. A small colony in e.-cen. Ariz., and an isolated record in n.-cen. Ariz. Western and Mexican subspecies.

MEXICAN MILK SNAKE

PL. 30; FIG. 69

Lampropeltis triangulum annulata

IDENTIFICATION: 24–30 in. (61–76 cm); record 41¼ in. (105.7 cm). A ringed milk snake with an abundance of black pigment. Black rings rather wide and not narrowing on the 1st row of scales. Red rings broad (14 to 26 in number). Belly mostly black (Fig. 69). Snout black (or virtually so). Scales *smooth;* anal *single.*

Found in a variety of habitats ranging from sand dunes to cultivated fields. **SIMILAR SPECIES:** (1) Coral Snakes have two warning colors — red and yellow — touching each other. Black separates the other colors in Mexican Milk Snake. (2) Scarlet and Ground Snakes have plain bellies. (3) Longnose Snake has the black areas sprinkled with yellow spots. **RANGE:** Cen. Texas through ne. Mexico. Mexican and Cen. and S. American subspecies.

The Mexican Milk Snake. The tricolored subspecies of the milk snake group, with their bewildering variations in color patterns, are favorites of herpetoculturalists, the people who breed snakes in captivity.

LOUISIANA MILK SNAKE

Lampropeltis triangulum amaura

IDENTIFICATION: 16–22 in. (41–56 cm); record 31 in. (78.7 cm). A brilliantly marked "mimic" of the venomous Coral Snake with 13 to 25 broad red crossbands on body. The red areas may cross the belly or may be encircled by black (Fig. 69); in the latter case they are best described as black-bordered red saddles extending well downward onto edges of belly plates. Snout mottled or speckled with black and white; rarely it may be as black as a Coral Snake's snout. Scales *smooth* and in 21 rows at midbody; anal *single*.

Usually found abroad only at night. Hides in such places as beneath stones or under bark of rotting logs or stumps. **SIMILAR SPECIES:** (1) The warning colors—red and yellow—touch in Coral Snakes; in Louisiana Milk Snake the black separates the other colors. (2) Scarlet and Ground snakes have plain whitish bellies. (3) Scarlet Kingsnake has plain red snout and only 19 rows of scales at midbody. **RANGE:** Sw. Ark. and se. Okla. to Gulf Coast of Texas; apparently absent from coastal La.

SCARLET KINGSNAKE

Lampropeltis triangulum elapsoides

IDENTIFICATION: 14–20 in. (36–51 cm); record 27 in. (68.6 cm). An extraordinary "mimic" of the venomous Eastern Coral Snake. But the snout is *red*, and the yellow rings are separated from the red by black. In southern Fla. the black rings may be enlarged mid-dorsally and cross the red rings. Rings normally continue across belly (Fig. 69). Scales *smooth*, in 19 rows at midbody; anal *single*. *Young:* 5–8 in. (13–20.3 cm) at hatching; light bands may be white instead of yellow.

A Scarlet Kingsnake baby emerging from the egg from which it has just hatched. Most egg-laying snakes deposit their clutches in moist, hidden environments and then abandon them. The young are on their own.

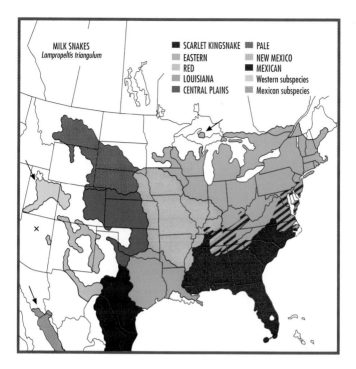

Secretive and adept at working its way beneath bark, logs, or other hiding places; seldom seen in the open except at night or after heavy rains. Commonly found in or near woodland habitats, pine especially. Often winters in pine stumps in the South. Food includes small snakes and lizards, baby mice, small fish, insects, and earthworms. **SIMILAR SPECIES:** (1) In Coral Snake (see Pl. 30) the two warning colors—red and yellow—touch each other; also the *snout is black.* (2) In Scarlet Snake the belly is plain white. (3) Ringed varieties of the Milk Snake have 21 or more scale rows at midbody. **RANGE:** Extr. s.-cen. Va. to the tip of Fla. (also Key West) and west to Mississippi R., thus chiefly in Coastal Plain but also occurring in more inland localities and to elevations of at least 2000 ft. (600 m) around edges of Appalachians; penetrates north into Tenn. and Ky. **NOTE:** The relationship of the Scarlet Kingsnake to the various races of the Milk Snake is uncertain. In the Cumberland and Interior Low Plateaus of Tenn. and Ky., and around the edges of the southern Appalachians, the Scarlet Kingsnake and Eastern Milk Snake occur together and maintain their identities as if they were full species, and some herpetologists believe that they should be accorded such status. Conversely, evidence has been presented that these two snakes intergrade in the lowlands and Piedmont from s. N.J. to ne. N.C. One of the most frequently occurring variations is shown as a presumed intergrade on Pl. 30. In La., Miss., w. Tenn., and Ky., no evidence has been presented that the Scarlet Kingsnake intergrades with western races of the Milk Snake. Much work is needed to determine the status of this strikingly colored snake.

PRAIRIE KINGSNAKE *Lampropeltis calligaster calligaster* PL. 29
IDENTIFICATION: 30–42 in. (76–106.7 cm); record 56 in. (142.7 cm). A blotched snake and one that may be troublesome to identify. Typically, back and tail are patterned with about 60 brown, reddish, or greenish, black-edged markings. Occasionally these are split in two down the back. There are two alternating rows of smaller dark markings on each side, but pairs of these may fuse together. The ground color is brownish gray to tan. In many older specimens the ground color darkens and the pattern becomes quite obscure, producing the dark variant that often is further characterized by the development of four longitudinal dusky stripes. Belly yellowish with squarish brown blotches. Scales *smooth*; anal *single. Young:* Strongly spotted; about 9–12 in. (23–30.6 cm) at hatching.

A resident of grassland prairies, open woodlands, and (farther east) patches of prairie and savannah in the midst of essentially forested country. **SIMILAR SPECIES:** (1) Great Plains Rat Snake bears a strong superficial resemblance to Prairie Kingsnake, but Rat Snakes have *keeled* scales and *divided* anals. (2) Glossy Snakes have plain white bellies. (3) In Milk Snakes the reddish blotches or rings are boldly surrounded by black, and there are *black* markings on belly. **RANGE:** W. Ind., cen. Ky., and nw. Miss. west through most of Kans., Okla., and e. Texas; isolated record in s. Texas.

MOLE KINGSNAKE PLS. 29, 31
Lampropeltis calligaster rhombomaculata
IDENTIFICATION: 30–40 in. (76–102 cm); record 47 in. (119.4 cm). A shiny, *smooth*-scaled serpent that may be patterned or not! Typical specimens have up to 71 rather small, *well-separated*, reddish brown, dark-edged spots down back and tail, and smaller and fainter spots on sides of body. The ground color is light to dark brown, sometimes with a greenish tinge but changing to a more yellowish hue on sides of body. Older specimens may lose virtually all their markings, resulting in a plain brown snake. Dusky lengthwise stripes may also develop, as in Prairie Kingsnake. Belly

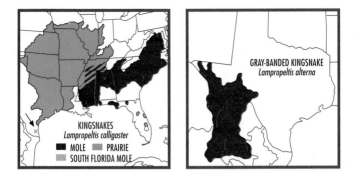

KINGSNAKES
Lampropeltis calligaster
■ MOLE ■ PRAIRIE
▨ SOUTH FLORIDA MOLE

GRAY-BANDED KINGSNAKE
Lampropeltis alterna

white or yellowish and checked, spotted, or clouded with brown. Scales *smooth;* anal *single. Young:* Boldly marked with well-separated brown or red spots (see Pl. 31); two lengthwise dark streaks on neck; about 6¾–9⅜ in. (17.2–23.8 cm) at hatching.

An accomplished burrower often turned up by the plow or during excavations. Occasionally appears on the surface, especially after heavy spring or summer rains. Ranges from Coastal Plain to at least the lower parts of Appalachians. Habitats include thickets, woodlots, cultivated fields, and even back yards in some suburban areas. **SIMILAR SPECIES:** (1) Corn Snake has *divided* anal, *keeled* scales, and underside of tail is usually striped (Fig. 66). (2) In Milk Snakes the dorsal blotches are large and close together, and belly is boldly marked with black. **RANGE:** Vicinity of Baltimore, Md., to e. La.; disjunct colonies in Fla. panhandle; intergrades with Prairie Kingsnake in s. Tenn., n. Ala., and n. Miss. **SUBSPECIES:** SOUTH FLORIDA MOLE KINGSNAKE, *Lampropeltis c. occipitolineata.* Similar to Mole Kingsnake, but adults retain the juvenile color pattern, have 75 or more dark-edged spots down back and tail, and display a network of dark lines on back of head. Disjunct colonies in cen. part of Fla. peninsula, north of Lake Okeechobee.

GRAY-BANDED KINGSNAKE *Lampropeltis alterna*　　PL. 32
IDENTIFICATION: 20–36 in. (51–90 cm); record 57¾ in. (147.1 cm). The *gray crossbands* on the body are the most constant feature of this highly variable snake. Other markings may consist solely of narrow black crossbands, or the black may be expanded, sometimes greatly, and it may include varying amounts of red or orange pigment. The narrow white lines bordering the black areas may be strikingly evident. Some specimens tend toward melanism, like the darkest of the three varieties shown on Pl. 32. Belly with

The Gray-banded Kingsnake varies more in coloration and pattern than any of our other serpents. (See Plate 32.)

black blotches that may fuse together. Eyes slightly protuberant; head noticeably wider than neck. Scales *smooth;* anal *single.* *Young:* Similar to adults, 7½–12⅜ in. (19–32.2 cm) at hatching.

This resident of the Chihuahuan Desert region lives in arid to semihumid habitats ranging from desert flats and canyons into mountains. Once considered rare, it is now known to be abundant but is seldom seen because of its secretive and nocturnal habits. Food is primarily lizards, but some small rodents are also probably eaten. This handsome serpent has a foul-smelling musk and a tendency to jerk spasmodically when handled. **SIMILAR SPECIES:** (1) In Texas Lyre Snake, pupil of eye is vertically elliptical in daylight, and anal plate is *divided.* (2) Milk Snakes have black-bordered red rings separated by areas of white or yellow (not gray). **RANGE:** Trans-Pecos region east to Edwards Co., Texas; south to ne. Durango and extr. w. Nuevo León.

SCARLET, LONGNOSE, AND SHORT-TAILED SNAKES: GENERA *Cemophora, Rhinocheilus,* AND *Stilosoma*

These serpents are allied to the members of the genus *Lampropeltis,* and the resemblance of the Scarlet Snakes in coloration and pattern to the ringed Milk Snakes is strikingly evident. Even the Longnose Snakes are similar, despite their speckled markings. The ranges of two of the genera are mutually exclusive (except in southern Texas), with *Cemophora* in the Southeast and *Rhinocheilus* in the West. The races of the latter extend, collectively, to California and Baja California and south to San Luis Potosí and Nayarit. The curiously attenuated *Stilosoma* is endemic to Florida.

An adult female Scarlet Snake from Highlands County, Florida. This serpent mimics the color and pattern of the venomous Eastern Coral Snake, with which it shares its range.

SCARLET SNAKE *Cemophora coccinea* **PLS. 30, 31; FIG. 69**
IDENTIFICATION: 14–20 in. (36–51 cm); record 32¼ in. (82.8 cm). The Coral Snake "mimic" with the plain whitish (or yellowish) belly. Snout *red* and pointed. The pattern is clean-cut in younger specimens; in adults, dark pigment may appear as small spots in the red and especially the whitish areas. Scales *smooth;* anal *single. Young:* From 5–7⁵⁄₁₆ in. (12.5–18.6 cm) at hatching.

Usually found in or near soils suitable for burrowing (sandy, loamy, etc.), in logs, beneath bark, etc.; seldom seen above ground except at night or after heavy rains. Occasionally unearthed during plowing or excavation work. Young mice and small snakes and lizards are killed by constriction. Snake eggs also are eaten. Small ones are swallowed whole, but larger eggs are seized at one end by the snake's jaws, which advance until the enlarged posterior maxillary teeth pierce the shell. A combination of vigorous chewing and pressure on the egg from a fold of the snake's body placed above it expels the egg's contents. **SIMILAR SPECIES:** (1) In venomous Coral Snakes, red and yellow rings touch and snout is black (Pls. 30 and 36). (2) In Scarlet Kingsnake and all Milk Snakes within its range, belly is heavily invaded by black pigment (Fig. 69). **RANGE:** Extr. s. Del. to tip of Fla.; west to La., e. Okla., and extr. e. Texas; disjunct colonies in s. Texas, N.J., and cen. Mo. **SUBSPECIES:** NORTHERN SCARLET SNAKE, *Cemophora c. copei* (Pls. 30 and 31). Upper labials normally 6; first black body blotch usually touching parietal scutes (at least in Atlantic coastal states). All of range except peninsular Fla. and s. Texas. FLORIDA SCARLET SNAKE, *Cemophora c. coccinea.* Similar but usually with 7 upper labials; first black body blotch separated from parietals by one to four scales. Peninsular Fla.

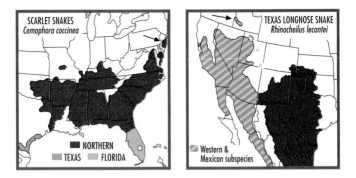

SCARLET SNAKES
Cemophora coccinea

■ NORTHERN
■ TEXAS ■ FLORIDA

TEXAS LONGNOSE SNAKE
Rhinocheilus lecontei

▨ Western &
Mexican subspecies

TEXAS SCARLET SNAKE, *Cemophora c. lineri*. Ventrals 184 or more (usually fewer in the other races); red blotches less brilliant than in eastern subspecies and with no black along their lower edges. Extr. s. Texas.

TEXAS LONGNOSE SNAKE   PL. 31
Rhinocheilus lecontei tessellatus

IDENTIFICATION: 22–32 in. (56–81 cm); record 41 in. (104.1 cm). A red, black, and yellow snake with a strongly speckled appearance. Head mostly black; snout red or pink and pointed, protruding, or even upturned; belly yellow or whitish with a few dark spots. *Scales under tail essentially in a single row*, but some are divided.

An adult Texas Long-nose Snake from Barber County, Kansas, eating a Prairie Racerunner.

Scales *smooth;* anal *single.* Vibrates tail when alarmed. *Young:* Speckling on sides of body may be only partially developed or virtually absent. Coloration paler in general than in adults—pink instead of red and whitish instead of yellow. About 6¼–10 in. (16.5–25.4 cm) at hatching.

SHORT-TAILED SNAKE
Stilosoma extenuatum

A resident chiefly of deserts and dry prairies. Nocturnal to a large extent, spending daylight hours secreted among rocks or debris or in mammal burrows or other underground retreats. Captives should be given shelters beneath which to hide or sand in which to burrow. Lizards are the chief food, but small rodents, lizard eggs, and insects are also eaten.

Occasional specimens perform a presumed defense display that may include a shifting of coils, twisting of body, and a smearing of blood, feces, and musk gland secretions over the snake and the captor's hands. Another behavioral display includes hiding the head beneath a body coil and waving the partially raised tail, which may concurrently smear a bloody fluid from the cloacal region onto the snake's body. **SIMILAR SPECIES:** (1) Scarlet Snake pattern consists of red saddles with black borders. (2) In the ringed Milk Snakes within its range, black pigment strongly invades the belly and there is no speckling on sides of body. Also, in *all* these snakes there is a *double row of scales under tail.* **RANGE:** Sw. Kans. to San Luis Potosí and west through N.M. and ne. Chihuahua. Western and Mexican subspecies.

SHORT-TAILED SNAKE *Stilosoma extenuatum* **PL. 31**

IDENTIFICATION: 14–20 in. (36–51 cm); record 25¾ in. (65.4 cm). An exceptionally slender spotted snake with a tail only 7–10% of total length. The small dark blotches number 50–80, are black or brown in coloration, and are separated along midline of back by areas of yellow, orange, or red. Belly strongly blotched with brown or black. Scales *smooth;* anal *single.*

A secretive burrower occurring chiefly in the dry "high" pinewoods of central Florida. Similar in habits to the Milk Snakes —vibrates tail when alarmed, strikes with a sneezelike hiss, is a constrictor, and primarily eats small snakes. **RANGE:** Fla. from Suwannee Co. south to Highlands Co.

"A difficult little snake" is a good way to describe any attempt to identify this species. It shows great individual variation in pattern throughout its wide range and is easily confused with similar small snakes in a number of other genera. Scales must be checked in many cases to be sure of identification.

GROUND SNAKE *Sonora semiannulata*   PL. 31; FIG. 70

IDENTIFICATION: 8½–12 in. (21.5–30.6 cm); record 18⅞ in. (48 cm). Plain, crossbanded, black-collared, or longitudinally striped specimens are sometimes found under the same rock. Further, plain individuals may be brown, gray, or orange, with or without a darkened head; those that are crossbanded may have bands of black, dark brown, light brown, or orange, with or without a broad orange or reddish middorsal stripe. Collared and crossbanded individuals are easily identified, but plain ones will be troublesome. Five common variations are shown on Pl. 31. Head is slightly wider than the neck, and this will help in distinguishing the Ground Snake from some of the other small brown or gray snakes; loreal scale (see Fig. 70) usually present, but sometimes fused with one of the adjacent scales. There is a tendency for each dorsal scale to be slightly darker (longitudinally) along its center; dorsal scales *smooth,* in 15 rows anteriorly and sometimes 14 posteriorly; anal *divided.* Belly plain white or yellowish, but underside of tail may be more colorful and display crossbands, although sometimes these are faint. *Young:* 3⅛–4¾ in. (8–12.1 cm) at hatching.

Found chiefly in the great open spaces of the plains and southwestern states, although it is a secretive snake most often discovered by overturning stones, boards, or trash, or by searching for it

GROUND SNAKE
A loreal scale separates second labial from prefrontal scale

BLACKHEAD SNAKE
No loreal; second labial touches, or almost touches, prefrontal scale (see text)

Fig. 70. *Heads of Ground* (Sonora) *and Blackhead* (Tantilla) *Snakes.*

at night. Feeds on small cen-
tipedes, scorpions, spiders,
and insects. **SIMILAR SPECIES:** (1)
Flathead, Blackhood, and
Blackhead Snakes lack any
crossbands or middorsal
stripes on the body, have a distinctly small head no wider
than neck, and lack a loreal
scale (see Fig. 70). (2) Earth
Snakes and Brown Snakes
have keeled scales. (3) In
Texas and Western Blind
Snakes, the belly scales are same size as dorsal scales. **RANGE:** Sw.
Mo. and s. Kans. to n. Mexico, west to Nev. and Calif. Disjunct
populations in n.-cen. Kans., and se. Colo. and adj. Okla., as well
as Ore., Idaho, Nev., Utah, and Baja California.

REAR-FANGED SNAKES: GENERA *Coniophanes, Ficimia, Gyalop-*
ion, Hypsiglena, Leptodeira, Tantilla, AND *Trimorphodon*

Fangs have evolved in the rear of the upper jaw, apparently independently, in a number of unrelated genera of the Family Colubridae in many parts of the world. Fortunately for us, none of ours is
so dangerous as the back-fanged Boomslang and Twig Snake of
Africa, bites from both of which have caused deaths in human
beings. Some of ours, like the Black-striped, Lyre, and Cat-eyed
Snakes, are venomous but scarcely dangerous to man; others, like
the Hooknose and Blackhead Snakes, have grooved teeth but no
well-developed venom system; still others, like the Night Snakes,
have venom but no grooves, or only slight indications of them.
These represent various stages in the evolutionary development of
the venom apparatus which, even in the dangerously poisonous
serpents, functions chiefly in the procurement of food.

The ranges of all these genera extend south into Mexico, and
most of them go much farther—*Coniophanes* to Peru, *Ficimia* to
Honduras, *Hypsiglena* to Costa Rica, *Leptodeira* to northern
Argentina and Paraguay, *Tantilla* to northern Argentina, and *Tri-*
morphodon to Costa Rica.

BLACK-STRIPED SNAKE   PL. 33
Coniophanes imperialis imperialis
IDENTIFICATION: 12–18 in. (30.6–45.7 cm); record 20 in. (50.8 cm).
The broad black or dark brown stripes alternate with stripes of tan
or brown that brighten abruptly at their anterior ends. A thin,

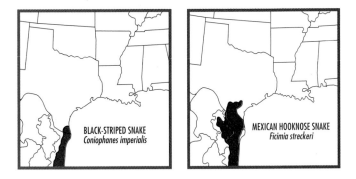

BLACK-STRIPED SNAKE
Coniophanes imperialis

MEXICAN HOOKNOSE SNAKE
Ficimia streckeri

whitish or yellowish line, extending from snout through top of eye, terminates near rear of head. These markings, plus a bright red or orange venter, assure identification. Scales *smooth;* anal *divided.*

A secretive, rear-fanged snake best sought by overturning piles of debris, heaps of rotting cactus, palm fronds, etc. It also takes refuge in deep cracks that form when soil dries out quickly under the torrid sun. Food includes small frogs, toads, lizards, and baby mice. **RANGE:** Extr. s. Texas to n. Veracruz. Mexican and Cen. American subspecies.

MEXICAN HOOKNOSE SNAKE *Ficimia streckeri*   PL. 33
IDENTIFICATION: 7–11 in. (18–28 cm); record 19 in. (48.3 cm). A combination of upturned snout, *smooth* scales, and relatively *little head pattern* identifies this species. Ground color pale to medium brown or gray. A dorsal pattern of narrow brown or olive crossbands or blotches numbering 33–60 on body; crossbands in many specimens reduced to transverse rows of small dark spots. In both Hooknose Snakes the snout, posterior to the "hook," is flattened or somewhat concave instead of bearing a dorsal keel as it does among the Hognose Snakes. Rostral in broad contact with frontal. Anal *divided.*

This nocturnal, burrowing serpent occasionally is seen above ground after rains, on freshly sprinkled lawns, along irrigation ditches, or in other places where water is present. Hooknose Snakes (of both species) make rather unsatisfactory captives. They should be provided with an inch or more of dry sand, into which they will promptly burrow out of sight. Food consists largely of spiders, but centipedes are also eaten. **SIMILAR SPECIES:** (1) Hognose Snakes have *keeled* scales. (2) In Western Hooknose Snake, dorsal markings are fewer in number but more prominent,

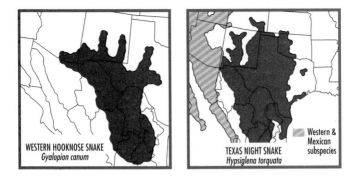

WESTERN HOOKNOSE SNAKE
Gyalopion canum

TEXAS NIGHT SNAKE
Hypsiglena torquata

Western & Mexican subspecies

the head is conspicuously patterned, and the rostral penetrates posteriorly to the prefrontals only. **RANGE:** S. Texas to Hidalgo and n. Veracruz.

WESTERN HOOKNOSE SNAKE *Gyalopion canum* PL. 33

IDENTIFICATION: 7–11 in. (18–28 cm); record 15⅒ in. (38.4 cm). Check for three things: (a) upturned snout; (b) *smooth* scales; and (c) a strongly marked pattern with the *crossbands on head* particularly prominent. There are 25–48 brown, dark-edged crossbars on body and 8–15 on tail. Ground color pale brown. Rostral in contact with *prefrontals. Anal divided.*

Largely a desert species, often found in areas where mesquite, creosote bush, and agave are dominant plants but also ascending into mountains at least to the pinyon-juniper zone. Food consists chiefly of spiders, but scorpions and centipedes also are eaten. Nocturnal and crepuscular.

A burrowing snake with the extraordinary habit of anal "popping." When touched in the field, it may undergo a series of gyrations as though writhing in agony, meanwhile extruding and retracting the lining of the cloaca through the vent to the accompaniment of a bubbling or popping sound. **SIMILAR SPECIES:** (1) Hognose Snakes have *keeled* scales. (2) Mexican Hooknose Snake has narrower but more numerous crossbands, its head markings are meager or virtually absent, and the rostral extends all the way to the frontal. **RANGE:** W. Texas and cen. N.M. to se. Ariz. and south to Zacatecas and San Luis Potosí.

TEXAS NIGHT SNAKE *Hypsiglena torquata jani* PL. 33

IDENTIFICATION: 14–16 in. (36–41 cm); record 20 in. (50.8 cm). A spotted snake with a bold elongated blotch on each side of the neck and another on the nape. A dark band backward and downward from eye. Pupil *vertically elliptical*. Body spots brown or dark gray; ground color light brown or grayish. Belly immaculate white or yellowish. Scales *smooth*; anal *divided*. *Young:* About 5–7 in. (12.5–18 cm) at hatching.

A resident of arid or semiarid country, prowling chiefly at night and often frequenting rocky regions. Small lizards are the principal food. Captives should be given sand or fairly dry soil in which to burrow, or stones or bark under which to hide. **RANGE:** S.-cen. Kans. and se. Colo. through N.M. and Texas and far south into Mexico; an isolated colony in ne. Texas. Western and Mexican subspecies.

NORTHERN CAT-EYED SNAKE   PL. 32
Leptodeira septentrionalis septentrionalis
IDENTIFICATION: 18–24 in. (45.7–61 cm); record 38¾ in. (98.4 cm). The *broad crossbands* (saddles) of dark brown or black extend almost completely across the back, and are usually in strong contrast with the light ground color, which varies from cream through yellow to reddish tan. Head broad, much wider than neck. Eye with *vertically elliptical* pupil (cat-eyed). Scales *smooth*; anal *divided*. *Young:* More boldly patterned than adults; ground color orange-tan; about 8½–9½ in. (21.5–24 cm) at hatching.

This snake, the northernmost representative of the genus *Leptodeira,* is equipped with grooved fangs toward the rear of the upper jaw for introducing venom into prey after it has been seized. The venom tends to benumb and immobilize the prey. The Cat-eyed Snake is big enough so that theoretically it might cause trouble if it swallowed a person's finger far enough to bring the fangs into play—a quite unlikely occurrence. It is best handled with care, however. Nocturnal, and likely to be found prowling in search of frogs near streams or other bodies of water. Sometimes climbs into bushes. **RANGE:** Extr. s. Texas to Veracruz and Hidalgo; an isolated colony in Coahuila. Related subspecies range southward through Mexico, Cen. America, and nw. S. America to Peru.

TEXAS LYRE SNAKE *Trimorphodon biscutatus vilkinsonii*   PL. 32
IDENTIFICATION: 18–30 in. (45.7–76 cm); record 41 in. (104.1 cm). The *dark brown body saddles,* 17–24 in number, are widest over the back, but they narrow to the width of only a scale or two on the lower sides. Similar but narrower markings on tail. Dorsal ground color light brown or gray. A few dark smudges on head represent remnants of the lyre-shaped pattern that is well-developed in some of the related subspecies. Belly white or gray to yellowish brown, and with a row of dark blotches down each side. *Pupil of eye vertically elliptical* and contracting to a tiny black slit

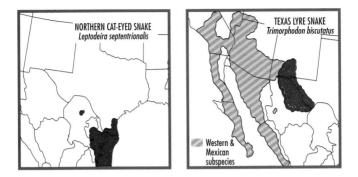

NORTHERN CAT-EYED SNAKE
Leptodeira septentrionalis

TEXAS LYRE SNAKE
Trimorphodon biscutatus

Western & Mexican subspecies

in bright light. Only snake in our area with an extra scale (the lorilabial) between the loreal and upper labials. Scales *smooth;* anal *divided. Young:* Similar to adults but more boldly patterned; about 8½ in. (21.5 cm) at hatching.

Another rear-fanged species that also should be handled with caution. A resident of rock piles and slides, rocky slopes and canyons, hiding in crevices by day and prowling by night. Lizards are the chief food, but small mammals, birds, and other snakes are also eaten. Vibrates tail when first caught. **SIMILAR SPECIES:** In Gray-banded Kingsnake pupil is circular and *anal is single.* **RANGE:** Big Bend region of Texas to s. N.M. and ne. Chihuahua. Western and Mexican subspecies.

CROWNED, FLATHEAD, BLACKHEAD, AND BLACKHOOD SNAKES: GENUS *Tantilla*

These small, secretive snakes have 15 rows of *smooth* scales throughout the length of the body, a *divided* anal, and most of them have black caps on their heads. There is no loreal, and the prefrontal scale may extend downward to meet the 2nd labial (Fig. 70). In other cases the tip of the postnasal may extend backward to meet the preocular, thus narrowly separating the 2nd labial from the prefrontal. The two conditions may occur in the same snake, one on each side of the head. Food includes centipedes and the larvae of insects that live underground. The genus ranges from the southern United States to northern Argentina.

SOUTHEASTERN CROWNED SNAKE   PL. 33
Tantilla coronata

IDENTIFICATION: 8–10 in. (20–25.4 cm); record 13 in. (33 cm). This black-headed snake has not only a black cap but also a light band

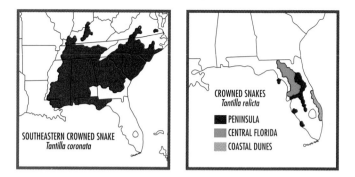

SOUTHEASTERN CROWNED SNAKE
Tantilla coronata

CROWNED SNAKES
Tantilla relicta

■ PENINSULA
■ CENTRAL FLORIDA
■ COASTAL DUNES

across rear of head, followed by a black collar three to five scales wide (Fig. 71). Remainder of dorsum is plain light brown or reddish brown; belly white or with a pinkish or yellowish tinge. Dark pigment usually extends downward from the head cap to or almost to the mouth, both under the eye and near back of head. Scales *smooth*; anal *divided*. *Young:* About 3 in. (7.5 cm) at hatching.

Habitats vary from the environs of swamps to dry wooded hillsides, and from wilderness areas to back yards. This snake is where you find it, and then almost always in hiding—under stones, in rotting logs, etc. Occurs at elevations from virtually sea level to 2000 ft. (600 m) or more in the southern Appalachians. **SIMILAR SPECIES:** (1) Most apt to be confused with Florida Brown Snake and *young* of other races of Brown Snakes, all of which also have dark heads followed by a light crossband, *but they have keeled scales* (a lens may be needed to see the keels in very small specimens). (2) Ringneck Snakes have brightly colored bellies— yellow, orange, or red—boldly marked with black spots (at least in southern subspecies). **RANGE:** S.-cen. Va. and sw. Ky. to the Fla. panhandle and the Florida parishes of Louisiana; isolated colonies in s. Ind. and adj. Ky., and in se. Va.

PENINSULA CROWNED SNAKE   FIG. 71
Tantilla relicta relicta

IDENTIFICATION: 7–9 in. (18–22.9 cm). Usually with a light crossband separating black head cap from black collar on neck (as in Southeastern Crowned Snake—see Fig. 71), but crossband often interrupted by black at midline. Most of head black, including labials. Head pointed and lower jaw partly countersunk into upper jaw. Scales *smooth*; anal *divided*. **SIMILAR SPECIES:** See Similar species under Southeastern Crowned Snake. **RANGE:** Peninsular Fla. in

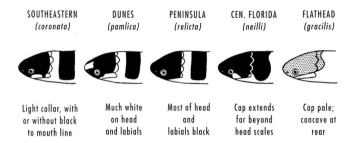

SOUTHEASTERN (coronata)	DUNES (pamlica)	PENINSULA (relicta)	CEN. FLORIDA (neilli)	FLATHEAD (gracilis)
Light collar, with or without black to mouth line	Much white on head and labials	Most of head and labials black	Cap extends far beyond head scales	Cap pale; concave at rear

Fig. 71. *Heads of Crowned and Flathead Snakes* (Tantilla).

scrub areas from Lake George, Marion Co., south in a narrow winding strip along the central ridge to Highlands Co. and west to Tampa Bay; isolated colonies in coastal scrub areas of Collier Co., along border between Charlotte and Sarasota cos., and on the Cedar Keys, Levy Co.

CENTRAL FLORIDA CROWNED SNAKE   PL. 33
Tantilla relicta neilli

IDENTIFICATION: 7–9 in. (18–23 cm); record 9¼ in. (24.1 cm). *Black of head and neck continuous*; black extends 3 to 8 scales behind parietal scutes (Fig. 71). Labials may be all black or with a whitish area posterior to eye. Head narrowly rounded (not pointed). Lower jaw not noticeably countersunk into upper jaw. Only one basal hook on each hemipenis (in males), a character shared by all races of *relicta*. Scales *smooth*; anal *divided*.

A secretive snake of the sandhills and moist hammocks of north-central Florida. **RANGE:** From Madison Co., in n. Fla., south to n. Polk Co. and the Hillsborough R.; east at least to the St. Johns R.

COASTAL DUNES CROWNED SNAKE   FIG. 71
Tantilla relicta pamlica

IDENTIFICATION: 7–8¼ in. (18–21.6 cm). The Crowned Snake with the most white on its head. In addition to the light crossband there are usually light areas on the snout, the temporal and parietal scutes, and the posterior labials. Black collar on neck about three scales wide. Dorsum reddish brown. Head pointed; lower jaw countersunk into upper. Scales *smooth*; anal *divided*.

A resident of relatively isolated coastal dunes and scrub areas of southeastern Florida. **RANGE:** Vicinity of Cape Canaveral south to s. Palm Beach Co., Fla.

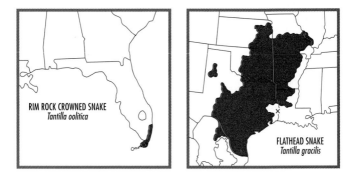

RIM ROCK CROWNED SNAKE
Tantilla oolitica

FLATHEAD SNAKE
Tantilla gracilis

RIM ROCK CROWNED SNAKE *Tantilla oolitica*   **NOT ILLUS.**
IDENTIFICATION: 7–9 in. (18–23 cm); record 11½ in. (29.2 cm). Best
identified by range; the only member of the Blackhead Snake
group (*Tantilla*) in extreme southern Florida. Head pattern similar to that of Central Florida Crowned Snake (Fig. 71). Black of
head continuous from snout to neck, except that specimens from
Key Largo may have a broken light crossband separating a black
head cap from a black collar. Each hemipenis (in males) with two
basal hooks instead of one as in all other kinds of *Tantilla* from
the Florida Peninsula. Scales *smooth*; anal *divided.*

A secretive snake more or less confined to sandy soils in flatwoods, hammocks, vacant lots, and pastures of the rim rock
(oolitic limestone) area paralleling the coast of extreme southeastern Florida. **RANGE:** Dade Co. south to Key Largo, Fla.

FLATHEAD SNAKE *Tantilla gracilis*   **PL. 33**
IDENTIFICATION: 7–8 in. (18–20.3 cm); record 9⅞ in. (24.9 cm). A
Blackhead Snake that usually doesn't have a black head! Head
normally slightly darker than body, but occasional specimens do
have quite dark heads; cap is *concave* at its posterior end (Fig.
71). A slender, shiny snake with a plain (unpatterned) dorsum of
some shade of brown—golden- or gray-brown to reddish brown.
Belly *salmon pink.* Six upper labial scales. Scales *smooth*; anal
divided. Young: Gray or brownish gray; about 3–3½ in. (7.5–9 cm)
at hatching.

A small, secretive, almost wormlike snake, completely inoffensive but adept at forcing its way through the fingers when held in
the hand. Normally found under rocks below which there is at
least some moisture. **SIMILAR SPECIES:** Lack of dorsal pattern makes
this snake easy to confuse with several other plain brown species.

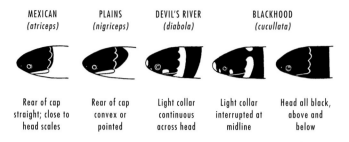

MEXICAN (atriceps)	PLAINS (nigriceps)	DEVIL'S RIVER (diabola)	BLACKHOOD (cucullata)

Rear of cap straight; close to head scales

Rear of cap convex or pointed

Light collar continuous across head

Light collar interrupted at midline

Head all black, above and below

Fig. 72. Heads of Blackhead and Blackhood Snakes (Tantilla).

(1) Brown Snake and the Rough Earth Snake have *keeled* scales. (2) Western Earth Snake has weak *keels* on at least some middorsal scales. (3) Ground Snake has cream or whitish belly and also usually has a loreal scale (Fig. 70). (4) Blind Snakes have belly scales same size as dorsal scales. (5) Plains Blackhead Snake has seven upper labials and the black cap, almost invariably prominent, usually extends farther posteriorly and is *convex* or pointed at rear (Fig. 72). **RANGE:** Extr. sw. Ill., Mo., and e. Kans. to s. Texas and Coahuila; disjunct population in nw. Texas; isolated record in extr. e. Texas.

▶LAINS BLACKHEAD SNAKE *Tantilla nigriceps*   PL. 33

IDENTIFICATION: 7–10 in. (18–25.4 cm); record 15⅟₁₆ in. (38.4 cm). The black cap is *convex* or even *pointed* at the rear, and it extends backward 2 to 5 scale lengths from the parietals (Fig. 72). Dorsum plain yellowish brown to brownish gray; belly whitish with a broad midventral pink area. Upper labial scales seven. First lower labials usually meet beneath chin (Fig. 73). Scales *smooth;* anal *divided.*

A Blackhead Snake of the southern Great Plains and arid lands to the south and west. Found under rocks, debris, and even dried cattle droppings, only rarely prowling in the open. **SIMILAR SPECIES:** (1) In the Flathead Snake, the upper labials are six, and in the few Flatheads with black caps, the rear of the dark area is *concave* (Fig. 71). (2) In the Southwestern Blackhead Snake, the first lower labials usually fail to meet beneath the chin (Fig. 73), and the posterior border of the black cap usually runs *straight* across and is followed by a subtle, narrow, light collar. (3) In the Mexican Blackhead Snake, the posterior border of the black cap is also usually *straight* across, and extends backward only 1 to 2 scale

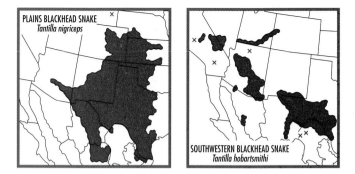

lengths from the parietals (Fig. 72). (4) Devil's River Blackhead Snake has a white collar followed by a broad black band (Fig. 72), and a plain white belly. (5) In the Blackhood Snake, the white collar is strongly interrupted by black or the entire head is black (Fig. 72), and the belly is uniform white. **RANGE:** Sw. Neb. to se. Ariz. and n. Mexico; an isolated record in e. Wyo.

SOUTHWESTERN BLACKHEAD SNAKE   FIG. 73
Tantilla hobartsmithi

IDENTIFICATION: 7–9 in. (18–23 cm); record 12⅜ in. (31.3 cm). The posterior edge of the black or dark brown cap is usually *straight* or *slightly convex*, extends backward only 1 to 3 scale lengths from the parietals, does not dip below the angle of the mouth, and is followed by a subtle, narrow, light collar. The tan to light brown dorsal body color is in striking contrast to the dark headcap. Chin and throat light gray, becoming reddish orange on the belly and tail. Upper labial scales seven. First lower labials usually fail to meet beneath chin (Fig. 73). Scales *smooth*; anal *divided*.

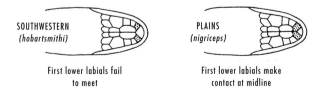

SOUTHWESTERN
(*hobartsmithi*)

First lower labials fail
to meet

PLAINS
(*nigriceps*)

First lower labials make
contact at midline

Fig. 73. *Scales on chins of Blackhead Snakes* (Tantilla).

Found in the open areas of the Southwest, and ascending canyons and arroyos into open forests. Look beneath logs, rocks, boards, and plant debris for this secretive snake. Food consists of centipedes, millipedes, and insects. **SIMILAR SPECIES:** (1) In the Flathead Snake the upper labials are six, and in the few Flatheads with black caps, the rear of the dark area is *concave*. (2) In the

MEXICAN BLACKHEAD SNAKE
Tantilla atriceps

Plains Blackhead Snake, the first lower labials usually meet beneath the chin (Fig. 73). (3) Devil's River Blackhead Snake has a white collar followed by a broad black band, and a plain white belly. (4) In the Blackhood Snake, the white collar is strongly interrupted by black or the entire head is black (Fig. 72), and the belly is uniform white. **RANGE:** Highly disjunct, from s.-cen. Texas and adj. n. Mexico north through Ariz. to w. Colo. and s. Utah, west to Calif., and s. to Sonora; isolated records in w. Coahuila, n. Ariz., and s. Calif. **NOTE:** The Southwestern Blackhead Snake (*hobartsmithi*) and the Mexican Blackhead Snake (*atriceps*), which follows, are strikingly similar in appearance, even to the shapes of their black heads, but the hemipenes of males are quite different. These two species are best identified by their ranges.

MEXICAN BLACKHEAD SNAKE *Tantilla atriceps*   PL. 33

IDENTIFICATION: 5–8 in. (12.5–20.3 cm); record 9⅛ (23 cm). The posterior edge of the black or dark brown cap is usually *straight or only slightly convex*, extends backward only 1 to 2 scale lengths from the parietals, and does not dip below the angle of the mouth (Fig. 72). Often a faint light line across the neck immediately posterior to the dark cap. The tan to light brown dorsal body color is in striking contrast with the dark headcap. Belly pink or red. Upper labial scales seven. First lower labials usually meet beneath the chin (Fig. 73) as in Plains Blackhead Snake. Scales *smooth*; anal *divided*.

This small, secretive snake occurs in a variety of habitats, ranging from wooded mountain canyons to desert flats. Moisture and shelter are necessities. It feeds on centipedes and insects. **SIMILAR SPECIES:** (1) In the Flathead Snake, the upper labials are six, and in the few Flatheads with black caps, the rear of the dark area is *concave* (Fig. 71). (2) In the Plains Blackhead Snake, the poster-ior border of the black cap is *convex or pointed* (Fig. 72), and extends

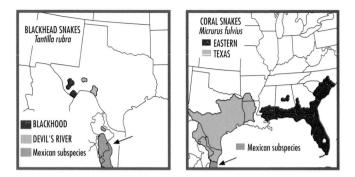

backward 2 to 5 scale lengths from the parietals. **RANGE:** Disjunct population in Duval and Kleburg cos. in extr. s. Texas; main portion of the range is in Mexico from cen. Coahuila south to n. San Luis Potosí and n. Zacatecas; an isolated colony in n. Tamaulipas.

DEVIL'S RIVER BLACKHEAD SNAKE   PL. 33
Tantilla rubra diabola
IDENTIFICATION: 8½–15 in. (21.5–38 cm); record 22¾ in. (58 cm). This snake not only has a black headcap but also a *light band* or collar across rear of head, followed by a black band 3½ to 4½ scales wide. A whitish spot on upper labials posterior to eye (Fig. 72). Rest of dorsum plain light brown or grayish brown. Belly white. Scales *smooth;* anal *divided.* **RANGE:** Known from two disjunct populations in the arid environs of the Pecos and Devil's river systems, Pecos and Val Verde cos., sw. Texas. Mexican subspecies.

BLACKHOOD SNAKE *Tantilla rubra cucullata*   PL. 33
IDENTIFICATION: 8½–15 in. (21.5–38 cm); record 25⅝ in. (65.4 cm). A black-headed snake with at least three different head patterns: (a) a black hood that covers both the dorsal and ventral surfaces of the head; (b) a ringneck variation that resembles the Devil's River Blackhead Snake except that the light neck ring is interrupted by black at its midpoint (Fig. 72); or (c) a ringneck variation in which the light neck ring is partially interrupted anteriorly by a black X with three black spots along the posterior margin. Remainder of dorsum plain light brown or grayish brown. Belly white. Scales *smooth;* anal *divided.* **RANGE:** Two disjunct populations in the Chisos and Davis mtns. of Trans-Pecos Texas.

These snakes are dangerously venomous. Although their small mouths and relatively short fangs make it difficult for them to bite most parts of the human anatomy (fingers or toes are vulnerable), their venoms are potent. They are strongly ringed with red, yellow, and black, or in the tropics with black and red or black and yellow. Coral Snakes range from the southern United States to central Argentina. The family is also widespread in the Old World, where it includes such notorious relatives as cobras, mambas, kraits, and tiger snakes.

EASTERN CORAL SNAKE   PL. 30; FIG. 69
Micrurus fulvius fulvius
IDENTIFICATION: 20–30 in. (51–76 cm); record 47¼ in. (120.7 cm). A shiny, "candystick" snake whose colored rings completely encircle the body. *Red and yellow rings touch.* End of snout black, followed by a yellow band across the head. Black ring on neck not touching the parietal scutes. Red rings dotted or spotted with black, the dark markings often concentrated into a pair of fairly large black spots in each red ring. Some specimens from southern Florida may entirely lack dark spots in the red rings. *Young:* Similarly patterned and colored; 7–9 in. (18–23 cm) at hatching.

Coral Snakes are usually secretive, but when they prowl it is normally by day, especially in early morning. Sometimes they may be discovered hiding under leaves or debris, in logs, palmetto stumps, etc. Habitats vary from well-drained pine woods and open, dry, or sandy areas, to such moister environments as pond and lake borders and in the (often) dense and jungly growths of hardwoods known in the South (Florida especially) as hammocks. Coral Snakes primarily eat slender lizards and small snakes. When suddenly restrained, a Coral Snake may thrust its tail upward with the tip curled into a ball that may momentarily be mistaken for the head. **SIMILAR SPECIES:** The venomous Coral Snakes are well-imitated serpents. Several of our harmless snakes also sport rings (or near-rings) of red, black, and yellow (or white). In all of them, however, black separates red from yellow. Think of a traffic light; red means *stop,* yellow means *caution.* If these two warning colors touch on the snake's body, it is poisonous. "Mimics" include the Scarlet Snake, Scarlet Kingsnake, and several of the Milk Snakes (Pl. 30). **RANGE:** Se. N.C. south, chiefly in lowlands, to extr. s. Fla. and Key Largo; west through Gulf States to w.-cen. Miss. and extr. e. La. Absent from much of the delta region of the lower Mississippi Valley; a disjunct colony in cen. Ala.

A newborn Texas Coral Snake with an egg from the same clutch. Coral snakes are the only venomous serpents in the United States and Canada that lay eggs.

TEXAS CORAL SNAKE *Micrurus fulvius tener*   **PL. 36; FIG. 69**
IDENTIFICATION: 20–30 in. (51–76 cm); record 47¾ in. (121.7 cm).
Similar to the Eastern Coral Snake, except that in the Texas subspecies the black pigment in the red rings is more widely scattered, and the black neck band extends far enough forward to
involve the posterior tips of the parietal scutes. *Young:* 6½–9⁷⁄₁₆ in.
(16.5–23.9 cm) at hatching.

In addition to inhabiting lowland areas, this race ascends onto
the Edwards Plateau of central Texas, where it may be found in
cedar brakes or rocky canyons, or on rocky hillsides. **SIMILAR SPECIES:**
(1) See the "mimics" and the Louisiana and Mexican Milk Snakes
on Pl. 30. (2) The crossbanded variants of the Ground Snake (Pl.
31) bear a remote resemblance to a Coral Snake, but they lack
the black snout and the broad black rings of this venomous
species, and their bellies are unmarked. (3) Longnose Snake has a
red snout and only a *single row of scales* under tail. **RANGE:** Sw. Ark.
and La. to w.-cen. Texas; south into Mexico. Mexican subspecies.

VIPERS: FAMILY VIPERIDAE
PIT VIPERS: SUBFAMILY CROTALINAE

All our dangerously poisonous serpents except the Coral Snakes
belong to this group. The Copperhead, Cottonmouth, and Rattlesnakes are members.

The subfamily name is derived from the deep facial pit on each
side of the head situated a little below midway between eye and
nostril (Fig. 18, opp. Pl. 34). The pit is a sensory organ that helps
the snake aim in striking at warm-blooded prey. Any serpent with
such a pit is poisonous, but this can be checked only on dead or

caged specimens. Don't approach live ones in the field close enough to see the pit. Also beware of handling freshly killed snakes. Reflex action is marked; even decapitated heads have been known to bite!

The scales under the tail are in only one row, at least anteriorly; the heads are distinctly wider than the necks; and the pupils of the eyes are vertically elliptical. A few nonpoisonous and rear-fanged snakes also have one or more of these characteristics.

Pit vipers range from southern Canada to southern Argentina and from extreme southeastern Europe through southern and central Asia and Malaysia. They, along with the true vipers of the Old World and the monotypic Azemiopinae of temperate mountainous southeastern Asia, constitute the Family Viperidae.

COPPERHEADS AND COTTONMOUTHS: GENUS *Agkistrodon*

These are the venomous "moccasins"—Copperheads being the so-called "highland moccasins" and Cottonmouths the "water moccasins." In referring to these snakes, however, the name "moccasin" should be studiously avoided, for it is misleading. Ignorant or uninformed persons apply the same term to the nonpoisonous Water Snakes. Members of the genus *Agkistrodon* have facial pits and all the other characteristics of the pit vipers. Scales are *weakly keeled*; anal *single*. When alarmed they rapidly vibrate their tails, producing a lively tattoo against a leaf, vegetation, or even the ground—whatever the tail may touch. The young at birth have bright yellow tail tips. The genus is repre-sented in North and Central America, Asia, Malaysia, and extremesoutheastern Europe north of the Caspian Sea.

Mice are the principal food of Copperheads, but they also eat small birds, lizards, small snakes, amphibians, and insects, especially cicadas (locusts). Cottonmouths eat all of these and, in fact, almost any animal their larger size enables them to swallow, but their mainstay is fishes. Their scientific name, *piscivorus,* means "fish-eating."

NORTHERN COPPERHEAD

PL. 34

Agkistrodon contortrix mokasen

IDENTIFICATION: 24–36 in. (61–90 cm); record 53 in. (134.6 cm). A *coppery-red head* and an hourglass pattern. Viewed from above, the dark chestnut crossbands are wide on the sides and narrow at the center of the back. Small, dark spots are frequently present between crossbands. Dark, rounded spots at sides of belly. Scales *weakly keeled*; anal *single*; a single row of scales under tail, at least anteriorly. *Young:* Paler; tail tip yellow; a *narrow* dark line through eye that divides the dark head from the pale lips; 8–9¾ in. (20.3–24.8 cm) at birth.

The Northern Copperhead has many aliases—"chunkhead," "highland moccasin," "pilot," "adder," etc. Natural camouflage renders it inconspicuous. Normally a quiet, almost lethargic snake, content to lie motionless or beat a dignified retreat. Once aroused, it strikes vigorously and may rapidly vibrate the tail. Rocky, wooded hillsides and mountainous areas are favorite habitats. Abandoned and rotting slab or sawdust piles, left in the wake of the itinerant, portable sawmill, are another; in these, Copperheads and other reptiles find shelter, food, and moisture. Copperheads are gregarious, especially in autumn, when they assemble at hibernating dens or denning areas, often in company with other species of snakes. **SIMILAR SPECIES:** (1) In Milk Snakes the large dorsal markings are *wide* at center of back; belly markings black and squarish. Eastern Milk Snake usually has *checkerboard* belly. (2) Hognose Snakes, besides having turned-up snouts, hiss and flatten their heads and necks. (3) Water Snakes seldom wander far from water and retreat into it when alarmed; their scales are *strongly* keeled. (4) In Fox Snakes, the markings consist of a series of large dark blotches flanked by a series of smaller blotches on each side. Great numbers of harmless snakes are killed in the mistaken belief they are Copperheads. If snake is dead, check for facial pits. (See also Pl. 34 and *Young* under Eastern Cottonmouth.) **RANGE:** Conn. to Ill. and Tenn.; south in uplands to n. Ga. and n. Ala.; isolated colonies in Mass. Intergrades over a broad area with the Southern Copperhead.

OSAGE COPPERHEAD *Agkistrodon contortrix phaeogaster* **PL. 34**
IDENTIFICATION: 24–36 in. (61–90 cm); record 40 in. (102 cm). The most northwestern Copperhead. Similar to the Northern Copperhead but with the dark crossbands in sharper contrast with the ground color, and *without small dark spots between them.* Crossbands are often edged with white. Tip of tail yellowish green (yellow in young). The gray to black belly markings blend together to produce a dusky, marbled, or clouded venter. Scales *weakly keeled; anal single. Young:* 7⁵⁄₁₆–10⅛ in. (18.6–25.6 cm) at birth.

Lives along rocky, wooded hillsides, brushy areas along creeks, and near abandoned farm buildings and sawmills. Like most Copperheads, it becomes nocturnal during the heat of the summer, prowling in search of its favorite food, mice. **SIMILAR SPECIES:** (1) Hognose Snakes have turned-up snouts, and hiss and flatten their heads and necks. (2) Water Snakes seldom wander far from water, and have *strongly* keeled dorsal scales and *divided* anal plates. **RANGE:** From e. Mo. west to e. Kans., and south to ne. Okla. Inter-

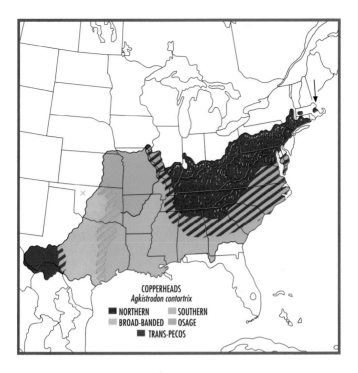

COPPERHEADS
Agkistrodon contortrix
■ NORTHERN ■ SOUTHERN
▨ BROAD-BANDED ■ OSAGE
■ TRANS-PECOS

grades with Southern Copperhead in s. Mo. and nw. Ark., with Northern Copperhead along the Mo.-Ill. border, and with Broad-banded Copperhead in ne. Okla.

SOUTHERN COPPERHEAD

Agkistrodon contortrix contortrix

IDENTIFICATION: 24–36 in. (61–90 cm); record 52 in. (132.1 cm). A *paler,* pinker counterpart of the Northern Copperhead. The dark markings are quite narrow across the back, giving the hourglasses a more wasp-waist appearance than in the northern race. Very often they are *broken* at middorsum, the two halves failing to meet. Scales *weakly keeled;* anal *single. Young:* Similar to young of Northern Copperhead but with pinched, often broken markings; 7–10 in. (18–25.4 cm) at birth.

This is mainly a snake of the lowlands, of low ground near swamps and cypress-bordered streams, but it also ascends into hilly regions. **SIMILAR SPECIES:** Baby Cottonmouths have a broad dark

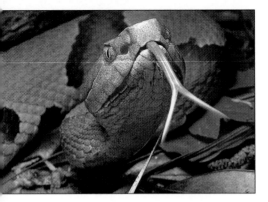

The deeply forked tongue of a Southern Copperhead extended for its full length. The tips gather chemical information that they transfer to a sensory organ in the roof of the mouth associated with taste and smell.

band through eye, and their body hues consist largely of dark browns. **RANGE:** S. Del. and adj. Md. south to extr. n.-cen. Fla., and west to se. Mo., se. Okla., and e. Texas; areas of intergradation with adjacent subspecies are wide in some parts of range.

BROAD-BANDED COPPERHEAD   PL. 34
Agkistrodon contortrix laticinctus

IDENTIFICATION: 22–30 in. (56–76 cm); record 37¼ in. (95 cm). The rich reddish brown or chestnut brown crossbands are almost as broad on the back as on the sides of the body. Tip of tail greenish gray. Scales *weakly keeled;* anal *single. Young:* Pattern contrasty, but of grays rather than rich browns; tip of tail yellow or greenish yellow; 7½–10 in. (19–25.4 cm) at birth. **RANGE:** N. Okla. to s.-cen. Texas; isolated record in nw. Okla.

TRANS-PECOS COPPERHEAD   PL. 34
Agkistrodon contortrix pictigaster

IDENTIFICATION: 20–30 in. (51–76 cm); record 32⅞ in. (83.5 cm). Superficially, this race resembles the Broad-banded Copperhead, but it differs chiefly in having a dark and strikingly patterned belly. Undersurface rich chestnut to almost black, but in sharp contrast with pale areas that: (a) extend downward from the dorsal ground color; and (b) appear in the form of inverted U's beneath each dark dorsal crossband. *Young:* 9⁹⁄₁₆–10¹³⁄₁₆ in. (24.2–27.5 cm) at birth.

This westernmost subspecies of the Copperhead lives in oases in the Chihuahuan Desert, in isolated populations that are relicts of a formerly much wider distribution. It normally occurs near permanent springs, in well-watered canyons, and in river-cane jungles bordering the Rio Grande, but it occasionally wanders

Rich chestnut cross-bands that continue in part on the belly are the hallmarks of the Trans-Pecos Copperhead. The facial pit to the left of the eye is an infrared-sensing receptor that aids in striking at prey.

into the adjacent desert during the rainy season. Relatively arid habitats are also utilized if they are near sources of water in canyons, hillside seepages, or even underground. **RANGE:** W. Texas from Crockett and Val Verde cos. through the Big Bend region and the Davis Mts.; extr. e. Chihuahua and n. Coahuila.

EASTERN COTTONMOUTH   PL. 34
Agkistrodon piscivorus piscivorus
   IDENTIFICATION: 30–48 in. (76–122 cm); record 74 in. (188 cm). A large, semiaquatic snake. Olive, brown, or black above; belly lighter. Crossbands with dark, more or less distinct borders; centers of crossbands often invaded by the lighter ground color. Details of pattern most evident in young and subadults; old adults may be completely dark and unpatterned. A dead specimen is easily distinguished from a water snake by its facial pits, *single* anal plate, and *single* row of scales under tail (Fig. 18, opp. Pl. 34). *Don't ever handle a live one!* Dorsal scales *weakly keeled. Young:* Strongly patterned with light-centered dark brown to brilliant reddish brown crossbands; a *broad dark band* through eye; tip of tail yellow; 8–13 in. (20.3–33 cm) at birth.
   Beware of any semiaquatic serpent within the range of the Cottonmouths. These very dangerous snakes closely resemble several of the nonpoisonous Water Snakes *(Nerodia)* and are difficult to tell from them in the field. Behavior offers some of the best clues. Cottonmouths often stand their ground or crawl slowly away. Water Snakes usually flee quickly or drop with a splash into the water. Cottonmouths vibrate tails when excited; Water Snakes do not. A thoroughly aroused Cottonmouth throws its head upward and backward and holds its mouth wide open, revealing a whitish interior—origin of the name Cottonmouth.

An Eastern Cotton-mouth (one of three subspecies) demonstrates the origin of its name. When alarmed it may arrange itself in a defensive coil and then hold its mouth open to reveal the cottony-white interior.

This is a snake of southern lowlands, a denizen of swamps, lakes, and rivers, of rice fields and ditches. Suns itself on branches, logs, or stones at water's edge and sometimes wanders away from its normal habitat in pursuit of food. Fish, frogs, salamanders, snakes, lizards, small turtles, baby alligators, birds, and small mammals are included on the menu. **SIMILAR SPECIES:** (1) The nonpoisonous water snakes (*Nerodia*) have *divided* anal plates, a *double* row of scales under tail, and *no* facial pits (Fig. 18, opp. Pl. 34). (2) Young Copperheads are more reddish than baby Cottonmouths, and they have a *narrow dark line* through eye. **RANGE:** Se. Va. to cen. Ga. Intergrades extensively with Florida Cottonmouth in s. S.C., s. Ga., se. Ala., and the western panhandle of Fla., and with the Western Cottonmouth in w. Ga., most of Ala., and e. Miss.

FLORIDA COTTONMOUTH   PL. 34
Agkistrodon piscivorus conanti

IDENTIFICATION: 30–48 in. (76–122 cm); record 74½ in. (189.2 cm). Similar to the Eastern Cottonmouth, but with *conspicuous head markings*—even in most large, dark individuals. A dark brown cheek stripe bordered above and below by a narrow, light line. Also a pair of dark stripes at front of lower jaw, and a pair of dark vertical lines at tip of snout. Behavior and habitat similar to that of Eastern Cottonmouth. **SIMILAR SPECIES:** See Fig. 18, opp. Pl. 34. **RANGE:** Extr. s. Ga. and all of peninsular Fla., including virtually all adjacent islands; apparently missing from the lower Keys despite an old record from Key West. See Eastern Cottonmouth for comments on intergradation.

WESTERN COTTON-
MOUTH
PL. 34

Agkistrodon piscivorus leucostoma

COTTONMOUTHS
Agkistrodon piscivorus

■ WESTERN ■ EASTERN
■ FLORIDA

IDENTIFICATION: 30–42 in. (76–106.7 cm); record 62 in. (157.5 cm). A smaller, darker, less well-patterned subspecies of the Cottonmouth. Belly dark brown or black, the dark dorsal crossbands (when evident) uniform or with dusky centers, and snout without clear-cut markings. Many specimens are plain black or dark brown with little or no trace of a pattern. *Young:* Strongly and brightly marked, but all pattern elements, including the dark cheek stripe, rapidly become far less conspicuous as the snake grows. A rare few retain markings into adulthood; most specimens become almost uniformly dark at an early age. From 6–11 in. (15.2–28 cm) at birth; tip of tail yellow.

Behavior the same as in Eastern Cottonmouth. The habit of holding the mouth open has earned it the names of "gapper" and "trapjaw," the latter in reference to speed with which mouth snaps shut if anything touches it. These names are prevalent in the Ozarks and adjacent regions. An extremely abundant snake in the swamps and bayous of Louisiana and other southern states. Also invades certain more upland areas of the Central Highlands and may be found in company of or hibernating with Rattlesnakes and Copperheads. **RANGE:** Extr. s. Ill. and w. Ky. to extr. sw. Ala.; west to Okla. and cen. Texas; isolated records in s. Ind., s.-cen. Tenn., and Rio Grande Valley. The two X-marks in Texas on the Cottonmouths map represent relict colonies, now extirpated, that survived well into the 19th century.

RATTLESNAKES: GENERA *Sistrurus* AND *Crotalus*

The rattle is the hallmark of these snakes. In adults it is an organ of loosely attached horny segments that strike against one another to produce a buzzing sound when the tail is vibrated rapidly. In the very young, the rattle is represented by a button. Later a new segment is added at each shedding time, the segments becoming progressively larger until the snake reaches adult size. Two to four new segments are normally added each year. The button remains at the end of the string unless it is lost through wear or breaking of the rather fragile rattle (see Fig. 19, opp. Pl. 35).

Because of the great disparity in size, the sounds made by the

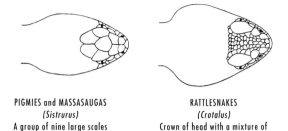

PIGMIES and MASSASAUGAS
(*Sistrurus*)
A group of nine large scales
(plates) on crown of head

RATTLESNAKES
(*Crotalus*)
Crown of head with a mixture of
large and small scales

Fig. 74. *Scales on tops of heads of Rattlesnakes* (Sistrurus *and* Crotalus).

different species vary greatly. In general, the largest Rattlesnakes produce the loudest, most sonorous tones. Buzzing is the best way to describe them, but the sounds have also been likened to those of escaping steam and the noise produced by cicadas ("locusts"). Rarely, a Rattlesnake may have no rattle—if the end of the tail has been chopped off by a person wielding a hoe or severed by some other enemy. Many other serpents, including Cottonmouths, Copperheads, and numerous nonpoisonous kinds, vibrate their tails rapidly when brought to bay. If their tails brush against dry leaves or other vegetation, the resultant sound is suggestive of a Rattlesnake.

The Pigmy Rattlesnakes and Massasaugas (*Sistrurus*) have a set of nine plates on the crowns of their heads, as do most nonpoisonous snakes. All our other rattlers (*Crotalus*) have their heads largely covered with small scales (see Fig. 74). The dorsal scales are *keeled* and the anal plate is *single*.

Rodents and birds are the chief foods, but frogs, lizards, etc., are also eaten, especially by the smaller kinds. Rattlesnakes occur only in the New World. There are about 30 species distributed from southern Canada to northern Argentina and Uruguay. They are found in all 48 of the contiguous states except Maine and Delaware but are most numerous, in variety of species and subspecies, in Mexico and the southwestern United States. In measuring Rattlesnakes the length of the rattle is *not* included.

EASTERN MASSASAUGA *Sistrurus catenatus catenatus*   **PL. 35**
IDENTIFICATION: 18½–30 in. (47.2–76 cm); record 39½ in. (100.3 cm). The "swamp rattler" or "black snapper." A spotted rattler

with a row of large black or dark brown blotches down the back and three rows of smaller dark spots on each side of body. Ground color gray or brownish gray. Belly black, irregularly marked with white or yellowish (Fig. 75). Some adults are jet-black, both above and below, with no trace of pattern save for a few light marks on chin and throat. Nine plates on crown of head

(Fig. 74). *Young:* Well patterned but paler than adults; 7½–9¹⁵⁄₁₆ in. (19–25.3 cm) at birth.

Wet prairies are the preferred habitat toward the western part of the range and bogs and swamps toward the east, but these snakes also occur in dry woodlands. Many individuals are mild-mannered, seldom rattling until thoroughly aroused. They may hide in crayfish holes or other underground cavities. At harvest times Massasaugas often turn up, sometimes in numbers, under shocks of grain where mice have congregated. Other food includes small birds, frogs, and snakes. **SIMILAR SPECIES:** Timber Rattlesnake has small scales on crown of head (Fig. 74). **RANGE:** W. N.Y. and s. Ont. to e. Iowa and extr. e. Mo.

WESTERN MASSASAUGA *Sistrurus catenatus tergeminus* **PL. 35**

IDENTIFICATION: 18–26 in. (45.7–66 cm); record 34¾ in. (88.3 cm). Similar to Eastern Massasauga but paler in coloration, with the dark brown blotches in strong contrast with the light gray or tan-gray ground color. Belly light with a few dark markings (Fig. 75).

WESTERN
(tergeminus)
Light in coloration

EASTERN
(catenatus)
Chiefly black

Fig. 75. Bellies of subspecies of the Massasauga (Sistrurus catenatus).

An adult Western Massasauga from Ellsworth County, Kansas. Noise from the rattle of this small rattlesnake is difficult to hear.

Young: Similar but often pinkish on venter and toward tip of tail; 7–9¼ in. (18–24 cm) at birth.

A snake of the plains and prairies, taking advantage of boggy areas and rocky outcrops where they exist. Lizards, small snakes, frogs, mice, and shrews have been recorded as food. **SIMILAR SPECIES:** (1) Western Pigmy Rattlesnake has a tiny rattle, slender tail, and usually a reddish stripe down center of back. (2) From all other rattlers within its range, the Western Massasauga may be distinguished by the group of nine plates on the crown of its head (Fig. 74). **RANGE:** Sw. Iowa and extr. nw. Mo. southwestward through cen. Texas to the Gulf; intergrades with the Eastern Massasauga in a disjunct colony in n.-cen. Mo., and with the Desert Massasauga along the Gulf Coast, in w.-cen. Texas, and in a disjunct colony in se. Colo. **SUBSPECIES:** DESERT MASSASAUGA, *Sistrurus c. edwardsii.* Smaller and more slender; max. about 21 in. (53 cm). Similarly patterned but paler, and with ventral surface nearly white and virtually (or completely) unmarked. Scale rows at midbody 23 (25 in Western Massasauga). Chiefly desert grasslands from w. Texas to se. Ariz.; also extr. s. Texas; isolated colonies in Coahuila and Nuevo León.

CAROLINA PIGMY RATTLESNAKE   PL. 35
Sistrurus miliarius miliarius

IDENTIFICATION: 15–21 in. (38–53 cm); record 25 in. (63.5 cm). The *tiny rattle,* sounding like the buzz of an insect, is scarcely audible more than a few feet away. It and the *slender tail* identify the pigmies or "ground rattlers." In this race the markings are clear-cut, there are one or two rows of dark lateral spots, and the venter is cream-colored, moderately flecked with brown or gray. Dorsal coloration brown or light gray; a middorsal russet stripe in many specimens. *Reddish variation:* In eastern North Carolina, chiefly between Pamlico and Albemarle sounds, the majority of specimens are reddish, ranging from orange or pinkish to brick red. Nine *plates* on crown of head (Fig. 74). *Young:* Tip of tail sulfur yellow; 5⅞–7½ in. (15–19 cm) at birth.

PIGMY RATTLESNAKES
Sistrurus miliarius
CAROLINA WESTERN
DUSKY

Behavior varies, depending on such factors as temperature and temperament. Some strike furiously; others are lethargic and do not even sound the rattle. Occurs in longleaf pine-scrub oak and longleaf-loblolly pine flatwood areas on the Atlantic Coastal Plain and in pine-oak woods farther west. Food (of all Pigmy Rattler subspecies) includes mice, lizards, snakes, and frogs. **RANGE:** E. N.C. to n.-cen. Ala.

DUSKY PIGMY RATTLESNAKE   PL. 35
Sistrurus miliarius barbouri
IDENTIFICATION: 15–22 in. (38–56 cm); record 31¼ in. (80.3 cm). This subspecies of the Pigmy Rattler has a *dusted appearance* caused by dark stippling that may largely obscure the markings, especially those on the head. A reddish brown middorsal stripe, prominent in many specimens, is subdued or only evident in the neck region in others. Usually three rows of dark lateral spots. Venter whitish, heavily blotched or flecked with black or dark brown; sometimes uniform brownish black, at least posteriorly. *Nine plates* on crown of head (Fig. 74). *Young:* Tail tip yellow; about 5⅝–7 in. (14.3–18 cm) at birth.

At home in flatwoods and in virtually all types of terrain where lakes and marshes abound. **RANGE:** Extr. s. S.C. to extr. se. Miss. and south to tip of Fla.

WESTERN PIGMY RATTLESNAKE   PL. 35
Sistrurus miliarius streckeri
IDENTIFICATION: 15–20 in. (38–51 cm); record 25⅛ in. (63.8 cm). *Tiny rattle* and *skinny tail.* Ground color light, usually pale grayish brown. The middorsal dark spots may be highly irregular in shape, but they often tend to form short transverse bars. One or two conspicuous rows of dark spots on each side of body. Reddish dorsal stripe sometimes absent. *Nine plates* on crown of head (Fig. 74). *Young:* About 5–7 in. (12.5–18 cm) at birth.

An adult Western Pigmy Rattlesnake from Barry County, Missouri.

Habitats are usually in areas where water is nearby—in river floodplains, swamps, marshes, and wet prairies. **SIMILAR SPECIES:** (1) Western Massasauga has much larger rattle and a tail of moderate size. (2) All other Rattlesnakes occurring within Western Pigmy's range have small scales on crown of head (Fig. 74). **RANGE:** S. Mo. and e. Okla. to the Gulf; a northeastward extension into w. Tenn. and sw. Ky.

TIMBER RATTLESNAKE *Crotalus horridus*   PL. 35; FIG. 76

IDENTIFICATION: 36–60 in. (90–152 cm); record 74½ in. (189.2 cm). Sometimes called the "banded," "velvet-tail," or "canebrake" rattler. Four major color variations: (a) *yellow variation:* black or dark brown crossbands on a ground color of yellow or brown; the crossbands, which may be V-shaped, break up anteriorly to form a row of dark spots down the back plus a row along each side of body; uplands of the Northeast; (b) *western variation:* black or dark brown crossbands on a ground color of gray, yellow, tan, or brown; a broad rusty middorsal stripe present; dark stripe present behind eye (Fig. 76); generally found west of the Mississippi River, from the Ozarks northward; (c) *southern variation:* black crossbands on a pinkish buff, pale gray, or tan ground color, with a broad, reddish middorsal stripe that splits the crossbands in half on the forward part of the body; broad dark stripe present behind eye (Fig. 76); lowlands of the South; and (d) *black* (melanistic) *variation:* a heavy stippling of black or very dark brown that hides much of the lighter pigment; completely black specimens are not unusual; uplands of the Northeast. *Young:* Always crossbanded, 7¾–16 in. (19.7–41 cm) at birth.

The only Rattlesnake in most of the Northeast. Still common in some mountainous regions, but completely extirpated in many areas where it was once numerous. During winter in the Northeast, Timber Rattlesnakes may congregate in dens to hibernate, often together with Copperheads and other snakes. Such dens, which once may have included a hundred or more rattlers, usually are in or near wooded rocky ledges with southern

TIMBER RATTLESNAKE
Crotalus horridus

exposures, where they can sun themselves in spring and autumn. During summer they scatter over the surrounding countryside but return to the den in the fall. In the Northeast, this is a snake of heavily timbered terrain, often found in second growth where rodents abound. In the South, it inhabits the lowlands, favoring cane thickets and swamplands. To the West it follows wooded stream valleys that extend out into the prairies. **SIMILAR SPECIES:** (1) Massasaugas and Pigmy Rattlesnakes have nine plates on crown of head instead of numerous small scales (Fig. 74); (2) both Diamondback Rattlesnakes have diamond markings instead of dark crossbands. **RANGE:** S.-cen. N.H. and the Lake Champlain region south to n. Fla., west to se. Minn. and cen. Texas. Inexplicably absent from sw. La.; isolated colonies on Lake Erie Is., and in s. Ont., se. New England, and n.-cen. N.C. (The map indicates the known historical distribution of the Timber Rattlesnake; it does not take into account areas in which it has been exterminated by the activities of human beings.)

A large adult Timber Rattlesnake from Jefferson County, Kansas. This snake was 56¾ inches long, from its snout to the end of the rattle.

The large Eastern Diamondback Rattlesnake easily ranks among the world's most dangerous snakes. Once common, especially in Florida, loss of habitat and persecution by human beings have greatly reduced its numbers.

EASTERN DIAMONDBACK RATTLESNAKE
Crotalus adamanteus

IDENTIFICATION: 33–72 in. (84–183 cm); record 96 in. (243.8 cm). An ominously impressive snake to meet in the field; suddenly finding yourself in close proximity to the compact coils, broad head, and loud, buzzing rattle is almost certain to raise the hair on the nape of your neck. The diamonds, dark brown or black in color, are strongly outlined by a row of cream-colored or yellowish scales. Ground color olive, brown, or almost black. Pattern and colors vivid in freshly shed specimens; dull and quite dark in those preparing to shed. Only rattler within its range with two prominent light lines on face and vertical light lines on snout. *Young:* 12–15 1⁄16 in. (30.6–38.1 cm) at birth.

At home in the palmetto flatwoods and dry pinelands of the South. Occasionally ventures into salt water, swimming to outlying Keys off the Florida coast. Individual dispositions vary. Some snakes will permit close approach without making a sound, whereas others, completely concealed in palmettos or other vegetation, will rattle when dogs or persons are 20 or 30 feet (6–9 m) away. Many stand their ground, but when hard pressed they back away, rattling vigorously but still facing the intruder. Frequently they take refuge in burrows of gopher tortoises, in holes beneath stumps, etc. Rabbits, rodents, and birds are eaten. **RANGE:** Coastal lowlands from se. N.C. to extr. e. La.; all of Fla., including the Keys.

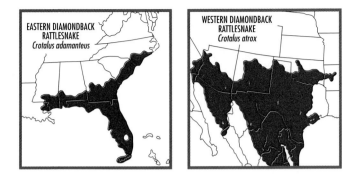

EASTERN DIAMONDBACK
RATTLESNAKE
Crotalus adamanteus

WESTERN DIAMONDBACK
RATTLESNAKE
Crotalus atrox

WESTERN DIAMONDBACK RATTLESNAKE
Crotalus atrox

IDENTIFICATION: 30–72 in. (76–183 cm); record 83⅞ in. (213 cm). Great size, a tendency to stand its ground, and the loud, buzzing rattle usually are sufficient identification. When fully aroused, it may raise the head and a loop of the neck high above the coils, gaining elevation for aiming and striking. The diamonds are not clear-cut, and the entire head and body may have a dusty appearance. General coloration brown or gray but sometimes with strong reddish or yellowish tones. Light stripe behind eye meets

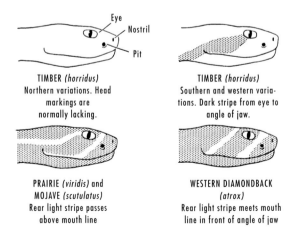

TIMBER *(horridus)*
Northern variations. Head
markings are
normally lacking.

TIMBER *(horridus)*
Southern and western variations. Dark stripe from eye to
angle of jaw.

PRAIRIE *(viridis)* and
MOJAVE *(scutulatus)*
Rear light stripe passes
above mouth line

WESTERN DIAMONDBACK
(atrox)
Rear light stripe meets mouth
line in front of angle of jaw

Fig. 76. *Sides of heads of Rattlesnakes* (Crotalus).

mouth line in front of angle of jaw (Fig. 76). *Tail strongly ringed with black and white or light gray ("coontail rattler"). Young:* Diamonds more sharply defined; 9¼–14 in. (24–36 cm) at birth.

A snake of the arid Southwest, occurring chiefly in the lowlands but also ascending into mountains to altitudes of 5000 ft. (1500 m) or more. At home on desert flats as well as in rocky cliffs and canyons. Food includes rabbits and such rodents as rats, mice, gophers, and ground squirrels. The Western Diamondback is responsible for more serious snakebites and fatalities than any other North American serpent. From the standpoint of sheer size, it and the Eastern Diamondback rank among the world's largest and most dangerous snakes. **SIMILAR SPECIES:** (1) In extreme western Texas (and westward) the Western Diamondback may be confused with the very similar Mojave Rattlesnake, which see for characteristics distinguishing the two species. (2) Prairie Rattler has light line behind eye passing *above* corner of mouth (Fig. 76). **RANGE:** W.-cen. Ark. and Texas to se. Calif.; south into n. Mexico; isolated populations in s. Mexico.

MOJAVE RATTLESNAKE *Crotalus scutulatus scutulatus* PL. 36

IDENTIFICATION: 24–36 in. (61–90 cm); record 51 in. (129.5 cm). Likely to be confused only with the Western Diamondback Rattler, but the Mojave normally has: (a) *black tail rings much narrower than white rings;* (b) light line behind eye passing above and beyond corner of mouth (Fig. 76); (c) whitish scales surrounding dark diamonds largely unicolored; (d) lower half of proximal (basal) segment of rattle paler than upper half; and (e) enlarged scales on snout and between supraoculars. Coloration variable; general appearance may be gray, greenish, or brownish, some specimens pale and others relatively dark. *Young:* About 10–11 in. (25.4–28 cm) at birth.

A snake of the desert; often found on open or brush- or grass-covered flats and on mountain slopes. Despite its similarity to the Western Diamondback, its venom is much more virulent, at least in some geographical portions of its range, a fact that makes the Mojave Rattler one of the most dangerous poisonous snakes in the United States. **SIMILAR SPECIES:** (1) Western Diamondback Rattlesnake has: (a) wider black tail rings; (b) light line from eye meeting mouth line (Fig. 76); (c) a diamond pattern that is often not clear-cut; (d) proximal segment of rattle same color throughout; and (e) small scales on snout and between supraoculars. Mojave Rattlesnakes in western Texas are often aberrant and one or more identification characters may approximate those of Western Diamondback. (2) Prairie Rattlesnake lacks "coontail" appearance of tail. **RANGE:** Extr. w. Texas including Big Bend region; s. Nev. and adj. Calif. to Querétaro. Mexican subspecies.

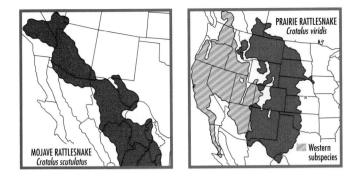

MOJAVE RATTLESNAKE
Crotalus scutulatus

PRAIRIE RATTLESNAKE
Crotalus viridis

Western subspecies

PRAIRIE RATTLESNAKE *Crotalus viridis viridis* PL. 36; FIG. 76

IDENTIFICATION: 35–45 in. (89–114 cm); record 57 in. (144.8 cm). A blotched rattlesnake with the blotches broad anteriorly, but narrow and joining with the lateral markings to form crossbands near the tail. Ground color usually greenish gray, olive-green, or greenish brown, but sometimes light brown or yellowish. The dark brown blotches are narrowly bordered with white. Two oblique light lines on head, the one behind eye passing above corner of mouth (Fig. 76). *Young:* About 8½–11 in. (21.5–28 cm) at birth.

A very abundant rattler (in some areas) that lives in the grasslands of the Great Plains but retreats in winter to dens in rocky outcrops and ledges. Also ascends into mountains, but only rarely above 8000 ft. (2400 m). This is the snake supposed to live in harmony with prairie dogs and burrowing owls, but, alas for the writers of fanciful fiction, young prairie dogs and owls make excellent meals for Prairie Rattlesnakes. **SIMILAR SPECIES:** (1) Tails of Mojave and Western Diamondback Rattlesnakes are strongly ringed with black and white. (2) In Western Diamondback, light line behind eye meets mouth line in front of angle of jaw (Fig. 76). (3) Western Massasauga has *nine plates* on crown of head instead of small scales (Fig. 74). (4) Rock Rattlesnakes have the dark crossbands far apart. **RANGE:** Extr. w. Iowa to the Rockies and beyond; s. Canada to n. Mexico; an isolated record in n.-cen. Kans. Western subspecies.

BLACKTAIL RATTLESNAKE *Crotalus molossus molossus* PL. 36

IDENTIFICATION: 30–42 in. (76–106.7 cm); record 49½ in. (125.7 cm). The "green rattler" of the central Texas uplands and westward. Characterized by three unique features: (a) black of the tail ends abruptly at body; (b) patches of light scales in dark crossbands; and (c) each scale unicolored. In most other Rattlesnakes

A Blacktail Rattlesnake on the defense, its tongue extended and its rattle at the ready. Coloration and pattern vary from one general region to the next within its range, but the black tail quickly identifies it.

the pattern cuts across the scales, so that many individual scales may be part dark and part light. Populations from upland areas, such as the Davis and Chisos mtns. of western Texas, tend to be dark in coloration. Specimens from farther west are often greenish yellow. *Young:* Similar, but with dark crossbands visible on tail; 6½–11¾ in. (16.5–29.7 cm) at birth.

An inhabitant of rock piles and slides, wooded canyons, and the vicinity of cliffs. **RANGE:** The Edwards Plateau of cen. Texas west to Ariz. and n. Mexico. Mexican subspecies.

MOTTLED ROCK RATTLESNAKE PL. 36
Crotalus lepidus lepidus

IDENTIFICATION: 18–24 in. (46–61 cm); record 30¼ in. (76.8 cm). A dusty-looking snake, the mottled effect being produced by a profuse stippling of dark pigment that may be so intense as to form pseudo-crossbands between the dark crossbars. General coloration may be gray, bluish gray, greenish gray, tan, brown, or pinkish. Examples of this snake from the Big Bend and Davis Mtns. are usually pink or buff, with 18–19 dark crossbars, while those from the Edwards Plateau-Stockton area are usually gray, with 22–23 dark crossbars. The dark crosslines, inconspicuous on forepart of body but progressively more prominent toward tail, may be brown or black but they vary in intensity from one specimen to the next. *A dark stripe from eye to angle of mouth. Young:* About 6½–8½ in. (16.5–21.5 cm) at birth.

A mountain-dwelling, rock-inhabiting Rattlesnake. Its menu is extremely varied; small rodents, lizards, small snakes, frogs, salamanders, and insects are included. **RANGE:** S.-cen. Texas west through Trans-Pecos region and south to San Luis Potosí; se. N.M. Mexican subspecies.

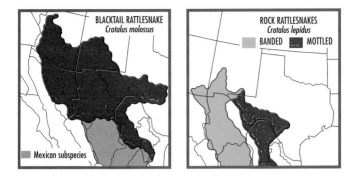

BLACKTAIL RATTLESNAKE
Crotalus molossus

Mexican subspecies

ROCK RATTLESNAKES
Crotalus lepidus
BANDED   MOTTLED

BANDED ROCK RATTLESNAKE   PL. 36
Crotalus lepidus klauberi

IDENTIFICATION: 15–24 in. (38–61 cm); record 32⅝ in. (82.9 cm). *A pattern of widely-spaced black or brown crossbars* throughout length of body and in strong contrast with the greenish to bluish green ground color of males, and gray to bluish gray ground color of females. For both sexes, relatively little dark spotting between crossbars (in comparison with the eastern subspecies, the Mottled Rock Rattlesnake). *No dark stripe from eye to angle of mouth.* *Young:* About 6¾–7¾ in. (17–19.6 cm) at birth; tail bright yellow at tip.

An inhabitant of rock slides and rocky hillsides, gorges, or stream beds in arid or semiarid terrain, chiefly in mountains. **RANGE:** Extr. w. Texas to w.-cen. N.M. and from se. Ariz. to Jalisco. Mexican subspecies.

The Banded Rock Rattlesnake, through much of its range, exhibits sexual dimorphism (see text). In both our kinds of rock rattlers there is a tendency for the body coloration to match or blend with the rocky habitat.

10

SALAMANDERS

ORDER CAUDATA

The Americas have far more kinds of salamanders than all the rest of the world put together. Those in our area range in size from dwarf species scarcely two inches long (5.1 cm) to giants like the Amphiumas that attain lengths of nearly four feet (1.2 m). The enormous family of lungless salamanders (Plethodontidae), almost exclusively confined to the New World, accounts for more than 230 of the 380-odd species of salamanders known to science.

Moisture is an absolute necessity for these creatures. Some kinds, including all the larger ones, are aquatic, but even the terrestrial species can survive only in damp environments. They hide by day and prowl by night. Observing salamanders consists largely of examining small streams and wet woodlands at night with flashlight or headlamp or, during daylight hours, overturning rocks, logs, or other objects beneath which they may hide.

Lizards are sometimes confused with salamanders, but lizards have scales on their bodies and claws on their toes. Salamanders have smooth or warty skins and are clawless. Because the tail is frequently damaged by accident or encounters with predators,

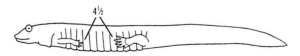

Fig. 77. Adpressed toes in salamanders. To count intercostal spaces, press limbs firmly against body.

herpetologists, in accumulating data for comparative studies, measure a *standard length,* the distance from tip of snout to posterior angle of vent (same as head-body length—see p. 141), as well as the *total length* (tip of snout to end of tail). The latter is a more useful measurement of the visual *real* size of a salamander, and is of more interest to the user of this Field Guide, but both are included in the accounts that follow. Salamanders, which are widely used for fish bait, are frequently liberated by anglers or bait dealers, and that often accounts for finding a species outside of its natural range.

Counting costal grooves (see p. 140) may be necessary for identifying some kinds of salamanders. Adpressing the toes (Fig. 77) is helpful in distinguishing between kinds that look alike but which have long legs and toes (or both) in one species and short ones in the other.

The best way of identifying many kinds of salamander larvae is to raise them until they transform into adults. They do well in aquariums (a minimum of one gallon of water for each specimen) if they are fed frequently with small, live, aquatic invertebrates, supplemented by crumbs of ground beef or canned dog food rich in meat. Large larvae are cannibalistic.

GIANT SALAMANDERS: FAMILIES CRYPTOBRANCHIDAE, PROTEIDAE, AMPHIUMIDAE, AND SIRENIDAE

North America boasts an assortment of big, bizarre salamanders that look more like bad dreams than live animals. Some are long, dark, and slender and resemble eels. Some permanently retain the larval form, bearing external gills throughout their lives. Others are flattened and suggest weird creatures crawling forth from the antediluvian slime. Since all are aquatic and nocturnal, few persons other than fishermen ever meet them in person. Periodically one or another is reported in the press as an animal "new to science." The erroneous belief that they are poisonous is widespread.

Many of these salamanders thrive in aquariums, but they should be provided with shelter in the form of flat rocks under which to crawl, or aquatic vegetation in which to hide. As in the care of aquarium fishes, the water must be kept from fouling and free from chlorine. A screened lid, tied or weighted down, should be provided; many specimens are persistent in their efforts to escape, at least during the first day or two. Many soon learn to eat small pieces of meat or liver or canned dog food.

Two of the families (Amphiumidae and Sirenidae) are confined to North America. The Proteidae (Waterdogs and Mudpuppies) also has a species in Europe, and the Cryptobranchidae (Hellbenders) has representatives in the Far East, including the enormous Japanese salamander that grows to a length of 5 feet (1.5 m). Not all members of these families are large: the Dwarf Siren (*Pseudobranchus*) is tiny (up to about 10 inches [25 cm] long) compared with its close relative, the Greater Siren, that attains a length in excess of 3 feet (.9 m).

The classification of the genus *Necturus*, several members of which are confusingly alike, needs study.

EASTERN HELLBENDER PL. 37
Cryptobranchus alleganiensis alleganiensis

IDENTIFICATION: 11¼–20 in. (29.2–51 cm). Records: Males 27 in. (68.6 cm); females 29⅛ in. (74 cm). A huge, grotesque, thoroughly aquatic salamander. Head flattened and each side of body with a wrinkled, fleshy fold of skin. Ground color usually gray, but varying from yellowish brown to almost black. Vague, scattered, and irregular dark or light spots may often be seen. No external gills in adult. *Young:* Numerous irregular dark spots that are conspicuous against light ground color; usually between 4 and 5 in. (10–12.5 cm) when they lose their external gills.

Almost always found in rivers and larger streams where water is running and ample shelter is available in the form of large rocks, snags, or debris. Hellbenders sometimes may be caught by *slowly* overturning or moving large rocks in clear, relatively shallow streams, and taking them by dip net or by hand. Since they are exceedingly slimy, the fingers must encircle the neck *and* immobilize both front legs on the first grab. Quite harmless, but many fishermen, believing them to be poisonous, will cut their lines

The large, thoroughly aquatic Eastern Hellbender has recently disappeared from a large part of its range. The silting and pollution of streams, resulting from activities of humankind, appear to be chiefly to blame.

and sacrifice their gear rather than unhook them. Captives will eat crayfish, earthworms, aquatic insects, and sometimes even pieces of meat. **SIMILAR SPECIES:** Adult Mudpuppies and Waterdogs have external gills, and so do larval specimens of other species. **RANGE:** S.-cen. N.Y. southwest to s. Ill., extr. ne. Miss., and northern parts of Ala. and Ga.; disjunct population in e.-cen. Mo.

HELLBENDERS
Cryptobranchus alleganiensis
■■■ EASTERN   ■ OZARK

OZARK HELLBENDER   PL. 37
Cryptobranchus alleganiensis bishopi

IDENTIFICATION: 11–22⅜ in. (28–56.8 cm). Much like the wide-ranging Eastern Hellbender but with the dark markings on the back much more conspicuous and in the form of *blotches* rather than spots. Lower lips heavily spotted with black (only lightly spotted or not at all in Eastern Hellbender). This form is best identified on basis of geography. **RANGE:** Sections of Black R. system and North Fork of White R. in se. Mo. and adj. Ark.

MUDPUPPY *Necturus maculosus*   PL. 37; FIGS. 20, 78

IDENTIFICATION: 8–13 in. (20–33 cm); record 19⅛ in. (48.6 cm). The gills, at maximum development, are like miniature ostrich plumes, dyed maroon and waving gracefully in the current. This, like all other members of its genus, is a permanent larva, retain-

Adults of the Red River Mudpuppy, like all members of the generic group Necturus, are neotenic. Although fully capable of reproduction, they retain the larval form, and the external gills are quite prominent.

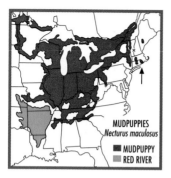

MUDPUPPIES
Necturus maculosus
■ MUDPUPPY
▨ RED RIVER

ing gills throughout life. *Four toes on each of the four feet.* Dark stripe through eye. General coloration gray or rust-brown to almost black; dorsum normally marked with rather indistinct, scattered, rounded, blue-black spots. Sometimes the spots are few in number, or, rarely, absent altogether; occasionally they fuse to form dorsolateral stripes. Belly grayish, with dark spots (Fig. 78) or sometimes plain gray. Tail fins often tinged with orange or reddish. *Larvae and young:* Normally striped; a broad middorsal dark stripe flanked on each side by a yellowish stripe (Fig. 20, opp. Pl. 37); a conspicuous dark stripe on side of body from gills to tip of tail. Occasionally the young are uniformly gray, without markings.

This salamander is a "mudpuppy" in the North, but southerners, not to be outdone in coining colorful names, refer to it and all its relatives as "waterdogs." Throughout much of Dixieland, "mudpuppy" is also used by country folk, but they reserve that name for adults of any of the Mole Salamanders (*Ambystoma*). Both names owe their origin, at least in part, to the erroneous belief that these animals bark.

Habitats include lakes, ponds, rivers, streams, and other permanent bodies of water; one was taken at a record depth of 90 ft. (27.4 m) in Green Bay, Wisconsin. Essentially nocturnal, but may also be active by day in muddy or weed-choked waters. Almost any small aquatic animal may be taken as food—fish, fish eggs, crayfish, aquatic insects, mollusks, etc. Size and condition of gills, although subject to individual variation, usually reflect environment. They are most likely to be large, bushy, and kept in motion if the water is foul or warm; usually they are small and contracted if the water is cool and contains considerable oxygen in solution. **SIMILAR SPECIES:** (1) Hellbenders have flat heads, folds of skin along sides, and adults lack external gills. (2) Gulf Coast Waterdog has very numerous dorsal spots, and dark stripe through eye may be absent or poorly developed. (3) Larvae of some Mole Salamanders (*Ambystoma*) grow large enough to be mistaken for Mudpuppies or Waterdogs (*Necturus*), but Mole Salamanders have five toes on each *hind* foot. **RANGE:** S. Quebec, Lake Champlain drainage, and e. N.Y., west to se. Manitoba and e. Kans., south to the Tennessee R. system; introduced in several places in New England; absent from much of northern Minn. and w. Wisc., as

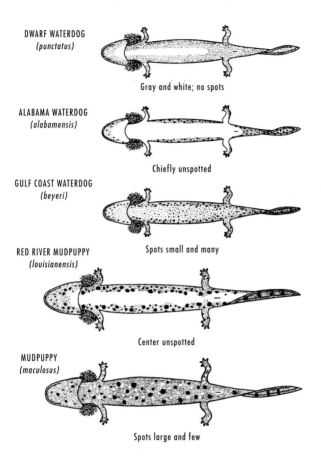

DWARF WATERDOG
(punctatus)

Gray and white; no spots

ALABAMA WATERDOG
(alabamensis)

Chiefly unspotted

GULF COAST WATERDOG
(beyeri)

Spots small and many

RED RIVER MUDPUPPY
(louisianensis)

Center unspotted

MUDPUPPY
(maculosus)

Spots large and few

Fig. 78. *Ventral patterns of several Waterdogs and the Mudpuppies* (Necturus).

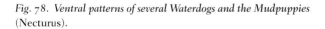

well as large areas of s. Tenn. and Ky.; also absent from the Adirondack area of n. N.Y. Apparently does not intergrade with the Red River Mudpuppy in Kans. and Mo. **SUBSPECIES:** MUD-PUPPY, *Necturus m. maculosus* (Pl. 37). As described and with range indicated above. RED RIVER MUDPUPPY, *Necturus m. louisianensis.* Ground color light yellowish brown or tan and with a broad, fairly distinct light stripe on each side of a darker mid-dorsal area. These markings are remnants of the juvenile pattern, which is striped like that of a young Mudpuppy. Dark spots begin to develop at an early age. Dorsum becomes gray in largest speci-mens, but dark spots remain clearly evident. Dark stripe through eye, extending from nostril to base of gills; center of venter gray-ish white, unmarked but tinged with pink (Fig. 78). Averages smaller than Mudpuppy; maximum length about 11 in. (28 cm). Arkansas R. and associated and adjacent drainage systems from se. Kans. and s. Mo. to n.-cen. La.

NEUSE RIVER WATERDOG *Necturus lewisi* **FIG. 79**

IDENTIFICATION: 6–9 in. (15.2–23 cm); record 10⅞ in. (27.6 cm). This Waterdog is strongly spotted both above *and below,* but markings tend to be fewer and smaller on the undersurfaces (Fig. 79). Spots dark brown or bluish black. Dorsal ground color rusty brown; ventral ground color dull brown or slate-colored. Dark line through eye. *Four* toes on all four feet. *Young:* Spotted, almost never plain or striped, but very small individuals some-times have a light middorsal stripe and dark sides with flecking. **SIMILAR SPECIES:** (1) Dwarf Waterdog is almost uniformly dark above and plain bluish white down center of belly (Fig. 78). (2) Larvae of Mole Salamanders have *five* toes on each *hind* foot. **RANGE:** Neuse and Tar R. systems, N.C.

Fig. 79. Pattern characteristics of the Neuse River Waterdog (Necturus lewisi). *The upper and lower surfaces are similarly patterned.*

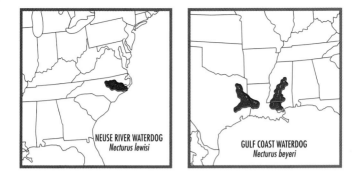

GULF COAST WATERDOG *Necturus beyeri* PL. 37; FIGS. 20, 28

IDENTIFICATION: 6¼–8¾ in. (15.9–22.2 cm). A profusely spotted Waterdog. Ground color dark brown, but appearing much lighter because of a multiplicity of tan spots that join to form an overlying, fine-meshed, netlike pattern. The round or oval spots, dark brown to almost black in color, are arranged in irregular rows or scattered at random. Belly invaded by spots and by dorsal ground color (Fig. 78). Dark stripe through eye in some specimens, absent in others. *Four* toes on all four feet. *Larvae and young:* Spotted, never striped (Fig. 20, opp. Pl. 37); dull yellow spots on head and body and in rows on edges of tail fin; dark spots develop as animal grows.

Chiefly in sandy, spring-fed streams. **SIMILAR SPECIES:** (1) Alabama Waterdog and Red River Mudpuppy both have at least the center of the venter unspotted. (2) Larvae of Mole Salamanders have *five* toes on each *hind* foot. **RANGE:** E. Texas to cen. La.; also through the Florida parishes of La. northward to cen. Miss.

ALABAMA WATERDOG *Necturus alabamensis* FIG. 78

IDENTIFICATION: 6–8½ in. (15.2–21.6 cm). A highly variable salamander in coloration and degree of spotting, depending both on age and geographic locality. Dorsum often reddish brown, but some individuals are russet, others are dark brown, and some may even be slaty black. Patternwise they may be nearly uniformly dark or have a spotted or mottled appearance. Dark spots fairly conspicuous in younger specimens (or in adults that have been poorly or long preserved), but they tend to coalesce and blend with the general dorsal ground color in older individuals. Small scattered light spots often present. Coloration paler on sides of body. *Center of belly unmarked* (Fig. 78), white to bluish white. Tips of digits whitish. Tail relatively short; dorsal fin low.

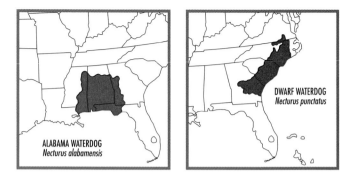

ALABAMA WATERDOG
Necturus alabamensis

DWARF WATERDOG
Necturus punctatus

Found chiefly in medium- to large-sized streams that have an abundance of hiding places—stones, bottom debris, and sunken snags and logs. **SIMILAR SPECIES:** (1) Gulf Coast Waterdog has the *entire venter spotted.* (2) Dwarf Waterdog lacks conspicuous markings of any kind. (3) Larvae of Mole Salamanders have *five* toes on each *hind* foot. **RANGE:** W. Ga. and the Fla. panhandle to e. Miss.

DWARF WATERDOG *Necturus punctatus*   **PL. 37; FIG. 78**
IDENTIFICATION: 4½–6¼ in. (11.5–15.9 cm); record 7⁷⁄₁₆ in. (18.9 cm).
A southeastern Waterdog with no conspicuous markings of any kind. Dorsum slate-gray to dark brown or black (sometimes purplish black) with a few small pale spots. Throat whitish. Central portion of belly bluish white, plain or partly invaded by the dorsal

The Dwarf Waterdog, the smallest member of the genus Necturus, differs from all the others in lacking large dark spots on both its back and venter. "Mudpuppy" and "Waterdog" are derived from colloquial names.

color (Fig. 78). *Four* toes on all four feet. *Young:* Always gray; may or may not be spotted.

Found in sluggish streams; prefers areas where the bottom is composed of masses of leaf litter and similar debris. **SIMILAR SPECIES:** (1) Neuse River Waterdog is conspicuously spotted. (2) Larvae of Mole Salamanders have *five* toes on each *hind* foot. **RANGE:** Coastal Plain from se. Va. to s.-cen. Ga.

TWO-TOED AMPHIUMA
Amphiuma means

TWO-TOED AMPHIUMA *Amphiuma means*   PL. 37

IDENTIFICATION: 14½–30 in. (36.8–76 cm); record 45¾ in. (116.2 cm). An "eel" with two pairs of tiny, useless-looking legs. *Two toes* on each limb. Dorsum dark brown or black; venter dark gray. No sharp change of color between back and belly. This is the "congo (conger) eel," "lamper eel," or "ditch eel" of fishermen and country folk. (The same names are often applied to the other species of *Amphiuma* and to both species of *Siren.*)

Almost completely aquatic, but occasionally moves overland through swamps on rainy nights. Habitats include ditches, sloughs, pools, ponds, rice fields, swamps, streams, etc. Many specimens utilize lairs in mud or jumbles of bottom debris, protruding their heads a short distance upward or outward from their hiding places while waiting for crayfish or other food to come along. Best sought at night in shallow water. A dip net with a deep bag, although rather awkward to use on such slippery elongated animals, is the safest tool with which to catch them unharmed. They can bite savagely. Another technique is to cover your hand with burlap sacking or wear a stout glove, grab the Amphiuma at midbody, and sling it out on land where you can work it into a bag. Food includes worms, insects, mollusks, crustaceans, small fish, snakes, frogs, and smaller Amphiumas. **SIMILAR SPECIES:** (1) See the other two kinds of Amphiumas—count toes. (2) Sirens have external gills and *no hind legs.* (3) True eels (fishes) have a fin at each side of head and no legs. **RANGE:** Coastal Plain from se. Va. to the southern tip of Fla. and west to se. Miss. and extr. e. La.

THREE-TOED AMPHIUMA *Amphiuma tridactylum*   PL. 37

IDENTIFICATION: 18–30 in. (45.7–76 cm); record 41¾ in. (106 cm). The Mississippi Valley representative of the Amphiuma group of species. *Three toes* on each limb. Dorsum dark brown and sharply

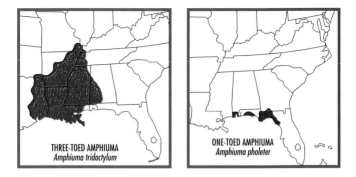

THREE-TOED AMPHIUMA
Amphiuma tridactylum

ONE-TOED AMPHIUMA
Amphiuma pholeter

set off from the much paler (light gray) venter. A dark throat patch.

An abundant salamander of bayous and ditches of the Mississippi delta region, of oxbows, lakes, and ponds, and in fact of almost any unpolluted muddy or mucky habitat throughout its range. **SIMILAR SPECIES:** See Similar Species under Two-toed Amphiuma. **RANGE:** Se. Mo., adj. Ky., and extr. se. Okla. to Gulf of Mexico.

ONE-TOED AMPHIUMA *Amphiuma pholeter*   PL. 37

IDENTIFICATION: 8½–12½ in. (21.5–32 cm); record 13 in. (33 cm). A dwarf Amphiuma with only *one toe* on each foot. Limbs and head proportionately shorter and eye proportionately smaller than in the other Amphiumas. Venter dusky and virtually same color as dorsum.

A secretive salamander of muck-bottomed stream floodplains and other mucky habitats where it feeds on insects and other invertebrates. **SIMILAR SPECIES:** In both the Two-toed and Three-toed Amphiumas the dorsum is distinctly darker than the venter. Occasional specimens of the two larger species may have only a single toe on one or more feet as a result of injury or fighting, but in such cases the maimed or regenerated condition of the limb is usually recognizable. **RANGE:** Disjunct; the Gulf Hammock region of the Fla. Peninsula and extr. sw. Ga. west through the Fla. Panhandle to Mobile Bay in sw. Ala.

GREATER SIREN *Siren lacertina*   PL. 37

IDENTIFICATION: 20–30 in. (51–76 cm); record 38¼ in. (97.8 cm). An "eel" with forelegs and external gills; these appendages are crowded together instead of being spread out along the slender

Close-up of head and appendages of the Greater Siren. The tiny foreleg, here elevated to show the four toes, is crowded close to the gills. There are no hind limbs. The long and slender sirens look like eels.

body. The legs, so small that they are easily hidden by the gills, have *four* toes each. General coloration olive to light gray, the back darker than sides, and the latter with rather faint greenish or yellowish dots and dashes. In some specimens circular, well-defined black spots may be seen on top of head, back, and sides. Belly with numerous small greenish or yellowish flecks. *Young:* A prominent light stripe on side of body plus a light dorsal fin make juveniles look superficially like Dwarf Sirens. Light markings disappear and young become almost uniformly dark as they approach maturity.

Lives in a large variety of essentially shallow-water habitats—ditches, weed-choked or muddy ponds, rice fields, streams with clear to turbid water, lakes, etc. Often these salamanders may be observed at night with the aid of a flashlight as they forage. Young ones may sometimes abound amid roots of water hyacinths. Sirens may yelp when caught, making a sound similar to that of a Green Treefrog heard calling in the distance. Crayfish, worms, mollusks, small fish, etc., are eaten, but Sirens also engulf quantities of aquatic vegetation in the course of swallowing animal food.

SIMILAR SPECIES: (1) True eels (which are fishes) have a fin at each side of neck and no legs or external gills. (2) Amphiumas also lack external gills, but they have *four* small legs, a pair aft as well as forward. (3) Dwarf Sirens have only *three* toes on each leg. (4) Difficulty will inevitably arise in trying to distinguish small Greater Sirens from adults of Eastern Lesser Siren—even experts have trouble. Eastern Lesser Siren lacks any pronounced light markings; counting costal grooves will help, these being 36–40 in Greater Siren (from armpit to anus), and 31–35 in East-

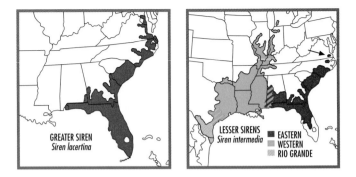

ern Lesser Siren. Counting costal grooves is always difficult on a live salamander. Let your Siren settle down in a flat-sided aquarium and don't touch it when you count. **RANGE:** Vicinity of Washington, D.C., to extr. s. Fla. and s. Ala.

LESSER SIREN *Siren intermedia* PL. 37

IDENTIFICATION: 7–27 in. (18–68.6 cm). Size varies — see subspecies. Similar to the Greater Siren in general appearance and in having external gills and two tiny front legs, each with *four* toes. General dorsal coloration dark brown to bluish black, sometimes olive-green. Darker specimens are virtually without markings, but in the lighter ones irregularly scattered black dots are discernible. *Young:* A red band across snout and along side of head. These markings disappear with age; older juveniles may be olive-green with tiny brown spots.

An Eastern Lesser Siren with gills and a foreleg in natural positions. Distinguishing between the two species of sirens may be difficult. Even experts sometimes have trouble. Read the text carefully for details.

This eel-like salamander spends the daylight hours burrowed in debris that accumulates at bottoms of ditches, ponds, and other bodies of shallow water. When and if the water dries up it descends into the mud, and when that, in turn, dries over, the Siren becomes entombed and must wait, sometimes for months, until the coming of rains. In preparation for estivation, skin glands secrete a substance that forms a dry, inelastic parchment-like cocoon covering the entire body (except the mouth), and which protects the animal from desiccation.

Sirens were named for a temptress of mythology, and not for the warning device used by emergency vehicles. They do make sounds, however, consisting of series of faint clicks that are emitted when other Sirens approach or when a specimen partially leaves a burrow in shallow water to gulp air at the surface. They also may utter shrill cries of distress, as when seized by a Water Snake. Food similar to that of Greater Siren. **SIMILAR SPECIES:** See Greater Siren. **RANGE:** N.C. to s.-cen. Fla.; west to e. and s. Texas and north in Mississippi Valley to Ind. and Ill.; isolated colonies (introduced?) in se. Va., ne. N.C., sw. Mich., and n. Ind. **SUBSPECIES:** EASTERN LESSER SIREN, *Siren i. intermedia* (Pl. 37). Plain black or brown above or with minute black dots sprinkled over dorsal surface and tail; venter uniformly dark but paler than dorsum; costal grooves 31–35; averages small, with a maximum length of 15 in. (38.1 cm). S. Atlantic and Gulf Coastal Plains to se. Miss.; intergrades with *nettingi* in w. Ala. and se. Miss. WESTERN LESSER SIREN, *Siren i. nettingi*. Olive or gray above with scattered, minute black spots; venter dark with numerous *light* spots; costal grooves 34–36; averages larger—record 19¾ in. (50.2 cm). Mississippi Valley; east to w. Ala. and west to e. Texas. RIO GRANDE LESSER SIREN, *Siren i. texana*. Gray or brownish gray above and marked with tiny black flecks; venter light gray but paler under gills and limbs, around vent, and behind the angles of jaws; costal grooves 36–38; size large—record 27 in. (68.6 cm). Lower Rio Grande Valley and n. Tamaulipas; intergrading with *nettingi* along and near Texas coast.

DWARF SIRENS: GENUS *Pseudobranchus*

These are small, aquatic, eel-like salamanders with external gills and tiny forelegs. Each foot bears *three* toes. All five subspecies are patterned with longitudinal stripes. As in the Waterdogs, the size of the gills depends on temperature and other conditions.

This is one of the groups of animals that has prospered by the introduction of the water hyacinth. Dwarf Sirens find food and shelter among the roots of these floating pests. A good collecting technique is to roll up masses of hyacinths or slide a large boxlike sieve of fine-mesh wire under a patch of them and carry them ashore. Careful sorting through the lot often may reveal Dwarf Sirens. (There is a good chance of finding small aquatic snakes at the same time.) When picked up or pinched, Dwarf Sirens may yelp faintly. Food includes aquatic insects and other invertebrates. The genus *Pseudobranchus* occurs only in the extreme southeastern United States. There is a single species, but there are several races.

NARROW-STRIPED DWARF SIREN   PL. 39; FIG. 80
Pseudobranchus striatus axanthus

IDENTIFICATION: 4¾–7½ in. (12.1–19 cm); record 9⅞ in. (25.1 cm). The only Dwarf Siren in which there are no sharply defined light stripes (Fig. 80). Entire animal looks muddy, and pattern details are obscure. Head terminates in a bluntly rounded snout. *Three* toes on each foot. **SIMILAR SPECIES:** Both Greater and Lesser Sirens have *four* toes on each foot. **RANGE:** Ne. and cen. Fla.

SLENDER DWARF SIREN   PL. 39; FIG. 80
Pseudobranchus striatus spheniscus

IDENTIFICATION: 4–6 in. (10–15.2 cm). A tiny, slender "eel" with a narrow, wedge-shaped snout, and two bright tan or yellow stripes on sides of body.

Dwarf Sirens of all races occur in a variety of shallow, freshwater habitats, including swamps, marshes, lime-sink ponds, and ditches, particularly those choked with vegetation. Best found by seining up and examining detritus from pond bottoms or by sifting through hyacinths. **SIMILAR SPECIES:** Greater and Lesser Sirens have *four* toes on each foot. Dwarf Sirens have only *three*. **RANGE:** S. Ga. and eastern two-thirds of Fla. panhandle. **SUBSPECIES:** All of these are strongly striped (Fig. 80). The stripes are most easily seen when the salamanders are submerged in water. Put them in a flat-sided aquarium when trying to identify the various subspecies. BROAD-STRIPED DWARF SIREN, *Pseudobranchus s. striatus.* Most strikingly patterned of all the races; a broad, dark brown middorsal stripe with a vague light line down its center and flanked on each side by a broad yellow stripe; belly dark but heavily mottled with yellow. Body short and stocky. Total length up to 8 in. (20.3 cm). S. S.C., se. Ga., and extr. ne. Fla. GULF HAMMOCK DWARF SIREN, *Pseudobranchus s. lustricolus.* A broad, dark middorsal stripe containing *within itself* three narrow, light stripes, the central one down ridge of back; two broad, sharply defined light stripes on each side of body, upper one orange-brown in coloration and lower one silvery white; belly black with light mottling; body relatively stout, snout blunt; length up to 8½ in. (21.6 cm). Gulf Hammock region on northwestern side of Fla. peninsula. EVERGLADES DWARF SIREN, *Pseudobranchus s. belli.* Similar in stripe pattern to Gulf Hammock race, but with the broad light stripes buff in color and belly gray; a small, slender subspecies with length up to 6 in. (15.2 cm). Southern third of Fla. peninsula.

DWARF SIRENS
Pseudobranchus striatus

■ SLENDER
■ BROAD-STRIPED
■ GULF HAMMOCK
■ NARROW-STRIPED
■ EVERGLADES

BROAD-STRIPED
(striatus)
Dark middorsal stripe
flanked by broad yellow one

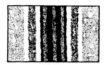

SLENDER
(spheniscus)
Two tan or yellow
stripes on each side

EVERGLADES
(belli)
Lateral stripe buff;
belly gray

GULF HAMMOCK
(lustricolus)
Three narrow yellow
stripes in dark middorsal
region; belly blackish

NARROW-STRIPED
(axanthus)
Dark stripes narrow,
subdued

Fig. 80. Diagrammatic patterns of subspecies of the Dwarf Siren (Pseudobranchus). Each diagram shows a section of skin removed from the animal and flattened out—dorsum in center, belly at sides.

Like moles, these amphibians stay underground most of their lives. But they congregate in numbers in temporary pools and ponds (one species uses streams) after early spring rains for courtship and deposition of eggs, activities that may be completed in one or just a few nights. The eggs may be laid in large clusters or in small groups, floating at the surface of the water or submerged and attached to sticks or debris. The method depends on the species. Some kinds breed in autumn; in the South, most egg-laying takes place in winter.

Finding specimens before or after the breeding season is largely a matter of chance. They may wander on rainy nights, but they take shelter before morning beneath boards, logs, stones, etc., unless they accidentally tumble into cellar window wells or ditches.

The larvae of some kinds grow to large size, retain their gills, remain permanently aquatic, and breed without developing all the adult characteristics. Such specimens technically are said to be neotenic; the Mexican Indians have given us the name "axolotl" for them (Fig. 21, opp. Pl. 38). Newly transformed salamanders of this genus are often difficult to identify.

Some of the Mole Salamanders bear a resemblance to certain of the lungless salamanders (Plethodontidae), but members of the latter family have a groove running from the nostril down to the lip—see p. 140. (A lens may be necessary to check this characteristic.) Mole Salamanders have five toes on each hind foot and four on each front foot.

The Family Ambystomatidae occurs throughout most of the United States and ranges from extreme southeastern Alaska, James Bay, and southern Labrador to the southern edge of the Mexican Plateau. Its members are widely studied as laboratory animals. In captivity adults are easily maintained in terrariums equipped with a few inches of damp earth. They will eat live earthworms and other invertebrates, and some can be trained to accept small pieces of meat. Larvae are easily raised in aquariums.

MOLE SALAMANDER *Ambystoma talpoideum*   **PL. 38**

IDENTIFICATION: 3–4 in. (7.5–10 cm); record 4¹³⁄₁₆ in. (12.2 cm). Head and feet seem too large for the rest of the animal. Ground color black, brown, or gray; pale flecks bluish white. *Young:* About 2³⁄₁₆–2¾ in. (5.6–7 cm) following metamorphosis.

A confirmed burrower, but occasionally found under logs or other objects in damp places. Chiefly confined to lowlands and

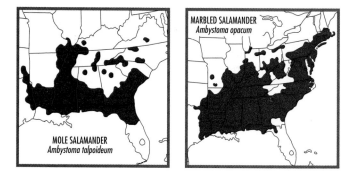

valleys. Often neotenic. **RANGE:** S.C. to n. Fla. and west to e. Texas and extr. se. Okla.; north in Mississippi Valley to s. Ill.; disjunct populations in Va., the Carolinas, Ga., Ala., Tenn., and Ky.

MARBLED SALAMANDER *Ambystoma opacum*   PL. 38

IDENTIFICATION: 3½–4¼ in. (9–10.7 cm); record 5 in. (12.7 cm). "Banded salamander" would be a good alternate name. The light markings, basically crossbands, are variable, being sometimes incomplete, running together, or enclosing dark spots. On rare occasions there may be a light stripe along or parallel to the mid-dorsal line. Markings gray in females, white in males; in both sexes they contrast strongly with the black components of the pattern and the plain black belly. *Newly transformed juveniles:* Scattered light flecks on a dorsal ground color of dull brown to black; about 1¾–2¹³⁄₁₆ in. (4.4–7.1 cm).

A pair of Marbled Salamanders, small stout-bodied members of the mole salamander family. Their markings may vary in width, arrangement, and number, but the pale components are whitish in males, gray in females.

This rather chunky salamander occurs in a variety of habitats, ranging from moist sandy areas to dry hillsides. Breeds in *autumn,* the female depositing her eggs in a low depression, which will be filled by the next good rain. Eggs, laid in a group but unattached to one another, do not hatch until covered with water. Until then they are guarded by female. **SIMILAR SPECIES:** Ringed and Flatwoods Salamanders are more slender, and their light rings or crossbands are narrow. **RANGE:** S. New England to n. Fla. and west to s. Ill., se. Okla., and e. Texas; disjunct colonies near southern perimeters of Lakes Erie and Michigan, as well as in sw. Mo. and along the northern border between Ohio and Ind.

RINGED SALAMANDER *Ambystoma annulatum* PL. 38

IDENTIFICATION: 5½–7 in. (1 4–1 8 cm); record 9⅜ in. (2 3.8 cm). Any of the rings may be incomplete, interrupted across the back, or represented solely by vertical light bars or elongated spots. Coloration variable from medium dark brown to almost black; rings may be buff, yellow, or whitish, sometimes not all the same color on same animal. A light gray, rather irregular stripe along lower side of body. Belly slate-colored, with small whitish spots. Head small. *Newly transformed juveniles:* About 2¾ in. (7 cm).

Seldom encountered except during or following medium to heavy autumn rains. These stimulate the salamanders into forming breeding congresses of scores or even hundreds in pools or shallow ponds. **SIMILAR SPECIES:** (1) Marbled Salamander is a shorter, stouter amphibian with a plain black belly, and its crossbands are broader and usually have a silvery appearance. (2) In Barred Tiger Salamander (and Marbled) black pigment extends uninterruptedly from back to belly. **RANGE:** Cen. Mo., n.-cen. and w. Ark., and e. Okla.

The Central Highlands—the Ozarks, Boston and Ouachita mountains and associated ranges—are collectively the homes of many unusual salamanders, including the strikingly marked Ringed Salamander, an autumn breeder.

RINGED SALAMANDER
Ambystoma annulatum

FLATWOODS SALAMANDER
Ambystoma cingulatum

FLATWOODS SALAMANDER *Ambystoma cingulatum* PL. 38

IDENTIFICATION: 3½–5 1/16 in. (9–12.9 cm). The dorsal markings are highly variable, ranging from a "frosted" or lichenlike appearance to a netlike (reticulated) pattern or a tendency to form a series of narrow light rings. Ground color black to chocolate black; markings gray or brownish gray. Belly black with scattered pearl-gray spots or with great numbers of tiny gray flecks that produce a salt-and-pepper appearance. *Newly transformed juveniles:* About 2¾ in. (7 cm).

An inhabitant of slashpine-wiregrass flatwoods. Often found under objects near the small, shallow cypress ponds characteristic of such areas. Eggs are scattered terrestrially in fall or early winter to await the arrival of rains. **SIMILAR SPECIES:** (1) Mabee's Salamander is often brownish and with the light flecks most conspicuous along the sides; not patterned all over as in the Flat-

The Flatwoods Salamander, a small slender member of the mole salamander group, varies greatly in color pattern. Some, like this one, may be crossbanded. Others bear frosted, netlike, or lichenlike patterns.

woods. If in doubt check jaw teeth; they are in a single row in Mabee's, in multiple rows in the Flatwoods Salamander. (2) Slimy Salamander (complex) has a groove from nostril to lip, and its skin-gland secretions stick like glue to one's fingers. **RANGE:** S. S.C. to n. Fla. and sw. Ala.

MABEE'S SALAMANDER *Ambystoma mabeei* PL. 38
IDENTIFICATION: 3–4 in. (7.5–10.2 cm); record 4¼ in. (11.4 cm). The *light specks* are palest and most conspicuous along the sides. Dorsal ground color chiefly deep brown to black; belly dark brown or gray. Note long toes and small head. Jaw teeth are in a single row.

Named for W. B. Mabee, who collected the first specimen made known to science. **SIMILAR SPECIES:** (1) Mole Salamander has a conspicuously large head. (2) Slimy Salamander (complex) has groove from nostril to lip. (3) Flatwoods Salamander is "frosted" or patterned all over, not just conspicuously along sides; if in doubt, check jaw teeth, which in the Flatwoods are in multiple rows. **RANGE:** Coastal Plain of the Carolinas and extr. se. Va.

SMALLMOUTH SALAMANDER *Ambystoma texanum* PL. 38
IDENTIFICATION: 4–5¼ in. (10–14 cm); record 7 in. (17.8 cm). Well named; both *mouth and head are small*. Ground color black or very dark brown. Usually a pattern of grayish lichenlike markings, but these are extremely variable in intensity. Many specimens have the markings concentrated on the back and upper sides. Some, especially toward the northeastern part of the range, are almost plain black. Texas specimens are very heavily speckled, with the light markings especially large and prominent on the lower sides.

A late winter and spring breeder, and frequently found at those seasons under logs, boards, or other debris near ponds or swamps, in river bottoms, or other situations where moisture is abundant. Known to hybridize with Blue-spotted and Tiger Salamanders. **SIMILAR SPECIES:** (1) Jefferson and Blue-spotted Salamanders have *much* longer toes and a longer snout and head. (2) Mole Salamander has a conspicuously large head. (3) Rule out any lungless salamander that may be similarly marked or colored by checking for groove from nostril to lip. **RANGE:** Extr. se. Mich., n. Ohio, and Pelee Island, Ont. (in Lake Erie), west to se. Neb. and south to the Gulf. Absent from much of the Central Highlands area in Mo. and Ark., and from coastal La.

STREAMSIDE SALAMANDER *Ambystoma barbouri* NOT ILLUS.
IDENTIFICATION: 4–5¼ in. (10–14 cm); record 6⅝ in. (16.8 cm). Identical to the Smallmouth Salamander, but it breeds in streams with

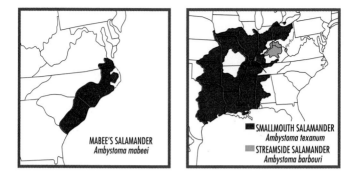

MABEE'S SALAMANDER
Ambystoma mabeei

■ SMALLMOUTH SALAMANDER
Ambystoma texanum
▨ STREAMSIDE SALAMANDER
Ambystoma barbouri

limestone bedrock (not in pools and ditches, as does the Small-mouth) and lays its eggs singly (not in clumps). Check the map— it is the only way to be sure of the identity of your catch. The lar-vae are much larger than those of the Smallmouth Salamander, and far fewer eggs are laid.

The Streamside Salamander inhabits upland forests in close proximity to streams. It migrates to breeding sites in the fall, and its prolonged breeding season lasts from early December to mid-April, regardless of rainfall (or lack of it). In contrast, the Small-mouth Salamander in the eastern part of its range has a compara-tively brief spring breeding season that occurs during early warm rains. **SIMILAR SPECIES:** See Smallmouth Salamander. **RANGE:** N.-cen. Ky., sw. Ohio, and se. Ind.; isolated colonies in sw. Ky. and w. W. Va.; isolated records (presumably of this salamander) along the Ohio R. in nw. W. Va. and se. Ohio.

EFFERSON SALAMANDER *Ambystoma jeffersonianum* **PL. 38**
IDENTIFICATION: 4¼–7 in. (10.7–18 cm); record 8¼ in. (21 cm). The *long toes, long snout,* and relatively slender build are the best things to look for in distinguishing this otherwise nondescript salamander from other members of the genus *Ambystoma*. Dorsal ground color dark brown or gray, with the belly distinctly paler than the sides. Small bluish flecks, chiefly on limbs and lower sides of body, are usually present. Bluish markings conspicuous on small adults; they may be virtually absent on large adults. South of its hybrid zone with the Blue-spotted Salamander (see Note below), this species has a *pale belly;* inside the hybrid zone its belly may be slightly darker, but with a *gray vent* that is always paler than in the Blue-spotted.

An early spring breeder. Named for Jefferson College, Canons-

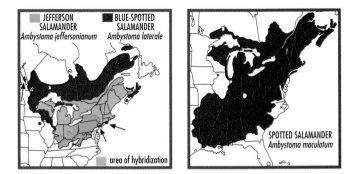

burg, Pa., hence indirectly for the excellent naturalist who attained the Presidency—Thomas Jefferson. **SIMILAR SPECIES:** See Blue-spotted Salamander. **RANGE:** South of a large area where it hybridizes with the Blue-spotted Salamander (see Note below), pure examples of this species are known from s. N.Y. southwest to w. Va., cen. Ky., and s. Ind. **NOTE:** The Jefferson and Blue-spotted Salamanders have been shown to hybridize over a wide area of the ne. U.S. and se. Canada, from Nova Scotia west to n. Wisc., and south to Ind. and Ohio (see map above). Within this area a bewildering array of colors and patterns may be exhibited by the hybrids and their parents, and certain identification to either species is extremely difficult. Previously it was thought that the salamanders in this region were composed of four entities, two bisexual (*laterale* and *jeffersonianum*) and two unisexual (parthenogenetic, all-female), and the latter two were also recognized as species. Recent studies have shown that continuous re-hybridization by fertilization, not parthenogenetic reproduction, takes place among Jefferson and Blue-spotted Salamanders, and recognition of the hybrids as species is not warranted. To identify whether you have a specimen (hybrid or pure) of the *Ambystoma laterale-jeffersonianum* complex, simply eliminate all the other known species of Mole Salamanders found within the range of this complex (see Similar Species under Blue-spotted Salamander below).

BLUE-SPOTTED SALAMANDER *Ambystoma laterale* **PL. 38**
IDENTIFICATION: 4–5½ in. (10–14 cm); record (probably a hybrid) 6⁵⁄₁₆ in. (16 cm). Many specimens would match the enamelware pots and dishpans of yesteryear, with their flecks and spots of white and blue on bluish black. The relatively long toes, blue to bluish-

white flecks on the back, and bluish-white spots on sides of trunk and tail, will usually distinguish this species from all others except the Jefferson Salamander (see below). Dorsal ground color black or bluish black. North of its hybrid zone with the Jefferson Salamander this species has a *black belly;* within the hybrid zone its belly may be slightly paler, but the area around the vent is usually *black.*

Breeds in spring in woodland ponds, ditches, etc., and occurs farther north than any other salamander in eastern North America. **SIMILAR SPECIES:** (1) Smallmouth and Streamside Salamanders have short snouts and short toes. (2) Slimy Salamander (complex) has groove from nostril to lip. (3) Jefferson Salamander has proportionately longer toes and grows much larger—to 8¼ in. (21 cm). The Blue-spotted normally is profusely marked with *spots,* whereas light markings in the virtually unicolored Jefferson are confined to bluish *flecks* on the limbs and along the sides. The Blue-spotted is a dark animal (ground color black or nearly so); the Jefferson may be dark brown, but it tends to be paler— brownish gray or lead-colored. Outside of the hybrid zone, examine the belly, which is black in the Blue-spotted Salamander and paler than the dorsum and sides in the Jefferson Salamander. Within the hybrid zone, look at the vent, which is surrounded by *black in the Blue-spotted,* and usually surrounded by *gray in the Jefferson.* **RANGE:** North of its hybrid zone with the Jefferson Salamander, pure examples of this species occur from the northern shore of the Gulf of St. Lawrence west across s. Canada to se. Manitoba, and south along the western edge of its range to ne. Ill. and adj. Ind; disjunct populations in Lab., s. Nova Scotia and adj. islands, e.-cen. Iowa, and along the western shore of Lake Winnipeg; small isolated colonies in e. Long Island and n. N.J.

SPOTTED SALAMANDER *Ambystoma maculatum* **PL. 38**
IDENTIFICATION: 4⅜–7¾ in. (11.2–19.7 cm); record 9¾ in. (24.8 cm). Up to 50 round, light spots, *yellow or orange* in coloration, arranged in an irregular *row* along each side of the back, from eye to tail tip. Dorsal ground color black, slate, or bluish black; *belly slate-gray.* Unspotted individuals are rare but probably occur throughout the range of the species. Young sometimes have a dark brown ground color.

An early spring breeder that, under stimulus of warm rains, sometimes makes mass migrations to woodland ponds. Occasionally found (from spring to autumn) beneath stones or boards in moist environments or during wet weather. **SIMILAR SPECIES:** Light spots on Eastern Tiger Salamander are irregular, often elongated, and extend far down on sides. The Tiger also has an *olive-yellow*

An adult Spotted Salamander from Stewart County, Tennessee. The arrival of this amphibian at its vernal pools and ponds is a sure sign of spring.

belly. **RANGE:** Nova Scotia and the Gaspé Peninsula to s.-cen. Ont.; south to Ga. and e. Texas. Absent from the Prairie Peninsula in Ill. and from most of s. N.J. and the Delmarva Peninsula. Isolated records from e. N.C. and nw. Ill.

EASTERN TIGER SALAMANDER PL. 38
Ambystoma tigrinum tigrinum

IDENTIFICATION: 7–8¼ in. (18–21 cm); record 13 in. (33 cm). The light spots, olive- or yellowish brown, are highly irregular in shape and distribution, and extend well downward on the sides. Dorsal ground color dull black to deep brown; *belly olive-yellow,* marbled with darker pigment.

A winter and very early spring breeder, usually congregating in deeper water than does the Spotted Salamander. Larvae are often common in farm ponds—until such ponds are stocked with fish! **SIMILAR SPECIES:** In the Spotted Salamander, the light spots form an irregular *row* and belly is gray. **RANGE:** Long Island to n. Fla. and s. Miss.; Ohio to Minn. and south to n. Ark. and to the Gulf through Ga.; absent from most of Appalachian uplands and lower Mississippi delta region; large disjunct population in e. Texas, and smaller isolated colonies in ne. Miss., ne. Minn., the upper peninsula of Mich., and in s. Ohio, adj. Ky., and w.-cen. Va.

BARRED TIGER SALAMANDER PL. 38
Ambystoma tigrinum mavortium

IDENTIFICATION: 6–8½ in. (15.2–21.5 cm); record 12⅞ in. (32.7 cm, neotenic). Either dark or light bars may extend upward from belly to midline of back. Highly variable, however, the light markings taking many shapes and forms but in general being larger in size and fewer in number than the light markings on the Eastern Tiger. Ground color black or dark brown; markings yellowish, bright on sides but diffused with darker pigment on back. Belly black and yellow.

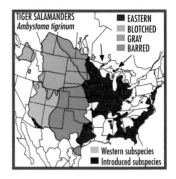

Occasionally neotenic, especially toward the west, where the immediate environs of a pond may become completely dry and inhospitable for a salamander. **SIMILAR SPECIES:** (1) Some specimens resemble Ringed Salamander. In the Barred Tiger, the head is larger and the dark pigment extends all the way from back to belly; in the Ringed the black is interrupted by a light grayish stripe along lower side of body. (2) Marbled Salamander has a solid black belly; Barred Tiger has a black and yellow belly. **RANGE:** Disjunct; cen. Neb. to s. Texas. **SUBSPECIES:** BLOTCHED TIGER SALAMANDER, *Ambystoma t. melanostictum*. A race in which the dark ground color (brown to black) is reduced to a network; light areas dull yellow and with indefinite borders. Slightly smaller on the average than the Barred Tiger. Frequently neotenic. Neb. to Wash. and s.-cen. Alberta. GRAY TIGER SALAMANDER, *Ambystoma t. diaboli*. Ground color light olive to dark brown; scattered small dark brown to black spots on back and sides. Frequently neotenic. Sw. Minn. to s. Manitoba and s. Sask. Western subspecies. **NOTE:** Tiger Salamanders, which have been widely transported as fish bait, are now established in so many localities that it is difficult to define natural ranges, particularly of the western races.

NEWTS: FAMILY SALAMANDRIDAE

Newts are not so slippery as most salamanders. Their skins are rougher and not slimy, and they do not slide easily through your fingers when you try to handle them. The costal grooves, which are prominent in most other salamanders, are indistinct.

Most newts are essentially aquatic. In the case of all the Eastern Newts (species *viridescens* and *perstriatus*), however, there is also a land stage, like the Red Eft form of the Red-spotted Newt. The larvae transform into efts, which remain ashore for one to three years; they then return to the water and change into the aquatic adults. Sometimes the land stage is omitted, and the larvae transform directly into adults, in which case remnants of the external gills may be retained. The tails of efts are almost round in cross section, and their skins are quite rough; the tails of adults are vertically compressed, and their skins are much smoother.

Natural food includes insects, leeches, worms, tiny mollusks and crustaceans, young amphibians, and frogs' eggs. Captive aquatic adults will eat small pieces of meat, but crumbs of canned dog food make a better balanced diet. Efts respond most readily to live insects. Few predators will eat newts, for their skin-gland secretions are toxic or at least irritating to mucous membranes.

There are three species in eastern North America. Other members of this large family, the Pacific Newts (genus *Taricha*), occur in British Columbia and the Pacific states (southeastern Alaska to southern California), and still other kinds inhabit Europe, North Africa, and Asia.

RED-SPOTTED NEWT PL. 39
Notophthalmus viridescens viridescens

IDENTIFICATION: 2¼–4¹³⁄₁₆ in. (5.7–12.2 cm); record 5½ in. (14 cm). Up to 21 red spots, variable in number and position, are present at all stages of the complex life history. The aquatic adults, although normally olive-green, may vary from yellowish brown to dark greenish brown. Their venters are yellow with small black spots. *Male:* Both the high tail fin and black excrescences on the hind legs disappear after the spring breeding season, but they may develop again as early as the following autumn. *Red Eft:* 1⅜–3⅜ in. (3.5–8.6 cm). Bright orange-red to dull red or orange, the most brilliantly colored ones usually occurring in moist, forested

The brilliantly colored Red Eft, the land form of the Red-spotted Newt. The skin gland secretions are distasteful, and many potential enemies avoid efts, which often wander freely in full sight during daylight hours.

mountains or other upland habitats. Individuals recently transformed from the larval to eft stage may be yellowish brown or dull reddish brown. Specimens transforming to adult form (or aquatic adults that have had to live out of water, as when ponds dry up) may be very dark, even almost black. Neoteny is rare.

EASTERN NEWTS
Notophthalmus viridescens

- ■ RED-SPOTTED
- ▨ CENTRAL
- ▨ BROKEN-STRIPED
- ■ PENINSULA

Ponds, small lakes, marshes, ditches, quiet portions of streams, or other permanent or semipermanent bodies of un-polluted water are the most frequent habitats during aquatic stages. This newt has been found at a depth of nearly 40 ft. (12 m) in Lake George, New York. Adults may be seen resting motionless or swimming about slowly in open water or crawling on the bottom or through vegetation. Often they remain active all winter and may be observed through the ice. The terrestrial efts, although avoiding direct sunlight, are extraordinarily bold, often walking about in the open on the forest floor in broad daylight. After summer showers in mountainous regions they sometimes may be seen by scores or even hundreds. In many areas, notably on the Coastal Plain, the land stage may be omitted, presumably in response to harsher environmental conditions. **SIMILAR SPECIES:** Most other small salamanders have slimy skins and conspicuous costal grooves. **RANGE:** Canadian Maritime Provinces to Great Lakes and south to cen. Ga. and Ala.

CENTRAL NEWT *Notophthalmus viridescens louisianensis* **PL. 39**

IDENTIFICATION: 2½–4 in. (6.4–10 cm); record 4¹⁵⁄₁₆ in. (12.5 cm). A small, more slender race of the Red-spotted Newt, but normally *without red spots*. If such spots are present they are small or only partly outlined by black. The dorsal ground color varies from olive-green to yellowish- or olive-brown and is sharply cut off from the yellow venter.

A newt of swales and swamplands, of woodland ponds and ditches, and of river bottoms in the South. The eft or land stage is uncommon in many areas in comparison with its abundance in the Red-spotted Newt. Neoteny is frequent on the southeastern Coastal Plain. **SIMILAR SPECIES:** See Red-spotted Newt. **RANGE:** Lake Superior region to e. Texas and east to s. S.C. This race intergrades with the Red-spotted subspecies over a broad area in Mich. and through the Deep South.

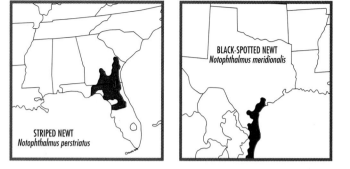

PENINSULA NEWT

PL. 39

Notophthalmus viridescens piaropicola

IDENTIFICATION: 3–4⅛ in. (7.5–10.5 cm). This is a dusky newt from Florida with a dark olive, dark brown, or almost black dorsum, and a venter finely peppered with black specks on a ground color of yellow or orange-yellow.

An inhabitant of ponds, ditches, swamps, and virtually any other standing body of water. Often abundant in canals or sloughs choked with hyacinths, or in submerged aquatic vegetation of cypress-bordered ponds. Terrestrial individuals, which are rare, may be found ashore under logs or debris. Neoteny is common. **RANGE:** Peninsular Fla.

BROKEN-STRIPED NEWT

PL. 39

Notophthalmus viridescens dorsalis

IDENTIFICATION: 2½–3¾ in. (6.4–9.5 cm). The black-bordered *red dorsolateral stripe is broken* in at least one or two places on head and trunk; it rarely extends onto tail. There may also be a row of small, red spots on lower sides of body and a light line down center of back. *Eft:* Reddish brown; red stripes not so strongly bordered by black as in the adults.

Found in pools, ponds, ditches, quiet portions of streams, etc.; the efts under logs, boards, or other shelters in damp places. **RANGE:** Coastal Plain in the Carolinas.

STRIPED NEWT *Notophthalmus perstriatus*

PL. 39

IDENTIFICATION: 2–4⅛ in. (5.1–10.5 cm). The *red dorsolateral stripe is continuous* on the trunk, but it may break into fragments on the head and tail. It varies in coloration from bright to dull red, but the red may be partly obscured by dusky pigment. The stripe is

Courtship in the Black-spotted Newt. The male's (above) cloaca is partly extruded in readiness to deposit a spermatophore that the female will later pick up with her cloaca to fertilize her eggs as they are laid.

dark-bordered, but not so boldly and evenly as in Broken-striped Newt. There may be a row of red spots along the side of body and a faint light stripe down center of back. Dorsal ground color olive-green to dark brown. Venter yellow, usually sparsely marked with black specks. *Eft:* Orange-red but also with red stripes like those of the adults.

Generally to be found in almost any body of shallow, standing water; the efts remain ashore but usually near such habitats. Neoteny occurs frequently. **RANGE:** S. Ga. and n. Fla.

BLACK-SPOTTED NEWT   PL. 39
Notophthalmus meridionalis meridionalis

IDENTIFICATION: 3–4⁵⁄₁₆ in. (7.5–11 cm). The large black spots—on both dorsum and venter—give this salamander its name. The yellowish stripes are wavy or uneven, and often there is a suggestion of a brown or russet stripe down the center of the back. No red spots. Venter bright orange to yellow-orange.

A resident of ponds, lagoons, and swampy areas—habitats that are not abundant in its rather arid homeland. **SIMILAR SPECIES:** Central Newt has much smaller dark spots and no stripes. **RANGE:** S. Texas and adj. Mexico. Mexican subspecies.

LUNGLESS SALAMANDERS: FAMILY PLETHODONTIDAE

Lungs are absent and respiration is accomplished through the skin and the lining of the mouth. There is a groove extending downward from the nostril to the edge of the mouth (the nasolabial groove—see p. 140), but this is so small that a lens may be needed to reveal it. In some forms there are cirri, downward projections from the nostrils beyond the mouth line, and the groove follows these.

To this family belong such abundant groups as the Dusky, Brook, and Woodland Salamanders and their allies (genera *Desmognathus* through *Haideotriton,* inclusive). The family ranges from southern Canada to Bolivia, and is also represented in Europe.

There are two subfamilies. One, the Desmognathinae, includes the Dusky *(Desmognathus),* Shovelnose *(Leurognathus),* and Red Hills *(Phaeognathus)* Salamanders. In all of these the lower jaw is relatively immovable, thus stiffening the forward portion of the body so the animal can more readily force its way under things. The salamander opens its mouth in large part by lifting the upper jaw and head. All other members of the group are classified in the Subfamily Plethodontinae. **NOTE:** Lungless salamanders have been intensively studied by herpetologists since the publication of the second edition of this Field Guide in 1975. Many new species have been discovered, especially "cryptic" ones whose genetic distinctness was established by biochemical, chromosomal, and morphometric techniques. A number of these new species look alike in life or so closely resemble others that exact identification is virtually impossible without recourse to complex laboratory studies. We have included all the new species, how-ever, and as many visual diagnostic characteristics about them as possible. It will be practical, in most cases, to depend heavily on geography and to call your specimen by the name of the one it most closely resembles from within the areas shown on the range map.

DUSKY SALAMANDERS: GENUS *Desmognathus*

Identifying these salamanders is like working with fall warblers— only worse! Added to changes in coloration and pattern associated with age and size are bewildering individual variations plus differences between one local population and the next. Short-cuts toward identification can be taken by ignoring color patterns at first and concentrating on three other things: (a) the shape of the tail; (b) sizes (of transformed animals); and (c) geography. Pay strict attention to ranges to eliminate species not found in your vicinity. *Then,* check patterns and do what professional herpetologists do—collect a small series to learn how much the population varies in the immediate area. Among them may be a specimen or two that will match the illustrations closely enough to furnish a clue.

There is usually *a pale diagonal line from eye to angle of jaw*

(Fig. 22, opp. Pl. 41). This may be absent, however, in old, dark adults or in those specimens where it is obscured by dark or light pigment. The hind legs are larger and stouter than the forelegs; the body is relatively short and stout. Dusky Salamanders are accomplished jumpers, often leaping several times their own length in their efforts to escape.

Members of this genus are found most commonly in or near brooks, rills, mountain cascades, springs, or seeps, but they are usually absent from larger streams where predatory fish occur. Collectively, they reach their greatest abundance in the Appalachian region. SIMILAR SPECIES: (1) In the Woodland Salamanders (*Plethodon*), the body is long and slender, there is no light line from eye to angle of jaw, and the hind legs are about the same size as the forelegs (Fig. 22, opp. Pl. 41). (2) The Shovelnose Salamander (*Leurognathus*) has smaller eyes and a more wedge-shaped head. (3) The Red Hills Salamander (*Phaeognathus*) has no light line from eye to angle of jaw, and it has 20–22 costal grooves (only 13–15 in Dusky and Shovelnose Salamanders). (4) The Mole Salamanders (*Ambystoma*) lack the naso-labial groove common to *Desmognathus* and all other lungless salamanders (Family Plethodontidae) — see illustrations on p. 140.

NORTHERN DUSKY SALAMANDER   PL. 41; FIGS. 81, 82
Desmognathus fuscus fuscus

IDENTIFICATION: 2½–4½ in. (6.4–11.5 cm); record 5⁹⁄₁₆ in. (14.1 cm). A medium-sized *Desmognathus* with a *keeled tail*; tail a little less than ⅖ total length, compressed and knife-edged above, and higher than wide at posterior edge of vent. Mouth line of adult males only slightly sinuous (Fig. 81). General coloration gray or brown, markings often not much darker than ground color. Pattern changes with age. The very young may have pairs of round yellowish dorsal spots bordered by a dark *wavy* band (Fig. 82); similar markings continue onto tail. The pattern breaks up as the animal ages, the darker remnants of it appearing as spots or

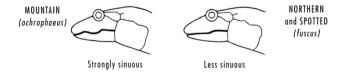

MOUNTAIN (*ochrophaeus*)		NORTHERN and SPOTTED (*fuscus*)
Strongly sinuous		Less sinuous

Fig. 81. Mouth lines of adult male Dusky Salamanders (Desmognathus).

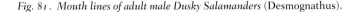

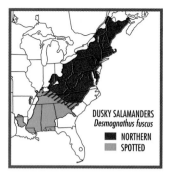

DUSKY SALAMANDERS
Desmognathus fuscus

■ NORTHERN
■ SPOTTED

streaks. Base of tail usually lighter (olive, yellowish, or bright chestnut) than rest of dorsum and bordered by dark scallops. Venter variable, but usually lightly mottled with gray or brown, sometimes heavily; dark pigment of sides of body may encroach on edges of belly.

Abundant in many localities, occurring in brooks, near springs, and in seepage areas. Perhaps most common along edges of small woodland streams where stones, chunks of wood, and miscellaneous debris provide ample shelter both for the salamanders and their food. Seldom wanders far from running or trickling water. **SIMILAR SPECIES:** See main heading for Dusky Salamanders for ways of distinguishing *Desmognathus* from species of other genera. Other members of Dusky group may be confusingly similar: (1) In the Mountain Dusky Salamander the *tail is round* (not knife-edged on top) and more tapering, and the mouth line in adult males is more sinuous (Fig. 81). (2) Seal Salamanders are larger as adults, and they usually have heavy black or dark brown dorsal spots and pale venters. (3) Blackbelly Salamander grows larger and has an ebony venter and two rows of conspicuous light dots on each side of body. (4) Shovelnose Salamander is strictly aquatic. Check ranges; Northern Dusky is the only member of its genus occurring in many parts of the North. **RANGE:** S. New Brunswick and s. Que. to se. Ind. and the Carolinas; distribution sporadic in the southern Appalachians. Altitudinally, from virtually sea level to high in the mountains.

SPOTTED DUSKY SALAMANDER   PL. 42
Desmognathus fuscus conanti

IDENTIFICATION: 2½–5 in. (6.4–12.7 cm). Anatomically similar to the Northern Dusky Salamander—size medium and with the tail moderately keeled above. More colorful and usually much more strongly patterned than northern race, and with remnants of the spotted juvenile pattern often evident in the adults. Frequently *6–8 pairs of golden or reddish golden dorsal spots* that are normally separate from one another, but which may fuse to form a light dorsal band with saw-toothed, wavy, or even straight dark margins. Coloration variable; specimens from some localities are much darker and with the dark markings much more prominent than in the one illustrated on Pl. 42. Line from eye to angle of jaw yellow or orange. Venter light but mottled with black and white (or gold) flecks. **SIMILAR SPECIES:** In specimens from southern localities check the gap between the adpressed toes (Fig. 77). In any Southern Dusky Salamander *(auriculatus)* with a head-body length of 2 in. (5.1 cm) or more there are 4½–5½ costal folds between the adpressed toes; in the Spotted Dusky *(conanti)* there are 2–4. **RANGE:** Extr. s. Ill., w. Ky. and w. Tenn. to the Gulf of Mexico and east to the Fla. panhandle and to the Fall Line in Ga.; also on Crowley's Ridge in ne. Ark. and in the Ouachita-Red River rolling lands of La. and extr. s. Ark.

SANTEETLAH DUSKY SALAMANDER   NOT ILLUS.
Desmognathus santeetlah

IDENTIFICATION: 2½–3¾ in. (6.4–9.5 cm). A medium-sized salamander, generally similar to but smaller and with a more subdued and somber pattern than the Northern Dusky Salamander. In adults, the dorsal pattern is often uniformly greenish brown, with occasional small red spots enclosed by dark borders; dorsolateral stripes sometimes present, although these are usually thin, and often interrupted. *Belly washed with yellow,* as are sides, which

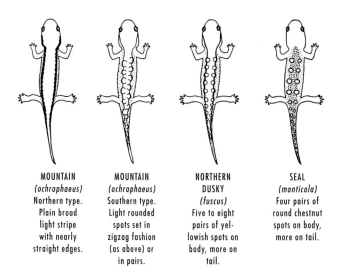

MOUNTAIN	MOUNTAIN	NORTHERN	SEAL
(ochrophaeus)	*(ochrophaeus)*	DUSKY	*(monticola)*
Northern type.	Southern type.	*(fuscus)*	Four pairs of
Plain broad	Light rounded	Five to eight	round chestnut
light stripe	spots set in	pairs of yel-	spots on body,
with nearly	zigzag fashion	lowish spots on	more on tail.
straight edges.	(as above) or	body, more on	
	in pairs.	tail.	

Fig. 82. *Dorsal patterns of young Dusky Salamanders* (Desmognathus).

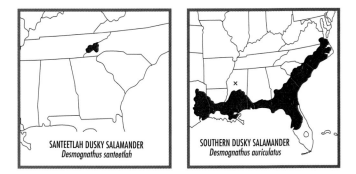

SANTEETLAH DUSKY SALAMANDER
Desmognathus santeetlah

SOUTHERN DUSKY SALAMANDER
Desmognathus auriculatus

exhibit a salt-and-pepper effect and have a ventrolateral row of light "portholes" between the front and hind legs. The tail is weakly keeled. Yellow line from eye to angle of jaw. *Young:* Normally with ten dorsal spots between the front and hind limbs.

A denizen of stream headwaters and seepage areas in the southern Appalachians, but restricted in those habitats to higher altitudes at elevations between 2220 and 5920 feet (677–1805 meters), where it feeds on small insects. **SIMILAR SPECIES:** (1) Northern Dusky Salamander usually has a bolder, brighter dorsal pattern edged with dark wavy dorsolateral stripes. (2) Mountain Dusky and Imitator Salamanders have gray bellies. Best identified by its restricted range. **RANGE:** Higher elevations of the Great Smoky and Unicoi mtns. of Tenn. and N.C., and the Great Balsam Mtns. of N.C.

SOUTHERN DUSKY SALAMANDER   FIG. 83
Desmognathus auriculatus

IDENTIFICATION: 3–5 in. (7.5–12.5 cm); record 6⅜ in. (16.3 cm). Tail stout at base; compressed posteriorly and knife-edged above. Best characterized as a dark salamander with a row of "portholes" between front and hind leg and along each side of tail. These consist of whitish or reddish spots, but they may be irregular in placement, arranged in a double row, or even obscure in the darkest specimens. General dorsal coloration dark brown or black; belly black or very dark brown but sprinkled with distinct white dots. There is much local variation in this salamander, and in some populations, notably among those living in ravine or spring habitats in peninsular Florida, certain individuals bear a reddish dorsal wash, producing the effect of a light middorsal stripe. In many areas in the South this species occurs sympatrically with the

Fig. 83. *Dorsal pattern variations and a side view of the Southern Dusky Salamander* (Desmognathus auriculatus).

Spotted Dusky Salamander; elsewhere they occupy different habitats; in a number of areas, especially on the outer Coastal Plain, the two species may hybridize.

Usually found near cypress ponds or in stagnant or nearly stagnant pools in river flood plains and coastal swamps; the environment is usually mucky and acidic from decomposition of organic material. **RANGE:** Chiefly on the outer Coastal Plain; se. Va. to cen. Fla. and west to e. Texas; an isolated record in n. cen. Miss.

OUACHITA DUSKY SALAMANDER   PL. 42; FIG. 84
Desmognathus brimleyorum

IDENTIFICATION: 3⅛–5½ in. (8–14 cm); record 7 in. (17.8 cm). A large, robust *Desmognathus* with the tail distinctly keeled and compressed near the tip. Young specimens look superficially like the Northern Dusky Salamander. Usually a row of faint pale spots along each side of body (Fig. 84) and another parallel row extending from foreleg to hind leg. General dorsal coloration brown or gray; belly pale and virtually unmarked, varying from pinkish white to yellowish but faintly stippled with very pale brownish pigment. *Large adult male:* Dorsum uniformly dark brown.

Juveniles and larvae hide under stones or in wet gravel at or below water level at streamside, and also in piles of small rocks. Adults are most often found in water beneath large boulders, in large rock piles, or along wet, rocky banks. This salamander is

Fig. 84. Dorsal view of a Ouachita Dusky Salamander (Desmognathus brimleyorum).

much more aquatic than terrestrial. Many specimens are infested with mites of the Family Trombiculidae, which may cause loss or fusing of toes or both. **RANGE:** Ouachita Mts. of Ark. and Okla.

BLACK MOUNTAIN SALAMANDER   NOT ILLUS.
Desmognathus welteri

IDENTIFICATION: 3–5 in. (7.5–12.5 cm); record 6¹¹⁄₁₆ in. (17 cm). A rather chubby salamander. Tail stout at base, but compressed and knife-edged above on posterior half. Resembles Seal Salamander, but belly is usually finely to heavily stippled with gray or brownish pigment on a whitish ground color. Dorsum pale to medium brown and patterned with small dark brown spots or streaks that, in some specimens, tend to surround paler areas. *No sharp lateral separation* of dorsal and ventral ground colors; the dark dorsal pigmentation fading gradually into the paler venter. A line of faint pale dots between legs on each side of body. *Tips of toes usually dark,* except in very young specimens.

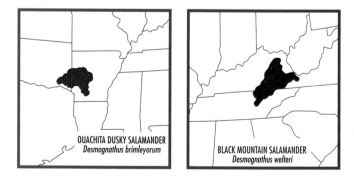

OUACHITA DUSKY SALAMANDER
Desmognathus brimleyorum

BLACK MOUNTAIN SALAMANDER
Desmognathus welteri

An aquatic salamander of mountain brooks, spring runs, and roadside puddles in wooded mountainous terrain. **SIMILAR SPECIES:** Seal Salamander usually has: (a) a distinct lateral separation between the dorsal and ventral coloration; and (b) venter lightly pigmented. **RANGE:** Much of e. Ky., adj. sw. Va., south into Tenn. Named for Big Black Mt. in Harlan Co., Ky.

SEAL SALAMANDER *Desmognathus monticola*   PL. 41; FIG. 82

IDENTIFICATION: 3¼–5 in. (8.3–12.5 cm); record 5⅞ in. (14.9 cm). A stout-bodied salamander. Tail compressed and knife-edged above near tip; approximately ¼ total length. Most specimens are *boldly patterned above,* but plain and quite *pale below;* usually a distinct lateral separation between dorsal and ventral pigmentation. Dorsum with strong black or dark brown markings on a ground of buff, gray, or light brown, the markings extremely variable — wormlike, netlike, or surrounding roughly circular areas of ground color. Some specimens patterned simply with scattered dark or light spots or streaks. Markings usually more strongly evident toward western part of range, and least so toward south, where adults may lose virtually all traces of pattern. Venter white in juveniles but becoming lightly and usually *uniformly* pigmented with gray or brown in old adults. Sometimes a *single* row of light dots on sides between legs. Old adults may be purplish brown, with dark markings few and obscure. *Young:* About four pairs of rounded chestnut or orange-brown spots down back (Fig. 82).

Wet spots in cool, well-shaded ravines and banks of mountain brooks are among the varied habitats utilized by this large, active species. Hides by day and may be found by overturning stones, bark, etc. Sometimes appears in the open in shady spots during daylight. At night, poised at the entrance to a burrow or perched atop a wet rock and illuminated by the observer's flashlight, its appearance suggests a miniature seal. **SIMILAR SPECIES:** (1) Northern Dusky Salamander has a light but mottled undersurface; also it is less pop-eyed than Seal Salamander. (2) Blackbelly Salamander has a black venter and *two* rows of small white dots along each side of body. (3) See also Black Mountain Salamander. **RANGE:** Mountainous and hilly regions from sw. Penn. to Ga. and Ala.;

SEAL SALAMANDER
Desmognathus monticola

a disjunct colony in the hill country of sw. Ala. and an isolated record in the extr. western tip of Fla. panhandle.

BLACKBELLY SALAMANDER PL. 41
Desmognathus quadramaculatus

IDENTIFICATION: 4–6⅞ in. (10–17.5 cm); record 8¼ in. (21 cm). A large, robust salamander of cascading southern mountain streams. Tail very stout at base, less than ½ total length, and knife-edged above. *Belly black* in adults; dark, but flecked with yellow in young. (Put your specimen in a bottle to see its underside.) Usually a conspicuous *double row of light dots* along each side of body. *Young:* Snout and feet often light in color, especially in southern part of range.

This salamander, the heaviest and bulkiest of the lungless group within our territory, is daring enough to pause in the open occasionally on a wet rock, even in sunshine! Abundant in boulder-strewn brooks; also found near waterfalls or other places where cold water drips or flows. Usually seeks shelter under rocks during daylight, but when these are lifted it dashes off instantly to plunge beneath the nearest stone or to swim vigorously away with *or against* the current. Trying to catch these agile amphibians is like going fishing with your bare hands. When caught, they may bite, a painless but surprising experience. **SIMILAR SPECIES:** (1) Old adults of other members of Dusky Salamander group may be almost uniformly dark (bellies included), but they do not attain so large a size and their tails are proportionately longer. (2) Shovel-nose Salamander has a long, sloping snout and small eyes. **RANGE:** S.-cen. W. Va. through mountains to Ga.; isolated records (not mapped) in cen. Ga. may have originated from the release of specimens distributed commercially as fish bait.

MOUNTAIN DUSKY SALAMANDER PL. 42; FIGS. 81, 82, 85,
Desmognathus ochrophaeus

IDENTIFICATION: 2¾–4 in. (7–10 cm); record 4⅜ in. (11.1 cm). A medium-sized *Desmognathus* with a *round tail;* tail about ½ total length and as wide as or even wider than its height at posterior edge of vent. Mouth line of adult males very sinuous (Fig. 81). Extraordinarily variable in coloration and pattern (several variations are shown on Pl. 42 and in Fig. 85). *A light line from eye to angle of jaw.*

In northern part of range specimens, including juveniles (Fig. 82), typically have a *straight-edged* light stripe down back and tail. The stripe may be yellow, orange, olive, gray, tan, brown, or reddish; it is flanked by very dark, sometimes black, pigment that usually fades into the mottled lower sides. A row of dark, often

BLACKBELLY SALAMANDER
Desmognathus quadramaculatus

MOUNTAIN DUSKY SALAMANDER
Desmognathus ochrophaeus

chevronlike, spots down center of back. Old individuals may be nearly plain dark brown and virtually without pattern.

In southern part of range *ochrophaeus* is highly variable. Some individuals resemble northern specimens, but the great majority have a *wavy* or *irregular* dorsal stripe, and they may be marked with large light areas that are remnants of the light spots set in paired or zigzag fashion down the backs of southern juveniles (Fig. 82). Coloration as diverse as in northern populations, but it may include individuals with red cheek and leg patches in the Nantahala Mts. and adj. Highlands Plateau.

More terrestrial than most other Dusky Salamanders, some-

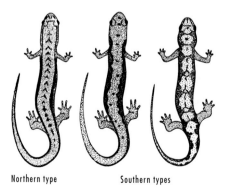

Northern type   Southern types

Fig. 85. *Variations in dorsal patterns of the Mountain Dusky Salamander* (Desmognathus ochrophaeus).

times wandering far out into the woods during wet weather. Normally found under stones, logs, leaves, etc., near springs, seepage areas, or streams, not actually in the water but where the ground is saturated. Often congregates in winter in large numbers in shaly seepage areas or near springs. Frequently found abroad at night, when it may climb trees and shrubs while foraging. **SIMILAR SPECIES:** (1) Two-lined Salamanders have bright yellow bellies and laterally compressed tails. (2) Woodland Salamanders have smaller hind legs and lack light line from eye to angle of jaw (Fig. 22, opp. Pl. 41). (3) Dusky (*fuscus*) and Seal (*monticola*) Salamanders have tails that are knife-edged above (no dorsal keel in *ochrophaeus*); mouth line of adult male Duskies is only slightly sinuous (Fig. 81). **RANGE:** Chiefly upland areas from Adirondack Mts., N.Y., to n. Ga. and ne. Ala.; isolated colonies in w.-cen. Ga. and ne. Ky. Occurs from a few hundred feet above sea level to the coniferous forests of the highest peaks of the southern Appalachians.

IMITATOR SALAMANDER *Desmognathus imitator* PL. 40

IDENTIFICATION: 2½–4 in. (6.4–10 cm); record 4⅜ in. (11 cm). A medium-sized salamander that "imitates" a variant of the Jordan's Salamander (*Plethodon jordani*) in having yellow, orange, or red cheek patches. Mature adult pattern usually consists of the distinctive cheek patches coupled with strongly undulating, often interrupted, dark dorsolateral stripes that lack a bold broad stripe between them; old adults are often black and patternless, and lack the colorful cheek patches. Tail rounded; belly gray; suggestion of dark line (instead of light) from eye to angle of jaw.

A resident of many habitats, including small streams, wet rock

The Imitator Salamander, a member of the dusky group (genus Desmognathus*), strongly resembles the redcheek variation of the extremely multipatterned Jordan's Salamander, a woodland species (genus* Plethodon*).*

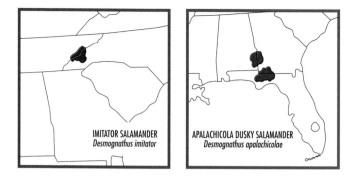

IMITATOR SALAMANDER
Desmognathus imitator

APALACHICOLA DUSKY SALAMANDER
Desmognathus apalachicolae

faces, and saturated gravel and leaf litter in seepages and springs; frequently found beneath rocks and rotten logs on forest floor. **SIMILAR SPECIES:** (1) Mountain Dusky Salamander usually has distinct, wavy dorsolateral stripes in the southern Appalachians, and lacks red, orange, or yellow cheek patches where its range coincides with the Imitator Salamander. (2) Two-lined Salamanders have bright yellow bellies. (3) Woodland Salamanders (*Plethodon*) have smaller hind legs. (4) Dusky and Seal Salamanders have tails that are knife-edged above (rounded in *imitator*). **RANGE:** Generally restricted to and found throughout the Great Smoky Mts. National Park of Tenn. and N.C. at elevations from 2950 ft. (900 m) to Clingman's Dome at 6640 ft (2024 m); also found outside the Park at Waterrock Knob, N.C.

APALACHICOLA DUSKY SALAMANDER   NOT ILLUS.
Desmognathus apalachicolae
IDENTIFICATION: 3¼–4 in. (8.3–10 cm). A medium-sized, robust salamander, similar to, but slightly larger than, southern populations of the Mountain Dusky Salamander; 10–14 pairs of light, round, coalescing dorsal blotches set off by black fringes, although old adults may be uniformly brown; belly immaculately white or smudged with a thin veneer of dark pigment; tail longer than body, round in cross-section, and tapering to a thin filament that is laterally compressed at the tip. *Young:* More boldly patterned than adults, with dorsal blotches washed with red, orange, or yellow.

During the day, this salamander may be found beneath debris along small streams in deep, moist ravines with steep walls and permanent seepages; at night it is active on the wet substrate and leaf litter in the same ravines. **SIMILAR SPECIES:** Southern Dusky Salamander has a black or very dark brown belly, sprinkled with white flecking. **RANGE:** Occurs in two disjunct areas, a northern population along the Ala.-Ga. border in the lower Chattahoochee and upper Choctawhatchee river drainages, and a southern one at the se. Ga.-Fla. border in the upper Apalachicola and Ochlockonee river drainages.

PIGMY SALAMANDER *Desmognathus wrighti*   **PL. 42, FIG. 86**

IDENTIFICATION: 1 ½–2 in. (3.8–5.1 cm). A tiny, bronzy mite of a salamander; one of our smallest species and a chiefly terrestrial one. Tail rounded; less than ¼ total length. A broad, light middorsal stripe, varying from reddish brown to tan in coloration; usually with a dark *herringbone* pattern down its center (Fig. 86). Silvery pigment along sides of body. Venter flesh-colored and unmarked except for gold pigment under the heart. *Top of head rugose*, snout especially. *Male:* Mental gland U-shaped (Fig. 87).

A resident chiefly of high spruce-fir forests of the Southern Appalachians. Best sought by day under moss and bark on rotting logs or beneath rotting wood or litter on the forest floor near seepage areas. At night, especially in foggy or rainy weather, it may become "arboreal," ascending trunks of trees as much as 6 or 7 ft. (2 m) above ground. There is no aquatic larval stage; transformation of larva takes place within the egg. **SIMILAR SPECIES:** In Seepage Salamanders *top of head is smooth* and mental gland (males only) is kidney-shaped (Fig. 87). **RANGE:** Elevations of 2750 to over 6500 ft. (800–2000+ m) from sw. Va. to near the Ga. line

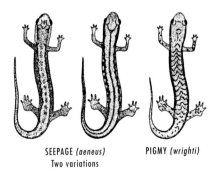

SEEPAGE *(aeneus)*   PIGMY *(wrighti)*
Two variations

Fig. 86. Dorsal patterns in Seepage and Pigmy Salamanders (Desmognathus).

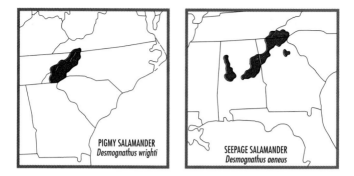

PIGMY SALAMANDER
Desmognathus wrighti

SEEPAGE SALAMANDER
Desmognathus aeneus

in sw. N.C.; known from Mt. Rogers, Whitetop, Grandfather, and Roan mts., the Black Mts., Cowee Mts., Great Smoky, Plott Balsam, and Great Balsam mts., Wayah Bald, and Standing Indian mt., all of which are within area shown on map.

EEPAGE SALAMANDER *Desmognathus aeneus* **FIGS. 86, 87**

IDENTIFICATION: 1¾–2¼ in. (4.4–5.7 cm). Another tiny salamander and an especially slender one. Tail rounded; about ½ total length. A wide, wavy to almost straight-sided pale dorsal stripe varying in coloration from yellow or tan to reddish brown. Stripe may be flecked or smudged with darker pigment that may suggest a herringbone pattern; sometimes a dark middorsal line that is continuous with a Y-shaped mark on head (Fig. 86). Sides dark where they meet the dorsal stripe, paler toward belly. Undersurfaces plain to mottled with brown and white. *Top of head smooth. Male:* Mental gland kidney-shaped (Fig. 87).

Most often encountered beneath damp leaf mold on the forest floor, near seepages, springs, or small streams. There is no aquat-

PIGMY
(*wrighti*)
Mental gland
large, U-shaped

SEEPAGE
(*aeneus*)
Mental gland
small, kidney-shaped

Fig. 87. *Chins of male Pigmy and Seepage Salamanders* (Desmognathus).

ic larval stage; terrestrial larvae transform in only a few days. **SIMILAR SPECIES:** See Pigmy Salamander. **RANGE:** Elevations of 700–4500 ft. (210–1400 m) from extr. sw. N.C. to e.-cen. Ala.; as low as 100 ft. (30 m) in an isolated colony in w.-cen. Ala.; a second isolated colony in ne. Ga.

SHOVELNOSE AND RED HILLS SALAMANDERS: GENERA
Leurognathus AND *Phaeognathus*

Salamanders of these two genera, together with the many kinds of Dusky Salamanders *(Desmognathus)*, constitute the Subfamily Desmognathinae. The genus *Leurognathus* was described in 1899, but the first specimen of *Phaeognathus* was not discovered until 1960 despite the fact that it attains the greatest length of any lungless salamander of our area. Both genera are confined to the southeastern United States.

SHOVELNOSE SALAMANDER
PL. 41; FIG. 88

Leurognathus marmoratus

IDENTIFICATION: 3½–5 in. (9–12.5 cm); record 5¾ in. (14.6 cm). Pattern and coloration dull and variable but blending beautifully with pebbles, leaves, and debris on bottoms of rocky streams. Dorsum black, brown, or gray and usually with two rows of irregular, often weakly indicated, pale-colored spots or blotches that vary in size, intensity, and coloration (gray, olive, yellowish, or whitish) from one local population to another. A pale, often poorly defined, line from eye to angle of jaw. Tail less than ¼ total length, compressed, and knife-edged above. Head flattened and wedge-shaped, the slope starting downward from a point *well behind* the rather small eyes.

An aquatic amphibian of mountain brooks that vary in size and amount of flow from trout streams to rills, but all of which offer an abundance of stones beneath which to hide. Small brooks with

DUSKY
Internal openings of nostrils clearly visible

SHOVELNOSE
Narrow slitlike openings
(often not visible)

Fig. 88. Roofs of mouths of Dusky (Desmognathus) *and Shovelnose* (Leurognathus) *Salamanders.*

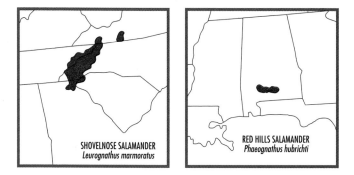

SHOVELNOSE SALAMANDER
Leurognathus marmoratus

RED HILLS SALAMANDER
Phaeognathus hubrichti

sandy or gravelly bottoms are a favorite habitat. In clear, quiet waters, if care is taken not to disturb it unduly (by lifting rocks slowly, for example), the Shovelnose tends to remain still or walk slowly and deliberately to another shelter. The Blackbelly Salamander, often present in same streams, normally *dashes* away. Food consists principally of the larval or nymphal stages of aquatic insects. **SIMILAR SPECIES:** Blackbelly Salamander and other members of the Dusky group tend to be more pop-eyed, and usually have a more conspicuous light line from eye to jaw. Check roof of mouth if in doubt. Internal openings of nostrils are rounded and clearly evident in Dusky Salamanders *(Desmognathus)*; they are slitlike and scarcely noticeable in Shovelnose Salamanders (Fig. 88). If you have to open a mouth, lift or prod the upper jaw *gently*; you are liable to damage the lower jaw or its musculature if you try to force it downward. **RANGE:** Elevations of 1000–5500 ft. (300–1700 m) from Whitetop Mt. in sw. Va. through w. N.C. and e. Tenn. to extr. ne. Ga. and adj. S.C.; also Floyd Co., Va.

RED HILLS SALAMANDER *Phaeognathus hubrichti*   PL. 41

IDENTIFICATION: 4–8 in. (10–20.3 cm); record 10¹⁄₁₆ in. (25.6 cm). This amphibian, the longest member of the Subfamily Desmognathinae, totally lacks distinctive markings. It is deep, dark brown all over except that the snout, jaws, and soles of the limbs are slightly paler. Body elongate, legs short; 20–22 costal grooves, and about 14 costal folds between the toes of the adpressed limbs; no light line from eye to angle of jaw.

A fossorial salamander that apparently is confined to cool, moist, forested ravines. It is rarely seen except at night at the mouths of its burrows, which are excavated chiefly in sandy loam over and around claystone rock. **SIMILAR SPECIES:** (1) Shovelnose and Dusky Salamanders are marked with a pale line from eye to angle of jaw, and they have only 13–15 costal grooves. (2) Slimy Salamanders (complex) are usually well sprinkled with light spots, and they normally have only 16 costal grooves. **RANGE:** The Red Hills formations of Ala. between the Alabama and Conecuh rivers.

WOODLAND SALAMANDERS: GENUS *Plethodon*

This group is widespread and abundant through the forested portions of eastern North America. In high, humid mountains in the South, specimens may be encountered at almost all seasons (except midwinter), but elsewhere they are easiest to find after spring or autumn rains. During hot, dry weather they either estivate or seek moisture in rock crevices or below ground. When it is damp or rainy, Woodland Salamanders prowl at night, and they often can be observed with the aid of a flashlight or headlamp. By day they hide in burrows, under stones or damp boards, or beneath a variety of other shelters where there is little danger of desiccation.

The Woodland Salamanders feed on a large variety of invertebrates, including earthworms and many kinds of insects, among them beetles with hard shells, ants with sharp stings, and bugs with bad smells. Most captives readily accept small live insects or tiny crickets, of which the latter are procurable at almost any tropical-fish supply store.

Eggs are laid in small clusters in damp logs, moss, etc., and complete development takes place within the egg; there is no aquatic larval stage as is the case among most other salamanders. Adult males of some species have a prominent large circular gland (the mental gland) under their chins.

The genus is strictly North American, with a large number of forms in our area and others in forested portions of far western states from northwestern California to British Columbia; also in mountains of northern Idaho and adj. Mont., and in n.-cen. N.M. **SIMILAR SPECIES:** (1) Mole Salamanders (*Ambystoma*) all lack the groove from the nostril to lip (use a lens). (2) Dusky Salamanders (*Desmognathus*), especially the kinds that wander far out into the forest, are often confused with Woodland Salamanders. Dusky Salamanders usually have a light line from eye to angle of jaw, and their hind legs are larger and stouter than their forelegs. Woodland Salamanders lack the light line, and *all four* limbs are about the same size (Fig. 22, opp. Pl. 41).

REDBACK SALAMANDER *Plethodon cinereus*   **PL. 40; FIG. 89**
  IDENTIFICATION: 2¼–4 in. (5.7–10 cm); record 5 in. (12.7 cm). *Two distinct variants:* (a) *redback*—a straight-edged reddish stripe

The two most prevalent color phases of the Redback Salamander, the redback (above) and the leadback. Either type may predominate in local populations. An abundant species in areas that remain wild within its range.

down back from base of head to tail, bordered by dark pigment that extends downward onto sides of body; (b) *leadback*—uniformly dark gray to black. (Some individuals are intermediate between the two.) In the redback, the stripe may be orange, yellow, or even light gray instead of red. Usually the stripe *narrows* slightly on base of tail. In some areas, redback and leadback variations are equally abundant; in others, one or the other may predominate; leadbacks may be rare or absent at high elevations.

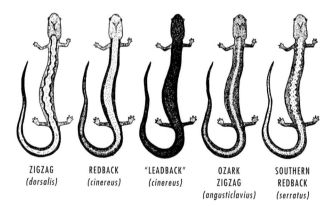

ZIGZAG	REDBACK	"LEADBACK"	OZARK ZIGZAG	SOUTHERN REDBACK
(dorsalis)	*(cinereus)*	*(cinereus)*	*(angusticlavius)*	*(serratus)*

Fig. 89. Dorsal patterns of small Woodland Salamanders (Plethodon).

Both variations have one outstanding character in common— bellies mottled with approximately equal parts of black and white (or yellow), producing a *salt-and-pepper* effect (Fig. 90). An all-red variation is found occasionally. Costal grooves usually 19, ranging from 17 to 22.

A terrestrial salamander, confined more or less to wooded or forested areas. Hides beneath all manner of objects, including chunks of tar paper or other trash, as well as logs, bark, stones, etc. On rainy nights it sallies forth in search of insects, sometimes even climbing small plants in its quest. The most ubiquitous salamander throughout the greater part of its range. **SIMILAR SPECIES:** (1) Ravine Salamander and Valley and Ridge Salamander (both colored the same as the leadback variation) are more slender, and their bellies look almost *uniformly dark* (Fig. 90). (2) See also Eastern Zigzag Salamander. **RANGE:** S. Que. and the Canadian Maritime Provinces to ne. Minn.; south to n. and e. N.C.; an isolated colony in s. N.C.

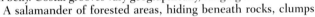

SOUTHERN REDBACK SALAMANDER   PL. 40; FIG. 89
Plethodon serratus

IDENTIFICATION: 3³⁄₁₆–4⅛ in. (8.1–10.5 cm). A *light middorsal stripe,* sometimes straight-edged or sometimes with saw-toothed edges whose "teeth" correspond with costal grooves (stripe widest above each groove and narrowest between them). Stripe may be orange or reddish and extend onto tail, rest of body dark gray to almost black—coloration, in general, like Redback Salamander's; occasional individuals may be dark and unpatterned (leadback variation). Red pigment is mixed with dark pigment on sides but not on belly. Costal grooves vary geographically, ranging from 18 to 21.

A salamander of forested areas, hiding beneath rocks, clumps

The Southern Redback Salamander has a fragmented range in several southern states. The specific name serratus *derives from the rather saw-toothed manner in which the red of the back meets the dark area on the sides.*

REDBACK SALAMANDER
Plethodon cinereus

SOUTHERN REDBACK SALAMANDER
Plethodon serratus

CHEAT MOUNTAIN SALAMANDER
Plethodon nettingi

PEAKS OF OTTER SALAMANDER
Plethodon hubrichti

SHENANDOAH SALAMANDER
Plethodon shenandoah

of moss, or under rotten logs. During the dry season it may be found near seeps and springs. **SIMILAR SPECIES:** Ozark Zigzag Salamander has red pigment as well as black and white on belly. **RANGE:** Four disjunct populations: mountains of w.-cen. Ark. and adj. Okla.; cen. and se. Mo.; cen. La.; and ne. Ga. and adj. Ala., Tenn., and N.C.

PEAKS OF OTTER SALAMANDER   NOT ILLUS.
Plethodon hubrichti

IDENTIFICATION: 3³⁄₁₆–4¹³⁄₁₆ in. (8.1–12.2 cm); record 5⅛ in. (13.1 cm). Dark brown dorsum covered with abundant brassy flecking and, less commonly, larger white spots. Sides with white spots; belly plain dark brown; chin with small white spots. Costal grooves usually 19, ranging from 18 to 20. Lacks a striped variation, but hatchlings have scattered small red spots on the dorsum.

A denizen of cool, moist forests at high elevations. **SIMILAR SPECIES:** (1) Redback Salamander has a *salt-and-pepper* belly. (2) Valley and Ridge Salamander has 20–21 costal grooves. **RANGE:** Peaks of Otter region of the Blue Ridge Mts., northeast of Roanoke, Va.

RAVINE SALAMANDER *Plethodon richmondi*   **PL. 41; FIG. 90**

IDENTIFICATION: 3–4½ in. (7.5–11.5 cm); record 5⅝ in. (14.3 cm). Like a lead-colored Redback Salamander but with a virtually plain dark belly and lightly mottled chin (Fig. 90). A *longer, more slender,* short-legged species—almost a worm with legs. Dorsal coloration seal-brown to nearly black but sprinkled with minute silvery-white and bronzy or brassy specks; very small, irregular white blotches on lower sides. Costal grooves 19–22.

Wooded *slopes* of valleys and ravines are preferred. Frequently found at high elevations in southern part of range. **SIMILAR SPECIES:**

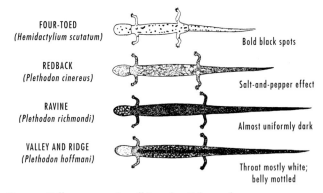

FOUR-TOED
(*Hemidactylium scutatum*)
Bold black spots

REDBACK
(*Plethodon cinereus*)
Salt-and-pepper effect

RAVINE
(*Plethodon richmondi*)
Almost uniformly dark

VALLEY AND RIDGE
(*Plethodon hoffmani*)
Throat mostly white;
belly mottled

Fig. 90. *Belly patterns of small Lungless Salamanders.*

(1) Redback Salamander has a *salt-and-pepper* belly (Fig. 90). (2) Eastern Zigzag Salamander, even in its dark variation, usually has some reddish or orange pigment showing on the undersurfaces. (3) Wehrle's and Jordan's Salamanders are much stouter-bodied and have proportionately larger legs. **RANGE:** W. Pa. to se. Ind.; south to nw. N.C. and adj. Tenn.

SHENANDOAH SALAMANDER   NOT ILLUS.
Plethodon shenandoah
IDENTIFICATION: 3–4⅜ in. (7.5–11 cm). Another salamander that exhibits two distinct variations, one with a narrow red or yellow middorsal stripe, the other unstriped and uniformly dark brown but usually with small, red, dorsal spots; sides with many white spots. Belly dark brown or black with a variable number of small white or yellow spots; chin usually more mottled than belly. Costal grooves usually 18, ranging from 17 to 19.

A resident of northwest-facing talus slopes at elevations above 2950 ft. (900 m). **SIMILAR SPECIES:** Redback Salamander has a *salt-and-pepper* belly. **RANGE:** Restricted in the Blue Ridge Mts. of Virginia to three peaks: The Pinnacles, Stony Man, and Hawksbill.

VALLEY AND RIDGE SALAMANDER   FIG. 90
Plethodon hoffmani
IDENTIFICATION: 3⁹⁄₁₆–4⅜ in. (9.1–11.2 cm); record 5⅜ in. (13.7 cm). Similar to the Ravine Salamander but with throat mostly white; belly dark but with a moderate amount of white mottling. Costal grooves usually 20–21.

This small salamander lives beneath flat stones and other objects on forested hillside slopes, where it occurs up to 4600 ft. (1402 m) in elevation. **RANGE:** Chiefly the Valley and Ridge physiographic province from the Susquehanna R. Valley in w.-cen. Pa., south to the New R. in Va. and W. Va.

RAVINE SALAMANDER
Plethodon richmondi

VALLEY & RIDGE SALAMANDER
Plethodon hoffmani

CHEAT MOUNTAIN SALAMANDER   PL. 40
Plethodon nettingi

IDENTIFICATION: 3–4 in. (7.5–10 cm); record 4⅜ in. (11.1 cm). Usually the dorsal surface is strongly sprinkled with *small brassy flecks* that extend onto the tail and are most numerous on or near the head, but some specimens lack these or are sprinkled also with silvery flecks or spots; flanks with larger, white spots. Dorsal ground color black or very dark brown; belly and throat plain dark slaty gray to black. Brassy flecks disappear in preserved specimens. Costal grooves usually 18, ranging from 17 to 19. Hatchlings have red dorsal pigment; no striped variation.

An inhabitant of spruce and mixed deciduous forests above 3150 ft. (960 m) elevation in the Cheat Mountains of West Virginia. Look for it beneath logs and rocks during the day; at night it actively searches for insects on the forest floor. **SIMILAR SPECIES:** (1) Redback Salamanders collected high in the Cheat Mountains have all been of the redback variation (not leadback), so reddish stripe in combination with *salt-and-pepper* belly will distinguish these. (2) Valley and Ridge Salamander has 20–21 costal grooves; throat mostly white. **RANGE:** E.-cen. W. Va.

WELLER'S SALAMANDER   *Plethodon welleri*   PL. 40

IDENTIFICATION: 2½–3⅛ in. (6.4–7.9 cm). In size and shape like a small leadback variation of the Redback Salamander. Upper surfaces with a profusion of dull *golden or silvery blotches* on a ground color of black. Belly varies from plain black to black with white spots. Costal grooves usually 16, ranging from 15 to 17.

Named for Worth Hamilton Weller, a promising young Cincinnati naturalist who lost his life while collecting salamanders on Grandfather Mt., N.C. in 1931. **RANGE:** Tri-state area—extr. ne. Tenn., Whitetop and Mt. Rogers, Va., and nw. N.C. From 2500 ft. (760 m) upward, but chiefly in spruce forests above 5000 ft. (1500 m).

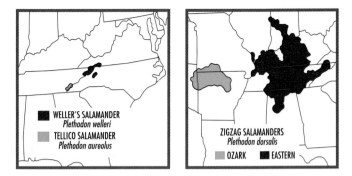

WELLER'S SALAMANDER
Plethodon welleri

TELLICO SALAMANDER
Plethodon aureolus

ZIGZAG SALAMANDERS
Plethodon dorsalis

OZARK   EASTERN

EASTERN ZIGZAG SALAMANDER
PL. 40; FIG. 89

Plethodon dorsalis dorsalis

IDENTIFICATION: 2½–3½ in. (6.4–9 cm); record 4⅜ in. (11.1 cm). "Zigzag" well describes the light dorsal stripe in many specimens; in others the angles are not so sharp, and "lobed" or "wavy" would be more accurate. The stripe varies from red to yellowish in coloration, and it may be straight for at least part of its length; it is *broadly* continued on the tail. *Belly includes a mottling of orange or reddish pigment.* This salamander also occurs in a dark variation. Costal grooves usually 18, ranging from 17 to 19.

Sometimes a woodland species, but also often found near springs or near mouths of caves. Ascends to elevations of 2500 ft. (760 m) in western approaches to Blue Ridge Mts. **SIMILAR SPECIES:** Redback Salamander has a straight dorsal stripe that *narrows* slightly on base of tail. Dark variations of Eastern Zigzag and Redback will offer difficulties. Unpatterned Zigzags have the dark pigment diffused, as though the dark borders of the light stripe had broken down and spread about. The dorsal coloration may be uniformly dark brown, reddish brown, or gray; dark Redbacks (leadbacks) are much darker, usually dark gray to black, and they have *salt-and-pepper* bellies without a mottling of red or orange pigment. **RANGE:** Extr. e.-cen. and s. Ill., and cen. Ind. south to n. Ala.; east to ne. Tenn. and adj. Va.

OZARK ZIGZAG SALAMANDER
FIG. 89

Plethodon dorsalis angusticlavius

IDENTIFICATION: 2⅜–3⅞ in. (6–9.8 cm). General coloration similar to that of the Eastern Zigzag Salamander. The narrow orange or reddish middorsal stripe may have indistinct edges, and it varies in width from one specimen to the next. Some individuals are uni-

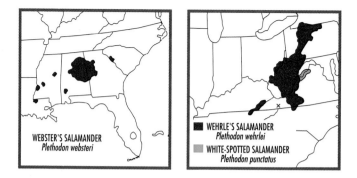

WEBSTER'S SALAMANDER
Plethodon websteri

■ WEHRLE'S SALAMANDER
Plethodon wehrlei
■ WHITE-SPOTTED SALAMANDER
Plethodon punctatus

formly dark. Costal grooves usually 18, ranging from 17 to 19.

This salamander prefers to live beneath rocks, rotten logs, and leaf litter, sometimes near the seeps of small streams. It is found also on steep hillsides and in or near caves. **SIMILAR SPECIES:** See Southern Redback Salamander. **RANGE:** The Central Highlands of sw. Mo., n. Ark., and ne. Okla.

WEBSTER'S SALAMANDER *Plethodon websteri*   **NOT ILLUS.**

IDENTIFICATION: 2¾–3³⁄₁₆ in. (7–8.2 cm). Identical in appearance to the Eastern Zigzag Salamander, even to the extent of having both striped and unstriped variations. Identify this salamander on the basis of geography—within the bulk of its range there is little else with which it can be confused. Costal grooves usually 18, ranging from 17 to 19.

A salamander of forested hillsides where it can be found beneath rocks and logs, as well as in leaf litter. Named for T. Preston Webster, a molecular biologist who first discovered the distinctness of this species. **SIMILAR SPECIES:** The range of the Eastern Zigzag Salamander overlaps that of Webster's Salamander in Jefferson County, Ala. At that locality, Webster's is normally striped and the Eastern Zigzag is normally unstriped. **RANGE:** E.-cen. Ala. and adj. Ga., with scattered, isolated colonies in w. S.C., sw. Ala., s. La., and at several localities in Miss.

WEHRLE'S SALAMANDER *Plethodon wehrlei*   **PL. 41**

IDENTIFICATION: 4–5¼ in. (10–13.3 cm); record 6⅝ (16.8 cm). Dark gray or dark brown with a row of irregular white, bluish-white, or yellowish spots and dashes along each side of body. Brassy flecking and a few very small white dots usually present. The middorsal area may lack conspicuous markings or it may be patterned with small *red, orange-red,* or *yellow* spots, often arranged in pairs. Some individuals from Tenn., Ky., and W. Va. exhibit two rows of large dorsal yellow spots. Specimens from the northern and western parts of the range usually are plain-backed, but those from farther south, the young especially, tend to be spotted with red. *Throat white or blotched with white;* white spots frequently extending backward onto breast. Belly and underside of tail uniformly gray. Webbing on hind foot often extending almost to tips of first two toes. Costal grooves usually 17, ranging from 16 to 18. *Dixie Caverns variation:* Ground color purplish brown and entire dorsum profusely frosted with small light flecks and bronzy mottling. Known from Dixie Caverns and Blankenship Cave near Roanoke, Va.

At home in upland forests; found under stones, in rotting logs, in deep rock crevices, or in the twilight zones of caves. Named for R. W. Wehrle of Indiana, Pa., a naturalist who collected many of the specimens from which the species was first described. SIMILAR SPECIES: (1) Easily confused with the Northern Slimy Salamander (*glutinosus*), which (at least where its range overlaps Wehrle's Salamander) normally has white spots scattered all over the dorsum, not just along sides; also, *glutinosus* usually has only 16 costal grooves, and its dark throat may be gray, but *not white.* (2) White-spotted Slimy Salamander (*cylindraceus*) has large, white dorsal spots and usually 16 costal grooves. (3) Jordan's Salamander has less extensive webbing on hind foot, no white or brassy spotting on sides or back (where it occurs with Wehrle's Salamander), and also usually 16 costal grooves. (4) Jefferson and other Mole Salamanders (*Ambystoma*) lack the groove from nostril to lip that is common to all Woodland Salamanders. RANGE: Extr. sw. N.Y. to most of W. Va., and south to w.-cen. Va. and adj. N.C. Isolated colony in se. Ky. and adj. ne. Tenn; isolated record in sw. Va.

WHITE-SPOTTED SALAMANDER   FIG. 91
Plethodon punctatus

IDENTIFICATION: 4–5 in. (10–12.5 cm); record 6¾ in. (17.1 cm). A close relative of Wehrle's Salamander but lacking the brassy flecking and red spots of that species, and with much larger numerous white or yellowish white dorsal spots. *Throat light, pinkish in life.* Costal grooves 17 or 18.

A resident of forested areas with extensive rock outcrops, where it feeds on small insects. SIMILAR SPECIES: White-spotted Slimy Salamander (*cylindraceus*) has large dorsal white spots, abundant lateral white or yellow spotting, usually 16 costal grooves, and much less webbing between the toes on the hind foot. RANGE: High elevations on Shenandoah and Great North mts. on the Va.-W. Va. border.

IDENTIFICATION: 4¾–6¾ in. (12.1–17.2 cm); record 8⅛ in. (20.6 cm). A complex of medium to large, chiefly black salamanders consisting of 13 genetically distinct species the status of which was determined by laboratory techniques. Many are virtually indistinguishable in the field, and for practical purposes can be considered simply as Slimy Salamanders. For those who are interested, we have listed the species by both scientific and common names below. For their geographical distributions check the map on p. 472. Most of these salamanders are well sprinkled with silvery white spots or brassy flecks or both, and the belly, although variable, is normally lighter than the dorsum. Costal grooves usually 16, rarely 15 or 17. Under the Similar Species section in the accounts of other Woodland Salamanders, we have included a few known specific external characters of those of the 13 species that may occur with them and which might be useful in identification.

These are the "sticky" salamanders whose skin-gland secretions cling to your hands like glue and almost have to wear off. (Some of the other large Woodland Salamanders are almost as bad.) Moist woodland ravines or hillsides are favorite habitats.

The various species, with their common names, are listed here in the alphabetical order of their scientific names.

WESTERN SLIMY SALAMANDER *Plethodon albagula.*
CHATTAHOOCHEE SLIMY SALAMANDER *P. chattahoochee.*
ATLANTIC COAST SLIMY SALAMANDER *P. chlorobryonis.*
WHITE-SPOTTED SLIMY SALAMANDER *P. cylindraceus.*
NORTHERN SLIMY SALAMANDER *P. glutinosus* (Pl. 41).
SOUTHEASTERN SLIMY SALAMANDER *P. grobmani.*
KIAMICHI SLIMY SALAMANDER *P. kiamichi.*
LOUISIANA SLIMY SALAMANDER *P. kisatchie.*
MISSISSIPPI SLIMY SALAMANDER *P. mississippi.*
OCMULGEE SLIMY SALAMANDER *P. ocmulgee.*
SAVANNAH SLIMY SALAMANDER *P. savannah.*
SEQUOYAH SLIMY SALAMANDER *P. sequoyah.*
SOUTH CAROLINA SLIMY SALAMANDER *P. variolatus.*

SIMILAR SPECIES: Combination of black dorsum with irregularly scattered white spots and/or brassy flecks will usually distinguish the members of this species complex from other dark salamanders that resemble it. Notable exceptions are the Cumberland Plateau and Southern Appalachian Salamanders. Like all large Woodland Salamanders, all members of this complex have a groove running downward from nostril to lip; the Jefferson and other Mole Salamanders (*Ambystoma*) lack this. **RANGE:** Overall for the complex,

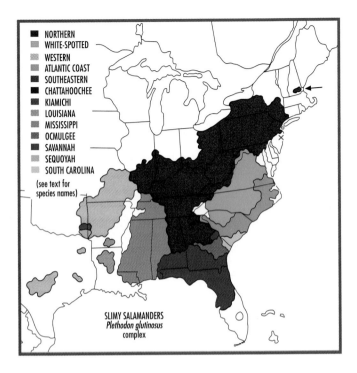

SLIMY SALAMANDERS
Plethodon glutinosus
complex

from extr. sw. Conn. and cen. N.Y. to cen. Fla. and west to Mo. and e. Okla.; isolated populations in s. N.H., s. Ark., n.-cen. La., and e. and s.-cen. Texas; isolated records from Ocean Co., N.J. Depend on geography to identify individual species of this complex.

TELLICO SALAMANDER *Plethodon aureolus*   **NOT ILLUS.**

IDENTIFICATION: 4–5¹⁵⁄₁₆ in. (10–15.1 cm). A black salamander with *abundant dorsal brassy spotting and flecking* and lateral white or yellow spots; chin usually lighter than the uniform slate gray belly. Costal grooves usually 16. At higher elevations in the ne. part of its range the dorsal spotting may be reduced or absent.

A salamander of lower mountain slopes and adjacent lowlands.
SIMILAR SPECIES: (1) Southern Appalachian Salamander (*teyahalee*) is larger and has *white* dorsal spots. (2) Jordan's Salamander (within range of Tellico Salamander) lacks lateral white spots and dorsal brassy spots. (3) The Northern Slimy Salamander (*glutinosus*) has

not been found within the range of the Tellico Salamander except at one site in extr. n. Polk Co., Tenn. **RANGE:** Between the Little Tennessee and Hiwassee rivers on the w. slopes of the Unicoi Mts. and nearby lowlands of ne. Polk and e. Monroe cos., Tenn., and nw. Graham and nw. Cherokee cos., N.C.

WELLER'S SALAMANDER
Plethodon welleri
TELLICO SALAMANDER
Plethodon aureolus

CUMBERLAND PLATEAU SALAMANDER
Plethodon kentucki

NOT ILLUS.

IDENTIFICATION: 3⅞–6⅝ in. (9.8–16.8 cm). A medium-sized, black salamander with small, sparse, and widely scattered dorsal white spots that exhibit very little brassy flecking; larger lateral white spots; *chin lighter than uniform slate gray belly,* and in adult breeding males the mental gland is quite large. Costal grooves usually 16.

Ridges of the Cumberland Plateau from 825–4070 ft. (250–1240 m). **SIMILAR SPECIES:** (1) Northern Slimy Salamander (*glutinosus*) populations that occur with the Cumberland Plateau Salamander are larger, have a *dark* chin, larger and more frequent dorsal spotting, and adult males have a smaller mental gland. (2) Where it occurs with the Cumberland Plateau Salamander, Wehrle's Salamander is patterned with large yellow spots, is dark gray or brown, and generally has light flecking and spotting confined to the sides of the body. **RANGE:** E. Ky., ne. Tenn., sw. Va., and W. Va. west of the New and Kanawha rivers.

SOUTHERN APPALACHIAN SALAMANDER
Plethodon teyahalee

NOT ILLUS.

IDENTIFICATION: 4¾–6¾ in. (12.1–17.2 cm); record 8³⁄₁₆ in. (20.7 cm). A large, black salamander with very small dorsal white spots and larger lateral white spots; *small red spots often present on legs;* belly uniform slate gray; chin usually lighter than belly. Costal grooves usually 16.

A salamander of the higher slopes of the Blue Ridge physiographic province. Named for Teyahalee Bald in the Snowbird Mts. of North Carolina. **SIMILAR SPECIES:** (1) Tellico Salamander (*aureolus*) is smaller, has *brassy* (not white) dorsal spots, and lacks small red spots on its legs. (2) Jordan's Salamander lacks dorsal white spots. (3) Only one member of the Slimy Salamander complex, the Northern Slimy Salamander *(glutinosus)*, has been found within the range of the Southern Appalachian Salamander, and only at one site in extr. n. Polk Co., Tenn. **RANGE:** West of the French Broad R. in sw. N.C., adj. Tenn., nw. S.C., and n. Rabun Co., Ga.

YONAHLOSSEE SALAMANDER

Plethodon yonahlossee   **PL. 40**

IDENTIFICATION: 4½–7 in. (11.5–18 cm); record 8¹¹⁄₁₆ in. (22.1 cm). A large and extremely handsome salamander, with a broad *red or chestnut stripe* down the back, extending from neck well onto base of tail. A stripe of light gray or whitish pigment *directly below* the red stripe. Head plain black or marked with light specks. Tail black. Underparts dark gray, belly often mottled with light spots. *Young:* Red dorsal spots in 4 to 6 pairs on a dark ground color; belly light. Costal grooves usually 16. *Bat Cave variation:* Black sometimes invades the red stripe to an appreciable extent, and the stripe may exhibit reduced chestnut pigment that may be confined to scattered flecks and blotches or both. Pale spotting concentrated on sides in large individuals. *Young:* Dorsum with 3–7 small chestnut spots; belly gray. Restricted to the Bat Cave area of Rutherford Co., N.C., at elevations of 1400–2600 ft. (430–790 m).

One of our most agile salamanders, darting away into forest litter, under any nearby log or rock, into the cool and moist crevices of rock outcrops, or down the long burrows it utilizes to move about beneath the surface. Named for the old Yonahlossee Road on Grandfather Mountain, N.C. **SIMILAR SPECIES:** Other red- or chestnut-backed salamanders (Redback Salamander and some individuals of Mountain Dusky Salamander) occurring within the range of the Yonahlossee Salamander have the red flanked on each side by *dark* instead of light pigment. **RANGE:** Southern Blue Ridge Mts., east and north of French Broad R. in sw. Va., w. N.C., and extr. e. Tenn.; elevations of 1400–5700 ft. (430–1700 m).

PIGEON MOUNTAIN SALAMANDER   **PL. 41**

Plethodon petraeus

IDENTIFICATION: 4½–6½ in. (11.5–16.5 cm); record 7³⁄₁₆ in. (18.3 cm). A large salamander with an adult dorsal pattern of reddish brown, brown, or olive-brown that extends onto the head and well beyond the base of the tail. Smaller individuals may have a dorsal pattern of 3–12 opposing or alternating reddish brown spots. Upper surfaces of head, legs, and body sparsely scattered with small light spots and brassy flecking. Sides black with white or yellowish spots and some brassy flecking. Undersurface of belly and tail

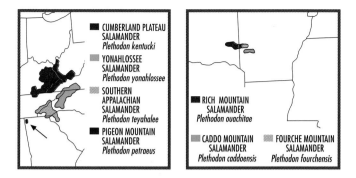

black; chin with reddish brown pigment or yellowish spotting; throat and chest with yellowish mottling. Toes thick, short, blunt, and flattened. Costal grooves usually 16, ranging from 15 to 17.

A salamander of limestone crevices on forested mountain slopes. **SIMILAR SPECIES:** (1) The Northern Slimy Salamander (*glutinosus*) has a black dorsum with variable white spots and flecks. (2) All Mole Salamanders (*Ambystoma*) lack a groove running downward from nostril to lip. **RANGE:** Restricted to Pigeon Mt., Walker Co., in nw. Ga. at elevations of 720–1640 ft. (220–500 m).

RICH MOUNTAIN SALAMANDER PL. 40
Plethodon ouachitae

IDENTIFICATION: 4–5 in. (10–12.5 cm); record 6¼ in. (15.9 cm). Extremely variable in coloration. A typical adult from Rich Mountain has varying amounts of chestnut pigment overlying the black dorsal ground color, as well as numerous small white specks and metallic-looking (brassy) flecks. Some of these pattern elements may be missing, however, and the chestnut pigment is reduced or lacking in populations from some of the adjacent mountains. Throat *whitish*; chest *dark*. Costal grooves usually 16.

A resident of forested ridges and slopes, where it lives beneath logs and woodland litter. **SIMILAR SPECIES:** (1) Where their ranges overlap, the Western Slimy Salamander (*albagula*) has a black dorsum liberally sprinkled with variable-sized white spots, and a dark chin. (2) Fourche Mountain Salamander has two irregular rows of large whitish dorsal spots on body (Fig. 91). **RANGE:** Rich Mt. and adjacent ridges of the Ouachita Range in w. Ark. and e. Okla. Hybridizes with Fourche Mountain Salamander at west end of Fourche Mountain.

WHITE-SPOTTED *(punctatus)*

FOURCHE MOUNTAIN *(fourchensis)*

Fig. 91. *Dorsal patterns of two Woodland Salamanders* (Plethodon) *with restricted ranges.*

FOURCHE MOUNTAIN SALAMANDER   PL. 40; FIG. 91
Plethodon fourchensis

IDENTIFICATION: 4¼–6 in. (11.5–15.2 cm); record 7 in. (17.8 cm). Formerly called the "Buck Knob" variation of the Rich Mountain Salamander. Look for the *two irregular rows of large whitish spots* down the back of the black body; a variable number of small white spots and brassy flecks scattered dorsally; yellowish white spots present on cheeks, legs, sides, and even a few on the dark belly. Chin *light.* Costal grooves usually 16.

A salamander of forested ridges and slopes, where it lives beneath rotten logs and woodland litter. **SIMILAR SPECIES:** (1) Western Slimy Salamander *(albagula)* is black with smaller, scattered white spots (never arranged in rows). (2) Rich Mountain Salamander usually has chestnut pigment dorsally. **RANGE:** Higher parts of Fourche and Irons Fork mts. in Polk and Scott cos., Ark.; from 1700 to 2400 ft. (520–730 m) in elevation.

CADDO MOUNTAIN SALAMANDER   PL. 40
Plethodon caddoensis

IDENTIFICATION: 3½–4 in. (9–10 cm); record 4⅜ in. (11.1 cm). A slender, black-and-white salamander somewhat similar to the Rich Mountain species but lacking the chestnut pigment of the latter. The black back and sides of the body are profusely marked with whitish spots that stand out less sharply than the Western Slimy

Salamander's spotting and the Rich Mountain Salamander's speckling. Brassy flecks scattered over back. *Throat light; chest light* (speckled black and white); belly dark. Costal grooves usually 16.

Prefers north-facing slopes, which are cooler and wetter during summer, and will often retreat to mines or burrow beneath talus slopes to escape the heat. **SIMILAR SPECIES:** Western Slimy Salamander *(albagula)* is more robust and has a *dark* throat and chest. **RANGE:** Restricted to the Caddo Mts. of Polk and Montgomery cos. in w. Ark.

JORDAN'S SALAMANDER *Plethodon jordani* PL. 40

IDENTIFICATION: 3½–5 in. (9–12.5 cm); record 7¼ in. (18.4 cm). (Northern individuals tend to be smaller than southern ones.) This salamander exhibits a bewildering array of colors and patterns and combinations of both. Specimens that match the red cheek, red leg, Metcalf's, and Clemson variations illustrated on Pl. 40 are easily identified as this salamander, but other variations may be mistaken for a number of Woodland Salamanders (see Similar Species, below). Many of these confusing specimens are black, either unmarked or with small white spots on cheeks and sides of body. General trends are as follows: red cheeks and red legs in the Great Smoky and Nantahala mts., respectively; lateral white spots in extr. sw. part of range; bellies dark in roughly se. half of range (bellies paler toward north and west); indications of brassy flecks strongest in nw. S.C. Costal grooves usually 16.

The humid, forested southern Appalachians are the home of this extraordinarily variable salamander. Habitats, which include forest litter, rotting logs, and mossy stone piles, range from near the summits of the highest mountains to as low as 700 ft. (210 m) in extreme nw. S.C. Northern populations are generally restricted to high altitudes. Named for David Starr Jordan, eminent ichthyologist and president of Stanford University. **SIMILAR SPECIES:** The following descriptions apply only to those areas where both Jordan's Salamander and the compared species are found together. (1) Northern *(glutinosus)* and White-spotted *(cylindraceus)* Slimy Salamanders usually are abundantly sprinkled with white spots *all over sides and dorsum.* (2) Tellico Salamander *(aureolus)* has

JORDAN'S SALAMANDER
Plethodon jordani

FOUR-TOED SALAMANDER
Hemidactylium scutatum

MANY-LINED SALAMANDER
Stereocheilus marginatus

brassy dorsal spots and *abundant white spotting on sides and legs.*
(3) Southern Appalachian Salamander (*teyahalee*) has *tiny* dorsal
white spots and *larger* lateral white spots, with small *red* spots
often present on legs; hybridizes with Jordan's Salamander in the
sw. part of its range. (4) Yonahlossee Salamander has a broad *red
or chestnut stripe* down the back. (5) Wehrle's Salamander has
small *red, orange-red, or yellow spots on back,* often arranged in
pairs. (6) Imitator Salamander (*Desmognathus*) has red, orange,
or yellow cheek patches, a dorsal pattern, a line from eye to angle
of jaw, and distinctly larger hind legs. (7) Mountain Dusky Salamander (also *Desmognathus*) may have reddish legs but usually
has a dorsal pattern, a line from eye to angle of jaw, and distinctly
larger hind legs. Knowledge of habitat helps. The Imitator and
Mountain Dusky Salamanders are usually found near springs,
edges of streams, in seepage areas, etc., whereas Jordan's Salamander is a resident of moist, humid forests, not necessarily near
water. **RANGE:** Highlands of sw. Va. and w. N.C. to extr. e. Tenn.,
extr. ne. Ga. and extr. nw. S.C.

FOUR-TOED, MANY-LINED, AND GREEN SALAMANDERS:
GENERA *Hemidactylium, Stereochilus,* AND *Aneides*

Salamanders of these three genera are not closely related and are
grouped here only for convenience. The first two are monotypic,
with *Hemidactylium* widely distributed in the East and *Stereochilus* restricted to a portion of the southeastern Coastal Plain.
The genus *Aneides* is represented in our area only by the Green
Salamander, but there are several species in the West that range,
collectively, from Vancouver Island, British Columbia, to northern Baja California; another occurs only in mountains of southern New Mexico. The generic standard common name for *Anei-

des is Climbing Salamanders, in reference to the arboreal and rock-climbing tendencies of several of the species.

GREEN SALAMANDER
Aneides aeneus

FOUR-TOED SALAMANDER   PL. 43; FIG. 90
Hemidactylium scutatum

IDENTIFICATION: 2–3½ in. (5.1–9 cm); record 4 in. (10.2 cm). Look for three things: (a) enamel-white belly boldly marked with *black spots* (unique among our salamanders—see Fig. 90); (b) four toes on *hind foot* as well as forefoot (most salamanders have *five* toes on each *hind foot*); (c) *marked constriction* at base of tail (if an enemy seized the tail, this is where it would break away from body).

Usually associated with sphagnum. Sphagnaceous areas adjacent to woods are common habitats, and so are boggy woodland ponds. The Four-toed Salamander is terrestrial when adult (like Woodland Salamanders), but its larvae are aquatic (like those of Dusky Salamanders). **SIMILAR SPECIES:** Dwarf Salamander also has four toes on all feet, but it lacks characteristics (a) and (c) above. **RANGE:** Highly disjunct; from Nova Scotia west to Wisc. and se. Okla., and south to e. La. and the panhandle of Fla.; isolated colonies in many states.

MANY-LINED SALAMANDER *Stereochilus marginatus* PL. 43
IDENTIFICATION: 2½–3¾ in. (6.4–9.5 cm); record 4½ in. (11.4 cm). Nondescript except for a series of narrow, indistinct, dark longitudinal lines on sides of body, and even these may be reduced to a few dark spots. In some specimens there are indistinct dark (or light) markings on the back. Most Many-lined Salamanders tend to be brown in general coloration, others may be dull yellow. Belly yellow with scattered dark specks. The small head and short tail are characteristic.

A denizen of pools and sluggish streams in swampy woodlands, best found by raking out dead leaves and other bottom debris. Essentially aquatic but sometimes uncovered by overturning logs near small streams or around woodland ponds. **RANGE:** Coastal Plain from se. Va. to Ga. and extr. n. Fla.

GREEN SALAMANDER *Aneides aeneus*   PL. 43
IDENTIFICATION: 3¼–5 in. (8.3–12.5 cm); record 5½ in. (14 cm). Our *only really green salamander.* Green, lichenlike markings on a dark ground color. Note square-tipped toes.

Few people have ever seen a Green Salamander in the field. Even carefully examining its normal rocky cliff habitat at night with headlamp or flashlight may reveal only an eye or body lying hidden in a deep crevice.

A cliff dweller. Narrow crevices on rock faces are a favorite habitat, provided rocks are damp but not wet, situated where the atmosphere is humid, and well protected from sun and direct rain. The flattened head and body are admirably adapted for getting about in tight places. Also sometimes found under stones, logs, or loose bark. Occasionally arboreal. **RANGE:** Appalachian region; sw. Pa., extr. w. Md., and s. Ohio to n. Ala. and extr. ne. Miss.; a disjunct area in sw. N.C. and adj. states; isolated colonies in cen. Tenn. and ne. W. Va.

SPRING, RED, AND MUD SALAMANDERS: GENERA *Gyrinophilus* AND *Pseudotriton*

These are chiefly red or salmon-colored salamanders, most of them patterned with black spots. All are at home in the water as well as in damp or soggy terrain. The Spring Salamanders (*Gyrinophilus*) like clear, cool water, and their habitats vary from forested seepage areas to rushing mountain brooks. Formerly they were called "purple salamanders," a name more appropriate for a badly preserved specimen than one of the orange- or salmon-colored living animals. Both the Red and Mud Salamanders (*Pseudotriton*) are red or reddish, and details must be checked carefully to tell them apart. Age also is important; young adults are brilliantly colored, whereas older specimens darken, and their patterns become obscure. The Reds prefer clear water, but the Muds usually are found in muddy places. Both genera occur only in eastern North America.

An adult Spring Salamander from Windham County, Vermont. This amphibian often frequents its namesake, the springs that seep into small streams.

SPRING SALAMANDER
(INCLUDING NORTHERN AND KENTUCKY)   PL. 42

Gyrinophilus porphyriticus (subspecies *porphyriticus* and *duryi*)

IDENTIFICATION: 4¾–7½ in. (12.1–19 cm); record 9⅛ in. (23.2 cm). The light line from eye to nostril is bordered below by gray pigment, but these markings usually are not overly conspicuous. The general dorsal coloration varies from salmon or light brownish pink to reddish. The ground color has a cloudy appearance, and the darker markings are vague — not clear-cut.

These are agile denizens of cool springs and mountain streams but are also likely to be found in any wet depression beneath logs, stones, or leaves in the surrounding forests. **SIMILAR SPECIES (AND SUBSPECIES):** (1) In other Spring Salamanders (subspecies *danielsi* and *dunni*) there is a conspicuous light *and dark* line from eye to nostril. (2) In Red and Mud Salamanders, such markings are completely absent, and the heads are rounded, thus lacking the distinct angle (canthus rostralis) along which the lines run from eye to nostril in Spring Salamanders. **RANGE:** Sw. Me. and s. Que. to n. Ala. and extr. ne. Miss.; an isolated colony in Hamilton Co., extr. sw. Ohio. **SUBSPECIES:** NORTHERN SPRING SALAMANDER, *Gyrinophilus p. porphyriticus* (Pl. 42). Salmon or light yellowish brown with reddish tinges, and with a mottled or clouded appearance; sides tend to be darker and to form a netlike pattern enclosing light spots; venter flesh-colored; small, scattered black spots on belly and throat and especially on margin of lower jaw in old specimens. Recently transformed young are salmon-red and with the darker mottlings not well developed. Specimens from southern localities may show evidences of intergradation with the other

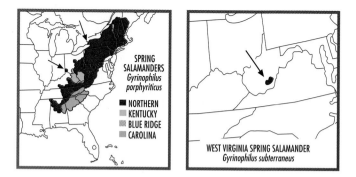

SPRING
SALAMANDERS
*Gyrinophilus
porphyriticus*

■ NORTHERN
■ KENTUCKY
▨ BLUE RIDGE
■ CAROLINA

WEST VIRGINIA SPRING SALAMANDER
Gyrinophilus subterraneus

races. Occupies most of the range of the species. KENTUCKY
SPRING SALAMANDER, *Gyrinophilus p. duryi*. Smaller; max.
length about 6¼ in. (16.5 cm). Dorsal coloration salmon-pink to
light brownish pink; small black spots usually arranged in a row
along each side of body, but sometimes scattered along sides or
(in some individuals) over all the dorsal surfaces. (Even when the
black spots are widely distributed, they are most strongly concentrated along the sides.) Venter flesh-colored and unmarked except
on lower lip and occasionally chin and throat. S. Ohio, e. Ky., w.
W. Va., and adj. Va.

SPRING SALAMANDER
(INCLUDING BLUE RIDGE AND CAROLINA)   PL. 42
Gyrinophilus porphyriticus (subspecies *danielsi* and *dunni*)
IDENTIFICATION: 5–7½ in. (12.5–19 cm); record 8⅟₁₆ in. (20.5 cm).
The white line from eye to nostril, *bordered below* by a conspicuous black or dark brown line, is the distinctive mark of these
races. There also may be a dark line above the white line, and in
many specimens this, too, is conspicuous. Dorsal coloration clear
reddish, salmon, or orange-yellow marked with black or brown
spots or flecks.
   Turning over a stone at a mountain spring and revealing one of
these brightly colored amphibians is an exciting experience. Also
found in seepage and wet forest areas, especially near edges of
mountain brooks. **SIMILAR SPECIES (AND SUBSPECIES):** In the subspecies
porphyriticus and *duryi*, lines from eyes to nostril are much less
prominent; a *light* line is present, but the dark line below it may
be obscure or virtually lacking. Such markings are completely
absent among Red and Mud Salamanders. **RANGE:** Southern
Appalachians and adj. Piedmont from N.C. to Ala. **SUBSPECIES:**

BLUE RIDGE SPRING SALAMANDER, *Gyrinophilus p. danielsi* (Pl. 42). Reddish or rich salmon color with scattered black spots on the back; specimens from high elevations have heavy dark speckling on chin. The Blue Ridge Province of w. N.C. and adj. Tenn. CAROLINA SPRING SALAMANDER, *Gyrinophilus p. dunni.* Orange-yellow to light reddish, profusely flecked with dark pigment; venter salmon pink, usually immaculate except for margins of jaws, which are mottled with black and white. Southern portion of Blue Ridge Province and the Piedmont from sw. N.C. to e.-cen. Ala.

WEST VIRGINIA SPRING SALAMANDER NOT ILLUS.
Gyrinophilus subterraneus

IDENTIFICATION: 4–7 in. (10–17.7 cm). A cave-dwelling salamander, closely related to but paler than the Spring Salamander (*porphyriticus*), and from which it differs in the following ways: body generally darker dorsally and lighter laterally; light line from eye to nostril indistinct. The eyes are very small, and adults retain the brownish-pink (almost flesh-colored) ground color and the light gray reticulated pattern seen in larval specimens. The larvae grow to a much larger head-body length (9.6 cm or longer) than do those of the Spring Salamander (8 cm or less).

Found in and along the cave stream, where it feeds on small invertebrates. **SIMILAR SPECIES:** Spring Salamanders (*porphyriticus*) found within the range of the West Virginia Spring Salamander have a distinct light line from eye to nostril, larger eyes, and a darker dorsal body color. **RANGE:** Found only in General Davis Cave, Greenbrier Co., se. W. Va.

TENNESSEE CAVE SALAMANDER PL. 39
Gyrinophilus palleucus

IDENTIFICATION: 3–7¼ in. (7.5–18.4 cm). Essentially a neotenic, cave-dwelling member of the Spring Salamander genus, although a few transformed adults have been found. Like most salamanders that spend their entire existence beneath the water, this one has external gills, lacks eyelids, and has small eyes (their diameter ¼ or less than the distance from anterior corner of eye to tip of snout). In larvae of Northern Spring Salamander, the diameter of eye is ⅓ or more of distance from eye to snout. **RANGE:** Caves of cen. and se. Tenn. and n. Ala. **SUBSPECIES:** PALE SALAMANDER, *Gyrinophilus p. palleucus* (Pl. 39). Coloration normally pale flesh-pink, except for the bright red external gills. Body pigmentation lacks dark spots. Caves along southeastern edge of Cumberland Plateau in n. Ala. and adj. Tenn. BIG MOUTH CAVE SALAMANDER, *Gyrinophilus p. necturoides.* Dark and heavily

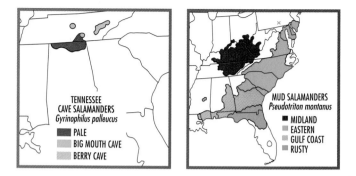

spotted dorsally; ground color russet-brown to deep brownish purple; spots roughly circular and blackish, extending from level of jaw to basal third of tail; venter pearl gray. Two isolated colonies, one in Rutherford Co. and another at Big Mouth Cave, Grundy Co., Tenn. BERRY CAVE SALAMANDER, *Gyrinophilus p. gulolineatus*. Grows larger, to 8¹⁵⁄₁₆ in. (22.7 cm). Similar but with a wider head, more spatulate snout, and a dark stripe or blotch on forward half of throat. From Roane Co. to McMinn Co. in e. Tenn.

EASTERN MUD SALAMANDER
PL. 42

Pseudotriton montanus montanus

IDENTIFICATION: 3–6½ in. (7.5–16.5 cm); record 8⅛ in. (20.7 cm). A red-colored salamander with a *brown* eye. Black spots round and well separated. Dorsum with a definite ground color that doesn't blend directly into the reddish of the lower sides and belly. Young specimens brightly colored, with sharply distinct spots and virtually unmarked venters. Older ones vary from light reddish brown to chocolate; their dorsal spots are larger and more numerous but tend to be inconspicuous against the darker backgrounds; undersurfaces often spotted or flecked with brown or black.

Occurs in the muddy environs of springs, muddy seeps along small streams, etc. It burrows into the muck in its efforts to escape and may take refuge in crayfish or other holes. **SIMILAR SPECIES:** (1) Mud and Red Salamanders are easily confused—even experienced herpetologists have trouble with them. Check color of iris; it normally is yellowish instead of brown in the Reds. Look at shape of head: in the Muds, snout is blunter and shorter in front of eyes. Habitat will help: Mud Salamanders usually live up to their names. (2) Spring Salamanders have a light and dark line from eye to nostril. **RANGE:** S. N.J. to the Carolinas and ne. Ga.; an old isolated record in s.-cen. Pa. from which the species was first described, but now probably extinct there. **SUBSPECIES:** MIDLAND MUD SALAMANDER, *Pseudotriton m. diastictus.* One of the most brilliantly colored salamanders in e. N. America. The ground color, coral pink or red to brown, is clearer and much brighter than in Eastern Mud Salamander; black spots fewer in number; undersurfaces unmarked except occasionally for a dark line on rim of lower jaw. S. Ohio and W. Va. to s. Tenn. and much of Ky. GULF COAST MUD SALAMANDER, *Pseudotriton m. flavissimus.* Averages smaller and more slender; max. length about 4¹¹⁄₁₆ in. (11.9 cm). A large number of small, well-separated round spots on a ground of clear, light brownish salmon; underside of head and trunk clear salmon pink. Extr. s. S.C. to extr. e. La.; an isolated colony in e.-cen. Miss.

RUSTY MUD SALAMANDER   PL. 42
Pseudotriton montanus floridanus

IDENTIFICATION: 2⅞–4¼ in. (7.3–10.7 cm); record 4⅝ in. (11.7 cm). The rustiest and one of the smallest of the Mud Salamanders. The virtually plain dorsum may be slightly mottled with indistinct darker areas and a few small, irregular, light pinkish spots. *No dark dots on back,* but there may be a few scattered ones atop tail. Streaking on sides highly irregular—a mixture of pinkish buff and rust color and sometimes with streaks or specks of black. Undersurfaces buffy and sparsely marked with small, irregular blackish spots.

Habitats include mucky seepage areas and small, shallow streams flowing through hardwood hammocks or mixed forests. **RANGE:** N. Fla. and s. Ga.

NORTHERN RED SALAMANDER   PL. 42
Pseudotriton ruber ruber

IDENTIFICATION: 4–6 in. (10–15.2 cm); record 7⅛ in. (18.1 cm). A red or reddish orange salamander with the uppersurfaces profusely dotted with irregular, rounded black spots. Iris of eye normally *yellow.* Margin of chin often flecked with black. *Old adults:* Dull purplish brown, the ground color darker and the spots larger and running together; black or brown spots on undersurfaces.

Look for the Northern Red Salamander under moss, stones, or other objects in or near springs or rills, even mere trickles, provided water is clear, cool, and not stagnant. Occurs in streams that flow through open fields and meadows as well as those through woods; streams with bottoms of sand, gravel, or rock usually are preferred. **SIMILAR SPECIES:** (1) Mud Salamanders have: (a) notice-

A young adult Northern Red Salamander from Walker County, Georgia. This is one of the most brightly colored salamanders in North America.

ably fewer and well-separated *circular* (or nearly circular) black spots; (b) their dorsal ground color is more sharply set off from the ventral coloration; and (c) their irises are *brown*. (2) Spring Salamanders have a light and dark line from eye to nostril. **RANGE:** S. N.Y. and Ohio to ne. Ala. (except in s. Blue Ridge, where related subspecies occur). **SUBSPECIES:** BLUE RIDGE RED SALAMANDER, *Pseudotriton r. nitidus.* Small; max. length about 4⅝ in. (12 cm). Coloration and pattern similar to Northern Red Salamander's but without black pigment on tip half of tail and little or none on chin; old adults retain their bright appearance. Elevations to more than 5000 ft. (1500 m), north and east of French Broad R., in s. Blue Ridge Mts.; Floyd Co., Va.

BLACKCHIN RED SALAMANDER   PL. 42
Pseudotriton ruber schencki
IDENTIFICATION: 2¾–4¾ in. (7–12.1 cm); record 5¾ in. (14.6 cm). A Red Salamander with a strong concentration of black pigment under the chin. (Black area much heavier and broader than narrow black flecking seen in some individuals of its related subspecies.) Tail spotted almost to tip.

Under logs, stones, moss, etc., in habitats ranging from open pastures to forests. **RANGE:** Elevations to more than 5000 ft. (1500 m), west and south of French Broad R., s. Blue Ridge Mts.

SOUTHERN RED SALAMANDER   PL. 42
Pseudotriton ruber vioscai
IDENTIFICATION: 3⅞–5¾ in. (9.8–14.6 cm); record 6⅜ in. (16.2 cm). A purplish, reddish, or salmon-colored salamander with a profusion

of white flecks, these largely concentrated on snout and sides of head. The purplish effect is produced by numerous fairly large, blue-black blotches. Undersurfaces light but with a profusion of small dark spots.

RED SALAMANDERS
Pseudotriton ruber
■ NORTHERN
■ BLACKCHIN
■ BLUE RIDGE
■ SOUTHERN

In and near springs, small streams, and in rotting, well-saturated logs. **RANGE:** S.-cen. S.C. to se. La. and sw. Ky.; intergrades with the northern subspecies through much of Ala.

BROOK SALAMANDERS: GENUS *Eurycea*

These are salamanders of small brooks, rills, springs, seepage areas, river-bottom swamps, and other small bodies of water where fish are absent or at a minimum. An alternate name might be "yellow salamanders," for yellowish pigment is found in most of them, at least on their undersurfaces. In many there are well-pronounced cirri (downward projections) from the nostrils in males during the breeding season. All species have aquatic larvae.

The Brook Salamanders may be readily separated into three groups:

1. Typical "brook" salamanders, such as the Northern Two-lined and Many-ribbed. These frequently wander well out into moist woodlands during wet weather and on humid nights.
2. The "long-tailed salamanders," which in the adult stage have tails considerably more than ½ their total lengths (juveniles have much shorter tails). These salamanders are essentially terrestrial but they swim readily; they include the Three-lined, Longtail, Dark-sided, and Cave Salamanders, the last three of which frequently are found in caves.
3. The "neotenic euryceas," which retain the larval form (with external gills) throughout life. These are completely aquatic and are difficult to distinguish from the larvae of salamanders that normally transform into a gill-less adult form. They occur in localities along or near the Balcones Escarpment in central Texas, where, fortunately, there are no other larval aquatic salamanders that would be confused with them.

The genus *Eurycea* occurs only in eastern and south central North America.

NORTHERN ■
TWO-LINED SALAMANDER
Eurycea bislineata
SOUTHERN ■
TWO-LINED SALAMANDER
Eurycea cirrigera
BLUE RIDGE ▨
TWO-LINED SALAMANDER
Eurycea wilderae

NORTHERN TWO-LINED SALAMANDER

Eurycea bislineata   **PL. 43**

IDENTIFICATION: 2½–3¾ in. (6.4–9.5 cm); record 4¾ in. (12.1 cm). The common yellow salamander of the Northeast. The two dark lines border a broad light middorsal stripe but often tend to break up into dots or dashes on tail. The dorsal coloration, always essentially yellow, may be brownish, greenish, bronzy, or bordering on orange. The broad light stripe down the back is usually peppered with small black spots that may join to form a narrow median dark line. Mottling on side of body varies in intensity from one specimen to the next; it may be so dark that it blends with dorsolateral line or it may be much reduced or virtually absent. Costal grooves 15–16; tail 55–60% of total length in adults.

Essentially a brookside salamander, hiding under all manner of objects at water's edge and running or swimming away vigorously when alarmed. Saturated areas near springs or seeps are also favorite habitats. In warm, wet weather, it may wander far out into nearby woodlands. **SIMILAR SPECIES:** (1) Examples of Blue Ridge Two-lined Salamanders that occur below 4000 feet (1200 m) and Southern Two-lined Salamanders have 14 costal grooves. Rely heavily on geography in distinguishing among the three species of Two-lined Salamanders. (2) Dusky Salamanders, some populations of which include yellowish specimens, have enlarged hind legs and a light stripe from eye to angle of jaw (Fig. 22, opp. Pl. 41). (3) Adult Longtail and Three-lined Salamanders are larger and have 13–14 costal grooves. (4) Cave Salamander is larger and has tail more than 60% of its total length. (5) Ground Skink (a lizard) has scales on its body and claws on its toes. **RANGE:** S. Que. to n. Va. and west to Ont. and cen. Ohio; isolated records in s. Lab.

SOUTHERN TWO-LINED SALAMANDER   NOT ILLUS.

Eurycea cirrigera

IDENTIFICATION: 2½–3¾ in. (6.4–9.5 cm); record 4⁵⁄₁₆ in. (11 cm). Similar to the Northern Two-lined Salamander but has 14 costal grooves instead of 15 or 16. During breeding season, males in some populations possess well-developed projections (cirri) downward from the nostrils, as in the Blue Ridge Two-lined Salamander. Tail 55–60% of total length in adults.

Members of the family Plethodontidae not only are lungless; they also have a nasolabial groove below each nostril. In breeding males of the Southern Two-lined Salamander, the grooves may pass beyond the lip on cirri.

A secretive salamander, hiding beneath all types of sheltering objects, including masses of wet leaves in creek or river swamps. **SIMILAR SPECIES:** (1) Brownback Salamander has short tail that is only about 50% of its total length. (2) See Similar Species under Northern Two-lined Salamander. **RANGE:** S. Va. west to e. Ill., and south to n. Fla. and e. La.; an isolated colony in ne. Ill.

BLUE RIDGE TWO-LINED SALAMANDER   PL. 43
Eurycea wilderae

IDENTIFICATION: 2¾–4¼ in. (7–10.7 cm); record 4¾ in. (12.1 cm). A salamander of the southern Appalachian highlands, often with colors and pattern more vivid than in the other Two-lined Salamanders. Populations at elevations below 4000 feet (1200 m) have 14 costal grooves, whereas those above usually have 15 or 16. Lines *broad and black* and normally breaking up into dots at about middle of tail. Adult males in some populations have conspicuous projections (cirri) downward from nostrils, a well-developed mental gland, and longer legs than females, whereas in other populations they lack these features but have broader heads than females during the breeding season.

Found in and near springs and rills, but wandering far out into the humid forests, at least at higher elevations. Within its range, abundant at all altitudes to the tops of tallest mountains. **SIMILAR SPECIES:** (1) Junaluska Salamander has a short tail only about 50% of its total length. (2) See Similar Species under Northern Two-lined Salamander. **RANGE:** Southern Appalachian Mts. from sw. Va. to n. Ga.

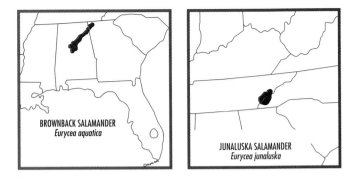

BROWNBACK SALAMANDER
Eurycea aquatica

JUNALUSKA SALAMANDER
Eurycea junaluska

BROWNBACK SALAMANDER *Eurycea aquatica* PL. 43

IDENTIFICATION: 2¼–3⅝ in. (6.4–9.2 cm). Resembles the Southern Two-lined Salamander, but its short tail equals only 50% of its total length. Body is short and stout, with sides of dusky black bordering a brownish dorsum that extends as a light band to the tip of the tail; legs short, with 2–4 costal grooves between adpressed limbs (see Fig. 77); belly yellow, virtually unmarked; 13–14 costal grooves.

A resident of springs and small streams. **RANGE:** Restricted to a narrow strip from Bibb Co. in cen. Ala., northeast in the Valley and Ridge Province to Whitfield Co. in extr. nw. Ga. **NOTE:** Some authorities contend this salamander should not be classified as a distinct species and that it actually represents aberrant individuals or populations of *Eurycea cirrigera*.

JUNALUSKA SALAMANDER *Eurycea junaluska* NOT ILLUS.

IDENTIFICATION: 3–4 in. (7.5–10 cm). Patterned more like a Dusky than a Brook Salamander. A mottled brownish dorsum; dorsolateral stripes, when present, broken into a series of thin wavy lines. Tail short, only about 50% of total length; limbs long, with no more than one costal groove between adpressed limbs (see Fig. 77); costal grooves 14. Sexually mature males have cirri and wider heads than females.

Lives beneath rocks, logs, and other debris in and along streams. Named for the Cherokee Indian Chief Junaluska, who was prominent in the history of the region. **SIMILAR SPECIES:** (1) Dusky Salamanders have enlarged hind legs and a light line from eye to angle of jaw. (2) Blue Ridge Two-lined Salamander has distinct dorsolateral stripes and a longer tail (55–60% of total length). (3) See Similar Species under Northern Two-lined Salamander. **RANGE:** Known from elevations below 2400 feet (730 m) along the Cheoah R. and its tributaries in Graham Co., N.C., along the Tellico R. in Monroe Co., Tenn., and along Fighting Creek in the Great Smoky Mts., Sevier Co., Tenn.

MANY-RIBBED SALAMANDERS
Eurycea multiplicata

■ GRAYBELLY
■ MANY-RIBBED

MANY-RIBBED SALAMAN-DER   PL. 43
Eurycea multiplicata multiplicata

IDENTIFICATION: 2½–3¼ in. (6.4–8.3 cm); record 3⁹⁄₁₆ in. (9 cm). A yellowish salamander without strong longitudinal dark stripes. Sides of body somewhat darker than middorsal area and often with a row of faint light spots. Undersurfaces plain bright yellow. Costal grooves 19 or 20.

Essentially an aquatic amphibian, hiding beneath stones, logs, and various other objects, both in and out of caves. Wanders short distances afield in wet weather. **SIMILAR SPECIES:** (1) Dwarf Salamander has only *four* toes on each *hind* foot. (2) Two-lined Salamanders are superficially similar, but their ranges do not overlap range of Many-ribbed. They and Dwarf Salamander have 16 or fewer costal grooves. **RANGE:** N.-cen. Ark. to se. Okla.

GRAYBELLY SALAMANDER   PL. 43
Eurycea multiplicata griseogaster

IDENTIFICATION: 1⅞–3¼ in. (4.8–8.3 cm); record 4¹⁄₁₆ in. (10.2 cm). A dark subspecies of the Many-ribbed Salamander, with a *gray* instead of yellow belly. Amount of tan on back variable, and middorsal area may consist of a longitudinal stripe paler than the adjacent sides. Costal grooves 19 or 20. Occasionally neotenic. **SIMILAR SPECIES:** (1) Ouachita Dusky Salamander has light line from eye to angle of jaw. (2) Darker specimens of Dwarf Salamander resemble Graybelly but they have only *four* toes on hind feet. **RANGE:** Sw. Mo. and adj. Ark. and Okla.; extr. se. Kans.

LONGTAIL SALAMANDER   PL. 43
Eurycea longicauda longicauda

IDENTIFICATION: 4–6¼ in. (10–15.9 cm); record 7¾ in. (19.7 cm). The only yellowish salamander with vertical black markings on the tail. These, although frequently varying from the herringbone or "dumbbell" theme, are usually conspicuous. The ground color also varies—from yellow to orange-red or even red. Some individ-

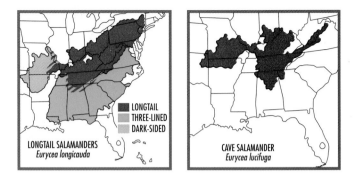

LONGTAIL
THREE-LINED
DARK-SIDED

LONGTAIL SALAMANDERS
Eurycea longicauda

CAVE SALAMANDER
Eurycea lucifuga

uals from scattered portions of the range have the black markings larger and more conspicuous. Costal grooves 13 or 14 in this and the two subspecies below. *Young:* Yellow; tail relatively short.

Found in or under rotting logs, under stones, in shale banks near seepages, under rocks at streamside, and frequently in caves. Also occurs in ponds in the limestone belt of northern N.J. **RANGE:** S. N.Y. to n. Ala. and se. Mo.

THREE-LINED SALAMANDER PL. 43
Eurycea longicauda guttolineata
 IDENTIFICATION: 4–6¼ in. (10–15.9 cm); record 7⅞ in. (20 cm). This is the southern member of the Longtail Salamander group and the only one with three dark stripes. Middorsal stripe may be broken into a series of elongated dark spots. Ground color varies

An adult Three-lined Salamander from Watauga County, North Carolina. This southern subspecies is the most distinctive race of the Longtail Salamander.

from yellow to tan. Belly mottled with greenish gray on a ground color of dull yellow.

In river-bottom swamps, wet ditches, seepage areas at springs and streamside; sometimes at considerable distances from water but always in a damp environment. **RANGE:** Va. to Fla. panhandle and Mississippi R. **NOTE:** Some authorities contend this salamander should be classified as a distinct species; it apparently does not intergrade with the Longtail Salamander in many places where their ranges overlap.

DARK-SIDED SALAMANDER PL. 43
Eurycea longicauda melanopleura
IDENTIFICATION: 3⅝–5⅞ in. (9.2–15 cm); record 6⅝ in. (16.8 cm). The dark stripes, one along each side of the body, are in strong contrast with a broad middorsal stripe that is essentially light in color but well marked with dark spots. Coloration varies. Dark pigment on sides is grayish in juveniles but changes to deep reddish brown in old adults. The light flecks and spots in the dark bands vary from light gray to yellow. The middorsal stripe ranges from bright yellow in juveniles through greenish yellow to dull brownish yellow in the largest individuals.

This is a cave salamander, occurring in the twilight zone of caverns and grottoes but also venturing far afield into the outer world. **RANGE:** Central Highlands and adj. areas; intergrading with the Longtail Salamander in Ill. and se. Mo.

CAVE SALAMANDER *Eurycea lucifuga* PL. 43
IDENTIFICATION: 4–6 in. (10–15.2 cm); record 7⅛ in. (18.1 cm). A reddish salamander with a *long* tail. Ground color variable, how-

An adult Cave Salamander from Cherokee County, Kansas. This amphibian lives in the twilight zones of caves and beneath the rock overhangs of small streams.

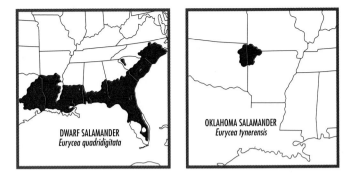

DWARF SALAMANDER
Eurycea quadridigitata

OKLAHOMA SALAMANDER
Eurycea tynerensis

ever, and ranging from dull yellow through orange to bright orange-red. (Young tend to be yellow, adults reddish.) The black spots are usually irregularly scattered, but sometimes they may form two or three longitudinal rows. Occasional specimens have the black markings especially large and conspicuous. Yellowish undersurfaces normally unspotted. Costal grooves 14 or 15. *Young:* Tail relatively short.

A favorite habitat is in the twilight zone of caves—near entrances, where the light is weak. There these salamanders, which are excellent climbers, move about on the formations and ledges, sometimes clinging solely by their prehensile tails. They also occur outside caves and may be discovered beneath logs, stones, or debris in wooded or fairly open places. **SIMILAR SPECIES:** (1) Three-lined and Dark-sided Salamanders have dark longitudinal markings. (2) Longtail Salamander usually has dark "dumbbells" or a herringbone pattern on sides of tail; also, its head is not so broad and flat as Cave Salamander's. **RANGE:** Limestone areas, Va. to Okla.

DWARF SALAMANDER *Eurycea quadridigitata*   PL. 43

IDENTIFICATION: 2⅛–3 in. (5.4–7.5 cm); record 3⁹⁄₁₆ in. (9 cm). *Four toes on hind feet* as well as forefeet. (Most other salamanders have five on each *hind* foot.) The dark dorsolateral stripe ranges from black through various shades of dark brown, and the amount of dark pigmentation on sides of body is quite variable. Many specimens have a middorsal row of small, dark spots; in others the row is short, broken, or absent. *Male:* With cirri during the breeding season.

A resident of low, swampy areas, where it hides under all types of shelter. **SIMILAR SPECIES:** Two-lined and Many-ribbed Salamanders are superficially similar, but both have *five* toes on their *hind* feet. **RANGE:** Chiefly in Coastal Plain from N.C. to Fla. and west to e. Texas; disjunct colony in S.C.

OKLAHOMA SALAMAN-DER *Eurycea tynerensis*   PL. 39

SAN MARCOS SALAMANDER
Eurycea nana

COMAL BLIND SALAMANDER
Eurycea tridentifera

IDENTIFICATION: 1¾–3⅛ in. (4.4–8 cm). The grayish appearance is caused by a heavy stippling and streaking of black over a cream-colored ground. Amount of dark pigment variable; may be most dense on sides, leaving a broad light stripe down back, or it may be heavy over all dorsal surfaces. Usually at least one row of small, light spots appears along each side of body (as many as three rows in small specimens). Belly pale, except where viscera or eggs show through body wall. *External gills present.* Tail fin low.

This neotenic salamander lives in small, gravelly creeks and springs, and may be found among stones or in vegetation growing in water. **SIMILAR SPECIES:** Larvae of Grotto Salamander have high tail fin and longitudinal streaks on sides of body. **RANGE:** Ne. Okla. and adj. corners of Ark. and Mo.

SAN MARCOS SALAMANDER *Eurycea nana*   PL. 39

IDENTIFICATION: 1½–2 in. (3.8–5.1 cm). Almost plain brown above, but with a row of yellowish flecks or spots down each side of back. Belly whitish or yellowish except where viscera and eggs (of females in season) show through translucent skin. *External gills present.*

A tiny neotenic species known only from the mats of algae carpeting the big spring pool that is the source of the San Marcos R., at San Marcos, Texas. **SIMILAR SPECIES:** (1) Texas Salamander is chiefly yellowish rather than brown. (2) Other neotenic salamanders of the general region are virtually white. **RANGE:** San Marcos, Hays Co., Texas.

TEXAS SALAMANDER *Eurycea neotenes*   PL. 39; FIG. 92

IDENTIFICATION: 2–4¼ in. (5.1–10.5 cm). Light brownish yellow in coloration, but mottled or flecked with darker pigment; a double row of light flecks on each side of body, at least in smaller specimens (lower row fades out in older ones). Belly and lower sides almost always white or cream, except where viscera or eggs may

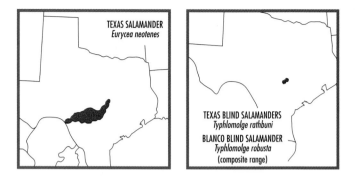

be seen through skin. Local populations vary in coloration, size, robustness, and head shape. Costal grooves 13–16. *External gills present.*

This neotenic salamander is a resident of springs, seeps, and small cavern streams along the Balcones Escarpment and on adjacent portions of the Edwards Plateau of south central Texas. **SIMILAR SPECIES:** (1) The Texas Blind, Blanco Blind, and Comal Blind Salamanders are virtually plain white and have flattened snouts. (2) San Marcos Salamander is plain brown with a single row of yellowish flecks or spots down each side of back. **RANGE:** Edwards Plateau area from vicinity of Austin to Val Verde Co., Texas.

COMAL BLIND SALAMANDER *Eurycea tridentifera* **FIG. 92**
IDENTIFICATION: 1 ½–2⅞ in. (3.8–7.3 cm). A white or slightly yellowish neotenic salamander with pink or red *external gills* and a large head that occupies about ⅓ of the entire head-body length. Snout

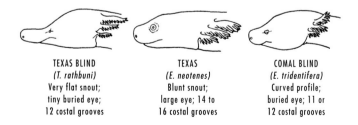

| TEXAS BLIND
(T. rathbuni)
Very flat snout;
tiny buried eye;
12 costal grooves | TEXAS
(E. neotenes)
Blunt snout;
large eye; 14 to
16 costal grooves | COMAL BLIND
(E. tridentifera)
Curved profile;
buried eye; 11 or
12 costal grooves |

Fig. 92. *Neotenic salamanders from Texas* (Typhlomolge *and* Eurycea).

depressed abruptly at about level of eyes. Traces of gray pigment in skin. Legs relatively long. Costal grooves 11 or 12. **SIMILAR SPECIES:** In Texas Blind Salamander, head is considerably more flattened (Fig. 92), snout is much more truncate (square-cut) when viewed from above, and legs are longer. **RANGE:** Known only from Honey Creek Cave, Comal Co., Texas.

BLIND SALAMANDERS: GENERA *Typhlomolge, Typhlotriton,* AND *Haideotriton*

These are residents of caves or underground streams that live in perpetual darkness and have no need for functional eyes. They are white or pinkish with an iridescent overwash, and their skins are so translucent that outlines of the darker internal organs are readily apparent through at least the lower sides and belly. Occasionally they are pumped to the surface or appear in the outflow from deep wells or springs, but otherwise one must seek them by becoming a spelunker (cave explorer), and often an aquatic one at that. Blind salamanders of this family (Plethodontidae) have been found only in limestone regions of the southern United States. A similar-looking blind species of a different family (Proteidae) occurs in Europe.

TEXAS BLIND SALAMANDER
PL. 39; FIG. 92
Typhlomolge rathbuni
    IDENTIFICATION: 3¼–4¼ in. (8.3–10.7 cm); record 5⅜ in. (13.7 cm). A ghostly salamander with toothpick legs and a strongly flattened snout (Fig. 92). Remnants of eyes appear as tiny dark dots buried under the skin. Costal grooves 12. *External gills present.*

The Texas Blind Salamander, a ghostly wraith that few people have ever met in the wild. It lives in water in fault caves along the Texas Balcones Escarpment and is occasionally pumped to the surface from deep wells.

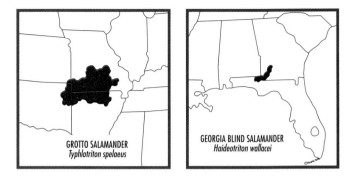

GROTTO SALAMANDER
Typhlotriton spelaeus

GEORGIA BLIND SALAMANDER
Haideotriton wallacei

This weird-looking amphibian occurs in cave waters at San Marcos, Texas, where a reserve has been set aside for its protection. **SIMILAR SPECIES:** (1) Most other neotenic salamanders of same general region bear at least some dark pigment, and their snouts are not so grotesquely flattened. (2) See Comal Blind Salamander. **RANGE:** Vicinity of San Marcos, Hays Co., Texas.

BLANCO BLIND SALAMANDER   NOT ILLUS.
Typhlomolge robusta

IDENTIFICATION: 4 in. (10.1 cm). A robust version of its ghostly relative, the Texas Blind Salamander; eyes much reduced; legs and body short; head flattened; costal grooves 12.

The rarest of North American salamanders, this amphibian is known from a single specimen obtained from beneath the bed of the Blanco River. **RANGE:** The ne. edge of the range of the Texas Blind Salamander near San Marcos, Hays Co., Texas.

GROTTO SALAMANDER *Typhlotriton spelaeus*   PL. 39

IDENTIFICATION: 3–4¾ in. (7.5–12.1 cm); record 5⁵⁄₁₆ in. (13.5 cm). The "ghost lizard" of Ozark caves and grottoes. The whitish or pinkish adults sometimes have faint traces of orange on tail, feet, and lower sides of body. Eyes show as dark spots beneath fused or partly fused eyelids. *No* external gills as adults. *Young:* The larvae have functional eyes and external gills; they are rather strongly pigmented, being brownish- or purplish gray with yellowish longitudinal flecks or dark streaks on the sides; *tail fin high.*

This is an extraordinary salamander that literally has two lives. First, as a larva it resides in mountain brooks and springs, and its activities are not unlike those of larvae of other species. Later it moves into a cave, loses fins and pigment, its eyes cease to func-

A larval Grotto Salamander from Missouri. This cave-adapted amphibian spends its entire adult life in darkness.

tion, the eyelids grow shut or nearly so, and it remains a blind troglodyte for the rest of its days. **SIMILAR SPECIES:** Larvae of several forms of Brook Salamanders (*Eurycea*) live in the same region but all have low tail fins, and their patterns tend to be in the form of stippling, networks, or lichenlike patches. **RANGE:** Central uplands; sw. Mo., extr. se. Kans., and adj. areas in Ark. and Okla.

GEORGIA BLIND SALAMANDER   FIG. 93
Haideotriton wallacei

IDENTIFICATION: 2–3 in. (5.1–7.6 cm). A pinkish-white and slightly opalescent salamander. External gills long, slender, and red. Head broad and long but not greatly flattened. In the young, eyes are represented by tiny, dark spots; in adults (Fig. 93) they may be invisible or virtually so. **RANGE:** Known from a deep well and several caves in sw. Ga. and adj. Fla.

Fig. 93. Georgia Blind Salamander (Haideotriton wallacei), *showing rounded snout, large gills, and lack of eye spots.*

TOADS AND FROGS

ORDER ANURA

Toads and frogs, which range, collectively, from above the Arctic Circle to virtually the southern tips of Africa, Australia, and South America and into many islands, including New Zealand, are the most widely distributed of all the amphibians. Nearly 3700 species are known.

The typical toad (*Bufo*) has a warty skin and short legs for hopping, and the typical frog (*Rana*) has a relatively smooth skin and long legs for leaping, but there are numerous variations among the other genera. Although there are no hard and fast rules for distinguishing "toad" from "frog," standardized common names, used in this Field Guide, are now widely accepted and make it easier to discuss and read about these small animals.

Our species advertise their presence by their calls, and some kinds are rarely seen except at breeding time. Eggs of most are laid in water. Each species has its own, often distinctive, mating call. These are best learned by listening to the records and cassettes listed on p.594. (The Folkways Record also includes other sounds made by frogs such as screams that are uttered when they are seized by enemies, territorial and rain calls, and various warning chirps or croaks. The latter are the release calls of males that reveal their sex when, during the excitement of mating time, one male may inadvertently grasp another.)

Most toads and frogs are best observed at night with the aid of a flashlight. Because the color or pattern of the concealed surfaces of the limbs are often of diagnostic value, some kinds must be in hand for identification. In arid regions or during prolonged droughts these amphibians may estivate for months at a time.

The tadpoles of more than a dozen kinds of toads and frogs are illustrated and described below (Figs. 110–124).

MEXICAN BURROWING TOAD

PL. 45

Rhinophrynus dorsalis

MEXICAN BURROWING TOAD
Rhinophrynus dorsalis

IDENTIFICATION: 2–2¾ in. (5.1–7 cm); record 3½ in. (8.9 cm). The *rotund body* and the *broad* reddish or orange middorsal stripe (buff in young specimens) are sufficient for identifying this toad, which barely enters the United States. Although it looks somewhat like a Narrowmouth Toad of giant size, it is the only living representative of its family, Rhinophrynidae. Tadpole: see Fig. 115.

When this amphibian is calling or alarmed, the body is so inflated with air that it resembles a miniature, somewhat flattened balloon with a small, triangular snout protruding from one side. Specimens are virtually never seen until heavy rains stimulate them to leave their burrows to form breeding choruses. **SIMILAR SPECIES:** Sheep Frog has a yellow *threadlike* middorsal line and a similar line on its belly. **VOICE:** A loud, low-pitched *wh-o-o-o-a,* much like a farmer commanding a mule to stop. **RANGE:** In the lowlands from extr. s. Texas to Yucatán and Honduras; west coast from the Río Balsas, Mexico, to Costa Rica.

SPADEFOOTS: FAMILY PELOBATIDAE

A single, sharp-edged, black spade on each hind foot enables a spadefoot to burrow vertically downward into sandy or other loose soil. This is the hallmark of the genus, but other characteristics include a rather smooth skin, parotoid glands absent or indistinct, and a pupil that is vertically elliptical when exposed to even a moderately bright light (Fig. 94).

In contrast, the true toads *(Bufo)* have *two* tubercles on the underside of each hind foot, one of which may be quite spadelike. They also have well-developed warts, ridges, and parotoid glands, and their pupils are horizontally oval (Fig. 94).

For distinguishing among the several spadefoots, two things should always be checked: (a) is the spade elongated and sickle-shaped or short and wedge-shaped (Fig. 95); and (b) is there a raised area (boss) between the eyes? (See Fig. 96.)

Spadefoots are explosive breeders, appearing suddenly, sometimes in great numbers, after heavy rains and at almost any time during the warm months of the year. In general, they are adapted

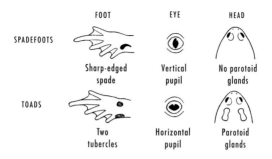

Fig. 94. *Characteristics of Spadefoots* (Scaphiopus) *and Toads* (Bufo).

for life in arid regions and can remain underground for weeks or even months at a time, but they often venture forth on damp or rainy nights. Breeding males have black pads or excrescences on their thumbs and first two fingers.

Many persons experience strong allergic reactions from handling spadefoots. These may take the form of violent sneezing, copious discharge of mucus from the nose, and watering of the eyes. As a precaution, wash your hands with soap or detergent to remove any skin-gland secretions they may have gotten on them from these amphibians, and keep your hands away from your face until you do.

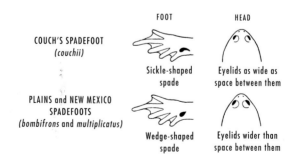

Fig. 95. *Characteristics of Spadefoots* (Scaphiopus).

A raised boss
between the eyes

No raised boss

CANADIAN TOAD *(hemiophrys)*
PLAINS SPADEFOOT *(bombifrons)*
HURTER'S SPADEFOOT *(hurterii)*

Most other species
of TOADS and
SPADEFOOTS

Fig. 96. Tops of heads of Toads (Bufo) and Spadefoots (Scaphiopus).

The genus *Scaphiopus*, occurring throughout a large part of the United States and from southwestern Canada to southern Mexico, is the only group of the family in the New World. Other genera are found in Europe, extreme northwestern Africa, Asia, and the East Indies.

EASTERN SPADEFOOT *Scaphiopus holbrookii holbrookii* PL. 44

IDENTIFICATION: 1¾–2¼ in. (4.4–5.7 cm); record 2⅞ in. (7.3 cm). The only spadefoot occurring east of the Mississippi R. Spade elongate and sickle-shaped. No boss between eyes. Two yellowish lines, one originating at each eye and running down back, are usually well in evidence. The two lines together may form a lyre-shaped pattern or resemble the outline of a somewhat misshapen hourglass. Normally there is an additional light line on each side

The Eastern Spade-foot, the only species of its group occurring east of the Mississippi. It is seldom seen, emerging from its burrow only after heavy rains or lengthy wet periods during the warmer months of the year.

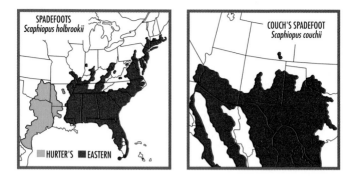

SPADEFOOTS
Scaphiopus holbrookii

■ HURTER'S ■ EASTERN

COUCH'S SPADEFOOT
Scaphiopus couchii

of body. Ground color some shade of brown (grayish- or blackish-brown or sepia). Some specimens may be almost uniformly dark gray to almost black.

Although this is a species of the forested East and Southeast, it is usually found in areas characterized by sandy or other loose soil —habitats that in some respects resemble those of the spadefoots of more arid regions to the west. **VOICE:** An explosive grunt, rather low-pitched, short in duration, but repeated at brief intervals. Some persons liken sound to call of a young crow. **RANGE:** S. New England to s. Fla. and some of the Keys; west to se. Mo., e. Ark., and e. La.; isolated colonies in w. Ind., s. and ne. W. Va., and sw. Va.; absent from many upland areas.

HURTER'S SPADEFOOT *Scaphiopus holbrookii hurterii* **PL. 44**
IDENTIFICATION: 1¾–2¼ in. (4.4–5.7 cm); record 3¼ in. (8.3 cm). The only spadefoot with a *boss* between the eyes (Fig. 96) and an *elongate* sickle-shaped spade. (The boss is actually a little farther back than the eyes.) General coloration often matches the garrison green uniforms of the U.S. Marine Corps, but it may vary from grayish green to a chocolate- or greenish brown, or to almost black. The two curved, light stripes on the back are often as conspicuous as those of the Eastern Spadefoot.

An inhabitant of wooded and savanna areas but also occurring in arid terrain in southern Texas. Named for Julius Hurter, Missouri herpetologist. **SIMILAR SPECIES:** (1) In Couch's and Eastern Spadefoots there is no boss between eyes. (2) In Plains and New Mexico Spadefoots the spade is *short,* rounded, and often wedge-shaped (Fig. 95). **VOICE:** A bleating note, slightly explosive and short in duration, each bleat lasting less than ¼ second. **RANGE:** W. Ark. and nw. La. to cen. Okla. and s. Texas; isolated colony in n.-cen. Ark.

A large adult Couch's Spadefoot, one of the more brightly colored members of the spadefoot family.

COUCH'S SPADEFOOT *Scaphiopus couchii*   PL. 44; FIG. 95

IDENTIFICATION: 2¼–2⅞ in. (5.7–7.3 cm); record 3½ in. (8.9 cm). A southwestern spadefoot with considerable yellowish pigmentation in the skin. Dorsal ground color varying from bright greenish yellow to dull brownish yellow; marked with a mottling or marbling of black, green, or dark brown. (Dark pattern may fade out during breeding season.) Spade *elongate* and often sickle-shaped. No boss between eyes. Diameter of eyelid about equal to distance between eyes (Fig. 95).

A species of shortgrass plains and also of mesquite savannahs and other arid or semiarid regions. Named for Darius Nash Couch, a professional soldier who collected many natural-history specimens in northeastern Mexico while on leave of absence from the Army during 1853. **SIMILAR SPECIES:** (1) Plains and New Mexico Spadefoots have *short* wedge-shaped spades and eyelids noticeably wider than distance between them (Fig. 95). (2) Hurter's Spadefoot has boss between eyes (Fig. 96). **VOICE:** A groaning bleat, suggestive of a goat or sheep unhappy at being tied. Each bleat relatively long, lasting ¼ to one second. **RANGE:** Cen. Texas and adj. Okla. to extr. se. Calif.; south to tip of Baja Calif. and to Nayarit, Zacatecas, and Querétaro; absent from highlands of w. Mexico; an isolated colony in se. Colo.

PLAINS SPADEFOOT *Scaphiopus bombifrons*   PL. 44; FIGS. 95, 96

IDENTIFICATION: 1½–2 in. (3.8–5.1 cm); record 2⁹⁄₁₆ in. (6.4 cm). Our only spadefoot with a pronounced *boss* between the eyes *plus* a *short*, rounded, often wedge-shaped spade. General coloration grayish or brownish, often with a greenish tinge; dark markings

An adult Plains Spadefoot in a defensive posture, puffed up to make it look larger, but also to make it more difficult to swallow.

brown or gray. Small tubercles on the dorsum may be noticeably yellowish or reddish. Four rather vague longitudinal light lines often present on back. Eyelids wider than distance between them (Fig. 95). Tadpole: see Fig. 111.

At home on the Great Plains and in regions of low rainfall; a species of the open grasslands, usually avoiding river bottoms and wooded areas. **SIMILAR SPECIES:** (1) Both Couch's and New Mexico Spadefoots lack a boss between eyes (Fig. 96). Also, in Couch's Spadefoot, the spade is *elongate* and space between eyes is about equal to width of an eyelid (Fig. 95). (2) See also Canadian Toad. **VOICE:** A short, rasping bleat repeated at intervals of ¼ to a full second, or a rasping snore, rather low-pitched and each trill lasting ½ to ¾ second. **RANGE:** Sw. Manitoba to s. Alberta and south to Chihuahua; follows Missouri R. Valley eastward across Mo.; a disjunct area in extr. s. Texas and ne. Mexico; isolated colonies in nw. Ark. and s.-cen. Colo.

NEW MEXICO SPADEFOOT *Scaphiopus multiplicatus* PL. 44

IDENTIFICATION: 1½–2 in. (3.8–5.1 cm); record 2½ in. (6.4 cm). The spade is *short* and wedge-shaped, and there is *no* boss between the eyes. General coloration dusky—gray, brown, dusky green, or sometimes almost black—with scattered spots and blotches of a darker color. The small tubercles on the dorsum may be reddish. Occasional specimens may have vague suggestions of longitudinal, light-colored lines. Eyelids wider than distance between them (Fig. 95). Skin produces an odor like unroasted peanuts.

At home in shortgrass plains and in playas and alkali flats of arid and semiarid regions; absent from extreme deserts. **SIMILAR SPECIES:** (1) Plains Spadefoot has boss between eyes (Fig. 96). (2)

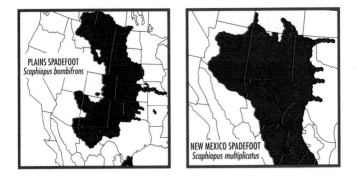

PLAINS SPADEFOOT
Scaphiopus bombifrons

NEW MEXICO SPADEFOOT
Scaphiopus multiplicatus

In Couch's Spadefoot the spade is *elongate*, and space between eyes is about equal to width of eyelid (Fig. 95). **VOICE:** A vibrant, metallic trill like running a fingernail along the stiff teeth of a large comb. Each trill lasts about ¾ to 1½ seconds. **RANGE:** W. Okla. and cen. Texas to Ariz. and far south into Mexico.

TROPICAL FROGS: FAMILY LEPTODACTYLIDAE

A very large family of the American tropics, with a few species ranging northward into Texas and the southwestern United States and two others introduced into Florida. Although some members of the family deposit their eggs in water, all but one of our species lay their eggs on land, and their tadpoles undergo complete metamorphosis in the egg. The exception is the White-lipped Frog, which builds a foam nest and has aquatic tadpoles. The family also occurs in Mexico, Central and most of South America, and is abundantly represented in the West Indies. Some authorities believe that many of the frogs of the Australian region also belong to this family, but others do not.

Disc is present in the BARKING FROG *(Eleutherodactylus a. latrans)* and the WHITE-LIPPED FROG *(Leptodactylus labialis)*

Fig. 97. Ventral disc in two species of tropical frogs.

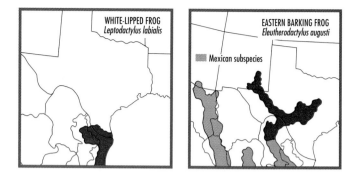

WHITE-LIPPED FROG *Leptodactylus labialis*   **PL. 45; FIG. 97**
IDENTIFICATION: 1⅜–2 in. (3.5–5.1 cm). A white or cream-colored
line on the upper lip and a distinct ventral disc (Fig. 97). Dorsolateral folds present. Ground color varies from gray to chocolate
brown. Number and size of dark dorsal spots also variable. Tadpole: see Fig. 116.

One of the several Mexican amphibians and reptiles that barely
enter the United States in extreme southern Texas. Found in a
wide variety of habitats, including roadside ditches, irrigated
fields, moist meadows, drains, etc. **SIMILAR SPECIES:** Spotted Chorus
Frog has no dorsolateral folds and also lacks a ventral disc. **VOICE:**
Throw-up, throw-up repeated continually and with a rising inflection at end of each call. Males call from cavities beneath hum-
mocks of grass or clods of dirt or in small pits as much as 3 in. (8
cm) deep. Breeding begins with onset of rainy season. Eggs are
laid in a foam nest constructed of glandular secretions from the
frogs, which are whipped into a froth that looks like beaten egg
white. The larvae live in the liquefied center of the nest until
rains enable them to swim into nearby pools. **RANGE:** Lower Rio
Grande Valley, Texas, to n. Venezuela.

EASTERN BARKING FROG   **PL. 45; FIG. 97**
Eleutherodactylus augusti latrans
IDENTIFICATION: 2½–3 in. (6.4–7.5 cm); record 3¾ in. (9.5 cm). A frog
that looks like a toad but has a smooth, dry skin (no warts). There
is a dorsolateral fold and a ventral disc similar to that of White-
lipped Frog (Fig. 97). The general coloration may vary from tan to
greenish and may include tones of pink or reddish brown. *Young:*
Often greenish and with a fawn-colored band across middle of
back.

A resident of limestone caves and ledges that rarely ventures out into the open, even during rains. When captured, as by snake or human being, it puffs itself up prodigiously. Sometimes called the "robber frog." **VOICE:** An explosive call, like the bark of a dog when heard at a distance but more of a guttural *whurr* at close range. The single note may be repeated at regular

GREENHOUSE FROG
Eleutherodactylus planirostris

intervals of 2 to 3 seconds. When females are grasped in the hand they may make a blaring screech. Breeds during rainy periods from late winter to May. **RANGE:** Cen. Texas to se. N.M. and n. Coahuila. Mexican and western subspecies.

GREENHOUSE FROG PL. 45
Eleutherodactylus planirostris planirostris

IDENTIFICATION: ⅝–1¼ in. (1.6–3.2 cm). A tiny immigrant, probably from Cuba. Two pattern phases: (a) *striped,* with longitudinal light stripes; and (b) *mottled,* with irregular dark and light markings. The general coloration is brown, but usually with distinct reddish tones. Eyes reddish; belly white. *Young:* With a tiny tail at hatching.

These minute frogs are terrestrial, seeking shelter by day or in dry weather beneath boards, leaves, trash, or other debris where there is some moisture. They normally move about only at night or in rainy weather. Often found in gardens, greenhouses, dumps, hardwood hammocks, gopher tortoise burrows, and small stream valleys. **VOICE:** Short, melodious, birdlike chirps, usually 4–6 in a series. Breeds during summer rainy season (May to September in n. Fla.). One of only two frogs east of Texas that lay their eggs on land. The eggs are deposited under damp vegetation or debris. Development takes place entirely in the egg; no free tadpole stage. **RANGE:** Introduced and now widespread in Fla.; isolated records in the Fla. panhandle and at New Orleans, La. Native to Cuba; also introduced in Jamaica, the Cayman Is., some of the Bahamas, and the vicinity of Veracruz, Mexico. Subspecies in Cuba and the Bahamas.

PUERTO RICAN COQUI *Eleutherodactylus coqui* PL. 45
IDENTIFICATION: 1–2¼ in. (2.5–5.8 cm). A small, brown or grayish brown frog with a bewildering variety of patterns. Upper body

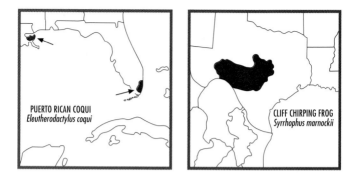

PUERTO RICAN COQUI
Eleutherodactylus coqui

CLIFF CHIRPING FROG
Syrrhophus marnockii

may exhibit one or more of the following: uniform brown or gray with no pattern, an ill-defined dark M between the shoulders, or two broad cream dorsolateral stripes irregularly bordered above and below with tiny black spots. Some individuals have a broad, cream band across the head between the eyes. Belly white or pale yellow, stippled with brown. Toe pads are large; no webbing between toes. Eye brown to golden. *Young:* With a tiny tail at hatching.

In its native range, a resident of trees, bromeliads, and beneath dead logs and leaf litter on the forest floor. In the United States, currently restricted to areas around greenhouses. Usually active only at night or on rainy days. **SIMILAR SPECIES:** Greenhouse Frog has reddish eyes. **VOICE:** A brief, two-note *co qui,* like the high-pitched chirp of a bird. Breeds year-round and, like the Greenhouse Frog, lays its eggs on land. Young develop in the egg; no free tadpole stage. **RANGE:** Introduced in South Miami and at Homestead, southern Fla., and at New Orleans, La.; also introduced on the Virgin Is. Native to Puerto Rico.

CLIFF CHIRPING FROG *Syrrhophus marnockii*   PL. 45
IDENTIFICATION: ¾–1½ in. (1.9–3.8 cm). Greenish in coloration but mottled with brown and clad in a smooth skin. Head proportionately quite large.

The flattened head and body facilitate rapid retreats into cracks and crevices of cliffs that mark the eastern and southern faces and occur in numerous other parts of the Edwards Plateau of central Texas. This small amphibian normally is active only at night. It leaps and hops as do other frogs, but it may also run when seeking shelter. **SIMILAR SPECIES:** Green Toad has a warty skin. **VOICE:** A cricketlike chirp or trill that may be heard throughout the

year. The mating call, given only when a female is present, is similar but clearer and sharper. Peak of breeding season is in April or May, but egg deposition may occur at any time from late February to early December. **RANGE:** S.-cen. Texas.

SPOTTED CHIRPING FROG *Syrrhophus guttilatus*   **PL. 45**

IDENTIFICATION: ¾–1¼ in. (1.9–3.2 cm). Similar to the Cliff Chirping Frog, but with a vermiculate (wormlike) dark pattern, a dark bar between the eyes, and a yellowish to brownish ground color.

Occurs in springs, canyons, and caves in the Chisos Mts., and in other areas where moisture is present in Brewster and Presidio cos.,Texas. Often runs when disturbed, instead of leaping or hopping. **VOICE:** A sharp, relatively short, whistle. **RANGE:** Big Bend region of Texas; also from se. Coahuila to Guanajuato; isolated colonies in w. Texas and Durango.

RIO GRANDE CHIRPING FROG   **PL. 45**
Syrrhophus cystignathoides campi

IDENTIFICATION: ⅝–1 in. (1.6–2.5 cm). A nondescript species, brown to grayish- or yellowish olive and with no distinctive field marks. But since it barely enters the United States from Mexico, it will cause little confusion except in extreme southern Texas. Dark line from nostril through eye usually not very prominent. Behavior will help. This little frog not only leaps and hops but also runs, and is very quick and adept at darting under cover.

An abundant species in the lower Rio Grande Valley that seems to thrive in the midst of civilization. At night it may appear on lawns or in flower beds or gutters, especially if some sprinkling has been going on. By day it hides under boards, debris, flower boxes, or other objects that offer both moisture and shelter.

More natural habitats include environs of palm groves, thickets, ditches, and resacas. **VOICE:** A cricketlike chirp, usually given erratically, not at regular intervals. Breeds in spring but may be heard during any of the warm months when irrigation is in progress. **RANGE:** Extr. s. Texas and ne. Mexico; isolated colonies (introduced) at Houston and San Antonio.

TOADS: FAMILY BUFONIDAE

The homely "hoptoad" is readily recognized as such, but telling the different kinds apart is quite another matter. Recourse must be made to checking the shapes and sizes of the shoulder (parotoid) glands and cranial ridges, the relative number and prominence of the warts, and differences in coloration and pattern. To complicate matters, certain species are known to hybridize with others. This unfortunate state of affairs undoubtedly has been aggravated by the human propensity for altering habitats and thus bringing animals together that had remained isolated for one reason or another during prehistoric times.

Toads in general have dry, warty skins, and they hop. Frogs of the genus *Rana,* as well as many other kinds, have moist, relatively smooth skins, and they leap. Only spadefoots (*Scaphiopus*) are likely to be confused with true toads (*Bufo*). For ways of telling the two genera apart see Fig. 94.

One does not get warts from touching toads, but their skin-

Rounded in most
of the species
within our area

Sausage-shaped in the
GREAT PLAINS *(cognatus),*
TEXAS *(speciosus),* and OAK
(quercicus) TOADS

Fig. 98. Male Toads (Bufo) with vocal sacs inflated (diagrammatic).

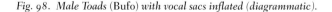

gland secretions are irritating to mucous membranes. Wash your hands after handling them, and keep your fingers away from your mouth and eyes until you do.

In the North, toads breed in the spring and, depending on weather conditions, at more or less the same time each year. In the South, they may mate more than once and, collectively, during almost any month. In the arid Southwest, where they occur in greatest variety, deposition of eggs usually depends on the advent of rain. Breeding males have dark nuptial pads on their thumbs and inner fingers. Throats of males are usually dark, ranging from black to dusky. The vocal sac in most species is round when inflated; in others it is sausage-shaped (Fig. 98). In most species the females grow larger than their mates. Individual toads may vary considerably in coloration, being dark at one time and light at another, depending on conditions of temperature, animation, etc. Small toads, especially those which have recently transformed, are often virtually impossible to identify.

The natural distribution of the family is nearly worldwide, except for Madagascar, Polynesia, and the Australian and polar regions. Toads of some species, however, notably *Bufo marinus*, have been introduced into various tropical regions by humankind in an effort to control insect pests.

AMERICAN TOAD *Bufo americanus*   PL. 44; FIG. 99

IDENTIFICATION: 2–3½ in. (5.1–9 cm); record 4⅜ in. (11.1 cm). The widespread and abundant "hoptoad" of the Northeast. Throughout the great bulk of its range, only Fowler's Toad is likely to be confused with it, but, unfortunately, the two sometimes hybridize. Despite considerable individual and local variation, the following

A pair of American Toads in amplexus, the male tightly grasping the larger female beneath him and fertilizing her eggs as she extrudes them. The eggs are deposited in water in long gelatinous double strands.

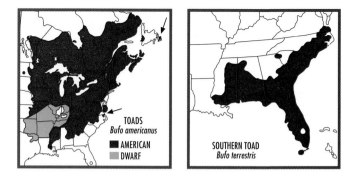

TOADS
Bufo americanus

■ AMERICAN
▨ DWARF

SOUTHERN TOAD
Bufo terrestris

points normally hold for the American Toad: (a) only *one or two large warts* in each of largest dark spots; (b) chest and forward part of abdomen *usually spotted* with dark pigment; (c) enlarged warts on tibia; and (d) parotoid gland either separated from the ridge behind the eye, or connected with it by a short spur (Fig. 99). A light middorsal stripe may or may not be present. Many American Toads are almost plain brown, but others, females especially, are gaily patterned. The general ground color varies through numerous shades of brown to gray or olive or brick red but may be ornamented by patches of yellow or buff or other light colors. Dark spots are brown or black, and warts vary from yellow, orange, or red to dark brown. Tadpole: see Fig. 112.

Habitats are legion, ranging from suburban back yards to mountain wildernesses. Requisites seem to be shallow bodies of water in which to breed (temporary pools or ditches or shallow portions of streams, for example), hiding places where there is some moisture, and an abundant supply of insects and other invertebrates for food. Toads of this and several other species do well in captivity if they have loose soil in which to burrow, water to soak in occasionally, plenty of live insects, and a minimum of handling. **SIMILAR SPECIES:** (1) See Fowler's Toad and Southern Toad. (2) Woodhouse's Toad has a plain belly, and its warts are more numerous and nearly all same size. **VOICE:** A rather long musical trill, one of the most pleasant sounds of early spring. Individual calls may last 6–30 seconds; trill rate about 30–40 per second. Breeds from March to July (the later dates at high altitudes or latitudes). **RANGE:** Maritime Provinces to se. Manitoba; south to Miss., adj. La., and e. Kans.; isolated colonies in se. N.D., ne. N.C., and Newf. **SUBSPECIES:** EASTERN AMERICAN TOAD, *Bufo a. americanus* (Pl. 44). As described and with range indicated

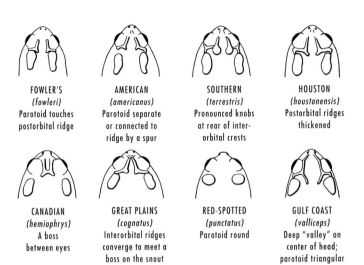

FOWLER'S	**AMERICAN**	**SOUTHERN**	**HOUSTON**
(fowleri)	*(americanus)*	*(terrestris)*	*(houstonensis)*
Parotoid touches postorbital ridge	Parotoid separate or connected to ridge by a spur	Pronounced knobs at rear of inter-orbital crests	Postorbital ridges thickened

CANADIAN	**GREAT PLAINS**	**RED-SPOTTED**	**GULF COAST**
(hemiophrys)	*(cognatus)*	*(punctatus)*	*(valliceps)*
A boss between eyes	Interorbital ridges converge to meet a boss on the snout	Parotoid round	Deep "valley" on center of head; parotoid triangular

Fig. 99. *Cranial crests and parotoid glands of various Toads* (Bufo).

above. DWARF AMERICAN TOAD, *Bufo a. charlesmithi*. Size much smaller; seldom exceeds 2½ in. (6.4 cm). Very often reddish in coloration; dorsal spots, when present, small and including only a single wart; venter only faintly spotted, or not at all. Call pitched about midway between calls of American and Southern Toads. Sw. Ind. and s. Ill. to e. Okla. and ne. Texas.

SOUTHERN TOAD *Bufo terrestris*   PL. 44; FIG. 99

IDENTIFICATION: 1⅝–3 in. (4.1–7.5 cm); record 4⁷⁄₁₆ in. (11.3 cm). Pronounced *knobs* and high cranial crests give the head a strongly sculptured appearance. Viewed in direct profile, large adults look almost horned. The two crests that run forward from the knobs tend to approach each other toward the snout (Fig. 99). General coloration usually some shade of brown but variable from red to black; with or without dark spots that contain one or two warts, or

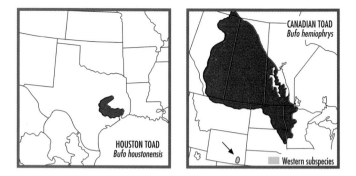

CANADIAN TOAD
Bufo hemiophrys

HOUSTON TOAD
Bufo houstonensis

Western subspecies

often more. There may be a light middorsal stripe, but this is often obscure, especially toward rear of back. *Young:* Knobs not well developed, but their future locations indicated by backward extensions from cranial crests.

The common toad of the South, particularly abundant in sandy areas. Like other toads, it becomes active at twilight, foraging well into the night. Daylight hours are spent chiefly in hiding, often in burrows of the animal's own making. **SIMILAR SPECIES:** None of our other toads has such pronounced cranial knobs. Most trouble will come in trying to identify young specimens. (1) Fowler's Toad has smaller, less elevated warts, and there are usually three or more in each large dark spot. (2) In Oak Toad, cranial crests are inconspicuous, and the light middorsal stripe is prominent. (3) In American Toad, even in young, there are no marked extensions backward from the interorbital crests (Fig. 99). **VOICE:** A shrill, musical trill almost an octave higher than that of American Toad. Duration of call varies from about 2 to 8 seconds. Trill rate rapid, about 75 per second. These toads breed in shallow water and may be heard from March to October, depending on locality and weather conditions. **RANGE:** Coastal Plain from extr. se. Va. to Mississippi R.; south throughout Fla. and on some of the lower Keys; isolated colony in extr. w. S.C.

HOUSTON TOAD *Bufo houstonensis*   FIG. 99

IDENTIFICATION: 2–2⅝ in. (5.1–6.7 cm); record 3⅛ in. (7.9 cm). An isolated relative of the American Toad that resembles it in most details of structure and voice. Cranial ridges quite thickened, especially those running across behind eyes. The dorsum bears a dark, mottled pattern that may be arranged in a vague herringbone fashion. The mottling is brown to black on a ground color of

The Houston Toad, an endangered species. Quite appropriately the Houston Zoo began breeding it in captivity to help save it. The remaining wild populations now seem to be stabilized and are being carefully monitored.

cream to purplish gray and with or without patches of dark green. Usually a middorsal light stripe present. Venter with numerous small dark spots. **SIMILAR SPECIES:** (1) In Woodhouse's Toad group (including Fowler's Toad), the parotoid gland touches cranial ridge behind eye (Fig. 99). (2) Gulf Coast Toad has a pronounced dark stripe along side of body and a deep valley between eyes. (3) In Texas Toad, both tubercles beneath hind foot have sharp cutting edges. **VOICE:** A piercing but rather musical trill, higher pitched than in American Toad but with about same trill rate (32 per second) and of 4–11 seconds duration. **RANGE:** Se. Texas.

CANADIAN TOAD *Bufo hemiophrys hemiophrys*   PL. 44

IDENTIFICATION: 2–3 in. (5.1–7.5 cm); record 3¼ in. (8.3 cm). The "Dakota toad." A far-northern species with a pronounced boss between eyes (similar to boss of Plains and Hurter's Spadefoots — see Fig. 96). The boss, which may be grooved on top, extends from snout as far back as level of rear margin of eyelids. Borders of parotoid glands indistinct and blending with skin. Ground color brownish or greenish, sometimes reddish. Warts brown or reddish. A light middorsal stripe. *Young:* Cranial crests absent; these develop later, eventually uniting to form the boss.

Considerably more aquatic than most toads. Frequently found along the shores of small lakes, in which it may take refuge by swimming well out into the water. **SIMILAR SPECIES:** (1) Woodhouse's Toad has pronounced cranial crests but normally lacks boss between eyes (at least in the eastern part of its range). (2) Dark spots of Great Plains Toad are large, contain many warts, and are distinctly light-bordered. (3) In American Toad the cranial crests

The Canadian Toad ranges chiefly through west-central parts of the country for which it is named. The raised, thickened crests between the eyes extend forward to form a boss, a rounded area on the snout. (See Fig. 99.)

are strongly evident. (The boss obscures them in Canadian Toad.) (4) In Plains Spadefoot, parotoid glands are lacking, and pupil of eye is vertical (horizontal in true toads). **VOICE:** A rather soft, low-pitched trill lasting 2–5 seconds and repeated two or three times a minute. Trill rate very rapid, about 90 per second. **RANGE:** Nw. Minn. and ne. S.D. northwest to the e. half of Alberta and into extr. s. Dist. of Mack. Western subspecies.

WOODHOUSE'S TOAD *Bufo woodhousii woodhousii* **PL. 44**
IDENTIFICATION: 2¼–4 in. (6.4–10 cm); record 5 in. (12.7 cm). Because it lacks any really distinctive markings, this large toad is best identified by a process of boiling down — by eliminating everything it couldn't be (see Similar Species, below). There is a *light middorsal stripe, cranial crests* are *prominent,* and *parotoid glands* are *elongate.* The dark dorsal spots contain from one to several warts, and the spots themselves are irregular and not so prominent as in some other species. Belly whitish or yellowish, usually completely unmarked but sometimes with a dark breast spot and dark flecks between forelegs. General coloration yellowish brown or gray, sometimes with an olive or greenish cast.

This amphibian, abundant in many localities, ranges from the grasslands of the Great Plains into the arid Southwest. Habitats include marshes and swales, river bottoms, mountain canyons, desert streams, and irrigated areas, plus urban and suburban back yards. It usually appears at night and often near lights, where insects abound and may be had for the gulping. Named for Samuel Washington Woodhouse, surgeon and naturalist of exploration expeditions to the Southwest in the mid-19th century. For-

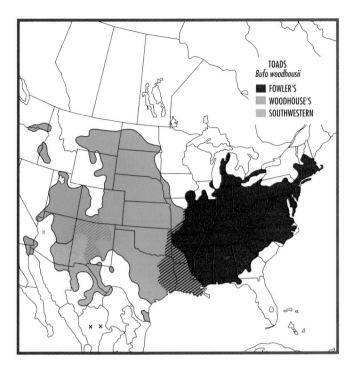

TOADS
Bufo woodhousii

■ FOWLER'S
▨ WOODHOUSE'S
▨ SOUTHWESTERN

merly called "Rocky Mountain toad." **SIMILAR SPECIES:** (1) Texas Toad has *no light middorsal stripe* and no (or virtually no) cranial crests. (2) Red-spotted Toad has *round* parotoids. (3) Canadian Toad has raised *boss* between eyes. (Woodhouse's Toads within our area normally lack such a boss.) (4) In the American Toad, there are numerous *dark markings on chest.* (5) Fowler's Toad, related sub-specifically to Woodhouse's Toad, has large, dark, well-defined dorsal spots, often six in number, and each containing three or more warts. **VOICE:** A nasal *w-a-a-a-h*, lasting 1 to 2½ seconds and rather like a sheep bleating in the distance. Call very similar to that of Fowler's Toad but somewhat lower in pitch. Breeds March to July, usually after rains, wherever there is shallow, standing or slightly moving water. **RANGE:** The Dakotas and Mont. to cen. Texas; west of the Rocky Mts. proper from n. Utah to cen. Ariz.; disjunct colonies in several states; an isolated record in w.-cen. Ariz. **SUBSPECIES:** SOUTHWESTERN WOODHOUSE'S TOAD, *Bufo w. australis.* A race with dark markings on the chest and in which the light middorsal stripe normally does not involve the snout.

Extr. w. Texas, chiefly in Rio Grande Valley; sw. N.M. and se. Ariz. south into Mexico; disjunct records from Durango; intergrades with *woodhousii* through a large part of N.M. and into adjacent states.

FOWLER'S TOAD *Bufo woodhousii fowleri* PL. 44; FIG. 99

IDENTIFICATION: 2–3 in. (5.1–7.5 cm); record 3¾ in. (9.5 cm). A typical Fowler's Toad has: (a) *three or more warts* in each of the largest dark spots; (b) a virtually *unspotted* chest and belly; (c) no greatly enlarged warts on tibia; and (d) a parotoid gland that touches cranial ridge behind eye (Fig. 99). There is some variation, but usually at least three of these characteristics are present. Many specimens have a single dark breast spot on an otherwise immaculate venter. The general dorsal coloration is brown, gray, or, more rarely, greenish or brick red. A light middorsal stripe.

An extremely abundant toad of the Atlantic Coastal Plain from Long Island to North Carolina. Farther inland its distribution is spotty, and it occurs chiefly in sandy areas, around shores of lakes, or in river valleys. In regions where their presence is not even suspected, these toads may appear suddenly in large numbers when warm, heavy rains follow a long period of drought. Named for S. P. Fowler, an early Massachusetts naturalist. **SIMILAR SPECIES:** (1) American Toad has: (a) only *one or two* large warts in each dark spot; (b) chest *spotted* with dark pigment; (c) enlarged warts on tibia; and (d) parotoid gland either separated from ridge behind eye or connected with it by a short spur. (2) Southern Toad has pronounced knobs at rear of cranial crests (see Fig. 99). (3) Gulf Coast Toad has broad, dark stripe along the side. **VOICE:** A short, unmusical bleat—a nasal *w-a-a-a-h*—lasting 1 to 4 sec-

An adult Fowler's Toad from Caldwell County, Kentucky. This is the eastern race of this species, which has the largest range of any toad in North America.

onds. Breeds from spring to mid-August, usually later than the American Toad in any given locality. Calls from ditches, temporary pools, or shallow margins of permanent bodies of water. **RANGE:** Cen. New England to Gulf Coast and west to Mich., nw. Ark., and e. La.; absent from southern part of Atlantic Coastal Plain and most of Fla. **NOTE:** Fowler's Toad is known to hybridize with

GULF COAST TOAD
Bufo valliceps

other species of toads. The offspring may show characteristics of both parents, and the calls of male hybrids may be intermediate and difficult or impossible to identify.

GULF COAST TOAD *Bufo valliceps valliceps*   PL. 44; FIG. 99

IDENTIFICATION: 2–4 in. (5.1–10 cm); record 5⅛ in. (13 cm). The broad, dark lateral stripe is usually so prominent that it alone may assure identification. It is bordered above by a light stripe, and there is also a light middorsal stripe. General dorsal coloration variable from almost black, with touches of rich orange, to yellow-brown with whitish spots. Cranial crests strongly developed and bordering a broad, rather deep "valley" down center of head; parotoid glands often triangular (Fig. 99). A rather flat toad; the normal resting posture tends to be more squat than in other species. *Male:* Throat clear yellowish green.

Roadside, railroad, or irrigation ditches are frequently utilized,

The vocal sac of a calling Gulf Coast Toad is rounded, and thus resembles the sacs of most of our other toads. The broad light lateral stripe is characteristic. Ranges southward to Costa Rica in Central America.

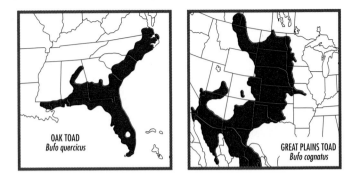

OAK TOAD
Bufo quercicus

GREAT PLAINS TOAD
Bufo cognatus

but Gulf Coast Toads also occur in a wide variety of other habitats, including coastal prairies, on barrier beaches bordering the Gulf of Mexico, and in all manner of places in towns and on the outskirts of cities—even in dumps and storm sewers. **VOICE:** A short trill, lasting 2–6 seconds and repeated several times at intervals of about 1–4 seconds. Call similar to that of American and Houston Toads but less musical. Might be likened to sound of a wooden rattle. Vocal sac a large, globular pouch reaching from chin to abdomen when inflated. Breeds March to September. **RANGE:** Extr. s. Miss., s. La., e.-cen. and s. Texas south to Costa Rica; disjunct populations in Big Bend region of Texas and on Ark.-La. border; isolated colony in s. Miss.; Mexican and Central American subspecies.

OAK TOAD *Bufo quercicus*   **PL. 46; FIG. 98**

IDENTIFICATION: ¾–1 ⁵⁄₁₆ in. (1.9–3.3 cm). An elfin toad clad in a tapestry of many colors. A conspicuous light middorsal stripe that may be white, cream, yellow, or orange; the four or five pairs of spots on the back are black or brown. Some warts are red, orange, or reddish brown. The ground color varies from pearl-gray to almost black, so that at times the Oak Toad is almost entirely black with very little pattern in evidence (except for light stripe).

An abundant amphibian of southern pine woods. Hides under all manner of objects but is much more active by day than other toads. **VOICE:** Like *peeping* of newly hatched chicks, high-pitched and earsplitting in large choruses. Breeding occurs in shallow pools, ditches, cypress and flatwoods ponds, etc., from April to October, depending on arrival of warm, heavy rains. *Vocal sac sausage-shaped* (Fig. 98). **RANGE:** Coastal Plain from se. Va. to e. La.; a northeastward extension in Ala.; south throughout Fla. and on some of the Keys.

In the Great Plains Toad the vocal sac is large and sausage-shaped. The shrill, piercing trill resembles the noise made by a riveting machine, and a single call sometimes may last for the better part of a minute.

GREAT PLAINS TOAD *Bufo cognatus* PL. 44; FIGS. 98, 99

IDENTIFICATION: 1⅞–3½ in. (4.8–9 cm); record 4½ in. (11.4 cm). Our only toad with *large* dark blotches, each blotch boldly bordered by light pigment and containing many warts. Ground color gray, brown, greenish, or yellowish. Blotches green, olive, or dark gray and bordered by light pigment. Some specimens have a narrow, light middorsal stripe. Cranial crests well apart toward the rear but extending diagonally forward to meet a boss on the snout (Fig. 99). *Young:* Crest between eyes in form of a V; dorsum may be dotted with small red tubercles.

This is a common toad of the "great open spaces," of broad grasslands, and the arid Southwest. It is an accomplished burrower and normally moves about only at night. Often found along irrigation ditches or in river bottoms or flood plains. **VOICE:** A shrill, piercing, metallic trill, suggestive of a riveting machine, sustained and often lasting 20 seconds or more. (Single calls of more than 50 seconds' duration are on record.) Trill rate 13–20 per second. The din of a large chorus is nerve-shattering. *Vocal sac sausage-shaped,* ⅓ the bulk of the toad when fully inflated (Fig. 98). Breeds April to September, usually May to July in northern part of range. **RANGE:** Great Plains from extr. sw. Manitoba to se. Alberta and south to n. and w. Texas; e.-cen. Utah to extr. se. Calif. and far south into Mexico; disjunct colony in s.-cen. Colo.

TEXAS TOAD *Bufo speciosus* PL. 44; FIG. 98

IDENTIFICATION: 2–3¼ in. (5.1–8.3 cm); record 3⅝ in. (9.2 cm). A chubby toad without distinctive features except on the underside of the foot, where the two tubercles are sharp-edged, often black,

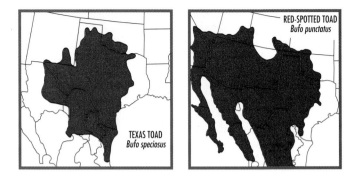

TEXAS TOAD
Bufo speciosus

and the inner one is *sickle-shaped*. No light middorsal stripe. Cranial crests indistinct or absent. Parotoid gland oval. General coloration gray, marked with yellowish-green or brown spots and pink, orange, or greenish warts.

Habitats include grasslands, cultivated areas, and mesquite-savannah associations. Sandy soils are preferred. All the obvious breeding sites are utilized—rain pools, cattle tanks, irrigation ditches, etc. **SIMILAR SPECIES:** (1) Red-spotted Toad has small, *round* parotoid glands, and its warts are buff or reddish. (2) In Giant Toad, parotoid gland is *very* large and extends far down on side of body. (3) In Woodhouse's Toad, cranial crests are prominent. **VOICE:** A continuous series of loud, explosive trills, each ½ second or more in length. Like a high-pitched riveting machine. Trill rate 39–57 per second, hence much more rapid than in Great Plains Toad. *Vocal sac sausage-shaped* and ⅓ the bulk of the toad when fully inflated (Fig. 98). Breeds April to September (with rains). **RANGE:** Sw. Okla., adj. Texas, and se. N.M. to Chihuahua, Coahuila, and cen. Tamaulipas.

RED-SPOTTED TOAD *Bufo punctatus*   **PL. 44; ; FIG. 99**
IDENTIFICATION: 1½–2¼ in. (3.8–6.4 cm); record 3 in. (7.6 cm). Our only toad with *round* parotoid glands (Fig. 99). Each gland is small, no larger than the eye. Cranial crests absent or only slightly developed. General coloration gray, light to medium brown, or pale olive; warts buff or reddish and sometimes set in small, dark blotches. No light stripe down back. Specimens from the limestones of the Edwards Plateau in central Texas are pale gray and virtually unmarked. A flattish toad, not so rotund as most other species.

In rough, rocky regions and open grasslands. Also a resident of the desert, but most typically found near springs, seepages, persistent pools along streams, cattle tanks, etc., throughout the arid Southwest. **SIMILAR SPECIES:** Other toads have elongated parotoid glands, well-defined cranial crests, or both. **VOICE:** A clear, musical trill, high and essentially on one pitch. Duration about 4–10 seconds; interval variable, sometimes longer or sometimes shorter than call itself. Breeds April to September, coincidentally with rains. Usually calls out of water, frequently on rocks at the water's edge. **RANGE:** Sw. Kans. and cen. Texas to se. Calif.; far south into mainland Mexico and to the southern tip of Baja Calif.

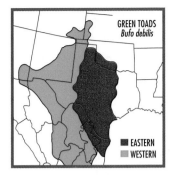

GREEN TOADS
Bufo debilis

■ EASTERN
▨ WESTERN

EASTERN GREEN TOAD *Bufo debilis debilis*   PL. 46

IDENTIFICATION: 1¼–2 in. (3.2–5.1 cm). The *bright green* coloration, in combination with the flattened head and body, makes the Green Toads easy to identify. Warts, including black ones, are numerous on the dorsal surfaces, although less conspicuous than in many other kinds of toads. Throat black or dusky in males, yellow or white in females.

A resident of relatively arid habitats; seldom seen abroad except during and after periods of heavy rain. Sometimes found under rocks. **SIMILAR SPECIES:** (1) Cliff Chirping Frog has smooth skin (no warts). (2) Skins of Strecker's and Spotted Chorus Frogs also lack prominent warts. **VOICE:** A shrill trill, almost with the insistence of an irate policeman's whistle, but not nearly so loud; of 5–6 seconds' duration at intervals of nearly same length. Louder and shriller than call of Narrowmouth Toad. Breeds from March to September — if rains occur during that period. Often calls at the bases of clumps of grass. **RANGE:** Nw. Texas and sw. Okla. to ne. Mexico.

WESTERN GREEN TOAD *Bufo debilis insidior*   PL. 46

IDENTIFICATION: 1¼–2⅛ in. (3.2–5.4 cm). Similar to the Eastern Green Toad, but green coloration is often paler. In western race: (a) black lines connect many of the round, black dots on dorsum; and (b) warts on parotoid glands and upper eyelids have black points (warts broad and flattened in eastern race).

Occurs in higher — usually above 2500 ft. (760 m) — and drier

A male Western Green Toad with its vocal sac inflated. The two kinds of green toads are small and western in distribution. The greenish dorsal coloration and flattened head and body are characteristic of both.

areas than its eastern counterpart. A resident largely of subhumid valleys, shortgrass prairies, and desert flats, where it is seldom seen except after heavy rains. **SIMILAR SPECIES:** See Eastern Green Toad. **VOICE:** A cricketlike trill held at one pitch and lasting about 3–7 seconds. Some persons liken the sound to that of an electric buzzer. **RANGE:** Chihuahuan Desert and adjacent regions from w. Kans. and se. Ariz. to Zacatecas and San Luis Potosí.

GIANT TOAD *Bufo marinus* PL. 44

IDENTIFICATION: 4–6 in. (10–15.2 cm); record 9⅜ in. (23.8 cm) in S. America; probably not over 7 in. (17.8 cm) in U.S.; females weigh up to 3.3 pounds (1.5 kg). A huge, brown toad that barely enters the United States. It is characterized by immense, deeply pitted parotoid glands extending far down sides of body.

Pools and arroyos in Rio Grande Valley, but occupying a wide variety of habitats in the tropics. The skin-gland secretions are

GIANT TOAD
Bufo marinus

highly toxic to dogs and other animals that may be foolish enough to bite one of these toads. **VOICE:** A slow, low-pitched trill, suggestive of the exhaust noise of a distant tractor. Breeding depends on advent of rains and may occur from early spring to autumn. **RANGE:** Extr. s. Texas and s. Sonora and south to and through the Amazon Basin in S. America; introduced into many tropical parts of the world and also at Miami, Fla., and vicinity, where it is now abundant in suburban areas and along canals of the region. Also established at Tampa on the Gulf Coast, and on Stock I. and Key West.

TREEFROGS AND THEIR ALLIES: FAMILY HYLIDAE

A large family (about 635 species) with representatives in all the habitable continents, including Australia. Within our area there are five genera: Treefrogs (*Hyla, Osteopilus,* and *Smilisca*), Cricket Frogs (*Acris*), and Chorus Frogs (*Pseudacris*). They are slim-waisted, usually long-limbed frogs, mostly of small size. Females grow much larger than males.

CRICKET FROGS: GENUS *Acris*

These are small, warty, nonclimbing members of the Treefrog family. They are subject to extreme variation in coloration and details of pattern, and may exhibit a myriad of combinations of black, yellow, orange, or red on a base of brown or green. Fortunately there are two pattern details that remain virtually constant:

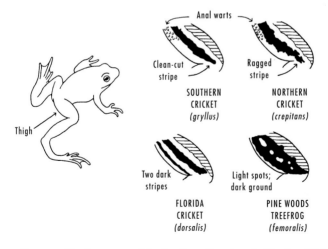

Fig. 100. Thigh patterns of Cricket Frogs (Acris) *and a Treefrog* (Hyla).

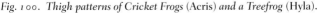

(a) a dark triangle or V-shaped spot between the eyes; and (b) a longitudinal dark stripe (or stripes) on the rear surface of the thigh (Fig. 100). Some of the Chorus Frogs (genus *Pseudacris*) may also show dark triangles between the eyes, but their skins are less warty and their toes are only slightly webbed (Fig. 101). The most positive check is the thigh stripe, which requires catching the frog and straightening out the leg to see it. Males have a single vocal pouch under the chin.

Behavior and habitat will help. These small, often very abundant, frogs elude their enemies by a quick succession of erratic hops, usually coming to rest just tantalizingly out of reach. They are at home in or near permanent bodies of shallow water that provide cover in the form of vegetation, either emergent or along the shore, and which are exposed to the sun during the greater part of the day. They are also found on the sandy, gravelly, or muddy bars and banks of small sluggish or intermittent streams.

The genus ranges from southeastern N.Y., the southern peninsula of Mich., and se. S.D. south to the tip of Fla. and ne. Mexico.

SOUTHERN CRICKET FROG *Acris gryllus gryllus* **PL. 46**
IDENTIFICATION: ⅝–1¼ in. (1.6–3.2 cm). A southern and lowland frog. Dark stripe on thigh usually clean-cut and between two well-defined light stripes; anal warts present (Fig. 100). Head pointed and hind legs proportionately longer than in the Northern Cricket Frog. Amount of webbing on toes less than in the northern species; the 1st toe is partly free of webbing and the 4th (longest) toe has the last three joints (phalanges) free (Fig. 101).

Chiefly a frog of the lowlands, of Coastal Plain bogs and ponds and river-bottom swamps. It follows river valleys northward into more upland regions, however. VOICE: Like a rattle or metal clicker — *gick, gick, gick, gick,* etc., in rapid succession. Breeds February to October, the actual time depending largely on rains. RANGE: Se. Va. to Gulf Coast and Mississippi R.

FLORIDA CRICKET FROG *Acris gryllus dorsalis* **FIG. 100**
IDENTIFICATION: ⅝–1 in. (1.6–2.5 cm). Similar to the Southern Cricket Frog except that there are *two* dark lines on rear of thigh and *no* anal warts.

A diminutive frog that makes its presence known by its clicking call. Breeding may occur during any month of the year. RANGE: Se. Ga., extr. sw. Ga., and sw. Ala. south to s. tip of Fla.

NORTHERN CRICKET FROG *Acris crepitans crepitans* **PL. 46**
IDENTIFICATION: ⅝–1⅜ in. (1.6–3.5 cm). A northern and upland frog. Dark stripe on thigh often not clean-cut, and it may have ragged

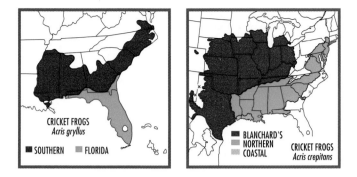

CRICKET FROGS
Acris gryllus
■ SOUTHERN ■ FLORIDA

■ BLANCHARD'S
■ NORTHERN
▓ COASTAL
CRICKET FROGS
Acris crepitans

edges (Fig. 100). Head blunt. Hind leg *short*; when it is extended forward along side of body the heel usually fails to reach snout. In the Southern Cricket Frog, heel usually extends beyond snout, but this is an average character and should not be relied upon in itself for separating these two species. Consider geographic origin of the specimen and check amount of webbing on hind foot. In the northern species the 1st toe is completely webbed and only 1½ to 2 joints (phalanges) of the 4th (longest) toe are free (Fig. 101). **VOICE:** *Gick, gick, gick, gick*, etc. Like two pebbles being clicked together, slowly at first but picking up speed and continuing for 20–30 or more beats. Breeds April to July; in northern part

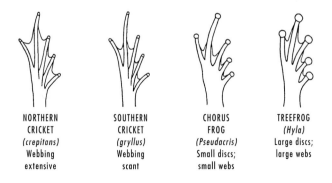

NORTHERN
CRICKET
(crepitans)
Webbing
extensive

SOUTHERN
CRICKET
(gryllus)
Webbing
scant

CHORUS
FROG
(Pseudacris)
Small discs;
small webs

TREEFROG
(Hyla)
Large discs;
large webs

Fig. 101. *Webbing and toe discs of two species of Cricket Frogs (Acris), and of Chorus Frogs and Treefrogs.*

of range this is one of the last frogs to get into full chorus. **RANGE:** Se. N.Y. to the Fla. panhandle and e. Texas; extinct on Long Island; an isolated record in S.C. **SUBSPECIES:** COASTAL CRICKET FROG, *Acris c. paludicola*. A smooth-skinned, distinctly pinkish frog overall, with an obscure dorsal pattern. Toe pads large; belly and throat pink, the latter not darkened during the breeding season in males as they are on the throats of males of the other subspecies. A resident of shallow pools in coastal marshes from sw. La. to se. Texas.

BLANCHARD'S CRICKET FROG PL. 46

Acris crepitans blanchardi

IDENTIFICATION: ⅝–1 ½ in. (1.6–3.8 cm). The western member of the group. Wartier, heavier, and bulkier than other Cricket Frogs. Dark stripe on thigh ragged (not clean-cut) and blending with the dark pigment above it and in the anal region. General coloration usually some shade of light brown or gray, with a tendency toward uniformity instead of the wide variety of strongly contrasting color patterns that are so prevalent in the other forms. Tadpole: see Fig. 118.

Named for Frank Nelson Blanchard, a herpetologist at the University of Michigan. **VOICE:** Like the clicking of pebbles in rapid succession. Breeds from February in southern part of range to late July farther north. **RANGE:** Mich. and Ohio to Nebr., extr. e. Colo., and most of Texas; the Pecos R. Valley in N.M. and the Río Sabinas Valley in Coahuila; an isolated colony in ne. Colo.; scattered records in Minn., N.M., and Texas.

An adult Blanchard's Cricket Frog from Riley County, Kansas. A chorus of this frog sounds like someone vigorously shaking a bag of marbles.

As their name implies, Treefrogs (or tree "toads") are well adapted for an arboreal existence. Their toes end in adhesive discs, and their long limbs and digits help them cling to twigs and bark. But only a few of them ascend high into trees. More common habitats include brushy thickets, swampland vegetation, moist woodlands, or even on the ground or burrowed in it.

Color changes are pronounced in some species, and the same frog may be gray at one time and green or brown at another, either patterned or plain-colored, depending on conditions of light, moisture, temperature, stress, or general activity. The young of several of the species may exhibit a plain bright green livery for long periods of time, rendering it difficult to tell them apart. It is sometimes helpful to leave a Treefrog undisturbed in a collecting bottle or, preferably, a terrarium for a few days; it eventually may change its pattern and coloration to match one of the illustrations on Pl. 47. Some species of Treefrogs have distinctive markings or coloration on the concealed surfaces of their hind legs, thus making capture imperative for close examination.

Chorus Frogs are often mistaken for Treefrogs, but their toe discs are smaller and the webbing between the toes is less well developed (Fig. 101).

Male Treefrogs have a vocal sac that looks like a round balloon under the throat when inflated. The only exceptions among the species in our area are the Mexican and Cuban Treefrogs, in which the single sac inflates more to each side than in the middle, thus producing a suggestion of a double sac.

Many captive Treefrogs will survive in terrariums for long periods of time if they are given a variety of live insects and other invertebrates to eat. Members of the genus *Hyla* occur virtually throughout the range of the entire Family Hylidae, except in Australia and New Guinea.

PINE BARRENS TREEFROG *Hyla andersonii* PL. 47

IDENTIFICATION: 1 ⅛–1 ¾ in. (2.8–4.4 cm); record 2 in. (5.1 cm). The lavender stripes, bordered by white and set against green make this beautiful little frog easy to identify. Considerable orange on concealed surfaces of legs.

A resident of the swamps, bogs, and brown, acid waters of the New Jersey pine barrens and the pocosins (shrub bogs) of the Carolinas. Rarely seen, however, unless one follows the call of a singing male to its source. **VOICE:** A nasal *quonk-quonk-quonk* repeated at a rate of about 25 times in 20 seconds (on warm nights; more slowly on cooler ones). Call similar to that of Green

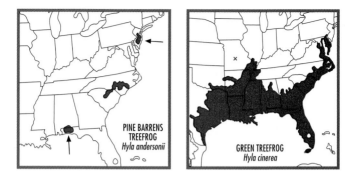

PINE BARRENS
TREEFROG
Hyla andersonii

GREEN TREEFROG
Hyla cinerea

Treefrog but lower in pitch and not audible for so great a distance. Breeds in late spring in New Jersey and from April to September farther south. **RANGE:** S. N.J.; se. N.C. and adj. S.C.; also occurs in the Fla. panhandle and extr. s.-cen. Ala.

GREEN TREEFROG *Hyla cinerea*   PL. 47

IDENTIFICATION: 1¼–2¼ in. (3.2–5.7 cm.); record 2½ in. (6.4 cm). Usually bright green, but the coloration is variable; it may be nearly yellow, as it often is when the frog is calling, or a dull greenish- or slate gray, as when it is hidden and inactive during periods of cool weather. Length of white or yellowish stripe along the side also variable; commonly it extends nearly to groin but may terminate farther forward or be longer on one side of body than on other. In some populations the lateral stripe may be very short or lacking entirely. The two Green Treefrogs illustrated on Pl. 47 represent the extremes of pattern. Many individuals have tiny, golden spots on their backs.

This is a "rain frog," a vernacular name shared by other members of the group, especially the Squirrel Treefrog. Some country people believe these amphibians are weather prophets, but, although they tend to sing mostly during damp weather, they may call as lustily before fair weather as before foul. Habitats include swamps, borders of lakes and streams, floating vegetation, or in fact almost any place well supplied with water or dampness. Occasionally enters brackish water. Green Treefrogs are frequent visitors to windows at night, where they seek insects attracted by lights. **SIMILAR SPECIES:** (1) Pine Barrens Treefrog is ornamented with lavender stripes and much orange on concealed surfaces of legs. (2) Squirrel Treefrog occasionally has a light lateral stripe, but the stripe's lower border is indistinct and not sharply defined as in

A calling Green Treefrog that has inhaled so much air to fill its vocal sac that even its abdomen is slightly expanded. The light lateral stripe varies in length and may be short or even absent in some individuals.

Green Treefrog; also Squirrel Treefrog is usually *brown* and will eventually return to that color from its temporary green livery. (3) Treefrogs of many species, especially young ones, may turn bright green, but most of them lack light stripes. **VOICE:** Bell-like, and the origin of the local names of "bell frog" and "cowbell frog." Call has a ringing quality, but is best expressed as *queenk-queenk-queenk* with a nasal inflection; may be repeated as many as 75 times a minute. Breeding calls may be heard from March to October in the far South (in spring farther north); the congresses are sometimes enormous, with hundreds or even thousands of males participating. **RANGE:** Delmarva Peninsula to southern tip of Fla. and on some of Keys; west through Gulf Coastal Plain to e. and s. Texas; north to extr. s. Ill.; isolated colony in s.-cen. Mo. Introduced in northwestern corner of P.R. **NOTE:** The Green and Barking Treefrogs hybridize in some areas; the offspring are stout-bodied, as in the Barking Treefrog, but they resemble the Green Treefrog in pattern.

BARKING TREEFROG
Hyla gratiosa   **PL. 47**

IDENTIFICATION: 2–2⅝ in. (5.1–6.7 cm); record 2¾ in. (7 cm). One of the larger, stouter Treefrogs —and the spottiest. The profuse round, dark markings usually persist, at least in part, through the various color changes, but they may disappear when the frog turns dark

BARKING TREEFROG
Hyla gratiosa

An adult Barking Treefrog from Marion County, Florida. A large colorful member of the treefrog genus Hyla.

brown or bright green or fades to tones of pale gray or yellow. At least some green pigment usually in evidence.

Both a high climber and a burrower, but also uses other habitats between these two extremes. In hot, dry weather, often takes shelter in sand or soil beneath roots or clumps of grass or other vegetation. **SIMILAR SPECIES:** Some Southern Leopard Frogs are profusely spotted, but they lack adhesive discs on toes. **VOICE:** This frog gets its name from its voice. A barking call of nine or ten raucous syllables is uttered from high in the treetops. The breeding call, given in or close to the water, is a single explosive *doonk* or *toonk* often repeated at intervals of one or two seconds. Breeds March to August. **RANGE:** N.C. to s. Fla. and e. La., chiefly in the Coastal Plain but also in many upland areas; isolated colonies in Del. and adj. Md., sw. Ky. and adj. Tenn., and in se. Va.; introduced in s. N.J., but now probably extinct there.

PINE WOODS TREEFROG *Hyla femoralis* PL. 47; FIG. 100

IDENTIFICATION: 1–1½ in. (2.5–3.8 cm); record 1¾ in. (4.4 cm). Here's a frog that simply must be caught to assure identification. There is a row of small orange, yellow, or whitish spots on the rear of the thigh (Fig. 100), but these are concealed when the animal is at rest, and when it leaps you cannot see them either. The deep reddish brown coloration is perhaps most common, but this frog may also be gray or greenish gray at times.

An arboreal acrobat that climbs high in the trees, but also frequents lower levels, even the ground. Commonly found in pine flatwoods and in or near cypress swamps. **SIMILAR SPECIES:** (1) Several other Treefrogs strongly resemble this one, but they all lack light spots on concealed portion of thigh. (2) Gray Treefrog and

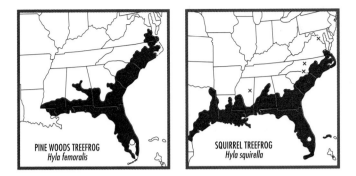

PINE WOODS TREEFROG
Hyla femoralis

SQUIRREL TREEFROG
Hyla squirella

Bird-voiced Treefrog both have a light spot below eye. **VOICE:** The "dot-and-dash" frog. Morse code done with a snore — no messages, but with the abandon of an amateur playing with a telegraph key. A large chorus sounds like a series of riveting machines all operating at once. Breeding calls may he heard from April to early September (March to October in Florida). **RANGE:** Coastal Plain, se. Va. to s. Fla. and e. La.

SQUIRREL TREEFROG *Hyla squirella*   PL. 47

IDENTIFICATION: ⅞–1⅝ in. (2.2–4.1 cm). Like a "chameleon" in its myriad variations of coloration and pattern. The same frog may be brown at one time and green at another, plain or spotted. Often, but not always, there is a spot or dark bar between the eyes. Also, there may be a light stripe along side of body. Identify by a process of elimination, ruling out any species it couldn't be. You had better catch it first!

Called a "rain frog" in many parts of the South. A ubiquitous animal that may appear suddenly in and around houses, even "dropping from the sky" as it falls from a tree during acrobatics while in pursuit of insects. Found in gardens, weed or brush tangles, woods, trees, vines — in fact, almost anywhere close to moisture, food, and a hiding place. **SIMILAR SPECIES:** (1) Pine Woods Treefrog has light, round spots on rear of thigh, and Cricket Frogs have hidden stripes on theirs (Fig. 100). (2) Gray and Bird-voiced Treefrogs have a light spot beneath each eye. (3) Spring Peeper has an X on its back. (4) Cuban Treefrog, in addition to its large size, is warty and has very large toe discs. (5) Ornate Chorus Frog sports a black spot on its flanks, and additional ones rise from groin. (6) Chorus Frogs, in general, have smaller toe discs and less webbing than Treefrogs (Fig. 101). (7) See also Green

Treefrog. **VOICE:** Ducklike, but slightly more nasal. A harsh trill or rasp repeated at a rate of 15–20 times in 10 seconds (during height of breeding season). The so-called rain call, usually voiced away from water, is a scolding rasp, quite squirrel-like. Breeds from March to October in Florida, April to August farther north. **RANGE:** Se. Va. to Fla. Keys; west to La. and along Texas coast to well south of Corpus Christi Bay; isolated records in Miss., N.C., and Va.; introduced and established on Grand Bahama in the Bahama Is.

GRAY TREEFROG *Hyla versicolor* and *Hyla chrysoscelis*   PL. 47

IDENTIFICATION: 1¼–2 in. (3.2–5.1 cm); record 2⅜ in. (6 cm). These two lookalike species of Treefrogs have long masqueraded as one. Only by their voices can you tell them apart in the field. For practical purposes it is sufficient to identify either species as a Gray Treefrog. The following characteristics are shared by both.

Size moderately large in comparison with most other members of the Treefrog family within our area. Coloration normally gray (or green), but subject to many variations. An individual frog may be gray, brown, green, pearl-gray, or even almost white, depending, at least in part, on changes in its activities or environment. Light spot beneath eye usually discernible. Concealed surfaces of hind legs *bright orange* (or golden yellow) mottled with black. Skin of back quite warty for a Treefrog, the warts very numerous but not so prominent or protuberant as in the average toad (*Bufo*). Tadpole: see Fig. 119.

Not often seen on ground or at water's edge, except in breeding season. Many forage aloft, chiefly in relatively small trees or shrubs that are near or actually standing in shallow bodies of water. Extremely well camouflaged when clinging to bark of a rough tree trunk, and often their presence is known only when they call. **SIMILAR SPECIES:** (1) Bird-voiced Treefrog closely resembles

GRAY TREEFROGS
Hyla versicolor
Hyla chrysoscelis
(composite range)

members of Gray Treefrog complex, but concealed surfaces of hind legs are washed with green or yellowish white instead of orange. Also, Bird-voiced has a rapid, ringing call instead of a trill. (2) The Squirrel Treefrog also resembles Gray Treefrog when both are in green livery; if in doubt allow frog to rest quietly until colors change or details of pattern appear. (3) See Canyon

An adult Gray Treefrog from Valley Forge, Pennsylvania. Recent studies have shown that two cryptic species occur in North America, but they are very difficult to identify except in the laboratory.

Treefrog, which occurs west of range of Gray Treefrog. **VOICE:** The call of the Gray Treefrog (without discrimination between the two species) has been variously likened to a musical trill, a resonant, flutelike trill, or a sound similar to the call of the red-bellied woodpecker. The calls of the two species are best described as a slow trill (*versicolor*) and a fast, higher-pitched trill (*chrysoscelis*). When the two are heard together, it is sometimes possible to distinguish between the males, but positive identification of the calls at other times depends on making tape recordings and analyzing them in the laboratory in conjunction with temperature data obtained in the field. The speed of the trills in both species is slowed when the weather is cool. **RANGE:** S. Me. to n. Fla. and west to s. Manitoba and cen. Texas; isolated colony in New Brunswick. The general limits of the complex as a whole are probably shown fairly accurately on the map, but detailed delineation of the distributional patterns of these two sympatric, sibling species must await (a) the accumulation and analysis of calls recorded in the field in a large number of localities and (b) the use of laboratory techniques to determine the chromosome numbers of individual frogs (including females); *versicolor* (tetraploid) has twice as many chromosomes as *chrysoscelis* (diploid).

BIRD-VOICED TREEFROG   *Hyla avivoca*   PL. 47

IDENTIFICATION: 1⅛–1¾ in. (2.8–4.4 cm); record 2¹⁄₁₆ in. (5.2 cm). A junior edition of the Gray Treefrog. Both species have a light spot under the eye, but in the Bird-voiced Treefrog the *concealed* portions of the hind legs are washed with pale *yellowish green to greenish- or yellowish white* instead of orange. General dorsal coloration gray, brown, or green.

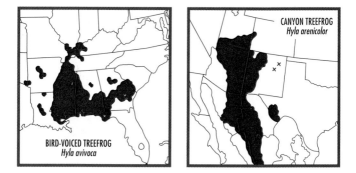

CANYON TREEFROG
Hyla arenicolor

BIRD-VOICED TREEFROG
Hyla avivoca

A resident of permanent wooded swamps—of tupelo, cypress, birch, buttonbush, and vine tangles—along many of the creeks and larger waterways of the South. **SIMILAR SPECIES:** See Gray Treefrog. **VOICE:** A ringing, birdlike whistle, *wit-wit-wit-wit* rapidly repeated 20 or more times. A single frog calling reminds one of whistling for a dog. Breeds from spring to late summer. **RANGE:** Extr. s. Ill. to La. and east to the Fla. panhandle, e.-cen. Ga. and adj. S.C.; isolated colonies in Ga., Ala., La., Ark., and Okla.

CANYON TREEFROG *Hyla arenicolor*   PL. 47

IDENTIFICATION: 1¼–2 in. (3.2–5.1 cm); record 2¼ in. (5.7 cm). A Treefrog of boulder-strewn canyon creeks of the arid Southwest and Mexico. General coloration brownish gray, often tinted with pink. Dorsal markings varying from dark or medium brown to greenish. Concealed surfaces of hind limbs orange-yellow. A dark bar below eye. Skin moderately rough. *Male:* Throat gray, brown, or black.

This well-camouflaged frog is sometimes seen at night perched on or between boulders along small, intermittent streams that retain at least some water throughout the year. Essentially an upland species in our area, but it follows streams, such as Limpia Creek in the Davis Mountains of western Texas, into lower and more arid terrain. **VOICE:** A series of short nasal notes—*ah-ah-ah-ah*—that sound much as a Gray Treefrog would if it called from inside a tin can. Breeds March to July or during autumn rains in drier parts of range. **RANGE:** Chisos and Davis mts. and canyons of Trans-Pecos Texas; s. Utah and extr. w. Colo. to Oaxaca; isolated records in ne. N.M.

CUBAN TREEFROG *Osteopilus septentrionalis*   PL. 47

IDENTIFICATION: Males 1½–3½ in. (3.8–9 cm); females 2–5 in. (5.1–12.5 cm); record 5½ in. (14 cm). An immigrant from the

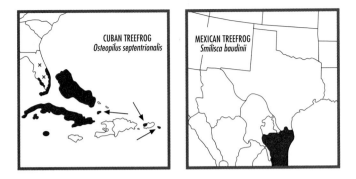

CUBAN TREEFROG
Osteopilus septentrionalis

MEXICAN TREEFROG
Smilisca baudinii

West Indies and the largest of our Treefrogs. The extra large toe discs and warty skin suffice for distinguishing adults from other frogs, but smaller specimens may offer trouble. This species has no line or stripe, light or dark, running through or under eye. General coloration variable, mostly through greens and bronzes. Tadpole: see Fig. 120.

Largely nocturnal, sometimes appearing near lights in search of insects. By day this large amphibian hides where there is moisture—in cisterns, drains, cellars, the axils of palms or banana trees, even on porches of houses in jardinieres or other containers holding potted plants that are watered daily. Don't put a Cuban Treefrog in a cage or terrarium with smaller frogs or toads. It may eat them. **VOICE:** Very suggestive of the snoring rasp of the Southern Leopard Frog, but less vigorous and usually higher pitched. The call has been described as a rasping snarl, the individual notes of which may vary at least through an octave. Vocal sac of male inflates toward each side to suggest a double pouch. **RANGE:** S. Fla. and the Keys; isolated records in peninsular Fla.; Cuba and the Isla de Pinos, the Bahamas and Cayman Is.; introduced on P.R. and St. Croix.

MEXICAN TREEFROG *Smilisca baudinii*   PL. 47

IDENTIFICATION: 2–2¾ in. (5.1–7 cm); record 3⁹⁄₁₆ in. (9 cm). The most constant markings are the light spot beneath the eye, a light spot at the base of the arm, and a dark patch running backward from the eardrum onto the shoulder. The dark patch usually persists during the most extreme color changes, changes that may produce a brown, very dark gray, or gray-green frog or, conversely, a pale yellow or pale gray one. Tadpole: see Fig. 121.

Occurs chiefly in subhumid regions. During dry season takes refuge underground, in damp tree holes, under tree bark or the outer sheaths of banana trees, etc. **VOICE:** Like the starting mechanism of an old car; a series of blurred notes—*heck* or *keck*—sometimes interspersed with chuckles. Also described as a series of short, explosive notes—*wonk-wonk-wonk*. Inflated vocal sac of male consists of a pair of bulges protruding downward and sideward from under throat. Breeds with advent of rain. **RANGE:** Atlantic and Pacific lowlands and adj. areas from extr. s. Texas and s. Sonora to Costa Rica.

CHORUS FROGS: GENUS *Pseudacris*

Many persons hear Chorus Frogs, but few ever see them. In the North these are vernal choristers that respond to the first warm rains as spring moves northward. In the South these are "winter frogs," their breeding season beginning at any time from November to late winter but usually in correlation with *cool* rains. They sing day and night in or near shallow, often temporary, bodies of water, sometimes in the open, but more often concealed in a clump of grass or other vegetation, where they are extremely difficult to find even when they advertise their presence by calling loudly. They are seldom encountered after the breeding season.

These are the "swamp treefrogs" or "swamp cricket frogs," small members of the Treefrog family that climb little and then only into weeds or low shrubs in pursuit of insects. Their toe discs are small, and the toes themselves are only slightly webbed (Fig. 101). A light line along the upper lip is common to most of them. Males have a single round vocal pouch that, when collapsed, is gray or brown over a cream or yellowish ground color.

The genus is strictly North American, ranging from the Gulf of Mexico to New York and southern Ontario in the East and from Arizona almost to the Arctic Circle in the West.

SPRING PEEPER *Pseudacris crucifer* PL. 46

IDENTIFICATION: ¾–1¼ in. (1.9–3.2 cm); record 1½ in. (3.7 cm). The dark cross on the back is usually in the form of an X, but more often than not an imperfect one. This small frog varies through shades of yellow, brown, gray, or olive, but it is not distinctly striped, mottled, or spotted like other members of its genus.

A frog of the woodlands that is especially abundant in areas of brushy second growth or cutover woodlots, if these are near small, temporary or semipermanent ponds or swamps. In general, these small singers tend to form their choral groups where trees or shrubs are standing in the water, or at least nearby. In contrast, other small choristers of both the genera *Pseudacris* and *Hyla* (Treefrogs) often choose open places for calling stations, although there is actually much overlap. Spring Peepers are seldom seen except in the breeding season, but they do occasionally wander through the woods by day in damp or rainy weather. Professional herpetologists, based on laboratory techniques, recently transferred the Spring Peeper from the genus *Hyla* to *Pseudacris*. **SIMILAR SPECIES:** Other members of the genus are distinctly striped, mottled, or spotted, and most have a light line along upper lip; (1) In Mountain Chorus Frog the dorsal markings may

SPRING
PEEPERS
Pseudacris crucifer

■ NORTHERN
■ SOUTHERN

resemble a crude X, but there is usually a well-defined dark triangle between the eyes. (2) Gray and Bird-voiced Treefrogs have a light spot beneath the eye. (3) Pine Woods Treefrog has rounded light spots on rear of thigh (Fig. 100). **VOICE:** A high, piping whistle, a single clear note repeated at intervals of about a second. There is a terminal upward slur, unlike the piping note of the Ornate Chorus Frog, which ends sharply. A large chorus of peepers heard from a distance sounds like sleigh bells. Some specimens utter a trilling peep that may be heard in the background of small choruses. **RANGE:** Canadian Maritime Provinces to n. Fla.; west to se. Manitoba and e. Texas; isolated record in extr. ne. Kans.; introduced in Cuba. **SUBSPECIES:** NORTHERN SPRING PEEPER, *Pseudacris c. crucifer* (Pl. 46). This race, occurring throughout almost all of range of species, is characterized by a plain or virtually plain belly. SOUTHERN SPRING PEEPER, *Pseudacris c. bartramiana*. Similar, but with belly strongly marked with dark spots. S. Ga. and n. Fla.

An adult male Spring Peeper from Missouri. This small amphibian is an enigma to herpetologists, because it exhibits some of the characteristics of Chorus Frogs (Pseudacris) and Treefrogs (Hyla).

Pseudacris triseriata triseriata

IDENTIFICATION: ¾–1½ in. (1.9–3.9 cm). Normally with three dark stripes down the back (Fig. 102). These typically are as broad and strong as the dark lateral stripe that runs from snout to groin and passes through the eye, but they are subject to variation. They may be broken or reduced to rows of dark spots or be lacking altogether. Middle stripe often forks into two parts posteriorly. A dark triangle or other dark figure may be present between eyes. Always a *light line along upper lip.* Dorsal ground color varies from pale gray to dark brown but may also be dull green or olive. Markings are darker gray or brown. Undersurfaces whitish, either plain or with a few dark spots on throat and chest. Tadpole: see Fig. 117.

Shallow bodies of water are required during the breeding season and for the development of tadpoles, but otherwise this frog survives in a wide variety of habitats, some of them surprisingly dry and greatly altered by human activities. Originally this was chiefly a frog of the prairies, but it has expanded its range to include agricultural lands and may even be heard in the environs of large cities and suburban areas, provided pollution is not too severe. **SIMILAR SPECIES:** (1) Spring Peeper *lacks* light line on lip and usually has a dark X on back. (2) Mountain Chorus Frog has only two dark dorsal stripes (Fig. 102), and they curve inward and may unite to form a crude X. (3) Spotted Chorus Frog has bright green spots or stripes. (4) Upland Chorus Frog, with which the Western Chorus Frog intergrades along a broad line through Mississippi Valley, will offer trouble. Both are variable, but the Western *usually* is strongly striped, whereas the Upland *usually* is spotted or weakly striped (Fig. 102). Striped specimens of Upland Chorus Frog have stripes rather thin and frequently broken, but the

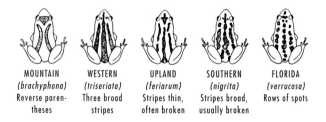

MOUNTAIN	WESTERN	UPLAND	SOUTHERN	FLORIDA
(brachyphona)	(triseriata)	(feriarum)	(nigrita)	(verrucosa)
Reverse paren-	Three broad	Stripes thin,	Stripes broad,	Rows of spots
theses	stripes	often broken	usually broken	

Fig. 102. Dorsal patterns of various Chorus Frogs (Pseudacris).

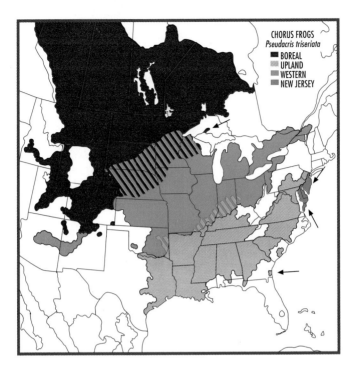

lateral stripe (one passing through eye) is broad and strong and usually points up the weakness of the dorsal pattern. In the Western, length of tibia is considerably less than ¼ length from snout to vent; in the Upland it is approximately half. Geography (point of origin of specimen) may offer best clue to identification (see map above). **VOICE:** A vibrant, regularly repeated *crreek* or *prreep* (roll the *r*'s), speeding up and rising in pitch toward the end. The sound may be roughly imitated by running a finger over approximately the last 20 of the *small* teeth of a good-quality pocket comb, rubbing the shortest teeth last. Breeds from February to June, the latest dates occurring in northernmost parts of range. **RANGE:** Extr. s. Que. and adj. N.Y. to Kans. and Okla.; a disjunct area in N.M. and Ariz.; isolated colony in sw. Okla. **SUBSPECIES:** NEW JERSEY CHORUS FROG, *Pseudacris t. kalmi*. Very similar but averaging more robust and usually with broad, well-defined dorsal stripes. Coastal Plain from Staten Island, N.Y., to southern tip of Delmarva Peninsula.

UPLAND CHORUS FROG

Pseudacris triseriata feriarum

IDENTIFICATION: ¾–1⅜ in. (1.9–3.5 cm); record 1½ in. (3.8 cm). A frog with an extremely variable pattern. The following are constant: (a) light line along the upper lip; (b) dark stripe from snout to groin and passing through eye. On the other hand, the middorsal pattern may be striped, partly striped, spotted—or even lacking. Basically there are three longitudinal dark stripes, but they are usually narrow and often broken up into streaks or rows of small spots (Fig. 102). Sometimes there are small, scattered spots or virtually no dark markings at all. A dark triangle between eyes (or a suggestion of one) is usually present. General coloration brown or gray. Undersurfaces cream-colored but often with dark stipplings on breast. Length of tibia about ½ length from snout to vent.

Grassy swales, moist woodlands, river-bottom swamps, and environs of ponds, bogs, and marshes are included among the habitats. This is an upland frog in the North, but it deeply invades the lowlands in the South. **SIMILAR SPECIES:** (1) In Brimley's Chorus Frog the lateral stripe (one passing through eye) is *black* and chest is boldly spotted. (2) In Southern Chorus Frog there are *black* stripes or rows of spots down back. (3) Ornate Chorus Frog has a black stripe from *snout to shoulder* followed by black spots along the side of body. (4) See also Similar Species under Western Chorus Frog. **VOICE:** A regularly repeated *crreek* or *prreep* similar to that of Western Chorus Frog. Usually calls from fairly open situations, as is also the case among all the other races of *triseriata*. Breeds from February to May in the North; during winter or early spring in the South. **RANGE:** N. N.J. to Fla. panhandle; west to e. Texas and se. Okla.; isolated colonies in coastal S.C. and se. Ga.

BOREAL CHORUS FROG *Pseudacris triseriata maculata* PL. 46

IDENTIFICATION: ¾–1⁷⁄₁₆ in. (1.9–3.7 cm). Northernmost of all the Chorus Frogs and the one with the shortest legs. Length of tibia is noticeably shorter than tibia of Western Chorus Frog, which in pattern and gross appearance is very similar. General coloration brown or greenish. The stripes, especially the middorsal one, may break up into rows of spots.

Short legs in frogs seem to be an adaptation for life in cold climates. Typical specimens have such abbreviated legs that they hop instead of making long leaps like their more southern relatives. This is a frog of marshy environs of far-northern ponds, lakes, and meadows and similar habitats in mountainous areas. **VOICE:** A regularly repeated *prreep, prreep* (roll the r's), much like call of Western Chorus Frog. **RANGE:** N. Ont. to vicinity of Great

Bear Lake in nw. Canada; south to Utah and n. N.M. and intergrading with Western Chorus Frog from n. Wisc. to Neb.; isolated colonies in se. Colo., ne. N.M., and on the n. border of N.M. and Ariz.

CHORUS FROGS
Pseudacris nigrita
■ SOUTHERN
▨ FLORIDA

SOUTHERN CHORUS FROG — PL. 46; FIG. 102
Pseudacris nigrita nigrita

IDENTIFICATION: ¾–1¼ in. (1.9–3.2 cm). Darkest of all the Chorus Frogs—the markings are usually black. The black stripe from snout to groin (and passing through eye) is prominent and continuous, but the three dorsal stripes have a strong tendency to break up into rows of large spots, especially the middle one, which usually forks into two rows posteriorly (Fig. 102). Ground color light gray, tan, or silvery and often so pale as to appear almost white in contrast with black markings. *Prominent white line along lip.* The snout in this frog and Florida Chorus Frog tends to be more pointed than snouts of other Chorus Frogs.

Habitats include pine flatwoods, wet meadows, roadside ditches, moist woodlands, etc. **SIMILAR SPECIES:** Cricket Frogs have prominent stripes on rear of thigh (Fig. 100). **VOICE:** A trill resembling the sound of a ratchet but with a musical quality. About 8 or 10 beats to each trill; trills are repeated at regular intervals. Breeds November to April. **RANGE:** E. N.C. to n. Fla. and se. Miss.

FLORIDA CHORUS FROG — PL. 46; FIG. 102
Pseudacris nigrita verrucosa

IDENTIFICATION: ¾–1¼ in. (1.9–3.2 cm). The only Chorus Frog with the upper lip chiefly black instead of white. Normally there is a series of black spots on the lip, but these may join together so that the light pigment is much reduced. The dark dorsal spots, normally arranged in three rows, seldom run together (Fig. 102).

A resident of varied habitats—ditches, swales, flatwoods ponds, the prairie lands of south-central Florida, and pine forests and sinkholes on the eastern edge of the Everglades. **SIMILAR SPECIES:** (1) Florida Cricket Frog has conspicuous stripes on rear of thigh (Fig. 100). (2) Young River Frogs have strongly webbed toes. **VOICE:** A regularly repeated rasping trill. Breeding is usually associated with fairly heavy rains and may occur during any month of year. **RANGE:** Fla. Peninsula.

An adult Spotted Chorus Frog from Butler County, Kansas. This is the gem of the prairie, a small brightly colored harbinger of spring on the western plains.

SPOTTED CHORUS FROG *Pseudacris clarkii* **PL. 46**

IDENTIFICATION: ¾–1¼ in. (1.9–3.2 cm). The only Chorus Frog garbed with patches of bright *green* that are rimmed with black. Two extremes of pattern are illustrated. Spotted specimens are by far the more common, and the spots are normally scattered, sometimes very numerous, and not arranged in rows. When stripes are present, they tend to be longitudinal. Almost always a *green triangle between eyes.* Dorsal ground color pale gray to grayish olive. Belly plain white.

An amphibian of the grassland prairies. Inactive during dry weather, but even when conditions of moisture are optimum it normally ventures abroad only at night or in the early evening. **SIMILAR SPECIES:** (1) Western Chorus Frog is normally brown or gray — but sometimes dull green or olive—and is patterned with stripes or with dark spots arranged in three longitudinal rows. (2) Strecker's Chorus Frog is larger, toadlike, and with a *black* stripe from snout to shoulder; it also usually has a dark spot below eye. (3) In the very much larger Crawfish Frog the spots are dark with *light* borders. **VOICE:** A rasping trill, *wrrank-wrrank-wrrank,* etc., rapidly repeated 20–30 or more times. Interval between notes is about equal to duration of notes themselves. Two males singing together, but with their calls alternating, sound like rapid sawing. Peak of season in April and May, but breeding may follow rains in virtually any month in southern part of range. **RANGE:** Cen. Kans. to s. Texas and extr. ne. Tamaulipas.

BRIMLEY'S CHORUS FROG *Pseudacris brimleyi* **PL. 46**

IDENTIFICATION: 1–1¼ in. (2.5–3.2 cm). A very changeable little frog that may fade to virtually plain brownish yellow except for the

SPOTTED CHORUS FROG
Pseudacris clarkii

BRIMLEY'S CHORUS FROG
Pseudacris brimleyi

bold black stripe down each side of the body. This stripe, extending without interruption from snout to groin and passing through eye, is always strongly evident. Middorsal stripes brown or gray and frequently much less evident than in frog shown on Pl. 46. Undersurfaces yellow and normally there are *dark spots on chest*. Markings on legs tend strongly to be longitudinal instead of forming crossbands. No dark triangle between eyes.

An early singer in the marshes, swamps, ditches, and wet open woods of the Coastal Plain. Named for Clement S. Brimley, North Carolina naturalist. **SIMILAR SPECIES:** (1) In Ornate Chorus Frog, there are bold black spots on sides and rising from groin. (2) In both Southern and Upland Chorus Frogs, middorsal stripes or spots are usually same color as lateral stripes. (3) See also Little Grass Frog. **VOICE:** A short, rasping trill, lasting less than a second and repeated a dozen times or more. Similar to call of Squirrel Treefrog, but the individual notes are shorter and more strongly accented at end. Breeds from February to April. **RANGE:** Se. Va. to e. Ga.

MOUNTAIN CHORUS FROG   PL. 46; FIG. 102
Pseudacris brachyphona

IDENTIFICATION: 1–1¼ in. (2.5–3.2 cm); record 1½ in. (3.8 cm). The frog with the reversed parentheses (Fig. 102). In some specimens the two curved stripes bend inward so far that they touch at center of back, producing a crude dark X. Occasionally, the stripes may be broken into spots. The dark triangle between the eyes is almost invariably present, and there is a white line on upper lip, as in most Chorus Frogs. Many specimens are "dirty" olive, and thus greener than the one illustrated on Pl. 46. Yellow pigment on concealed and lower surfaces of legs.

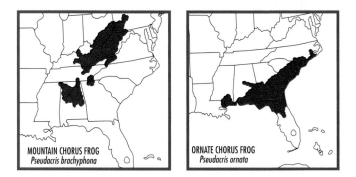

MOUNTAIN CHORUS FROG
Pseudacris brachyphona

ORNATE CHORUS FROG
Pseudacris ornata

Like a miniature Wood Frog in habits, leaping power, and gross appearance. A woodland species ranging upward to elevations of at least 3500 ft. (1100 m), occurring chiefly on forested slopes and hilltops, and often at long distances from water. Breeds in small, shallow bodies of water in woods or at its edge—in ditches, pools along streams or those that form below hillside springs.
SIMILAR SPECIES: (1) Spring Peeper, which normally has a fairly clearcut dark X on back, lacks white line on lip. (2) In both the Upland and Western Chorus Frogs the dorsal pattern consists basically of *three* longitudinal stripes; if stripes are broken into spots, as is often the case, then the spots are usually arranged in *three* rows. (3) Wood Frog has dorsolateral ridges. **VOICE:** A rasp like that of Western Chorus Frog, but given more rapidly, higher in pitch, and more nasal in quality. Sounds like a wagon wheel turning without benefit of lubrication. Breeds February to April, depending upon latitude and altitude. **RANGE:** Disjunct. The main portion of the range from sw. Pa. and se. Ohio to n. Tenn.; a second population in n.-cen. Ala. and adj. parts of Tenn. and Miss.; a small area in n. Ga. and adj. se. Tenn. and sw. N.C.

ORNATE CHORUS FROG *Pseudacris ornata* PL. 46
IDENTIFICATION: 1–1¼ in. (2.5–3.2 cm); record 1⁷⁄₁₆ in. (3.7 cm). More like the creation of an imaginative artist than a real live frog. A black, masklike stripe running through the eye. *Dark spots on sides and near groin.* Yellow in groin and numerous small yellow spots on concealed portions of legs. Coloration highly variable— the individual frog may change from almost plain black to silvery white or to the brilliant colors shown on Pl. 46. The reddish brown coloration is the most common. *Young:* Pattern details not well developed.

Habitats include cypress ponds, pine barren ponds, flooded meadows, and flatwoods ditches—plus their environs. **SIMILAR SPECIES:** (1) Strecker's Chorus Frog is larger and stouter, more toadlike, with a particularly stout foreleg and a dark spot below eye. (2) Among all other Chorus Frogs whose ranges overlap this species (Brimley's, Upland, Southern, and Florida), the pattern consists of longitudinal dark stripes or rows of spots, and there are no conspicuous, light-bordered black spots along sides. **VOICE:** A series of shrill, birdlike peeps, or like the ring of a steel chisel struck by a hammer, 65–80 times a minute. Similar to Spring Peeper's call but quicker and lacking Peeper's terminal slur. Calls during late fall, winter, and early spring. **RANGE:** Coastal Plain from N.C. to e. La.; south through much of n. Fla.

STRECKER'S CHORUS FROG *Pseudacris streckeri* PL. 46

IDENTIFICATION: 1–1⅝ in. (2.5–4.1 cm); record 1⅞ in. (4.8 cm). Largest and chubbiest of the Chorus Frogs. The stout hand and forearm are quite toadlike. A dark, often black, masklike stripe from snout to shoulder that may continue as a series of dark spots along the side. General coloration highly variable—gray, hazel, brown, olive, or green, the dorsal markings sometimes even dark brown or black. The dark spot below the eye, present in most specimens, is variable in size; in some it may be little more than an upward bulge from the narrow, dark line bordering the upper lip.

This frog utilizes a wide variety of habitats, including moist, shady woods, rocky ravines, environs of streams, lagoons, and cypress swamps, sand prairies, and even cultivated fields. Named for John K. Strecker, a naturalist long associated with Baylor University. **SIMILAR SPECIES:** In all other Chorus Frogs occurring within the range of this species, there is a *continuous* light line along the upper lip. **VOICE:** Very similar to that of Ornate Chorus Frog. Clear and bell-like, a single and quickly repeated note. In strong chorus the effect is of a rapidly turning pulley wheel badly in need of greasing. Calls during and after rains from November to May, with peak of season in January and February in southern part of range. **RANGE:** Extr. s.-cen. Kans. south through Texas to the Gulf; isolated colonies in s. Texas, w. Okla., and the upper Mississippi R. Valley of Ark., Mo., and Ill. **SUBSPECIES:** STRECKER'S CHORUS FROG, *Pseudacris s. streckeri* (Pl. 46). Dark stripe through eye and dark spots along side of body in strong contrast with ground color; considerable yellow or orange-yellow pigment in groin. Most of range stated above. ILLINOIS CHORUS FROG, *Pseudacris s. illinoensis.* Dark lateral stripe is usually poorly developed in this pale-colored race; little or no yellow pigment in groin and

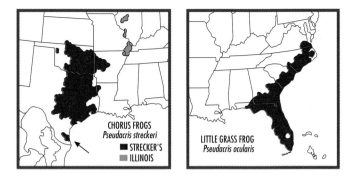

CHORUS FROGS
Pseudacris streckeri
■ STRECKER'S
■ ILLINOIS

LITTLE GRASS FROG
Pseudacris ocularis

dorsum never green. The stout forelimbs are well adapted for burrowing forward in sand. Unlike toads (*Bufo*) and spadefoots
(*Scaphiopus*) that dig with their hind limbs and drop or back into
a hole, the Illinois Chorus Frog uses its hands and goes in head
first. Chiefly in sand prairies and cultivated fields of se. Mo. and
adj. Ark.; also in w.-cen. and sw. Ill.

LITTLE GRASS FROG *Pseudacris ocularis*   PL. 46
IDENTIFICATION: ⁷⁄₁₆–⅝ in. (1.1–1.6 cm); record ¹¹⁄₁₆ in. (1.7 cm). Tini-
est North American frog. The dark line passing through the eye
and onto side of body is constant, and although this may be variable in length, it is the most reliable characteristic. Usually a narrow, dark middorsal stripe starting as a triangle between eyes and
extending to anal region. Another dark, narrow stripe separates
the middorsal color from the lighter ground color of the sides.
General coloration extremely variable—tan, brown, greenish,
pink, or reddish. Chest white or yellowish. Toes slightly webbed.
    An elfin Chorus Frog whose climbing is restricted to low vege-
tation. Moist, grassy environs of ponds and cypress bays are
favorite habitats. **SIMILAR SPECIES:** Most persons upon seeing or cap-
turing this minute amphibian for the first time mistake it for the
young of some other species. (1) A dark lateral stripe passing
through the eye is also the most conspicuous pattern element in
the larger Brimley's Chorus Frog, but that species usually has a
spotted chest. (2) Cricket Frogs have stripes on the rear of their
thighs (Fig. 100). **VOICE:** A tinkling, insectlike call—*set-see, set-see*
—so high and shrill that some people have difficulty hearing it.
May breed any month of year in Fla.; from January to September
farther north. **RANGE:** Se. Va. to southern tip of Fla.; inland to edge
of the Piedmont and to extr. se. Ala.

Narrowmouth Toads: Family Microhylidae

Two closely related genera, found only in North and Central America, represent this family in our area. These are *Gastrophryne* (Narrowmouth Toads) and *Hypopachus* (Sheep Frogs). They are small, plump amphibians with short limbs, pointed heads, and a *fold of skin across the back of the head*. Males almost always have dark throats, females light ones. They are very secretive, hiding by day but venturing forth at night when the weather is warm and damp. In trying to escape they usually resort to running instead of leaping, but intersperse their gait with short hops of an inch or two or more. Once fully aroused they are difficult to catch, darting into the nearest crack or crevice and disappearing. Food consists very largely of insects, such as small beetles, termites, and especially ants. They are occasionally found at night feeding at the openings of ant hills. The fold of skin across the head can move forward to wipe away any insects that may attack the eyes. Other members of the family occur in Mexico, Central and South America, Africa, Asia, the Indo-Australian archipelago, and northern Australia.

EASTERN NARROWMOUTH TOAD
PL. 45; FIG. 103

Gastrophryne carolinensis

IDENTIFICATION: ⅞–1¼ in. (2.2–3.2 cm); record 1½ in. (3.8 cm). Shape and general appearance alone are usually enough to identify this small frog. (Confusion could only occur in e. Okla., extr. w. Ark., and e. Texas, where the range overlaps that of the Great Plains Narrowmouth Toad.) The general coloration varies through shades of gray, brown, or reddish, and the same frog may

An Eastern Narrowmouth Toad. Members of its group are anomalous and don't resemble the average toad or frog. The body is rotund, the head narrow and sharp-pointed and, as its name implies, the mouth is small.

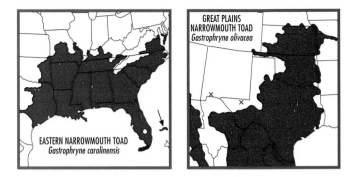

EASTERN NARROWMOUTH TOAD
Gastrophryne carolinensis

GREAT PLAINS
NARROWMOUTH TOAD
Gastrophryne olivacea

change from one color to another, depending on its environment and activities. The pattern illustrated on Pl. 45 — a broad, dark middorsal area flanked by broad light stripes — is very frequently obscured (often completely) by patches, spots, and mottlings of dark or light pigment. *Belly strongly mottled* (Fig. 103). *Key West variants:* Middorsal area only a little darker than the light dorsolateral stripes and separated from them by an irregular dark line. About half the Narrowmouth Toads on Key West and adjacent Keys are marked in this fashion, about one-fourth are tan with virtually no pattern (like *olivacea*), and the rest are similar to mainland specimens, but usually much more reddish. Tadpole: see Fig. 113.

A wide variety of habitats are utilized, but all have two things in common — shelter and moisture. Margins of bodies of water are good places in which to look for them. Usually found by overturning boards, logs, or other shelters, or raking through vegetable debris, abandoned sawdust piles, etc. **SIMILAR SPECIES:** (1) Great Plains Narrowmouth Toad has only a few dark spots on its back or no pattern at all; its venter is unspotted. (2) See also Sheep Frog. **VOICE:** Like the bleat of a lamb and occasionally with a very short preliminary *peep*. The call has a vibrant quality, something like an electric buzzer, and lasts for about ½–4 seconds. Breeding sites are chiefly in shallow water, but deep-water situations also are used if covered by a dense floating mat of vegetation. The males usually call from within clumps of plants with their bodies floating free but with their forelimbs resting on a stem. Rains initiate breeding, which may occur any time between early April and October in the South but is limited to midsummer in northern part of range. **RANGE:** S. Md. to Fla. Keys; west to Mo. and e. Texas; introduced on Grand Bahama I. and at Nassau on New Providence I., Bahama Is.

Gastrophryne olivacea

IDENTIFICATION: ⅞–1½ in. (2.2–3.8 cm); record 1⅝ in. (4.1 cm). The oddly shaped body and the absence, or near absence, of pattern make this an easy frog to identify. Adults vary from tan to gray or olive green, depending on their activities, environment, etc. Dorsum sometimes has scattered small black spots. Belly light and unmarked, or virtually so (Fig. 103). *Young:* Dark brown with a conspicuous dark, leaflike pattern that may occupy half the width of the back. The dark pattern disappears and the general coloration becomes paler as frog grows in size.

A resident of grasslands, marshy sloughs, and rocky, open-wooded slopes. Toward the west it ranges widely through the Chihuahuan and Sonoran deserts. Hides beneath rocks, boards, debris, etc., in damp places or after rains, but also takes shelter in rodent and reptile burrows and in cracks of drying mud. These Narrowmouth Toads sometimes are found in burrows of tarantulas, where they are apparently unmolested and presumably derive protection from the presence of the big spiders. Their skin-gland secretions may be distasteful to potential enemies. Keep your fingers out of your mouth and away from your eyes after handling any Narrowmouth Toad, or you may experience a sharp burning sensation that may last an hour or more. Sometimes called the "ant-eating toad" in reference to its favorite food. **SIMILAR SPECIES:** (1) Eastern Narrowmouth Toad has strongly patterned dorsum, and its belly is mottled with dark pigment. (2) Sheep Frog and Mexican Burrowing Toad have light lines down centers of their backs. **VOICE:** A distinct but very short *peep* followed by a buzz like

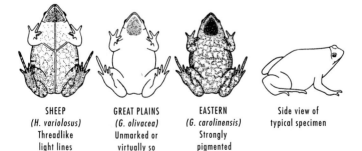

| SHEEP
(*H. variolosus*)
Threadlike
light lines | GREAT PLAINS
(*G. olivacea*)
Unmarked or
virtually so | EASTERN
(*G. carolinensis*)
Strongly
pigmented | Side view of
typical specimen |

Fig. 103. Venters of Sheep Frog (Hypopachus) and Narrowmouth Toads (Gastrophryne).

SHEEP FROG
Hypopachus variolosus

that of an angry bee. To some ears the buzz may sound like the bleat of a sheep but higher in pitch and with much less volume. Duration of call about 1–4 seconds. Breeding begins upon arrival of heavy rains and may take place at any time from March to September. **RANGE:** Se. Neb. and Mo. south to Tamaulipas and San Luis Potosí; west through most of Texas and n. Mexico to w.-cen. Chihuahua and ne. Durango; a large disjunct western population from extr. s.-cen. Ariz. south along the Pacific Coast of Mexico to Nayarit; isolated records in w. Texas and sw. N.M.

SHEEP FROG *Hypopachus variolosus* PL. 45; FIG. 103

IDENTIFICATION: 1–1½ in. (2.5–3.8 cm); record 1¾ in. (4.4 cm). The Narrowmouth Toad with the yellow streak down its back. There is a similar light, threadlike line down the dark mottled belly with extensions outward across the chest toward the arms (Fig. 103). *Two prominent metatarsal tubercles* (spades on the heel). Tadpole: see Fig. 114.

Remains secreted most of the year beneath partly buried objects (such as fallen palm trees), in burrows, or in the trash of packrat nests. **SIMILAR SPECIES:** Both Narrowmouth Toads have only a *single metatarsal tubercle.* **VOICE:** A sheeplike bleat lasting about two seconds and seldom repeated at less than 15-second intervals. Males call while floating in the water, sometimes with their forelimbs resting on a stem. Breeding is initiated by rains or flooding of the frogs' habitat by irrigation. **RANGE:** S. Texas and near Alamos, Sonora; continuous range from cen. Nuevo León and cen. Sinaloa to Costa Rica. (Some of the Mexican populations lack the yellow stripe.)

TRUE FROGS: FAMILY RANIDAE

These are the typical frogs. In general they are long-legged, narrow-waisted, and rather smooth-skinned, with fingers free and toes joined by webs. Check for the presence or absence of dorsolateral ridges (see p. 140), which are raised longitudinal folds of glandular tissue. Males of some species have paired vocal pouches situated at the sides of the throat; others have a pouch or pouches positioned under the throat (Fig. 104). Voice is not entirely restricted to males; females of several species scream loudly when captured, and other vocal sounds have been reported. Breeding males have the bases of their thumbs enlarged, and their forearms are swollen. Sex among adults of the Bullfrog and Green Frog groups is easily determined by looking at the tympanum (see footnote opposite Pl. 48).

The family occurs in all continents except Antarctica. The big genus *Rana,* with about 270 species and most of them in the Old World, is the only North American representative. From this genus come the frogs' legs of commerce. The Leopard and Pickerel Frogs, and the Gopher and Crawfish Frogs, are discussed under separate headings.

BULLFROG *Rana catesbeiana*   **PL. 48; FIGS. 105, 106**
IDENTIFICATION: 3½–6 in. (9–15.2 cm); record 8 in. (20.3 cm). Our largest frog. Plain or nearly plain green above, or with a netlike pattern of gray or brown on a green background. Venter whitish, often mottled with gray and with a yellowish wash, especially on throats of adult males. *No dorsolateral ridges on trunk;* ridges end near eardrum. In the southeastern part of its range the Bullfrog may be heavily patterned with dark gray or brown; some individu-

| Paired external pouches, swelling into spheres above arms | Pouch or pouches internal; throat and sides of body expanding |

Fig. 104. Two types of vocal sacs in True Frogs (Rana).

A *Bullfrog eating a small water snake. Conversely, large water snakes eat bullfrogs. This voracious predator, unwisely introduced in many of the western states, has decimated the local semiaquatic faunas.*

als, especially from Florida, are almost black above and heavily mottled below.

Aquatic and preferring larger bodies of water than most other frogs. A resident of lakes, ponds, bogs, sluggish portions of streams, cattle tanks, etc.; usually seen at water's edge or amidst vegetation or snags among which it can hide. Small streams are also utilized where better habitats are lacking.

This big, voracious amphibian will eat virtually anything that moves and that it can swallow. Humans have been responsible for introducing it into many areas, notably in our western states. Once established in such alien habitats, it promptly reduced or even extirpated local populations of native, semiaquatic amphibians and reptiles, such as frogs of other species, garter snakes, and small turtles. **SIMILAR SPECIES:** (1) Green Frog and Bronze Frog have *dorsolateral* ridges. (2) In Pig Frog, the hind feet are webbed virtually to tips of toes (Fig. 105); the Bullfrog has them less fully webbed, and the 4th toe extends well beyond the web. (3) River Frog has light spots on lips. **VOICE:** A vibrant, sonorous series of bass notes best stated as *jug-o'-rum.* A single internal vocal sac, forming a flattened pouch under the chin when inflated. Breeds late April to July; February to October in the South. **RANGE:** N.S. to cen. Fla.; west to Wisc. and across the Great Plains to the Rockies. The natural western limits are now hopelessly confused because of the introduction of Bullfrogs into a vast number of localities as far west as B.C. and Calif.; also introduced in Mexico, Cuba, Jamaica, etc.

RIVER FROG *Rana heckscheri*   **PL. 48; FIG. 106**
IDENTIFICATION: 3¼–4⅝ in. (8.3–11.7 cm); record 6⅛ in. (15.5 cm). A large, greenish black frog with *conspicuous light spots on lips,*

these usually largest on lower jaw and often producing a scalloped effect along edge of upper lip. Skin often rugose. Venter medium to dark gray (sometimes almost black), marked with light spots or short wavy lines. Usually a pale girdle outlining groin (Fig. 106). *No dorsolateral ridges. Young:* With reddish eyes.

RIVER FROG
Rana heckscheri

A frog of river swamps and swampy shores of ponds and bayous. Adults are not particularly wary and are easily observed at night. **SIMILAR SPECIES:** (1) Pig Frog and Bullfrog lack light lip spots, and their venters are pale with dark markings; Pig Frog also has light line or row of light spots along rear of thigh. (2) Bronze Frog and Green Frog, which often show pale spots on lips, especially in young adults, have *conspicuous dorsolateral ridges.* **VOICE:** A deep, sonorous rolling snore; also a snarling, explosive grunt. Breeds April to August. A single internal vocal pouch. **RANGE:** Se. N.C. to n.-cen. Fla. and se. Miss.

PIG FROG *Rana grylio*   **PL. 48; FIG. 105**

IDENTIFICATION: 3¼–5½ in. (8.3–14 cm); record 6⅜ in. (16.2 cm). A "bullfrog" with a rather narrow and pointed head and with the hind feet fully webbed. The *4th toe webbed virtually to its tip* (Fig.

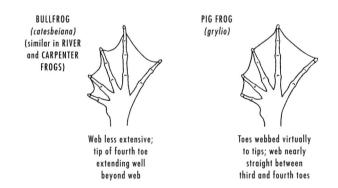

BULLFROG
(catesbeiana)
(similar in RIVER
and CARPENTER
FROGS)

PIG FROG
(grylio)

Web less extensive; tip of fourth toe extending well beyond web

Toes webbed virtually to tips; web nearly straight between third and fourth toes

Fig. 105. *Toe webbing in the Pig Frog and other True Frogs (Rana).*

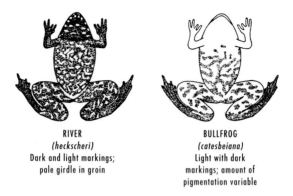

RIVER
(heckscheri)
Dark and light markings;
pale girdle in groin

BULLFROG
(catesbeiana)
Light with dark
markings; amount of
pigmentation variable

Fig. 106. *Venters of River Frog and Bullfrog* (Rana).

105). Pattern and coloration variable; olive to blackish brown and with prominent, scattered dark spots. Venter white or pale yellow with a netlike pattern of brown, dark gray, or black on thighs; a similar dark pattern extending well forward on underside of body in some specimens. A light line or row of light spots across rear of thighs. (Carpenter Frog has similar markings on rear of thighs.) *No dorsolateral ridges. Young:* Superficially like adult Carpenter Frogs.

Strongly aquatic; at the edges of lakes, marshes, and cypress bays, in water-lily prairies, or amid other emergent or floating vegetation. Shy and difficult to approach except at night with the aid of a light. **SIMILAR SPECIES:** (1) In Bullfrog, River, and Carpenter Frogs the webs are less extensive and the *4th toe extends well beyond the web* (Fig. 105). (2) Bronze, Leopard, Pickerel, Crawfish, and Gopher Frogs have *dorsolateral ridges*. **VOICE:** Like the guttural grunt of a pig. Choruses sound like a herd of swine; very large groups produce a continuous roar. Males float high in the water when calling. There is only a single internal vocal pouch, but an extension at each side gives it a three-sectional effect (with throat and sides expanded somewhat like right-hand frog in Fig. 104). **RANGE:** S. S.C. to extr. s. Fla. and extr. se. Texas; introduced on Andros and New Providence is. in the Bahamas.

CARPENTER FROG *Rana virgatipes*   **PL. 48**
IDENTIFICATION: 1 ⅝–2 ⅝ in. (4.1–6.7 cm). The light stripes, four in all, the lack of dorsolateral ridges, and the Coastal Plain distribution

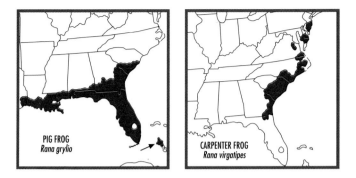

PIG FROG
Rana grylio

CARPENTER FROG
Rana virgatipes

are usually sufficient to identify this frog, except within range of Pig Frog (see Similar Species, below).

Sometimes called the "sphagnum frog" because of a close association with sphagnum bogs. It may also be found in stands of emergent, grasslike vegetation. In such habitats it is difficult to stalk, especially since its color blends so well with the acid, brown-stained waters of the bogs. In more open habitats it may be seen at the water's surface with only the head exposed. When approached, the head vanishes downward but may reappear seconds later a few feet away. **SIMILAR SPECIES:** Young Pig Frogs may have suggestions of pale, longitudinal dorsal stripes, but their 4th toes are webbed virtually to their tips; the 4th toe extends well beyond web in Carpenter Frog (Fig. 105). **VOICE:** *Pu-tunk', pu-tunk', pu-tunk'*. Like two carpenters hitting nails a fraction of a second apart. Several variations on this theme. Large choruses resemble a corps of workers hammering away. Breeds April to August. Vocal pouches paired, spherical when inflated (Fig. 104). **RANGE:** Coastal Plain, s. N.J. to Okefenokee Swamp region of Ga. and adj. Fla.; a disjunct colony in Va.

FLORIDA BOG FROG *Rana okaloosae* PL. 48

IDENTIFICATION: 1⅜–1¾ in. (3.5–4.4 cm); record 1¹⁵⁄₁₆ in. (4.9 cm). Smallest of our True Frogs and the one with the most restricted range. Unspotted dorsum yellow-green to dark brown; distinctive light dorsolateral ridges stop short of groin; scattered light ventrolateral spots. Tympanum brown; upper lip greenish yellow; throat yellow; belly with dark, wormlike markings; eye copper-colored. Toes of each hind foot extend well beyond the extremely reduced webbing.

An amphibian that lives in or along clear, shallow, freshwater seeps and shallow, boggy overflows of small streams, frequently near lush beds of sphagnum moss. **SIMILAR SPECIES:** (1) Bullfrog, Pig

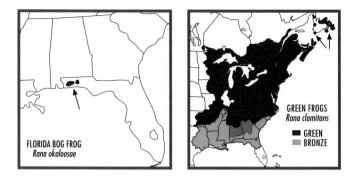

GREEN FROGS
Rana clamitans

■ GREEN
■ BRONZE

FLORIDA BOG FROG
Rana okaloosae

Frog, and River Frog lack dorsolateral ridges and grow to a much larger size. (2) Southern Leopard Frog has distinctive dorsal spots. (3) Bronze Frog is larger, has more extensive webbing on hind feet, and has the center of tympanum elevated. **VOICE:** Call most closely resembles that of the Carpenter Frog but is a series of single, rather than paired, guttural *chucks.* Breeds throughout the warmer months, from April to August. **RANGE:** Known only from Okaloosa and Santa Rosa cos. in western Fla.

BRONZE FROG *Rana clamitans clamitans*   **PL. 48**

IDENTIFICATION: 2⅛–3 in. (5.4–7.5 cm); record 3⅜ in. (8.7 cm). A southern frog with a plain brown or bronzy back. The green of the upper lips is often lacking. Venter white but with dark, wormlike markings. In some males the throat is washed with light yellow. Dorsolateral ridges *ending on body,* not reaching groin. Center of tympanum elevated. *Young:* Numerous dark dorsal spots; venter with heavy brown or black, wormlike markings.

A secretive frog, taking shelter in logs and stumps, in crevices in limestone sinks, etc.; habitats include swamps, bayheads, wet hammocks, and environs of streams. **SIMILAR SPECIES:** (1) The northern subspecies, the Green Frog, has markings in strong contrast with ground color. (2) Bullfrog, Pig, River, and Carpenter Frogs lack dorsolateral ridges. (3) In Pickerel and Southern Leopard Frogs there is a light line on upper jaw, and dorsolateral ridges extend to groin. **VOICE:** A twanging, explosive baritone note; usually a single *clung* or *c'tung,* but sometimes repeated rapidly three or four times. Two (internal) vocal pouches; the throat and sides expand when the frog is calling (Fig. 104). Breeds April to August. **RANGE:** Coastal Plain from s. N.C. to n.-cen. Fla. and west to e. Texas; north in Mississippi Valley to about mouth of Ohio R.

The Bronze Frog is the southern counterpart of the widespread Green Frog. In both subspecies the determination of sex is simplified by the size of the tympanum (eardrum), which is larger than the eye in males.

GREEN FROG *Rana clamitans melanota* PL. 48

IDENTIFICATION: 2¼–3½ in. (5.7–9 cm); record 4¼ in. (10.8 cm). Highly variable — may be more brown than green. Green to greenish brown above, dark brown or grayish dorsal spots or blotches usually present and often numerous. Venter white but usually some dark spots or mottling under legs and head. Throat of adult male bright yellow. Dorsolateral ridges *ending on body,* not reaching groin. Center of tympanum elevated. *Young:* Numerous small dark dorsal spots; venter mottled. Tadpole: see Fig. 124.

An abundant frog that throughout a large part of its range may be found wherever there is shallow fresh water — in springs, rills, creeks, and ditches, and along edges of lakes and ponds. In many regions, however, it is characteristically a frog of brooks and small streams. **SIMILAR SPECIES:** (1) The Bullfrog has no dorsolateral ridges. (2) Leopard and Pickerel Frogs have a light line on upper jaw, and their dorsolateral ridges extend to groin. (3) Check Mink Frog. Green Frogs from Canada and northernmost parts of United States are likely to be very dark, with a profusion of black or dark brown markings. Such frogs *strongly resemble* Mink Frog. **VOICE:** Like a loose banjo string and rather explosive, either a single note or repeated three or four times, the notes progressively less loud. A pair of vocal pouches, not evident externally. When the frog is croaking, the throat and sides of body expand considerably (Fig. 104). Breeds April to August. **RANGE:** Maritime Provinces to N.C.; west to Minn. and e. Okla., but absent from a large part of Ill. and adj. Ind.; introduced in Newf.; also introduced (not shown on map) in British Columbia, Wash., and Utah. **NOTE:** Green Frogs sometimes are blue. The normal yellow pigment component of

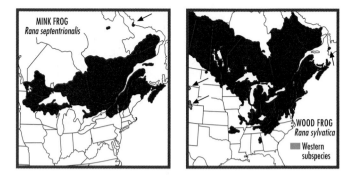

the skin may be sparse or lacking, resulting in a partially or almost completely blue dorsum. Blue Leopard Frogs and Bullfrogs have also been reported.

MINK FROG *Rana septentrionalis*   **PL. 48; FIG. 107**

IDENTIFICATION: 1⅞–2¾ in. (4.8–7 cm); record 3 in. (7.6 cm). The skin produces an odor like the scent of a mink (or rotten onions) when the frog is rubbed or handled roughly. Webbing on toes of hind feet *extends to last joint of 4th toe and to tip of 5th toe.* The dorsolateral ridges may be absent, partially developed, or even prominent. The dorsal pattern may be mottled or spotted (Fig. 107). Dark spots often round and variable in size; in some frogs they dominate the pattern, in others the ground color is most conspicuous. Dark markings on dorsal surfaces of *hind legs* in

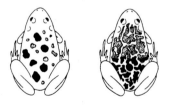

Fig. 107. Variations (diagrammatic) in dorsal patterns of the Mink Frog (Rana septentrionalis), showing spotted and mottled types.

The northern Mink Frog occurs chiefly in eastern and midwestern Canada, although it also enters some of our northern states. It gets its common name because its skin produces an odor said to be like that of a mink.

form of irregular blotches, each with its long axis *more or less paralleling long axis of leg.*

A frog of the North, found along watercourses but especially partial to borders of ponds and lakes or the cold waters near the mouths of streams that empty into them. Look for it where water lilies are plentiful and where it can venture well out from shore by hopping from pad to pad. **SIMILAR SPECIES:** Likely to be confused only with Green Frog, which often occurs abundantly with and strongly resembles Mink Frog. In Green Frog, *hind legs are crossbanded.* That species also lacks minklike odor, always has dorsolateral ridges, and webbing fails to reach tip of 5th toe and barely passes beyond second joint of the 4th. **VOICE:** A burred and rather deep *cut-cut-cut-cut-cut,* more rapid than but suggestive of the Carpenter Frog's "hammer blows." Breeds June to August. Vocal pouches paired. **RANGE:** S. Lab. and Maritime Provinces to Minn. and se. Manitoba; south to n. N.Y. and n. Wisc.; isolated colonies in n. Que. and n. Lab.

WOOD FROG *Rana sylvatica* PL. 48

IDENTIFICATION: 1 ⅜–2 ¾ in. (3.5–7 cm); record 3 ¼ in. (8.3 cm). The frog with the robber's mask. A dark patch extending backward from the eye is always discernible despite pronounced variations in coloration of the body, even in the same specimen; the gamut runs from pink through various shades of brown to almost black. Specimens from far northern localities (Quebec to British Columbia and Alaska to as far south as Colorado) may have a prominent, light middorsal stripe. Toward the northern portions of the range, the hind legs of the Wood Frog become proportion-

An adult Wood Frog from Indiana. Note the dark mask through the eye, characteristic of this frog.

ately shorter, and specimens resemble toads in appearance and hopping abilities. Tadpole: see Fig. 122.

Usually encountered in or near moist wooded areas in United States and Canada; often wanders considerable distances from water. In the far North it may occur wherever there is shallow water for breeding, even in tundra ponds. **VOICE:** A hoarse clacking sound that suggests the quack of a duck. Has little carrying power. Shorter, less loud and less deep, but otherwise resembling voice of Northern Leopard Frog. Appears very early, often heard calling before ice is completely off the ponds. An explosive breeder, the eggs being laid all in the course of a very few days and the adults then disappearing from the ponds instead of lingering, sometimes for weeks, as do many other kinds of frogs. Paired lateral vocal sacs. **RANGE:** Lab. to Alaska; south in the East to the southern Appalachians. Isolated colonies in the Central Highlands, e.-cen. Ala., nw. N.D., and w. Newf. Ranges farther north than any other North American amphibian or reptile. Western subspecies.

LEOPARD AND PICKEREL FROGS: *Rana pipiens,*
Rana utricularia, AND THEIR RELATIVES; *Rana palustris*

Five species of frogs belonging to this group, all medium in size and strongly spotted, occur within our area. They maintain their identities in virtually all localities, even where they occur together, but hybridization between some pairs of species has been reported in a few places. The Pickerel Frog, with its squarish spots and bright orange or yellow on the concealed surfaces of the hind legs, can usually be identified with ease. The four Leopard

Frogs are another matter, but fortunately their ranges are almost mutually exclusive, and geography—knowing the place where the specimen was collected or observed—is very helpful. Check the ranges (see maps on pp. 567 and 569), and go on from there.

The dorsolateral folds are continuous to the groin in two of the Leopard Frogs; they are interrupted just anterior to the groin and are offset inward in the other two (Fig. 108). Further separation of the members of the group depends on examination of males or listening to their mating calls. When the vocal sacs are at rest, as they are most of the time, they are invisible in the Northern Leopard Frog, but in the other three species the area surrounding the sac is differentiated by the presence of dark pigment or a roughening of the skin, or the collapsed sac may be clearly visible. (When inflated, the vocal sacs form paired pouches in all the Leopard Frogs—Fig. 104.) Mating calls, with approximate pulse rates at 60°F (15.5°C), are given for each of the four Leopard Frogs in the accounts that follow. (The rates are more rapid at higher temperatures and less so at lower ones.) Most males in two of the species have vestigial oviducts, whereas males of the other two species lack them. Dissection is required, of course, to check this additional means of identification.

The classification of Leopard Frogs has achieved some stability in the last decade and a half. Studies are still needed, however, on their distribution and ecology. Where two species occur in the same general geographic area, do they normally occupy distinctive habitats? Have they been brought together in some places, where they may hybridize, as a result of the human disturbance of habitats? Why are Leopard Frogs apparently absent from many sizable areas where *Rana palustris* is widespread, whereas they occur abundantly with the Pickerel Frog in a large number of oth-

Interrupted and
inset medially
(blairi and
berlandieri)

Not interrupted
near groin
(pipiens and
utricularia)

Fig. 108. *Dorsolateral ridges in four species of Leopard Frogs* (Rana).

er localities? Also, taxonomic studies are needed to determine the status of populations of Leopard Frogs in Florida.

NORTHERN LEOPARD FROG *Rana pipiens* PL. 48; FIG. 108

IDENTIFICATION: 2–3¼ in. (5.1–9 cm); record 4⅜ in. (11.1 cm). A brown or green frog with two or three rows of irregularly placed dark spots between conspicuous dorsolateral ridges. Spots *rounded and with light borders;* adjacent spots may run together. Numerous additional rounded dark spots on sides. A light line on upper jaw. *No* distinct light spot on center of tympanum. *Male:* Vocal sacs visible only when calling; vestigial oviducts usually present. Tadpole: see Fig. 123.

In parts of Minnesota and adjacent states, a small percentage of the Leopard Frog population consists of two aberrant types of patterns: (a) black spots greatly reduced in number or even completely absent, except for a spot behind each elbow; or (b) ground color between spots strongly invaded by dark pigment. These were once thought to be subspecies, but they are merely mutations of the Northern Leopard Frog. The spotted one looks superficially like the Northern Crawfish Frog.

This is the "meadow frog," at least in summertime, a name earned by its wanderings well away from water. Leopard Frogs have long been used as laboratory animals. **SIMILAR SPECIES:** (1) Pickerel Frog has squarish dark spots, and concealed surfaces of its hind legs are bright yellow or orange. (2) Crawfish Frog is squat and stubby in appearance. (3) In other species of Leopard Frogs, vocal sacs, when at rest, are visible in males. **VOICE:** Mating call a long, deep rattling snore interspersed with clucking grunts that may be single or of two or more syllables; call duration more than

An adult Northern Leopard Frog. Once the common frog dissected in high school and college biological classes, this amphibian is now scarce throughout much of its range.

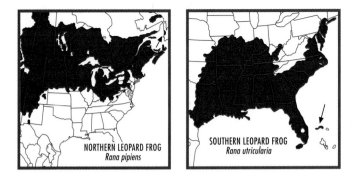

NORTHERN LEOPARD FROG
Rana pipiens

SOUTHERN LEOPARD FROG
Rana utricularia

a second (usually three); pulse rate about 20 a second. Breeds March to May in the more humid parts of its range. **RANGE:** S. Que. west to extr. s. Dist. of Mack.; south to Pa. and Ky. in the East (isolated records in Md. and W. Va.); west to Pacific states, and south, in the West, to Nev., Ariz., and N.M. (isolated colonies in e. Colo. and s. N.M.); introduced in w. Newf. and extensively in the West, particularly Calif.; disjunct colony in Labrador.

SOUTHERN LEOPARD FROG *Rana utricularia*   **PL. 48**

IDENTIFICATION: 2–3¼ in. (5.1–9 cm); record 5 in. (12.7 cm). Similar to the Northern Leopard Frog, but differing from the latter as follows: (a) usually a distinct light spot in center of tympanum; (b) longer, pointed head; and (c) only a few dark spots on sides of body. A light line along upper jaw. General coloration green or brown or a combination of both. Number of dark dorsal spots highly variable (occasionally completely absent); spots often longitudinally elongated. *Male:* Vocal sacs lie loose at angle of jaw when at rest, but are distinctly spherical when inflated (Fig. 104); vestigial oviducts absent, except in males from the Florida peninsula. Also, in Florida males, the vocal sacs may fold inward out of sight when not inflated.

In all types of shallow, freshwater habitats, and even entering slightly brackish marshes along coasts. Ventures well away from water in summer, when weeds and other vegetation provide shelter and shade. **SIMILAR SPECIES:** (1) Pickerel Frog has squarish dark spots, and concealed surfaces of hind legs are bright yellow or orange. (2) Gopher and Crawfish Frogs have fat, chunky bodies and rounded, nonpointed snouts. (3) If specimen is from an area of overlap with one of the other Leopard Frogs, check characteristics of the other species. **VOICE:** Mating call a short, chuckle-like, guttural trill; pulse rate usually fewer than 13 a second. Breeds in early spring in the North; in any month in the South. **RANGE:** Long Island and extr. s. N.Y. to s. Fla. (and some of the *lower* Keys); west to e.-cen. Texas and north in Mississippi Valley to se. Kans., Mo., cen. Ill., Ind., and extr. s. Ohio. **NOTE:** Specimens from Florida are designated as a separate race, the FLORIDA LEOPARD FROG, *Rana utricularia sphenocephala,* in the most current technical publication on Leopard Frogs. Some professional herpetologists have followed this arrangement, but others have not. Further studies are needed to clarify the status and name of these frogs in Florida.

PLAINS LEOPARD FROG *Rana blairi*   PL. 48; FIG. 108

IDENTIFICATION: 2–3¾ in. (5.1–9.5 cm); record 4⅜ in. (11.1 cm). Similar to the Northern Leopard Frog but averaging stockier and with a relatively shorter head and a *distinct* light line along upper jaw. Ground color of body usually brown. Nearly always a light spot on tympanum; usually a dark snout spot. Considerable yellow in groin and to some extent on ventral surface of thigh. *Dorsolateral ridges interrupted just anterior to groin and inset medially* (Fig. 108). *Male:* Vocal sac area small (when deflated), but longitudinally roughened below light labial stripe; no vestigial oviducts.

The Leopard Frog of the plains and prairies. Widespread in many parts of its range but restricted to remnants of the Prairie Peninsula toward the east. Breeds with the onset of warm rains, at least in the less humid parts of the range. **SIMILAR SPECIES:** See Northern Leopard Frog. **VOICE:** Mating call usually two or three distinctly spaced abrupt guttural notes best described as *chuck-chuck* or *chuck-chuck-chuck,* and delivered at a pulse rate of

An adult Plains Leopard Frog from Douglas County, Kansas. This frog is adapted to the marshes and streams of western prairies.

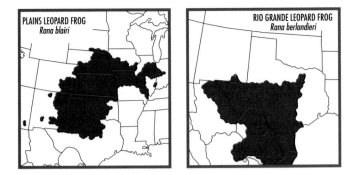

about three a second. **RANGE:** W. Ind. to se. S.D. and e. Colo.; south in the West to cen. Texas; isolated colonies in se. Ill., N.M., and se. Ariz.

RIO GRANDE LEOPARD FROG *Rana berlandieri*   **PL. 48**
IDENTIFICATION: 2¼–4 in. (5.7–10 cm); record 4½ in. (11.4 cm). Similar to our other Leopard Frogs, but more pallid. Light line along upper jaw less prominent than in the other species and usually incomplete anterior to eye. *Dorsolateral ridges interrupted just anterior to groin and inset medially* (Fig. 108). *Male:* Vocal sac, when not inflated, collapses inward into a pouch, the external opening of which appears as a dark slit. Vestigial oviducts present, except in specimens from Trans-Pecos Texas.

This frog is well adapted to arid conditions. It is an explosive breeder, ready to take advantage of the rains when they come, hence it may spawn during almost any month of the year. Watercourses, even intermittent ones, and cattle tanks are frequented, but it may appear suddenly, at the onset of rain, in regions where its presence is not even suspected. **SIMILAR SPECIES:** See Southern and Plains Leopard Frogs. **VOICE:** Mating call a short, guttural trill, more rapid than that of Southern Leopard Frog and with shorter pulses (13 or more a second). **RANGE:** Cen. and w. Texas and extr. s. N.M. south into Mexico.

PICKEREL FROG *Rana palustris*   **PL. 48**
IDENTIFICATION: 1¾–3 in. (4.4–7.5 cm); record 3⁷⁄₁₆ in. (8.7 cm). A frog with square spots arranged in two parallel rows down the back. These dark markings and similar ones on the sides have the unevenness of squares drawn freehand; the edges are irregular and often curved, but the spots definitely are not circular. Adja-

PICKEREL FROG
Rana palustris

cent squares may join to form rectangles or long, longitudinal bars. *Bright yellow or orange on concealed surfaces of hind legs.* A light line along upper jaw. Prominent dorsolateral ridges extending to groin. Venter plain whitish in northern populations, but usually mottled or marbled with dark pigment in Coastal Plain specimens. *Young:* With a metallic luster but without bright colors under the legs; lower lip clouded with dark pigment.

Typically a species of cool, clear water in the North—in sphagnum bogs, rocky ravines, and meadow streams but also occupying a wide variety of other habitats. In the South it occurs in the relatively warm, turbid, and often tea-colored waters of Coastal Plain and floodplain swamps. Wanders well out into grassy fields or weed-covered areas in summer. Often found in the twilight zones of caves. Few snakes will eat Pickerel Frogs, probably because the skin-gland secretions make them distasteful. **SIMILAR SPECIES:** In the Leopard Frogs, the dark dorsal spots are circular or oval, and there is no bright yellow or orange on the concealed surfaces of the legs (except in Plains Leopard Frog). **VOICE:** A steady, low-pitched snore of 1 or 2 seconds' duration but with little carrying power. Males very often call while completely submerged in water. Two vocal pouches. Breeds March to May. **RANGE:** Canadian Maritime Provinces to the Carolinas; west to se. Minn. and e. Texas; large gaps in the range, especially toward the south and in prairie portions of Ohio, Ind., and Ill.

CRAWFISH AND GOPHER FROGS: *Rana areolata* AND *Rana capito*

Frogs of stubby appearance—short, plump bodies, large heads, and relatively short legs. Nocturnal, normally spending the daylight hours underground in burrows or tunnels, in holes beneath stumps, etc. Both the Florida and Dusky races of the Gopher Frog utilize the burrows of the Gopher Tortoise; the Crawfish Frog often uses the abandoned burrows of the lobsterlike crawfish. The breeding seasons of both species occur in the spring, the dates often being correlated with the occurrence of heavy rains. Males have lateral vocal pouches that are enormous when inflated, each approaching the size of the frog's head.

IDENTIFICATION: 2¼–3 in. (5.7–7.5 cm); record 3⅝ in. (9.2 cm). A stubby appearance plus rounded, dark dorsal *spots encircled by light borders.* Coloration highly variable, depending on conditions of temperature, activity, etc. Chin and throat unspotted except at sides; belly immaculate whitish (Fig. 109). Dorsum often smooth or nearly so. Males may have yellow or greenish yellow on their dorsolateral ridges and on the concealed surfaces of the limbs.

Not restricted to crawfish holes, but often found in those that have lost their chimneys and contain water. Other habitats include small mammal burrows, holes in roadside banks, and in storm or drainage sewers. **SIMILAR SPECIES:** (1) Leopard Frogs have longer bodies and proportionately longer legs, and they lack the stubby, squat appearance of Crawfish Frogs. (2) Pickerel Frog has squarish spots. (3) Gopher Frog has pigmented ventral surfaces (Fig. 109), and lacks light-bordered dorsal spots. **VOICE:** A loud (often chuckling) deep snore with considerable carrying power. Large choruses sound like a sty full of hogs at feeding time. Breeds February to June. **RANGE:** Sw. Ind. to s. Iowa and se. Kansas and south to the Gulf of Mexico. **SUBSPECIES:** SOUTHERN CRAWFISH FROG, *Rana a. areolata* (Pl. 48). As described above. Se. Okla. and sw. Ark. south to Gulf of Mexico. NORTHERN CRAWFISH FROG, *Rana a. circulosa.* Somewhat larger; length to 4½ in. (11.4 cm). Head shorter and broader, dorsolateral ridges more prominent, and dorsum rougher. Sw. Ind. and e. Kans. south to ne. Okla. and s.-cen. Miss.

CRAWFISH
(areolata)
Largely unmarked

GOPHER
(capito)
Pigmented, often
heavily

Fig. 109. Venters of the Crawfish Frog (Rana areolata) *and two races of the Gopher Frog* (Rana capito capito *and* R. c. sevosa). *In a third race, the Florida Gopher Frog* (R. c. aesopus), *the belly is usually unmarked posteriorly.*

CRAWFISH FROGS
Rana areolata
🟦 NORTHERN
⬛ SOUTHERN

GOPHER FROGS
Rana capito
🟦 DUSKY 🟩 FLORIDA
⬛ CAROLINA

DUSKY GOPHER FROG

Rana capito sevosa   **PL. 48**

IDENTIFICATION: 2½–3½ in. (6.4–9 cm); record 3⅞ in. (9.8 cm). Warts always prominent but variable in shape—circular, elongate-oval, or in long ridges. Dorsal coloration also variable, but always dark and ranging from virtually uniform black to a pattern of reddish brown or dark brown spots on a ground of gray or brown. Ventral surfaces spotted, at least from chin to midbody (Fig. 109). **SIMILAR SPECIES:** (1) River Frog has white spots on lips. (2) In the Crawfish Frog, the belly is immaculate, and dark dorsal spots are rounded and encircled by *light borders*. **VOICE:** A deep snore or like the distant roar of an outboard motor; more continuous and hoarser than the guttural notes of the Southern Leopard Frog. **RANGE:** Gulf Coast, w. Fla., and adj. Ala. to extr. e. La.; isolated colonies in cen. and se. Ala. **SUBSPECIES:** CAROLINA GOPHER FROG, *Rana c. capito*. Warts smaller, closer together, and almost pavementlike in arrangement (like Belgian blocks on an old-fashioned street, but very much in miniature). Dorsal spots inconspicuous. Ventral surfaces heavily marked with dark flecks that produce a clouded or marbled pattern. *Young:* Less spotting on ventral surfaces, especially on abdomen, where it may be lacking entirely. Coastal Plain of the Carolinas and e.-cen. Ga.

FLORIDA GOPHER FROG   *Rana capito aesopus*   **PL. 48**

IDENTIFICATION: 2¾–3¾ in. (7–9.5 cm); record 4¼ in. (10.8 cm). The light ground color has earned this species the name of "white frog." The coloration varies from creamy white to brown through various shades of yellow or purplish. The black or dark brown markings are irregular in shape and not encircled by light borders. Dorsum may be smooth or slightly warty. Chin and throat spotted; belly usually unmarked posteriorly. Males may have yellow on the dorsolateral ridges, on the warts, along upper jaw, and in armpits and groins. Specimens from the Lake Wales Ridge in Polk and Highland cos., Fla., are dwarfed in size—average length 2¼ in. (6.4 cm).

This short, plump frog sometimes may be seen several feet (about 1 m) back from the entrance of Gopher Tortoise burrows during daylight hours, but it is best sought at night, when it ventures forth to feed. **VOICE:** A deep, roaring snore. Large choruses produce an effect like that of pounding surf. Breeds in spring toward northern part of its range, but from February until autumn farther south. **RANGE:** Coastal Plain, s. Ga. to s. Fla.; an isolated colony in w.-cen. Ga.

A SAMPLING OF TADPOLES

Many herpetologists have tended to neglect tadpoles, not only because they are difficult to identify, but also because they pass through many different stages in the development from egg to adult form. Here are drawings of representative species of a dozen genera, shown as they appear just before the growth of their hind legs. Various parts of their bodies and mouthparts are labeled in Fig. 110, below. The illustrations that follow were prepared from preserved specimens, the mouthparts by examination under the microscope—the only way to see them accurately. All are of species that live and metamorphose in water; a few other kinds develop on land within the egg (see text).

In the descriptions that follow, the number and placement of labial tooth rows are given as fractions. For example, 2/3 means there are two rows (anterior labial tooth rows) on the upper lip and three rows (posterior labial tooth rows) on the lower lip. If you attempt identification, study the drawings below and refer to

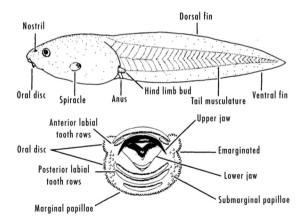

Fig. 110. Generalized drawing of a tadpole showing parts of body (top) and mouthparts (bottom).

the Glossary. Also, remember that Figs. 111–124 portray only a sampling of the many different kinds of toad and frog tadpoles occurring within our area. Be sure, by referring to the maps, that you eliminate other species that do not live where you found the tadpole.

Total lengths are given only as a general reference. Temperatures and other environmental factors cause tadpoles to grow at different rates, so measurements vary. Information on tadpoles in general may be found among the publications listed near the end of the References.

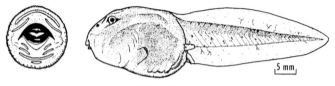

PLAINS SPADEFOOT

Fig. 111.

PLAINS SPADEFOOT *Scaphiopus bombifrons*   **P. 505**
Total length 1 %6–1 ⅞ in. (4–4.8 cm). Body/tail length ratio 1:1.4. A deep-bodied tadpole; body broadest just behind eyes. Eyes dorsal; nostrils small and closely spaced. Tail fin clear and of medium height; tail musculature with pigment. Oral disc round; marginal papillae small, unpigmented, completely bordering disc. Upper jaw cuspate; lower jaw notched. Labial tooth rows 2/4 to 4/6.

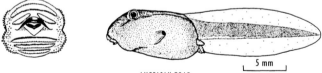

AMERICAN TOAD

Fig. 112.

AMERICAN TOAD *Bufo americanus*   **P. 513**
Total length ¾–1 in. (1.8–2.4 cm). Body/tail length ratio 1:1.3. A dark tadpole. Body somewhat flattened. Eyes small and dorsal; nostrils small. Tail fin low, without pigment, and rounded at tip. Tail musculature without pigment along ventral edge. Oral disc emarginated at jaw edges; without marginal papillae anteriorly and posteriorly. Jaws serrated; upper jaw slightly cuspate; lower jaw notched. Labial tooth rows 2/3.

EASTERN NARROWMOUTH TOAD | 5 mm |

Fig. 113.

EASTERN NARROWMOUTH TOAD **P. 551**
Gastrophryne carolinensis

Total length 1–1 3/16 in. (2.5–3 cm). Body/tail length ratio 1 :1.7. Body noticeably flattened. Eyes lateral. Oral disc replaced by labial flaps with a median notch. Nostrils not present until late in development. A single spiracle present and located ventral to anus. Intestinal coil not visible. Tail fin low, pigmented along dorsal and ventral edges of musculature. Large, light blotches on sides and belly, extending onto tail.

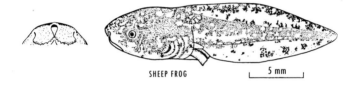

SHEEP FROG | 5 mm |

Fig. 114.

SHEEP FROG *Hypopachus variolosus* **P. 554**

Total length 3/4–7/8 in. (1.8–2.2 cm). Body/tail length ratio 1 :1.6. Body flattened. Eyes lateral; nostrils absent until late in development. Oral disc replaced with labial flaps having a medial notch and scalloped edges. Intestinal coil slightly visible. Tail fin pigmented along dorsal edge. Spiracle single and located below anus. Some light blotches on body and tail musculature.

MEXICAN BURROWING TOAD | 5 mm |

Fig. 115.

MEXICAN BURROWING TOAD *Rhinophrynus dorsalis* **P. 501**

Total length 1 1/8–1 3/8 in. (2.8–3.5 cm). Body/tail length ratio 1 :1.4. Body noticeably flattened. Eyes lateral. Tail fin low and not pigmented. Intestinal coil visible. A spiracle is present on both sides. Oral disc replaced with a fleshy, terminal mouth surrounded by barbels. No medial notch on upper lip.

WHITE-LIPPED FROG

Fig. 116.

WHITE-LIPPED FROG *Leptodactylus labialis*   **P. 508**

Total length 1 1/16–1 1/4 in. (2.6–3.2 cm). Body/tail length ratio 1 :1.8. Head and body heavily pigmented. Tail fin low, tapering to a fine point. Intestinal coil visible. Oral disc not emarginated; papillary border showing a wide dorsal gap. The lower jaw is small. Labial tooth rows 2/3.

WESTERN CHORUS FROG

Fig. 117.

WESTERN CHORUS FROG   **P. 542**

Pseudacris triseriata triseriata

Total length 1 1/16–1 3/16 in. (2.6–3 cm). Body/tail length ratio 1 :2. Intestinal coil visible. Tail musculature unicolored. Dorsal tail fin higher than ventral fin. Tail fin clear or weakly pigmented. Oral disc emarginated at jaw edges and ventrally. Third posterior labial tooth row (if present) shorter than 1st and 2nd rows. Labial tooth rows 2/2 or 2/3.

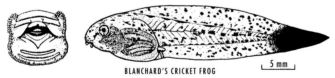

BLANCHARD'S CRICKET FROG

Fig. 118.

BLANCHARD'S CRICKET FROG   **P. 530**

Acris crepitans blanchardi

Total length 1 1/8–1 1/2 in. (2.7–3.8 cm). Body depressed dorsoventrally. Eyes dorsolateral; nostrils large. Up to one half of spiracle tube free from body wall. Intestinal coil visible. Tail fin faintly mottled; dorsum of tail musculature banded. Large part of tail tip black. Oral disc slightly emarginated at jaw edges. Labial tooth rows 2/2.

GRAY TREEFROG

Fig. 119.

GRAY TREEFROG *Hyla versicolor* **P. 536**

Total length 1¼–1½ in. (3.2–3.8 cm). Body/tail length ratio 1:2. Intestinal coil visible. Middle of tail fin high and heavily mottled with black; often washed (in life) with red or orange. Tail ends in a well-developed flagellum. Oral disc slightly emarginated at jaw edges. Jaws serrated; lower jaw narrow. Labial tooth rows 2/3.

CUBAN TREEFROG

Fig. 120.

CUBAN TREEFROG *Osteopilus septentrionalis* **P. 538**

Total length 1¹⁄₁₆–1¼ in. (2.6–3.2 cm). Body/tail length ratio 1:1.5. Body heavily pigmented; intestinal coil visible. Tail fin moderately pigmented; tail musculature with large, light areas anteriorly. Oral disc elongated and emarginated ventrally. Labial tooth rows 2/4.

MEXICAN TREEFROG

Fig. 121.

MEXICAN TREEFROG *Smilisca baudinii* **P. 539**

Total length 1¹⁄₁₆–1¼ in. (2.6–3.2 cm). Body/tail length ratio 1:1.5. Body heavily pigmented. Intestinal coil visible. Tail fin clear or showing some veins dorsally. Tail musculature lightly pigmented. Oral disc not emarginated; papillary border with small gap anteriorly. Some submarginal papillae present. Upper jaw with long lateral processes; lower jaw large. Labial tooth rows 2/3.

WOOD FROG

5 mm

Fig. 122.

WOOD FROG *Rana sylvatica*   **P. 563**

    Total length 1⅝–1⅞ in. (4.2–4.8 cm). Body/tail length ratio 1:1.8.
No distinct markings on body. Intestinal coil partially visible. Tail
fin rounded dorsally, tapering to a fine point. Faint, small markings on tail fin. Oral disc emarginated; large papillae present.
Labial tooth rows 3/4.

NORTHERN LEOPARD FROG

5 mm

Fig. 123.

NORTHERN LEOPARD FROG *Rana pipiens*   **P. 566**

    Total length 1¾–2⅛ in. (4.5–5.4 cm). Body/tail length ratio 1:1.5.
Body moderately pigmented. Intestinal coil visible. Fin and tail
musculature weakly pigmented. Oral disc emarginated at jaw
edges. Lower jaw large. A few large submarginal papillae present.
Labial tooth rows 2/3.

GREEN FROG

5 mm

Fig. 124.

GREEN FROG *Rana clamitans melanota*   **P. 561**

    Total length 2¹⁵⁄₁₆–4 in. (7.4–10 cm). Body/tail length ratio 1:1.8.
Tail fin with dark mottling; less on body where a few dark markings are present. Intestinal coil not visible. Oral disc strongly
emarginated; marginal papillae large, flattened and heavily pigmented. Upper jaw slightly cuspate. Labial tooth rows 2/3.

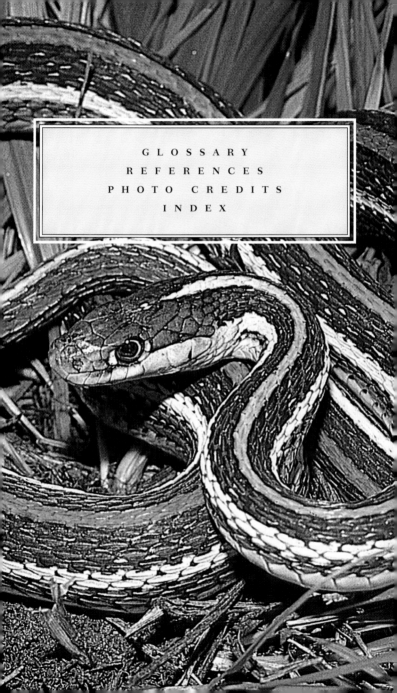

GLOSSARY
REFERENCES
PHOTO CREDITS
INDEX

GLOSSARY

For names of scales and other anatomical nomenclature, see pp. 138–141.

ALLOPATRIC. A term applied to two or more populations that occupy mutually exclusive, but usually adjacent, geographical areas.

AMBIENT TEMPERATURE. The temperature of the environment surrounding the animal in question.

AQUATIC. Frequenting water, or living or growing in water. Technically, only animals that have gills for extracting oxygen from water are aquatic, whereas others, such as turtles and water snakes, are semiaquatic.

ATTENUATED. Thin or slender.

AZYGOUS. Odd, not paired.

BARBELS. Small, fleshy, usually downward projections of skin on the chin and/or throat (in some kinds of turtles and the tadpoles of the Mexican Burrowing Toad).

BOSS. A raised, rounded area; in toads, a rounded eminence on the midline of the head between the eyes or on or near the end of the snout.

CANTHUS ROSTRALIS. The ridge from the eye to the tip of the snout that separates the top of the muzzle from the side.

CARAPACE. The upper shell of a turtle.

CIRRI. Downward projections from the nostrils in males of certain lungless salamanders. The naso-labial groove extends downward to near the tip of each cirrus.

CLINE. A gradual change in a variable characteristic.

CLOACA. The common chamber into which the urinary, digestive, and reproductive canals discharge their contents, and which opens to the exterior through the anus.

COSTAL GROOVES. Vertical grooves on the flanks of salamanders. The spaces between grooves are called costal folds.

CRANIAL CRESTS. The raised ridges on the heads of toads—interorbital (between the eyes) or postorbital (behind the eyes).

CREPUSCULAR. Active at twilight and/or dawn.

CUSP. A toothlike projection on the jaw of a turtle.

CUSPATE. Possessing an enlarged point at the middle of the upper jaw (in certain tadpoles and turtles).

DIMORPHISM. Difference in form, color, or structure between members of the same species. The sexes may be different or there may be two color phases of the same sex (dichromatism).

DORSAL. Of or pertaining to the upper surface.

DORSAL GAP. The area above the upper lip of tadpoles where the oral disc ends.

DORSOLATERAL. Neither directly down the center of the back nor at the side of the body, but more or less intermediate between the two.

DORSUM. The entire upper surface of an animal.

EMARGINATED. Indented, as on either side of the oral disc of some kinds of tadpoles.

ENDEMIC. Confined to, or indigenous in, a certain area or region.

ESTIVATION. A state of inactivity during prolonged periods of drought or high temperatures, usually while the animal is in seclusion.

EXCRESCENCE. A natural outgrowth of the epidermis (the outer layer of the skin), as on the limbs or digits of amphibians during the breeding season.

EXTRALIMITAL. Occurring outside the geographical area covered by this Field Guide.

FEMORAL PORES. Small openings, containing a waxlike material, on the underside of the thighs in some lizards.

FLAGELLUM. An extension of the tail of some tadpoles that is capable of moving independently from the rest of the tail.

FORM. A species or a subspecies; a distinct, identifiable population.

FOSSORIAL. Adapted for digging.

FRACTURE PLANES. Zones of softer tissue in the tail bones of some species of lizards that permit the tail to break off easily when it is seized by an enemy.

GRANULES. Very small, flat scales.

GRAVID. Bearing eggs or young, ordinarily in the oviducts.

GROWTH RINGS. Concentric subcircular areas on the scutes of some turtles. Each ring represents a season's growth. Rings, if present, are most evident in young turtles; they are usually not countable in adults.

GULAR. On or pertaining to the throat. Also the most anterior scutes (or scute) on a turtle's plastron.

HEMIPENES. The copulatory organs of males. There are two such organs in snakes and lizards, but only a single penis in turtles and crocodilians. (Singular: hemipenis.)

KEEL. A ridge down the back (or along the plastron) of a turtle. Also, a longitudinal ridge on a dorsal scale in certain snakes.

LABIAL. Of or pertaining to the lip.

LABIAL TOOTH ROWS. Rows of tiny, horny projections on the lips of tadpoles.

LATERAL. Of or pertaining to the side.

MELANISM. Abundance of black pigment, sometimes resulting in an all-black or nearly all-black animal; opposite of albinism.

MENTAL GLAND. A gland, often large, situated on the chins of some kinds of salamanders. The secretion of the gland is sexually stimulating to females of the same species.

METAMORPHOSIS. A change of form or structure, as when a tadpole transforms into a frog or toad.

MIDDORSAL. Of or pertaining to the center of the back.

MIDVENTRAL. Of or pertaining to the center of the abdomen.

MONOTYPIC. The only representative of its group, such as a genus with only one species.

NASO-LABIAL GROOVE. A groove extending downward from the nostril and across the lip in the lungless salamanders.

NEOTENIC. Mature and capable of reproduction but retaining the larval form, appearance, and habits.

OCELLI. Round, eyelike spots.

ORAL DISC. Fleshy parts of a tadpole's mouth.

PAPILLAE. Small, nipple-like protuberances.

PARAVERTEBRAL STRIPE. A stripe lying to one side but paralleling the midline of the back.

PAROTOID. One of a pair of external wartlike glands on the shoulder, neck, or back of the eye in toads; enlarged and prominent in many species.

PARTHENOGENESIS. Reproduction without fertilization by a male element.

PHALANGES. The bones of the toes. (Singular: phalanx.)

PLASTRON. The lower shell of a turtle.

PREOCULAR. Anterior to the eye.

POSTOCULAR. Behind the eye.

PROCESS. An extension of a structure or organ.

RACE. Subspecies.

RUGOSE. Wrinkled or warty.

SCALE PITS. Tiny depressions on the posterior portions of the dorsal scales in some kinds of snakes.

SCUTE. Any enlarged scale on a reptile; sometimes called "shield" or "plate."

SERRATE. Having projections in the shape of the teeth of a saw. Jaws of some tadpoles may be serrated.

SIBLINGS. Offspring of same parents, but not necessarily at same birth.

SIBLING SPECIES. Two or more species presumably derived from a common parental stock. They often resemble one another closely and may occur together or replace each other geographically.

SPATULATE. Flat and rounded at tip; shaped like the blade of a kitchen spatula.

SPIRACLE. A tubelike external opening, on the left side in most kinds of tadpoles, for the exit of respiratory water.

SUBCAUDALS. The scales beneath the tail; in a double row in most snakes, but in a single row in others. Sometimes shortened to "caudals."

SUBOCULAR. Beneath the eye.

SUPRAOCULAR. Above the eye.

SUPRAORBITAL SEMICIRCLE. A row of small scales separating the supraoculars from the median head scutes in certain lizards.

SUTURE. A seam; the boundary between scales or scutes.

SYMPATRIC. A term applied to two or more populations that occupy identical or broadly overlapping geographical areas.

TAXON. The technical term for a unit or category, i.e., for a species, subspecies, genus, family, etc. (Plural: taxa.)

TAXONOMY. The science of the classification of animals or plants.

TIBIA. The leg (of toads and frogs) from heel to knee.

TROGLODYTE. A cave dweller.

TUBERCLES. Small, knoblike projections.

TUBERCULATE. With raised projections.

TYMPANUM. The eardrum.

VENTER. The entire undersurface of an animal.

VENTRAL. Of or pertaining to the lower surface.

VOCAL SAC. An inflatable pouch on the throat or at the sides of the neck in male toads and frogs; single in most species, but paired in others.

NOTE: For the definition of other words and terms used in herpetology see: Peters, James A. 1964. *Dictionary of Herpetology.* New York: Hafner Publishing Co.

REFERENCES

This Field Guide is designed to present general information about the reptiles and amphibians of our area, but limitations of space prohibit the inclusion of many details that would be of interest to persons wishing to know more about the herpetofauna of their home region or the places they visit on vacation. Many state, regional, and general books and booklets have been published, some of which can be readily obtained through any good bookstore. Others, especially those that are now out of print, must be sought by visiting a library, zoo, or natural history museum. The list below is a generally comprehensive review of the pertinent literature.

GENERAL

Ballinger, Royce E., and John D. Lynch. 1983. *How to Know the Amphibians and Reptiles.* Dubuque, Ia.: Wm. C. Brown.

Bartlett, Richard D. 1988. *In Search of Reptiles and Amphibians.* New York: E. J. Brill.

Bellairs, Angus. 1970. *The Life of Reptiles.* 2 vols. New York: Universe Books.

Bishop, Sherman C. 1947. *Handbook of Salamanders.* Ithaca, N.Y.: Comstock.

Blair, Albert P., and Fred R. Cagle. 1968. *Vertebrates of the United States.* 2nd ed. (See amphibians and reptiles). New York: McGraw-Hill.

Carr, Archie. 1952. *Handbook of Turtles.* Ithaca, N.Y.: Cornell Univ. Press.

———. 1963. *The Reptiles.* New York: Time, Inc.

Cochran, Doris M. 1961. *Living Amphibians of the World.* Garden City, N.Y.: Doubleday.

Collins, Joseph T. 1990. *Standard Common and Current Scientific*

Names for North American Amphibians and Reptiles. 3rd ed. Society for the Study of Amphibians and Reptiles.

Conant, Roger. 1981. *Reptile Study* (merit badge pamphlet). Irving, Texas: Boy Scouts of America.

Duellman, William E., and Linda Trueb. 1986. *Biology of Amphibians.* New York: McGraw-Hill.

Ernst, Carl H., and Roger W. Barbour. 1973. *Turtles of the United States.* Lexington: Univ. Press of Kentucky.

Fitch, Henry S. 1970. *Reproductive Cycles in Lizards and Snakes.* Lawrence, Kansas: Univ. Kansas Mus. Nat. Hist. Misc. Publ. No. 52.

Frost, Darrel R. (ed.). 1985. *Amphibian Species of the World.* Lawrence, Kansas: Allen Press.

Gloyd, Howard K. 1940. *The Rattlesnakes, Genera Sistrurus and Crotalus.* Chicago Academy of Sciences Spec. Publication No. 4. (Reprinted in 1978 by the Society for the Study of Amphibians and Reptiles.)

Goin, Coleman J., Olive B. Goin, and George R. Zug. 1978. *Introduction to Herpetology.* San Francisco: W. H. Freeman.

Halliday, Tim R., and Kraig Adler (eds.). 1986. *The Encyclopedia of Reptiles and Amphibians.* New York: Facts on File.

Iverson, John B. 1986. *A Checklist with Distribution Maps of the Turtles of the World.* Richmond, Ind.: Paust Printing.

Kauffeld, Carl F. 1957. *Snakes and Snake Hunting.* Garden City, N.Y.: Hanover House.

———. 1969. *Snakes: The Keeper and the Kept.* New York: Doubleday.

King, F. Wayne, and Russell L. Burke (eds.). 1989. *Crocodilian, Tuatara, and Turtle Species of the World.* Washington, D.C.: Assoc. Systematics Collections.

Klauber, Laurence M. 1972. *Rattlesnakes: Their Habits, Life Histories, and Influence on Mankind.* 2nd ed. 2 vols. Berkeley and Los Angeles: Univ. California Press.

Mattison, Christopher. 1982. *The Care of Reptiles and Amphibians in Captivity.* England: Blandford Press.

Minton, Sherman A., Jr., and Madge Rutherford Minton. 1969. *Venomous Reptiles.* New York: Scribner's.

———. 1973. *Giant Reptiles.* New York: Scribner's.

Murphy, James B., and Joseph T. Collins (eds.). 1980. *Reproductive Biology and Diseases of Captive Reptiles.* Society for the Study of Amphibians and Reptiles.

Neill, Wilfred T. 1971. *The Last of the Ruling Reptiles.* New York: Columbia Univ. Press.

Oliver, James A. 1955. *The Natural History of North American Amphibians and Reptiles.* Princeton, N.J.: Van Nostrand.

Pope, Clifford H. 1955. *The Reptile World.* New York: Knopf.

Porter, Kenneth R. 1972. *Herpetology*. Philadelphia: Saunders.

Pritchard, Peter C. H. 1979. *Encyclopedia of Turtles*. Neptune, N.J.: T.F.H. Publications.

Schmidt, Karl P., and Robert F. Inger. 1957. *Living Reptiles of the World*. Garden City, N.Y.: Hanover House.

Scott, Norman J., Jr. (ed.). 1982. *Herpetological Communities*. Washington, D.C.: U.S. Fish and Wildlife Service Wildlife Res. Report 13.

Seigel, Richard A., Joseph T. Collins, and Susan S. Novak (eds.). 1987. *Snakes: Ecology and Evolutionary Biology*. New York: Macmillan. (Obtainable from McGraw-Hill).

Smith, Hobart M. 1946. *Handbook of Lizards*. Ithaca, N.Y.: Comstock.

Williams, Kenneth L. 1988. *Systematics and Natural History of the American Milk Snake, Lampropeltis triangulum*. 2nd ed. Milwaukee Public Mus. Publication.

Wright, Albert Hazen, and Anna Allen Wright. 1949. *Handbook of Frogs and Toads*. 3rd ed. Ithaca, N.Y.: Comstock.

——. *Handbook of Snakes*. 3 vols. (including bibliography). Ithaca, N.Y.: Comstock.

Zappalorti, Robert T. 1976. *The Amateur Zoologist's Guide to Turtles and Crocodilians*. Harrisburg, Pa.: Stackpole Books.

REGIONAL

NEW ENGLAND

DeGraaf, Richard M., and Deborah D. Rudis. 1983. *Amphibians and Reptiles of New England*. Amherst: Univ. Massachusetts Press.

SOUTHEAST

Jackson, Jeffrey J. 1983. *Snakes of the Southeastern United States*. Athens: Univ. Georgia.

Martof, Bernard S., William M. Palmer, Joseph R. Bailey, and Julian R. Harrison III. 1980. *Amphibians and Reptiles of the Carolinas and Virginia*. Chapel Hill: Univ. North Carolina Press.

WEST

Shaw, Charles E., and Sheldon Campbell. 1974. *Snakes of the American West*. New York: Knopf.

Stebbins, Robert C. 1985. *A Field Guide to Western Reptiles and Amphibians*. 2nd ed. Boston: Houghton Mifflin.

PACIFIC NORTHWEST

Nussbaum, Ronald A., Edmund D. Brodie, Jr., and Robert M. Storm. 1983. *Amphibians and Reptiles of the Pacific Northwest*. Moscow: Univ. Idaho Press.

CANADA

Bleakney, Sherman. 1958. *A Zoogeographical Study of the Amphi-*

bians and Reptiles of Eastern Canada. Natl. Mus. of Canada Bull. No. 155.

Cook, Francis R. 1967. *An Analysis of the Herpetofauna of Prince Edward Island.* Natl. Mus. of Canada Bull. No. 212.

——. 1984. *Introduction to Canadian Amphibians and Reptiles.* Ottawa: Natl. Mus. of Canada.

Froom, Barbara. 1972. *The Snakes of Canada.* Toronto: McClelland and Stewart, Ltd.

——. 1976. *The Turtles of Canada.* Toronto: McClelland and Stewart, Ltd.

——. 1982. *Amphibians of Canada.* Toronto: McClelland and Stewart, Ltd.

Gilhen, John. 1984. *Amphibians and Reptiles of Nova Scotia.* Halifax: Nova Scotia Mus.

Green, David M., and R. Wayne Campbell. 1984. *The Amphibians of British Columbia.* British Columbia Prov. Mus. Handbook No. 45.

Gregory, Patrick T., and R. Wayne Campbell. 1984. *The Reptiles of British Columbia.* British Columbia Prov. Mus. Handbook No. 44.

Logier, E. B. S. 1958. *The Snakes of Ontario.* Univ. Toronto Press.

——, and G. C. Toner. 1961. *Check List of the Amphibians and Reptiles of Canada and Alaska.* Contrib. Royal Ontario Mus. of Zool. and Palaeon. No. 53.

Preston, William B. 1982. *The Amphibians and Reptiles of Manitoba.* Winnipeg: Manitoba Mus. of Man and Nature.

MEXICO

Smith, Hobart M., and Rozella B. Smith. 1971 (Vol. 1) and 1973 (Vol. 2). *Synopsis of the Herpetofauna of Mexico.* Augusta, W. Va.: Eric Lundberg.

——. 1976 (Vols. 3 and 4), 1977 (Vol. 5), and 1979 (Vol. 6). *Synopsis of the Herpetofauna of Mexico.* North Bennington, Vt.: John Johnson.

Smith, Hobart M., and Edward H. Taylor. 1966. *Herpetology of Mexico: Annotated Checklists and Keys to the Amphibians and Reptiles.* Ashton, Md.: Eric Lundberg. (A reprint of Bulletins 187, 194, and 199 of the U.S. National Museum of Natural History with a list of subsequent taxonomic innovations.)

WEST INDIES

Henderson, Robert W., and Albert Schwartz. 1984. *A Guide to the Identification of the Amphibians and Reptiles of Hispaniola.* Milwaukee Public Mus. Spec. Publ. Biol. and Geol. No. 4.

Schwartz, Albert, and Robert W. Henderson. 1985. *A Guide to the Identification of the Amphibians and Reptiles of the West Indies Exclusive of Hispaniola.* Milwaukee Public Mus.

By States

ALABAMA

Linzey, Donald W. 1979. *Snakes of Alabama*. Huntsville, Ala.: Strode Publishers.

Mount, Robert H. 1975. *The Reptiles and Amphibians of Alabama*. Auburn: Auburn Univ., Ala.

ARKANSAS

Dowling, Herndon G. 1957. *A Review of the Amphibians and Reptiles of Arkansas*. Fayetteville: Univ. Arkansas Mus. Occasional Papers No. 3.

COLORADO

Hammerson, Geoffrey A. 1982. *Amphibians and Reptiles in Colorado*. Denver: Colorado Div. of Wildlife.

CONNECTICUT

Babbitt, Lewis Hall. 1937. *The Amphibia of Connecticut*. Hartford: State Geol. and Nat. Hist. Survey Bull. No. 57.

Lamson, George Herbert. 1935. *The Reptiles of Connecticut*. Hartford: State Geol. and Nat. Hist. Survey Bull. No. 54.

Petersen, Richard C., and Robert W. Fritsch, II. 1986. *Connecticut's Venomous Snakes*. Hartford: State Geol. and Nat. Hist. Survey Bull. No. 111.

FLORIDA

Ashton, Ray E., Jr., and Patricia Sawyer Ashton. 1988 (Part One, *The Snakes*, 2nd ed.), 1985 (Part Two, *The Lizards, Turtles, and Crocodilians*), and 1988 (Part Three, *The Amphibians*). *Handbook of Reptiles and Amphibians of Florida*. Miami: Windward Publishing.

Carr, Archie, and Coleman J. Goin. 1955. *Guide to the Reptiles, Amphibians, and Freshwater Fishes of Florida*. Gainesville: Univ. Florida Press.

Duellman, William E., and Albert Schwartz. 1958. *Amphibians and Reptiles of Southern Florida*. Gainesville: Bull. of the Florida State Mus. No. 3.

Iverson, John B. 1989. The Distributions of the Turtles of Florida. *Florida Scientist*, Vol. 52, No. 2.

McDiarmid, Roy W. (ed.). 1978. *Rare and Endangered Biota of Florida*. Volume Three. Amphibians and Reptiles. Gainesville: Univ. Presses of Florida.

Wilson, Larry David, and Louis Porras. 1983. *The Ecological Impact of Man on the South Florida Herpetofauna*. Lawrence, Kansas: Univ. Kansas Mus. Nat. Hist. Spec. Publ. No. 9.

GEORGIA

Williamson, Gerald K., and Robert A. Moulis. 1979. *Distribution of Georgia Amphibians and Reptiles in the Savannah Science Museum*. Savannah: Savannah Science Mus. Spec. Publ. No. 1.

ILLINOIS

Smith, Philip W. 1961. *The Amphibians and Reptiles of Illinois.* Urbana: Illinois Nat. Hist. Survey, Vol. 28, Art. 1.

INDIANA

Minton, Sherman A., Jr. 1972. *Amphibians and Reptiles of Indiana.* Indianapolis: Indiana Academy of Sci. Monograph No. 3.

IOWA

Christiansen, James L., and Reeve M. Bailey. 1986. *The Snakes of Iowa.* Des Moines: Iowa Conserv. Commission.

Christiansen, James L., and Russell R. Burken. 1978. *The Endangered and Uncommon Reptiles and Amphibians of Iowa.* Cedar Falls: Iowa Academy of Science.

KANSAS

Caldwell, Janalee P., and Joseph T. Collins. 1981. *Turtles in Kansas.* Lawrence, Kansas: AMS Publishing.

Collins, Joseph T. 1982. *Amphibians and Reptiles in Kansas.* 2nd ed. Lawrence, Kansas: Univ. Kansas Mus. Nat. Hist. Pub. Ed. Series No. 8.

KENTUCKY

Babcock, Jan V. 1977. *Endangered Plants and Animals of Kentucky* (see pp. 75-92 on amphibians and reptiles). Lexington: College of Engineering, Univ. Kentucky.

Barbour, Roger W. 1971. *Amphibians and Reptiles of Kentucky.* Lexington: Univ. Press of Kentucky.

LOUISIANA

Dundee, Harold A., and Douglas A. Rossman. 1989. *The Amphibians and Reptiles of Louisiana.* Baton Rouge: Louisiana St. Univ. Press.

Keiser, Edmund D., Jr., and Larry David Wilson. 1979. *Checklist and Key to the Amphibians and Reptiles of Louisiana.* 2nd ed. Lafayette, La.: Lafayette Nat. Hist. Mus. Tech. Bull. 1.

MARYLAND

Harris, Herbert S., Jr. 1975. *Distributional Survey (Amphibia/Reptilia): Maryland and the District of Columbia.* Baltimore: Bull. of the Maryland Herpetological Society, Vol. 11, No. 3.

MICHIGAN

Holman, J. Alan, and James H. Harding. 1977. *Michigan's Turtles.* Lansing: Michigan State Univ. Mus. Educ. Bull. No. 3.

Holman, J. Alan, James H. Harding, Marvin M. Hensley, and Glenn R. Dudderar. 1989. *Michigan Snakes. A Field Guide and Pocket Reference.* Lansing: Michigan State Univ. Mus. and Cooperative Extension Service.

Ruthven, Alexander G., Crystal Thompson, and Helen T. Gaige. 1928. *The Herpetology of Michigan.* Ann Arbor: University Museums, Univ. Michigan Handbook Ser. No. 3.

MINNESOTA

Karns, Daryl R. 1986. *Field Herpetology Methods for the Study of Amphibians and Reptiles in Minnesota.* Occasional Paper No. 18. Minneapolis: Univ. Minnesota Bell Mus. Nat. Hist.

Lang, Jeffrey W. 1982. *The Reptiles and Amphibians of Minnesota: Distribution Maps, Habitat Preferences, and Selected References.* Minnesota Dept. of Natural Resources.

Moriarty, John J. 1987. *Distribution Maps for Reptiles and Amphibians of Minnesota.* Minneapolis: Minnesota Herpetological Society, Bell Mus. Nat. History.

MISSISSIPPI

Cliburn, J. William. 1976. *A Key to the Amphibians and Reptiles of Mississippi with Guides to Their Study.* 4th ed. Jackson: Mississippi Mus. of Nat. Science.

Lohoefener, Ren, and Ronald Altig. 1983. *Mississippi Herpetology.* Mississippi State Univ. Research Center Bull. No. 1, Mississippi State Univ.

MISSOURI

Johnson, Tom R. 1987. *The Amphibians and Reptiles of Missouri.* Jefferson City: Missouri Dept. Conservation.

MONTANA

Black, Jeffrey H. 1970. *Amphibians of Montana.* Helena: Montana Fish and Game Dept.

———. 1970. *Turtles of Montana.* Helena: Montana Fish and Game Dept.

Thompson, Larry S. 1982. *Distribution of Montana Amphibians, Reptiles, and Mammals.* Helena: Montana Audubon Council.

NEBRASKA

Lynch, John D. 1985. *Annotated Checklist of the Amphibians and Reptiles of Nebraska.* Lincoln: Transactions of the Nebraska Academy of Science Vol. 13.

NEW HAMPSHIRE

Oliver, James A., and Joseph R. Bailey. 1939. *Amphibians and Reptiles of New Hampshire.* Concord: Biol. Survey of the Connecticut Watershed.

NEW JERSEY

Trapido, Harold. 1937. *The Snakes of New Jersey: A Guide.* Newark, N.J.: Newark Museum.

NEW MEXICO

Baltosser, William H., Howard Campbell, J. William Eley, John P. Hubbard, and C. Gregory Schmitt. 1985. *Handbook of Species Endangered in New Mexico* (sections on Amphibians and Reptiles). Santa Fe: New Mexico Dept. of Game and Fish.

Degenhardt, William G., and James L. Christiansen. 1974. Distribution and Habitats of Turtles in New Mexico. *Southwestern Naturalist,* Vol. 19, No. 1.

NEW YORK

Bishop, Sherman C. 1941. *The Salamanders of New York.* Albany: New York State Mus. Bull. No. 324.

NORTH CAROLINA

Huheey, James E., and Arthur Stupka. 1967. *Amphibians and Reptiles of Great Smoky Mountains National Park.* Knoxville: Univ. Tennessee Press.

Palmer, William M. 1974. *Poisonous Snakes of North Carolina.* Raleigh, N.C.: State Mus. of Nat. History.

NORTH DAKOTA

Wheeler, George C., and Jeanette Wheeler. 1966. *The Amphibians and Reptiles of North Dakota.* Grand Forks: Univ. North Dakota Press.

OHIO

Conant, Roger. 1951. *The Reptiles of Ohio.* 2nd ed. Notre Dame, Ind.: American Midland Naturalist.

Pfingsten, Ralph A., and Floyd L. Downs (eds.). 1989. *Salamanders of Ohio.* Columbus: Bull. Ohio Biol. Survey, Vol. 7, No. 2.

Walker, Charles F. 1946. *The Amphibians of Ohio. Part I. The Frogs and Toads.* Columbus: Ohio State Mus. Sci. Bull. Vol. 1, No. 3.

OKLAHOMA

Black, Jeffrey H., and Gregory Sievert. 1989. *A Field Guide to Amphibians of Oklahoma.* Oklahoma City: Okla. Dept. Wildlife Conservation.

Carpenter, Charles C., and James J. Krupa. 1989. *Oklahoma Herpetology: An Annotated Bibliography.* Norman: Univ. Oklahoma Press.

Sievert, Gregory, and Lynnette Sievert. 1988. *A Field Guide to the Reptiles of Oklahoma.* Oklahoma City: Okla. Dept. Wildlife Conservation.

Webb, Robert G. 1970. *Reptiles of Oklahoma.* Norman: Univ. Oklahoma Press.

PENNSYLVANIA

McCoy, C. J. 1982. *Amphibians and Reptiles in Pennsylvania.* Pittsburgh: Carnegie Mus. Nat. Hist. Spec. Publ. No. 6.

SOUTH DAKOTA

Fishbeck, Dale W., and James C. Underhill. 1959. *A Check List of the Amphibians and Reptiles of South Dakota.* Vermillion, S.D.: Proceedings of the South Dakota Academy of Sci. Vol. 38.

Melius, Michael M. 1987. *Plants and Animals Rare in South Dakota. A Field Guide.* Hermosa, S.D.: Ornate Press.

Over, William H. 1923. *Amphibians and Reptiles of South Dakota.* Vermillion, S.D.: South Dakota Geol. and Nat. Hist. Survey Bull. No. 12.

TENNESSEE

Huheey, James E., and Arthur Stupka. 1967. *Amphibians and Reptiles* of *Great Smoky Mountains National Park.* Knoxville: Univ. Tennessee Press.

Sinclair, Ralph, Will Hon, and Robert B. Ferguson. 1965. *Amphibians and Reptiles in Tennessee.* Nashville: Tennessee Game and Fish Commission.

TEXAS

Dixon, James R. 1987. *Amphibians and Reptiles of Texas.* College Station: Texas A & M University Press.

Easterla, David A. 1975. *The Amphibians and Reptiles of Big Bend National Park, Texas.* Big Bend Natural History Association.

Garrett, Judith M., and David G. Barker. 1987. *A Field Guide to Reptiles and Amphibians of Texas.* Austin: Texas Monthly Press.

Raun, Gerald G., and Frederick R. Gehlbach. 1972. *Amphibians and Reptiles in Texas.* Dallas: Dallas Mus. of Nat. Hist. Bull. No. 2.

Tennant, Alan. 1984. *The Snakes of Texas.* Austin: Texas Monthly Press.

Vermersch, Thomas G., and Robert E. Kuntz. 1986. *Snakes of South Central Texas.* Austin: Eakin Press.

VIRGINIA

Linzey, Donald W., and Michael J. Clifford. 1981. *Snakes of Virginia.* Charlottesville: Univ. Press of Virginia.

Tobey, Franklin J. 1985. *Virginia's Amphibians and Reptiles: A Distributional Survey.* Purcellville, Va.: Virginia Herpetological Society.

WEST VIRGINIA

Green, N. Bayard, and Thomas K. Pauley. 1987. *Amphibians and Reptiles in West Virginia.* Pittsburgh: Univ. Pittsburgh Press.

WISCONSIN

Vogt, Richard Carl. 1981. *Natural History of Amphibians and Reptiles of Wisconsin.* Milwaukee: Milwaukee Public Museum.

WYOMING

Baxter, George T., and Michael D. Stone. 1985. *Amphibians and Reptiles of Wyoming.* 2nd ed. Cheyenne: Wyoming Fish and Game Dept.

IDENTIFICATION OF TADPOLES AND LARVAE

Identification of frog tadpoles and salamander larvae to species is virtually impossible in the field. For individuals interested in this aspect of the lives of amphibians, contact a herpetologist at the nearest museum or university. The references listed below, designed for use in a laboratory, may also be of some help.

Altig, Ronald. 1970. A Key to the Tadpoles of the Continental United States and Canada. *Herpetologica,* Vol. 26, no. 2.

——, and Patrick H. Ireland. 1984. A Key to Salamander Larvae and Larviform Adults of the United States and Canada. *Herpetologica,* Vol. 40, no. 2.

Ireland, Patrick H., and Ronald Altig. 1983. Key to the Gilled Salamander Larvae and Larviform Adults of Arkansas, Kansas, Missouri, and Oklahoma. *Southwestern Naturalist,* Vol. 28, no. 3.

Orton, Grace L. 1952. Key to the Genera of Tadpoles in the United
States and Canada. *American Midland Naturalist,* Vol. 47.

SOUND RECORDINGS OF FROG AND TOAD CALLS

Bogert, Charles M. *Sounds of North American Frogs: the Biological
Significance of Voice in Frogs.* (Record or cassette; 92 calls of 50
species of frogs and toads; accompanied by a profusely illustrated
essay on the subject.) Produced by Folkways Records, N.Y. Distributed by Rounder Records, Cambridge, Mass., and Smithsonian Folkways Records, Rockville, Md.

Johnson, Tom R. *Talking Toad and Frog Poster and Cassette.* (20-
minute cassette of 20 kinds of Missouri toads and frogs.) Jefferson City: Missouri Department of Conservation.

Kellogg, Peter Paul, and Arthur A. Allen. *Voices of the Night.* Sounds of
Nature series. (Record; calls of 34 kinds of toads and frogs of
eastern North America.) Boston: Houghton Mifflin for Cornell
Laboratory of Ornithology.

Turcotte, W. H. *Mississippi Frog Songs.* (30-minute cassette of 28
kinds of Mississippi frogs and toads.) Jackson: Mississippi
Department of Wildlife Conservation.

JOURNALS

Herpetological Review. Published quarterly by the Society for the
Study of Amphibians and Reptiles, Inc. Membership also
includes subscription to the quarterly *Journal of Herpetology* and,
with additional payment, receipt of annual accounts of the *Catalogue of American Amphibians and Reptiles,* a series of loose-leaf
reviews of species and genera, each prepared by a specialist. The
SSAR also publishes *Herpetological Circulars* and *Contributions
to Herpetology.* Both of these are available at reduced rates to
members. Contact SSAR, Department of Zoology, Miami University, Oxford, Ohio 45056.

Herpetologica and *Herpetological Monographs.* Published by the Herpetologists' League, Inc., 1041 New Hampshire Street,
Lawrence, Kans. 66044.

Copeia. Published quarterly by The American Society of Ichthyologists
and Herpetologists, Inc., Florida State Museum, University of
Florida, Gainesville, Fla. 32611.

PHOTO CREDITS

SUZANNE L. COLLINS: Alligator Snapping Turtle, Three-toed Box Turtle, Ornate Box Turtle, Common Map Turtle, Red-eared Slider, Eastern River Cooter, Western Painted Turtle, Northern Earless Lizard, Northern Prairie Lizard, Texas Horned Lizard, Prairie Racerunner, Broadhead Skink, Great Plains Skink, Northern Prairie Skink, Slender Glass Lizard, Florida Water Snake, Graham's Crayfish Snake, Redbelly Snake, Plains Garter Snake, Checkered Garter Snake, Western Ribbon Snake, Lined Snake, Smooth Earth Snake, Eastern Hognose Snake, Western Hognose Snake, Rough Green Snake, Smooth Green Snake, Bullsnake, Scarlet Snake, Texas Longnose Snake, Eastern Coral Snake, Western Massasauga, Western Pigmy Rattlesnake, Timber Rattlesnake, Spotted Salamander, Spring Salamander, Northern Red Salamander, Three-lined Salamander, Cave Salamander, Grotto Salamander, Couch's Spadefoot, Plains Spadefoot, Fowler's Toad, Blanchard's Cricket Frog, Barking Treefrog, Gray Treefrog, Spring Peeper, Spotted Chorus Frog, Wood Frog, Northern Leopard Frog, Plains Leopard Frog.

TOM R. JOHNSON: Western Spiny Softshell, Brown Anole, Broad-banded Water Snake, Eastern Yellowbelly Racer, Banded Rock Rattlesnake, Canadian Toad, Mink Frog.

CRAIG MCINTYRE: Gray-banded Kingsnake, Gulf Coast Toad.

WILLIAM B. MONTGOMERY: Houston Toad.

DON SIAS: American Alligator, Red-eared Sliders and Painted Turtles, Green Anole, Variable Skink, Corn Snake, Southern Copperhead, American Toad, Great Plains Toad, Western Green Toad, Green Treefrog, Bullfrog.

R. W. VAN DEVENDER: Florida Worm Lizard, Mississippi Green Water Snake, Western Coachwhip, Schott's Whipsnake, Trans-Pecos Rat Snake, Mexican Milk Snake, Scarlet Kingsnake, Trans-Pecos Copperhead, Eastern Cottonmouth, Diamondback Rattlesnake,

Blacktail Rattlesnake, Eastern Hellbender, Red River Mudpuppy, Dwarf Waterdog, Greater Siren, Lesser Siren, Marbled Salamander, Ringed Salamander, Flatwoods Salamander, Red-spotted Newt, Black-spotted Newt, Imitator Salamander, Redback Salamander, Southern Redback Salamander, Green Salamander, Southern Two-lined Salamander, Texas Blind Salamander, Eastern Spadefoot, Eastern Narrowmouth Toad, Bronze Frog.

INDEX

This index has been organized to avoid repetition of such words as "salamander," "turtle," and "lizard" scores of times. In looking for common names, work backward. If you wish to find the entry for "Mountain Dusky Salamander," for example, look under "Salamander" first, then for the subdivision headed "Dusky," and finally for the word "Mountain." In the case of scientific names, look for the genus first, and then the species or subspecies.

This is primarily a species index, but there are also headings for each order, suborder, family, subfamily, and genus.

References to the text are in lightface type. Plate numbers are in **BOLDFACE**; plate numbers appear only after the common names of the animals.

THE PETERSON SERIES®

PETERSON FIELD GUIDES®

BIRDS

ADVANCED BIRDING (39) North America 53376-7
BIRDS OF BRITAIN AND EUROPE (8) 66922-7
BIRDS OF TEXAS (13) Texas and adjacent states 92138-4
BIRDS OF THE WEST INDIES (18) 67669-X
EASTERN BIRDS (1) Eastern and central North America
　91176-1
　EASTERN BIRDS' NESTS (21) U.S. east of Mississippi River 48366-2
　　　HAWKS (35) North America 44112-9
　　　WESTERN BIRDS (2) North America west of 100th meridian
　　　and north of Mexico 91173-7
　　　　WESTERN BIRDS' NESTS (25) U.S. west of Mississippi
　　　　River 47863-4
　　　　MEXICAN BIRDS (20) Mexico, Guatemala, Belize, El
　　　　Salvador 48354-9
　　　　WARBLERS (49) North America 78321-6

FISH

PACIFIC COAST FISHES (28) Gulf of Alaska to Baja California 33188-9
ATLANTIC COAST FISHES (32) North American Atlantic coast 39198-9
FRESHWATER FISHES (42) North America north of Mexico 91091-9

INSECTS

INSECTS (19) North America north of Mexico
　91170-2
BEETLES (29) North America 91089-7
EASTERN BUTTERFLIES (4) Eastern and central North
　America 90453-6
WESTERN BUTTERFLIES (33) U.S. and Canada west of 100th meridian, part of
　northern Mexico 41654-X
EASTERN MOTHS North America east of 100th meridian 36100-1

MAMMALS

MAMMALS (5) North America north of Mexico 91098-6
ANIMAL TRACKS (9) North America 91094-3

ECOLOGY

EASTERN FORESTS (37) Eastern North America 92895-8
CALIFORNIA AND PACIFIC NORTHWEST FORESTS (50) 92896-6
ROCKY MOUNTAIN AND SOUTHWEST FORESTS (51) 92897-4
VENOMOUS ANIMALS AND POISONOUS PLANTS (46) North America north of
　Mexico 35292-4

PETERSON FIELD GUIDES® continued

PLANTS

EARTH AND SKY

REPTILES AND AMPHIBIANS

SEASHORE

AUDIO AND VIDEO

EASTERN BIRDING BY EAR
cassettes 50087-7
CD 71258-0
WESTERN BIRDING BY EAR
cassettes 52811-9
CD 71257-2
EASTERN BIRD SONGS, Revised
cassettes 53150-0
CD 50257-8
WESTERN BIRD SONGS, Revised
cassettes 51746-X
CD 51745-1

PETERSON'S MULTIMEDIA GUIDES: NORTH AMERICAN BIRDS
(CD-ROM for Windows) 73056-2

PETERSON FLASHGUIDES™

ATLANTIC COASTAL BIRDS	79286-X
PACIFIC COASTAL BIRDS	79287-8
EASTERN TRAILSIDE BIRDS	79288-6
WESTERN TRAILSIDE BIRDS	79289-4
HAWKS	79291-6
BACKYARD BIRDS	79290-8
TREES	82998-4
MUSHROOMS	82999-2
ANIMAL TRACKS	82997-6
BUTTERFLIES	82996-8
ROADSIDE WILDFLOWERS	82995-X
BIRDS OF THE MIDWEST	86733-9
WATERFOWL	86734-7
FRESHWATER FISHES	86713-4

WORLD WIDE WEB: http://www.petersononline.com

PETERSON FIELD GUIDES can be purchased at your local
    bookstore or by calling our toll-free number, (800) 225-3362.

When referring to title by corresponding ISBN number,
preface with 0-395.